COBOL

by Design

Gary Klein
Louisiana Tech University

Malú Cabrera

FRANKLIN, BEEDLE & ASSOCIATES INCORPORATED
8536 SW St. Helens Drive, Suite D
Wilsonville, Oregon 97070
(503) 682-7668

Dedication

A Nuestro Hijo, Stefan Galen

Publisher	**Jim Leisy**
Manuscript Editor	**Sheryl Rose**
Production Manager	**Bill DeRouchey**
Production	**Tom Sumner**
Cover Design	**Neo Nova**
Cover Photograph	**Ian Shadburne**
Manufacturing	**Malloy Lithographing**
	Ann Arbor, Michigan

Rights and Permissions
Franklin, Beedle & Associates Incorporated
8536 SW St. Helens Drive, Suite D
Wilsonville, Oregon 97070

Printed in the United States of America

Library of Congress Cataloging-in-Publication Data

Klein, Gary (Gary S.)
    COBOL by design / Gary Klein, Malú Cabrera.
        p.   cm.
    Includes index.
    ISBN 0-938661-60-4
    1. COBOL (Computer program language) 2. Business--Data
processing.   I. Cabrera, Malú.   II. Title.
HF5548.5.C2K54   1993
   650 '.0285'5133--dc20   93-18268
                                              CIP

PREFACE

Our primary goal in preparing this text is to emphasize program design rather than language syntax. Good program design is the result of structured design discipline, good programming habits, and knowledge of language limitations. Thus, our emphasis on program design is complemented by teaching the principles of structured design and coding of programs. Good programming habits are stressed and all examples highlight these practices. Lastly, sufficient COBOL is presented to enable students to implement the design structures.

The basis of our orientation is unique for a programming text. Our premise is that the COBOL language is not an end in itself, but the means for implementing program solutions. We feel that any programming language is easier to learn and use if the student has a problem-solving perspective. Our emphasis is on teaching the proper skills needed to develop structured programs; therefore the COBOL language is presented in the context of program purpose and program structure. Design proficiency is a critical first step in achieving programming proficiency.

Although newer languages are in use, COBOL has remained a popular choice for many business applications. Some people have written off COBOL as a dead language only to be surprised at its resiliency. In the information systems of the future, other languages will fill the needs of more advanced applications. However, COBOL remains an effective and dynamic language that has many structure and file features appropriate to business applications. It also serves as an excellent tool for the study of program design.

This text embodies the classroom principles used in an introductory COBOL course that conforms to IS2 of the ACM Information Sciences Curriculum and CIS-2 and CIS-3 of the DPMA Model Curriculum. The material is appropriate for individuals who are computer literate, whether or not they have had a previous programming course.

The first ten chapters are meant to be covered in sequence. Chapter 7 is optional, although highly recommended. The last five chapters are designed to be covered in any sequence and each is dependent only on the first ten chapters. This arrangement allows the instructor the flexibility of choosing the material to cover, as well as its order. The supplemental material in the appendices includes references for flowchart symbols, a reserved word list, and a COBOL statement reference.

To help the student place programming in perspective, Chapter 1 presents the environment within which business information systems are developed. This context enables the student to understand the contribution of programming to the overall organizational goals, and to understand the importance of developing program design before code.

Actual program design is discussed in Chapter 2. Two design tools, the program hierarchy chart and Nassi-Schneiderman charts, are presented and their use in creating structured programs is illustrated. The student is made aware of the principles of functional decomposition, top-down design, and the use of limited program structures. These design tools are then used throughout the book in all program examples and program design discussions. We have included the use of structured English to complement the explanation of more complex logic. Flowcharts are included in an appendix for all case programs developed throughout the text. Flowcharts are an effective graphic for explanation purposes and therefore useful in learning, but for valid reasons have fallen into disfavor for program design purposes.

Following the presentation of the environment and design principles, Chapter 3 exposes the student to a complete COBOL program to illustrate the interrelationship of program design, documentation, and code. In addition, the general rules and language structure of COBOL are presented in this chapter. A simple but complete example program is presented to enable students to write simple report programs using the example program as a pattern. A case study further reinforces the chapter discussion and provides an additional sample program.

In Chapters 4 through 6 the COBOL language is presented in terms of data and program structures. We hold that in learning a programming language, the preferred approach is to describe the statements in terms of their function. This approach reinforces the problem-solving approach and permits the student to treat program design independently of the language, supporting our premise that languages are the means for implementing the designs. A case study at the end of each chapter shows the student how to apply the COBOL statements learned.

Chapter 7 covers program integrity, which is composed of debugging, testing, and common organizational operating controls. It provides students with a structured approach toward finding and correcting errors and offers recommendations on commonly used techniques. Debugging features of the COBOL language are presented. The importance of testing is stressed and practices used by organizations are discussed.

Report generation, sequential file updating, and table manipulation are some of the more commonly used program structures in the business setting. The program designs for these three common applications are presented in Chapters 8 through 10. These designs are effective and are in actual use by many organizations. The additional COBOL necessary for these tasks is presented in terms of the design, providing a solid foundation on which to base advanced COBOL features such as the SORT statement, advanced editing, and the SEARCH statement.

Throughout the text we emphasize the importance of documenting the program design by accompanying complete program examples with pertinent documentation. This emphasis makes the examples easier to study and understand. In Chapter 11, we further our discussion of documentation and tie it to the maintenance phase of an information system. Maintenance is presented as a crucial ingredient in the life of any program.

We stress the principles of good design throughout. In Chapter 12, the student is first introduced to the principles of evaluating this design by discussing coupling, cohesion, and other measures of effective program design. Subroutines are presented as a means for improving the design of a program and as a way to reduce the amount of code required in a complete system. The coverage of subroutines is also a critical feature of any course that teaches COBOL as a language for interactive programming, since many interactive functions are handled through subroutine calls to other languages.

Programmer productivity is a necessary goal in current organizational settings. One of the better productivity tools is the COBOL Report Writer feature. Chapter 13 discusses how this feature can eliminate a large section of a program's logical structure, thus saving design and coding time. This feature is often overlooked because of perceived coding difficulties. We present only a subset of the Report Writer feature in order to overcome this impression. However, it is possible to produce the majority of reports with the selected subset.

Chapter 14 covers direct access file concepts and explains their role in improving the performance of an information system. Furthermore, these file structures are very important in creating modern interactive programs. Since program design is affected by the change to direct access files, these changes in program design are explored within the context of file and program structures.

There is no doubt that interactive programs make up the majority of new business programs. Although many software developers have extended COBOL to handle interactive systems, the 1985 ANSI COBOL standards do not include many of the desirable functions. Still, it is quite possible to duplicate desirable interactive features with available COBOL statements. In Chapter 15 the general characteristics of interactive systems are presented first. We then cover the COBOL statements necessary to support many desired features of an interactive system.

An instructor's manual is available to qualified adopters. The instructor's manual includes tips on course organization and management, a detailed topic outline with chapter objectives, answers to questions in the text, transparency masters of selected figures from the text, and three semesters of program assignments. Test data for the assignments, sample programs for the assignments, output from the assignments, case study programs, and case study test data are all available on a separate diskette to qualified adopters of the text.

Throughout the text we have used the masculine gender to conform to the general rules of grammar. Our intent is to include both sexes in such references. "He" refers to "he or she" and "his" refers to "his or her" unless otherwise warranted by the context.

Acknowledgments

To the reviewers of this book, whose insights and suggestions are greatly appreciated:

Larry Cobb, Alabama State University
Mary Curtis, Louisiana State University
Dick Fisher, Miami University
Dr. Mo Adam Mahmood, University of Texas at El Paso
Mike Payne, Purdue University
Behrooz Seyed-Abbassi, University of North Florida
Dr. G.W. Willis, Baylor University

TABLE OF CONTENTS

PERSPECTIVES

1.1 COBOL in Perspective
 Business Problems
 The System Development Life Cycle
 Case Study: CDL's System Development Life Cycle
 Summary
 Exercises

COBOL is one of the most widely used business programming languages. Developed specifically to meet the needs of the business community, COBOL is a tool that facilitates the implementation of solutions to typical business situations. It is important that the student who is learning COBOL develop an understanding of the reasons COBOL was developed and the framework in which COBOL is used.

1.1 COBOL in Perspective

A group of computer professionals representing the U.S. government, computer manufacturers, universities, and users met in 1959 and 1960 at the request of the Department of Defense to develop a computer language oriented to business programming but complete enough for widespread use in nonbusiness situations. This group of professionals, named the Conference on Data Systems Languages (CODASYL), tried to create for programming of business-oriented problems a standardized language that was machine-independent and utilized a syntax that closely resembled English. The result was a computer language named *COBOL*, an acronym for COmmon Business-Oriented Language. This novel, high-level language, oriented to the problem and not to the computer, specified the problem-solving logic in procedural statements rather than machine-oriented instructions. Though criticized from its beginning, COBOL succeeded in becoming the most extensively used programming language for business applications.

COBOL has certain advantages that have not yet been attained by other programming languages. Occasionally updated to incorporate new hardware and software features, it supports structured programming concepts and utilizes an English-like syntax. Its popularity is reflected in the portability of its programs and programmer experience. Companies often outgrow their existing computer systems and have to upgrade to more sophisticated ones. If the programs are written in COBOL, the conversion is easier than if they were written in a less standardized language. For users of smaller systems who may not have existing COBOL programs, manufacturers usually provide translators that automatically convert programs written in assembly, RPG, or some language other than COBOL.

Resource requirement estimates for COBOL programming projects are easier to derive and also more accurate because of the widespread experience with the language. This experience also makes it less difficult to hire new or replacement programmers, something that cannot be underestimated in a field where the shortage of trained personnel is well documented. It is advantageous for both the organizations hiring programmers and the programmers seeking employment.

As hardware has improved and as the use of COBOL has increased, enhancements to improve its usefulness have been incorporated into the COBOL standards. These standards are maintained by the American National Standards Institute (ANSI) and the standard versions of COBOL are called American National Standard (ANS) COBOL. Many changes were reflected in the update from the 1968 version to the 1974 version of ANS COBOL with further enhancements in the 1985 version. Such response to a changing environment in a standardized way has kept COBOL a productive language.

The use of an English-like structure and syntax enhances the functionality of COBOL and produces code that is easy to read and maintain. Although COBOL must still be coded by a programmer, almost anyone can understand the logic in well-written code. This facilitates the communication of the program purpose and reduces the need for extensive explanations via comments in the code. The similarity to English makes COBOL easier to learn and understand, and provides a self-documentation feature that is extremely important in the maintenance phase of program development.

COBOL is very efficient in the processing of business applications that are characterized by the handling of many data files and the generation of many reports. In general, business systems do more summarization of data than they do computation on the data. COBOL allows handling of various file structures and easy specification of the data contained in them.

Because of its business orientation, COBOL is a valuable tool for implementing problem solutions in the form of applications programs that provide managers with information to solve business problems. By increasing his awareness of business problem situations, the programmer can better contribute to the success of an organization.

1.1.1   Business Problems

In a business organization, problems are events that raise questions for consideration or solution, thereby requiring decisions on the part of a manager. When defined in this way, a problem can be an actual malfunction in the operation of the organization, an opportunity to be exploited, or a simple event requiring a minor task to be performed. Problems can range from the desirable, such as dispersing the cash from a windfall profit, to the ordinary, such as deciding on the advertising budget for a new product, to the distressing, such as encountering a cash-out situation when many bills are due.

Business problems occur at all levels of decision making in an organization. At the highest level, strategic decisions involve major risks and investments for a company, such as introducing a new car line. Strategic problems tend to be unstructured and abstract. Often the information needed to support the decision-making process is unavailable. Tactical decisions involve the middle level of the decision framework and include situations with shorter time frames, such as selecting a long-distance telephone carrier. Problems affecting the day-to-day tasks of an organization represent the lowest level of decision making and call for operational decisions such as authorizing overtime to complete a specific job. Operational problems are usually very structured. The decisions to be made are of a concrete nature and the data required to support them are readily available. Programs written in COBOL are ideally suited to this last category of decision making.

The business problem solver is first and foremost a decision maker and is often a manager within the company. A business's success is directly related to the resolution of its problems by the decision maker. Successful firms have a history of good problem solving; unsuccessful firms do not. Many factors affect the solution of problems. Figure 1.1 shows that problems may arise through the operations of the company or from external entities such as a major customer or the government. For example, when a production problem must be solved, the manager must often decide if cost or productivity is the more important objective. In trying to solve the problem in the most beneficial way, the decision maker may find that the environment restricts the solutions available. For example, the tax structure restricts the way paychecks are computed. The manager must review the available information to arrive at the best solution to the problem and to meet organizational goals.

Figure 1.1   *Forces Acting on a Decision Maker*

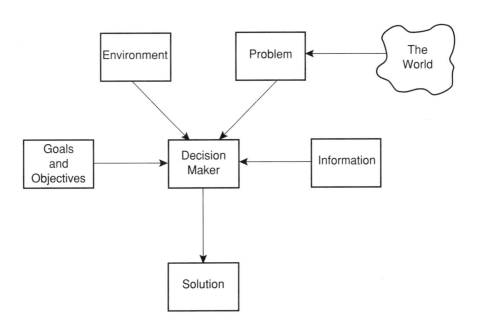

A key factor in making educated decisions is the availability of good information. Not all data available are worth examining or retaining. "Goodness" may be measured by the ability of the information to improve the quality of a problem solution by reducing uncertainty. "Good" information is valid, timely, relevant, and understandable. Therefore, data must have value to merit consideration in a decision. Their value depends on an ability to generate quality information that, in turn, makes a difference to the problem solver.

For example, information such as the cash flow status of the company would allow a manager to make an educated investment decision. Additional information concerning the riskiness of different investment alternatives would further improve the decision. A reliable stock forecast would increase the manager's knowledge and enable him to analyze the alternatives, allowing him to formulate a better solution. The availability of information, even good information, does not, of course, guarantee that the manager will arrive at the best solution, but it does increase the chances that he will make more educated and therefore better decisions.

In a business, an information system collects, stores, and processes data in order to report information to the problem solver. Figure 1.2 shows these functions. Business systems support the problem-solving process and improve the quality of decisions by improving the quality of information through increased speed, accuracy, and quantity. Because of the importance of information systems, a descriptive structured design process, known as the life cycle, was developed to help organize all of the steps in building a system.

1.1.2   The System Development Life Cycle

The programmer represents a crucial link in a chain of events leading from the identification of a problem, progressing through identifiable developmental phases, and culminating in a working solution. To be successful, the programmer must realize how his job fits into the entirety of a business solution. This is best accomplished by identifying the context in which business systems are developed. Our discussion is not meant as an extensive treatise on the subject but only as an overview.

The development of a business system proceeds through a systematic process known as the system development life cycle. It provides the framework which represents an idealized flow of events during the creation and implementation of business systems. These activities are summarized in Figure 1.3. Each function of the life cycle can be isolated and sequenced, thus providing a descriptive model that aids our understanding of the system development process. However, in actual developmental settings the steps in the life cycle are highly interrelated and their boundaries not always clearly defined. Some steps may require repetition based on their evaluation and feedback. At each stage of the life cycle, management should review the project and decide whether it meets its objectives and whether it should continue. Since considerable resources are committed in each subsequent activity, this evaluation is crucial. The later a project is rejected, the greater the resources that will have been wasted. Even though the ideal situation is rarely achieved in the real world, the life cycle provides guidelines for the development of information systems. Furthermore, it defines how the required tasks, including the tasks of the COBOL programmer, are interrelated.

Figure 1.2   ***Flow of Data in Business Information Systems***

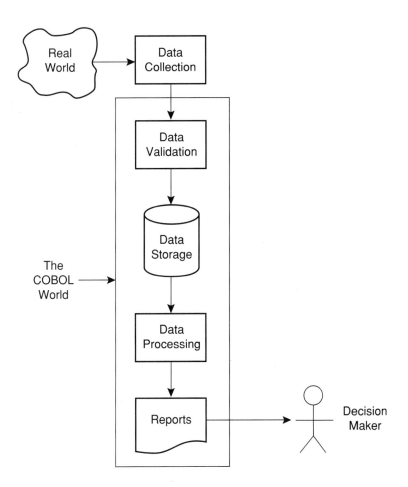

Figure 1.3   The Business System Development Life Cycle

Phase	Description
Problem recognition	Identify and document the business problem.
Feasibility study	Determine the technical, operational, and economic feasibility of solving the problem. Evaluate several alternatives.
Logical analysis	Make a detailed study of the system. Identify all inputs, outputs, and procedures. Understand the needs of the user and determine the requirements of the system before design begins.
Physical design	Develop the detailed specifications for the system.
Programming	Design, code, and test the programs required by the new system.
Implementation	Test the new system to ensure that specifications are met. Train the users of the system and convert the data. Put the new system into use.
Maintenance	Improve and correct the system throughout the remainder of its useful life.

Problem Recognition. With information systems, problems that can be solved with improved information performance are examined. Information performance can be enhanced through improvements in the accuracy of the information provided, the speed at which information is provided, and the availability of essential information. For example, if the tax structure changes, information currently being gathered by the company becomes inaccurate and changes in the information system must be made. If a company's manual order processing is months behind, a computerized system may alleviate the backlog, prevent future bottlenecks, and increase customer satisfaction. It is also possible that an existing information system functions well, yet does not provide all the information upper-level management requires for its decision-making activities.

However, before any work can be performed in solving a business problem, the problem must be correctly identified and documented. *Problem identification* involves the interaction between systems personnel, known as analysts, and the current users of the system under study.

The initial investigations should yield some broad objectives for the system and should identify the perceived benefits of any proposed system. Thus a preliminary investigation should formally define and document the problem.

Often an apparent problem is only a symptom of the real problem. For example, the absence of the newspaper from your doorstep in the morning is the symptom of an apparent problem. The actual problem may be that you forgot to pay the bill for last month's subscription or that the carrier is ill. Identifying the true nature of the problem will determine the success of the remaining steps in the life cycle. Once the problem has been identified, the organization can begin working collectively toward its solution. If the problem is not correctly identified, the rest of the system, including the programs, will not solve it.

Feasibility Study. The goal of the *feasibility study* is to determine the technical, economic, and operational practicality of solving the business problem with an automated information system. For example, if solutions require the use of unavailable equipment or do not fit into the corporate structure, they should be eliminated or deferred for further study. In this stage, a more thorough study of the existing system and the proposed new system determines whether the benefits of the new system can be realized within the technical and operational environment of the business. The existing system is studied to find its strengths and weaknesses, and its scope is identified. User involvement is decisive in identifying major goals and requirements for the proposed system. These specifications are then used to develop alternative system solutions to the business problem, and their benefits and drawbacks are evaluated.

The feasibility study should be a survey. It should identify workable solutions that merit more comprehensive analyses. If a system meets all the feasibility criteria, it is more likely to be implemented as planned. To progress beyond this point in the development of a system without such a study courts disaster. This may be exemplified by a programmer trying to code a program that is technically infeasible or by seeing his program discarded when found operationally infeasible. The feasibility study should filter the proposed solutions so that only those with a high probability of success are undertaken. Thus the feasibility study is important not only to the success of the system but also to the economic stability of the company.

Logical Analysis. The problem recognition and feasibility studies can be thought of as systems planning stages that precede the actual development of a system. By the end of the feasibility study, a company has decided that the new system can be implemented. The next step is to identify the requirements to be met by the new system. This involves a comprehensive study of the required operations of the system, the association of the parts composing the system, and the relationships of the system with other systems and its operating environment. It involves gathering additional information from the users about what the system does, what the users need, and what restrictions the system must meet. How the problem can be solved is not considered during this stage. Similarly, such specific implementation issues as program identification and file design are left for later steps.

The goal of logical analysis is to define the flow of information that will best solve the information requirements of the user. It involves detailing the flow of information through the company and documenting it. Sources of information are identified as inputs to the system. Data sources may be external, such as a customer placing an order, or internal, such as an employee filing a time card. The inputs are traced through the system and all operations on the data such as summarizing, updating, or filing are identified. Files and reports are identified as to content and recipient, and data volume and retention policies are determined.

The systems analyst uses diverse tools during the analysis task to promote a complete understanding of the problem and provide working documents that become the functional specifications of the system. The specifications are generally refinements of the goals and objectives identified in prior activities of the life cycle that define the functions to be performed. Some of the most commonly used structured systems analysis tools include data flow diagrams, system dictionaries, and data structure diagrams. A data flow diagram (DFD) shows the processes in a system and the data that pass among them. It identifies the data stores and the sources and destinations of data. A system dictionary defines all the data identified in the DFD by specifying the structure of the files, records, and fields. It may include information such as their physical storage device and the method of accessing them. Data structure diagrams illustrate detailed data structures and the associations among the data items. In subsequent stages of the life cycle, the analyst or programmer uses the documentation provided by the analysis tools to design and structure the new system. Many of these documentation tools are automated, often as part of an analysis and design aid known as Computer Assisted Systems Engineering (CASE).

Physical Design. The physical design task involves taking the logical analysis specifications and deriving the technical aspects of the new system, that is, the hardware and software specifics. Once the analyst completes the physical design he essentially has a blueprint that provides the framework of the new system. In deriving the physical design, the analyst follows an iterative, or repetitive, process in which he transforms and augments the functions specified in the logical analysis phase until they specify how they are to meet the goals of the system.

During this step the analyst details the input and output requirements of the system. He specifies the input and output file layouts, sizes, content, access methods, and storage media; he also determines data descriptions, report formats, and generation frequency. If dialogues and menus are to be used for human-machine communication in the system, there are additional design considerations. These may include screen formats, data-validation and error-handling rules, and message and "help" dialogues. These factors necessarily influence programming considerations.

Programming. During the *programming* activity the design is translated into a processing logic executable by a computer. The program specifications provided by the design task are refined, the complete program documentation regarding the program structure is developed, and the programs are generated and tested. In many business programming environments, especially at the operational level, this means writing and testing COBOL programs.

It is imperative that programmers understand and interpret the functional specifications derived in the design activity. Various tools exist to record these specifications. One of the most common is the hierarchy chart. In some companies, hierarchy charts are developed during the design step of the life cycle, but in others programmers develop their own. In either case, the programmer must be familiar with this structuring tool in order to develop his programs or to interpret an inherited design. Hierarchy charts illustrate program structure by showing the program's functions and their interrelationships level by level from the most general to the most specific. They do not show the sequence of execution nor do they detail external characteristics such as file structure. We will emphasize the construction and use of hierarchy charts throughout this book.

To develop the program logic necessary to accomplish the functions required by the system, the programmer specifies the control structure of a program, that is, how the functions within the program should be sequenced to comprise a solution. In this book we use the Nassi-Schneiderman chart as the standard logic specification tool. The programmer can then use the program logic developed to write the code in the selected programming language. Good program design documents allow an almost direct translation into program statements so that the coding process becomes an almost clerical task. Once the coding is complete, the program is tested to ensure that the design specifications are met and that the bugs have been detected and corrected.

Implementation. The goal of *implementation* is to attain an operational system and ensure that it is running smoothly. Before giving final acceptance the user tests the system, ensuring that all individually developed programs properly perform their function as a whole and that they conform to his needs.

At this time users are trained in the use of the system, the readying of system inputs, and the interpretation of the system outputs. Once they are trained, the stage is set for converting to the new system. Conversion requires that old data be translated to the new formats and that the old system be replaced with the new one.

Maintenance. *Maintaining* a system means keeping the system up-to-date and in good condition. Because of the dynamism of the environment in which businesses operate, it is estimated that a system's lifetime is about five years. Considering that system development accounts for an average of one year and system maintenance for the remainder of its productive life, it is easy to see that the maintenance activity will require much of the programming effort.

Changes to an operational system are often made to adapt it to new environments. These modifications constitute routine maintenance. Other changes result from program errors appearing after implementation of a system and are often the result of improper testing. Since these errors may have a detrimental effect on the production environment, they require quick fixes and are considered emergency maintenance. Changes resulting from users' requests for refinements to improve system performance or for additional functionality are termed system enhancements. Enhancements are a type of maintenance that is commonplace throughout the life of the system.

Even though maintenance comprises a considerable portion of a system's life cycle, in most data processing shops it is often viewed as a necessary evil. Maintenance consumes valuable personnel resources that must be diverted from new systems development. Furthermore, maintenance costs are increasing not only because of the increasing cost of personnel but also the volume of new systems being put into production. No wonder companies are looking for increased programmer productivity as a means of decreasing the resources expended in this stage. With good system design and complete documentation, programs should be more easily maintained and modified.

An inevitable fact is that as a system ages, its maintenance will consume more and more resources, its cost of upkeep will begin to outweigh its benefits, and the system will become obsolete. As the system fails to meet the requirements of the user, the problem will be recognized and a new system development life cycle will begin.

This text concentrates on the physical design and programming phases of the life cycle. We provide appropriate linkages to prior and later phases. This recognition of the entire process permeates the case studies presented at the end of each chapter. Our heroine is an information systems professional responsible for the entire development process. Her examples embody the practice of good design, clearly written code, and a perspective of the entire problem.

Case Study: CDL's System Development Life Cycle

Compact Discs for Less (CDL) is a mail order retailer that caters to owners of compact disc players. Lately, the owner of CDL has noticed a large number of complaints from his customers caused by a growing backlog of orders and increased double billings.

The owner undertook a minor investigation that revealed a more accurate picture of the situation. When CDL was established, few people owned compact disc players and CDL maintained its accounts receivable and inventory files manually. As the price of compact disc players dropped rapidly, CDL's sales jumped dramatically. Soon the company was deluged with orders and the inventory records lagged far behind in reflecting true stock levels. In addition, the accounts receivable file required frequent updates that became hard to handle manually.

Problem Recognition. Rapidly increasing sales might not be considered a problem for a company. But in the case of CDL, sales are growing too quickly for the accounts receivable department to process billings using the current system. Although an immediate and simple solution could be developed, it might not be the best one or even a feasible one. For instance, the simplest solution would be for CDL to reject orders. Yet, from a profit standpoint, this solution makes no sense.

In analyzing the situation, it becomes apparent that the customer complaints are merely symptoms of the real problem, whose source is twofold: an inadequate accounts receivable system and an order-processing system that cannot sustain rapid growth. The owner decides that CDL might be a perfect candidate for a computerized business system.

Feasibility Study. Because of the perceived seriousness of the situation and his lack of experience in automated information systems, CDL's owner hires Charlene Hilton, a programmer/analyst, to conduct the feasibility study and, if warranted, to continue with the systems development. Charlene begins her feasibility study by interviewing the owner to pinpoint the long-term commitments and growth goals he has for the company. Once she has documented the company goals, Charlene speaks with the accounts receivable clerk, Fred Newman, to determine his accounting information needs. Charlene then approaches Harriet Goodman, the inventory control clerk, to determine what information she requires to maintain up-to-date inventory records. Through the interviews Charlene obtains enough data to achieve a general level of understanding of the existing system and to outline the information requirements of its users.

Logical Analysis. Having received the go-ahead for system development, Charlene proceeds to perform a detailed study of the system in which she identifies the flow of information within the organization and determines the functions, inputs, outputs, and files necessary to meet the users' requirements. During this step, she further identifies the contents of each input document, report, and file currently used. These content descriptions will be used in later phases of the life cycle to design the physical characteristics of the system. They will also be used when conferring with the users of the system to confirm the accuracy of the new system design.

Physical Design. Since Charlene is both the programmer and the analyst, the remainder of the steps tend to blend together. During this phase Charlene develops a system flowchart that shows how the functions and the physical characteristics of the new system are to be implemented. A *system flowchart* represents the physical flow of data between files and programs. Appendix A lists the various system flowchart symbols and their meanings. Figure 1.4 shows the system flowchart for the order-entry process developed by Charlene. Note that it also identifies the individual programs needed. In Figure 1.4:

    (a) Payments and orders are entered into CDL's business system and

    (b) are saved on a tape file.

    (c) The tape file is used by a program called "Categorize Daily Mail" to determine three input disk files (d, e, and f):

    (d) payments that contain all required information,

    (e) orders received, and

    (f) payments that do not provide adequate information to be applied to the customer accounts.

    (g) The orders are extended to verify complete information and quantities and to store them

    (h) on a disk file

    (i) which is validated

    (j) against a file containing in-stock information.

    (k) Invalid orders are reported to the appropriate clerks

    (l) and billing information is generated for the valid orders.

    (m) The billing information is used to update

    (n) an inventory file,

    (o) issue purchase requests, and

    (p) update the customer accounts receivable

    (q) file stored on disk.

    (r) The updated file

    (s) is used to create

    (t) a listing of account information.

Figure 1.4*   *CDL's Preliminary Business Information System

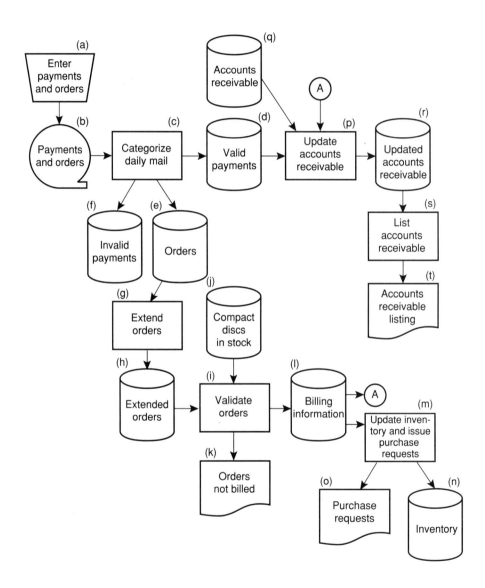

Using the physical characteristics of the system and the information obtained during the logical analysis activity, Charlene begins to design the layouts of the inputs, outputs, and files. Each one must have exact specifications for each item it contains. Charlene then writes detailed program summaries for each program identified in the system flowchart. When the physical design is complete, Charlene prepares a documentation package containing all the specifications. These documents will be used in the programming activity to design and code the programs.

Summary

COBOL is an acronym for COmmon Business-Oriented Language. It was developed as a high-level programming language oriented to business applications. COBOL continues to be a popular language because of its standardization, its continuing evolution, its support of structured programming principles, and the relative simplicity afforded by its English-like structure and syntax. It will continue to be popular because of its many advantages in solving business problems and because of the investment companies have in COBOL programs.

In a business organization, problems are defined as events that require decisions by management. Business problems occur at various levels of decision making and vary in complexity, seriousness, and urgency. The success of business organizations is directly related to their problem-solving abilities.

Another element contributing to success is the worthwhile information a company has at its disposal. Information must be timely, relevant, and understandable and must make a difference to the decision maker in order to be worthwhile. The goal of business information systems is to improve a company's problem-solving ability by improving the quality of information.

Business information systems proceed through a systematic process known as the system development life cycle. It consists of seven phases: problem recognition, feasibility study, logical analysis, physical design, programming, implementation, and maintenance. The programmer must realize that the program is a link in a complex process that requires many resources and much dedicated time by many individuals. The system development life cycle identifies the context within which the programmer realizes these activities.

Key Terms

COBOL	logical analysis	maintenance
system development life cycle	physical design	system flowchart
problem identification	programming	
feasibility study	implementation	

Exercises

1.1 "Good" information is:
    a.   valid.
    b.   timely.
    c.   relevant.
    d.   understandable.
    e.   all of the above

1.2   A programmer can better contribute to the success of an organization by:
     a.   focusing on the main goal of producing working programs.
     b.   increasing his awareness of business problem situations.
     c.   refining his COBOL coding skills to facilitate shorter, more concise programs.

1.3   COBOL programming is ideally suited for abstract and unstructured strategic problems. True or false?

1.4   A business's success is directly related to the resolution of its problems by the:
     a.   company charter.
     b.   decision-maker.
     c.   lawyer.
     d.   maintenance supervisor.

1.5   The programmer represents the *first* link in a chain of events leading from identification of a problem to the culmination of a working solution. True or false?

1.6   The availability of information guarantees that the decision maker will arrive at the best solution to a problem. True or false?

1.7   COBOL continues to be popular because of its:
     a.   individualization.
     b.   continuing evolution.
     c.   support of structured programming principles.
     d.   A and C
     e.   B and C
     f.   all of the above

1.8   COBOL is occasionally updated to incorporate newer hardware and software features. True or false?

1.9   Business systems:
     a.   support the problem-solving process.
     b.   improve the quality of decisions.
     c.   improve the quality of information.
     d.   none of the above
     e.   A and B
     f.   all of the above

1.10   An information system _____, _____, and _____ data in order to report information to the problem solver.
     a.   holds, displays, retrieves
     b.   creates, updates, saves
     c.   collects, stores, processes
     d.   manipulates, edits, translates

1.11   Resource requirements estimates for COBOL programming projects are complicated to derive because of usually lengthy program size. True or false?

1.12   It is impossible to convert assembly, RPG, or other languages into COBOL by translator programs or otherwise. True or false?

1.13   The acronym COBOL stands for what words?

1.14   A key factor in making decisions is the availability of _____.

1.15   The _____ provides the framework that represents an idealized flow of events during the creation and implementation of business systems.

1.16   _____ illustrate(s) program structure by showing the program's functions and interrelationships level by level from most general to most specific.

1.17   _____ graphically organize(s) program functions so that a computer can execute them.

1.18   COBOL is very efficient in the processing of _____ applications, which are characterized by the handling of many _____ and the generation of many _____.

1.19   The steps of the system development lifecycle are (in correct order):

1. _____

2. _____

3. _____

4. _____

5. _____

6. _____

7. _____

1.20   Why is the quality of data available for a particular business problem important to the decision maker?

2

DESIGNING
STRUCTURED PROGRAMS

Structured programs are those developed within the disciplined, organized framework of structured programming. Some writers may limit the definition of structured programming to the sphere of source-code logic; we have chosen to define it in broader terms. As used in this text, *structured programming* encompasses two primary aspects of program development: design and coding.

Structured programs are designed using structured design methodologies. Their logic is developed using a limited number of control structures, and their code is written using the COBOL statements that implement these control structures. Structured programs are easy to code, test, and maintain. These benefits can be translated into increased programmer productivity and greater program accuracy.

As you become more aware of the impact of program design on your coding effort, we are certain that it will provide further motivation for mastering the structuring techniques discussed in this chapter.

2.1   Developing the Program Structure

At the dawn of the computer era, machines were costly, had small memories, and ran slowly. Because programmers were concerned with program efficiency from the standpoint of size and speed, they concentrated on making their programs use less memory and run more quickly. In those days, hardware costs were more significant than were programming costs. But today advancements in computer technology have lowered hardware costs, increased memory size, and multiplied processing speeds.

However, programming costs have not decreased. Demands for automated business systems and software costs have increased to the point where software now represents the major part of business system development costs. Programming philosophy is now aimed at increasing programmer productivity to control software development and software maintenance costs.

Various methods and techniques have been developed to control program complexity and produce programs that are easy to read, understand, code, debug, and modify. Programs are designed following an organized methodology that yields more rigid designs. These programs can then be understood not only by the programmers who code them but also by the programmers who need to correct or modify them.

Structured program design helps reduce costs during the developmental phases of the life cycle as well as later during maintenance. It is a methodology for taking a statement of the program requirements produced in the analysis phase and developing a plan for their implementation on a computer. At the end of the design phase this plan can be coded and tested.

Structured system design methodologies offer a disciplined approach to developing the structure and logic needed to write programs. The goal of program structuring is to produce an understandable, dependable, durable, and efficient solution that works correctly. It serves to develop a blueprint of the solution prior to specifying the detailed processing requirements. Program structuring is facilitated by segmentation and the use of structuring tools.

2.1.1   *Controlling Complexity through Segmentation*

Structured program design strives to minimize the complexity of programs by segmenting them into subunits called *modules* and organizing these modules into hierarchies. The idea of segmentation is not new. For years business organizations have used the concepts of specialization and division of duties.

Each module is defined to accomplish a single function within the program. To illustrate this concept, let us consider the automobile. The automobile is one complete system whose objective is to transport people and things from one place to another. However, it is built from a set of subsystems or components, each of which has an identifiable function. If one of the major components, such as the engine, is removed from the system, the automobile cannot function.

An automobile consists, among other things, of an engine module, a transmission module, a steering mechanism module, a drive train module, and four wheel modules. If any of these components fails, the entire system comes to a halt. To repair the system, however, only the failed component need be repaired or replaced. For example, when a tire goes flat only one tire module needs to be replaced, not the entire automobile. The engineer who designs engines may do so with little knowledge of how transmissions work. Because the car is modularized, each component can be treated individually, yet the functioning of the automobile as a whole depends on the unified functioning of its components.

Like the automobile, a computer program is simpler to understand if it is segmented into modules having defined functions. One method of partitioning a program into modules is called functional decomposition. Some general guidelines should be followed in this process. First, each module should carry out one well-defined piece of the program. For example, if one of the requirements of a company payroll system is to print paychecks, a single module should print the paychecks without doing any other tasks. Second, the function of the module should be easy to understand even though it may be complicated to implement. For example, the concept that a module's function is to compute reorder quantities in an inventory control program is easy to grasp even though the actual computations may be complex. Third, the connections between modules should be as simple and minimal as possible so that modules are as independent as possible. For example, suppose one module computes a total purchase amount and another module computes the sales tax. Only the purchase amount should be provided to the sales tax computation module by the total purchase module since it requires no other information.

In structured program design, segmenting the program into understandable units helps control a program's complexity. It also results in simpler designs with easy-to-understand modules. Functional decomposition is not the only technique available for partitioning a program. Other methods include transaction analysis, which derives the program structure using data structure diagrams, and transform analysis, which does so using data flow diagrams. These methodologies require greater background knowledge, however, and are usually covered in analysis and design courses.

Once the various functions of a program have been identified, they must be organized. Structured design uses a hierarchical organization. *Hierarchies* are patterns of organization. Matter itself is a set of units arranged in hierarchical fashion. Matter is composed of molecules which are composed of atoms. Atoms are composed of neutrons, protons, and electrons, which may be further decomposed into other components.

Large organizations such as businesses, churches, and governments are also organized into hierarchies. In these organizations there are definite relationships of superiority and subordination. Figure 2.1 shows the organization chart for CDL. The owner of the company, Ron Owens, is depicted at the top of the organization chart. Although he is responsible for all the subordinates in his company, he formally communicates only with the vice presidents directly below him. The vice presidents, in turn, communicate with the managers directly below them and with the owner directly above them. The vice presidents are subordinates of the owner and superiors of the managers. Each vice president controls and is responsible only for his subordinates, and does not communicate (officially) with the subordinates of the other vice presidents. These lines of control may be followed to the bottom level of the organization, with all but the owner having a superior, and all but the lowest level workers having subordinates.

Figure 2.1   **Compact Discs for Less Organization Chart**

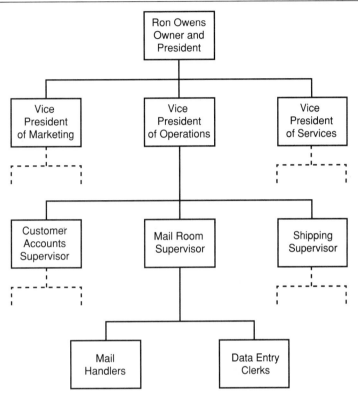

In organizing the program modules, we wish to follow a similar hierarchical pattern with definite lines of control. By studying the organization chart we can derive some general guidelines for doing so. First, managers coordinate the work of their subordinates and should not perform any of the lower-level work themselves. For example, the secretaries type letters and the janitors sweep floors. In programs, the higher-level modules should coordinate the work of their subordinate modules. These worker modules perform such tasks as locating records in a file or computing required values. Second, managers should provide subordinates with only as much information as the subordinates need to do their jobs. This avoids bogging down the subordinates with irrelevant details and allows better performance of the job. A module in a program should provide only the data a subordinate module requires to perform its function. This avoids errors and often results in a more efficient program. Third, every individual should have a well-defined responsibility, and tasks should be allocated to the proper individual. In a program, each module should have a well-defined function, and each task should be assigned to the proper module.

2.1.2   Using Graphic Tools: The Hierarchy Chart

In this text we use the hierarchy chart as the tool for designing a program's structure. *Hierarchy charts* partition a program into modules and organize the modules into a hierarchy by identifying the program functions level by level from the most general to the most specific. Furthermore, they demonstrate the implied relationship among the modules without showing the sequence of execution or specifying external characteristics such as file structures. Only the factors necessary to designing the program structure are considered. When completed, the hierarchy chart represents the framework or structure of the program in a graphic rather than a narrative form. The hierarchy chart in Figure 2.2 depicts a simple program that lists those sales representatives whose expense accounts exceed a certain dollar amount and prints the total number of such overspenders. Each box represents a module, and the position of the modules indicates their relationship. The top module, "Report Excess Accounts," is the superior of the three tasks in the second level. The subordinate modules are all necessary to perform the overall function of the superior module and are all controlled by the superior module. The second-level module "Find Overspenders" requires and controls three different tasks, namely "Read Employee Record," "Compare Expense Account," and "Print Report Line."

Figure 2.2   Expense Account Program Hierarchy Chart

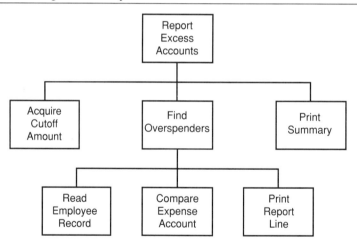

Benefits of the Hierarchy Chart. One of the advantages of the hierarchy chart is its graphic nature. In one glance you have an overall view of the program, its organization, and major functions. Because of its pictorial quality, a hierarchy chart facilitates communication between the designer and the user of the system, or among the implementers of the system.

Since the hierarchy chart is developed in the design phase, it assures that some valuable documentation is produced in the development process. And, because the hierarchy chart is such an integral part of the design process, it is more likely to remain current. Not only is this a big plus in itself, but when the program requires maintenance such documentation can save much time and effort.

Designing the Hierarchy Chart. It is important to remember that the hierarchy chart shows the partitioning of the program into modules and how they are organized to accomplish the overall function. Each module must be described in terms of the function it performs. Program details such as headings, decisions, sequencing, and variable names are excluded from the hierarchy chart. Our only concern is with the program structure and function. Furthermore, hierarchy charts imply no order of execution by the arrangement of the modules. They do, however, show the general *flow of control* of the program.

Examine the program specifications in Figure 2.3. This program is to produce an inventory report of current stock and to indicate the items that need to be reordered or whose orders are overdue. In addition, the program should calculate totals for key variables and display them at the end of the report. Notice that certain details such as the report layout and the input file layouts are missing from the program specifications. Although these items are needed to code the program, they are not necessary to develop the hierarchy chart. Remember that the *physical* characteristics of the program are ignored; so the missing information is irrelevant at this point.

Figure 2.3   **An Inventory Status Program Specification**

PROGRAM SUMMARY

TITLE: *Inventory Listing*

PREPARED BY: *Fred Joe Baker*

DATE: *6-19-93*

FILES USED		
FILE NAME	MEDIA	ORGANIZATION
Inventory	*Disk*	*Sequential*

DESCRIPTION

Produce a report listing the current stock in inventory. Indicate inventory items requiring reordering and items that have orders outstanding and are past due. At the end of the report, display the total number of items needing reordering, and the total number of items whose orders are past due.

Past due items are any items whose order was placed over 30 days ago. An item requires reordering when the quantity on hand is less than the reorder point. These data items all appear on the Inventory File.

Developing the First Level. In creating a hierarchy chart, begin by drawing a box at the top of the page to depict the function of the program as a whole, as in Figure 2.4. This top module is considered to begin and end the program and represents the highest level of functional decomposition. In developing the rest of the hierarchy chart we will partition each function into component functions, level by level, progressing from an overview of the problem to more specific detail. Proceeding in this fashion is referred to as *top-down design* and is an inherent part of structured programming. In contrast, the approach wherein all the detailed tasks in a program are first identified and then organized to accomplish the overall function of the program is known as bottom-up design. Good design methodology espouses the principles of top-down design. This approach enables one to keep a tight rein on the flow of control and allows the division of complex modules into two or more simpler modules.

Figure 2.4   *First and Second Levels of Inventory Status Hierarchy Chart*

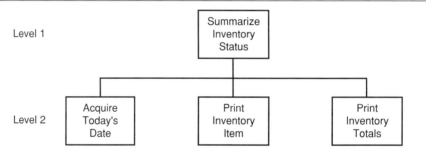

Bottom-up design does not allow for this simplification and leads to difficulty when the modules are integrated into a hierarchy chart. It is analogous to having to build an automobile given a box of parts and no instructions.

Each module should have a meaningful name that summarizes its function. In general, module names are composed of a verb representing the action accomplished by the module, a noun that describes the entity or data affected, and one or two adjectives that clarify that entity. Although this may seem a bit simplistic, it is almost always sufficient. In our example an appropriate name for the top-level module might be "Summarize Inventory Status."

Developing the Second Level. To develop the second level in the program hierarchy chart, we use a pattern of decomposition in wide use today. It is based on temporal considerations and yields three subordinate modules. We begin by determining the one primary function that must be performed repetitively in order to accomplish the overall function of the program. In this example, it is the printing of a line of detail for each inventory item. Let us call this module "Print Inventory Item" and sketch the corresponding box as in Figure 2.4. Next, consider the function that must be performed before the inventory item lines are printed. It is acquiring the date used to determine whether an order is overdue. Call this module "Acquire Today's Date" and sketch it in front of the repetitive primary module. The third module in the second level is the function that must be accomplished after the inventory item lines are printed. In this case it is printing the report summary. The module "Print Inventory Totals" completes the second level of decomposition. This three-module decomposition approach at the second level is very useful, and it allows for some of the restrictions certain languages place on design. For example, some languages require that variables be initialized prior to their use in calculations to ensure correctness of computations. The approach we have taken usually results in simpler code, while still yielding a good design. Often, deciding between structuring guidelines may involve a trade-off between better structure and better code. In all but the rarest of cases, better structure should take priority over ease of coding.

Developing the Lower Levels. Having defined the second-level modules, we can continue our functional decomposition. The module, "Print Inventory Item," can be subdivided into four simpler functions: reading the individual inventory record, determining the item's status, maintaining inventory totals, and printing the data associated with the item. These modules are sketched and named in Figure 2.5, thereby adding a third level to the hierarchy chart and providing even more detail. "Read Inventory Record" describes the task of obtaining the inventory record from the file of records. "Determine Item Status" describes the task of determining whether an item order is overdue or if the item requires reordering. "Maintain Inventory Totals" keeps the running totals that are to be printed at the end of the report and "Print Single Item" describes the task of transferring a single item's information to the printer.

Figure 2.5   *Inventory Status Hierarchy Chart, Levels 1–3*

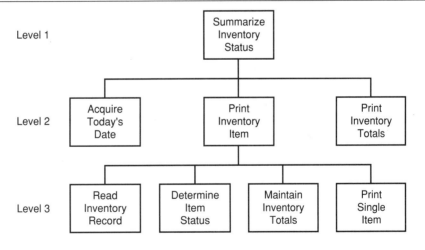

Further decomposition of the module "Determine Item Status" yields two subordinate modules, each of which performs one task: testing the reorder point and checking for past due orders. We sketch the modules "Check Reorder Point" and "Check Past Due Orders" as a fourth level of decomposition as shown in Figure 2.6. At this time it seems that further segmentation might be redundant so we stop. Suppose, however, that the programmer has been given more detailed program specifications requiring that headings be printed at the top of each page of the report. He would need to modify the hierarchy chart to incorporate this function. He could, for instance, divide the module "Print Single Item" into two subordinate modules named "Print Page Headings" and "Print Single Inventory Item" to control the printing of the headings and the individual item data, respectively.

Figure 2.6   *Complete Inventory Status Hierarchy Chart*

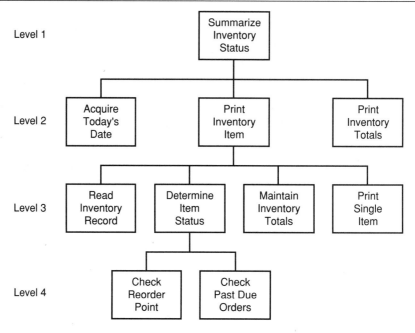

The segmentation process should continue until the program has been defined into its component functions to such a level that it is understandable and clear. If the designer is overzealous, the segmentation can be carried to extremes, resulting in modules of one line of code. Moderation is a good rule to follow. Segment the problem until it is understandable and its modules perform well-defined functions.

As design progresses from one level to the next, the flow of control passes to lower levels but it always returns to the next higher level. In Figure 2.6, the module "Summarize Inventory Status" passes control to "Print Inventory Item," which passes control either to one of its own subordinates or back to its immediate superior. A module may not pass control to its peers or to the subordinates of other modules. In Figure 2.6, "Acquire Today's Date" could not pass control to "Print Inventory Item" or "Print Single Item," for example.

Large hierarchy charts may extend to multiple pages. When this occurs, place the first and second levels of the hierarchy chart on the first page and each second-level module along with its subordinate modules on a separate page. Figure 2.7 illustrates a multiple-page hierarchy chart. Most organizations and instructors have definite notational standards, but some leave it up to the individual designer. No matter what standards you use, apply them consistently.

Figure 2.7   ***Interpage Hierarchy Chart with Duplicate Modules***

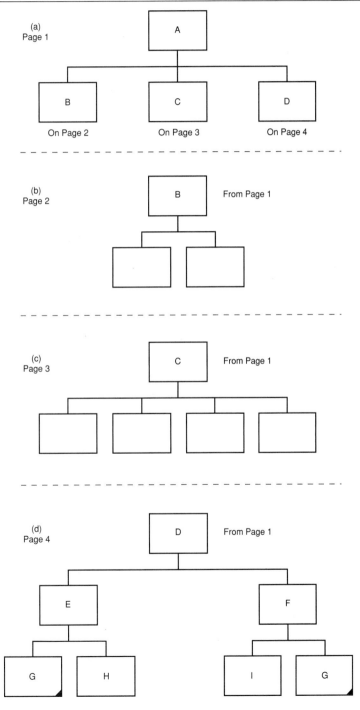

Hierarchy charts of programs in which the same function is performed under the control of different superiors result in duplicate modules. These are called common modules and are denoted by shading the lower right corner of the rectangles representing them as illustrated in Figure 2.7d. An advantage of signifying common modules is that if a module has subordinate detail, that detail need only be sketched once in the hierarchy chart.

2.1.3   *Evaluating the Hierarchy Chart*

Once the program structure has been completed, it is ready for review. Whether the review involves presenting your design to a manager, programming team, or user, the guidelines for reviewing the hierarchy chart are essentially restatements of the design guidelines. They are directed at analyzing whether a program design is sound. The following is a set of criteria for evaluating the quality of your design.

Understandability. The name of a module should be descriptive and should summarize the function it performs. Are the words in the module name used in a clear manner? For example, does one module "Compute Federal Withholdings" and another "Read Inventory Record"? Are the hierarchy chart levels distinguishable? Are common modules shaded? Is it easy to follow the hierarchy chart from one page to another? In essence, could another programmer, your manager, or the user follow your design?

Span of Control. One criterion for determining possible design problems involves the number of subordinates controlled by a module or its *span of control*. The number of subordinate modules should be small. This does not mean that larger spans of control might not be warranted. However, it does send a signal that functional decomposition should be reviewed. Conversely, a span of control of one might indicate an overzealous decomposition, with the subordinate module performing the same function as its boss, as illustrated in Figure 2.8. A good rule of thumb is to allow approximately two to seven subordinates for a module. The number of subordinates may be reduced by dividing the controlling module or by combining subordinate modules, as shown in Figure 2.9. It may be increased by further functional decomposition.

Figure 2.8   *Redundant Decomposition*

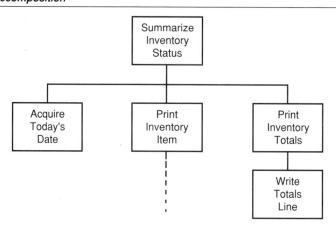

Figure 2.9   ***Reducing the Number of Subordinate Modules***

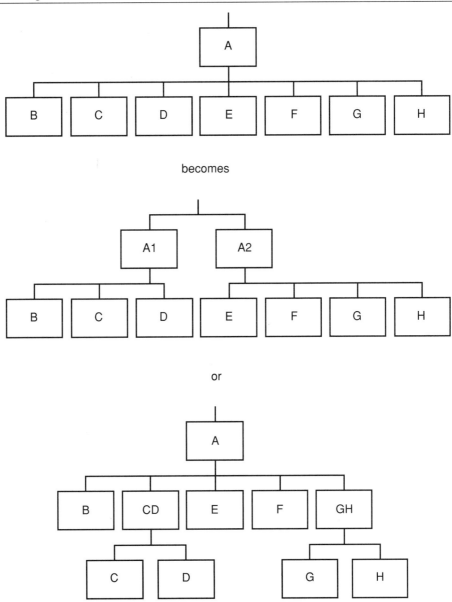

Component Size. Module size is a function of the number of lines of code. Although a module may be conceptually simple, it may require many instructions. According to structured programming guidelines, a module usually should have less than 50 COBOL statements to remain manageable. Unfortunately, there is no magic formula for predicting the number of statements needed to code the function of a given module. Therefore, it may be necessary to revise a hierarchy chart during the coding process. It is also desirable to have separate modules containing the input or output statements for accessing a file. These will appear as common modules in the hierarchy chart.

Flow of Control. To maintain proper flow of control, control must flow from the higher levels to the lower levels and return to the next higher level. This should be reflected by the placement of the modules on the hierarchy chart. For example, Figure 2.10 is a hierarchy chart of "Summarize Inventory Status" of Figure 2.6, but the modules have been rearranged so that the subordination of modules is incorrect. The figure illustrates a problem with the flow of control. The module "Determine Item Status" appears as a second-level module. Since control passes from the first-level modules to the second-level modules, the item status information that is printed in the module "Print Single Item" will not be available until after "Print Single Item" has been performed. Design problems involving flow of control are often hard to spot. One of the simplest ways to verify that the flow of control in a hierarchy chart is accurate is to examine each module and ask whether the information required to perform its function is available from its superior or from its subordinate modules. If not, there is an error in the design.

Figure 2.10   Design Flaws in Inventory Status Hierarchy Chart

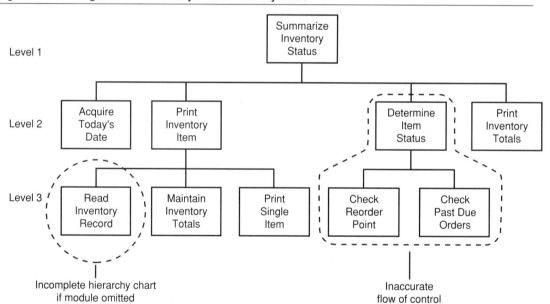

Completeness. *Completeness* ensures that all the tasks required to perform the program requirements are accounted for. Progressing level by level and starting at the top, ask whether the current module's immediate subordinates define all the tasks required by it. If not, the hierarchy chart is incomplete. For example, if the module "Read Inventory Record" were not included on the flowchart in Figure 2.10, the module "Print Inventory Item" would not have the information required to perform its function of printing an inventory item. The hierarchy chart would therefore be incomplete.

Data Hiding. *Data hiding* measures the independence of modules. Each module should work apart from the other modules without allowing them to see the data being acted upon. Thus the modules hide their data. Modules will exhibit a high degree of independence if the amount of data transferred between them is minimized because their functions will not be dependent on data from other modules. This independence allows a programmer to concentrate on a single module without worrying about what functions the other modules are performing. It also reduces the amount of effort needed for testing, debugging, and maintenance. By isolating the functions of a program into independent modules, the program performs in a manner analogous to the components in an automobile.

Although it is impossible to structure a program in which modules are completely independent from each other, whatever data are required by a module should be provided by one of its subordinates or its superior. Figure 2.11 shows two hierarchy charts exhibiting different degrees of data hiding. Figure 2.11a shows the module "Print Error Message" as a subordinate of module "Edit Inventory Record." However, an error message to be printed by "Print Error Message" can be generated by either module "Edit Type 1 Record" or module "Edit Type 2 Record" so that when "Print Error Message" is performed it may not necessarily print all appropriate messages. Furthermore, data are being provided by a peer module. Figure 2.11b corrects this problem by segmenting each edit module into a test module and an error message printing module. "Print Error Message" is now subordinate to the edit modules, and the appropriate error message will be generated by its direct superior.

Figure 2.11   *Data Hiding*

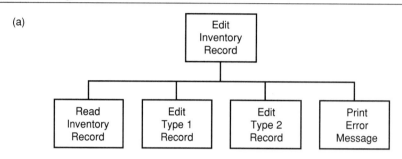

(a)

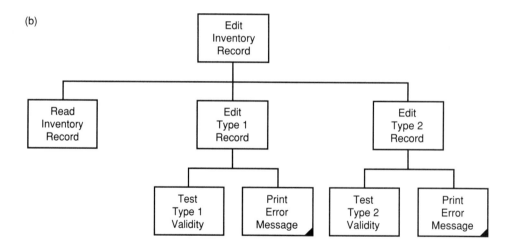

(b)

Functionality. Effective top-down program design yields modules that perform only one function. This *functionality* leads to clarity in design and ease of maintenance. By indicating one module for each task, a module can be developed and coded separately from all other tasks. In addition, if a certain function in the program is incorrect, the programmer can identify the source of the error by examining the particular module performing the function in error. If more than one function appears in a module, the designer is in effect hiding the functionality of each task. Data should be hidden, but tasks should not.

Each module in the hierarchy chart of Figure 2.6 depicts a single function to be performed and reflects the functionality in its module name. If a module name contains two subjects or two verbs, it is usually a telltale sign that the module does not perform a single function and should be further partitioned. For example, if the module "Determine Item Status" in Figure 2.6 were named "Check Reorder Point and Past Due Orders" and it had no subordinates, the name would indicate that the module performed multiple functions. By examining the module names, the programmer can estimate the singleness of functionality of each module.

Once you have reviewed the hierarchy chart and made any necessary modifications you are ready to specify the program logic needed to round out your design. This step is known as *detailed program design.*

2.2   *Developing the Detailed Program Design*

Recall that at the end of the design phase we should be able to code and test the plan we have developed. However, the hierarchy chart provides only the overall structure of the program. In order to fill in the detail needed to actually write the code, the modules in the hierarchy chart must be transformed into logic specifications. Several tools exist for this purpose, among them the flowchart, Nassi-Schneiderman charts, and structured English. We will concentrate on Nassi-Schneiderman (N-S) charts to specify program logic because of their graphical nature and because they restrict program logic to specific elemental structures. First, however, we review the other approaches which will be used to supplement N-S charts in certain examples.

2.2.1   *The Flowchart as a Design Tool*

A *flowchart* provides a representation of the program solution by graphically illustrating the sequence of steps necessary to accomplish a task. These steps are denoted by special flowcharting symbols that are connected by arrows indicating the direction of flow of logic. The meanings of these symbols, also known as "blocks," are shown in Appendix A.

The flowchart in Figure 2.12 represents a simplified process to compute social security taxes. A flowchart is read from top to bottom following the direction of flow. A terminal symbol (a) indicates the beginning of the program. Notice that we have inserted the name of the task in the symbol. Next an I/O symbol (b) indicates that the gross pay amount is input from an external source. A second I/O symbol (c) indicates that the year-to-date salary is to be input. A decision symbol (d) indicates that the path to follow depends on whether or not the maximum annual social security tax has been deducted. Since there are two possible outcomes, there are two possible paths that can be followed. If the condition is **TRUE**, the **TRUE** branch is followed. Then another I/O symbol (e) indicates that the program should write a message stating that no tax is due this period. If the condition is **FALSE**, the **FALSE** branch is followed. A process box (f) states that the necessary computations for determining the social security tax need to be made, and an I/O box (g) indicates that the social security tax due is to be written to an output file. A connector (h) merges the two branches of logic. From now on they will follow the same logic flow. Finally, a terminal symbol (i) indicates the logical end of the task.

Figure 2.12   **Flowchart for Determining Social Security Taxes**

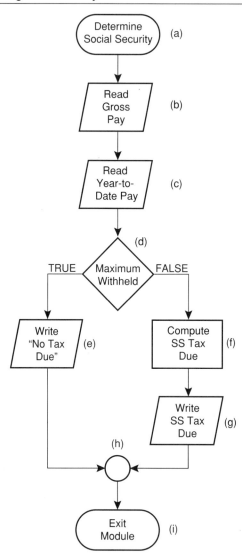

2.2.2   *Structured English as a Design Tool*

Flowcharts require careful construction and much space. A more compact form for defining procedural logic is structured English, often called "pseudocode" because of its similarity to some programming languages. *Structured English* uses narrative notation to represent the flow of operations in a program. There is no universal standard for writing structured English. Therefore, its detail depends on the individual programmer's style. For example, the flowchart example in Figure 2.12 might appear in structured English as follows:

```
DETERMINE-SOCIAL-SECURITY:
        READ GROSS-PAY;
        READ YEAR-TO-DATE-PAY;
        IF maximum amount is withheld THEN
                WRITE "no tax due" message;
        ELSE
                COMPUTE SS-TAX-DUE;
                WRITE SS-TAX-DUE;
        END-IF;
EXIT DETERMINE-SOCIAL-SECURITY.
```

A diagram tool such as a flowchart or Nassi-Schneiderman chart reveals the logic structure of a program more clearly than structured English; however, structured English can clarify an algorithm. In this book, Nassi-Schneiderman charts, defined in the following section, will be used as the main logic documentation technique, but will be supplemented by structured English and flowcharts when complex algorithms are used.

2.2.3   Nassi-Schneiderman Charts

Flowcharts have the major advantage of being graphical depictions of the logic associated with a program. However, they often inspire poor design because they do not place restrictions on the flow of logic and can lead to unstructured designs and code. With this design criticism in mind, *Nassi-Schneiderman charts* (N-S charts) were designed to replace traditional flowcharts with a charting method that allows a more structured view of the flow of logic.

Figure 2.13 shows an N-S chart for the logic in Figure 2.12. The N-S chart is a box, intended to represent a single page, showing the program logic of a single module. It is read from the top down to determine sequence. Different courses of action for decisions are shown by different columns under a triangle. Other notations will be introduced in the following section.

Figure 2.13   Nassi-Schneiderman Chart for Determining Social Security Taxes

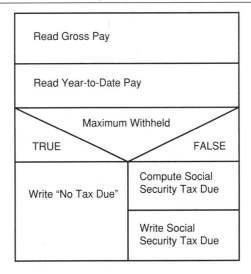

2.2.4   *Basic Design Constructs*

To develop understandable and reliable program logic, structured programming limits the number of building blocks a programmer may use. These building blocks are concerned with the control logic of a program and are commonly known as *control structures* or *constructs*. The limitation on the number of constructs encourages programming discipline, promotes simplicity, and speeds coding, debugging, and maintenance. With fewer control structures, programs have fewer possibilities for error and programmer productivity is increased.

The allowable control structures are the *sequence, selection*, and *iteration* constructs. These are illustrated in Figure 2.14 with N-S charts and structured English. The sequence control structure depicts actions that are to be executed in order of occurrence. For example, if you want to go swimming, you may put on your swimsuit, put on your goggles, and jump into the pool. These actions are executed in a certain order. The selection structure allows a choice between two courses of action based on the outcome of a specific condition. For example, in choosing whether to go for a bike ride or to play racquetball, your deciding factor might be the weather. The iteration construct allows cycling through a course of action until some condition is met. For example, you might continue to swim laps until the pool closes. All program logic may be designed and implemented using these three control structures and combinations of the three.

To maintain logical independence, each construct may have only one entry point and one exit point. Furthermore, the combination of constructs must follow the single entry/single exit rule. With this restriction the logic for each module can be specified without affecting the logic in another module. Since the modules will be logically independent, large programs can be divided and coded by more than one programmer.

Using the three primitive control structures and following the single entry/single exit rule ensures that program control will flow as indicated in the hierarchy chart: from the top to the bottom and back up. Each module in the hierarchy chart will have a separate logical design composed of a combination of the three control structures. Control will flow from the beginning to the end of the program with no skipping around or backtracking. In this way the complexity of the program logic is controlled just as the complexity of the program structure was controlled through segmentation.

The Sequence Construct. The concept of sequence, or the execution of one task after another, is integral to structured design. Many functions in the business world require that a series of uninterrupted steps be performed in a specified order. Figure 2.14a illustrates the sequence structure as a series of actions in the N-S chart and a series of flowchart symbols connected without any decision symbols between them. Figure 2.15 shows the charts of a sequential process that computes the total bill for birdseed at a retail outlet. The first step determines the quantity of birdseed bought by a customer, the next step calculates the total amount of the purchase, the third step calculates the sales tax, and the fourth step determines the amount to be collected from the customer.

Figure 2.14 **The Sequence, Selection, and Iteration Constructs**

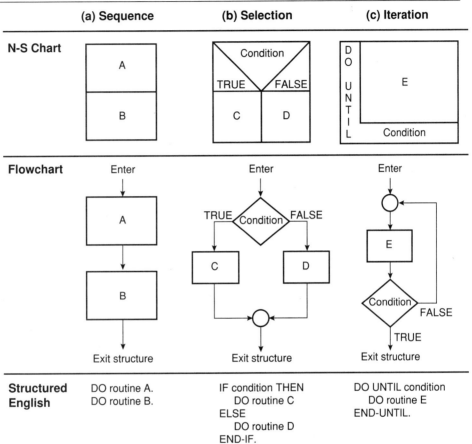

	(a) Sequence	**(b) Selection**	**(c) Iteration**
N-S Chart	A / B	Condition / TRUE / FALSE / C / D	DO UNTIL / E / Condition
Flowchart	Enter → A → B → Exit structure	Enter → TRUE Condition FALSE → C / D → Exit structure	Enter → E → Condition FALSE / TRUE → Exit structure

Structured English	DO routine A.
	 DO routine B.
		IF condition THEN
		     DO routine C
		 ELSE
		     DO routine D
		 END-IF.
			DO UNTIL condition
			     DO routine E
			 END-UNTIL.

Figure 2.15 **Charts of a Sequential Structure to Determine Total Amount Due**

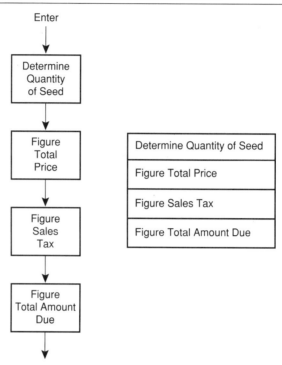

The sequence structure is the most elementary of the three control structures because it has no variations. Most computational, input, and output tasks are represented in sequence form. Many modules in the lower levels of a hierarchy chart often represent sequences of tasks. In the hierarchy chart shown in Figure 2.16, examine the modules that have no subordinates. "Initialize Payroll Totals" involves setting many variables to their starting values in a sequential fashion. "Print Payroll Summary" is a sequence construct that formats the print lines and sends the information to the printer. The module "Get Employee Record" reads in the information from the input device and saves the data in memory.

Figure 2.16   Hierarchy Chart for Payroll Program

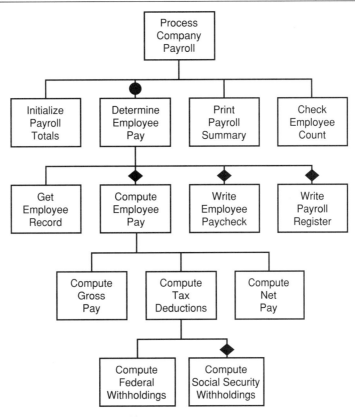

The Selection Construct. It is often necessary to vary the sequence of tasks within a program to handle the different situations that arise. The selection structure makes it possible to select one of two courses of action based on the results of testing a condition. The selection construct in Figure 2.14b shows the condition as a decision block and the two courses of action as processes C and D. If the condition is TRUE, the branch containing process C is selected; if the condition is FALSE, the branch with process D is selected. Only two courses of action may be specified in the selection structure. Once either branch is traversed, control returns to a common point, denoted by a connector symbol in the flowchart and a bottom bar in the N-S charts, before exiting the construct.

Assume that in the example of the company selling birdseed, different pricing structures apply to retail and wholesale customers. Figure 2.17 illustrates that the customer bill computation is different for each type of customer. If the customer purchases birdseed for noncommercial purposes, he is billed at the retail rate and tax must be charged on the sale. If the customer qualifies as a wholesaler, he gets a 10 percent discount and no tax is charged. After the computation of the total costs by one or the other branch of logic, control leaves the selection structure at one exit point and flows to the next process, which computes the amount due.

Figure 2.17   Charts of a Selection Process for Determining the Total Amount Due

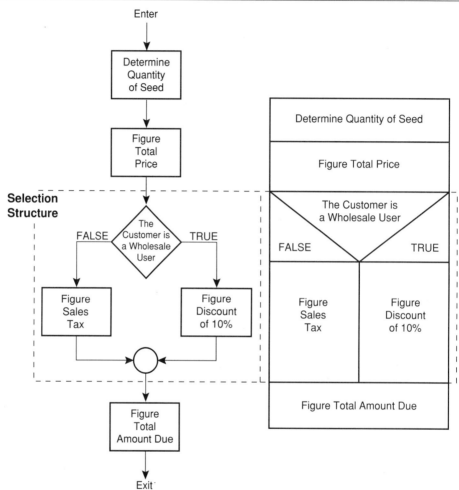

It is possible that one of the actions following a condition will be null. In this case, control passes to the single exit point of the selection construct. In the example of the birdseed company, assume that, owing to a revision in state law, the company must now charge tax to all customers. The charts in Figure 2.18 reflect this change. Notice that an action (10 percent discount) is required only if the condition is TRUE. If it is FALSE, control merely passes to the next activity, the computation of the tax. Notice that the N-S chart has a hyphen to denote that no action is taken. Similarly, one could use the word "null" to indicate a null path, or simply leave the box blank.

Figure 2.18   *Selection Structure with Null Path for Determination of Total Amount Due*

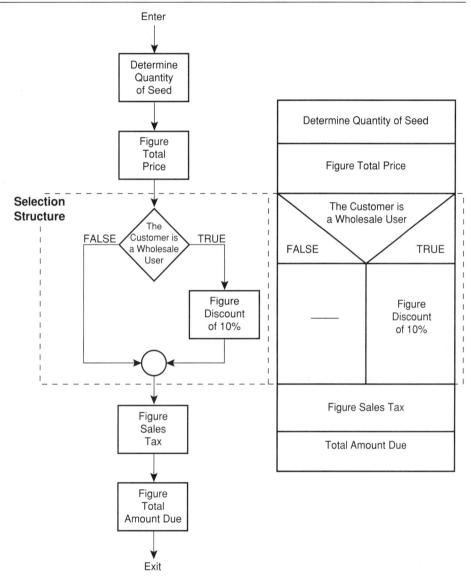

Several modules in the hierarchy chart in Figure 2.16 involve the use of the selection construct. In the module "Check Employee Count" we must determine whether the number of paychecks produced matches the number of employees. The selection construct for this module is illustrated in Figure 2.19. Based on the result of the comparison, the appropriate message is displayed. The selection construct would also be used in "Compute Tax Deductions" to determine whether module "Compute Social Security Withholdings" should be executed. The condition would be whether the maximum annual amount of social security tax had already been withheld.

Figure 2.19   A Selection Structure in the Payroll Program

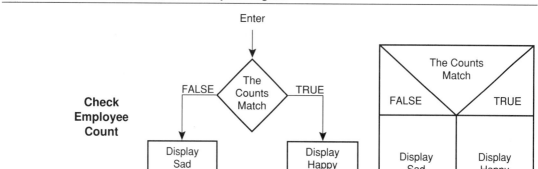

A condition should be stated so that it can be evaluated as either TRUE or FALSE. Even mathematical comparisons can be worded as TRUE/FALSE conditions. In Figure 2.19 the condition is phrased so that it can be answered with a TRUE or FALSE response rather than as a question requiring a yes/no or equal/not-equal answer. TRUE/FALSE responses ensure that the selection construct is well designed by limiting to two the number of actions that may be taken.

It is possible to vary and augment the basic selection process by combining it with the other basic constructs as long as there are only two outcomes for each condition and the single entry/single exit rule is not violated. Figure 2.20a illustrates an example in which the action specified for a true condition is a simple sequence construct. Figure 2.20b shows that the outcome of a condition may be another selection construct. Other combinations of sequence and selection control structures are illustrated in Figure 2.20c and 2.20d.

Here we will introduce a minor variation on the hierarchy chart that helps simplify the design of the program logic. It involves adding a distinguishing mark above a module on the hierarchy chart to identify the logical construct that controls it. In Figure 2.16 we use a solid decision block above the module "Compute Employee Pay" to indicate that a selection construct describes the control logic needed to perform it.

The Iteration Construct. The third control structure for representing program logic is the iteration construct. It provides the means for representing repetitions of certain logic or *loops*. When we developed the second level of the example hierarchy chart in Figure 2.6, one of the guidelines we used was to identify the primary function to be done repeatedly. We use the iteration construct to represent this function because the same program logic is to be repeated. A basic iteration construct is depicted in Figure 2.14c.

Figure 2.20   *Various Selection Structures*

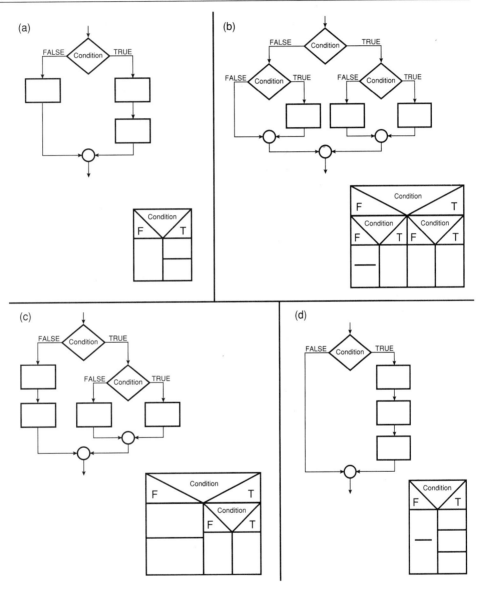

Some variation on the iteration structure may be necessary to control the repetition of the logic. For example, it might be necessary to repeat the logic *until* a condition is true. This variation would be appropriate for a situation in which a program accepts input from a user until the user provides a valid entry. This variation of the iteration structure is called the *DO UNTIL* construct.

Its charts are shown in Figure 2.21a. In other situations it might be more appropriate to repeat certain steps as long as a specific condition exists. For example, in preparing a manual payroll the clerk would have to stay as long as there are still checks to be written. In other words, while there are still checks to write, the clerk cannot leave. This variation of the iteration is known as the *DO WHILE* construct. Its charts are shown in Figure 2.21b. The difference may seem subtle, but comparing the two flowcharts should clarify it. In the DO UNTIL, the iterative process is performed at least once before the condition is tested. But when the condition is met the process ceases to be performed. In the DO WHILE the condition is tested *before* any processing is attempted, thereby allowing the process to be bypassed. Furthermore, the DO UNTIL construct exits when the condition is TRUE; the DO WHILE exits when the condition is FALSE. Figure 2.21 also shows the notational differences between DO WHILEs and DO UNTILs for N-S charts. (The use of the words "do until" and "do while" in the notation are not common practice and will be used only in this chapter to accustom the reader to the different notations.)

Figure 2.21   *Variations of the Iteration Structure*

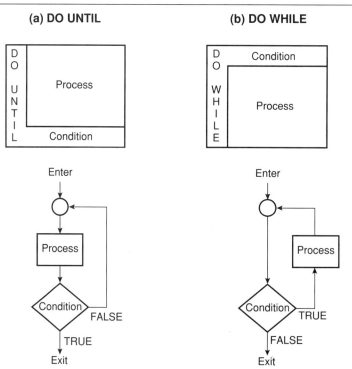

(a) DO UNTIL   ### (b) DO WHILE

Assuming that in the example of the birdseed company there may be multiple customers waiting to pay, the DO WHILE iteration construct is the appropriate one for determining the dollar amount due. The charts in Figure 2.22 show that the condition is first tested to determine whether or not to perform the tasks. As long as there is a customer waiting to pay, the cashier at the birdseed company has to compute the amount owed by the customer. When there are no longer any customers waiting to pay, the cashier may perform other tasks; he may "leave" the construct. If no customer ever buys anything at the birdseed company, the cashier will never need to determine the amount owed. Figure 2.23 shows that the DO UNTIL is improper in this situation, since it would result in an error if no customer was waiting to pay.

Figure 2.22   *An Iteration Structure for Determining the Total Amount Due*

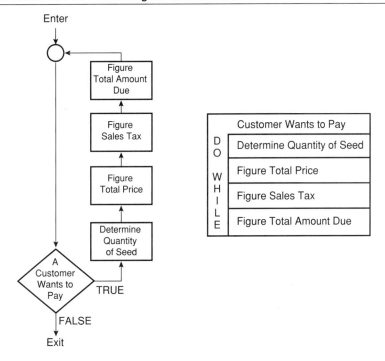

Figure 2.23   *Improper Use of the DO UNTIL*

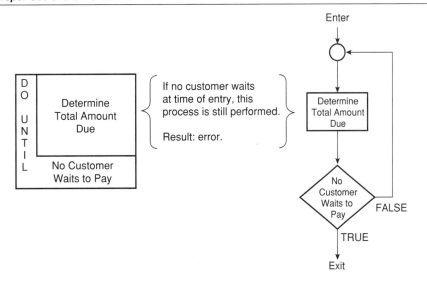

The distinction between the DO WHILE and the DO UNTIL constructs becomes important when the execution of the tasks in the iteration is based on the presence of a predetermined condition. For example, assume we are writing a program in which a player tries to guess the number between 1 and 10 that the computer has randomly generated. If the player guesses correctly, the game ends; otherwise the player must enter another guess. The simpler iteration construct for this game would be the DO UNTIL, since the player has to enter at least one guess before the game can end. Suppose, however, that we use the DO WHILE structure to represent this game. It would be necessary to set the condition variable (guess) to a value other than 1 through 10 before entering the DO WHILE construct. This way the termination condition would be properly initialized for the first pass through the iteration. Figure 2.24a illustrates the proper charts for implementing the game with a DO WHILE construct. If the initialization is ignored as in Figure 2.24b, it could end the game prematurely if the existing value of the variable happened to meet the condition. It could also cause unpredictable results if the test variable contained garbage. The possibility of such errors must be taken into account when designing programs.

Figure 2.24c implements the program with a DO UNTIL construct. Notice that in contrast to Figure 2.24a fewer chart symbols were required to perform the same job. This results in a program that is shorter, simpler, and easier to maintain.

In the hierarchy chart of the payroll program in Figure 2.16 the repetitive program logic is controlled by an iteration construct. This is depicted by a filled-in circle above module "Determine Employee Pay." The variation of the iteration construct in this case is the DO UNTIL. The charts for the module "Process Company Payroll" are illustrated in Figure 2.25. Recall that only the "Determine Employee Pay" module requires repetition, since the pay must be calculated for every employee. The iteration will be performed until there are no more employees needing to be paid.

Sequence and selection constructs may be combined with iteration constructs to describe processes adequately. Well-developed hierarchy charts result in associated logic charts that are composed only of sequence, selection, and iteration constructs. Although the number of combinations of constructs is unlimited, it is best to keep the structures simple.

Figure 2.24   *Using the DO WHILE Structure to Design a DO UNTIL*

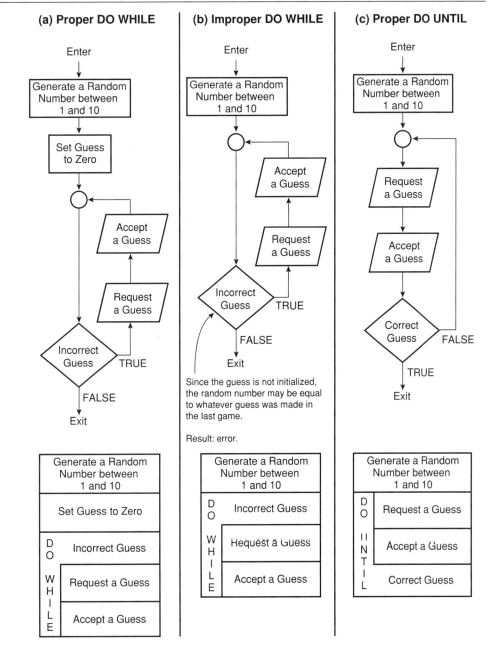

Figure 2.25   *Charts for the Module "Process Company Payroll"*

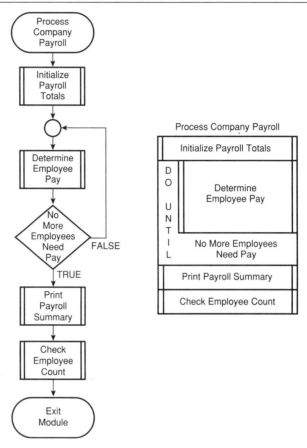

2.2.5   *Developing N-S Charts from the Hierarchy Chart*

To design the program logic, you must develop an N-S chart (or flowchart) for the hierarchy chart with the help of the program specifications. The first step is to number each module on the hierarchy chart. The numbering plan should retain the hierarchical relationship of the modules. A common numbering technique is to leave the top module unnumbered, then begin assigning the second-level modules of the hierarchy chart numbers in increments of 1000. Each second-level module's subordinates are then numbered in increments of 100 within the thousands designation of their immediate superior. Thus, the subordinates of module 2000 would be labeled 2100, 2200, and so on. The fourth-level subordinate modules in the hierarchy chart are numbered by tens within the hundreds designation of their immediate superior, and the fifth-level subordinate modules are numbered by ones within the tens designation of their immediate superior. If there are more than five levels in the hierarchy chart, begin numbering the second level modules in increments of ten thousands, or begin assigning letters to the numbers at the lower levels to differentiate them. If there are very few levels in the hierarchy chart, begin numbering the high-level modules with smaller numbers. If a module appears in more than one place in the hierarchy chart, assign it only one number, preferable at the first occurrence of the module, and use that number throughout. Figure 2.26 shows the numbered hierarchy chart for the payroll problem.

Figure 2.26   Module Numbering Scheme for the Payroll Program

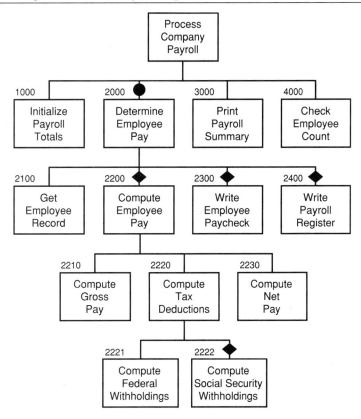

The module number becomes part of the name of the module. This implies that the complete module name is used in the N-S charts. For example, the module "Compute Employee Pay" in Figure 2.26 becomes "2200 Compute Employee Pay" in the program documentation and in the code. This allows for easy cross referencing.

The next step is to develop the N-S chart for each module. This involves translating a module's subordinates into the appropriate N-S chart symbols and showing the flow of control within the module with combinations of the three basic control structures.

The charts of the superior modules show the way in which they control subordinate modules. In Figure 2.25 the "Process Company Payroll" chart is a combination of sequence constructs that controls modules "Initialize Payroll Totals," "Print Payroll Summary," and "Check Employee Count," and an iteration construct that controls the module "Determine Employee Pay." This corresponds to the construct symbols depicted on the hierarchy chart in

Figure 2.26. Each subordinate module in the flowchart is depicted by a process block with double lines indicating that it is defined elsewhere. Double lines are used only on the N-S charts when module numbers are not yet assigned, as in Figure 2.25.

In developing the charts, draw one chart on a page and follow the numbering sequence of the hierarchy chart. This facilitates locating the chart for a specific module. The N-S charts representing the complete program design for the hierarchy chart in Figure 2.26 are illustrated in Figure 2.27.

Figure 2.27   N-S Charts for the Payroll Program

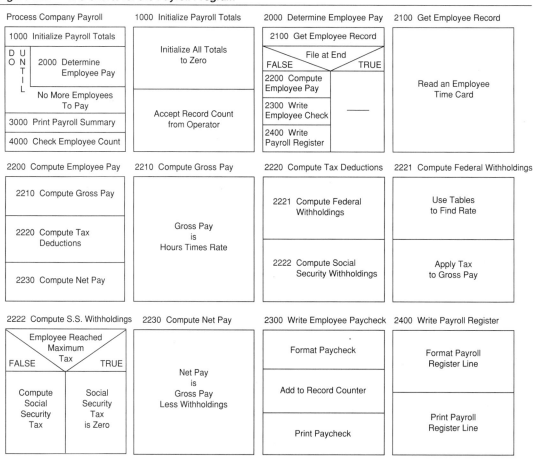

Figure 2.27   *(continued)*

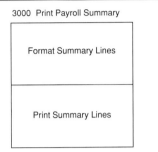

3000 Print Payroll Summary

Format Summary Lines

Print Summary Lines

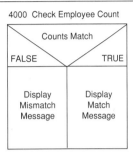

4000 Check Employee Count

Counts Match

FALSE   TRUE

Display
Mismatch
Message

Display
Match
Message

The program structure and the detailed program design for the payroll program are now complete. They are represented by the hierarchy chart and the N-S charts, respectively. Now, all that is needed to code the program are the report and record layouts.

2.3   *Examining the Program Design*

A good programmer carefully examines his design to determine its fitness and accuracy. Flaws in design translate into problematic programs, and the cost of correcting errors rises as the development of the system proceeds to later phases in the life cycle. It is therefore vital that the design be appropriate and correct.

In many business environments it is so important to review an application's design that formal evaluation procedures known as walkthroughs have been instituted. We will discuss these shortly. However, even if no such formal procedures exist, the programmer can take steps in this direction. In fact, it is wise to do so in preparation for a formal walkthrough.

It is probably better to review your design after not looking at it for a day or two; otherwise, you might be too familiar with it to detect any shortcomings. This also helps you to start without preexisting assumptions. Begin by reviewing your hierarchy chart. Does it conform to the criteria listed in the section on evaluating the hierarchy chart? If not, now is the time to revise it. Remember that any changes to the hierarchy chart will also result in changes to the N-S charts.

Once you are satisfied that your program structure is adequate, examine the N-S charts. Verify that the module names correspond to the chart names. Have you accounted for all the modules? Does each chart's logic perform the required tasks? Go through each iteration structure at least three times: the first, last, and "middle" times through it. Verify that a module does not call itself. This situation, known as recursion, is not allowed in COBOL. Figures 2.28a and 2.28b demonstrate how N-S charts can indicate recursion by having a module control its own execution or by controlling the execution of a second module that returns the favor.

Figure 2.28   **Examples of Recursion**

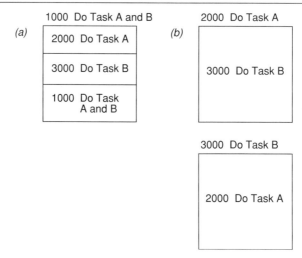

Try to devise "exception" situations and determine how your program is equipped to handle them. For example, does your program allow for faulty data? Does it disallow them? Correct them? Often, with the help of the user, you can identify "exception" situations that "could not possibly happen" and devise alternatives for dealing with them.

Once you have reviewed your own logic you are ready for more formal examinations of your design. A formal method of scrutinizing programs is the *structured walkthrough*. It is a meeting held to discuss a particular system or program in an effort to identify problems. The rationale for structured walkthroughs is that many heads are better than one, like "brainstorming sessions" in the computer room with your fellow students in an effort to find a problem. Unlike these impromptu sessions, structured walkthroughs are formal, well-organized meetings; like them, they involve peer review. The goal of walkthroughs is to find flaws in the program design. Since several programmer-reviewers are involved, flaws are identified more quickly.

Walkthroughs are used to review a project during the various steps of the development process. They may concentrate on program specifications, program design, code, test data, test results, and documentation. In design walkthroughs systems analysts, users, and programmers review the system structure and detect flaws, weaknesses, unclear logic, and omissions.

Case Study: CDL's Categorize Daily Mail

One of the programs Charlene identified for the new system for the CDL company involves editing an input file containing the orders and the payments received by the mail department. Figure 2.29 provides the program requirements, and Figure 2.30 shows the layouts of the input and output files.

Figure 2.29 **Program Specifications for "Catergorize Daily Mail"**

PROGRAM SUMMARY

TITLE: *Categorize Daily Mail*

PREPARED BY: *C. Hilton*

DATE: *6-19-93*

FILES USED

FILE NAME	MEDIA	ORGANIZATION
Payments and Orders	Tape	Sequential
Invalid Payments	Disk	Sequential
Orders	Disk	Sequential
Valid Payments	Disk	Sequential

DESCRIPTION

Customer payments and orders are keyed in by clerks, and a code to distinguish them is automatically attached.

The program must write order records to an order file, and payment records to a valid payments file only if the payment amount is more than $0.00. Otherwise they should be written to an invalid payments file.

Figure 2.30   *CDL's Record Layouts for Orders and Payments*

RECORD LAYOUT SHEET

Record Name: *Order/Payment*		File Name: *Orders and Payments*			
Prepared By: *C. Hilton*		Date: *6-22-93*			
Key Fields:		Organization: *Sequential*			
Field	Description	Type*	Length	Decimal	
Code	*"P" for Payment, "O" for Order*	*A*	*1*		
Amount	*Amount of Payment or Order*	*N*	*8*	*2*	
Customer #	*A unique customer ID*	*N*	*6*	*0*	
Check #	*The check ID*	*A*	*8*		
Compact Disc #	*The CD's stock number*	*N*	*6*	*0*	
Quantity	*The number ordered*	*N*	*2*	*0*	
Order #	*A preprinted number from order form*	*N*	*6*	*0*	

* A = alphanumeric
  N = numeric

RECORD LAYOUT SHEET

Record Name: *Order*		File Name: *Order*			
Prepared By: *C. Hilton*		Date: *6-22-93*			
Key Fields:		Organization: *Sequential*			
Field	Description	Type*	Length	Decimal	
Customer #	*A unique customer ID*	*N*	*6*	*0*	
Compact Disc #	*The stock number for the CD*	*N*	*6*	*0*	
Quantity	*The number ordered*	*N*	*2*	*0*	
Order #	*A preprinted order form number*	*N*	*6*	*0*	

* A = alphanumeric
  N = numeric

Figure 2.30   (continued)

RECORD LAYOUT SHEET

Record Name: *Payments*			File Name: *Valid/Invalid Payments*		
Prepared By: *C. Hilton*			Date: *6-22-93*		
Key Fields:			Organization: *Sequential*		
Field	Description		Type*	Length	Decimal
Customer #	*A unique customer ID*		*N*	*6*	*0*
Payment amount	*$*		*N*	*8*	*2*
Check ID	*The check number*		*A*	*8*	

* A = alphanumeric
  N = numeric

The program should separate new orders from payments and prepare multiple output files for use in later programs. The payments are to be edited and written to one of two output files depending on whether they are valid or invalid. In developing the hierarchy chart, recall that the first-level module designates the program's overall function and its name should reflect that. Therefore it is called "Categorize Daily Mail." To begin our functional decomposition, we first identify the primary function to be done over and over. This is the task of separating the daily mail into orders and payments. Therefore, module "Separate Daily Mail" appears as the second module in the second level of Figure 2.31. Before the primary function can be executed, the program must obtain the first record. Module "Read Mail Record" accomplishes this task and appears as the first module on the second level of the hierarchy chart.

Figure 2.31   *First Two Levels of the Hierarchy Chart for CDL's "Categorize Daily Mail" Program*

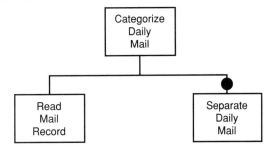

Examination of the module "Separate Daily Mail" reveals that it can be segmented into three submodules. "Edit Daily Payment" examines the items identified as payments, "Write Daily Order" prepares the customer orders for output, and "Read Mail Record" makes the next mail item available. These breakdowns appear as the third level of the hierarchy chart and are illustrated in Figure 2.32.

Figure 2.32   First Three Levels of the Hierarchy Chart for the "Categorize Daily Mail" Program

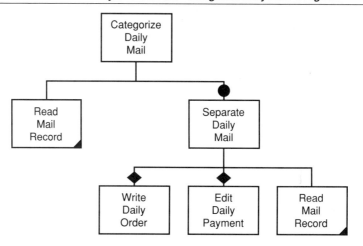

Module "Edit Daily Payment" can be further subdivided into the tasks needed for dealing with the two edit conditions: error detected or no error detected. Thus, the module "Edit Daily Payment" is segmented into the modules "Write Valid Payment" and "Write Invalid Payment." These modules are added and the final hierarchy chart is numbered. This is illustrated in Figure 2.33. The hierarchy chart represents the structure from which the program logic can be designed and coded. Figure 2.34 contains the N-S charts for each module.

Figure 2.33 **Complete Hierarchy Chart for the "Categorize Daily Mail" Program**

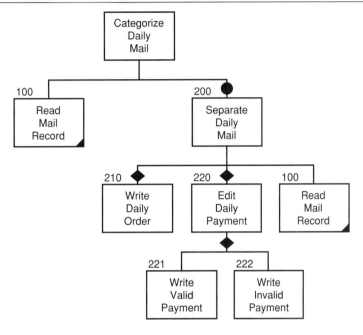

Figure 2.34 **N-S Charts for CDL's "Categorize Daily Mail" Program**

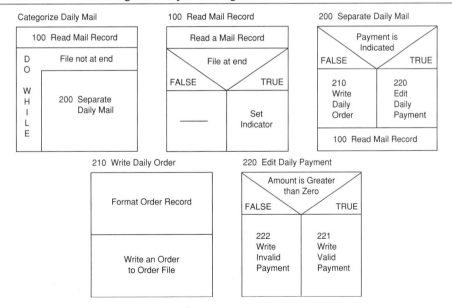

Figure 2.34   *(continued)*

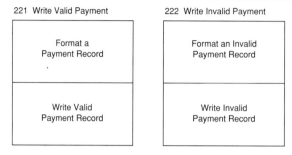

221 Write Valid Payment

Format a Payment Record
Write Valid Payment Record

222 Write Invalid Payment

Format an Invalid Payment Record
Write Invalid Payment Record

Summary

Structured programs are designed and coded using a disciplined, organized approach. Such programs are easier to code, test, and maintain, factors that contribute to increased programmer productivity. The goal of structured design methodologies is twofold: to develop the structure of the program solution and to specify that logic for subsequent coding.

One tool of structured design is the hierarchy chart. The hierarchy chart represents the framework of the program. The program is partitioned into functional modules in a top-down fashion, providing greater detail as one progresses from the higher levels to the lower levels. The hierarchy chart also represents the flow of control in the program. Control passes from superior modules to subordinate modules and returns to superiors. Once the hierarchy chart is complete, it should be evaluated for fitness and accuracy using criteria such as understandability, span of control, component size, flow of control, completeness, data hiding, and functionality.

The detailed design of the program is developed by translating the modules of the hierarchy chart into N-S charts. In the detailed design phase the programmer limits the number of structures used to specify the flow of control to three basic constructs: sequence, selection, and iteration. The sequence structure is used to depict actions to be executed in order of occurrence, the selection structure allows branching based on some condition, and the iteration construct allows the specification of repetitions.

Once the detailed logic is completed, it must be examined to ensure that the N-S charts accomplish their purpose, that they are complete, and that they conform to structured programming principles.

Key Terms

structured programs	completeness	selection
modules	data hiding	iteration
functional decomposition	functionality	DO UNTIL
hierarchy	detailed program design	DO WHILE
hierarchy chart	flowcharts	structured walkthrough
flow of control	structured English	
top-down design	Nassi-Schneiderman charts	
common modules	constructs (control structures)	
span of control	sequence	

Hints for Avoiding Errors

1. Take ample time during each step of the design process. Rushing through one step will lead to multiple errors in the following steps.
2. Select a notation to use in your logical design documentation and use it consistently to prevent confusion.
3. Develop several designs for a program and evaluate the merits of each. This decreases the need for later revisions.

Exercises

2.1   Develop a hierarchy chart describing the coursework requirements for a degree in your
       academic major.

2.2   Develop a hierarchy chart for the program specification in Figure 2.35.

Figure 2.35   **Program Specifications for Exercise 2.2**

PROGRAM SUMMARY

TITLE: *Summarize Payroll*

PREPARED BY: *Rookie Programmer*

DATE: *6-19-93*

FILES USED

FILE NAME	MEDIA	ORGANIZATION
Payroll File	*Disk*	*Sequential*

DESCRIPTION

Produce a report for the payroll dept. that summarizes yearly earnings, hours worked for the year for each active employee of the company, and salary statistics on programmers as a group. At the end of the report display the number of active employees on the payroll file, their average yearly earnings, the total number of active programmers, and the highest, lowest, and average yearly salary of active programmers.

Hourly and salaried employees are differentiated by a "pay indicator" code which indicates whether the employee's pay is a yearly salary or the hourly pay rate. The yearly earnings of hourly workers need to be computed.

Employees work 50-week years.

The letters "PG" are the first two characters of the "job code" for programmers.

Zero ("0") is the "status" code for inactive employees.

2.3 Complete the design specifications for the program described in Figure 2.3 by developing the N-S charts.

2.4 In a hierarchy chart the flow of control from one module to another is in the following sequence: inferior modules to superior modules to low-level modules and then back to the next inferior module. True or false?

2.5 The goal of structured design methodologies is to develop the _____ and specify the _____ of the program.
  a. logic charts, files
  b. content, length
  c. hierarchy, modules
  d. structure, logic

2.6 A condition is tested *before* the iteration process is performed in the:
  a. DO WHILE construct.
  b. DO UNTIL construct.
  c. DO AFTER construct.

2.7 Bottom-up design is an inherent part of structured programming. True or false?

2.8 Nested logic structures are illegal in structured programming and should be avoided at all costs. True or false?

2.9 The _____ rule restricts a module's structure so that it does not affect the logic in another module.
  a. multi entry/multi exit
  b. multi entry/single exit
  c. single entry/multi exit
  d. single entry/single exit

2.10 What tools use the hierarchy chart as a guide in developing the logic specifications for a program?
  a. Nassi-Schneiderman diagrams
  b. pseudocode
  c. flowcharts
  d. Warnier-Orr diagrams
  e. B and C
  f. A and C
  g. all of the above

2.11 In the detailed program design a programmer should not generate flowcharts from the hierarchy chart because of the possibility of future changes, but should create them from scratch using previous experience. True or False?

2.12 What are the proper steps a programmer should take in evaluating a program design?
  a. Match hierarchy and flowcharts, walkthrough, relax.
  b. Sort flowcharts, fine-tune hierarchy, allow break period, revise, walkthrough.
  c. Walkthrough, revise, examine flowcharts, review hierarchy.
  d. Allow break period, review hierarchy, examine flowcharts, walkthrough.
  e. Allow break period, walkthrough, review hierarchy, allow break period, examine flowcharts.

2.13   The hierarchy chart also represents the _____ of _____ in a program.
- a. framework, items
- b. physical requirements, logic
- c. flow, control
- d. flow, data

2.14   The three basic design constructs are:
- a. _____
- b. _____
- c. _____

2.15   _____, a measure of module independence, involves modules working separately and apart from each other.

2.16   According to structured programming, a module should usually be less than _____ COBOL statements in length in order to remain manageable.

2.17   An advantage of _____ is that if a module has subordinate detail, that detail need only be sketched once in the hierarchy chart.

2.18   The _____ structure allows branching based on some condition.

2.19   Draw an N-S chart for any module so that it exhibits all three design constructs.

2.20   Why should a programmer spend time devising "exception" conditions to predetermine a program's operating results?

2.21   Explain the importance of modularity from a programmer's point of view.

THE STRUCTURE
OF COBOL

Programming languages consist of elements that are related to each other in an organized pattern, and COBOL is no exception. You must understand the structure of COBOL before you can code COBOL programs. This chapter presents a complete picture of the COBOL language by providing a few basic rules and a first look at a simple subset of COBOL statements.

3.1   *An ANS COBOL Sample Program*

Figure 3.1 describes a sample program that lists employees who have earned a total wage of more than $75,000 for the year. The program reads the data from a master payroll file and prints the employee data for those who exceed the cutoff amount. Figure 3.2 shows how the data are arranged on the payroll master file. Figure 3.3 shows the format for the report to be output; in the figure the Xs represent character data and the Zs represent numeric data. For simplicity we have eliminated information such as headings and totals from the report.

Figure 3.1   Program Description

PROGRAM SUMMARY
TITLE: *List Excessive Salaries*
PREPARED BY: *J. Joeps*
DATE: *6-15-93*

FILES USED		
FILE NAME	MEDIA	ORGANIZATION
Payroll Master File	*Disk*	*Sequential*
Excessive Salary Listing	*Printer*	*Sequential*

DESCRIPTION

A report is required to discover the highest paid employees. If the total year to date wages (salary plus bonus) is more than $75,000, print the employee's ID number, name, and wages on a listing.

Figure 3.2   Record Layout

RECORD LAYOUT SHEET

Record Name: *Payroll*		File Name: *Payroll Master*		
Prepared By: *J. Joeps*		Date: *6-11-93*		
Key Fields: *Employee - ID-number*		Organization: *Sequential*		
Field	Description	Type*	Length	Decimal
Employee ID	The number uniquely identifying	N	4	0
	each employee			
Name	The name of the employee	A	20	
Address	The street address of the employee	A	20	
City	Employee city of residence	A	13	
State	Employee state of residence	A	2	
Zip code	Employee zip code of residence	N	5	0
SSN	Social security number	N	10	0
Phone	Employee's home phone	N	10	0
Federal tax	Year to date taxes withheld	N	10	2
SS tax	Year to date Social Security paid	N	10	2
Salary	Year to date salary	N	10	2
Bonus	Year to date bonus paid	N	10	2
Monthly	Monthly salary	N	10	2
Department	Employee's department	A	4	

* A = alphanumeric
  N = numeric

3.1.2   The Hierarchy Chart

In Chapter 2 we stressed the importance of program design and introduced the hierarchy chart as one of the design tools we will be using throughout the text. The hierarchy chart for our example program appears in Figure 3.4. The top-level module represents the entire program. The name of the program and the top module is "List Excessive Salaries." It is decomposed into the two modules "Read Payroll Master File" and "Produce Employee Wages." The first of these modules acquires the first record from the master file. The presence or absence of a first record will determine whether the iterative task of the second module needs to be conducted. The occurrence of the single read task before entering the repetitive module in the second level is a common technique known as the prime read. We will discuss the prime read in depth in a later section of this chapter.

Figure 3.3   *Printer Layout*

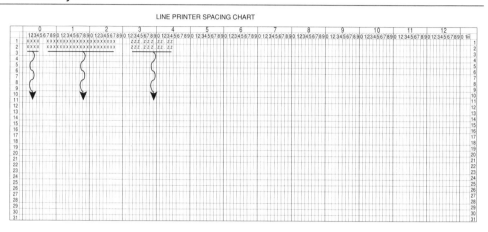

Figure 3.4   *Hierarchy Chart for "List Excessive Salaries" Program*

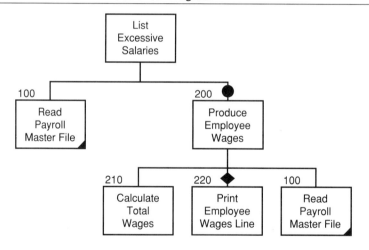

The repetitive module "Produce Employee Wages" is the heart of the design. This module directs the actions of its three subordinate modules, which "Calculate Total Wages" for every employee, "Print Employee Wages Line" based on a selection criterion, and "Read Payroll Master File" to obtain the next payroll record. We now number the modules and proceed to the detailed design phase.

3.1.2   The Logic Charts

Figure 3.5 contains the Nassi-Schneiderman charts and flowcharts corresponding to the "List Excessive Salaries" program hierarchy chart. Recall that the logic charts give a step-by-step account of what is needed to accomplish a module's overall task. The "List Excessive Salaries" module first performs "100-Read-Payroll-Master-File," and then performs "200-Produce-Employee-Wages" while the employee file is not at end. To review, the top module in the program consists of one sequence construct followed by an iteration construct.

Module "200-Produce-Employee-Wages" performs "210-Calculate-Total-Wages," which calculates the total wages earned by an employee followed by a selection structure in which "220-Print-Employee-Wages-Line" is performed based on a comparison between the employee's wages and the constant 75,000. The module "100-Read-Payroll-Master-File" is then performed to obtain the next employee record.

Modules "100-Read-Payroll-Master-File," "210-Calculate-Total-Wages," and "220-Print-Employee-Wages-Line," which are also detailed in Figure 3.5, outline how the logic accomplishes the module's task. Once all modules have been charted the program may be coded.

3.1.3   The COBOL Code

The complete COBOL program is shown in Figure 3.6. As you look through the code, several features and patterns will become evident. We will mention them briefly in the following pages, but the details will be discussed throughout the rest of the book.

Figure 3.5   *N-S Charts and Flowcharts for "List Excessive Salaries" Program*

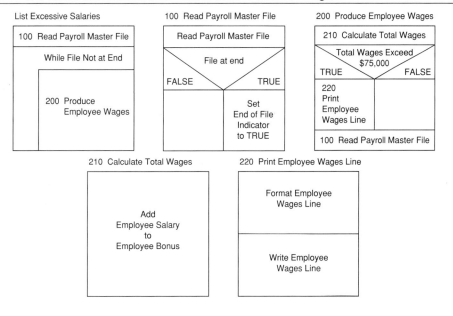

Figure 3.5 (continued)

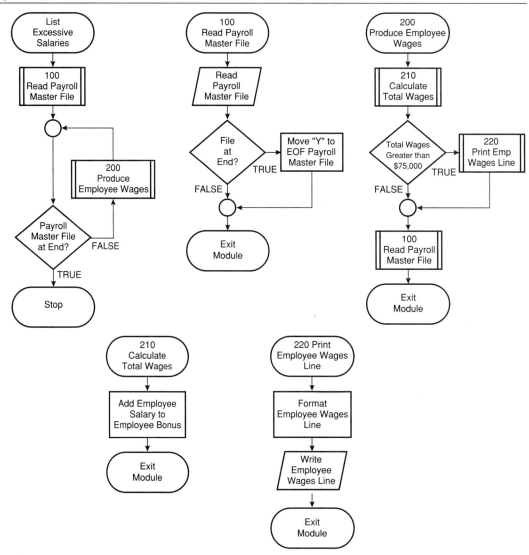

Figure 3.6   "List Excessive Salaries" Listing

```
1 IDENTIFICATION DIVISION.
2
3 PROGRAM-ID. LIST-EXCESS-SALARIES.
4* PRODUCE A LIST OF EMPLOYEES WHOSE
```

Figure 3.6   *(continued)*

```
 5* SALARIES AND BONUS EXCEEDS $75,000
 6 AUTHOR. NEWT JAMES.
 7 INSTALLATION. IRS.
 8 DATE-WRITTEN. JULY 30,1996.
 9 DATE-COMPILED. 14-Jan-90 14:24.
10 SECURITY. CONFIDENTIAL.
11
12
13 ENVIRONMENT DIVISION.
14
15 CONFIGURATION SECTION.
16
17 SOURCE-COMPUTER. GENERIC-COMPUTER.
18 OBJECT-COMPUTER. GENERIC-COMPUTER.
19
20 INPUT-OUTPUT SECTION.
21
22 FILE-CONTROL.
23     SELECT PAYROLL-MASTER-FILE ASSIGN TO S-PAY.
24     SELECT EXCESS-SALARY-LIST-FILE ASSIGN TO PRINTER.
25
26
27 DATA DIVISION.
28
29 FILE SECTION.
30
31 FD  PAYROLL-MASTER-FILE
32     LABEL RECORDS ARE STANDARD.
33
34 01  PAYROLL-REC.
35     05  PMF-EMPLOYEE-ID-NUMBER        PIC 9(4).
36     05  PMF-EMPLOYEE-NAME             PIC X(20).
37     05  FILLER                        PIC X(80).
38     05  PMF-YEAR-TO-DATE-SALARY       PIC 9(8)V99.
39     05  PMF-YEAR-TO-DATE-BONUS        PIC 9(8)V99.
40     05  FILLER                        PIC X(14).
41
42 FD  EXCESS-SALARY-LIST-FILE
43     LABEL RECORDS ARE STANDARD.
44
45 01  EMPLOYEE-WAGES-LINE.
46     05  EWL-EMPLOYEE-ID-NUMBER        PIC 9(4).
47     05  FILLER                        PIC X(4).
```

Figure 3.6   *(continued)*

```
48       05   EWL-EMPLOYEE-NAME              PIC X(20).
49       05   FILLER                         PIC X(4).
50       05   EWL-WAGES                      PIC ZZZ,ZZZ,ZZZ.ZZ.
51
52  WORKING-STORAGE SECTION.
53
54  01   END-OF-FILE-INDICATORS.
55       05   EOF-PAYROLL-MASTER-FILE        PIC X VALUE "N".
56
57  01   TOTAL-FIELD.
58       05   TOT-WAGES                      PIC 9(9)V99.
59
60
61  PROCEDURE DIVISION.
62
63  LIST-EXCESSIVE-SALARIES.
64       OPEN INPUT PAYROLL-MASTER-FILE.
65       OPEN OUTPUT EXCESS-SALARY-LIST-FILE.
66       PERFORM 100-READ-PAYROLL-MASTER-FILE.
67       PERFORM 200-PRODUCE-EMPLOYEE-WAGES
68           UNTIL EOF-PAYROLL-MASTER-FILE = "Y".
69       CLOSE PAYROLL-MASTER-FILE.
70       CLOSE EXCESS-SALARY-LIST-FILE.
71       STOP RUN.
72
73  100-READ-PAYROLL-MASTER-FILE.
74       READ PAYROLL-MASTER-FILE
75           AT END MOVE "Y" TO EOF-PAYROLL-MASTER-FILE.
76
77  200-PRODUCE-EMPLOYEE-WAGES.
78       PERFORM 210-CALCULATE-TOTAL-WAGES.
79       IF TOT-WAGES > 75000.00
80           PERFORM 220-PRINT-EMPLOYEE-WAGES-LINE.
81       PERFORM 100-READ-PAYROLL-MASTER-FILE.
82
83  210-CALCULATE-TOTAL-WAGES.
84       ADD  PMF-YEAR-TO-DATE-SALARY  PMF-YEAR-TO-DATE-BONUS
85           GIVING TOT-WAGES.
86
87  220-PRINT-EMPLOYEE-WAGES-LINE.
88       MOVE SPACES TO EMPLOYEE-WAGES-LINE.
89       MOVE PMF-EMPLOYEE-ID-NUMBER TO
90           EWL-EMPLOYEE-ID-NUMBER.
```

Figure 3.6   *(continued)*

```
91      MOVE PMF-EMPLOYEE-NAME TO EWL-EMPLOYEE-NAME.
92      MOVE TOT-WAGES TO EWL-WAGES.
93      WRITE EMPLOYEE-WAGES-LINE.
```

3.2   *COBOL Syntax*

All programming languages have rules known as language syntax that govern the writing of programs. In writing COBOL code we will use the program documentation to develop syntactically correct programs.

3.2.1   *The Hierarchy of COBOL Syntax*

The COBOL language has a hierarchical structure. In general, a COBOL program is composed of divisions. Divisions are composed of sections, and sections are composed of paragraphs. Paragraphs, in turn, are composed of a series of sentences or entries. Sentences and entries contain statements made up of clauses, which in turn are made up of words. Figure 3.7 illustrates the general hierarchical structure of COBOL syntax.

Each COBOL program is made up of four required divisions. The IDENTIFICATION DIVISION identifies the program; the ENVIRONMENT DIVISION describes the computer configuration; the DATA DIVISION describes the data, files, and temporary work areas being used; and the PROCEDURE DIVISION specifies the instructions for the processing logic. The DIVISIONS occur on lines 1, 13, 27, and 61 of the code in Figure 3.6.

Divisions are made up of sections, but not all divisions require sections. Sections are used whenever the syntax dictates their inclusion, or when the programmer requires them. The FILE SECTION (line 29 of Figure 3.6) describes the program's files. *Paragraphs* represent minor segments of the SECTIONs. Some paragraphs are required in every program; others are developed by the programmer to represent the modules on the hierarchy chart. The paragraph "210-CALCULATE-total wages" appears in the design of Figure 3.5 and the code of Figure 3.6.

As in the English language, COBOL paragraphs are composed of sentences. *Sentences* are sequences of one or more statements ending with a period. Each statement is a syntactically correct combination of words including an action word or verb. COBOL *statements* may be conditional or imperative. In a *conditional* statement the action is taken based on whether some condition is true or false. In an *imperative* statement the action is taken unconditionally. Lines 79 and 80 of the COBOL code of Figure 3.6 are a complete sentence. They are also a single conditional statement in which an action is taken only when the total wages condition is satisfied.

In some instances paragraphs are composed of *entries*, which are conceptually similar to sentences but follow a different grammar. Statements and entries are composed of *clauses*. Clauses are fragments of code that may be combined with other fragments to make up a statement, an entry, or a sentence. Line 85 of Figure 3.6 is a clause indicating where the result of an addition (Line 84) is to be stored.

Figure 3.7   *The Syntax Hierarchy of COBOL*

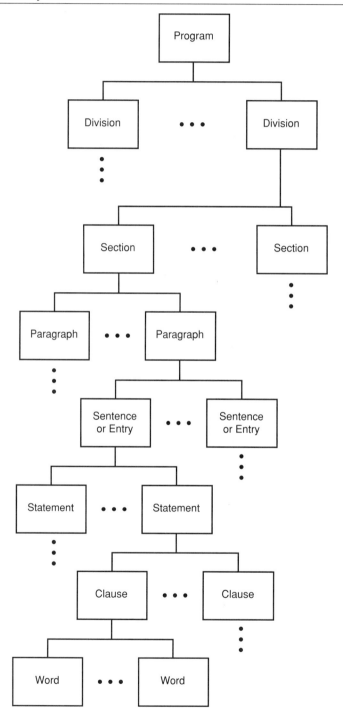

Words are the smallest unit of COBOL snytax. They are used in a manner analogous to English in order to construct clauses, statements, sentences, and paragraphs. Words must be separated by spaces or valid combinations of spaces and punctuation characters such as commas, parentheses, and quotation marks. Some words have special meanings in COBOL. They are known as *reserved words* and may be used by the programmer in a restricted fashion. Some examples of reserved words are READ, CLOSE, INSPECT. Appendix B contains a list of COBOL reserved words.

3.2.2   Names

Programmers must create their own *names* to identify files, data items, paragaphs, and sections, among others. The rules for constructing names are:

1. Names may be up to 30 characters long.
2. Names may be composed only of alphabetic characters, numeric digits, and hyphens (-).
3. Names may not begin or end with a hyphen.
4. Names must have at least one alphabetic character, except for paragraph names.
5. Reserved words cannot be used as names.

The generous character allotment and the hyphen allow programmers to make up longer, more meaningful names. Figure 3.8 illustrates some examples of good and poor names.

Figure 3.8   Name Usage in COBOL

Poor Name	Good Name
FROGGY	PART-NAME-INDEX
INPUT-FILE	CUSTOMER-ADDRESS-FILE
CSZ	CITY-STATE-ZIP
DATE-1	BILLING-DATE
ENDIT	EOF-INDICATOR-INVOICES
DOLLARS-PD	PAST-DUE-AMOUNT
GET-RECORD	READ-CUSTOMER-FILE

3.2.3   Literals

In some cases a programmer may wish to use literals in a program. A literal is a word whose value is the same as the characters making up the word. Literals may be numeric or nonnumeric. The following statement is from the program in Figure 3.6:

```
IF TOT-WAGES > 75000.00 PERFORM 220-PRINT-EMPLOYEE-WAGES-
LINE.
```

The word 75000.00 is a numeric literal. Nonnumeric literals are defined by enclosing the character string making up the literal in quotation (") marks. The example from the sample program:

```
READ PAYROLL-MASTER-FILE AT END MOVE "Y" TO
       EOF-PAYROLL-MASTER-FILE.
```

contains the character literal "Y". Its value does not change throughout the execution of the program. The rules for constructing literals are:

1. *Numeric literals* (a) may be composed of one or more numeric characters, an optional decimal point, and/or an algebraic sign. (b) The decimal point may not be the rightmost character. (c) If present, the algebraic sign must be the leftmost character.

2. *Nonnumeric literals* (a) may be up to 160 characters long and be delimited by quotation marks. (b) Any character in the machine's character set may appear in the character string. (c) A quotation mark inside the nonnumeric literal may be represented by two contiguous quotation marks.

3.2.4   Coding Forms

In order to facilitate the coding of COBOL programs, special reprinted forms exist that remind the programmer of the language format. Nowadays, text editors are commonly used that have the required margins and indentations preset to the proper columns. However, since a textbook is currently limited to paper, we will use the coding form in our examples. Figure 3.9 is a blank COBOL coding form that illustrates the general format of COBOL instructions. The coding form is divided into 80 columns. Each column corresponds to the column positions in a line at the visual display terminal. ANS standards specify that statements be keyed in the format indicated by the form, but many computers allow simplifications such as predetermined, automatic tabs during input and automatic line sequencing. Check your system's documentation guide for details.

Figure 3.9   **COBOL Coding Form**

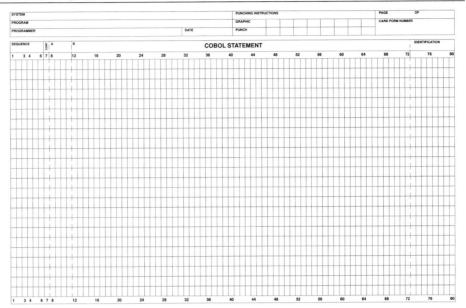

The first six columns of the coding form are used for sequence numbers. Sequence numbers are a holdover from the days of punched cards when a dropped card deck could spell disaster unless some method for resequencing them was provided. So the sequence numbers in columns 1 to 6 served that purpose. Now, however, sequence numbers are automatically generated by the COBOL compiler to serve as reference points.

Comments are indicated by placing an asterisk (*) in column 7. Comments appear on the source listing but are ignored by the compiler. Comment lines may appear anywhere in the source program. The columns labeled 73 to 80 on the coding form are reserved for an eight-character comment. This is another holdover from the days of punched cards when columns 73 to 80 usually contained the name of the program on every card. These columns are ignored by many COBOL compilers and are automatically filled by others.

Columns 8 through 72 are reserved for the actual program code. Column 8 represents margin A and column 12 margin B. The *margins* define where certain coding structures begin. For simplicity we call columns 8 to 11 area A and columns 12 to 72 area B. The margin usage will become clear as you study the COBOL commands.

Each line on the coding form should represent one line at the terminal screen. Since COBOL commands are usually longer than those of other languages, they often extend to more than one line. In order to maintain readability, you should divide the statement onto successive lines at word breaks. For example,

```
READ PAYROLL-MASTER-FILE
    AT END MOVE "Y" TO EOF-PAYROLL-MASTER-FILE.
```

illustrates this method of maintaining readability and consequently making the program easier to debug.

The coding form divides the area following margin B into segments of four columns. Four is not a magic number in COBOL, but this has become an accepted amount of indentation for statement continuation. This is illustrated in lines 64, 66, 74, 78, and 84 of the sample program in Figure 3.6. Portions of the sample program are shown in Figure 3.10 as they would appear on a coding form.

Figure 3.10   COBOL Code for "List Excessive Salaries" Program

Figure 3.10   (continued)

SYSTEM		PUNCHING INSTRUCTIONS		PAGE	OF
PROGRAM		GRAPHIC		CARD FORM NUMBER	
PROGRAMMER	DATE	PUNCH			

```
SEQUENCE  A  B                        COBOL STATEMENT                           IDENTIFICATION
1   3 4  6 7 8  12    16    20    24    28    32    36    40    44    48    52    56    60    64    68    72    76    80

              200-PRODUCE-EMPLOYEE-WAGES.
                  PERFORM 210-CALCULATE-TOTAL-WAGES.
                  IF  TOT-WAGES  >  75000.00
                      PERFORM 220-PRINT-EMP-WAGES-LINE.
                  PERFORM 100-READ-PAYROLL-MASTER-FILE.

              210-CALCULATE-TOTAL-WAGES.
                  ADD  PMF-YEAR-TO-DATE-SALARY  TO  PMF-YEAR-TO-DATE-BONUS
                      GIVING  TOT-WAGES.

              220-PRINT-EMP-WAGES-LINE.
                  MOVE  SPACES  TO  EMPLOYEE-WAGES-LINE.
                  MOVE  PMF-EMPLOYEE-ID-NUMBER  TO  ESL-EMPLOYEE-ID-NUMBER.
                  MOVE  PMF-EMPLOYEE-NAME  TO  ESL-EMPLOYEE-NAME.
                  MOVE  TOT-WAGES  TO  ESL-WAGES.
                  WRITE  EMPLOYEE-WAGES-LINE.
```

3.2.5   Format of COBOL Syntax

Just as in natural languages there are rules of syntax that dictate how words may be arranged to form phrases and sentences, so too COBOL's syntax dictates the specific positioning of words within clauses, statements, or sentences. The following example indicates how the COBOL statement formats are illustrated in most COBOL reference manuals.

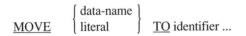

MOVE   { data-name / literal }   TO identifier ...

The *MOVE* statement transfers data from one memory location to another. The format for the MOVE statement and for all COBOL statements conforms to the following notation rules:

1. Reserved words are shown in capital letters.
2. If the reserved word is required for a clause, the word is underlined.
3. If a word is capitalized but not underlined, the programmar can include it in the clause at his discretion.
4. All punctuation characters shown in the format are required.
5. Words in lowercase characters indicate information that must be supplied by the

programmer.
6. Words between brackets [ ] indicate a clause that is optional.
7. Words between braces { } indicate that one and only one of the enclosed clauses must be included.
8. The ellipsis symbol (...) indicates that a clause may be repeated as often as required by the programmer.

Thus, for the MOVE statement, the words MOVE and TO are required. A data-name or literal must be specified after the word MOVE. Multiple identifiers may appear after the word TO. Appendix C contains the COBOL language in this format for quick reference to its correct syntax.

3.2.6   Syntax Errors

Violating the rules of COBOL syntax results in syntax errors that are detected during compilation of the program.

Desk Checking. *Desk checking* your program can help you detect syntax errors even before you compile the program. Desk checking includes reviewing your program code for obvious errors. Some of the things to look for include:

1. Correct spelling of reserved words and division, section, and paragraph names. Cross-check paragraph names to the hierarchy chart's module names.
2. Punctuation, including periods, hyphens, quotation marks, and spaces.
3. Verifying that file, record, and data-names are defined and that they are spelled correctly.
4. Checking alignment, verifying that statements begin and end in the proper columns.

Desk checking for syntax errors should be a little more than a perfunctory inspection but not an in-depth examination of your program code. The compiler can do a faster, more thorough job of finding syntax errors, but a quick review reflects some professionalism on your part and cuts down on the number of times your program has to be compiled. Each compilation requires computer resources, but more importantly it requires your time for reviewing the results. Often one error may result in multiple errors throughout the program, thus causing a display of pages and pages of error messages that could have been avoided by a simple examination prior to compilation.

Correcting Syntax Errors. During compilation the compiler will generate diagnostic messages when it encounters syntax errors. These diagnostics are printed or displayed along with the source program code and serve to identify the cause or nature of the problem. Although most messages are self-explanatory, a complete list may be found in your system's COBOL documentation.

Here are a few guidelines for correcting the errors flagged by the compiler:

1. Approach each diagnostic in sequence. Correcting early diagnostics many times has the effect of clearing up later error conditions.
2. If a diagnostic does not make sense, check the punctuation and syntax of the previous line of code. If this does not help, go on to the next diagnostic. It might clear up the previous error condition.
3. If a diagnostic is still unclear, check the correct format of the statement of entry being referenced.
4. If you just can't figure out a message, skip it this time.
5. Once you have made a complete pass of the diagnostics and corrected as many errors as you can, recompile the program. Some of your previous "errors" may be gone if they were caused by prior, now-corrected errors.
6. If you still get messages that are unclear to you, it is time to refer to the COBOL reference manual provided with your compiler.

3.3   *The Four COBOL Divisions*

To explain a very basic subset of COBOL, we will use the example program in Figure 3.6 for purposes of illustration. Lines 1, 13, 27, and 61 identify four groupings of a COBOL program known as divisions. There are four required divisions: IDENTIFICATION, ENVIRONMENT, DATA, and PROCEDURE. All four appear in that order in all programs. The IDENTIFICA-TION DIVISION contains the name of the program and other documentation. The ENVIRON-MENT DIVISION describes the computer facilities and those aspects that depend on the hardware used. The DATA DIVISION defines the data used by the program and their hierarchical relationships. It is developed from file layouts and printer layouts that specify the format of the data. The PROCEDURE DIVISION conducts the sequential, iterative, and selective tasks that are associated with a program and specified in the hierarchy chart and the Nassi-Schneiderman charts. DIVISIONs all begin in area A.

3.3.1   *IDENTIFICATION DIVISION*

The IDENTIFICATION DIVISION is the shortest of all the COBOL DIVISIONs. Its purpose is to identify the program and its related listings. The first noncomment line of code in a COBOL program must be the words IDENTIFICATION DIVISION followed by a period. The syntax for the entire division is:

IDENTIFICATION DIVISION.
PROGRAM-ID. program-name.
[AUTHOR. [comment entry]]
[INSTALLATION. [comment entry]]
[DATE-WRITTEN. [comment entry]]
[DATE-COMPILED. [comment entry]]
[SECURITY. [comment entry]]

The PROGRAM-ID paragraph is the only mandatory item in the IDENTIFICATION DIVISION and must be the first paragraph in each program. The words PROGRAM-ID, as with all paragraph names, begin in area A and are followed by a period. Program-name is any programmer-specified name that follows the naming conventions of COBOL and is unique within the system. This name identifies the source code, object code, and associated program listings.

The remaining paragraphs of this division are optional, but they are useful for purposes of documentation. If used, they begin in area A and are followed by a *comment-entry* that ends with a period. Comment-entries can be continued on subsequent lines simply by writing the rest of the comment-entry anywhere in area B of the subsequent lines. Rules for constructing comment-entries in the IDENTIFICATION DIVISION are:

1. Any combination of characters from the machine's character set may be used.
2. Comment-entries may exceed one line.
3. Comment-entries do not affect the program. They are ignored by the compiler.

The AUTHOR paragraph allows the programmer to specify his name. The INSTALLATION paragraph is used to identify the location where the program is written. The DATE-WRITTEN paragraph indicates the day the program was coded. The DATE-COMPILED paragraph is the date of the current compilation into which most computers will place the actual compilation date. The last comment entry is the SECURITY paragraph, which is used to indicate how sensitive the program is to tampering.

The complete IDENTIFICATION DIVISION from the "List Excessive Salaries" program is:

```
IDENTIFICATION DIVISION.
PROGRAM-ID. LIST-EXCESSIVE-SALARIES.
* PRODUCE A LIST OF EMPLOYEES WHOSE
* SALARIES AND BONUSES EXCEED $75,000
AUTHOR. NEWT JAMES.
INSTALLATION. IRS.
DATE-WRITTEN. JULY 30, 1996.
DATE-COMPILED.
SECURITY. CONFIDENTIAL.
```

The lines with an asterisk are comment lines that briefly describe the purpose of the program.

3.3.2   ENVIRONMENT DIVISION

It is now possible to have complete independence from the machine environment. However, COBOL isolates most machine-dependent features in the ENVIRONMENT DIVISION. These entries would have to be changed in going from one machine environment to another.

The format for the ENVIRONMENT DIVISION is:

ENVIRONMENT DIVISION.
[CONFIGURATION SECTION.

```
[SOURCE-COMPUTER. [source-computer-entry.]]
[OBJECT-COMPUTER. [object-computer-entry.]]
[INPUT-OUTPUT SECTION.
FILE-CONTROL.
        {file-selection-entry} . . . ]]
```

The optional CONFIGURATION SECTION identifies the computer system being used. Two paragraphs are optional in this SECTION, the *SOURCE-COMPUTER* paragraph, which identifies the computer on which the program is compiled, and the *OBJECT-COMPUTER* paragraph, which identifies the computer on which the program runs. Depending on the system the programmer is using, the computer-entries may be names provided by the computer manufacturer or may be comment-entries that are ignored by the compiler. Consult your system's COBOL reference manual to determine the correct entries.

The INPUT-OUTPUT SECTION of the ENVIRONMENT DIVISION contains the necessary information for controlling the transfer of data between external devices and the program. Within the INPUT-OUTPUT SECTION the FILE-CONTROL paragraph identifies each file and provides related information. The simplified format of a file-section-entry is:

SELECT file-name ASSIGN TO implementor-name

The SELECT clause names each file of data and associates it with an external medium. The file-name is a unique name supplied by the programmer. Implementor-name identifies the storage medium for the file and is dependent on the machine being used. The proper device names can be found in your system's COBOL reference manuals. The following is an example of a SELECT clause from the "List Excessive Salaries" program:

```
SELECT EXCESS-SALARY-LIST-FILE ASSIGN TO PRINTER.
```

This means that any output sent to the file Excess-Salary-List-File will be sent to the hardware device known as a PRINTER.

Each file used in the program, including the reports sent to the printer, must have a SELECT clause. However, these entries may appear in any order within the FILE-CONTROL paragraph. You should take care to assign the files meaningful names, since the file-name used in the SELECT clause will be used throughout the program. For example, the name PAYROLL-MASTER-FILE is more descriptive than IN-FILE. We recommend that you append the suffix -FILE to the name you choose.

The ENVIRONMENT DIVISION for the "List Excessive Salaries" program is:

```
ENVIRONMENT DIVISION.
CONFIGURATION SECTION.
SOURCE-COMPUTER. GENERIC-COMPUTER.
OBJECT-COMPUTER. GENERIC-COMPUTER.
INPUT-OUTPUT SECTION.
```

```
FILE-CONTROL.
      SELECT PAYROLL-MASTER-FILE ASSIGN TO S-PAY.
      SELECT EXCESS-SALARY-LIST-FILE ASSIGN TO PRINTER.
```

3.3.3   DATA DIVISION

The *DATA DIVISION* describes the characteristics of the data read in, transformed, or written by a program. Each file, record, and data item must be defined in the DATA DIVISION. For now, we will cover only enough of the DATA DIVISION to understand the sample program in Figure 3.6. The format is:

DATA DIVISION.
[FILE SECTION.   ]
[{file-description entry}...]
[WORKING-STORAGE SECTION.   ]
[{working-data-item-description entry}...]

The FILE SECTION gives the characteristics of the input and output files. The WORKING-STORAGE SECTION defines most other items required by a program.

FILE SECTION. Every file that appears in a SELECT clause of the ENVIRONMENT DIVISION must be defined in the FILE SECTION. This is accomplished through the file description (FD) paragraph and an 01 level record description. The format for the FD is:

DATA DIVISION.
FILE SECTION.
FD file-name

$$\text{LABEL} \quad \left\{ \begin{array}{ll} \underline{\text{RECORDS}} & \text{ARE} \\ \underline{\text{RECORD}} & \text{IS} \end{array} \right\} \quad \left\{ \begin{array}{l} \underline{\text{STANDARD}} \\ \underline{\text{OMITTED}} \end{array} \right\} .$$

The FD entry begins in area A and ends with a period. It contains the name of the file as it appears in the SELECT clause. The required LABEL RECORD clause defines whether label records in the file exist. Label records are physical records generated by the system at the beginning and end of a file in order to provide information such as file-name, creation date, expiration date, and other documentation. They are not part of the file's data. They are analogous to a label glued to a notebook cover. Each computer system generates its own label records. COBOL is not concerned with their contents, only with their presence or absence. STANDARD implies that the labels exist and conform to the specifications of the particular system. OMITTED indicates that there are no labels for this file.

The FD and 01 entries for PAYROLL-MASTER-FILE in the "List Excessive Salaries" program are:

```
FD    PAYROLL-MASTER-FILE
      LABEL RECORDS ARE STANDARD.
01    PAYROLL-REC.
```

```
05    PMF-EMPLOYEE-ID-NUMBER          PIC 9(4).
05    PMF-EMPLOYEE-NAME               PIC X(20).
05    FILLER                          PIC X(80).
05    PMF-YEAR-TO-DATE-SALARY         PIC 9(8)V99.
05    PMF-YEAR-TO-DATE-BONUS          PIC 9(8)V99.
05    FILLER                          PIC X(14).
```

The 01 entry appearing below the FD represents a single record type in the file. From the program example,

```
01    PAYROLL-REC.
```

indicates that the file layout is to be described for an individual record. The 05 entries below the 01 record entry are the individual items that make up the record. The 05 entries have a direct correspondence to the file layout in Figure 3.2. Thus,

```
05    PMF-EMPLOYEE-ID-NUMBER   PIC 9(4).
```

is the first item in each record. The item is called PMF-EMPLOYEE-ID-NUMBER. The *PICTURE* clause PIC 9(4) indicates that it is numeric, as indicated by the 9, and that it is four positions long, as indicated by the 4 in parentheses. This exactly meets the specifications on the file layout given in Figure 3.2.

The second item is

```
05    PMF-EMPLOYEE-NAME  PIC X(20).
```

This means that the second item in each record is the employee name. The employee name has PIC X(20), which means it is a character field, indicated by the X, and is 20 positions long. This description is obtained directly from the file layouts that form part of the program specifications (Figure 3.2).

The next entry is

```
05    FILLER        PIC X(80):
```

It indicates that the next 80 positions in the record are not important to the program. Therefore, they are FILLER. Now compare the rest of the record with the file layout.

A similar analysis is applicable to the 01 entry for the printed report and the report layout given in Figure 3.3. Each position in the 01 record description represents a column on the report layout form. Thus,

```
05    EWL-EMPLOYEE-ID-NUMBER   PIC 9(4).
```

indicates that the first four positions on the report layout are to be occupied by the numeric customer number. The FILLER positions represent the spaces between the output items.

The final entry,

```
05    EWL-WAGES    PIC ZZZ,ZZZ,ZZZ.ZZ.
```

indicates that the value of the wages is to be edited. The decimal point and commas will be inserted automatically. The Z signifies that leading zeros will be printed as spaces, so that a value such as 000100000.00 would print as 100,000.00.

WORKING-STORAGE SECTION. The *WORKING-STORAGE SECTION* of the DATA DIVISION defines other fields used by the program, fields that are not part of input or output files. For the "List Excessive Salaries" program, the WORKING-STORAGE SECTION is as follows:

```
WORKING-STORAGE SECTION.
01   END-OF-FILE-INDICATORS.
     05   EOF-PAYROLL-MASTER-FILE        PIC X VALUE "N".
01   TOTAL-FIELD.
     05 TOT-WAGES                        PIC 9(9)V99.
```

In this example the 01 entries are not record names for files. Instead, the 01 entries are used to relate their subordinate items logically. If more than one file required an EOF indicator, that indicator would be added below the entry:

```
05 EOF-PAYROLL-MASTER-FILE              PIC X VALUE "N".
```

The end-of-file indicator serves to denote when all the input records in the payroll master file have been read. The *VALUE* clause sets the indicator to the value "N", for "NO! The end of the file has not yet been encountered!"

We need a temporary item to hold the total wages earned for each employee. Such an entry would be described as an 05 entry under the 01 entry:

```
01    TOTAL-FIELD.
```

If others were needed, they would also be described as TOT-WAGES 05 entries. In the line

```
05    TOT-WAGES        PIC 9(9)V99.
```

the V in the PIC entry for TOT-WAGES designates where the position of the decimal point is assumed to be during computations and storage. Thus TOT-WAGES is 11 numeric digits long with 9 digits before the decimal point and 2 digits after the decimal point.

3.3.4   *PROCEDURE DIVISION*

The fourth and last division in a COBOL program is the *PROCEDURE DIVISION*. It contains the actual instructions that direct the computer in the solution of a given problem. In this part, the Nassi-Schneiderman charts that were developed during the program design are translated into commands that carry out the logic.

Every paragraph in the PROCEDURE DIVISION has a name supplied by the programmer. The paragraph name must conform to the naming rules of COBOL. Paragraph names begin in area A and end with a period. Notice that the paragraphs in the PROCEDURE DIVISION of Figure 3.6 directly represent the modules of the hierarchy chart of Figure 3.4.

The sentences of a paragraph correspond to the Nassi-Schneiderman charts for each module. As we review the PROCEDURE DIVISION and compare it with the charts in Figure 3.5, you will probably be able to discern what each statement is doing. It is in the PROCEDURE DIVISION that the English-like syntax of COBOL becomes more noticeable. In this chapter we limit our discussion of the COBOL commands to a general survey of the statements used in the sample program.

Module "List-Excessive-Salaries." The first paragraph in the PROCEDURE DIVISION is LIST-EXCESSIVE-SALARIES, which is also the top module in the hierarchy. The code for this module is as follows:

```
LIST-EXCESSIVE-SALARIES.
    OPEN INPUT PAYROLL-MASTER-FILE.
    OPEN OUTPUT EXCESS-SALARY-LIST-FILE.
    PERFORM 100-READ-PAYROLL-MASTER-FILE.
    PERFORM 200-PRODUCE-EMPLOYEE-WAGES
        UNTIL EOF-PAYROLL-MASTER-FILE = "Y".
    CLOSE PAYROLL-MASTER-FILE.
    CLOSE EXCESS-SALARY-LIST-FILE.
    STOP RUN.
```

The OPEN Statement. An *OPEN* statement, required for each file used in the program, prepares the file for processing but performs no logical program function. Thus, OPEN statements usually appear in the first paragraph as part of the main module, but they are usually not included in the documentation. For example, notice that the N-S chart for the module does not indicate the OPEN statements.

The Simple PERFORM Statement. The *PERFORM* statement causes the named paragraph to be executed. Once the named paragraph is executed, control returns to the statement immediately following the PERFORM. Thus, PERFORM 100-READ-PAYROLL-MASTER-FILE causes all sentences in paragraph 100-READ-PAYROLL-MASTER-FILE to be executed, then hands control to the next statement, PERFORM 200-PRODUCE-EMPLOYEE-WAGES UNTIL EOF-PAYROLL MASTER = "Y". The simple PERFORM is a form of sequence structure.

The PERFORM UNTIL Statement. The *PERFORM UNTIL* statement represents the iteration structure. The named paragraph will be executed UNTIL the condition stated is met. For example:

```
PERFORM 200-PRODUCE-EMPLOYEE-WAGES
    UNTIL EOF-PAYROLL-MASTER-FILE = "Y".
```

implements an iteration that is to be done multiple times. The number of times is determined by the condition state of the UNTIL clause. In the PERFORM UNTIL statement, the condition is first tested. If it is true, control passes to the statement immediately following the PERFORM statement. In other words, 200-PRODUCE-EMPLOYEE-WAGES is not executed. If the condition is false, the paragraph will be executed. Control returns to the PERFORM statement so that the condition can be tested again. The module is repeatedly PERFORMed UNTIL the condition is true. This is exactly the requirement of the iteration structure called for in the N-S chart of module "List-Excessive-Salaries" and indicated on the hierarchy chart above module "200-Produce-Employee-Wages."

The CLOSE Statement. Each opened file must be closed. As with the OPEN, the *CLOSE* does not contribute to the logical solution of a problem and does not appear in the documentation. The CLOSE statement represents the final link in processing a file. The CLOSE refers to the same file-name that appears in the SELECT, FD, and OPEN. This bond between the ENVIRON-MENT DIVISION, the DATA DIVISION, and the PROCEDURE DIVISION is illustrated in Figure 3.11.

Figure 3.11   File Name Usage

```
 1 IDENTIFICATION DIVISION.
 2
 3 PROGRAM-ID. LIST-EXCESS-SALARIES.
 4* PRODUCE A LIST OF EMPLOYEES WHOSE
 5* SALARIES AND BONUS EXCEEDS $75,000
 6 AUTHOR. NEWT JAMES.
 7 INSTALLATION. IRS.
 8 DATE-WRITTEN. JULY 30,1996.
 9 DATE-COMPILED. 14-Jan-90 14:24.
10 SECURITY. CONFIDENTIAL.
11
12
13 ENVIRONMENT DIVISION.
14
15 CONFIGURATION SECTION.
16
17 SOURCE-COMPUTER. GENERIC-COMPUTER.
18 OBJECT-COMPUTER. GENERIC-COMPUTER.
19
20 INPUT-OUTPUT SECTION.
21
22 FILE-CONTROL.
23     SELECT PAYROLL-MASTER-FILE ASSIGN TO S-PAY.
24     SELECT EXCESS-SALARY-LIST-FILE ASSIGN TO PRINTER.
25
26
27 DATA DIVISION.
28
29 FILE SECTION.
30
31 FD  PAYROLL-MASTER-FILE
32     LABEL RECORDS ARE STANDARD.
33
34 01  PAYROLL-REC.
35     05  PMF-EMPLOYEE-ID-NUMBER        PIC 9(4).
36     05  PMF-EMPLOYEE-NAME             PIC X(20).
37     05  FILLER                        PIC X(80).
38     05  PMF-YEAR-TO-DATE-SALARY       PIC 9(8)V99.
39     05  PMF-YEAR-TO-DATE-BONUS        PIC 9(8)V99.
40     05  FILLER                        PIC X(14).
41
42 FD  EXCESS-SALARY-LIST-FILE
43     LABEL RECORDS ARE STANDARD.
44
45 01  EMPLOYEE-WAGES-LINE.
46     05  EWL-EMPLOYEE-ID-NUMBER        PIC 9(4).
47     05  FILLER                        PIC X(4).
48     05  EWL-EMPLOYEE-NAME             PIC X(20).
49     05  FILLER                        PIC X(4).
50     05  EWL-WAGES                     PIC ZZZ,ZZZ,ZZZ.ZZ.
51
52 WORKING-STORAGE SECTION.
53
54 01  END-OF-FILE-INDICATORS.
55     05  EOF-PAYROLL-MASTER-FILE       PIC X VALUE "N".
56
57 01  TOTAL-FIELD.
58     05  TOT-WAGES                     PIC 9(9)V99.
59
60
61 PROCEDURE DIVISION.
62
63 LIST-EXCESSIVE-SALARIES.
64     OPEN INPUT PAYROLL-MASTER-FILE.
65     OPEN OUTPUT EXCESS-SALARY-LIST-FILE.
66     PERFORM 100-READ-PAYROLL-MASTER-FILE.
67     PERFORM 200-PRODUCE-EMPLOYEE-WAGES
68         UNTIL EOF-PAYROLL-MASTER-FILE = "Y"
69     CLOSE PAYROLL-MASTER-FILE.
70     CLOSE EXCESS-SALARY-LIST-FILE.
71     STOP RUN.
72
73 100-READ-PAYROLL-MASTER-FILE.
74     READ PAYROLL-MASTER-FILE
75         AT END MOVE "Y" TO EOF-PAYROLL-MASTER-FILE.
76
77 200-PRODUCE-EMPLOYEE-WAGES.
78     PERFORM 210-CALCULATE-TOTAL-WAGES.
79     IF TOT-WAGES > 75000.00
80         PERFORM 220-PRINT-EMPLOYEE-WAGES-LINE.
81     PERFORM 100-READ-PAYROLL-MASTER-FILE.
82
83 210-CALCULATE-TOTAL-WAGES.
84     ADD  PMF-YEAR-TO-DATE-SALARY  PMF-YEAR-TO-DATE-BONUS
85         GIVING TOT-WAGES.
86
87 220-PRINT-EMPLOYEE-WAGES-LINE.
88     MOVE SPACES TO EMPLOYEE-WAGES-LINE.
89     MOVE PMF-EMPLOYEE-ID-NUMBER TO
90         EWL-EMPLOYEE-ID-NUMBER.
91     MOVE PMF-EMPLOYEE-NAME TO EWL-EMPLOYEE-NAME.
92     MOVE TOT-WAGES TO EWL-WAGES.
93     WRITE EMPLOYEE-WAGES-LINE.
```

The STOP RUN. The *STOP RUN* indicates that the program has finished. The computer will proceed to its next job when the STOP RUN is encountered.

Module "100-Read-Payroll-Master-File." The module contains a single *READ* statement:

```
READ PAYROLL-MASTER-FILE
      AT END MOVE "Y" TO EOF-PAYROLL-MASTER-FILE.
```

The READ statement is the primary input statement in COBOL. It causes a single record to be made available in the record area associated with a file. In the example a single record is read into PAYROLL-REC and made available to the program. The AT END clause tells the computer what action to take when the end of the file is encountered. In the example program, the end-of-file indicator is set to "Y" for "YES! I have encountered the file's end!"

Module "200-Produce-Employee-Wages." The new type of statement encountered in the module "200-Produce-Employee-Wages" is:

```
IF TOT-WAGES > 75000.00
      PERFORM 220-PRINT-EMPLOYEE-WAGES-LINE.
```

The COBOL *IF* statement represents the selection structure. Notice that there are two different courses of action that can be taken based on whether the condition TOT-WAGES > 75000.00 is true or false. If the condition is true, module "220-Print-Employee-Wages-Line" is performed. If the condition is false, the module is bypassed. The selection structure is indicated on the hierarchy chart in Figure 3.4 by the filled-in diamond above the module "220-Print-Employee-Wages-Line."

Module "210-Calculate-Total-Wages." The only statement in module 210 is:

```
ADD PMF-YEAR-TO-DATE-SALARY PMF-YEAR-TO-DATE-BONUS
      GIVING TOT-WAGES.
```

The *ADD* statement represents a simple sequence structure. The execution of this statement causes the computer to add the bonus and salary amounts and store the sum in the data item named TOT-WAGES.

Module "220-Print-Employee-Wages-Line." The code for paragraph 220-PRINT-EMPLOYEE-WAGES-LINE is:

```
MOVE SPACES TO EMPLOYEE-WAGES-LINE.
MOVE PMF-EMPLOYEE-ID-NUMBER TO EWL-EMPLOYEE-ID-NUMBER.
MOVE PMF-EMPLOYEE-NAME TO EWL-EMPLOYEE-NAME.
MOVE TOT-WAGES TO EWL-WAGES.
WRITE EMPLOYEE-WAGES-LINE.
```

The Nassi-Schneiderman chart for the module, from Figure 3.5, contains only sequence constructs. In other words, the code contains only statements that do not disrupt the program's flow of control.

The MOVE Statement. The MOVE statements at the start of the module transfer data from one data item to another. The first MOVE sentence:

```
MOVE SPACES TO EMPLOYEE-WAGES-LINE.
```

fills the output area with blanks. This clears the output area of any old data. The remaining MOVE statements transfer data to the output area from their respective sources. If the input record contained the values of 3412 for the employee ID number, "John Fredrick" for the employee name, and 80,000 for TOT-WAGES, these values would appear in EWL-EMPLOYEE-ID-NUMBER, EWL-EMPLOYEE-NAME and EWL-WAGES after the MOVEs had been executed.

The WRITE Statement. The *WRITE* statement causes one record to be written to the output file. In the example program the record corresponds to a line of print. Notice that in Figure 3.12 the WRITE statement refers to the record name associated with the file description for EXCESS-SALARY-LIST-FILE. All other file commands examined so far have referred to the file-name.

Overview. The top module, the first paragraph, is executed first. The files are opened by the OPEN statements. Next the PERFORM statement passes control to the paragraph 100-READ-PAYROLL-MASTER-FILE, which reads the first record of the file.

Control then returns to the PERFORM UNTIL statement in the first paragraph. The PERFORM UNTIL statement will repeatedly pass control to paragraph 200-PRODUCE-EMPLOYEE-WAGES until the end-of-file is reached, at which time the CLOSE statements are executed. The STOP RUN statement ends the processing.

Each time paragraph 200-PRODUCE-EMPLOYEE-WAGES is executed, it passes control to paragraph 210-CALCULATE-TOTAL-WAGES, which calculates the employee's wages, then to the IF statement, which determines whether control passes to paragraph 220-PRINT-EMPLOYEE-WAGES-LINE or to the following statement. If the dollar amount exceeds the cutoff, paragraph 220-PRINT-EMPLOYEE-WAGES-LINE, which sends the required data to an output file, is executed. Control then passes to paragraph 100-READ-PAYROLL-MASTER-FILE, which brings in a successive record to process and checks for the end of file.

Figure 3.12 *Record Name Usage*

```
 1 IDENTIFICATION DIVISION.
 2
 3 PROGRAM-ID. LIST-EXCESS-SALARIES.
 4* PRODUCE A LIST OF EMPLOYEES WHOSE
 5* SALARIES AND BONUS EXCEEDS $75,000
 6 AUTHOR. NEWT JAMES.
 7 INSTALLATION. IRS.
 8 DATE-WRITTEN. JULY 30,1996.
 9 DATE-COMPILED. 14-Jan-90 14:24.
10 SECURITY. CONFIDENTIAL.
11
12
13 ENVIRONMENT DIVISION.
14
15 CONFIGURATION SECTION.
16
17 SOURCE-COMPUTER. GENERIC-COMPUTER.
18 OBJECT-COMPUTER. GENERIC-COMPUTER.
19
20 INPUT-OUTPUT SECTION.
21
22 FILE-CONTROL.
23     SELECT PAYROLL-MASTER-FILE ASSIGN TO S-PAY.
24     SELECT EXCESS-SALARY-LIST-FILE ASSIGN TO PRINTER.
25
26
27 DATA DIVISION.
28
29 FILE SECTION.
30
31 FD  PAYROLL-MASTER-FILE
32     LABEL RECORDS ARE STANDARD.
33
34 01  PAYROLL-REC.
35     05  PMF-EMPLOYEE-ID-NUMBER      PIC 9(4).
36     05  PMF-EMPLOYEE-NAME           PIC X(20).
37     05  FILLER                      PIC X(80).
38     05  PMF-YEAR-TO-DATE-SALARY      PIC 9(8)V99.
39     05  PMF-YEAR-TO-DATE-BONUS       PIC 9(8)V99.
40     05  FILLER                      PIC X(14).
41
42 FD  EXCESS-SALARY-LIST-FILE
43     LABEL RECORDS ARE STANDARD.
44
45 01  EMPLOYEE-WAGES-LINE.          ◄
46     05  EWL-EMPLOYEE-ID-NUMBER      PIC 9(4).
47     05  FILLER                      PIC X(4).
48     05  EWL-EMPLOYEE-NAME           PIC X(20).
49     05  FILLER                      PIC X(4).
50     05  EWL-WAGES                   PIC ZZZ,ZZZ,ZZZ.ZZ.
51
52 WORKING-STORAGE SECTION.
53
54 01  END-OF-FILE-INDICATORS.
55     05  EOF-PAYROLL-MASTER-FILE      PIC X VALUE "N".
56
57 01  TOTAL-FIELD.
58     05  TOT-WAGES                   PIC 9(9)V99.
59
60
61 PROCEDURE DIVISION.
62
63 LIST-EXCESSIVE-SALARIES.
64     OPEN INPUT PAYROLL-MASTER-FILE.
65     OPEN OUTPUT EXCESS-SALARY-LIST-FILE.
66     PERFORM 100-READ-PAYROLL-MASTER-FILE.
67     PERFORM 200-PRODUCE-EMPLOYEE-WAGES
68         UNTIL EOF-PAYROLL-MASTER-FILE = "Y".
69     CLOSE PAYROLL-MASTER-FILE.
70     CLOSE EXCESS-SALARY-LIST-FILE.
71     STOP RUN.
72
73 100-READ-PAYROLL-MASTER-FILE.
74     READ PAYROLL-MASTER-FILE
75         AT END MOVE "Y" TO EOF-PAYROLL-MASTER-FILE.
76
77 200-PRODUCE-EMPLOYEE-WAGES.
78     PERFORM 210-CALCULATE-TOTAL-WAGES.
79     IF TOT-WAGES > 75000.00
80         PERFORM 220-PRINT-EMPLOYEE-WAGES-LINE.
81     PERFORM 100-READ-PAYROLL-MASTER-FILE.
82
83 210-CALCULATE-TOTAL-WAGES.
84     ADD  PMF-YEAR-TO-DATE-SALARY  PMF-YEAR-TO-DATE-BONUS
85         GIVING TOT-WAGES.
86
87 220-PRINT-EMPLOYEE-WAGES-LINE.
88     MOVE SPACES TO EMPLOYEE-WAGES-LINE.
89     MOVE PMF-EMPLOYEE-ID-NUMBER TO
90         EWL-EMPLOYEE-ID-NUMBER
91     MOVE PMF-EMPLOYEE-NAME TO EWL-EMPLOYEE-NAME.
92     MOVE TOT-WAGES TO EWL-WAGES.
93     WRITE EMPLOYEE-WAGES-LINE.
```

3.4   *Structured COBOL Coding*

Every programmer has an individual style. This is one manifestation of his creativity. Structured programming seeks to contain this creativity within the bounds of the principles described in the preceding chapter. These principles include deriving the programs from structured designs, restricting control logic to the three basic constructs, and adhering to the one entry/one exit rule.

The use of structured methodologies in the development of the program logic leads naturally to *structured code*. This is not to say that a programmer's creativity is stifled or that structured programs begin resembling each other, just as writing guidelines do not restrict the creativity of writers. It does, however, serve to contain the code so that it is easier to write, understand, and maintain. Following are some additional guidelines for improving programming style.

3.4.1   *The COBOL Priming Read*

Very rarely should a physical consideration influence the choice of control structures used in a program. However, the physical format of sequential files does influence the logic structure used to read them. Sequential files are very common. They always contain at least one record, even if it is one indicating that the file is "empty." This record is known as the end-of-file record. It is important, when handling sequential files, that the program not process this record. To accomplish this, it is necessary to read the first record of the file to determine whether it is a data record or an end-of-file record. If it is an end-of-file record, we have an end-of-file condition. If not, the data records can be processed until the *end-of-file condition* occurs. If we implemented the main iteration module with a PERFORM UNTIL statement, there would be no way for the programmer to know if the first record was a data record unless a READ had been issued before the iteration was entered. To implement a sequential file in COBOL we must PERFORM an initial READ prior to entering the PERFORM UNTIL iteration structure since the PERFORM UNTIL tests the condition prior to executing the paragraph. In other words, the first record must be READ before the main iteration control structure is entered. This results in the addition of an extra subordinate module to the second-level module that prepares things for the main processing loop. This initial READ is very common in COBOL programs and is usually referred to as a *priming read* or *initializing read*. Essentially, it readies the file for processing and ensures that the last record of the file is processed without requiring additional code. This is shown in the hierarchy chart of Figure 3.4 and reflected in the COBOL code in Figure 3.6.

3.4.2   *Tying the Code to the Documentation*

One of the basic rules of programming is to follow the documentation when coding. This implies that the code must have a direct relationship with the hierarchy charts, the Nassi-Schneiderman charts, and the file layouts. Paragraph names should reflect the module names in the hierarchy chart, either by having the same name or, if the module names are too long, by incorporating the module number and some abbreviated form of the module name.

When each module is coded, the statements in the paragraph should follow the logic shown in the module Nassi-Schneiderman charts. A block on a Nassi-Schneiderman chart may become more than one sentence of code, but the overall module logic sequence must remain identical to that of the design. Code the modules in numerical order so that the paragraphs associated with the Nassi-Schneiderman charts are easy to locate. "Top-down code" will evolve from a top-down design, but coding the paragraphs in numerical sequence in the program improves readability. The sample program in Figure 3.6 is tied in this fashion to the program documentation in Figures 3.2 through 3.5.

3.4.3   Observing Naming Conventions

Selecting meaningful names for files, data items, and paragraphs is very important for clarity in the code. We have already mentioned the importance of labeling paragraphs with the names of the modules in the hierarchy charts. File names should reflect the content of the file rather than the physical device on which they reside and should be followed by the suffix -FILE. For example, INVENTORY-FILE is much more descriptive than IN-TAPE. Record names should be suffixed by -REC or, for printer output files, by -LINE. The individual data items subordinate to the 01 level entry should be prefixed by the initials of the file or record to which they belong, whichever is more meaningful. In Figure 3.6, lines 34–39 and 45–50 exemplify this convention.

Data element names should reflect their contents or use. A data-name such as RETAIL-PRICE gives more information than does the name DOLLARS. To illustrate how senseless names destroy the intelligibility of a program, examine Figure 3.13. It depicts the sample program from Figure 3.6 using meaningless names. Notice how even this simple program has become hard to follow.

Figure 3.13   Use of Poor Names

```
 1 IDENTIFICATION DIVISION.
 2
 3 PROGRAM-ID. LIST-IT.
 4*PRODUCE A LIST OF EMPLOYEES WHOSE
 5*SALARIES AND BONUS EXCEEDS $75,000.
 6 AUTHOR. NEWT JAMES.
 7 INSTALLATION. IRS.
 8 DATE-WRITTEN. JULY 30,1991.
 9 DATE-COMPILED. 14-Jan-90 15:13.
10 SECURITY.   CONFIDENTIAL
11
12
13 ENVIRONMENT DIVISION.
14
15 CONFIGURATION SECTION.
16
17 SOURCE-COMPUTER. GENERIC-COMPUTER.
18 OBJECT-COMPUTER. GENERIC-COMPUTER.
19
20 INPUT-OUTPUT SECTION.
21
22 FILE-CONTROL.
23     SELECT INPUT-FILE ASSIGN TO S-PAY.
24     SELECT OUTPUT-FILE ASSIGN TO PRINTER.
25
```

Figure 3.13   (continued)

```
26
27 DATA DIVISION.
28
29 FILE SECTION.
30
31 FD  INPUT-FILE
32      LABEL RECORDS ARE STANDARD.
33
34 01  READ-LINE.
35      05  SOME-NUMBER          PIC 9(4).
36      05  NAM                  PIC X(20).
37      05  FILLER               PIC X(80).
38      05  SALARY               PIC 9(8)V99.
39      05  BONUS                PIC 9(8)V99.
40      05  FILLER               PIC X(14).
41
42 FD  OUTPUT-FILE
43      LABEL RECORDS ARE STANDARD.
44
45 01  PRINT-STUFF.
46      05  OTHER-NUMBER         PIC 9(4).
47      05  FILLER               PIC X(4).
48      05  PERSON-NAME          PIC X(20).
49      05  FILLER               PIC X(4).
50      05  TOO-MUCH-MONEY       PIC ZZZ,ZZZ,ZZZ.ZZ.
51
52 WORKING-STORAGE SECTION.
53
54 01  FROGGY           PIC X VALUE "N".
55
56 01  ALL-THE-DOUGH    PIC 9(9)V99.
57
58
59 PROCEDURE DIVISION.
60
61 DO-IT-ALL.
62      OPEN INPUT INPUT-FILE.
63      OPEN OUTPUT OUTPUT-FILE.
64      PERFORM 100-READ-SOMETHING.
65      PERFORM 200-MAKE-SECRET-LIST-APPEAR
66           UNTIL FROGGY = "Y".
67      CLOSE INPUT-FILE.
68      CLOSE OUTPUT-FILE.
```

Figure 3.13   *(continued)*

```
69      STOP RUN.
70
71 100-READ-SOMETHING.
72      READ INPUT-FILE
73           AT END MOVE "Y" TO FROGGY.
74
75 200-MAKE-SECRET-LIST-APPEAR.
76      PERFORM 210-NUMBER-CRUNCH.
77      IF ALL-THE-DOUGH > 75000.00
78          PERFORM 220-KICK-IT-OUT.
79              PERFORM 100-READ-SOMETHING.
80
81 210-NUMBER-CRUNCH.
82      ADD SALARY-BONUS GIVING ALL-THE-DOUGH.
83
84 220-KICK-IT-OUT.
85      MOVE SPACES TO PRINT-STUFF.
86      MOVE SOME-NUMBER TO OTHER-NUMBER.
87      MOVE NAM TO PERSON-NAME.
88      MOVE ALL-THE-DOUGH TO TOO-MUCH-MONEY.
89      WRITE PRINT-STUFF.
```

3.4.4   *Avoiding GO TO Statements*

One important premise in structured coding is the avoidance of GO TO statements. GO TO statements represent unconditional branching. In COBOL, GO TO statements transfer control to another paragraph, but control does not return to the paragraph issuing the GO TO statement. Therefore, control can be indiscriminately passed among the paragraphs of the program.

Trying to follow the control logic of a program full of GO TO statements results in much confusion. Figure 3.14 is a version of the program in Figure 3.6 using GO TO statements rather than PERFORM statements to transfer control. Notice again how complex a simple program has become.

Figure 3.14   *"List Excessive Salaries" Program with GO TO Usage*

```
00001      IDENTIFICATION DIVISION.                      GOTO0010
00002                                                    GOTO0020
00003      PROGRAM-ID. LIST-EXCESS-SALARIES.             GOTO0030
00004      *PRODUCE A LIST OF EMPLOYEES WHOSE            GOTO0040
00005      *SALARIES AND BONUS EXCEEDS $75,000           GOTO0050
00006      AUTHOR. NEWT JAMES.                           GOTO0060
00007      INSTALLATION. IRS.                            GOTO0070
00008      DATE-WRITTEN. JULY 30,1996.                   GOTO0080
```

Figure 3.14 *(continued)*

```
00009        DATE-COMPILED. 14-Jan-90 14:24.                              GOTO0090
00010        SECURITY. CONFIDENTIAL.                                      GOTO0100
00011                                                                     GOTO0110
00012                                                                     GOTO0120
00013        ENVIRONMENT DIVISION.                                        GOTO0130
00014                                                                     GOTO0140
00015        CONFIGURATION SECTION.                                       GOTO0150
00016                                                                     GOTO0160
00017        SOURCE-COMPUTER. GENERIC-COMPUTER.                           GOTO0170
00018        OBJECT-COMPUTER. GENERIC-COMPUTER.                           GOTO0180
00019                                                                     GOTO0190
00020        INPUT-OUTPUT SECTION.                                        GOTO0200
00021                                                                     GOTO0210
00022        FILE-CONTROL.                                                GOTO0220
00023            SELECT PAYROLL-MASTER-FILE ASSIGN TO S-PAY.              GOTO0230
00024            SELECT EXCESS-SALARY-LIST-FILE ASSIGN TO PRINTER.        GOTO0240
00025                                                                     GOTO0250
00026                                                                     GOTO0260
00027        DATA DIVISION.                                               GOTO0270
00028                                                                     GOTO0280
00029        FILE SECTION.                                                GOTO0290
00030                                                                     GOTO0300
00031        FD  PAYROLL-MASTER-FILE                                      GOTO0310
00032            LABEL RECORDS ARE STANDARD.                              GOTO0320
00033                                                                     GOTO0330
00034        01  PAYROLL-REC.                                             GOTO0340
00035            05  PMF-EMPLOYEE-ID-NUMBER          PIC 9(4).            GOTO0350
00036            05  PMF-EMPLOYEE-NAME               PIC X(20).           GOTO0360
00037            05  FILLER                          PIC X(80).           GOTO0370
00038            05  PMF-YEAR-TO-DATE-SALARY         PIC 9(8)V99.         GOTO0380
00039            05  PMF-YEAR-TO-DATE-BONUS          PIC 9(8)V99.         GOTO0390
00040            05  FILLER                          PIC X(14).           GOTO0400
00041                                                                     GOTO0410
00042        FD  EXCESS-SALARY-LIST-FILE                                  GOTO0420
00043            LABEL RECORDS ARE STANDARD.                              GOTO0430
00044                                                                     GOTO0440
00045        01  EMPLOYEE-WAGES-LINE.                                     GOTO0450
00046            05  EWL-EMPLOYEE-ID-NUMBER          PIC 9(4).            GOTO0460
00047            05  FILLER                          PIC X(4).            GOTO0470
00048            05  EWL-EMPLOYEE-NAME       PIC X(20).                   GOTO0480
00049            05  FILLER                 PIC X(4).                     GOTO0490
00050            05  EWL-WAGES              PIC ZZZ,ZZZ,ZZZ.ZZ.           GOTO0500
00051                                                                     GOTO0510
00052        WORKING-STORAGE SECTION.                                     GOTO0520
00053                                                                     GOTO0530
00054        01  END-OF-FILE-INDICATORS.                                  GOTO0540
00055            05  EOF-PAYROLL-MASTER-FILE  PIC X VALUE "N".            GOTO0550
00056                                                                     GOTO0560
00057        01  TOTAL-FIELD.                                             GOTO0570
```

Figure 3.14   (continued)

```
00058          05   TOT-WAGES                    PIC 9(9)V99.                    GOTO0580
00059                                                                            GOTO0590
00060                                                                            GOTO0600
00061     PROCEDURE DIVISION.                                                    GOTO0610
00062                                                                            GOTO0620
00063     LIST-EXCESSIVE-SALARIES.                                               GOTO0630
00064          GO TO 900-INITIALIZATION.                                         GOTO0640
00065     END-OF-PROGRAM.                                                        GOTO0650
00066          GO TO 1000-TERMINATION.                                           GOTO0660
00067                                                                            GOTO0670
00068     100-READ-PAYROLL-MASTER-FILE.                                          GOTO0680
00069          READ PAYROLL-MASTER-FILE                                          GOTO0690
00070               AT END GO TO END-OF-PROGRAM.                                 GOTO0700
00071          GO TO 210-ADD.                                                    GOTO0710
00072                                                                            GOTO0720
00073     150-IF.                                                                GOTO0730
00074          IF TOT-WAGES > 75000.00 GO TO 200-PRINT-EMP-WAGES-LINE.           GOTO0740
00075          GO TO 100-READ-PAYROLL-MASTER-FILE.                               GOTO0750
00076                                                                            GOTO0760
00077     200-PRINT-EMP-WAGES-LINE.                                              GOTO0770
00078          MOVE SPACES TO EMPLOYEE-WAGES-LINE.                               GOTO0780
00079          MOVE PMF-EMPLOYEE-ID-NUMBER TO EWL-EMPLOYEE-ID-NUMBER.            GOTO0790
00080          MOVE PMF-EMPLOYEE-NAME TO EWL-EMPLOYEE-NAME.                      GOTO0800
00081          MOVE TOT-WAGES TO EWL-WAGES.                                      GOTO0810
00082          WRITE EMPLOYEE-WAGES-LINE.                                        GOTO0820
00083          GO TO 100-READ-PAYROLL-MASTER-FILE.                               GOTO0830
00084                                                                            GOTO0840
00085     210-ADD.                                                               GOTO0850
00086          ADD PMF-YEAR-TO-DATE-SALARY PMF-YEAR-TO-DATE-BONUS                GOTO0860
00087               GIVING TOT-WAGES.                                            GOTO0870
00088          GO TO 150-IF.                                                     GOTO0880
00089                                                                            GOTO0890
00090     900-INITIALIZATION.                                                    GOTO0900
00091          OPEN INPUT PAYROLL-MASTER-FILE.                                   GOTO0910
00092          OPEN OUTPUT EXCESS-SALARY-LIST-FILE.                              GOTO0920
00093          GO TO 100-READ-PAYROLL-MASTER-FILE.                               GOTO0930
00094                                                                            GOTO0940
00095     1000-TERMINATION.                                                      GOTO0950
00096          CLOSE PAYROLL-MASTER-FILE.                                        GOTO0960
00097          CLOSE EXCESS-SALARY-LIST-FILE.                                    GOTO0970
00098          STOP RUN.                                                         GOTO0980
```

In a large program the use of GO TO statements is extremely confusing to someone who will have to maintain the program. COBOL provides the capability of constructing most programs without GO TO statements. Later we will discuss those rare instances when the GO TO statement is necessary.

3.4.5   *Observing Code Spacing Guidelines*

No code spacing standards have been established for COBOL programs by any agency, but certain guidelines for line spacing and indentation exist that help improve program readability.

Paragraphs should be separated by one or more blank lines to facilitate finding them in the code. As a matter of fact, blank lines may be inserted in COBOL code at any point. New divisions and sections should also be separated from other code by several blank lines or positioned at the top of a new page of the program listing. DATA DIVISION 01 entries should also be preceded by a blank line.

Most COBOL compilers support the use of a slash (/) in the continuation column to force a page break on subsequent listings. This may be used to advantage by placing a slash in column 7 when defining a division or section, in effect listing that division or section on a new page.

Indentation of code on succeeding lines should exhibit uniformity throughout the program. Use tabs of four columns for each successive indentation. Many systems allow tabs to be set automatically to facilitate this process. Indenting lines of code makes the code easier to read, and thus easier to debug and modify. Statements and sentences that use more than one line should have their extra lines indented. For example,

```
IF MASTER-QTY-ON-HAND IS LESS THAN MASTER-ORDERING-POINT
    MOVE MASTER-INVENTORY-RECORD TO REORDER-RECORD
    WRITE REORDER-RECORD.
```

The examples used throughout the book will serve as guidelines. Most companies and instructors have established standards that programmers must follow. If not, determine indentation and spacing standards for your programs and follow them consistently.

Case Study: CDL's Categorize Daily Mail Revisited

The Categorize Daily Mail program hierarchy charts and Nassi-Schneiderman charts from the previous chapter are replicated in Figure 3.15. We discussed the design aspects in the last chapter. In this chapter we will see how Charlene uses the file layouts, hierarchy chart, and Nassi-Schneiderman charts to write the COBOL code shown in Figure 3.16.

Figure 3.15   *"Categorize Daily Mail" Program Documentation*

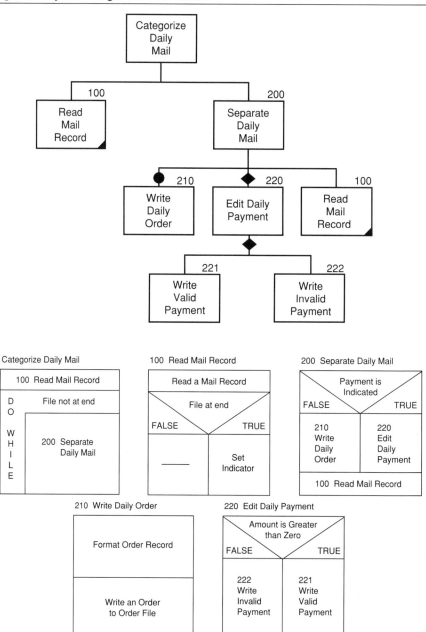

Figure 3.15   (continued)

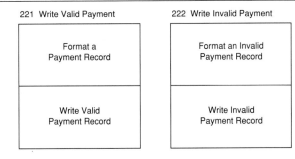

Figure 3.16   "Categorize Daily Mail" COBOL Code

```
 1 IDENTIFICATION DIVISION.
 2 PROGRAM-ID.  CATEGORIZE.
 3*  THIS PROGRAM TAKES A FILE WITH ORDERS AND PAYMENTS PROCESSED
 4*  BY THE CLERKS IN THE MAIL ROOM AND SEPARATES THEM INTO ORDERS,
 5*  VALID PAYMENTS AND INVALID PAYMENTS.
 6 AUTHOR.         C HILTON.
 7 DATE-WRITTEN.   6-22-85.
 8 DATE-COMPILED. 15-Jan-90 04:39.
11 ENVIRONMENT DIVISION.
12
13 CONFIGURATION SECTION.
14 SOURCE-COMPUTER.  GENERIC-COMPUTER.
15 OBJECT-COMPUTER.  GENERIC-COMPUTER.
16
17 INPUT-OUTPUT SECTION.
18 FILE-CONTROL.
19     SELECT PAYMENTS-AND-ORDERS-FILE ASSIGN TO DISK
20         ORGANIZATION IS SEQUENTIAL.
21     SELECT VALID-PAYMENTS-FILE ASSIGN TO DISK
22         ORGANIZATION IS SEQUENTIAL.
23     SELECT INVALID-PAYMENTS-FILE ASSIGN TO DISK
24         ORGANIZATION IS SEQUENTIAL.
25     SELECT ORDERS-FILE ASSIGN TO DISK
26         ORGANIZATION IS SEQUENTIAL.
27
28
29
30 DATA DIVISION.
31
```

Figure 3.16   *(continued)*

```
32 FILE SECTION.
33
34 FD   PAYMENTS-AND-ORDERS-FILE
35       LABEL RECORDS ARE STANDARD.
36
37 01   PAYMENT-OR-ORDER-REC.
38       05  PAO-CODE                      PIC X.
39       05  PAO-PAYMENT-AMOUNT            PIC 9(6)V99.
40       05  PAO-CUSTOMER-NUMBER           PIC 9(6).
41       05  PAO-CHECK-NUMBER              PIC X(8).
42       05  PAO-ORDER-INFORMATION.
43           10  PAO-CD-STOCK-NUMBER       PIC 9(6).
44           10  PAO-QUANTITY-ORDERED      PIC 99.
45           10  PAO-ORDER-NUMBER          PIC 9(6).
46
47
48 FD   VALID-PAYMENTS-FILE
49       LABEL RECORDS ARE STANDARD.
50
51 01   VALIDATED-PAYMENT-REC.
52       05  VP-CUSTOMER-NUMBER     PIC 9(6).
53       05  VP-PAYMENT-AMOUNT      PIC 9(6)V99.
54       05  VP-CHECK-NUMBER        PIC X(8).
55
56
57 FD   INVALID-PAYMENTS-FILE
58       LABEL RECORDS ARE STANDARD.
59
60 01   INVALID-PAYMENT-REC.
61       05  IP-CUSTOMER-NUMBER     PIC 9(6).
62       05  IP-PAYMENT-AMOUNT      PIC 9(6)V99.
63       05  IP-CHECK-NUMBER        PIC X(8).
64
65
66 FD   ORDERS-FILE
67       LABEL RECORDS ARE STANDARD.
68
69 01   ORDER-REC.
70       05  O-CUSTOMER-NUMBER         PIC 9(6).
71       05  O-ORDER-INFORMATION.
72           10  O-CD-STOCK-NUMBER     PIC 9(6).
73           10  O-QUANTITY-ORDERED    PIC 99.
```

Figure 3.16 **(continued)**

```
74          10  O-ORDER-NUMBER        PIC 9(6).
75
76
77 WORKING-STORAGE SECTION.
78
79 01  END-OF-FILE-INDICATORS.
80      05  EOF-PAYMENTS-AND-ORDERS  PIC X(5) VALUE "FALSE".
81
82
83
84 PROCEDURE DIVISION.
85
86 CATEGORIZE-DAILY-MAIL.
87      OPEN INPUT PAYMENTS-AND-ORDERS-FILE
88      OPEN OUTPUT ORDERS-FILE.
89      OPEN OUTPUT VALID-PAYMENTS-FILE.
90      OPEN OUTPUT INVALID-PAYMENTS-FILE.
91      PERFORM 100-READ-MAIL-RECORD.
92      PERFORM 200-SEPARATE-DAILY-MAIL
93          UNTIL EOF-PAYMENTS-AND-ORDERS EQUAL "TRUE ".
94      CLOSE PAYMENTS-AND-ORDERS-FILE.
95      CLOSE ORDERS-FILE.
96      CLOSE VALID-PAYMENTS-FILE.
97      CLOSE INVALID-PAYMENTS-FILE.
98      STOP RUN.
99
100 100-READ-MAIL-RECORD.
101     READ PAYMENTS-AND-ORDERS-FILE
102         AT END MOVE "TRUE " TO EOF-PAYMENTS-AND-ORDERS.
103
104 200-SEPARATE-DAILY-MAIL.
105     IF PAO-CODE EQUAL "O" PERFORM 210-WRITE-DAILY-ORDER
106     ELSE PERFORM 220-EDIT-DAILY-PAYMENT.
107     PERFORM 100-READ-MAIL-RECORD.
108
109 210-WRITE-DAILY-ORDER.
110     MOVE PAO-CUSTOMER-NUMBER   TO O-CUSTOMER-NUMBER.
111     MOVE PAO-ORDER-INFORMATION TO O-ORDER-INFORMATION.
112     WRITE ORDER-REC.
113
114 220-EDIT-DAILY-PAYMENT.
115     IF PAO-PAYMENT-AMOUNT IS GREATER THAN ZERO
```

Figure 3.16   *(continued)*

```
116              PERFORM 221-WRITE-VALID-PAYMENT
117         ELSE PERFORM 222-WRITE-INVALID-PAYMENT.
118
119  221-WRITE-VALID-PAYMENT.
120         MOVE PAO-CUSTOMER-NUMBER TO VP-CUSTOMER-NUMBER.
121         MOVE PAO-PAYMENT-AMOUNT  TO VP-PAYMENT-AMOUNT.
122         MOVE PAO-CHECK-NUMBER    TO VP-CHECK-NUMBER.
123         WRITE VALIDATED-PAYMENT-REC.
124
125  222-WRITE-INVALID-PAYMENT.
126         MOVE PAO-CUSTOMER-NUMBER TO IP-CUSTOMER-NUMBER.
127         MOVE PAO-CHECK-NUMBER    TO IP-CHECK-NUMBER.
128         MOVE ZERO                TO IP-PAYMENT-AMOUNT.
129         WRITE INVALID-PAYMENT-REC.
```

Within the PROCEDURE DIVISION the program is modularized to correspond to the hierarchy chart. For example, the hierarchy chart module "220-Edit-Daily-Payment" begins on line 114. Each module of the hierarchy chart has a corresponding section of code that implements its associated Nassi-Schneiderman chart. This primary relationship between design and code is a fundamental precept of structured programming. As you learn the COBOL language, we will stress the relationship between design and code.

Charlene used the file descriptions to develop the FD and 01 record descriptions for each file. For example, the Invalid Payments File has three items: the customer number, the payment amount, and the check number. These items along with their PICTURE clauses appear in the FILE SECTION of the DATA DIVISION under the record named INVALID-PAYMENT-REC. Charlene uses the standard of suffixing all file names with -FILE and all record names with -REC. The data-names are as descriptive as possible and are prefixed by the initials of the file-name. Thus IP-CHECK-NUMBER is the eight-character check number in a record of the INVALID-PAYMENTS-FILE.

In the PROCEDURE DIVISION Charlene coded each paragraph directly from the Nassi-Schneiderman charts. For example, the paragraph 200-SEPARATE-DAILY-MAIL and the N-S chart module "200-Separate-Daily-Mail" are identical. The first task in the module is to determine if the input record is an order or a payment. If the record is an order, the paragraph to write to the order file is performed; otherwise the module to edit a payment is performed. The last task done by paragraph 200-SEPARATE-DAILY-MAIL is to execute 100-READ-MAIL-RECORD to acquire the next input record.

In order to determine if the program functions properly, Charlene tests the program. She creates an input file of test data as shown in Figure 3.17. After running the program she examines the three output files, as shown in Figure 3.18, to determine whether the results are exactly as expected.

Figure 3.17   *Test Data for "Categorize Daily Mail"*

```
O00000000454345        85434578467899
O00000000289837        43213401467900
O00000000436789        87578803467901
P00000000546787a678654400000000000000
P00010000765436B987654600000000000000
```

Figure 3.18   *Test Results for "Categorize Daily Mail"*

```
Valid Payments File Result
76543600010000B9876546


Invalid Payments File Result
54678700000000A6786544


Orders File Results
45434585434578467899
28983743213401467900
43678987578803467901
```

Summary

COBOL has a hierarchical structure. Programs consist of four divisions: the IDENTIFICA-TION, ENVIRONMENT, DATA, and PROCEDURE divisions. Divisions are composed of sections, sections of paragraphs, and paragraphs of sentences or entries. Statements form sentences, and statements and entries are composed of clauses that are made up of words, the smallest language element in COBOL.

The IDENTIFICATION DIVISION identifies a COBOL program. The ENVIRONMENT DIVISION describes the computer configuration used. The DATA DIVISION describes the data, files, and temporary work areas used in the program. The PROCEDURE DIVISION specifies the actual problem-solving logic of the program.

To write structured COBOL programs, the programmer follows certain guidelines. First, he uses structured tools and techniques for developing the program design such as hierarchy charts and Nassi-Schneiderman charts. He follows the design documentation when coding. He uses meaningful names for files, data elements, and paragraphs in the code and uses spaces, blank lines, and indentation liberally. He uses the three primitive control structures and avoids unconditional branching statements like the GO TO statement.

Key Terms

division	IDENTIFICATION DIVISION	PICTURE (PIC)
section	PROGRAM-ID	WORKING-STORAGE SECTION
paragraph	program-name	VALUE
sentence	comment-entry	PROCEDURE DIVISION
statement	ENVIRONMENT DIVISION	OPEN
conditional	CONFIGURATION SECTION	PERFORM
imperative	SOURCE-COMPUTER	PERFORM UNTIL
entry	OBJECT-COMPUTER	CLOSE
clause	INPUT-OUTPUT SECTION	STOP RUN
word	FILE-CONTROL	READ
reserved word	SELECT	IF
name	file-name	ADD
literal	implementor-name	WRITE
comment	DATA DIVISION	structured code
margin	FILE SECTION	end-of-file-condition
MOVE	file description (FD)	priming read (initializing read)
desk checking	label records	

Hints for Avoiding Errors

1. Do not panic. There is always a learning curve associated with any new task, and learning a new programming language is no exception. It is important that you remain calm even in the face of deadlines. Corollary: Start assignments as soon as you can.

2. Be certain you understand the problem. Read the program specifications thoroughly and thoughtfully several times. Resolve any questions by speaking with the author of the specifications. Realize that good problem definition is hard work and takes time.

3. Think before beginning the programming tasks. Evaluate several program structure designs. You will save time in coding and debugging.

4. Review your logic to determine if the program design works "in principle." It is much easier to make corrections and changes at this level.

5. Use the design to generate the code. It is much easier to develop accurate code from a structured design rather than from memory.

6. Keep complete documentation. The hierarchy chart, Nassi-Schneiderman charts, and comments within the code are crucial to the maintenance of the program. Never assume that you will have the time to document the program after it is complete. Documenting programs often helps you locate errors in the logic before you even begin to code. If you make changes to the program, change the documentation.

7. Do not use tricky codes in order to speed up processing. Processing time is less expensive than programming time, and tricks make the code hard to change when changes are required.

8. Do not be afraid to start over. When a program is cumbersome, full of errors, full of corrections, or poorly designed, it is best to begin again. Do not try to patch a bad program. Write a good one.
9. Follow the guidelines for structured COBOL programming style. Your program will be easier to handle.

Exercises

3.1   Develop the hierarchy chart and Nassi-Schneiderman charts for the program described in Figure 3.19.

3.2   Alter the program design of Figures 2.26 and 2.27 to incorporate the priming read.

3.3   Using the same file structure of Exercise 3.1, develop the complete design to produce a listing of students who are classified as seniors (more than 90 hours earned).

3.4   Using your limited COBOL knowledge and the code in Figure 3.6 as a guide, write the code of Exercise 3.3.

3.5   The _____ DIVISION provides the necessary algorithms to execute the program.

3.6   A PERFORM statement is an unconditional branch. True or false?

3.7   Which of the following statements is correct?
      a. A hierarchy chart illustrates program logic.
      b. A hierarchy chart illustrates the relationship between modules.

3.8   A user-defined name may contain the $ character. True or false?

3.9   The _____ SECTION specifies the characteristics of the computer involved in the compilation and execution of the program.

3.10 A coding hierarchy for COBOL is:
      a. Divisions, sections, sentences, comments, paragraphs.
      b. Divisions, sections, paragraphs, sentences, statements, verbs.
      c. Divisions, paragraphs, sections, words.

3.11 Excluding comment statements, a COBOL program is coded using:
      a. Columns 12 to 72.
      b. Margin A through margin B.
      c. Margin A through column 72.
      d. Margin B through column 80.

3.12 Reserved words
      a. may be used by the programmer to define variables.
      b. have a predefined meaning in the COBOL language.
      c. are used only in the PROCEDURE DIVISION.

3.13 Which structure is not valid in structured design?
      a. the selection
      b. the sequence
      c. the unconditional branch
      d. the iteration

Figure 3.19   Program Specifications for Exercise 3.1

PROGRAM SUMMARY
TITLE:
PREPARED BY:
DATE:

FILES USED		
FILE NAME	**MEDIA**	**ORGANIZATION**
Fall 93 Students	Disk	Sequential

DESCRIPTION *A program is needed to perform sequential processing on a student file at a state college. The program should provide: a student listing with appropriate headings, total number of records read, average number of credits being taking, total tuition of students based on in-state = $60/credit, out-of-state = $120/credit.*

RECORD LAYOUT SHEET

Record Name:		File Name: *Fall 93 Students*			
Prepared By:		Date:			
Key Fields: *Student ID number*		Organization: *Sequential*			
Field	Description	Type*	Length	Decimal
Student ID No.	Student identifier number	N	6	
Major	Student's academic major	A	4	
Hours taken	Total academic hours earned	N	3	
Accum. credits	Total academic credits earned	N	3	
Hours curr. taking	Hours attempted this semester	N	2	
Residency	Residence status	A	3	

* A = alphanumeric
 N = numeric

3.14 Which statement in COBOL represents the iteration construct?
    a. IF
    b. PERFORM UNTIL
    c. READ
    d. PERFORM

3.15 Which statement in COBOL represents the selection structure?
    a. IF
    b. PERFORM UNTIL
    c. READ
    d. PERFORM

3.16 Which are not valid COBOL data-names?
    a. ACCOUNTS-DUE
    b. SELECT
    c. HEAD-OF-DEPT
    d. PAST-DUE-AMOUNT
    e. FORTUNE-500

Use the following COBOL statement syntax to answer Exercises 3.17 through 3.20

$$\underline{ADD} \quad \left\{ \begin{array}{l} \text{literal} \\ \text{identifier-1} \ldots \end{array} \right\} \quad \underline{TO} \quad \{\text{identifier-m}\}\ldots$$

3.17 The word ADD is required in this statement. True or false?
3.18 Only one field may be specified for the result. True or false?
3.19 Multiple fields must be specified after the word ADD. True or false?
3.20 The word TO is optional in this statement. True or false?
3.21 Reserved words can never be used for other purposes by the programmer, even if they are part of a data-name and are separated by hyphens (-). True or false?
3.22 COBOL is very flexible as a fourth-generation language allowing the programmer to place statements anywhere within the file regardless of column positions. True or false?
3.23 COBOL's name length restriction allows the programmer to use meaningful, descriptive names to identify data items and program features. True or false?
3.24 Which of the following is the correct order of COBOL syntax from highest to lowest levels?
    a. divisions, sections, paragraphs, statements, clauses, words
    b. divisions, sections, paragraphs, phrases, statements, words
    c. sections, divisions, departments, paragraphs, statements, clauses
    d. divisions, statements, paragraphs, clauses, words, letters
3.25 The _Data DIVISION_ specifies the temporary work areas to be used in a COBOL program.
    a. IDENTIFICATION DIVISION
    b. ENVIRONMENT DIVISION
    c. DATA DIVISION
    d. PROCEDURE DIVISION

3.26   As in BASIC and FORTRAN, structured COBOL programming makes extensive use of the GO TO statement. True or false?

3.27   Spaces, blank lines, and indentation should be liberally used throughout a COBOL program. True or false?

3.28   It is best to:
      a.   produce the N-S charts first and then develop the hierarchy chart at the same time the code is generated.
      b.   create the hierarchy and then generate N-S charts from the completed code.
      c.   generate working, completed code and then tailor the documentation to match its specifications.
      d.   always develop a complete program design before generating code directly from the documentation.

3.29   What is the best descriptive name below for a file record that is to be used as an output line to an employee payroll listing?
      a.   EMPLOYEE-PAYROLL-DETAIL-LINE
      b.   FILE-OUTPUT-FORMAT
      c.   PAYROLL-REC

3.30   Comments are indicated by placing an asterisk in column 8. True or false?

3.31   It is not acceptable programming practice to divide statements onto successive lines at mid-word breaks. True or false?

3.32   In the COBOL notation, all reserved words are:
      a.   italicized.
      b.   capitalized.
      c.   underlines.
      d.   lower-case.
      e.   enclosed in brackets

3.33   Which structure is not supported by COBOL syntax?
      a.   the sequence
      b.   the selection
      c.   the unconditional branch
      d.   the iteration
      e.   all of the above
      f.   none of the above

3.34   Which statement in COBOL represents the unconditional iteration construct?
      a.   GO TO
      b.   PERFORM
      c.   IF
      d.   PERFORM UNTIL
      e.   A and C
      f.   none of the above

3.35   Which statement in COBOL represents a DO WHILE iteration construct?
      a.   GO TO
      b.   PERFORM
      c.   IF
      d.   PERFORM UNTIL
      e.   B and D
      f.   none of the above

3.36   _____ can help detect syntax and logic errors before you compile the program.

3.37   The _____ clause names each file of data and associates it with an external medium.

3.38   The two statements that must appear at the start of every COBOL program are:

      a. _____
      b. _____

3.39   _____ is the notation used to describe the syntax of a statement that performs a COBOL priming read.

3.40   Literals may be _____ or _____. (One-word answers for each blank).

For Exercises 3.41 through 3.43 refer to the following code:

```
MAIN-LOGIC.
   ─ OPEN INPUT.
     MOVE 0 TO NUM-HOLD.
     MOVE 0 TO NUM-TOTAL.
     PERFORM 100-MAIN-PROCESS UNTIL NUM-HOLD > 5.
     GO TO 300-END.
100-MAIN-PROCESS.
     MOVE 1 TO NUM-HOLD.
     IF NUM-HOLD > 0 ADD 3 TO NUM-HOLD.
     IF NUM-HOLD < 3 MOVE NUM-HOLD TO NUM-TOTAL.
300-END.
     STOP RUN.
```

3.41   Is anything wrong with the syntax for the statements in MAIN-LOGIC? If so, what is (are) the error(s)?

3.42   What will be the final value of NUM-TOTAL?

3.43   Create an N-S chart that illustrates the logic in module 100-MAIN-PROCESS.

3.44   Can the three primitive control constructs be implemented in COBOL code? Explain.

3.45   Defend this statement: "COBOL coding forms are useful in program design and are a good addition to a program's documentation."

4

ORGANIZATION OF DATA

The major task of business information systems is the processing of data. Data are organized into hierarchical structures; understanding these data structures is essential for any programmer. In the business environment, most applications involve the processing of data for use in decision making. For example, a report showing the status of inventory items would enable a decision maker to order the correct items.

Our objective in this chapter is to familiarize you with some of the data structures supported in COBOL. Understanding these structures is critical to writing successful programs. Data structures form the basis for generating sophisticated reports, updating files, choosing among file structures, and managing internal tables.

4.1   General Structure of Data

Data are nothing more than facts about entities such as objects or individuals. In other words, data are the raw materials for the process of producing information. To be meaningful, however, data must be organized in a way that specifies the interrelationships among the data elements. This organization is known as the structure of data. The highest level of data for our purposes is the file. *Files* are large collections of related data.

Files are composed of *records* representing the collection of all the facts about a single entity. For example, all the facts kept about a student comprise a student record. Physically, records are a collection of the characters comprising the fields. In *sequential files* data records are usually ordered in the file in a sequence determined by a small part of the record known as a *key*. In the case of student records, the key might be the student's social security number. Sequential files must be read in the same key order in which the records are stored.

Sequential files are not new to you. When you type in your program at the keyboard, you are creating a sequential file of program-line records. The program is stored and later compiled in the same order in which it is arranged. When your program writes a report to the printer, you are creating a sequential file of report lines. These "lines" will be in the order in which you generate them in the program. This file is eventually written to the printer.

A sequential file is usually stored in a predetermined order. For example, employee records might be stored in alphabetical order by name or in numerical order by social security number. The key is used to order the file, and it is usually the prime identifier for processing the records in the file. If an employee file is arranged in alphabetical order, the employees' paychecks are likely to be generated in alphabetical order also, but the social security number could be used to change the order in which the paychecks are produced, resulting in a different paycheck sequence. In a payroll application, the order of the paychecks would be the same as the order of employees in the file, unless special processing changed that order before printing.

Records are composed of elementary data units known as data items or fields. A data item represents an individual fact or attribute of an entity. For example, your name, age, and classification in school are facts or attributes about you. In this case, you are the entity. If we want to generalize, we could say that name, age, and classification are facts about an entity known as student. Data items are in turn made up of a combination of *characters*. Figure 4.1 shows the general structure of data used in the text.

4.2   COBOL Data Hierarchy

Using the simplified assumption that a file is the most global view of data in COBOL, we can begin identifying the components of the COBOL data hierarchy. Figure 4.2 illustrates this hierarchy. The top level represents the most inclusive unit of data in a COBOL program, the file. The file is composed of records. A record is the data unit for input and output operations. Within a file, several different records may exist serving different purposes. For example, although all the records in a personnel file are personnel records, there might be a mixture of salaried and hourly employees. Since the information that is applicable to each type of employee might differ because of differing payroll, benefit, and hiring considerations, it does not make sense to force the same record structure on these different employee types unless the contents of each record are identical.

Figure 4.1   *The General Structure of Data*

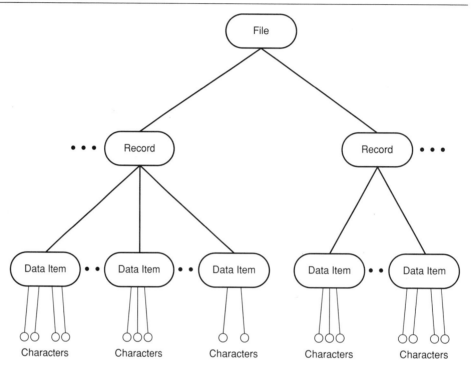

In COBOL terminology, a data item is the unit of data for a COBOL program. Recall that in the general discussion of the structure of data we mentioned the same terminology. In the general data hierarchy of Figure 4.1 a data item was actually the smallest unit of recognizable data, also referred to as a field. In COBOL, however, a data item may be a field, a series of fields, or even an entire record. In other words, we could consider an entire record one long field, if that is adequate for our program needs. This could be the case when the information contained in the record does not need to be accessed individually. For example, in describing a print file we could specify the entire print line as one record containing one field, 120 characters long.

This is not usually the case, however, and records often must be subdivided into groups of logically related information. Groupings relate items of a similar nature to each other. In a personnel file one grouping of data items would be used to identify the individual. This grouping might contain items such as the name, address, social security number, and home phone number of the employee. Another group might contain the payroll information such as the amount of salary paid to date for the year, the amount of FICA withheld for the year, and the amount of insurance premiums withheld for the year. Each group may be composed of *subgroups*, which is a further logical subdivision of a group. For example, an employee identification grouping might have a subgroup representing the employee's address.

Figure 4.2   **Data Hierarchy for Files in COBOL**

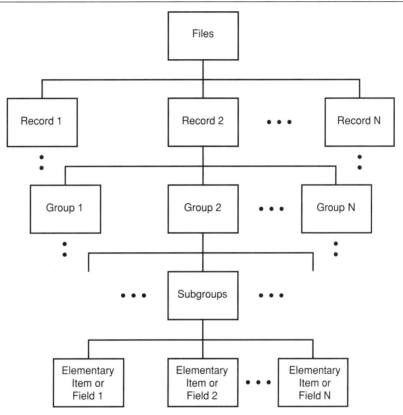

In COBOL the lowest-level data items are called *elementary items*. These are items that cannot be further subdivided for purposes of the program. In the example of the employee address subgroup the elementary items are street address, city, state, and zip code. Each elementary item must have a single name by which it is referenced. It will also have a description specifying its length and type.

Figure 4.3 contains the record layout for a file named "Customer Credit File." Note that although each field or data item is identified on the record layout form, the logical data groupings are not. The information contained in the record layout describes the physical contents of the record but says nothing about the interrelationships between the fields. In this case the programmer would need to segment the record into logical groupings.

Figure 4.3   Customer Credit Record Layout

RECORD LAYOUT SHEET

Record Name: Customer Credit		File Name: Customer Credit File			
Prepared By: G. Gibson		Date: 6-12-93			
Key Fields: Customer Identifier		Organization:			
Field	Description	Type*	Length	Decimal	
Customer identifier	The unique number representing	N	5	0	
	a customer				
Customer name	Company or individual name	A	30		
Cust. address1	First line of mailing address	A	30		
Cust. address2	Second line of mailing address	A	30		
Cust. city		A	15		
Cust. state	Must be U.S. postal code	A	2		
Cust. zip		N	5	0	
Cust. phone	(area code) prefix – #	N	10	0	
Latest purch. date	Date last order received	N	6	0	
Latest purch. amt.	Amount of last order	N	8	2	
Latest pmt. date	Date of last payment	N	6	0	
Latest pmt. amt.	Amount of last payment	N	8	2	
Credit code	Indicate prepay, COD, or credit	A	1		
Credit limit	Maximum allowable credit	N	8	2	
Balance	Amount currently owed—this also	N	8	2	
	allows for a credit balance				

* A = alphanumeric
  N = numeric

Figure 4.4 on pages 114-115 shows a possible COBOL data structure for the record layout in Figure 4.3. Let us examine this structure. First of all, notice that the record contents may be segmented into two major categories: customer identification information and credit information. We therefore choose this logical segmentation for the first set of groupings. The identification information group is made up of four items: the customer identifier number, the customer name, the customer phone number, and the customer address. The first three items in this breakdown need not be subdivided further and are therefore considered elementary items. The customer address may be further subdivided into five elementary items representing the first and second address lines, the city, state, and zip code.

For the credit information decomposition, the first segmentation includes the current credit status and the most recent transactions. The transaction information includes such data as the latest purchase and/or the latest payment amount and the date of the transaction. We therefore segment it into four data items representing the latest purchase date, latest purchase amount, latest payment date, and latest payment amount at the next level of decomposition. We can then further subdivide each date into the elementary items latest purchase month, latest purchase day, latest purchase year, and latest payment month, latest payment day, and latest payment year. We complete the logical data hierarchy by decomposing the current credit status into three elementary items representing the credit code, credit limit, and account balance.

When the user or analyst has not specified the structure of the program data, their logical segmentation becomes subjective, with the result that each programmer may end up with a different specification of the data structure. Unlike the design of the program hierarchy chart, there are no specific guidelines for this purpose. In general, experience and common sense will dictate the decomposition. If the programmer is familiar with the purposes of the program, he may deduce how the data are to be used. For example, if the user needs a report on the age of accounts receivable, the payment dates should probably be divided into their month, day, and year components. The resulting data structures should have enough segmentation to provide flexibility for future program requirements. However, seemingly endless subdivisions are unnecessary and complicate the program logic and readability. Keep the number of elementary items assigned to a single group down to a manageable number.

4.3   *Defining Data Files in COBOL*

Once the programmer has defined the structure of the data, he must transform the data structure into COBOL entries in the DATA DIVISION. The FILE SECTION in the DATA DIVISION contains the specifications for each file and the description for each record in the file.

4.3.1   *File Description*

The file description (FD) paragraph appears in the FILE SECTION of the DATA DIVISION. The name of each file described in an FD entry must correspond to the name used in the SELECT clause in the ENVIRONMENT DIVISION. Even reports that are to be sent to the printer are considered files and must have FD entries. The simplified format and rules for the FD entry are:

1.   The file-name must conform to COBOL naming rules.
2.   The file-name must appear as part of a SELECT clause.

The LABEL RECORDS clause indicates the presence or absence of label records. These labels almost always have a standard format, so the FD entry for such files would be *LABEL RECORDS STANDARD*. However, files for unit record devices such as printers do not have labels at all, so the LABEL clause would be *LABEL RECORDS OMITTED*. Complete file descriptions might be as follows:

```
FD    INVENTORY-MASTER-FILE
      LABEL RECORDS STANDARD.

FD    INVENTORY-REPORT-FILE
      LABEL RECORDS OMITTED.
```

4.3.2   Levels of Groupings in COBOL

Before we investigate how to specify the records, groups, and elementary items in COBOL, we need to see how level numbers are used to indicate the hierarchical relationships among elements in a data structure. In a data hierarchy, a *level number* represents the level of "depth" that a specific group or elementary item occupies within the overall structure. Level numbers may be taken from the set 01 through 49. They indicate the hierarchical relationships between elementary items and group items.

Figure 4.4   Customer Credit File Data Hierarchy

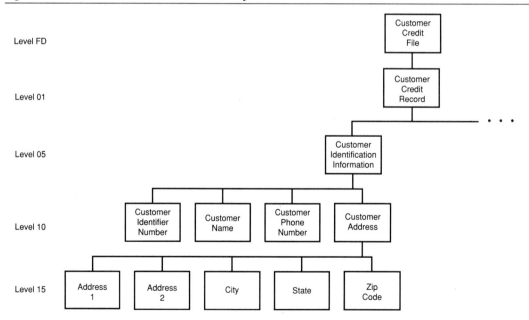

On the data hierarchy shown in Figure 4.4 we have assigned level numbers for each level of depth shown on the chart. Level numbers must represent progressively larger numbers as one proceeds from the record level to the elementary item level. Level numbers are usually assigned in increments of five to allow for possible later insertion of intermediate levels that might be needed. All data items subordinate to the same group must have the same level number. Data items with successively higher-level numbers form part of the group identified by the preceding lower-level number. Note how these rules apply to the data hierarchy of Figure 4.4.

4.3.3   Data Description Entries

Data description entries describe the elements of a data structure and their relationships. The level numbers used in the data hierarchy chart become the level numbers used in the data description entries in the FILE SECTION.

Figure 4.4   **(continued)**

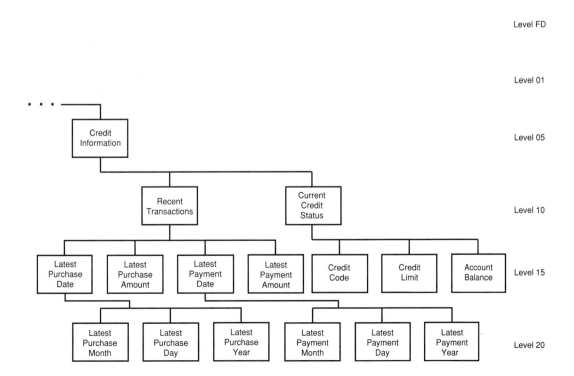

Records. Level number 01 is reserved for the record level in the FILE SECTION. Level number 01 must begin in area A and be followed by at least two spaces. The record-name immediately follows and must begin in area B. For clarity and ease of identification we will use the suffix -REC, -RECORD, or -LINE as part of the record-name. Formats for records are as follows:

When the record is divided into groups:

01   Record-name.

When the record is treated as an elementary item:

$$01 \quad \text{Record-name} \quad \left\{ \begin{array}{c} \underline{\text{PIC}} \\ \underline{\text{PICTURE}} \end{array} \right\} \quad \text{IS character-string.}$$

The record-name must be unique. The use of PICTURE will be discussed later in this chapter.

Groups and Elementary Items. Groups and elementary items are preceded by a level number other than 01. For consistency and readability we will code these levels within area B. Each additional higher-numbered level will be coded four spaces to the right of the previous level number. In this way all level numbers that are the same will begin at the same indentation. The clause associated with an entry will be indented four spaces from the beginning of its corresponding level number. This practice adds to the readability of the code and organizes the appearance of the data in a logical structure. Furthermore, the items that are immediately subordinate to the group item or record being described must be adjacent to each other and have the same level number. Following are the rules for the use of COBOL level numbers 01–49:

1. Level number 01 must begin in the margin A area.
2. Level numbers 02–49 may begin in the margin A area, but the associated data-names must appear after margin B.
3. At least one space must follow the level numbers 02–49.
4. Each level number must have a data item.
5. Items in the same group must be adjacent to one of the group members in the record layout.

The format for a group item description entry is:

Level number   Group-name   [<u>VALUE</u> IS literal-1].

1. The level number must follow level number rules.
2. The group-name must follow COBOL name rules.
3. Literal-1 may be a nonnumeric literal or a figurative constant.

The VALUE clause permits an initial value to be assigned to the group item. Although this feature is not useful when describing group items in the FILE SECTION since the value would be destroyed the first time we read from or wrote to a file, it is very useful when used in conjunction with WORKING-STORAGE entries. These will be discussed later.

The format for describing an elementary item is:

[VALUE IS literal-1].

1. The level number must follow level number rules.
2. The data-name must follow COBOL name rules.
3. Literal-1 may be a literal or a figurative constant.

The PICTURE clause defines the data type and length of the data item as specified in the record layout. We shall study it in detail subsequently.

Figure 4.5 contains the record description entry for the customer credit record data structure. It describes the group and elementary items that make up the record and shows their relationships. Notice that the COBOL entries follow the data hierarchy chart of Figure 4.4.

The successive indentation of the level numbers and their corresponding entries depict the item groupings within the record so that the correspondence to Figure 4.4 is graphically followed. CUSTOMER-CREDIT-RECORD is coded with the level number 01. The two main subgroups of the record, CCF-CUSTOMER-IDENTIFICATION and CCF-CREDIT-INFORMATION, are coded as 05 level-number entries and begin in the same margin. CCF-CURRENT-CREDIT-STATUS, CCF-RECENT-TRANSACTIONS, and CCF-CUSTOMER-ADDRESS are further subdivided. Notice that the level-15 data items making them up are coded consecutively under each group item and are indented four spaces.

In the description entry there is no implied relationship among non-adjacent groups with the same level numbers. For example, there is no relationship between CCF-CITY and CCF-LATEST-PAYMENT-AMOUNT other than that they are part of the same record. The fact that they both use level number 15 is strictly coincidental in this case and results from the fact that they each form part of two different level-10 entries.

Figure 4.5   COBOL Entries for the Customer Credit Data Structure

```
SYSTEM                                          PUNCHING INSTRUCTIONS              PAGE      OF
PROGRAM                                         GRAPHIC                           CARD FORM NUMBER
PROGRAMMER                          DATE        PUNCH

SEQUENCE    C  A  B              COBOL STATEMENT                                       IDENTIFICATION
                O
1   3 4  6 7 8   12   16   20   24   28   32   36   40   44   48   52   56   60   64   68   72   76   80

         FD   CUSTOMER-CREDIT-FILE
              LABEL RECORDS ARE STANDARD.

         01   CUSTOMER-CREDIT-RECORD
              05   CCF-CUSTOMER-IDENTIFICATION
                   10   CCF-CUSTOMER-IDENTIFIER              PICTURE   9(5).
                   10   CCF-CUSTOMER-NAME                    PICTURE   X(30).
                   10   CCF-CUSTOMER-ADDRESS
                        15   CCF-ADDRESS-1                   PICTURE   X(30).
                        15   CCF-ADDRESS-2                   PICTURE   X(30).
                        15   CCF-CITY                        PICTURE   X(15).
                        15   CCF-STATE                       PICTURE   X(2).
                        15   CCF-ZIP-CODE                    PICTURE   9(5).
                   10   CCF-CUSTOMER-PHONE                   PICTURE   9(10).
              05   CCF-CREDIT-INFORMATION.
                   10   CCF-RECENT-TRANSACTIONS.
                        15   CCF-LATEST-PURCHASE-DATE.
                             20   CCF-LATEST-PURCHASE-MONTH  PICTURE   99.
                             20   CCF-LATEST-PURCHASE-DAY    PICTURE   99.
                             20   CCF-LATEST-PURCHASE-YEAR   PICTURE   99.
                        15   CCF-LATEST-PURCHASE-AMOUNT      PICTURE   9(6)V99.
```

```
SYSTEM                                          PUNCHING INSTRUCTIONS              PAGE      OF
PROGRAM                                         GRAPHIC                           CARD FORM NUMBER
PROGRAMMER                          DATE        PUNCH

SEQUENCE    C  A  B              COBOL STATEMENT                                       IDENTIFICATION
                O
1   3 4  6 7 8   12   16   20   24   28   32   36   40   44   48   52   56   60   64   68   72   76   80

                        15   CCF-LATEST-PAYMENT-DATE.
                             20   CCF-LATEST-PAYMENT-MONTH   PICTURE   99.
                             20   CCF-LATEST-PAYMENT-DAY     PICTURE   99.
                             20   CCF-LATEST-PAYMENT-YEAR    PICTURE   99.
                        15   CCF-LATEST-PAYMENT-AMOUNT       PICTURE   9(6)V99.
                   10   CCF-CURRENT-CREDIT-STATUS.
                        15   CCF-CREDIT-CODE                 PICTURE   X.
                        15   CCF-CREDIT-LIMIT                PICTURE   9(6)V99.
                        15   CCF-BALANCE                     PICTURE   S9(6)V99.
```

Naming Conventions. In COBOL, records, group items, and elementary items are called data items because each one represents a unit of data, regardless of its inclusiveness. A record is a unit of data that includes all its groups and elementary items. In similar fashion, a group item includes its component subgroups and elementary items. For example, a date may be composed of the data elements month, day and year. If month, day and year are not further subdivided, these data items are called elementary items and represent the least inclusive unit of data. Often it is necessary to reference parts of a COBOL unit of data. To do so, larger units of data are decomposed into groups and elementary item components. We can readily see the difficulty in updating customers' accounts if the unit of data were limited to the entire record. It would be quite difficult to access the part of this unit representing the account balance.

Implicit in the ability to reference the elements of a unit of data is the requirement for a way to specifically address them. This is done by assigning each data item that will serve as a data unit a programmer-supplied name. The data-names must conform to COBOL naming conventions. Furthermore, for readability and clarity the names should be meaningful in the context of the program and the application. In Figure 4.5 we formed the data-names by combining the names used in the data hierarchy chart of Figure 4.4 with an appropriate prefix. This prefix may identify the files or the record of which the data items form a part. In our case we formed the prefix CCF by using the initials of the Customer Credit File. The prefix CCR for Customer Credit Record would have been just as appropriate.

Regardless of the prefix selected, it works as an identifier and a distinguisher. Often multiple files are used within a single program, and if the same data item name appears it is difficult to distinguish among the files without some simple means such as a prefix. For example, in an inventory update program we might have one file of inventory items and another file with additions or deletions from the inventory. It is quite likely that a stock number and a description for each stock item would appear in both files. Adding a prefix to each data-name differentiates that data item and identifies the record or file to which the item belongs. For example, MF-STOCK-NUMBER could represent the inventory item's stock number on the master file, while BT-STOCK-NUMBER would represent the inventory item's stock number on the business transactions file. Using prefixes not only ensures the uniqueness of data-names but also makes the code easier to follow in the program. Prefixes should be used for all data-names that are part of a larger structure.

Sometimes the use of a duplicate data-name is unavoidable. To differentiate among items with identical names COBOL requires that any references to the duplicate name be qualified. This is done by referring to the data-name in the context in which it appears. This concept is already familiar to you. For example, in order to differentiate between two baseball players whose names are Slugger Moshmann, you qualify their names by mentioning their team. The second baseman is Slugger Moshmann of the Los Angeles Dodgers and the shortstop is Slugger Moshmann of the St. Louis Cardinals. In this way you ensure their uniqueness.

The COBOL format for qualifying data-names is:

$$\text{data-name-1} \quad \left[\left\{ \begin{array}{c} \underline{\text{IN}} \\ \underline{\text{OF}} \end{array} \right\} \text{ data-name-2} \right] \ldots \left[\left\{ \begin{array}{c} \underline{\text{IN}} \\ \underline{\text{OF}} \end{array} \right\} \text{ file-name} \right]$$

Data-name-1 is the data-name being qualified. Data-name-2 and file-name are the qualifiers. Each qualifier must be one level higher than the data-name it qualifies and must form part of the same data hierarchy. One must continue specifying qualifiers until the data-name can be made unique. Since each file name must be unique, this would represent the highest-level qualifier.

The Reserved Word FILLER. We mentioned above that in order to reference a data item it had to have a name. However, on some occasions it is only necessary to reference certain fields of a record and to ignore others. COBOL provides a means for specifying an elementary item that is not to be referenced directly by using the reserved word *FILLER*. The format for the data description entry then becomes:

$$\text{level-number FILLER} \left\{ \begin{array}{l} \underline{\text{PIC}} \\ \underline{\text{PICTURE}} \end{array} \right\} \text{IS character-string}$$

[<u>VALUE</u> IS literal-1].

The use of FILLER is especially handy in describing input records in which certain fields should be skipped. For example, a program that lists the number of dependents of each employee does not (and probably should not) have access to the salary fields. The data description entry for the record might then use FILLER to "describe" that particular field. FILLER is an optional word and is not necessary as of the 1985 standard. However, using it helps to clearly indicate an unnamed area.

The PICTURE Clause. Recall that data description entries for elementary items have a PICTURE clause that specifies their length and data type. The reserved word PICTURE, which may be abbreviated PIC, appears after the data name in the entry.

In COBOL each elementary item is stored in memory as defined by the character string following the PICTURE clause. The data type is specified by the character A, 9, or X, which defines whether the data item is alphabetic, numeric, or alphanumeric, respectively. *Alphabetic data items* include the letters A to Z and the space. They are treated as alphanumeric data by most COBOL compilers. *Numeric data items* allow only the digits 0 to 9 and are used in computations as well as input and output. *Alphanumeric data items* include any character that is part of the alphabet, a numeric digit, or a special character in the computer's character set.

In defining the data type and length of an item, the programmer specifies one data type character per character occurring in the field, but he may not mix data types. For example, if the elementary item is composed of four digits, its PICTURE clause would be PIC 9999. A more compact way to specify the length of an elementary item is to denote data type with one occurrence of the data-type character and follow it by a digit in parentheses that indicates the length of the field. Figure 4.5 demonstrates this notation to specify the description of the elementary items. There are two advantages to this notation. First, it provides a shorthand way of specifying the data type and length and reduces errors when longer item lengths are specified. Second, since COBOL does not allow character strings longer than 30 characters, it would not be possible to describe such an elementary item without the shorthand version. For example, we can describe a data item 50 alphanumeric characters long as PIC X(50). The length specification of a data item indicates its length in characters and the number of memory positions needed to hold the data item. Thus a PICTURE clause such as PIC X(4) indicates that the item is four alphanumeric characters long and reserves four memory positions.

Numeric items are defined by using 9 as the data type character, followed by the length specification. Thus in Figure 4.5, the entry

```
15  CCF-ZIP-CODE     PIC 9(5).
```

specifies that the elementary item is five characters long and reserves five memory positions for it. In COBOL a numeric data item may not exceed 18 digit positions. However, even with this restriction we can still specify some very large and some very small numbers.

Numeric items may have additional specification requirements such as algebraic sign and decimal point placement, which may be indicated with operational characters. The operational character *S* indicates the presence of an algebraic sign. Any numeric item that might take on a negative value should have an algebraic sign. Otherwise, if a number becomes negative, its sign will be lost. The algebraic sign is specified by placing an S as the leftmost character in the data item description. PIC S9(6) indicates that the data item is a signed numeric field six positions long. The sign does not take up an extra memory position.

The capital letter *V* represents an assumed decimal point within a numeric data item. It is specified by placing a V where the location of the decimal point is assumed. The character V merely specifies the position of the decimal point. It does not require a place in memory nor does it appear physically in the data item. V acts as a placeholder. A data item defined as PIC 9(5)V99 indicates a numeric field seven positions long, with two of those positions to the right of the decimal and five to the left. Assuming that the contents of the data item described above is 1234567, it implies that the value of the item is 12345.67. If the description were PIC 9(3)V9(4), the value would be 123.4567. Both operational characters, V and S, may be used in describing a numeric item. The entry for CCF-BALANCE at the end of Figure 4.5 illustrates this.

Since we know the length of elementary items, it follows that we can determine the overall length of a group or record by adding the character positions of the elementary items subordinate to it. For example, in Figure 4.5, the character length of the group item CCF-CURRENT-CREDIT-STATUS is 17 and the record CUSTOMER-CREDIT-RECORD is 172, or 17 memory locations and 172 memory locations, respectively.

Specifying the correct length of elementary data items is critical in COBOL. If an item is longer than the length specified by the PICTURE clause, it will not be stored correctly. If a data value is shorter than the PICTURE clause specifies, COBOL will pad the data item so that it fills to the required length. This automatic filling does not change the value of the elementary item, merely its length. Figure 4.6 shows some examples of how specific values will be stored for various COBOL PICTURE lengths.

4.3.4   *Data Description Entries in the WORKING-STORAGE SECTION*

In the FILE SECTION of the DATA DIVISION we describe and set aside memory positions for each file and consequently for input and output records. Once a record has been written to a file or a new record has been read from a file, the data items that were set up in the FILE SECTION are no longer available to the programmer. The WORKING-STORAGE SECTION of the DATA DIVISION serves to describe data items not associated with input/output media. In essence it sets aside room for the data items needed for the duration of the program. As a result, total areas, work areas, literals, and other temporary data items are defined in the WORKING-STORAGE SECTION. Constants are also defined in this section. The data description entries in WORKING-STORAGE follow the same conventions as those in the FILE SECTION. The format for describing data items is:

Figure 4.6   **Examples of COBOL Data Storage**

Value		Saved as
For PIC X(8)	TODAY	T O D A Y
	YESTERDAY	Y E S T E R D A
	TOMORROW	T O M O R R O W
For PIC 9(5)	100	00100
	−250	00250
	472314	72314
	423.14	00423
For PIC 99V99	150	50V00
	21.3	21V30
	−.321	00V32
	.0001	00V00
For PIC S9(3)	100	100+
	−250	250−
	−4271	271−
	−13.25	013−
For PIC S99V99	10	10V0+
	−25	25V0−
	18.2	18V2+
	−17.3	17V3−

V represents an implied decimal point that uses no space in memory
+ , − represent algebraic signs that use no space in memory

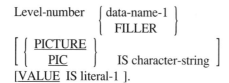

The VALUE Clause. The VALUE clause allows the programmer to specify the initial value for any data item. A VALUE clause also defines the constants used in a program. For a group item literal-1 is a nonnumeric literal or a figurative constant. For elementary items literal-1 is any literal or figurative constant. However, the VALUE clause literal must match the PICTURE clause description in type and size. In the example

```
01  WS-SALES-TAX-RATE    PIC 9V9(5)   VALUE   0.06125.
```

the entry defines a sales tax rate constant as having the value 6.125 percent. Another use of the VALUE clause is to define the initial value of an elementary character item. This is very useful for initializing variables. In the end-of-file indicator

```
01  WS-EOF-FLAG   PIC X(3)   VALUE   "NO".
```

the variable WS-EOF-FLAG is initialized to the value "NO".

Figurative Constants. The initial values of variables may also be specified with figurative constants. A *figurative constant* is a constant whose name represents its value. For example, the figurative constant ZERO(S) represents one of many instances of the numeric digit zero (0). The number of instances the figurative constant represents is determined by its context. In the example

```
01  WS-CUSTOMER-COUNTER   PIC 99   VALUE ZERO.
```

there are two instances of a zero since WS-CUSTOMER-COUNTER is defined as having a length of two. Figure 4.7 lists the figurative constants and the values they represent. SPACE(S) represents a space (blank) character. HIGH-VALUE(S) represents character data that are considered to be higher than any other value that can be stored in a field that size. Thus an alphanumeric data item filled with HIGH-VALUES will always test greater than any other alphanumeric data item except another one containing HIGH-VALUES. LOW-VALUE(S) serves a similar purpose except that it represents the lowest possible value. QUOTE(S) represents the quotation character. It cannot, however, be used instead of a quotation character to delimit a nonnumeric literal. The figurative constant ALL is very handy. It is always used with a nonnumeric literal or another figurative constant except itself. When used with a nonnumeric literal it indicates one or more instances of the character string represented by the literal. When used with another figurative constant it is redundant and is only employed to enhance readability. For example, if a data item has the following,

```
PIC X(10)     VALUE ALL   "-".
```

it means that all 10 characters of the data item are set to hyphens (-).

The singular and plural forms of the figurative constants are identical and interchangeable. Choose the form that improves readability. Figurative constants may be used in place of literals in many places in the program.

The code in the following example,

```
01  WS-CUSTOMER-TOTALS.
    05  WS-CUSTOMER-TOT-PURCHASES  PIC S9(5)V99  VALUE ZERO.
    05  WS-CUSTOMER-TOT-RETURNS    PIC S9(5)V99  VALUE ZERO.
```

initializes the two totals variables WS-CUSTOMER-TOT-PURCHASES and WS-CUS-TOMER-TOT-RETURNS to a value of zero. Figure 4.8 contains further examples of how figurative constants fill different data items.

Figure 4.7   *COBOL Figurative Constants and their Values*

Alphanumeric Figurative Constants	
SPACE, SPACES	One or more space characters
HIGH-VALUE, HIGH-VALUES	One or more characters of the highest position in a sorting sequence
LOW-VALUE, LOW-VALUES	One or more characters of the lowest position in a sequence
QUOTE, QUOTES	One or more quote characters
ZERO, ZEROS, ZEROES	One or more zero characters
Numeric Figurative Constant	
ZERO, ZEROS, ZEROES	The value of zero
Repeating Figurative Constant	
{ALL CHARACTER-LITERAL-STRING}	Repeats the literal string to fill the length of the data item

Figure 4.8   ***Results of Using Figurative Constants***

	Figurative constant	Result stored
For PIC X(6)	SPACE	☐☐☐☐☐☐
	ZEROS	0 0 0 0 0 0
	QUOTE	" _ _ _ _ _
	ALL "A"	A A A A A A
	ALL "JO"	J O J O J O
	ALL "FRED"	F R E D F R
For PIC 9(5)	ZEROS	0 0 0 0 0
For PIC 9(3)V99	ZEROS	0 0 0 0 0 ↑ Implied Decimal

Simple Editing. COBOL provides special features for formatting data items into a more readable format. *Editing* transforms data items by replacing, suppressing, or inserting characters in a field. Edited data items are defined in the DATA DIVISION of a program by using editing characters to indicate the editing operations to be performed on a data item. Then when the data item is moved to the edited item, the editing takes place automatically. Thus, much of the formatting for individual data items is easily specified in COBOL.

Figure 4.9 shows how unedited data would appear on a report. Notice that the readability and even the meaning of the data may be lost if editing is not performed. A programmer would want to print an actual decimal point where one existed in an item. He may do this by specifying in the description of the edited data item a period (.) in the position where he wants the decimal point to appear. For example, PICTURE 999.99 specifies an edited data item containing an explicit decimal point between the third and fourth character positions. The edited data item would then be printed. By printing the decimal point one can adequately account for dollars and cents in a price field. The explicit decimal point occupies a memory position and indirectly changes the data item from numeric to alphanumeric. This means that the program cannot use edited data in computations. Edited data are intended for display or printing purposes. Figure 4.10 shows how the data items from Figure 4.9 would be displayed when edited for decimal points.

Figure 4.9   Display Format of Numeric Data Items

Picture	Value	Displayed
9(4)	1324	1324
9(4)	34	0034
9(4)	0	0000
99V99	3.24	0324
99V99	18.72	1872
99V99	.01	0001
99V99	0	0000

Figure 4.10   Display Format Using Decimal Point

Picture	Value	Displayed
9(4)	1324	1324
9(4).99	34	0034.00
9(4)	0	0000
99.99	3.24	03.24
99.99	18.72	18.72
99.99	.01	00.01
99.99	0	00.00

Another editing feature allowed in COBOL is the suppression of leading zeros in numeric data items. By withholding the display of numerically nonsignificant zeros, number values appear more natural in a report or on a terminal screen. To accomplish this, the character Z is used in place of the data type character 9 in the PICTURE clause of the edited item beginning with the leftmost character and continuing for as many positions as desired. If the Z editing character is used, any leading zero in the specified position of the data item will be replaced by a blank when displayed. For example, PIC ZZZ9.99 will suppress zeros in the tens, hundreds, and thousands positions. If zeros appear in the units position in the value of the item or to the right of the decimal point, they will still be printed. For example, if the value of the numeric item is 0000.00, then 0.00 will still be exhibited.

Figure 4.11 shows the results displayed by replacing the leading 9s with Zs in the PICTURE clauses of the edited items. Zeros to the right of the decimal point are not replaced unless the value of the data item is zero. For example, if the value of a data item is 0.005, the edited item with a PICTURE Z.ZZZ would display .005. However, if the value is 0.000, it would display all spaces. Edited data items may combine the explicit decimal point and leading zero suppression. Figure 4.12 shows some examples.

Figure 4.11   *Display Format Using Zero Suppression*

Picture	Value	Displayed
Z(4)	1324	1324
Z(4)	0034	34
Z(4)	0000	

Figure 4.12   *Display Format Using Decimal Point and Zero Suppression*

Picture	Value	Displayed
ZZ.ZZ	03.24	3.24
ZZ.ZZ	18.72	18.72
ZZ.ZZ	00.01	.01
ZZ.ZZ	00.00	

Print Layouts. The WORKING-STORAGE SECTION allows a simple way for a programmer to format business reports. Since a single report may include headings, detail lines, and summaries, different formats are needed to specify them. COBOL provides a simple method for describing the different formats in the WORKING STORAGE SECTION.

In general, the programmer specifies a single record description for the print file in the FILE SECTION. This record represents one entire print line. In the example

```
FD      STUDENT-LIST
        LABEL RECORDS ARE OMITTED.
01      SL-PRINT-LINE            PICTURE X(120).
```

the record description entry has the level number 01 and follows the FD entry for the print file. This entry defines the entire record as a single elementary item, and its length as the length of one print line. The different report line formats are then described through different data item descriptions in the WORKING-STORAGE SECTION and are transferred to the print record. The print record is then written to the print file. Let us see how this is done with an example.

Figure 4.13 represents a simple one-page report that is to be printed as part of a program summarizing the status of an accounts receivable file. Notice that there are five different formats for the report lines. We have four heading lines: the first has the report title, the second has the company name, the third has the date of the report, and the fourth has the column headings. The fifth format describes the actual total values. Figure 4.14 illustrates the DATA DIVISION entries needed to represent this report. The first five 01 record entries in the WORKING-STORAGE SECTION represent the five different print line formats. This is a good example of the usefulness of FILLER entries and VALUE clauses. Note, too, the use of leading zero suppression in the items ARAR-TOTAL-ITEMS, ARAR-NEW-ITEMS, ARAR-30-DAY-ITEMS, and ARAR-60-DAY-ITEMS. We will study report formatting in detail in Chapter 8.

Figure 4.13   Sample Report Layout

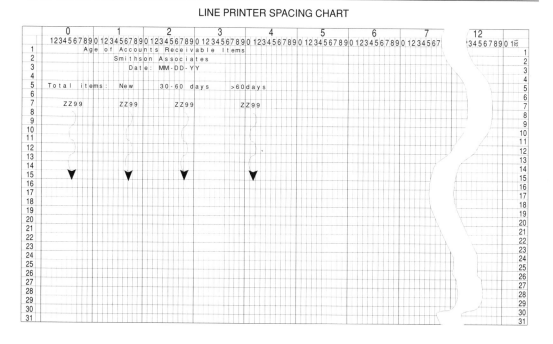

Figure 4.14   *COBOL Code for Sample Report*

```
FD   AR-AGE-REPORT
     LABEL RECORDS ARE OMITTED.
01   AR-AGE-LINE        PIC X(120).


     WORKING-STORAGE SECTION.

01   ARAR-REPORT-TITLE.
     05 FILLER              PIC X(30) VALUE SPACES.
     05 FILLER              PIC X(32) VALUE.
                    "AGE OF ACCOUNTS RECEIVABLE ITEMS".
01   ARAR-COMPANY-NAME
     05 FILLER              PIC X(36) VALUE SPACES.
     05 FILLER              PIC X(19) VALUE.
                    "SMITHSON ASSOCIATES".
01   ARAR-REPORT-DATE.
     05 FILLER              PIC X(39) VALUE SPACES.
     05 FILLER              PIC X(6)  VALUE "DATE:".
     05 ARAR-MONTH          PIC 99.
     05 FILLER              PIC X(1)  VALUE "-".
     05 ARAR-DAY            PIC 99.
     05 FILLER              PIC X(1)  VALUE "-".
     05 ARAR-YEAR           PIC 99.
```

```
01   ARAR-COLUMN-HEADINGS.
     05 FILLER              PIC X(25) VALUE SPACES.
     05 FILLER              PIC X(14) VALUE "TOTAL ITEMS".
     05 FILLER              PIC X(8)  VALUE "NEW".
     05 FILLER              PIC X(12) VALUE "30-60 DAYS".
     05 FILLER              PIC X(10) VALUE ">60 DAYS".

01   ARAR-AGE-SUMMARIES.
     05 FILLER              PIC X(28) VALUE SPACES.
     05 ARAR-TOTAL-ITEMS    PIC ZZ99.
     05 FILLER              PIC X(6)  VALUE SPACES.
     05 ARAR-NEW-ITEMS      PIC ZZ99.
     05 FILLER              PIC X(6)  VALUE SPACES.
     05 ARAR-30-DAY-ITEMS   PIC ZZ99.
     05 FILLER              PIC X(8)  VALUE SPACES.
     05 ARAR-60-DAY-ITEMS   PIC ZZ99.

01   AGE-REPORT-TOTALS
     05 ART-TOTAL-ITEMS     PIC 9(4) VALUE ZERO.
     05 ART-NEW-ITEMS       PIC 9(4) VALUE ZERO.
     05 ART-30-DAY-ITEMS    PIC 9(4) VALUE ZERO.
     05 ART-60-DAY-ITEMS    PIC 9(4) VALUE ZERO.
```

Computational Fields. Many programs maintain running totals or items containing intermediate results during computations. For example, in a payroll program the total number of weekly
hours worked is an intermediate result obtained by summing the number of hours worked each
day and is used to compute gross pay. In our accounts receivable aging report it is necessary to
have four counters to keep track of the number of accounts in each account age category. Since

they are temporary variables needed only for the report, they are described in the WORKING-STORAGE SECTION. In Figure 4.14 the level 01 entry called AGE-REPORT-TOTALS represents a totals record. This is decomposed into four elementary items, one for each total required in the report. The entries reserve memory for the data items and allow us to reference them. Notice that the elementary items are prefixed by ART- in order to distinguish their logical connections. Often, TOT- is used as a prefix for totals. The counters have been initialized to zero with VALUE clauses.

Indicators. *Indicators* are data items used to preserve the status of a program, that is, its condition at a particular time. Other names for indicators are switches and flags. A common example is an end-of-file indicator. It is set by the programmer when a file has reached its end and is tested by the program to control processing. Indicators are usually used with binary conditions. For example, the end-of-file indicator is set to the value "NO" until the end of the file is reached. At that time the value of the indicator is set to "YES".

Indicators are described in WORKING-STORAGE. It is helpful to group them under a single 01 level entry in order to provide a common location for their definition. Indicator names should be meaningful. End-of-file indicator names should be prefixed by EOF- followed by the file name. For example,

```
01     EOF-INDICATORS.
       05     EOF-INVENTORY-FILE   PIC XXX VALUE "NO".
       05     EOF-CUSTOMER-FILE    PIC XXX VALUE "NO".
```

are the end-of-file indicators for two files named INVENTORY-FILE and CUSTOMER-FILE.

Case Study: CDL's Extend Customer Orders

When CDL receives an order, the cost of each item is computed by extending the unit price information and adding the postage. This information is then used to create a new Extended Orders file. The program requirements and record layouts are shown in Figures 4.15 and 4.16 respectively.

Figure 4.15 **CDL's "Extend Customer Orders" Program Specifications**

PROGRAM SUMMARY

TITLE: *Extend Customer Orders*

PREPARED BY: *C. Hilton*

DATE: *6-28-93*

FILES USED		
FILE NAME	MEDIA	ORGANIZATION
Orders	*Disk*	*Sequential*
Extended orders	*Disk*	*Sequential*

DESCRIPTION

The customer orders were separated by the Categorize Daily Mail program.

The price field of the order will contain the price of a single CD if it is a discount item. If it is a standard priced item, the amount is initially set to zero. The retail standard price (currently $16.95) should replace the zero.

The total order price should be determined as follows: Item price times quantity plus postage and handling costs.

Postage and handling is computed at a bulk rate in groups of 5 items plus a single unit rate for the remaining items. Current rates: Bulk is $3.95; single is $1.24.

Total number of CDs ordered, total dollar value of CDs ordered, total dollar value of all orders, and total number of orders processed should be computed and displayed on the terminal.

Figure 4.16   *Record Layouts for CDL's "Extend Customer Orders" Progam*

RECORD LAYOUT SHEET
Revised

Record Name: *Order*		File Name: *Orders*		
Prepared By: *C. Hilton*		Date: *6-28-93*		
Key Fields:		Organization: *Sequential*		
Field	Description	Type*	Length	Decimal
Customer #	*A unique customer ID*	*N*	*6*	*0*
Compact Disc #	*The stock number for the CD*	*N*	*6*	*0*
Quantity	*The number ordered*	*N*	*2*	*0*
Order Number	*A preprinted order form number*	*N*	*6*	*0*
CD Price	*Price of the CD*	*N*	*8*	*2*

* A = alphanumeric
   N = numeric

RECORD LAYOUT SHEET

Record Name: *Order*		File Name: *Extended Orders*		
Prepared By: *C. Hilton*		Date: *6-28-93*		
Key Fields:		Organization: *Sequential*		
Field	Description	Type*	Length	Decimal
Customer #	*Customer ID*	*N*	*6*	*0*
Compact Disc #	*CD Stock number*	*N*	*6*	*0*
Quantity	*The number ordered*	*N*	*2*	*0*
Extended Price	*The full amount to be billed*	*N*	*8*	*2*
Order Number	*Preprinted order ID*	*N*	*6*	*0*

* A = alphanumeric
   N = numeric

Figure 4.17   Data Hierarchy Chart for "Extend Customer Orders" Program

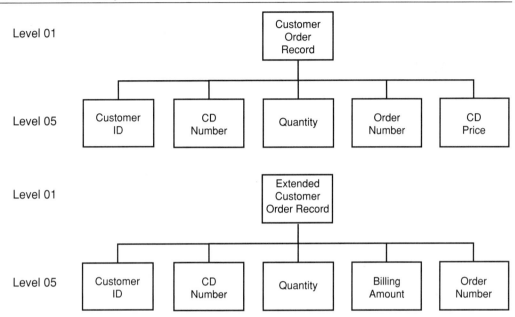

Charlene draws the data hierarchy chart in Figure 4.17 to describe the data record structure for the program. Using these charts she codes the first three COBOL DIVISIONs of the program in Figure 4.18.

Figure 4.18   First Three COBOL Divisions for "Extend Customer Orders" Program

```
IDENTIFICATION DIVISION.

PROGRAM-ID.  EXTEND-ORDERS.
THIS PROGRAM TAKES THE ORDERS SEPARATED BY THE CATEGORIZE DAILY
MAIL PROGRAM AND EXTENDS THE AMOUNT TO BE BILLED THE CUSTOMER

AUTHOR.       C HILTON
DATE-WRITTEN.  JUNE 29, 1993
DATE-COMPILED. JUNE 29, 1993



ENVIRONMENT DIVISION.

CONFIGURATION SECTION.
SOURCE-COMPUTER.  GENERIC-COMPUTER.
OBJECT-COMPUTER.  GENERIC-COMPUTER.
```

Figure 4.18   *(continued)*

```
INPUT-OUTPUT SECTION.

FILE-CONTROL.
    SELECT ORDERS-FILE ASSIGN TO DISK
        ORGANIZATION IS SEQUENTIAL.
    SELECT EXTENDED-ORDERS-FILE ASSIGN TO DISK
        ORGANIZATION IS SEQUENTIAL.


 DATA DIVISION.

 FILE SECTION.

 FD   ORDERS-FILE
      LABEL RECORDS ARE STANDARD.

 01   CUSTOMER-ORDER-REC.
      05   CO-CUSTOMER-ID    PIC 9(6).
      05   CO-CD-NUMBER      PIC 9(6).
      05   CO-QUANTITY       PIC 99.
      05   CO-ORDER-NUMBER   PIC 9(6).
      05   CO-CD-PRICE       PIC 9(6)V99.

 FD   EXTENDED-ORDERS-FILE
      LABEL RECORDS ARE STANDARD.

 01   EXTENDED-CUSTOMER-ORDER-REC.
      05   ECO-CUSTOMER-ID     PIC 9(6).
      05   ECO-CD-NUMBER       PIC 9(6).
      05   ECO-QUANTITY        PIC 99.
      05   ECO-BILLING-AMOUNT  PIC 9(6)V99.
      05   ECO-ORDER-NUMBER    PIC 9(6).

 WORKING-STORAGE SECTION.

 01   WORK-AREA.
      05   WA-BULK-MAIL      PIC 99.
      05   WA-SINGLE-MAIL    PIC 99.
      05   WA-SHIPPING-COST  PIC 9(6)V99.
      05   WA-CD-COST        PIC 9(6)V99.
      05   WA-COMBINED-COST  PIC 9(6)V99.

 01   CONTROL-TOTALS.
```

Figure 4.18   *(continued)*

```
      05   CT-NUMBER-OF-CDS        PIC  9(5).
      05   CT-NUMBER-OF-ORDERS     PIC  9(5).
      05   CT-SHIPPING-COST        PIC  9(10)V99.
      05   CT-OVERALL-COST         PIC  9(10)V99.

  01  END-OF-FILE-INDICATORS.
      05   EOF-ORDERS PIC X(5) VALUE "FALSE".

  01  COSTING-CONSTANTS.
      05   CC-BULK-RATE            PIC  99V99 VALUE 3.95.
      05   CC-SINGLE-RATE          PIC  99V99 VALUE 1.24.
      05   CC-STANDARD-CD-PRICE PIC  99V99 VALUE 16.95.
```

Summary

Business information systems are often referred to as data processing systems because the programs manipulate and transform data into information needed for making business decisions. Understanding the hierarchical structure of data will facilitate this data processing and form the basis for more complex topics.

Data are facts about entities. In order to be meaningful, they must be organized. In general, the data unit is called a data item or field. Records are collections of data items; files are collections of records. Data structures represent the logical organization of data, and it is this organization that is important to COBOL.

In COBOL, the highest hierarchical grouping of data is the file. Sequential files, which are common in business applications, store records in an order specified by a key or control field. COBOL files may be decomposed logically into records, groups, subgroups, and elementary items. Grouping allows us to relate similar items to each other.

Files are described in the FILE SECTION of the DATA DIVISION using FD (file description) entries. Records, groups, subgroups, and elementary items are also described in the FILE SECTION. They are given level numbers to indicate their position in the data hierarchy. All data items that are referenced must have names. It is important to assign them meaningful names for clarity. Furthermore, data-names must be unique. One way to accomplish this is through a prefix designating the file of which it is a part. Another way is through the use of qualifiers. The programmer specifies successively higher-level groups to which the data item belongs until the data-name is unique.

Elementary items are described with PICTURE clauses that define the type and length of the data item. Data item types include alphabetic, numeric, and alphanumeric. Length specifies how many characters long a data item is in order to reserve that number of memory positions for it. Other features that can be specified for numeric items are the algebraic sign and the implied decimal point placement. The operational characters S and V, respectively, are used for these purposes.

COBOL provides the WORKING-STORAGE SECTION for defining temporary work areas, constants, and detailed record formats of records described in the FILE SECTION. WORKING-STORAGE items are described in the same manner as data items in the FILE SECTION. Two data description entry features that are very useful in the WORKING-STORAGE SECTION are the reserved word FILLER and the VALUE clause. FILLER is used to describe elementary items that need not be referenced directly. A common use is in the description of report formats. VALUE clauses allow the programmer to specify the initial or constant value of the data item. This is useful for specifying report formats and for initializing variables.

COBOL also allows data item descriptions to be edited. By specifying the desired editing characters, decimal points can be printed and nonsignificant leading zeros may be suppressed. This allows data to be displayed in a more readable form.

Key Terms

data	subgroup	item
file	elementary item	9
record	LABEL RECORDS STANDARD	S
sequential file	LABEL RECORDS OMITTED	V
key	level number	figurative constants
data item	FILLER	editing
field	alphabetic data item	indicators
characters	numeric data item	
group	alphanumeric data	

Hints for Avoiding Errors

1. COBOL is very sensitive to spaces between words. Be certain that each word is separated by one or more spaces from its preceding and following words.
2. Remember that constants, values, layouts, and flags should appear in the WORKING-STORAGE SECTION. COBOL allows you to place them in the FILE SECTION, but they will be lost after the first time they are referenced.
3. The file names used by the program must be identical in the SELECT clause, the FD entry, and the PROCEDURE DIVISION. Unrecognized file names will cause many syntax errors.

Exercises

4.1   Develop the hierarchy chart, Nassi-Schneiderman charts, and DATA DIVISION for the program described by the specifications in Figures 4.19, 4.20, and 4.21.

Figure 4.19 Program Specifications for Exercise 4.1

TITLE: *Payroll Listing*

PREPARED BY: *C. Trap*

DATE: *6-30-93*

FILES USED

FILE NAME	MEDIA	ORGANIZATION
Payroll history	Disk	Sequential
Old employee list	Printer	Sequential

DESCRIPTION

Management wants a list of employees who have been with the company since the year 1971. Start on a new page and generate a report that looks like Figure 4.20. The input record is in Figure 4.21.

Figure 4.20 Report Layout for Exercise 4.1

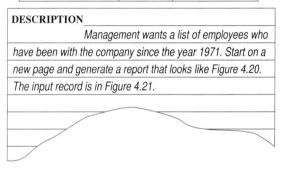

LINE PRINTER SPACING CHART

Figure 4.21   *Record Layout for Exercise 4.1*

RECORD LAYOUT SHEET

Record Name: *Payroll History Record*		File Name: *Payroll History*			
Prepared By: *J. Joeps*		Date: *6-18-93*			
Key Fields: *Employee ID*		Organization: *Sequential*			
Field	Description	Type*	Length	Decimal
Employee ID	Unique numeric ID for each emp.	A	8	
Emp. last name		A	15	
Emp. first name		A	15	
Job code	Job classification, seniority level	A	3	
Job title		A	10	
Pay indicator	Hourly vs. salaried	A	1	
Pay Rate		N	8	2
Status indicator	Active employee 0, 1	N	1	
Y-T-D gross pay		N	8	2
Y-T-D hrs. worked		N	5	1
Department	Current area where emp. is assigned	A	3	
Date of birth	MMDDYY	A	6	
Sex	M, F	A	1	
Date of hire	MMDDYY	A	6	
Insurance code	Policy identifier	A	1	
Marital status	Single, married, divorced, head of household	A	1	
Employee street		A	15	
Employee city		A	10	
Employee state		A	2	
Employee zip		A	5	

4.2   Develop a data hierarchy and DATA DIVISION entries to describe all the data items on:
   a.   your driver's license.
   b.   a credit card.
   c.   your transcript.
   d.   your textbooks needed for the semester.

4.3   A(n) _____ is a data item that is not further subdivided.

4.4   Create a PICTURE clause for each of the following:
   a.   a seven-digit numeric field.   9(7)
   b.   a three-digit signed numeric field with two decimal places.   S9V99
   c.   a four-character alphanumeric field.   X(4)

4.5   The WORKING-STORAGE SECTION may not be used to:
   a.   store intermediate results.
   b.   initialize a variable.
   c.   set up output lines.
   d.   define files.

4.6 Which of the following is a valid data-name?
    a. NET PAY
    b. NUMBER-
    c. HRS-WORKED

4.7 The end-of-file condition indicates that the next record is the last record on the file. True or false?

4.8 Which is not a valid figurative constant?
    a. ALL "HJG"
    b. SPACES
    c. COMMA
    d. QUOTE

4.9 Which PICTURE clause specifies a numeric variable?
    a. 9.99
    b. V99
    c. ZZ9
    d. Z9V99

4.10 PICTUREs of numeric computational items may not contain a
    a. V
    b. S
    c. 9
    d. .

4.11 The VALUE of the literal .86 stored in a PIC 99V99 elementary item would appear in unedited form as
    a. .86
    b. 00.86
    c. 0086
    d. 86

4.12 Group items _____ PICTURE clauses.
    a. must have
    b. must not have
    c. may have

4.13 Which reserved word is used to indicate an absence of LABEL RECORDS?
    a. LESS
    b. OMITTED
    c. STANDARD

For Exercises 4.14 through 4.17, use the following possible answers.
    a. Record
    b. Elementary item
    c. Group
    d. File
    e. Data Item

4.14 Which represents a collection of data records?

4.15 Which is a synonym for field?

4.16 Which is a named collection of one or more elementary items?

4.17 Which is the smallest item recognized in COBOL?

4.18   An 01 level may represent
    a.   a record entry in the FILE SECTION.
    b.   an elementary item in the FILE SECTION.
    c.   a group item in WORKING-STORAGE.
    d.   all of the above

4.19   Data items are defined in the _____ DIVISION but used in the
    _____ DIVISION.

4.20   A record entry that consists of only an 01 entry should have which of the following?
    a.   a VALUE clause
    b.   a name and a PICTURE clause
    c.   an 05 level

4.21   Files are described in the _____ SECTION of the
    _____ DIVISION using _____entries.
    a.   WORKING-STORAGE, DATA, group
    b.   FILE, DATA, data description
    c.   FILE, DATA, file description

4.22   Specifying the correct length of elementary data items is really an afterthought in COBOL. True or false?

4.23   Each qualifier must be one level higher than the data-name it qualifies. True or false?

4.24   The use of prefixes:
    a.   ensures uniqueness of data-names.
    b.   makes code easier to follow.
    c.   should be used for all data-names that are part of a larger structure.
    d.   all of the above

4.25   A sequential file is usually stored in an undetermined order. True or false?

4.26   The reserved word FILLER cannot be used by the programmer to ignore certain data fields in an input file record. All fields must be specified for COBOL. True or false?

4.27   PICTUREs of edited numeric items may not contain a
    a.   V
    b.   Z
    c.   .
    d.   9

4.28   It is useful to use the VALUE clause in describing group items in the FILE SECTION since the item's value can be permanently specified even though multiple READS and/or WRITES may occur. True or false?

4.29   The value of 55574.74 stored in a PIC 9(5)V9 elementary item would appear in unedited form as:
    a.   055574
    b.   555747
    c.   55574.7
    d.   05557.4

4.30   The clause PIC S9(6) indicates that the data item is an edited numeric field six positions long. True or false?

4.31   If a data item is longer than the field used to describe it, COBOL will automatically pad the field so that it will accommodate the data item. True or false?

4.32 The value 1050104 stored in PIC ZZ,ZZZ.99, if printed out, would appear as:
    a. 50,104.00
    b. 1,5.04
    c. 10,501.04

4.33 _____ are the raw materials for the process of producing information.

4.34 PIC 9(3)V99 indicates that the item is _____ positions long and reserves _____ memory positions.

4.35 A(n) _____ is a constant whose name represents its value.

4.36 _____ are data items used to preserve a program's condition at a particular time.

4.37 _____ allows the programmer to relate similar data items to each other.

4.38 _____ represents character data that is considered to be higher than any other value that can be stored in a field of a particular size.

4.39 The figurative constant _____ is always used with a nonnumeric literal and indicates one or more instances of the character string represented by the literal.

4.40 What is wrong with this data structure?

```
05 GROUP-ITEM          PICTURE X(23).
04 SUB UNIT-1     PICTURE V.
04 SUB UNIT-2     PICTURE Z99.
04 SUB UNIT-3     PICTURE X9.
   02 SUB-SUB-UNIT-1    PICTURE A(0)
   02 SUB-SUB-UNIT-2    PICTURE A(8).
```

4.41 Why are business information systems often referred to as data processing systems?

4.42 Why is it important to understand the hierarchical organization of data and how it relates to COBOL?

4.43 Explain the importance of grouping data items.

4.44 How does editing data help a decision maker?

PROCESSING DATA

The dynamism of a business organization is reflected in the volatility of its data items. Data migrate from one file to another; they are updated, operated on, and otherwise manipulated to provide value to the business organization. These data processes are vital for the operation of the business. Information systems process data into information and control its flow through an organization.

5.1   *Aspects of Handling Data*

Within an organization there is an entire spectrum of information generating tasks. Some programs manipulate files to keep them current. Others verify the contents of input data for accuracy. Still other programs store new information in files and retrieve existing information to aid managers in making decisions. Programs may read entire files to summarize their contents or they may compute an individual employee's pay and allot a percentage of it to taxes, stock option plans, and health insurance. From the subtle to the obvious, data handling is at the heart of information systems.

Data handling aspects may be categorized into input/output, data movement, arithmetic operations, and program control. By dividing them in this way, we can more readily picture the tasks that fall under each category and, later, associate with them their related COBOL instructions.

5.1.1   *Input/Output*

Input/output aspects of data handling refer to those operations in which data are transferred between external devices and internal memory storage. Input operations copy the data from an external device, such as disk or tape, to an area of memory storage known as the *input area*. These data replace the current contents of the input area, thereby becoming available to the program for further processing. Conversely, output operations transfer data from the *output area* of storage to an external device.

Input/output data handling allows input records to be read and made available to the program, and output records to be written to printers, tape, or disk. Even operations that involve external devices for both input and output have to be accomplished through operations involving internal memory as an intermediary step.

Input/output operations are necessary to transfer entire files between devices. For example, standard operating procedures in most data processing shops require that disk files be backed up to tapes that are stored in a safe place. Figure 5.1 shows a system flowchart for the backup operation. Such a procedure is nothing more than a series of input/output operations in which individual records are transferred from the input device to storage to the output device. When data entry clerks enter data from source documents to files that will serve as input to later processes, the input/output aspects of data handling are involved.

Figure 5.1   System Flowchart for File Transfer

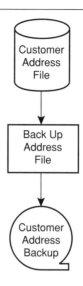

The data involved may be current data or historical information. They may be temporary if they are needed only as an intermediate step in a process, or they may be permanent data to be used as reference information.

5.1.2   Data Movement

Data movement involves transferring data from one location in memory to another. Data may be moved unchanged. Often, however, data are moved to produce information in a usable format. For example, when a manager requires reports involving data contained in a file, the program may move data in the input area to another area that is formatted so that it is easier to read. Reports in which leading zeros are changed to blanks and decimal points, commas, and dollar signs are inserted are much more readable than reports with cluttered output. Figure 5.2 shows an example of how data movement may produce more readable information.

Figure 5.2   Data Movement for Formatting Output

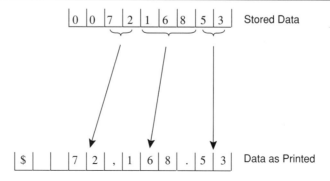

We previously classified the transferring of data between external devices under the I/O aspects of data handling. This, of course, is because data must be transferred from an input medium to storage before they can be output to another medium. It may be necessary to convert from one form to another, however, and this is accomplished by moving data from one area in memory to another.

It may be necessary to perform data movements in order to save the contents of a certain storage area. This is especially important when certain operations are to be performed on the data, altering their value and thereby destroying their initial values. As an example, in preparing customer statements one would want to save the beginning balance before applying payments and purchases to compute the new balance. Moving data in this case implies relocating them in memory.

5.1.3   Arithmetic Operations

In many cases it is necessary to perform arithmetic operations on data to produce information. Arithmetic operations include addition, subtraction, multiplication, and division. For example, payroll calculations for determining gross pay and net pay involve many arithmetic manipulations.

5.1.4   Program Control

If a program is to be realistic, there must be some way of altering its path. In a structured environment the selection and iteration structures transfer control when a specified condition is met. For example, branching might occur if the result of some arithmetic computation is zero or if two fields in memory are equal. In either case the transfer of control depends on the results of a comparison of data. Such transfers of control are known as conditional branches.

5.2   Input/Output COBOL Statements

Input/output (I/O) instructions in COBOL are related to the tasks necessary to ready the files to be used in the program. They specify the input or output operations to be performed.

5.2.1   The OPEN Statement

The OPEN statement causes the computer system to perform certain file preparation procedures. In the simplest case it checks whether the device is ready. In essence, the OPEN statement makes a file available for processing. Therefore, any file that is to be read or written must first be opened. The OPEN statement format and rules are:

$$\text{OPEN} \left\{ \begin{array}{l} \underline{\text{INPUT}} \\ \underline{\text{OUTPUT}} \\ \underline{\text{I/O}} \end{array} \right\} \quad \text{File-name} \dots$$

1. An OPEN statement must be executed for a file before any statement references that file, except for cases of the SORT and MERGE statements.

2.   The file-name must appear in an FD and in a SELECT clause.
3.   An OPEN file cannot be opened.

File-name defines the file that is to be opened. This file-name is the same as the one appearing in the ENVIRONMENT DIVISION in the SELECT clause and in the DATA DIVISION as an FD entry.

The OPEN statement further designates whether a file is to be used as an INPUT file or an OUTPUT file. *INPUT* files are used for getting input records. *OUTPUT* files are used for producing output records. *I/O* files are used for both and are discussed in a later chapter. For example,

```
OPEN INPUT SUPPLIER-ACCTS-FILE.
```

indicates that the file SUPPLIER-ACCTS-FILE is to be used as input to the program.

Even though the OPEN statement format allows more than one file to be specified, we recommend that you use a separate OPEN statement for each file. In this way, each OPEN statement is an independent sentence rather than one sentence with multiple clauses. This makes the code more readable and easier to modify when changes occur. For example,

```
OPEN INPUT CUSTOMER-ACCTS-FILE.
OPEN OUTPUT CUSTOMER-REPORT-FILE.
```

is more readable than

```
OPEN INPUT CUSTOMER-ACCTS-FILE, OUTPUT
CUSTOMER-REPORT-FILE.
```

Other examples of OPEN statements are illustrated in lines 76 and 77 of the program in Figure 5.3. This program, which lists the names of those employees who are union members, is developed from the documentation contained in Figures 5.4 through 5.6.

Figure 5.3   *Simple Input and Output Program*

```
  1  IDENTIFICATION DIVISION.
  2  PROGRAM-ID. EMPLOYEE-LIST.
  3 *    THE PROGRAM USES THE EMPLOYEE FILE TO PRODUCE
  4 *    A LIST OF EMPLOYEE NAMES
  5
  6
  7  ENVIRONMENT DIVISION.
  8
  9  CONFIGURATION SECTION.
 10  SOURCE-COMPUTER. GENERIC-COMPUTER
 11  OBJECT-COMPUTER. GENERIC-COMPUTER
 12
 13  INPUT-OUTPUT SECTION.
 14  FILE-CONTROL.
 15      SELECT EMPLOYEE-FILE ASSIGN TO DISK.
 16      SELECT EMPLOYEE-LIST-FILE ASSIGN TO PRINTER.
 17
 18
 19  DATA DIVISION.
 20
 21  FILE SECTION.
 22
 23  FD EMPLOYEE-FILE
 24     LABEL RECORDS ARE STANDARD.
```

```
 25
 26  01 EMPLOYEE-RECORD.
 27      05  EF-NUMBER        PIC X (10).
 28      05  EF-NAME          PIC X (30).
 29      05  EF-UNION-CODE    PIC X.
 30      05  FILLER           PIC X (90).
 31
 32  FD EMPLOYEE-LIST-FILE
 33     LABEL RECORDS ARE OMITTED.
 34
 35  01 EL-REPORT-LINE PIC X (120).
 36
 37
 38  WORKING-STORAGE SECTION.
 39
 40  01 ELRL-REPORT-TITLE
 41      05  FILLER  PIC X(20) VALUE "EMPLOYEE LISTING".
 42
 43  01 ELRL-COMPANY-NAME.
 44      05  FILLER  PIC X(20) VALUE "HAZGOOD BOLT SUPPLY".
 45
 46  01 ELRL-REPORT-DATE.
 47      05  FILLER  PIC X(6)  VALUE "DATE".
 48      05  ELRL-MM PIC XX.
```

Figure 5.3   (continued)

```
SEQUENCE                                    COBOL STATEMENT                                          IDENTIFICATION
49        05   FILLER    PIC X      VALUE  "-".
50        05   ELRL-DD PIC XX.
51        05   FILLER    PIC X      VALUE  "-".
52        05   ELRL-YY PIC XX.
53
54   01   ELRL-COLUMN-HEADING.
55        05   FILLER    PIC X(10)  VALUE  SPACES.
56        05   FILLER    PIC X(10)  VALUE  "EMPLOYEES".
57
58   01   ELRL-DIVIDER.
59        05   FILLER    PIC X (30)  VALUE ALL  "-".
60
61*  ALL PREVIOUS ENTRIES IN WORKING STORAGE ARE LAYOUTS FOR
62*  THE EMPLOYEE LISTING.   THE FOLLOWING ARE VARIABLES.
63
64   01   TODAYS-DATE.
65        05   TD-YY     PIC XX.
66        05   TD-MM     PIC XX.
67        05   TD-DD     PIC XX.
68
69   01   END-OF-FILE-INDICATORS.
70        05   EOF-OF-FILE    PIC X(5)  VALUE  "FALSE".
71
72
```

```
SEQUENCE                                    COBOL STATEMENT                                          IDENTIFICATION
73   PROCEDURE DIVISION.
74
75   PRODUCE-EMPLOYEE-LIST.
76        OPEN INPUT EMPLOYEE-FILE.
77        OPEN OUTPUT EMPLOYEE-LIST-FILE.
78        PERFORM 10-READY-EMPLOYEE-LIST.
79        PERFORM 20-PRINT-EMPLOYEE UNTIL EOF-EMPLOYEE-FILE = "TRUE".
80        CLOSE EMPLOYEE-FILE.
81        CLOSE EMPLOYEE-LIST-FILE.
82        STOP RUN.
83
84   10-READY-EMPLOYEE-LIST.
85        PERFORM 11-FORMAT-TODAYS-DATE.
86        PERFORM 12-WRITE-LISTING-HEADINGS.
87        PERFORM 13-READ-EMPLOYEE-RECORD.
88
89   11-FORMAT-TODAYS-DATE.
90        ACCEPT TODAYS-DATE FROM DATE.
91        MOVE TD-YY TO ELRL-YY.
92        MOVE TD-MM TO ELRL-MM.
93        MOVE TD-DD TO ELRL-DD.
94
95   12-WRITE-LISTING-HEADINGS.
96        WRIE EL-REPORT-LINE FROM ELRL-REPORT-TITLE
```

Figure 5.3   (continued)

SYSTEM			PUNCHING INSTRUCTIONS							PAGE	OF	
PROGRAM			GRAPHIC							CARD FORM NUMBER		
PROGRAMMER		DATE	PUNCH									

```
SEQUENCE  CONT  A  B                    COBOL STATEMENT                                    IDENTIFICATION

  97              AFTER ADVANCING PAGE
  98          WRITE EL-REPORT-LINE FROM ELRL-COMPANY-NAME.
  99          WRITE EL-REPORT-LINE FROM ELRL-REPORT-DATE.
 100          WRITE EL-REPORT-LINE FROM ELRL-COLUMN-HEADING
 101              AFTER ADVANCING 2 LINES.
 102          WRITE EL-REPORT-LINE FROM ELRL-DIVIDER.
 103
 104     13-READ-EMPLOYEE-RECORD.
 105          READ EMPLOYEE-FILE
 106              AT END MOVE "TRUE" TO EOF-EMPLOYEE-FILE.
 107
 108     20-PRINT-EMPLOYEE.
 109          IF EF-UNION-CODE = "U" PERFORM 21-LIST-SINGLE-EMPLOYEE.
 110          PERFORM 13-READ-EMPLOYEE-RECORD.
 111
 112     21-LISTR-SINGLE-EMPLOYEE.
 113          MOVE EF-NAME TO EL-REPORT-LINE.
 114          WRITE EL-REPORT-LINE.
```

Figure 5.4   **Hierarchy Chart for "Employee List" Program**

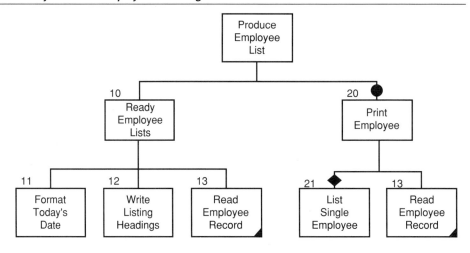

Figure 5.5   **N-S Charts for "Employee List" Program**

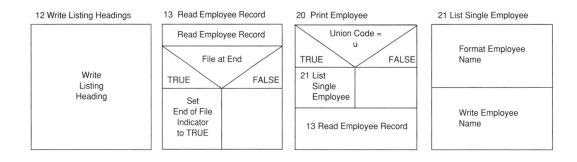

Figure 5.6   **Report Layout for "Employee List" Program**

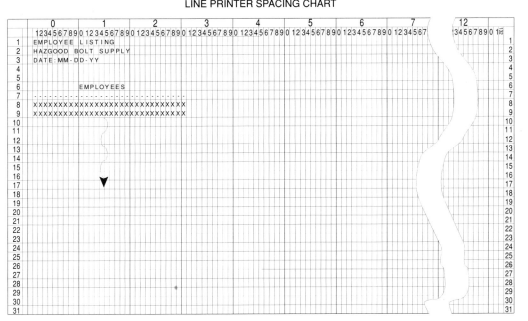

LINE PRINTER SPACING CHART

5.2.2   *The READ Statement*

The READ statement causes the computer to read one input record from the specified input file and place the contents in its input storage area, thus making it available for processing. The input area is defined in the FILE SECTION by an 01 record description. The format and rules for the sequential READ statement are:

READ file-name [NEXT] RECORD [INTO data-name]

       AT END imperative-statement-1 . . .
       [NOT AT END imperative-statement-2]
       [END-READ]

1. Multiple statements may appear as part of the AT END clause.
2. The READ statement is terminated by a period or the END-READ.
3. The file-name must appear in a SELECT clause.
4. The file must first be opened as INPUT.
5. The INTO option transfers the record read to the data-name specified.

The file named by the READ statement must have been previously opened as an INPUT file. The *INTO* clause allows the record to be transferred to a WORKING-STORAGE SECTION data item, as well as to the input area associated with the file's record description. In essence, this allows the program to specify a detailed description of the record in the WORKING-STORAGE SECTION instead of in the FILE SECTION. The data then appear in both locations. The COBOL sentence

```
READ NEW-CUST-FILE INTO WS-CUSTOMER-DETAIL

    AT END MOVE "YES" TO CUST-EOF-FLAG.
```

reads a record from NEW-CUST-FILE, brings the data to the memory area specified by the record entry of NEW-CUST-FILE, and also copies the record to the WORKING-STORAGE data item WS-CUSTOMER-DETAIL.

The last record in a sequential file does not contain data. Instead it contains a code that signals the hardware that the file contains no more records. The computer can detect the code, causing what is known as an *end-of-file condition*. The *AT END* clause allows the programmer to specify what action is to be taken when the end of the file is reached. Imperative-statement-1 and imperative-statement-2 may be one or more statements that tell the computer what action is to be taken unconditionally when the end-of-file record is read. The AT END clause must be terminated by a period, an END-READ delimiter, or the NOT AT END clause. The following READ statement:

```
READ CUST-ACCT-FILE
     AT END MOVE "Y" TO EOF-CUST-ACCT-FILE.
```

causes one record to be read from the file. When the end-of-file record is encountered, the program moves a value of "Y" to the data item EOF-CUST-ACCT-FILE.

In the above example the AT END clause contains a statement that sets an indicator usually defined in the WORKING-STORAGE SECTION. In Figure 5.3, EOF-EMPLOYEE-FILE on line 70 is the data item used for this purpose. The AT END clause of the READ statement in line 106 sets the indicator to "TRUE" when the end of the file is detected. This allows the rest of the program to know that the last record has been read. The PERFORM UNTIL statement in line 79 uses the indicator to terminate the iteration when the last record has been processed.

5.2.3   *The ACCEPT Statement*

The *ACCEPT* statement is used to input low-volume data, usually data such as dates. It is used extensively in interactive systems to acquire input from an operator or user at a terminal. The format and rules of the ACCEPT are:

ACCEPT DATA-NAME [FROM mnemonic-name]

1. Data-name must be in the WORKING-STORAGE SECTION.
2. The mnemonic-name must conform to specific system standards or be programmer-defined.

Data-name specifies the receiving field. This area must be defined and described in the DATA DIVISION. If the *FROM* option is used, mnemonic-name depends on the implementor and you must consult your system documentation for details. The statement

```
ACCEPT RUN-DATE FROM CONSOLE.
```

acquires the date from the operator at the console (assuming CONSOLE is the valid mnemonic-name for the system we are using) and stores it in RUN-DATE.

If the FROM option is not used, the input data will be obtained from the system's logical input device, which may be either the user's or the operator's terminal. For a particular system, the statement

```
ACCEPT EMPLOYEE-ID.
```

will transfer data input at the terminal and store it in the data element EMPLOYEE-ID.

A second format of the ACCEPT statement may be used to obtain values maintained by the operating system. The format and rules of this ACCEPT are:

$$\text{ACCEPT} \quad \text{data-name} \quad \text{FROM} \quad \begin{Bmatrix} \underline{\text{DATE}} \\ \underline{\text{DAY}} \\ \underline{\text{TIME}} \end{Bmatrix}$$

1. DATE is an elementary item with an implied PICTURE of 9(6)V. The format is
    YYMMDD where YY is the year in the century, MM is the two-digit month code,
    and DD is the day of the month. For example, July 15, 1985, is 850715.
2. DAY is an elementary item with an implied PICTURE of 9(5)V. The format is
    YYDDD. YY is the year in the century, DDD is a 3-digit number from 1 to 366
    representing the day in the year. For example, August 15, 1985, is 85227.
3. TIME is an elementary item with an equivalent PICTURE of 9(8)V. The format is
    HHMMSSuu. HH is the hour on a 24-hour clock; MM is the minutes after the
    hour; SS is the seconds after the minutes. uu is hundredths of seconds. For ex-
    ample, 10:15 A.M. is 10150000.
4. Data-name specifies the receiving field that is to receive the desired system-
    maintained value. The receiving field may be numeric, numeric edited, or alphanu-
    meric.
5. DATE, DAY, and TIME are reserved words in COBOL and may not be used as
    data-names by the programmer.

DATE, *DAY*, and *TIME* may not be referenced directly in the program except by the
ACCEPT, but the data-name specified in the ACCEPT statement may be referenced. Assume
the following data description:

```
05   WS-TODAY                    PICTURE 9(6).
```

Then the following statement:

```
ACCEPT WS-TODAY FROM DATE.
```

obtains the date from the system and stores it in the data item WS-TODAY. The date in WS-
TODAY will have the same format as DATE: YYMMDD. If this format is not appropriate for
use in the program, the data-name into which it is accepted should be formatted to allow
manipulation of the date. If we use the following description for the data-name:

```
01   WS-TODAYS-DATE.
        05   WS-TD-YEAR                      PICTURE XX.
        05   WS-TD-MONTH                     PICTURE XX.
        05   WS-TD-DAY                       PICTURE XX.
```

and we obtain the date with the statement

```
ACCEPT WS-TODAYS-DATE FROM DATE.
```

then each elementary item can be referenced directly. We may now manipulate the year, month,
and day separately. This comes in very handy for writing dates on reports. A complete example
of this process is in the code of Figure 5.3. Line 90 accepts the system date into lines 64 through
67. The statements in lines 91 through 93 then transfer the date to the output area.

5.2.4   *The WRITE Statement*

The WRITE statement transfers the data stored in the output area to the output device. The format and rules for the WRITE statement are:

WRITE record-name [<u>FROM</u> data-name-1]

$$
\left[\left\{ \begin{array}{l} \underline{\text{AFTER}} \\ \underline{\text{BEFORE}} \end{array} \right\} \text{ADVANCING} \left[\begin{array}{l} \left\{ \begin{array}{l} \text{data-name-2} \\ \text{literal} \end{array} \right\} \left\{ \begin{array}{l} \text{LINE} \\ \text{LINES} \end{array} \right\} \\ \underline{\text{PAGE}} \end{array} \right] \right]
$$

[<u>END-WRITE</u>]

1. The record-name must be described in the FD entry of the file opened for OUTPUT.
2. After a WRITE is executed, the data are no longer available in the record's area.
3. The FROM option transfers the data from data-name-1 to record-name prior to writing the record.
4. If the ADVANCING clause is omitted, the default is after advancement of <u>one line.</u>
5. The literal or data-name-2 in the ADVANCING clause must be a nonnegative integer less than 100.
6. The WRITE is terminated by a period or the END-WRITE clause.

Notice that we specify a record-name in the WRITE statement, whereas a file-name is specified in the READ statement. It is important to keep this difference in mind. In COBOL we READ files and WRITE records. Record-name refers to the 01 record description appearing in the DATA DIVISION under the FD entry of its corresponding file. For example, assume the following file is defined in the FILE SECTION of the DATA DIVISION:

```
FD    INV-REPORT-FILE
      LABEL RECORDS ARE OMITTED.
01    INV-REPORT-LINE    PIC X(120).
```

To write out the information to the file we use the statement

```
WRITE INV-REPORT-LINE.
```

This transmits the data to the output file according to the format specified in the 01 description of INV-REPORT-LINE.

The FROM clause is comparable in use to the INTO option of the READ statement. If used, the FROM option causes the contents of data-name-1 in WORKING-STORAGE to be transferred to the output area designated by record-name in the FILE SECTION, and then be written to the output file. For example, assume the following:

```
FD  CUST-REPORT-FILE
    LABEL RECORDS ARE OMITTED.
01  CUST-REPORT-LINE                          PIC X(100).


WORKING-STORAGE SECTION.


01  WS-REPORT-DETAIL                           PIC X(100).
```

The statement

```
WRITE CUST-REPORT-LINE FROM WS-REPORT-DETAIL.
```

transfers the contents of WS-REPORT-DETAIL to the record CUST-REPORT-LINE and then writes it to CUST-REPORT-FILE. This eliminates having to code the transference. Its usefulness will become more apparent when we write reports. It essentially allows the programmer to define the detailed specification of the output in the WORKING-STORAGE SECTION. When the WORKING-STORAGE data-name is specified in the FROM clause, the output data are transferred from WORKING-STORAGE to the print record, and then the record is written to the print file.

Many business applications involve the generation of reports, and COBOL offers a variety of features that facilitate this process. In addition to the FROM clause the WRITE statement provides other optional clauses that aid in writing print files. The *ADVANCING* clause allows the programmer to specify vertical spacing on a report. The AFTER specification indicates that the line is to be printed after the specified line or page advance is executed. For example, by specifying AFTER ADVANCING PAGE the current record will be printed at the top of the next page. Using AFTER ADVANCING 3 LINES causes the printer to print the current record on the third line after the line on which the last record was printed. Any integer literal or previously defined integer elementary item may be used to specify the number of lines to be skipped. If the ADVANCING clause is not used, COBOL assumes that one line is to be advanced. The program in Figure 5.3 contains WRITE statements in lines 96 to 102 that highlight many of the options of this statement. The resulting output from the example would be:

```
LINE   1               EMPLOYEE LISTING
       2               HAZGOOD BOLT SUPPLY
       3               DATE: 06-15.85
       4
       5               EMPLOYEES
       6               _____
```

5.2.5   *The DISPLAY Statement*

The *DISPLAY* verb is used to output low-volume data. It provides the capability of outputting a message without defining a file. The format and rules of the DISPLAY are as follows:

DISPLAY $\begin{Bmatrix} \text{data-name} \\ \text{literal} \end{Bmatrix}$ ... [UPON mnemonic-name]

[with NO ADVANCING]

1. The mnemonic-name must be a standard system name or be defined by the programmer.
2. Each data item named and each literal will be sent to the device in the listed order.
3. The literals may be alphanumeric, figurative constants (except ALL), and numeric literals.
4. Some systems will not display signed numeric items correctly. (Check your reference manual.)
5. The NO ADVANCING CLAUSE will cause the next display to begin at the immediate next position.
6. If the NO ADVANCING CLAUSE is omitted, the next displayed item will be on the next available line.

The contents of data-name or the value of literals are sent to a hardware device. The UPON option specifies the device on which the message will be displayed. If not specified, the output is sent to the default device. The default device is dependent on the system you are using. Assuming that the default device is the user's terminal, the statement:

```
DISPLAY STOCK-ON-HAND.
```

would output the contents of STOCK-ON-HAND to the user's terminal. The statement

```
DISPLAY "INVALID CUSTOMER FILE".
```

would output the literal to the user's terminal.

5.2.6   *The CLOSE Statement*

Once a file has been processed, it should be closed. The format and rules for the CLOSE statement are:

RELEASES RESOURCE

CLOSE file-name ...

1. A CLOSE may be issued only to OPEN files.
2. The file-name must be one that appears in an FD and SELECT clause.

Notice that there is no need to specify whether the file was used for input or output. In line 80 of the program in Figure 5.3 the statement

```
CLOSE EMPLOYEE-FILE.
```

terminates the processing of the EMPLOYEE-FILE. The CLOSE statement causes a file to be unavailable for further processing and causes the computer to perform any necessary housekeeping functions. We recommend that you use one CLOSE statement for each file you are closing.

5.3   Data Movement

To transfer data from an input area to an output area, or to place a special value in a data item, it is necessary to move data within memory. The basic COBOL instruction that accomplishes this is the MOVE instruction.

5.3.1   The MOVE Statement

The MOVE verb transfers data to one or more data items. The format and rules for the MOVE statement are:

$$\underline{\text{MOVE}} \quad \begin{Bmatrix} \text{data-name-1} \\ \text{literal} \end{Bmatrix} \quad \underline{\text{TO}} \text{ data-name-2} \dots$$

The following table summarizes many of the rules applicable to the MOVE statement, (other rules will be discussed in Chapter 8):

data-name-2: Receiving Item

data-name-1 Sending Item	Alphanumeric	Numeric with Decimal	Numeric without Decimal	Numeric Edited
Alphanumeric	Rule 1	Rule 5	Rule 5	Rule 5
Numeric with Decimal	Rule 4	Rule 2	Rule 2	Rule 2
Numeric without Decimal	Rule 1	Rule 3	Rule 2	Rule 3

1. The receiving item accepts the sending item and left-justifies. The rightmost characters are truncated if the sending field is larger than the receiving field. The rightmost characters are converted to spaces in the receiving field if the receiving field is longer than the sending field. Numeric signs are not moved.
2. The decimal points are aligned. The value is transferred. The rightmost digits after the decimal point are lost if the sending field has more places after the decimal point. The leftmost digits are lost if the sending field has more places before the

decimal. Extra positions are zero filled unless editing specifies otherwise. If both fields are signed, the sign is moved. If only the receiving field is signed, a positive sign is inserted. If only the sending field is signed, the absolute value is moved.
3. The decimal in the sending field is assumed to be after the rightmost digit. Rule 2 is then followed.
4. This MOVE is not allowed.
5. The sending field is assumed to be unsigned with the decimal after the rightmost position. Rule 2 is then followed. Note that this move can result in character data in a numeric field and should be used with care.

The *sending area*, data-name-1, remains unchanged after the execution of a MOVE statement. Data-name-2, following TO, is the *receiving item* that indicates the area whose contents are replaced by the data in the sending item. For example, in

```
MOVE "YES" TO WS-EOF-CUST-FILE.
```

the literal YES replaces the contents of WS-EOF-CUST-FILE. In

```
MOVE SF-STUDENT-NAME TO WS-NAME-OUT.
```

the contents of SF-STUDENT-NAME replace the contents of WS-NAME-OUT, and both fields will contain the same data after the MOVE. The example

```
MOVE ZEROS TO WS-TOTAL-MIS-MAJORS.
```

initializes the counter WS-TOTAL-MIS-MAJORS by replacing its contents with a value of zero. If a figurative constant is moved to a data item, the data item must be defined as numeric or alphanumeric depending on whether the figurative constant is numeric or alphanumeric. For example, if the receiving item is defined as PIC 9(8)V99, then the statement

```
MOVE ZEROS TO MONTHLY-SALES-TOTAL.
```

initializes MONTHLY-SALES-TOTAL to zero. Figure 5.7 shows some examples of values resulting from the execution of various MOVE statements. Lines 91, 92, and 93 in Figure 5.3 move the current date to the report for printing.

Figure 5.7   Results of MOVE Statements

	Sending		Receiving
Picture	Contents	Picture	Contents
X(4)		J	A	C	K		X(4)		J	A	C	K	
X(4)		J	O	H	N		X(3)		J	O	H	
X(4)		F	R	E	D		X(5)		F	R	E	D			
X(6)		0	6	1	5	8	5		9(6)		0	6	1	5	8	5	
X(5)		6	1	5	8	5		9(6)		6	1	5	8	5			
X(7)		0	0	6	1	3	8	5		9(6)		0	0	6	1	3	8	

Sending Picture	Sending Contents	Receiving Picture	Receiving Contents
9(3)V99	231V00	9(3)V9(3)	231V00
9(3)V99	012V12	9(3)V9	012V1
9(3)V99	125V13	9V9	5V1
9(3)V99	180V11	9(6)	000180
9(4)	1032	9(3)	032
9(4)	1032	9(4)	1032
9(4)	1032	9(5)	01032
9(4)	1032	9(4)V99	1032V00
9(4)	1032	99V99	32V00

5.4   Arithmetic Operations

Business applications often require computations such as calculation of income taxes and determination of sales forecasts. COBOL provides the arithmetic statements for manipulating data in calculations.

5.4.1   The COMPUTE Statement

The *COMPUTE* statement is the most versatile arithmetic statement. It allows the programmer to specify multiple arithmetic calculations in a way similar to familiar arithmetic notation. The format for the COMPUTE statement and the rules for forming the statement are:

COMPUTE data-name-1 . . . = arithmetic-expression

1. Operators in the arithmetic expression must be preceded and followed by one or more spaces.
2. The COMPUTE statement must be used if exponentiation is desired.
3. The result of the calculation is stored in the data items written to the left of the equal sign.
4. Data-name-1 must be an elementary numeric item or an elementary numeric edited data item. The calculated value is placed here and is edited according to the data-name-1 item PICTURE.

The arithmetic-expression following the equal (=) sign may be a combination of numeric data items, literals, and the arithmetic operators. The arithmetic operators and their order of precedence are:

( )　Parentheses
-　Unary minus signs (negative values)
**　Exponentiation
*　Multiplication
/　Division
+　Addition
-　Subtraction

1. Arithmetic expressions within parentheses are calculated first (innermost before outermost).
2. Unary minus signs are evaluated.
3. Exponentiation is performed in right-to-left order.
4. Multiplication and division operations are performed from left to right in order of occurrence.
5. Addition and subtraction operations are performed from left to right in order of occurrence.

In the following example,

```
COMPUTE WS-NET-PAY = WS-HOURLY-RATE * NUM-HOURS -

       WS-DEDUCTIONS
```

deductions are to be subtracted from the product of hourly rate and number of hours worked. The resulting value is to be stored in the item WS-NET-PAY.

The value of the arithmetic expression is determined using the standard order of evaluation outlined above. This order of precedence states that parenthetical expressions, that is, the operations within parentheses, are evaluated first. If more than one pair of parentheses appears in the expression, the operations proceed from the innermost to the outermost set. For example, the order of evaluation in

$$(\ C \ + \ (A*B) \ ) \ * \ E$$
$$\underbrace{\qquad}_{(1)}$$
$$\underbrace{\qquad\qquad}_{(2)}$$
$$\underbrace{\qquad\qquad\qquad}_{(3)}$$

indicates that (1) A is multiplied by B, (2) the product is added to C, and (3) this sum is multiplied by E. Parentheses not only alter the order of calculations but also serve to clarify complex expressions. Use them to make your code more readable.

Unary minus signs are evaluated next followed by exponentiation operations in right-to-left order. Multiplication and division are next in left-to-right order of operator appearance. And finally, addition and subtraction are done in left-to-right order of operator appearance. Figure 5.8 illustrates the order of evaluation of a complex COBOL expression.

Figure 5.8   Order of Arithmetic Operations

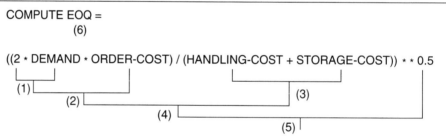

```
COMPUTE EOQ =
        (6)

((2 * DEMAND * ORDER-COST) / (HANDLING-COST + STORAGE-COST)) * * 0.5
```

Order of operations

1. 2 * Demand
2. Result of (1) * order-cost
3. Handling-cost + storage-cost
4. Result in (2) divided by result in (3)
5. Result in (4) * * .5
6. Store the result from (5) in (6)

When the computed value is stored in the result field, the decimal points are aligned in a manner analogous to the alignment of sending and receiving fields in a MOVE statement. All positions after the decimal are stored by truncating any digits to the right of the decimal point that do not fit into the result area. Positions before the decimal point are stored so that the leftmost digits are truncated if the PICTURE clause in the receiving field is not large enough. If the receiving field is too large, the extra positions are filled with zeros. Figure 5.9 illustrates the effects of field size on the value of the results. Notice that the danger in specifying a tiny result field is the loss of the most significant digits.

Figure 5.9   *Decimal Alignment in Stored Values*

Result	Picture	Stored Value
315.127	9(5)	00315
315.127	9(5)V99	00315V12
317.999	99V99	17V99
00.001	99V99	00V00
−32.77	99V99	32V77

5.4.2   *The ADD Statement*

The ADD statement adds two or more numeric data items and stores the resulting sum. There are two different formats for the ADD statement: the ADD TO and the ADD GIVING. The format and rules of the ADD TO statement are:

$$\underline{\text{ADD}} \quad \left\{ \begin{array}{l} \text{data-name-1} \\ \text{literal-1} \end{array} \right\} \ldots \underline{\text{TO}} \text{ data-name-m...}$$

1. An ADD statement must contain at least two elementary numeric items.
2. When the TO option is used, the values of the operands before the word TO are added together. Their sum is then added to the current value of each data-name mentioned after the word TO. The receiving item(s) contain the computed result(s).
3. Resultant sums are not edited with the TO option.
4. Decimal points are aligned.

The ADD TO adds the contents of the data item(s) and literals specified before the TO clause to each data item(s) specified in the TO clause and stores the result in the data item(s) specified in the TO clause. For example,

```
ADD 1 TO WS-TOTAL-COUNT.
```

adds 1 to whatever value is contained in WS-TOTAL-COUNT and stores the new value in WS-TOTAL-COUNT, destroying the old value of WS-TOTAL-COUNT.

Keep in mind that when the TO format is used, all the data elements and literals are added together and the resulting sum replaces the value of data-name-m while the contents of data-name-1/literal-1 remain unchanged. For example, the statement

```
ADD INTEREST TO BAL-FORWARD.
```

would proceed in the following way:

```
DATA ELEMENT:         INTEREST        BAL-FORWARD
BEFORE ADD TO:        510.37          8332.78
AFTER ADD TO:         510.37          8843.15
```

The format and rules of the ADD GIVING statement are:

ADD $\left\{ \begin{array}{l} \text{data-name-1} \\ \text{literal-1} \end{array} \right\}$ $\left\{ \begin{array}{l} \text{data-name-2} \\ \text{literal-2} \end{array} \right\} \ldots$

GIVING data-name-m . . .

1. An ADD statement must contain at least two elementary numeric items.
2. The word GIVING must not be written in the same statement as TO.
3. When the GIVING option is used, there must be at least 2 operands preceding the word GIVING. The sum may be edited according to data-name-m's PICTURE and may be an elementary numeric item or an elementary numeric edited item.
4. Decimal points are aligned.

The ADD GIVING adds all the data items and literals specified before the GIVING clause and stores the result in the data-name(s) specified by the GIVING clause. For example,

```
ADD  FED-INCOME-TAX STATE-INCOME-TAX GIVING
     TOT-INCOME-TAX.
```

adds the values of the data items FED-INCOME-TAX and STATE-INCOME-TAX and stores the sum in TOT-INCOME-TAX. Any previous value in TOT-INCOME-TAX is lost. The data-name specified after GIVING may refer to either a numeric or a numeric edited item. The statement

```
ADD REG-PAY OVERTIME-PAY GIVING TOT-PAY.
```

proceeds as follows:

```
DATA ELEMENT:         REG-PAY   OVERTIME-PAY   TOT-PAY
BEFORE ADD GIVING:    800       250            unknown
AFTER ADD GIVING:     800       250            1050
```

When the computer executes ADD statements, it automatically makes the decimal point alignment and takes the signs into account. Thus the programmer does not have to worry about the actual PICTURE clause of each data item, only that of the resulting item. Be aware that if the resulting value has more digits to the right or to the left of the decimal point than the receiving item, truncation will occur. If the result is smaller than the size of the receiving field, the extra positions will be zero-filled in the same fashion as with the MOVE statement. If the result is negative and the resulting data item is unsigned, the sign will be lost.

ADD statements are used in situations requiring only additions. These situations include keeping record counts, page counts, control totals, or summary totals. If more than just simple addition is required, the COMPUTE statement should be used.

5.4.3   *The SUBTRACT Statement*

The *SUBTRACT* verb performs subtraction of a single numeric data item or of the sum of two or more numeric data items from a specified data item and stores the difference. The format is very similar to the ADD statement format, and there are two versions: the SUBTRACT FROM and the SUBTRACT GIVING. The format and rules for the SUBTRACT FROM are:

SUBTRACT $\left\{ \begin{array}{l} \text{data-name} \\ \text{literal} \end{array} \right\}$ ... <u>FROM</u> data-name-m ...

1. All operands must be elementary numeric items.
2. When the FROM option is used, the values of the operands before the word FROM are added together. Their sum is then subtracted from the current value of each identifier mentioned after the word FROM. The receiving item(s) contain the computed result(s).
3. Each data-name must refer to an elementary numeric item.

In the SUBTRACT statement, the data items listed before the FROM are added and the resulting sum is subtracted from the data item(s) specified in the FROM clause. The result replaces the value of the data item(s) specified in the FROM clause. For example,

```
SUBTRACT UNION-DUES TOT-WITHHOLD FROM PAY.
```

subtracts the sum of the UNION-DUES and TOT-WITHHOLD from the data item PAY and stores the result in PAY, replacing PAY's previous contents.

The format and rules for the SUBTRACT GIVING statement are:

SUBTRACT $\left\{ \begin{array}{l} \text{data-name-1} \\ \text{literal-1} \end{array} \right\}$ ... <u>FROM</u> $\left\{ \begin{array}{l} \text{data-name-m} \\ \text{literal-m} \end{array} \right\}$

<u>GIVING</u> data-name-n . . .

1. All operands must be elementary numeric items.
2. Each data-name must refer to an elementary numeric item, except the identifier following the word GIVING, which may be a numeric edited item.

If the SUBTRACT GIVING format is used, the value of the result is stored in the data item(s) specified in the GIVING clause. For example,

```
SUBTRACT UNION-DUES TOT-WITHHOLD FROM PAY GIVING NET-PAY.
```

subtracts the sum of UNION-DUES and TOT-WITHHOLD from PAY and stores the result in the data item NET-PAY. Whatever value was in PAY is not changed, but the contents of NET-PAY are replaced. As with the ADD statement, the SUBTRACT is usually used when only the subtract operation is needed; otherwise the COMPUTE statement is used.

5.4.4   The MULTIPLY Statement

The *MULTIPLY* statement performs the multiplication of two numeric data items and stores the product. Its two formats are very similar to those of the ADD and SUBTRACT statements: the MULTIPLY BY and the MULTIPLY GIVING. The two format versions of the MULTIPLY statement are given below.

Format 1:

$$\underline{\text{MULTIPLY}} \quad \left\{ \begin{array}{l} \text{data-name-1} \\ \text{literal-1} \end{array} \right\} \quad \underline{\text{BY}} \quad \text{data-name-2} \ldots$$

Format 2:

$$\underline{\text{MULTIPLY}} \quad \left\{ \begin{array}{l} \text{data-name-1} \\ \text{literal-1} \end{array} \right\} \quad \underline{\text{BY}} \quad \left\{ \begin{array}{l} \text{data-name-2} \\ \text{literal-2} \end{array} \right\}$$

$$\underline{\text{GIVING}} \text{ data-name-3} \ldots$$

1. All operands must be elementary numeric items.
2. The result specified by the <u>GIVING</u> clause may be a numeric or numeric edited item.

If the MULTIPLY BY version is used, the data item that appears before BY is multiplied by the data item specified in the BY clause. The result is stored in the data item in the BY clause, replacing its previous contents. If more than one item is specified in the BY clause, the data item specified before BY is multiplied by each BY clause data item in turn, and that product replaces each item's contents. In this example,

```
MULTIPLY SALES-AMOUNT BY TAX RATE.
```

the product of the sales value and rate is computed and stored in TAX-RATE, destroying TAX-RATE's previous contents. Using the MULTIPLY BY format can create confusion as to where the result is stored. A simple rule for remembering where the results of a computation are stored is that the last data item specified is the one changed as a result of executing the operation. For example, in the statement

```
MULTIPLY TAX-RATE BY SALES-AMOUNT.
```

the computed tax will be stored in SALES-AMOUNT and will destroy its previous contents!
    Be careful when using the MULTIPLY BY statement with literals. Consider the following

statement for calculating state sales tax:

```
MULTIPLY 0.06125 BY SALES-AMOUNT.
```

The result will be stored in SALES-AMOUNT, and as long as you remember what value is stored in SALES-AMOUNT you will avoid confusion (and errors!). Since the order of the operands seems so unnatural, we recommend that you always use the MULTIPLY GIVING format when using a MULTIPLY statement. It avoids confusion and does not alter the values of the items being multiplied. An even simpler technique is to use the COMPUTE statement instead of the MULTIPLY statement.

If the MULTIPLY GIVING format is used, the product is stored in the data item(s) specified in the GIVING clause. For example,

```
MULTIPLY SALES-AMOUNT BY TAX-RATE GIVING SALES-TAX.
```

calculates the product and replaces the contents of SALES-TAX. The contents of both SALES-AMOUNT and TAX-RATE remain unchanged.

5.4.5   The DIVIDE Statement

The final arithmetic statement provided by COBOL is the *DIVIDE* statement. It has three formats, the DIVIDE INTO, the DIVIDE GIVING, and the DIVIDE GIVING REMAINDER. For all three formats the rules are that the operands must be elementary items and that division by zero results in a SIZE ERROR condition (which we will discuss shortly). The format and rules of the DIVIDE INTO are:

DIVIDE $\left\{ \begin{array}{l} \text{data-name-1} \\ \text{literal-1} \end{array} \right\}$ <u>INTO</u> data-name-2 . . .

1. All data items must be elementary numeric items.
2. Truncation of the result follows numeric MOVE rules.

In using the DIVIDE INTO format, data-name-1 or literal-1 specifies the divisor (denominator) and data-name-2 in the INTO clause specifies the dividend (numerator). The resulting quotient is stored in the data item specifying the dividend. For example,

```
DIVIDE 0.9 INTO TOT-SALES-AMOUNT.
```

performs the division of the literal 0.9 into the value stored in TOT-SALES-AMOUNT and stores the result in TOT-SALES-AMOUNT, replacing its previous contents. If multiple dividends are specified, the operation is conducted for each one and the results are stored in multiple destinations in the same way as in the MULTIPLY statement.

The DIVIDE GIVING format is:

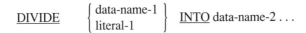

<u>DIVIDE</u> $\left\{ \begin{array}{l} \text{data-name-1} \\ \text{literal-1} \end{array} \right\}$ $\left\{ \begin{array}{l} \underline{\text{BY}} \\ \underline{\text{INTO}} \end{array} \right\}$ $\left\{ \begin{array}{l} \text{data-name-2} \\ \text{literal-2} \end{array} \right\}$

<u>GIVING</u> data-name-3 . . .

If the DIVIDE INTO GIVING format is used, the resulting quotient is stored in data-name-3 specified in the GIVING clause, and the contents of both operators remain unchanged. Data-name-3 may be a numeric or numeric edited elementary item.

A special feature of the DIVIDE GIVING statement is that the programmer may determine the order of specifying the divisor and the dividend by choosing between the reserved words BY and INTO. If DIVIDE BY GIVING is used, the first operand is the dividend and the second operand is the divisor. The resulting quotient is then stored in the data item(s) specified in the GIVING clause. This "interchangeability" of dividend and divisor is convenient, since it allows one to express the division in the terms one has learned. For example, the statement

```
DIVIDE QUANTITY INTO GROSS-COST GIVING UNIT-COST.
```

is equivalent to

```
DIVIDE GROSS-COST BY QUANTITY GIVING UNIT-COST.
```

The DIVIDE BY format always requires a GIVING clause. If the GIVING clause were not used, the result might not be saved because the divisor can be a numeric literal, which does not reserve memory accessible by the programmer.

Another COBOL feature allows the programmer to obtain the remainder resulting from a DIVIDE operation. This is accomplished by using a REMAINDER clause in the DIVIDE GIVING statement. The format of the DIVIDE GIVING REMAINDER statement is:

$$\underline{\text{DIVIDE}} \quad \left\{ \begin{array}{c} \text{data-name-1} \\ \text{literal-1} \end{array} \right\} \quad \left\{ \begin{array}{c} \underline{\text{BY}} \\ \underline{\text{INTO}} \end{array} \right\} \quad \left\{ \begin{array}{c} \text{data-name-2} \\ \text{literal-2} \end{array} \right\}$$

<u>GIVING</u> data-name-3
<u>REMAINDER</u> data-name-4

Using the DIVIDE GIVING REMAINDER format, data-name-4 specifies the storage location where the value of the remainder will be saved. The *REMAINDER* feature is especially desirable in business applications where the remainder is used for data validation purposes. The DIVIDE GIVING REMAINDER format is the only format of the DIVIDE statement that allows the program to save the remainder value.

Like the ADD, SUBTRACT, and MULTIPLY statements, the DIVIDE statement should be used only when division is the only operation being performed in a computation or when it is necessary to save the remainder. Otherwise the COMPUTE statement should be used. A program can be shortened by replacing consecutive ADDs, SUBTRACTs, MULTIPLYs, and DIVIDEs by a single COMPUTE statement. For example,

```
ADD A TO B.
ADD C TO D.
DIVIDE D INTO B.
MULTIPLY B BY E.
SUBTRACT F FROM E.
SUBTRACT G FROM E.
MULTIPLY E BY E GIVING Q.
```

can be replaced by

```
COMPUTE Q = ((A + B)/(C + D) * E - F - G) ** 2.
```

The COMPUTE statement is not only shorter, it is also easier to follow because we have been trained to specify arithmetic operations through symbolic notation rather than through English sentences.

5.4.6   *Arithmetic Statement Options*

Several optional clauses may be used with the COBOL arithmetic statements: the ROUNDED clause, the ON SIZE ERROR clause, the NOT ON SIZE ERROR clause, and the conditional delimiters. Figure 5.10 illustrates the formats of arithmetic statements incorporating these options.

Figure 5.10   *COBOL Arithmetic Statements*

— halfADjust

COMPUTE data-name [ROUNDED] = arithmetic-expression

[ON SIZE ERROR imperative-statement-1)

[NOT ON SIZE ERROR imperative-statement-2]

[END COMPUTE]

ADD { data-name-1 / literal-1 } . . . TO data-name-m [ROUNDED]

[ON SIZE ERROR imperative-statement-1]

NOT ON SIZE ERROR imperative-statement-2]

[END-ADD]

ADD { data-name-1 / literal-1 } { data-name-2 / literal-2 } . . .

GIVING data-name-m [ROUNDED] . . .

[ON SIZE ERROR imperative-statement-1]

[NOT ON SIZE ERROR imperative-statement-2]

[END-ADD]

SUBTRACT { data-name-1 / literal-1 } . . . FROM data-name-m [ROUNDED]

Figure 5.10   *(continued)*

[ON <u>SIZE</u> <u>ERROR</u> imperative-statement-1]

[<u>END</u> <u>SUBTRACT</u>]

<u>SUBTRACT</u> {data-name-1}... <u>FROM</u> {data-name-m}
{literal-1 }   {literal-m }

<u>GIVING</u> data-name-n [<u>ROUNDED</u>]...

[ON <u>SIZE</u> <u>ERROR</u> imperative-statement-1]

[<u>NOT</u> ON <u>SIZE</u> <u>ERROR</u> imperative-statement-1]

[<u>END-SUBTRACT</u>]

MULTIPLY {data-name-1} <u>BY</u> data-name-2 [<u>ROUNDED</u>]...
{literal-1 }

[ON <u>SIZE</u> <u>ERROR</u> imperative-statement-1]

<u>NOT</u> ON <u>SIZE</u> <u>ERROR</u> imperative-statement-2]

[<u>END-MULTIPLY</u>]

MULTIPLY {data-name-1} <u>BY</u> {data-name-2 }
{literal-1 }   {literal-2 }

<u>GIVING</u> {data-name-3} [<u>ROUNDED</u>]...

[ON <u>SIZE</u> <u>ERROR</u> imperative-statement-1]

<u>NOT</u> ON <u>SIZE</u> <u>ERROR</u> imperative-statement-2]

[<u>END-MULTIPLY</u>]

DIVIDE {data-name-1} <u>INTO</u> data-name-2 [<u>ROUNDED</u>]...
{literal-1 }

[ON <u>SIZE</u> <u>ERROR</u> imperative-statement-1]

<u>NOT</u> ON <u>SIZE</u> <u>ERROR</u> imperative-statement-2]

Figure 5.10   *(continued)*

[END-DIVIDE]

$$DIVIDE \begin{Bmatrix} \text{data-name-1} \\ \text{literal-1} \end{Bmatrix} \begin{Bmatrix} \underline{BY} \\ \underline{INTO} \end{Bmatrix} \begin{Bmatrix} \text{data-name-2} \\ \text{literal-2} \end{Bmatrix}$$

$\underline{GIVING}$ {data-name-3} [$\underline{ROUNDED}$] . . .

$\underline{REMAINDER}$ data-name-4

[ON $\underline{SIZE}$ $\underline{ERROR}$ imperative-statement-1]

$\underline{NOT}$ ON $\underline{SIZE}$ $\underline{ERROR}$ imperative-statement-2]

[END-DIVIDE]

The ROUNDED Clause. The *ROUNDED* option is used to round the operation's resulting value by adding 5 to the digit immediately following the rightmost digit of the result if the value is positive or subtracting 5 if the value is negative. For example, in the statement

```
ADD FICA TO DEDUCTIONS ROUNDED.
```

the sum of FICA and DEDUCTIONS will be rounded before being stored in DEDUCTIONS. Assume that the calculated result for an arithmetic expression is 32.123, and the value is to be stored in a data item with a PIC 99V99. The resulting value will be saved as 32.12, with or without rounding. However, if the value is 53.246, it will be saved as 53.24 without rounding, but as 53.25 with rounding.

The ON SIZE ERROR Clause. The *ON SIZE ERROR* clause allows a programmer to test for two conditions during computations: division by zero and loss of significant digits. Division by zero is an illegal operation, and any attempt to do so will result in a SIZE ERROR condition. In all other operations, if the result of a computation exceeds the size of the resulting data item, thereby causing the leftmost digits of the integer portion to be truncated, it results in a SIZE ERROR condition. The general format for use of the ON SIZE ERROR (and its complement) is:

[ON $\underline{SIZE}$ $\underline{ERROR}$ imperative-statement-1]
[$\underline{NOT}$ ON $\underline{SIZE}$ $\underline{ERROR}$ imperative-statement-2]

The ON SIZE ERROR clause causes the computer to execute the specified imperative-statement when a SIZE ERROR condition is encountered (or not).

If the ON SIZE ERROR clause is not used, the results may be severe. In the case of division by zero, most computers will stop executing the program altogether. In the case of digit truncation, the data item containing the result will not reflect the correct value. Such an error may go undetected and produce faulty reports or bad data on permanent files.

By specifying the ON SIZE ERROR clause, the programmer can direct the activities to be carried out should the condition occur. If a SIZE ERROR is detected, it triggers the execution of the imperative-statement specified in the clause and the result field is not changed. If no error occurs, the program continues its normal execution sequence or uses the action specified by the NOT ON SIZE ERROR clause. Generally the imperative-statement should perform some error routine. At the very least it should print an appropriate message.

Determining the Size of the Result Field. There are no COBOL rules for determining the size of the data item that will hold the results of arithmetic computations. It is therefore important that you know the application for which the program is written and some key factors such as the size of incoming data fields and how large calculation results have been in the past. With some logic and a few rules of thumb you should be able to make some educated estimates about the size of result fields.

When two fields are added, the result will be no longer than the length of the largest operand plus 1. If the addition is in an iteration, it is important that you know approximately how many times the addition is to be performed. For example, if you are adding a five-digit field into some result area each time an iteration is executed, then knowing something about the number of times the iteration is expected to be performed can indicate how big to make the result field. You can apply the rule of thumb used for calculating length of result fields in multiplication operations.

In multiplication operations the product of an m-digit field and an n-digit field is at most $(m + n)$ digits long. For example, 99999 multiplied by 99 is equal to 9899901, a seven-digit result.

In subtraction there are only two operands at any one time and their difference cannot contain more digits than the largest item, plus one digit. For example, if we are subtracting a two-digit field from a five-digit field, the difference cannot have more than six digits.

For division, the remainder and the quotient can be as large as the dividend. If decimal points occur in the divisor, the largest result may be determined using the inverse of the smallest value as an m-digit field, using the dividend as an n-digit field, and applying the multiplication rule.

Conditional Delimiters. Statements having optional conditions as part of their syntax are accompanied by an optional word to delimit the scope of the statement. The READ and WRITE have the END-READ and END-WRITE delimiters that have the effect of terminating the most recent READ or WRITE and all its associated conditional clauses. A period will terminate a statement as well as a delimiter, but a period will terminate *every* unfinished statement whereas a conditional delimiter terminates a single unfinished statement. All arithmetic statements have conditions as options in their syntax and all have conditional delimiters as an optional way to terminate the statement, as can be seen in Figure 5.10.

5.5　*Program Control Statements*

The statements that control the logic of a program are those that can alter the sequence of instructions. In COBOL these are the IF, PERFORM, PERFORM UNTIL, and STOP RUN statements.

5.5.1　*The IF Statement*

The IF statement directly supports the selection construct in COBOL. It evaluates a condition and continues execution based on the results of the evaluation. The condition used in the IF statement may vary from a simple comparison involving one relation to be evaluated to a complex one involving many relations and computations. The format and rules for the IF statement are:

IF condition-1 then
$$\left\{ \begin{array}{l} \text{statement-1} \dots \\ \underline{\text{NEXT SENTENCE}} \end{array} \right\}$$

$$\left[\left\{ \begin{array}{l} \underline{\text{ELSE}} \text{ statement-2} \dots \quad [\text{END-IF}] \\ \underline{\text{ELSE}} \underline{\text{ NEXT}} \underline{\text{ SENTENCE}} \\ \underline{\text{END-IF}} \end{array} \right\} \right]$$

1.　If condition-1 is true, the ELSE clause is ignored.
2.　If condition-1 is false, the statements associated with the ELSE clause are executed.
3.　Statement-1 and statement-2 may be one of a series of COBOL statements.
4.　The NEXT SENTENCE clause causes the program to pass control to the sentence immediately following the sentence containing the IF.
5.　The ELSE NEXT SENTENCE may be omitted if it is the last statement in the IF sentence.
6.　The IF statement is terminated by a period or the END-IF.

Figure 5.11 shows how the COBOL IF statement is related to the selection structure. The IF statement tests the value of a condition, executes statement-1 if it is true and statement-2, following the ELSE clause, if it is false. In the statement

```
IF END-FILE-FLAG = "YES"

        MOVE RECORD-COUNT TO REC-COUNT-OUT
        MOVE RESTOCK-COUNT TO RESTOCK-COUNT-OUT
ELSE
        PERFORM 2100-READ-INVENTORY-FILE.
```

two MOVEs will be executed if the condition END-FILE-FLAG = "YES" is true; otherwise the PERFORM statement will be executed. Line 109 in figure 5.3 shows the use of an IF statement to determine whether or not to print employee data based on a union code.

Figure 5.11   The COBOL Implementation of the Selection Control Structure

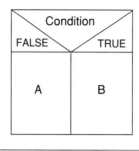

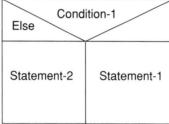

5.5.2   Relation Conditions

The most common conditional expression in COBOL is the *relation condition*. The relation condition compares two items and determines the truth value of the stated relationship between them. For example, two values may be compared to see if they are equal or if one is less than or greater than the other.

The format and rules for a relation condition are:

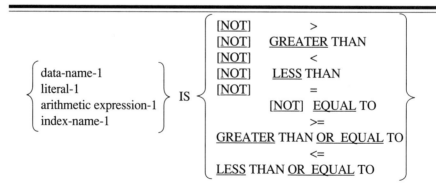

$$\left\{ \begin{array}{l} \text{data-name-2} \\ \text{literal-2} \\ \text{arithmetic-expression-2} \\ \text{index-name-2} \end{array} \right\}$$

1   Each operator (>, <, =, >=, <=) must be preceded and followed by a space.
2.   Both operands (data-names, literals, expressions) cannot be literals.
3.   Arithmetic expressions follow the construction rules of the COMPUTE statement.

Usually the relational symbols are preferred in the code. Examples are:

```
BALANCE-DUE > 25.00
AGE < 30
EOF-AR-OPEN-ITEMS = "FALSE"
```

When the computer evaluates a relation condition between numeric operands, the comparison is termed a *numeric comparison*. The length of the data items is not important in determining the truth value of the conditional expression; the comparison is based solely on the algebraic value of the numbers being compared. For example, 285.6887 is less than 286. Both operands, however, must be numeric items. When an arithmetic expression is used, the expression is evaluated prior to any comparisons. The same arithmetic rules used by the COMPUTE statement are used in the arithmetic expressions.

When nonnumeric operands are compared, the comparison is called a *nonnumeric comparison*. In this case the computer will determine the value of the relation condition based on the collating, or sorting, sequence of the computer's character set. The specific sequence may vary from machine to machine. Generally, however, uppercase letters are ordered in alphabetical sequence and numeric digits in counting sequence. For example, C is less than M and the character 1 is less than the character 8. Figure 5.12 shows a common collating sequence for a character set. Note that the special characters have the lowest values, i.e., they come first in the sorting sequence, followed by the numeric digits and finally by the alphabetic characters. Therefore, in a comparison of 1XYZ and AXYZ, 1XYZ would be considered to have a lower value than AXYZ and would test to be less than AXYZ.

Figure 5.12   Collating Sequence for a Portion of the ASCII Character Set

b	A	Q
(	B	R
)	C	S
,	D	T
.	E	U
/	F	V
0	G	W
1	H	X
2	I	Y
3	J	Z
4	K	
5	L	
6	M	
7	N	
8	O	
9	P	

When performing nonnumeric comparisons, the computer makes the operands appear to be of equal length by treating the shorter of the two operands as if the rightmost characters were all spaces. The comparison then proceeds on a character-by-character basis from left to right until the first unequal character is encountered. This occurrence determines the order of the two operands. If no unequal character is found, the two data items are considered to be equal. Figure 5.13 illustrates several examples of nonnumeric comparisons.

Figure 5.13   Character Relation Condition Result

1st Operand	IS	2nd Operand
ABCD	<	ABCDE
ABCD	>	ABCb
1934	<	193A
DFGb	=	DFG
JOHNbbEV	<	JOHNbbEZ
ABCbD	<	ABCDb
AB3	>	AB
AB3	<	ABC

b Denotes a blank character

5.5.3   The PERFORM Statement

The PERFORM verb transfers control to and executes a named set of instructions. Control returns to the statement following the PERFORM.

The simplest format of the PERFORM statement is the following:

PERFORM [procedure-1]

1. Procedure-1 is the name of a paragraph or section in the PROCEDURE DIVI-SION.
2. Procedure-1 may not contain a PERFORM of itself or of any procedure that PERFORMs Procedure-1.

In the following example

```
PERFORM 1000-GET-INV-RECORD.

CLOSE INV-FILE.
```

program control passes to paragraph 1000-GET-INV-RECORD, the paragraph is executed, and control then returns to the CLOSE statement. The program in Figure 5.3 uses many PERFORMs, including lines 85 through 87.

The PERFORM statement may be used as an imperative statement as in the following example:

```
COMPUTE WS-ORDER-TOTAL =
      WS-ORDER-TOTAL + CURRENT AMT
      ON SIZE ERROR
            PERFORM ERROR-ROUTINE.
```

The *range* of a PERFORM includes all the statements from the first statement executed to the last statement, inclusively. If a PERFORM statement is included within the range of another PERFORM, the PERFORM statements are *nested*. COBOL allows the nesting of PERFORM statements as long as the range of one PERFORM statement is wholly included in or wholly excluded from the range of the other PERFORM statement and as long as recursion is avoided. Following are some examples of nested PERFORMs:

```
VALID:
            PERFORM 100-TAXES.
                  .
                  .
                  .
      100-TAXES.
          PERFORM 120-SOCIAL-SECURITY.
          PERFORM 140-STATE.
INVALID:

      150-TEST-NUMERIC.
          PERFORM 160-TEST-DEDUCTION.
      160-TEST-DEDUCTION.
          PERFORM 150-TEST-NUMERIC.
```

5.5.4   *The PERFORM UNTIL Statement*

The PERFORM UNTIL statement implements the iteration construct in COBOL. It allows the continual execution of a set of instructions until a certain condition is met. The format and rules of the PERFORM UNTIL are as follows:

PERFORM [procedure-1]

$$\left[\text{with } \underline{\text{TEST}} \quad \left\{ \begin{array}{c} \underline{\text{BEFORE}} \\ \underline{\text{AFTER}} \end{array} \right\} \right] \underline{\text{UNTIL}} \text{ condition-1}$$

[imperative-statement-1 ... END-PERFORM]

1. Procedure-1 may be either a paragraph or section in the PROCEDURE DIVISION.
2. Procedure-1 may not contain a PERFORM of itself or of any procedure containing a PERFORM of procedure-1. *(RECURRSION)*
3. If procedure-1 is used, imperative-statement-1 and the END-PERFORM may not be used. The reverse also holds.
4. The WITH TEST option defaults to BEFORE.

The condition is used to control the number of times an iteration is performed. In the following example,

```
PERFORM 1000-PROCESS-INV-RECORD UNTIL EOF-INV-FILE = "Y".
```

paragraph 1000-PROCESS-INV-RECORD will be executed until there are no more records in the inventory file. At that point control will return to the statement following the PERFORM UNTIL. Line 79 in Figure 5.3 uses a PERFORM UNTIL to repeat a process while records remain in the input file.

In the PERFORM UNTIL statement the condition is tested first unless the AFTER option is specified. If the condition is true, control passes to the statement immediately following the PERFORM statement. In other words, procedure-1 is not executed. If the condition is false, procedure-1 will be executed and control will return to the PERFORM statement so that the condition can be tested again. Procedure-1 will continue to be performed until the condition is true. Therefore, it is possible to execute the procedure zero, one, or multiple times.

Figure 5.14 illustrates how the PERFORM UNTIL WITH TEST BEFORE statement functions in COBOL. Note that the PERFORM UNTIL WITH TEST BEFORE implements the iteration structure a little differently from the DO WHILE and DO UNTIL versions. Figure 5.15 illustrates the differences among these constructs and the COBOL statements needed to implement them. The WITH TEST AFTER option allows direct implementation of the DO UNTIL structure, as shown in Figure 5.15. An example would be:

```
PERFORM 110-FORMAT-LINES WITH TEST AFTER UNTIL EOF-MASTER = "TRUE".
```

Figure 5.14　**Flowchart of COBOL PERFORM UNTIL Statement**

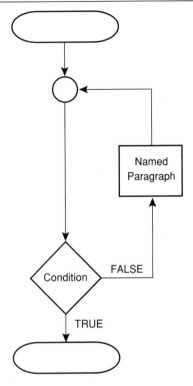

Figure 5.15   COBOL Implementation of Three Iteration Constructs

DO WHILE
code: PERFORM **A**
UNTIL NOT Condition

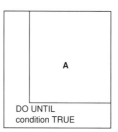

DO UNTIL
code: Perform **A**
Perform **A** UNTIL Condition
or: PERFORM **A** WITH
TEST AFTER UNTIL
Condition

COBOL PERFORM UNTIL WITH TEST
BEFORE
code: PERFORM **A**
UNTIL Condition

The option to specify one or more imperative statements is allowed in place of a procedure name. This is known as an in-line PERFORM. It allows the programmer to remove unnecessary short paragraphs by bringing the statements in the paragraph in-line with the PERFORM. However, paragraphs are a function of the logical design of the program. The logical design of a program should not be violated in order to save a few lines of code. The match between logical design and program code should always be preserved.

5.5.5   The STOP RUN Statement

The STOP RUN statement terminates the execution of a program and returns control to the operating system. The general format is:

STOP RUN

Case Study: CDL's Extend Customer Orders

To process the customer orders received by CDL, the cost of each item must be determined by extending its price information, adding postage and handling charges, and storing the extended order on a new file. Figure 5.16 gives the specifications for CDL's "Extend Customer Orders" program. It reads the file with the customer orders and extends the amount owed on each item ordered. Furthermore, the accounting department has requested that the program provide control totals for dollar amounts, number of orders, and number of CDs ordered. These are to be visually checked at the operator's terminal by a qualified person from the accounting department.

Figure 5.16   *CDL's "Extend Customer Orders" Program Specifications*

PROGRAM SUMMARY

TITLE: *Extend Customer Orders*

PREPARED BY: *C. Hilton*

DATE: *6-28-93*

FILES USED		
FILE NAME	MEDIA	ORGANIZATION
Orders	*Disk*	*Sequential*
Extended orders	*Disk*	*Sequential*

DESCRIPTION
The customer orders were separated by the Categorize Daily Mail program.
The price field of the order will contain the price of a single CD if it is a discount item. If it is a standard priced item, the amount is initially set to zero. The retail standard price (currently $16.95) should replace the zero.
The total order price should be determined as follows: Item price times quantity plus postage and handling costs.
Postage and handling is computed at a bulk rate in groups of 5 items plus a single unit rate for the remaining items. Current rates: Bulk is $3.95; single is $1.24.
Total number of CDs ordered, total dollar value of CDs ordered, total dollar value of all orders, and total number of orders processed should be computed and displayed on the terminal.

The amount of each order is determined as specified in the program summary. The record layout of the orders file was modified recently to reflect changes in the requirements of the program that created it. The revised file layout appears in Figure 5.17 along with the extended order file layout.

Figure 5.17   Record Layouts for CDL's "Extend Customer Orders" Program

RECORD LAYOUT SHEET
Revised

Record Name: *Order*		File Name: *Orders*		
Prepared By: *C. Hilton*		Date: *6-28-93*		
Key Fields:		Organization: *Sequential*		
Field	Description	Type*	Length	Decimal
Customer #	*A unique customer ID*	*N*	*6*	*0*
Compact disc #	*The stock number for the CD*	*N*	*6*	*0*
Quantity	*The number ordered*	*N*	*2*	*0*
Order number	*A preprinted order form number*	*N*	*6*	*0*
CD price	*Price of the CD*	*N*	*8*	*2*

* A = alphanumeric
   N = numeric

RECORD LAYOUT SHEET

Record Name: *Order*		File Name: *Extended Orders*		
Prepared By: *C. Hilton*		Date: *6-28-93*		
Key Fields:		Organization: *Sequential*		
Field	Description	Type*	Length	Decimal
Customer #	*Customer ID*	*N*	*6*	*0*
Compact disc #	*CD Stock number*	*N*	*6*	*0*
Quantity	*The number ordered*	*N*	*2*	*0*
Extended price	*The full amount to be billed*	*N*	*8*	*2*
Order number	*Preprinted order ID*	*N*	*6*	*0*

* A = alphanumeric
   N = numeric

Figure 5.18 **Hierarchy Chart for CDL's "Extend Customer Orders" Program**

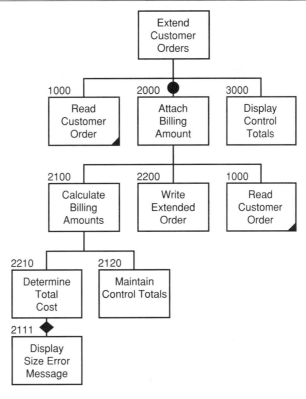

The hierarchy chart for accomplishing the above is presented in Figure 5.18. The repetitive module carries out the task of extending the customer orders and is designated as "2000-Attach-Billing-Amount." Prior to this task, we must do a priming read to obtain the first order record. This is accomplished by "1000-Read-Customer-Order." Once the repetition of order extensions is completed, we need to display the control totals. Module "3000-Display-Control-Totals" will do this task.

Module "2000-Attach-Billing-Amount" is subdivided into three subordinate modules. The first one, "2100-Calculate-Billing-Amount," calculates the order cost and is further divided into the modules "2110-Determine-Total-Cost" and "2120-Maintain-Control-Totals." Module "2110-Determine-Total-Cost" performs the billing calculations, and its subordinate module "2111-Display-Size-Error-Message" displays a warning message at the operator's console if significant digit truncation results from the calculations. Charlene carefully calculated the sizes of the fields for the computation results and considers that the probability of exceeding them is extremely low. Therefore, she will only display a simple error message. In real business situations, however, error routines are more complete. They might display the contents of the items in error, flag erroneous records, or even stop the execution of the program in an orderly manner.

Module "2120-Maintain-Control-Totals" keeps running totals of the number of CDs ordered, the total dollar value of the CDs ordered, the dollar value of all orders, and the total number of orders processed. Module "2200-Write-Extended-Order" is the next third-level task, which creates the new extended orders file, and module "1000-Read-Customer-Order" obtains the next record from the orders file.

Using the hierarchy chart, Charlene developed the Nassi-Schneiderman Charts illustrated in Figure 5.19. The completed program is shown in Figure 5.20. The test data and results are in Figure 5.21.

Figure 5.19   **N-S Charts for CDL's "Extend Customer Orders" Program**

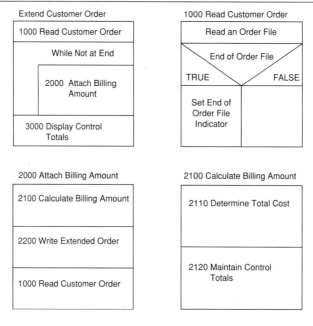

Figure 5.19 *(continued)*

2110 Determine Total Cost

Unit Price is set to zero	
TRUE	FALSE
Move Standard Price into Unit Price	
Compute Total Price	
Size Error Encountered	
TRUE	FALSE
2111 Display Size Error Message	
Compute Shipping Cost	
Size Error Encountered	
TRUE	FALSE
2111 Display Size Error Message	
Compute Total Cost	
Size Error Encountered	
TRUE	FALSE
2111 Display Size Error Message	

2111 Display Size Error Message

Display Size Error Message

2120 Maintain Control Totals

Increment Order Counter
Add to CD Total
Add Order Cost to Overall Total

2200 Write Extended Order

Format an Extended Order Record
Write an Extended Order Record

3000 Display Control Totals

Display Count of Orders
Display Number of CDs
Display Total Shipping Costs
Display Overall Costs

Figure 5.20   COBOL Code for CDL's "Extend Customer Orders" Program

```
 1 IDENTIFICATION DIVISION.
 2 PROGRAM-ID.  EXTEND-ORDERS.
 3*  THIS PROGRAM TAKES THE ORDERS SEPARATED BY THE CATEGORIZE DAILY
 4*  MAIL PROGRAM AND EXTENDS THE AMOUNT TO BE BILLED THE CUSTOMER
 5 AUTHOR.        C HILTON
 6 DATE-WRITTEN.  JUNE 29, 1995
 7 DATE-COMPILED. 24-Jan-90 09:30.
10 ENVIRONMENT DIVISION.
11
12 CONFIGURATION SECTION.
13 SOURCE-COMPUTER.  GENERIC-COMPUTER.
14 OBJECT-COMPUTER.  GENERIC-COMPUTER.
15
16 INPUT-OUTPUT SECTION.
17 FILE-CONTROL.
18     SELECT ORDERS-FILE ASSIGN TO DISK
19         ORGANIZATION IS SEQUENTIAL.
20     SELECT EXTENDED-ORDERS-FILE ASSIGN TO DISK
21         ORGANIZATION IS SEQUENTIAL.
22
23
24 DATA DIVISION.
25
26 FILE SECTION.
27
28 FD  ORDERS-FILE
29     LABEL RECORDS ARE STANDARD.
30
31 01  CUSTOMER-ORDER-REC.
32     05  CO-CUSTOMER-ID    PIC 9(6).
33     05  CO-CD-NUMBER      PIC 9(6).
34     05  CO-QUANTITY       PIC 99.
35     05  CO-ORDER-NUMBER   PIC 9(6).
36     05  CO-CD-PRICE       PIC 9(6)V99.
37
38 FD  EXTENDED-ORDERS-FILE
39     LABEL RECORDS ARE STANDARD.
40
41 01  EXTENDED-CUSTOMER-ORDER-REC.
42     05  ECO-CUSTOMER-ID   PIC 9(6).
43     05  ECO-CD-NUMBER     PIC 9(6).
44     05  ECO-QUANTITY      PIC 99.
```

Figure 5.20   (continued)

```
45      05   ECO-BILLING-AMOUNT   PIC 9(6)V99.
46      05   ECO-ORDER-NUMBER     PIC 9(6).
47
48 WORKING-STORAGE SECTION.
49
50 01   WORK-AREA.
51      05   WA-BULK-MAIL       PIC 99.
52      05   WA-SINGLE-MAIL     PIC 99.
53      05   WA-SHIPPING-COST   PIC 9(6)V99.
54      05   WA-CD-COST         PIC 9(6)V99.
55      05   WA-COMBINED-COST   PIC 9(6)V99.
56
57 01   CONTROL-TOTALS.
58      05   CT-NUMBER-OF-CDS       PIC 9(5)      VALUE ZERO.
59      05   CT-NUMBER-OF-ORDERS    PIC 9(5)      VALUE ZERO.
60      05   CT-SHIPPING-COST       PIC 9(10)V99  VALUE ZERO.
61      05   CT-OVERALL-COST        PIC 9(10)V99  VALUE ZERO.
62
63 01   END-OF-FILE-INDICATORS.
64      05   EOF-ORDERS PIC X(5) VALUE "FALSE".
65
66 01   COSTING-CONSTANTS.
67      05   CC-BULK-RATE           PIC 99V99 VALUE 3.95.
68      05   CC-SINGLE-RATE         PIC 99V99 VALUE 1.24.
69      05   CC-STANDARD-CD-PRICE   PIC 99V99 VALUE 16.95.
70
71
72 PROCEDURE DIVISION.
73
74 EXTEND-CUSTOMER-ORDER.
75      OPEN INPUT ORDERS-FILE.
76      OPEN OUTPUT EXTENDED-ORDERS-FILE.
77      PERFORM 1000-READ-CUSTOMER-ORDER.
78      PERFORM 2000-ATTACH-BILLING-AMOUNT UNTIL EOF-ORDERS = "TRUE ".
79      PERFORM 3000-DISPLAY-CONTROL-TOTALS.
80      CLOSE ORDERS-FILE.
81      CLOSE EXTENDED-ORDERS-FILE.
82      STOP RUN.
83
84 1000-READ-CUSTOMER-ORDER.
85      READ ORDERS-FILE AT END MOVE "TRUE " TO EOF-ORDERS.
86
```

Figure 5.20   (continued)

```
87 2000-ATTACH-BILLING-AMOUNT.
88      PERFORM 2100-CALCULATE-BILLING-AMOUNT.
89      PERFORM 2200-WRITE-EXTENDED-ORDER.
90      PERFORM 1000-READ-CUSTOMER-ORDER.
91
92 2100-CALCULATE-BILLING-AMOUNT.
93      PERFORM 2110-DETERMINE-TOTAL-COST.
94      PERFORM 2120-MAINTAIN-CONTROL-TOTALS.
95
96 2110-DETERMINE-TOTAL-COST.
97      IF CO-CD-PRICE = ZERO
98          MOVE CC-STANDARD-CD-PRICE TO CO-CD-PRICE.
99      COMPUTE WA-CD-COST = CO-CD-PRICE * CO-QUANTITY
100         ON SIZE ERROR PERFORM 2111-DISPLAY-SIZE-MESSAGE.
101     DIVIDE 5 INTO CO-QUANTITY GIVING WA-BULK-MAIL
102         REMAINDER WA-SINGLE-MAIL
103         ON SIZE ERROR PERFORM 2111-DISPLAY-SIZE-MESSAGE.
104     COMPUTE WA-SHIPPING-COST = WA-BULK-MAIL * CC-BULK-RATE
105         + WA-SINGLE-MAIL * CC-SINGLE-RATE
106         ON SIZE ERROR PERFORM 2111-DISPLAY-SIZE-MESSAGE.
107     COMPUTE WA-COMBINED-COST = WA-SHIPPING-COST + WA-CD-COST
108         ON SIZE ERROR PERFORM 2111-DISPLAY-SIZE-MESSAGE.
109
110 2111-DISPLAY-SIZE-MESSAGE.
111     DISPLAY "   ".
112     DISPLAY "SIZE ERROR FOUND DURING COMPUTATIONS!".
113
114 2120-MAINTAIN-CONTROL-TOTALS.
115     ADD 1                TO CT-NUMBER-OF-ORDERS.
116     ADD CO-QUANTITY      TO CT-NUMBER-OF-CDS.
117     ADD WA-SHIPPING-COST TO CT-SHIPPING-COST.
118     ADD WA-CD-COST       TO CT-OVERALL-COST.
119     ADD WA-SHIPPING-COST TO CT-OVERALL-COST.
120
121 2200-WRITE-EXTENDED-ORDER.
122     MOVE CO-CUSTOMER-ID   TO ECO-CUSTOMER-ID.
123     MOVE CO-CD-NUMBER     TO ECO-CD-NUMBER.
124     MOVE CO-QUANTITY      TO ECO-QUANTITY.
125     MOVE CO-ORDER-NUMBER  TO ECO-ORDER-NUMBER.
126     MOVE WA-COMBINED-COST TO ECO-BILLING-AMOUNT.
127     WRITE EXTENDED-CUSTOMER-ORDER-REC.
128
```

Figure 5.20 **(continued)**

```
129 3000-DISPLAY-CONTROL-TOTALS.
130     DISPLAY " ".
131     DISPLAY "THE NUMBER OF ORDERS IS "  CT-NUMBER-OF-ORDERS.
132     DISPLAY "THE NUMBER OF CDS ORDERED IS " CT-NUMBER-OF-CDS.
133     DISPLAY "THE TOTAL SHIPPING COSTS ARE " CT-SHIPPING-COST.
134     DISPLAY "THE TOTAL AMOUNT BILLED IS " CT-OVERALL-COST.
```

Figure 5.21 *Test Data and Results for CDL's "Extend Customer Orders" Program*

```
TEST DATA FOR EXTEND ORDERS PROGRAM:
7654875430981298765400000000
5498717453280183486500001095
5438769654380576543200000999
6340981543219064398710000000


EXTENDED ORDER TEST RESULTS - OUTPUT FILE

7654875430981200021378987654
5498717453280100001219834865
5438769654380500005390765432
6340981543219000012105643987


SCREEN RESULTS FOR EXTENDED ORDERS PROGRAM TEST

SIZE ERROR FOUND DURING COMPUTATIONS!
THE NUMBER OF ORDERS IS 00004
THE NUMBER OF CDS ORDERED IS 00108
THE TOTAL SHIPPING COSTS ARE 0000008667
THE TOTAL AMOUNT BILLED IS 0000040092
```

The test results show the program functions correctly. The totals and extended amounts are all as expected. The last record shows how an ON SIZE ERROR yields unpredictable results. Charlene notes that she should confer with management on a better way to handle errors that result from entering a price that is too high. She also notes that she will have to improve the appearance of the displayed control totals. For that, she'll have to refer to Chapter 8 of her old COBOL text.

Summary

It is necessary to manipulate available data to generate information for the business organization. In this chapter we discussed the several aspects of handling data in the information process. The first aspect, the input and output of data, involves the transference of data between external devices and memory. Data movement transfers data within memory, as when the contents of data items are moved to format reports or to save their original values. Data computations perform arithmetic operations on the data. Such operations are used in business applications for file updating, data validation, and other computations. Program control allows the sequencing of instructions to carry out the purpose of the program.

COBOL supports all aspects of data handling. Input/output aspects are handled through the OPEN, CLOSE, READ, WRITE, ACCEPT, and DISPLAY statements. OPEN and CLOSE are file preparation statements. ACCEPT and DISPLAY are used for low-volume input and output, and READ and WRITE are used for large-volume input and output.

Data movement is accomplished using the MOVE statement. This allows us to set data items to certain values, edit data to change them into a more visually pleasant format, and save values that are changed in the program.

Arithmetic statements—ADD, SUBTRACT, MULTIPLY, DIVIDE, and COMPUTE— are used for calculations on numeric data. The COMPUTE statement is generally used for specifying multiple arithmetic operations to be performed. The operations are denoted by the arithmetic operators $**, /, *, +, -$, representing exponentiation, division, multiplication, addition, and subtraction, respectively. These operators have an order of precedence dictating which operations are carried out first. However, parentheses alter this order and are evaluated first. The ADD, SUBTRACT, MULTIPLY, and DIVIDE statements should be used when the designated operation is the only one being performed or when the remainder in a division needs to be saved. Otherwise the COMPUTE statement should be used, since it is so versatile and the program code is easier to follow.

Result values may be rounded using the ROUNDED clauses to minimize the effects of truncation. Furthermore, COBOL has an ON SIZE ERROR option to flag the situation in which significant digits are truncated because of inadequate length of the result data item. This option allows the programmer to specify the action to be taken if a SIZE ERROR occurs.

Control over the execution of the program instructions is accomplished by the IF, PERFORM, PERFORM UNTIL, and STOP statements. The IF statement implements the selection construct in COBOL, allowing one of two paths of logic to be taken based on some condition. The PERFORM statement identifies a set of instructions to be executed once. The PERFORM UNTIL statement implements the iteration construct in COBOL and controls the number of times a loop is executed by testing some condition. The STOP RUN statement terminates the execution of a program.

Key Terms

input area	FROM	MULTIPLY
output area	DATE	DIVIDE
data movement	DAY	REMAINDER
INPUT	TIME	ROUNDED
OUTPUT	ADVANCING	ON SIZE ERROR
I/O	DISPLAY	relation condition
INTO	sending area	nonnumeric comparison
end-of-file condition	receiving item	range
AT END	COMPUTE	nested
ACCEPT	SUBTRACT	

Hints for Avoiding Errors

1. Be certain that all variables are initialized to their proper starting values.
2. Make sure all arithmetic resultant fields are large enough to contain the computed results.
3. All items used in computations must be numeric items. That means that the PICTURE clauses may contain only the characters 9, V, or S.
4. Data items used as counters, such as page counters, should not have an implied decimal point in their PICTURE clauses. They should be integers.
5. Remember the precedence order of the arithmetic operators in the COMPUTE statement. If in doubt about any arithmetic expression, use parentheses to indicate the proper order. A few "unnecessary" parentheses may even contribute to the clarity and readability of the code.
6. When a program maintains counts or totals, this function should be isolated in a separate module. This segments the function and provides more structured code.
7. Use the ON SIZE ERROR clause for critical final values. Whenever possible, the program should continue with the rest of its tasks.
8. Rather than relying on the ON SIZE ERROR clause for intermediate or temporary values, use a PICTURE clause that will be large enough.
9. Specify a sign whenever subtraction is involved in a computation, when one of the initial values is a signed field, or when there is any possibility that a value may be negative.
10. After a WRITE statement is issued to a record, the data in the record are no longer available. Do not design or code a program to use the record information that has already been written to a file.
11. The MOVE statement will function under extreme conditions but may not yield the expected results. It is up to you to be certain that the field types are proper and the lengths of the fields match.
12. When using the MOVE statement to move numeric data, remember that the data are truncated to fit into the receiving field. Also remember that if the receiving field has no sign and the sending field does, the sign will be lost.

Exercises

5.1   An employee file has records of the following format:

Field	Length	Format
Social security number	10	Numeric
Name	30	Alphanumeric
Hourly wage	6	Numeric (2 decimal)
Union code	1	Alphanumeric
Year-to-date wages	8	Numeric (2 decimal)
Date of hire	8	MM/DD/YYYY
Date of termination	8	MM/DD/YYYY
Department	4	Alphanumeric

Design and code a program that produces a list of active employees (active employees have a termination date of zero) and their weekly wages for a standard 40-hour week. Develop your own print layout. Be certain to include the social security number, name, hourly wage, and weekly wage on each line of the report. Add a line at the end of the report to show the total weekly wage for the company. Also add a line for average YTD wages paid to union members, nonunion members, and all employees. (Union code = "Y" for union member and "N" for non-members.)

5.2   For the employee record layout of Exercise 5.1, design a report which lists the terminated employees (terminated employees have a nonzero termination date). Design and code the program. The listing should include social security number, name, date of hire, and date of termination. Print year-to-date wages if the termination date is in the current year. Also print a summary line that shows the total year-to-date wages of terminated employees and the total number of terminated employees.

5.3   Use the employee record layout of Exercise 5.1 to design a report, design a program, and code a program that lists all union members in the accounting department (department = ACCT). The listing should include the name and YTD wages of the employees listed. If the employee has been terminated (nonzero termination date) then *only* print the date of termination, otherwise print the date of hire. Indicate on the report which date is included for each employee.

5.4   Replace all the COMPUTE statements in Figure 5.20 with the required ADD, SUBTRACT, MULTIPLY, and DIVIDE replacements. Which code is easier to follow? Are any of the replacements desirable in terms of program clarity?

5.5   Explain the order of arithmetic operations in the COMPUTE statement.

5.6   Which statement is incorrect?

        a.   SUBTRACT TAX FROM GROSS.

        b.   SUBTRACT QUANTITY 10 FROM TOTAL.

        c.   SUBTRACT TAX FROM 0.02.

5.7   When using the ROUNDED clause with a result field containing two decimal places, what value will be stored if the result is 26.0345?

    a.   26.00

    b.   26.03

    c.   26.04

    d.   26.0345

5.8   Let X = 1, Y = 2, Z = 3. What are the final values of X, Y, Z after executing both of these statements?

```
ADD X Y TO Z.
ADD Y TO Z GIVING X.
```

5.9   Let A = 5, B = 3, C = 4, D = 2, E = 27, F = 9. What is the value of A after executing this statement?

```
COMPUTE A = (B + C) * * D + E - 18 / F - 24.
```

5.10   Which of the following statements does not preserve the original values of the operand?

    a.   ADD A B C GIVING C.

    b.   SUBTRACT TAXES FROM PAY.

    c.   MULTIPLY LEVEL BY 10 GIVING HOURS.

    d.   DIVIDE TOTAL BY COUNT GIVING AVERAGE.

    e.   COMPUTE AVERAGE = TOTAL-NUMBER / PEOPLE.

5.11   Which data types and literal types may be used in computations?

5.12   Create a PICTURE clause for each of the following:

    a.   7-digit signed numeric field

    b.   3-digit unsigned numeric field with 2 places after the implied decimal point

    c.   3-digit integer with full zero suppression

    d.   6-digit real number with two places after the actual decimal point and zero suppression before the decimal point

5.13   Given the statements:

```
MOVE 2 TO A.
MOVE 8 TO B.
MOVE 50 TO C.
MOVE 10 TO D.
ADD A TO D.
ADD B D GIVING A.
SUBTRACT A D FROM C.
DIVIDE 2 INTO C.
MULTIPLY B BY C GIVING D.
ADD 5 TO A B C D.
```

what are the values of A, B, C, D?

5.14   Show the result of the statement

```
MOVE 8976.876 TO FIELD-A.
```

when FIELD-A has the PICTURE
   a.   ZZZZ.ZZ
   b.   ZZZZ.99
   c.   9999.999
   d.   99V99
   e.   ZZZZZ

5.15   What conditions cause an ON SIZE ERROR?

5.16   The resulting field in an arithmetic operation may only be a numeric elementary item. True or false?

5.17   The statement

```
WRITE PRINT-LINE FROM GRINITZ
```

has the same result as which two other COBOL statements?

5.18   Before a file is read, what COBOL statement must be used?

5.19.   Given the statements:
```
01 FIELD-1 PIC X(6) VALUE "ALASKA".
01 FIELD-2 PIC X(7) VALUE "INDIANA".
```
After the statement MOVE FIELD-2 TO FIELD-1 is executed, what value will FIELD-1 have?

5.20   Given the statements:
```
01   GARBAGE-COLLECTION.
   05   FILLER  PIC XXX.
   05   A          PIC XX.
   05   B.
        10   C   PIC X.
        10   D   PIC 999.
```

After the statement MOVE "WXYZ" TO GARBAGE-COLLECTION is executed, what value will A contain? C? D?

5.21   Using the same data definitions as in Question 5.20, what will the contents of each data item be after all three of the following MOVE statements are executed:

```
MOVE SPACES TO GARBAGE-COLLECTION.
MOVE ALL "PQR" TO B.
MOVE D TO A.
```

5.22   Which of the following commands is correct to close files ALPHA and BETA?
   a.   CLOSE ALPHA AND BETA.
   b.   CLOSE ALPHA BETA.
   c.   CLOSE INPUT ALPHA OUTPUT BETA.
   d.   CLOSE FILES.

5.23   Data handling aspects can be categorized as:
       a.   input/output (I/O).
       b.   data movement.
       c.   translation operations.
       d.   program control.
       e.   A, B, and D
       f.   B, C, and D
       g.   all of the above

5.24   The ACCEPT statement is used:
       a.   to input low-volume data.
       b.   to obtain data such as dates.
       c.   extensively in interactive applications.
       d.   all of the above

5.25   The CLOSE statement is an option since COBOL automatically closes all files being used upon execution of the STOP RUN command. True or false?

5.26   A statement that moves numeric data with decimal to an alphanumeric receiving field is allowed in COBOL. True or false?

5.27   The COMPUTE statement must be used in operations that involve exponentiation. True or false?

5.28   The code:

```
ADD OLD-BALANCE TO NEW-CHARGES GIVING NEW-BALANCE.
```

is a syntactically correct COBOL statement. True or false?

5.29   What is the format of a DATE maintained by a computer operating system?
       a.   YYMMDD
       b.   DDMMYY
       c.   YYDDD
       d.   DDDYY

5.30   COBOL supports all aspects of data handling except certain arithmetic operations. True or false?

5.31   Given:

```
ITEM-1 PIC 9(6).
ITEM-2 PIC X(5).
```

And the execution of:

```
MOVE ITEM-1 TO ITEM-2.
```

What will be the value of ITEM-2 if ITEM-1's value is 558766?
       a.   MOVE not allowed
       b.   58766
       c.   55876

5.32   It is possible to "double-column" reports in COBOL using the WRITE . . . BEFORE clause. True or false?

5.33   Which statement below is correct in COBOL?
      a.   DIVIDE FIRST-NUMBER SECOND-NUMBER
          GIVING THIRD-NUMBER.
      b.   DIVIDE FIRST-NUMBER BY SECOND-NUMBER
          REMAINDER THIRD-NUMBER.
      c.   DIVIDE FIRST-NUMBER GIVING THIRD-NUMBER
          INTO SECOND-NUMBER.
      d.   DIVIDE FIRST-NUMBER INTO SECOND-NUMBER
          GIVING THIRD-NUMBER REMAINDER EXTRA-NUMBER.

5.34   Truncation of result values from arithmetic operations is of no concern since COBOL allocates room for "spill over" in memory when executing computations. True or false?

5.35   In multiplication operations, the product of an m-digit field and an n-digit field is at most _____ digits long.
      a. $m * n$
      b. $m + n$
      c. $n - m$
      d. $mn2$

5.36   _____ involves transferring data from one memory location to another.

5.37   _____ statements in COBOL are related to the tasks necessary to ready the files to be used in the program.

5.38   The _____ statement transfers the data stored in the output area to the output device.

5.39   The _____ verb provides the capability of outputting a message without defining a file.

5.40   _____ and _____ are two optional clauses that may be used with the COBOL arithmetic statements.

5.41   The _____ statement evaluates a condition and continues execution based on the results of the evaluation of the condition.

5.42   The _____ statement identifies a set of instructions to be executed once as opposed to the _____ statement, which controls the number of times a loop is executed by testing some condition.

5.43   If a PERFORM statement is included within the range of another PERFORM, the PERFORM statements are said to be _____.

6

ADVANCED METHODS
FOR PROGRAM CONTROL

Several COBOL implementations of the three primitive control structures of structured design have been explored in previous chapters. The COBOL support of these structures has been direct but rather rigid. In this chapter we will study some COBOL statements that allow more programmer control over the sequence of execution within a program. We will continue to utilize the three control structures, but some complexities will be introduced to provide more flexibility. The sample customer discount classification program in Figure 6.1 will be used to highlight many of the features discussed in this chapter. The code is developed from the specifications in Figures 6.2, 6.3, and 6.4. The design for the code is in Figure 6.5 and 6.6.

Figure 6.1   ***Customer Discount Classification Program***

```
 1 IDENTIFICATION DIVISION.
 2 PROGRAM-ID.  CUSTOMER-DISCOUNT-CLASSIFY.
 3*  THIS PROGRAM TAKES THE BILLS FROM THE PRIOR MONTH AND
 4*  COMPUTES THE DISCOUNT RATE FOR THE FOLLOWING MONTH
 5 AUTHOR.        SELF.
 6 DATE-WRITTEN.  JUNE 29, 1995.
 7 DATE-COMPILED. 08-Jul-95 04:03.
10 ENVIRONMENT DIVISION.
11
12 CONFIGURATION SECTION.
13 SOURCE-COMPUTER.  GENERIC-COMPUTER.
14 OBJECT-COMPUTER.  GENERIC-COMPUTER.
15
16 INPUT-OUTPUT SECTION.
17 FILE-CONTROL.
18     SELECT CUSTOMER-BILL-FILE ASSIGN TO DISK
19         ORGANIZATION IS SEQUENTIAL.
20     SELECT CUSTOMER-CLASS-LIST ASSIGN TO PRINTER
21         ORGANIZATION IS SEQUENTIAL.
22
23
24 DATA DIVISION.
25
26 FILE SECTION.
27
28 FD  CUSTOMER-BILL-FILE
29     LABEL RECORDS ARE STANDARD.
30
31 01  CUSTOMER-BILL-REC.
32     05  CB-CUSTOMER-NBR   PIC 9(3).
33     05  CB-CUSTOMER-NAME  PIC X(15).
34     05  CB-PURCHASE-AMT   PIC 9(6)V9(2).
35
36 FD  CUSTOMER-CLASS-LIST
37     LABEL RECORDS ARE OMITTED.
38
39 01  CUSTOMER-CLASS-LINE PIC X(80).
40
41 WORKING-STORAGE SECTION.
42
43 01  DUPLICATE-BILL.
44     05  DB-CUSTOMER-NBR   PIC 9(3).
```

Figure 6.1 (continued)

```
45      05  DB-CUSTOMER-NAME  PIC X(15).
46      05  DB-PURCHASE-AMT   PIC 9(6)V9(2).
47
48 01  TODAYS-DATE.
49      05  TD-MM               PIC 9(2).
50      05  TD-DD               PIC 9(2).
51      05  TD-YY               PIC 9(2).
52
53 01  END-OF-FILE-INDICATORS.
54      05  EOF-BILLS PIC X(5) VALUE "FALSE".
55      88  MORE-BILLS VALUE "FALSE".
56      88  NO-MORE-BILLS VALUE "TRUE".
57
58 01  DOLLAR-COMPUTATIONS.
59      05  DC-TOTAL-DOLLAR-PURCHASES  PIC 9(8)V9(2)   VALUE ZERO.
60          88  TOT-POINTS-0     VALUE 0.00 THRU 99.99.
61          88  TOT-POINTS-1     VALUE 100.00 THRU 499.99.
62          88  TOT-POINTS-2     VALUE 500.00 THRU 999.99.
63          88  TOT-POINTS-3     VALUE 1000.00 THRU 4999.99.
64          88  TOT-POINTS-4     VALUE 5000.00 THRU 99999999.99.
65      05  DC-NUMBER-OF-PURCHASES     PIC 99           VALUE ZERO.
66      05  DC-AVERAGE-DOLLAR-PURCHASES PIC 9(6)V9(2)    VALUE ZERO.
67          88  AVG-POINTS-0     VALUE 0.00 THRU 49.99.
68          88  AVG-POINTS-1     VALUE 50.00 THRU 99.99.
69          88  AVG-POINTS-2     VALUE 100.00 THRU 199.99.
70          88  AVG-POINTS-3     VALUE 200.00 THRU 999999.99.
71      05  DC-POINTS                  PIC 99          VALUE ZERO.
72      05  DC-DISCOUNT-RATE           PIC 99          VALUE ZERO.
73
74
75 01  CUSTOMER-CLASSIFICATION-REPORT.
76      05  CCR-HEADING-1.
77          10  FILLER PIC X(28) VALUE SPACE.
78          10  FILLER PIC X(40) VALUE "WHOLESALE SEAFOOD DISCOUNTS".
79      05  CCR-HEADING-2.
80          10  FILLER PIC X(30) VALUE SPACE.
81          10  FILLER PIC X(13) VALUE "MONTH ENDING ".
82          10  CCR-DATE.
83              15  CCR-MM PIC 99.
84              15  FILLER PIC X  VALUE "/".
85              15  CCR-DD PIC 99.
86              15  FILLER PIC X  VALUE "/".
```

Figure 6.1   *(continued)*

```
 87              15  CCR-YY PIC 99.
 88      05  CCR-HEADING-3  PIC X(80) VALUE SPACE.
 89      05  CCR-HEADING-4.
 90          10  FILLER PIC X(5)  VALUE SPACE.
 91          10  FILLER PIC X(8)  VALUE "CUST #".
 92          10  FILLER PIC X(18) VALUE "CUSTOMER NAME".
 93          10  FILLER PIC X(12) VALUE "TOT PURCHASE".
 94          10  FILLER PIC X(12) VALUE "AVG PURCHASE".
 95          10  FILLER PIC X(10) VALUE "POINTS".
 96          10  FILLER PIC X(15) VALUE "DISCOUNT AMT".
 97      05  CCR-DETAIL-LINE.
 98          10  FILLER             PIC X(8)  VALUE SPACE.
 99          10  CCR-CUSTOMER-NBR   PIC 9(3).
100          10  FILLER             PIC X(3)  VALUE SPACE.
101          10  CCR-CUSTOMER-NAME  PIC X(18).
102          10  CCR-TOT-PURCHASES  PIC Z(8).99.
103          10  FILLER             PIC X(4)  VALUE SPACE.
104          10  CCR-AVG-PURCHASES  PIC Z(6).99.
105          10  FILLER             PIC X(6)  VALUE SPACE.
106          10  CCR-POINTS         PIC Z9.
107          10  FILLER             PIC X(6)  VALUE SPACE.
108          10  CCR-DISCOUNT-PCT   PIC Z9.
109
110
111 PROCEDURE DIVISION.
112
113 CUSTOMER-DISCOUNT-CLASS.
114     OPEN INPUT  CUSTOMER-BILL-FILE.
115     OPEN OUTPUT CUSTOMER-CLASS-LIST.
116     PERFORM 100-PREPARE-CUSTOMER-CLASS.
117     PERFORM 200-CLASSIFY-SINGLE-CUSTOMER UNTIL NO-MORE-BILLS.
118     CLOSE CUSTOMER-BILL-FILE.
119     CLOSE CUSTOMER-CLASS-LIST.
120     STOP RUN.
121
122 100-PREPARE-CUSTOMER-CLASS.
123     PERFORM 110-READ-CUSTOMER-BILL.
124     IF MORE-BILLS
125         PERFORM 120-WRITE-REPORT-HEADINGS
126         MOVE CUSTOMER-BILL-REC TO DUPLICATE-BILL
127     END-IF.
128
```

Figure 6.1 *(continued)*

```
129 110-READ-CUSTOMER-BILL.
130     READ CUSTOMER-BILL-FILE
131         AT END MOVE "TRUE" TO EOF-BILLS
132                  MOVE 999 TO CB-CUSTOMER-NBR
133     END-READ.
134
135 120-WRITE-REPORT-HEADINGS.
136     ACCEPT TODAYS-DATE FROM DATE.
137     MOVE TD-MM TO CCR-MM.
138     MOVE TD-DD TO CCR-DD.
139     MOVE TD-YY TO CCR-YY.
140     WRITE CUSTOMER-CLASS-LINE FROM CCR-HEADING-1
141         AFTER ADVANCING PAGE.
142     WRITE CUSTOMER-CLASS-LINE FROM CCR-HEADING-2.
143     WRITE CUSTOMER-CLASS-LINE FROM CCR-HEADING-3.
144     WRITE CUSTOMER-CLASS-LINE FROM CCR-HEADING-4.
145     WRITE CUSTOMER-CLASS-LINE FROM CCR-HEADING-3.
146
147 200-CLASSIFY-SINGLE-CUSTOMER.
148     PERFORM 210-ACCUMULATE-CUSTOMER-BILLS WITH TEST AFTER
149         VARYING DC-NUMBER-OF-PURCHASES FROM 1 BY 1
150             UNTIL CB-CUSTOMER-NBR NOT = DB-CUSTOMER-NBR.
151     PERFORM 220-DETERMINE-DISCOUNT-CLASS.
152     PERFORM 230-PRINT-CUSTOMER-CLASS.
153
154 210-ACCUMULATE-CUSTOMER-BILLS.
155     PERFORM 211-ADD-SINGLE-BILL.
156     PERFORM 110-READ-CUSTOMER-BILL.
157
158 211-ADD-SINGLE-BILL.
159     ADD CB-PURCHASE-AMT    TO DC-TOTAL-DOLLAR-PURCHASES.
160     MOVE CUSTOMER-BILL-REC TO DUPLICATE-BILL.
161
162 220-DETERMINE-DISCOUNT-CLASS.
163     COMPUTE DC-AVERAGE-DOLLAR-PURCHASES ROUNDED =
164         DC-TOTAL-DOLLAR-PURCHASES / DC-NUMBER-OF-PURCHASES.
165     IF TOT-POINTS-1
166         ADD 1 TO DC-POINTS
167     ELSE IF TOT-POINTS-2
168             ADD 2 TO DC-POINTS
169         ELSE IF TOT-POINTS-3
170                 ADD 3 TO DC-POINTS
```

Figure 6.1   *(continued)*

```
171                 ELSE IF TOT-POINTS-4
172                     ADD 4 TO DC-POINTS.
173     IF AVG-POINTS-1
174         ADD 1 TO DC-POINTS
175     ELSE IF AVG-POINTS-2
176             ADD 2 TO DC-POINTS
177          ELSE IF AVG-POINTS-3
178                  ADD 3 TO DC-POINTS.
179     EVALUATE DC-POINTS
180         WHEN 0 MOVE 0  TO DC-DISCOUNT-RATE
181         WHEN 1 MOVE 1  TO DC-DISCOUNT-RATE
182         WHEN 2 MOVE 2  TO DC-DISCOUNT-RATE
183         WHEN 3 MOVE 4  TO DC-DISCOUNT-RATE
184         WHEN 4 MOVE 7  TO DC-DISCOUNT-RATE
185         WHEN 5 MOVE 10 TO DC-DISCOUNT-RATE
186         WHEN 6 MOVE 15 TO DC-DISCOUNT-RATE
187         WHEN 7 MOVE 20 TO DC-DISCOUNT-RATE
188     END-EVALUATE.
189
190 230-PRINT-CUSTOMER-CLASS.
191     MOVE DB-CUSTOMER-NBR            TO CCR-CUSTOMER-NBR.
192     MOVE DB-CUSTOMER-NAME           TO CCR-CUSTOMER-NAME.
193     MOVE DC-TOTAL-DOLLAR-PURCHASES  TO CCR-TOT-PURCHASES.
194     MOVE DC-AVERAGE-DOLLAR-PURCHASES TO CCR-AVG-PURCHASES.
195     MOVE DC-POINTS                  TO CCR-POINTS.
196     MOVE DC-DISCOUNT-RATE           TO CCR-DISCOUNT-PCT.
197     WRITE CUSTOMER-CLASS-LINE FROM CCR-DETAIL-LINE.
```

Figure 6.2 *Narrative Description of Customer Classification*

All customer bills are saved in a file for a month (see Figure 6.4). A discount classification is produced at the end of the month which lists each customer and its discount class (see layout in Figure 6.3). Discount classes are determined by a system of points based on total dollar purchases by a customer for the month and average purchase size for a customer in the prior month. Points are accumulated as follows:

MONTH TOTAL $	POINTS TO ADD
<100	0
≥100 but <500	1
≥500 but <1000	2
≥1000 but <5000	3
≥5000	4

PLUS:

AVERAGE PURCHASE$	POINTS TO ADD
<50	0
≥50 but ≤100	1
≥100 but ≤200	2
≥200	3

Discount classes are then determined as follows:

POINTS	%DISCOUNT NEXT MONTH
0	0
1	1
2	2
3	4
4	7
5	10
6	15
7	20

Records in the file appear in customer groups, that is, all records for a customer appear prior to the first record for the next customer. Note that 999 is not a valid customer number.

Figure 6.3   *Printer Layout for Customer Classification*

LINE PRINTER SPACING CHART

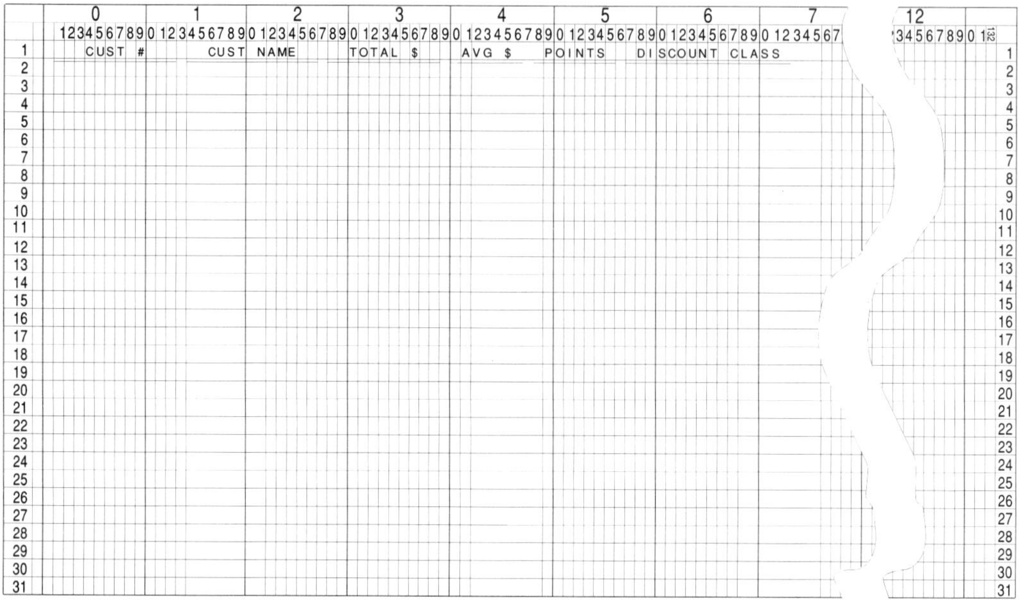

Figure 6.4   *Record Layout for Customer Classification*

RECORD LAYOUT SHEET

Record Name:		File Name:			
Prepared By:		Date:			
Key Fields:		Organization:			
Field	Description	Type*	Length	Decimal
Customer #		*N*	*3*	
Name		*A*	*15*	
Purchase #		*N*	*8*	*2*

* A = alphanumeric
  N = numeric

Figure 6.5   Hierarchy Chart for Customer Classification

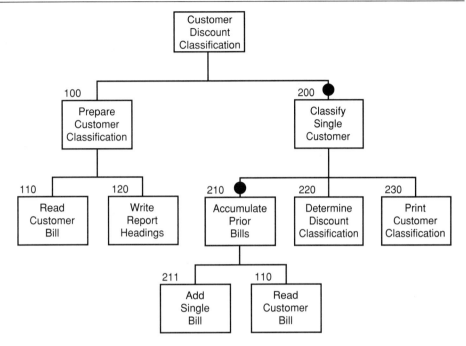

Figure 6.6   N-S Charts for Customer Classification

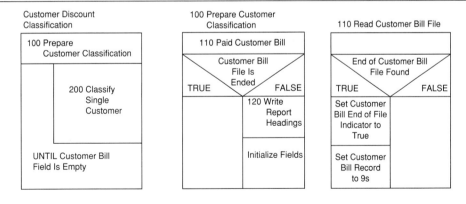

Figure 6.6   *(continued)*

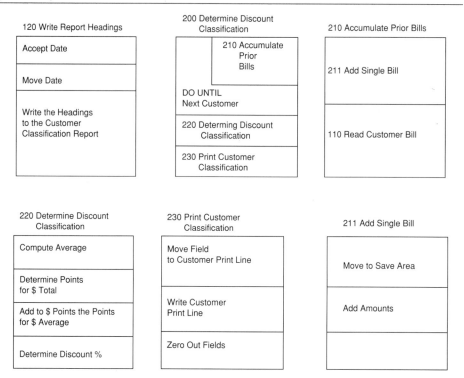

A couple of unique design problems are seen in this program. First, groups of records must be combined before a line on the report is printed. Second, multiple cases exist (i.e. a seven-point scale) for the classification scheme, whereas programs in prior chapters were restricted to binary decisions (i.e., True vs. False). The second situation of multiple cases is handled by nesting the selection structure, as seen in paragraph "220-DETERMINE-DISCOUNT-CLASS" of Figure 6.1. This nested structure will be described in depth later in the chapter, since COBOL has direct ways of handling nested selection structures.

The first problem is more complex, requiring that multiple customer records be combined into a single customer record prior to printing the required information. This problem is handled by a nested iteration structure as can be seen in the hierarchy chart of Figure 6.5. The module "200-CLASSIFY-SINGLE-CUSTOMER" is a repetitive process to deal with all customers. Since each customer may have multiple, adjacent records, a second iterative construct is required to accumulate the information for each customer. This is done by module "210-ACCUMU-LATE-PRIOR-BILLS." COBOL does not directly address nested iterations but they are easily handled by using nested PERFORM statements, as seen in lines 117 and 148 of Figure 6.1.

6.1 *Expanding Conditional Expressions*

In the selection and iteration constructs conditional statements control the flow of execution of the program. The truth or falsity of a conditional expression determines the program path to be followed. A conditional expression may contain one or more conditions to be tested. These conditions are assertions whose truth value can be determined by the computer. For example, X = Y is a condition to which a truth value can be assigned.

Two COBOL statements that use conditional expressions are the IF statement (Line 124 of Figure 6.1) and the PERFORM UNTIL statement (Line 117 of Figure 6.1). The IF statement evaluates a condition; the program executes the proper set of instructions depending on whether the condition is true or false. In the PERFORM UNTIL statement the conditional expression is first tested. If the condition is true, no transfer of control takes place; it passes to the statement following the PERFORM statement. If the condition is false, the specific paragraph is executed and the condition is tested again.

Other COBOL statements in which the action taken is based on whether a specific condition is true or false are considered *conditional statements*. For example, the READ . . . AT END is a conditional statement in which the condition is the detection of the end-of-file record (see Lines 130 and 131 of Figure 6.1). The arithmetic statements become conditional statements if the ON SIZE ERROR clause is used. In this case the condition tested is whether a result value exceeds the size of the result field. Statements that specify an action to be taken without condition, such as OPEN, MOVE, and CLOSE statements, are referred to as *imperative statements*.

When we first studied the IF and PERFORM UNTIL statements, we saw some simple examples of conditions that, when tested, allowed the program to follow different paths. However, it is not always possible to determine the course of action with such simple conditional expressions, and combinations of conditions may be needed. For example, a business gives its customers bad credit ratings if their account balances exceed $1,500.00 or their last payments are 2 months overdue. It may be necessary to specify conditions within conditions, as when a firm has different courses of action based on multiple seniority levels of its employees.

6.1.1 *Simple Conditions*

A simple condition is made up of only one condition. Simple conditions fall into four main categories: relation conditions, class conditions, sign conditions, and condition-names. Recall that relation conditions compare two values to determine if they are equal, if one is less than the other, or if one is greater than the other. The other conditions increase the types of comparisons that can be conducted and allow greater program flexibility.

Class Conditions. The *class condition* determines whether an item is numeric or alphabetic. An item is considered to be numeric if it is composed only of the digits 0 through 9 and an optional algebraic sign. If any letters or special characters appear in it, the data item is not numeric. An item is considered alphabetic if it contains only the letters A through Z and spaces. Figure 6.7 shows the truth values resulting from testing for a numeric class condition using different classes of PICTURE clauses and data items for standard COBOL. Certain manufacturers may implement the test in a non-standard fashion; so review your system documentation to be sure. From Figure 6.7 one can determine that the resulting truth values depend on the PICTURE of the data item being tested. The algebraic sign may cause the programmer difficulty if not accounted for in its PICTURE description. Figure 6.8 shows the contents of some data items and their appropriate classifications in standard COBOL.

Figure 6.7   Truth Values for Numeric Class Condition

	Value of a data item is		
PICTURE of data item is	Not numeric	Signed numeric	Unsigned numeric
Unsigned numeric or alphanumeric	FALSE	FALSE	TRUE
Signed numeric	FALSE	TRUE	Computer-dependent
Alphanumeric	FALSE	FALSE	TRUE

Figure 6.8   Sample Truth Values for Class Conditions

Picture	Value	Numeric	Alphabetic
X(5)	94312	TRUE	FALSE
X(5)	X4132	FALSE	FALSE
X(5)	XXYZZ	FALSE	TRUE
X(5)	bXYZb	FALSE	TRUE
9(3) or S9(3)	72B	FALSE	N/A
9(3) or S9(3)	72b	FALSE	N/A
9(3)	932	TRUE	N/A
9(3)	−132	FALSE	N/A
9(3)	+120	FALSE	N/A
S9(3)	−120	TRUE	N/A
S9(3)	+132	TRUE	N/A

b represents a space
N/A means the test is not allowed

The format and rules for the class condition are:

---

data-name-1   IS   [NOT] $\left\{ \begin{array}{l} \underline{\text{NUMERIC}} \\ \underline{\text{ALPHABETIC}} \end{array} \right\}$

1. The alphabetic test is not valid for a numeric data item.
2. The numeric test cannot be conducted for group items whose elementary items have algebraic signs.   S99

Class conditions are very useful for validating input data. For example, since many computers will stop program execution if arithmetic operations are attempted on nonnumeric data, it would be much more efficient to avoid such an operation in the first place. This can be accomplished by testing for a numeric class condition on input fields that should be numeric. In this way, a program would not try to credit a customer's account for "$kjh mm." Similarly, city names and state abbreviations are composed of alphabetic characters. Therefore, a state input as "I9" is an error since it contains a numeric character. But the programmer can easily test for such errors using class conditions. Such a test may appear:

```
IF REPORT-CUTOFF-DATE IS NOT NUMERIC PERFORM 135-DATE-ERROR.
```

Figure 6.9 illustrates the use of class conditions in an iterative structure and in a selection structure to specify the path of control to be followed by the program. In Figure 6.9a the terminal operator is asked to key in a data item until the value is numeric. In Figure 6.9b the class condition performs an error routine when a numeric value appears in the data item entered as a city field.

Figure 6.9   *Class Conditions in the Iteration and Selection Structures*

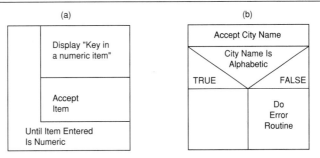

Sign Conditions. The *sign condition* tests only numeric or signed numeric data items to determine if the value is negative, zero, or positive. The format of the sign condition is:

$\left\{ \begin{array}{l} \text{data-name} \\ \\ \text{arithmetic-expression} \end{array} \right\}$ IS   [NOT] $\left\{ \begin{array}{l} \underline{\text{POSITIVE}} \\ \underline{\text{NEGATIVE}} \\ \underline{\text{ZERO}} \end{array} \right\}$

Figure 6.10 illustrates a selection construct controlled by a sign condition. The program reads a customer account record. If a positive balance is found, the program proceeds to issue balance due statements to the offending customers. In this example the sign rather than the magnitude of the item determines the course of action. The code may appear:

```
IF BALANCE-DUE IS POSITIVE PERFORM 10-SEND-BALANCE-DUE-NOTICE.
```

Figure 6.10   ***A Selection Structure Using the Sign Condition***

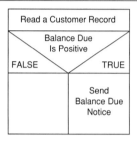

Condition-Name Conditions. *Condition-name conditions* may be used instead of relation conditions. Condition-names are defined in the DATA DIVISION following the data items that are to be tested for specific values. For example, suppose that in a payroll file employees have a code of "U" if they are union members and "E" (exempt) if they are not. A condition-name could be assigned to each value the union code field could take on. The format and rules for entering the condition-name in the DATA DIVISION are:

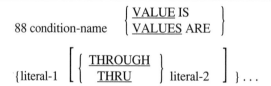

1. All condition-names must be level 88 entries.
2. Condition-name entries must immediately follow the entry for which the condition applies.
3. The literals may be listed in sequence or have a range specified with the THROUGH clause.

For the preceding example, the definition of the condition-names is:

```
DATA DIVISION.
          .
          .
          .
FILE SECTION.
          .
          .
          .
    05 EMP-UNION-CODE            PIC X.
       88  UNION                 VALUE "U".
       88  EXEMPT                VALUE "E".
```

Condition-names specify the value(s) against which the programmer wishes to test. The *level 88* entries follow the PICTURE clause of the associated data item that is to be tested. In our example it is EMP-UNION-CODE. This data item is known as the conditional variable. The truth or falsity of the condition-name depends on the value of the conditional variable. For example, if EMP-UNION-CODE contains "U", UNION is true and EXEMPT is false. One or more level 88 condition-names may be associated with each conditional variable.

For example, in:

```
05 PAY-CODE                  PIC 9.
    88  SALARIED             VALUE 0.
    88  HOURLY               VALUES 1 THRU 3.
    88  OVERTIME             VALUES 1 2.
    88  REGULAR              VALUE 3.
```

PAY-CODE is the conditional variable, and the tested values for this data item are defined by the level 88 condition-names. When PAY-CODE is zero, the condition-name SALARIED will have a value of true, and all other condition-names following PAY-CODE will have a value of false. A truth table of the condition-names for all values of PAY-CODE is:

CONDITION	VALUE				
	0	1	2	3	4-9
SALARIED	T	F	F	F	F
HOURLY	F	T	T	T	F
OVERTIME	F	T	T	F	F
REGULAR	F	F	F	T	F

Condition-names are used in the PROCEDURE DIVISION instead of a relation condition. For example, the truth values associated with PAY-CODE are accessed in the PROCEDURE

DIVISION merely by referring to the appropriate condition-name. Instead of writing the statement

```
IF PAY-CODE = 3
    PERFORM 100-COMPUTE-REGULAR PAY.
```

we may substitute the statement

```
IF REGULAR
    PERFORM 100-COMPUTE-REGULAR-PAY.
```

Although the savings in code may not be substantial, other benefits are derived from the use of condition-names. The first benefit is added clarity in the code. For example, the statement IF REGULAR . . . is easier to read and makes more sense than the statement IF PAY-CODE = 3 . . . . The second reason is that multiple conditions may be reduced to a single condition. This is the case of the condition-names HOURLY and OVERTIME. The third and perhaps most important benefit is that constants are removed from the PROCEDURE DIVISION. This is very advantageous. In the above example, if the codes ever change or new codes are added, the level 88 entries can be easily located and modified since they are defined in only one location within the program. Otherwise, if the program referred to the condition-name SALARIED 20 times, the code would need to be changed in all 20 locations where it is referenced in the PROCEDURE DIVISION.

Extensive use is made of 88 level entries in the program of Figure 6.1. Lines 55, 56, 60 through 64, and 67 through 70 all define level 88 entries. These are used to replace conditions in Lines 117 and 124 and extensively in module "220-DETERMINE-DISCOUNT-CLASS."

Negation. Any simple condition may be negated by placing the reserved word NOT before the condition. *NOT* is a logical unary operator. It negates the condition with which it is associated. This has the effect of reversing the outcome of the condition test. Thus, to reverse the truth or falsity of any simple condition the format is as follows:

$$
\underline{NOT} \quad \left\{ \begin{array}{l} \text{Relation-Condition} \\ \text{Class-Condition} \\ \text{Sign-Condition} \\ \text{Condition-Name} \end{array} \right\}
$$

In COBOL the reserved word NOT simply reverses the truth value of the condition stated. An example is:

```
IF NOT REGULAR PERFORM 200-COMPUTE-SALARY-PAY.
```

6.1.2   Compound Conditions

The conditions cited above were simple conditions. Each one involved only a single expression in the PROCEDURE DIVISION, and in all but the condition-name condition there was a single comparison. However, business applications often require combinations of two or more simple conditions to determine the proper course of action. These combinations of conditions, termed *compound conditions*, are formed by linking simple conditions with the logical operators AND, OR, and NOT. AND and OR require two operands. NOT is a unary operator and requires one operand. The format and rules for forming compound conditions are:

[NOT]   condition-expression-1

$$\left[\left\{ \begin{array}{l} \underline{\text{AND}} \\ \underline{\text{OR}} \end{array} \right\} \text{[NOT] condition-expression-2} \right] \dots$$

1. The condition expressions may be any valid condition, including a compound condition.
2. The NOT must precede the entire condition expression.
3. Parentheses may be used to indicate order of truth evaluation.

Compound conditions are often used in the sequence and iteration structures to control the sequence of operations within a program. For example, in Figure 6.11a the file merge process is repeated until both files being processed have reached their end-of-file records. Figure 6.11b controls whether a program sends out a "prepayment required" notice based on the creditworthiness of the customer as determined by a compound condition. As examples:

```
PERFORM 100-FILE-MERGE UNTIL EOF-BILLS = "TRUE" AND EOF-CUSTOMERS.

IF PAST-DUE = "TRUE" OR LIMIT-EXCESS = "TRUE" PERFORM 120-PRE-PAY.
```

Figure 6.11   Compound Conditions in the Iteration and Selection Structures

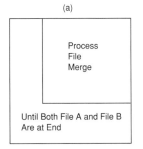
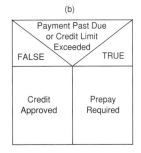

The AND Operator. When the *AND* operator is invoked, the simple conditions joined by AND are evaluated for their truth or falsity. Only if both simple conditions are true is the compound condition true. The following truth table illustrates the outcome of a compound condition using the AND operator:

Condition-1	True	True	False	False
Condition-2	True	False	True	False
Condition-1 AND Condition-2	True	False	False	False

To determine whether an employee is both male and over 45 years old, the compound condition would appear as follows:

```
EMPLOYEE-SEX = "M" AND EMPLOYEE-AGE > 45 .
```

The OR Operator. The *OR* operator indicates that the compound condition is true if either or both of the simple relations are true. The truth table for the OR operator is:

Condition-1	True	True	False	False
Condition-2	True	False	True	False
Condition-1 OR Condition-2	True	True	True	False

To decide if an employee is a member of the accounting department or of the sales department, the compound condition would be:

```
EMPLOYEE-DEPT = "ACCT" OR EMPLOYEE-DEPT = "SALE"
```

The NOT Operator. In complex conditions the NOT operator applies to the condition of which it forms a part. For example,

```
NOT A AND B
```

reverses the truth value of A but does not affect the truth value of B. If the NOT operator is to apply to the entire complex condition, the complex condition must appear in parentheses. For example,

```
NOT (A AND B)
```

negates the truth value of the expression A AND B. As in arithmetic expressions used in the COMPUTE statement, parentheses can alter and clarify the order of precedence in the evaluation of a condition. Therefore, use them sensibly. Examine the truth table below to see how the position of the NOT operator alters the truth value of the various conditions.

Condition A	True	True	False	False
Condition B	True	False	True	False
A AND B	True	False	False	False
A OR B	True	True	True	False

NOT A AND B	False	False	True	False
NOT A OR B	True	False	True	True
A AND NOT B	False	True	False	False
A OR NOT B	True	True	False	True
NOT A AND NOT B	False	False	False	True
NOT A OR NOT B	False	True	True	True
NOT (A AND B)	False	True	True	True
NOT (A OR B)	False	False	False	True

Evaluating Compound Conditions. Compound conditions themselves may be compounded in order to form even more complex conditions. The following precedence rules are used to evaluate their truth value:

1. The innermost parentheses are considered before the outermost.
2. Arithmetic expressions are reduced to single values. *before condition takes place*
3. All single conditions are evaluated.
4. All NOTs are evaluated from left to right.
5. All ANDs are evaluated from left to right.
6. All ORs are evaluated from left to right.

Figure 6.12 presents an example of how a compound condition would be evaluated. The result is true.

Figure 6.12   *Truth Evaluation of a Compound Condition*

Assume   A = 3   B = 4   C = 8   D = −1   E = 4   and EOF is TRUE

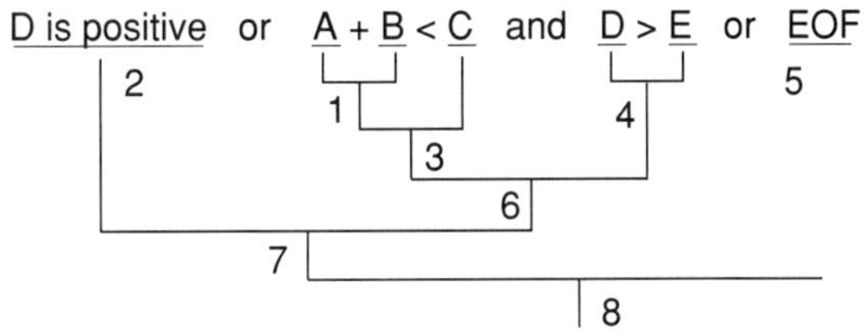

D is positive   or   A + B < C   and   D > E   or   EOF

6.2   *Nested Selection Constructs*

In a selection control structure only two courses of action are possible. But we have mentioned before that the basic constructs may be combined. Therefore, it is possible that each course of action in a selection construct contains another selection control structure. One selection structure within another selection structure is known as a *nested selection structure* or construct. Each selection construct in the structure represents a level of nesting. For example, we might initially want to divide employees into two groups: those who earn more than $25,000 and those who earn $25,000 or less. Of those earning more than $25,000 we might want to subdivide them into those who earn between $25,000 and $50,000 and those who earn more than $50,000. Figure 6.13 illustrates this structure. In this example there are two levels of nesting in the selection structure. However, nesting may reach higher levels. Be aware, however, that as the number of nested selection constructs increases, the complexity of the program increases.

Figure 6.13   *A Selection Structure with Two Levels of Nesting*

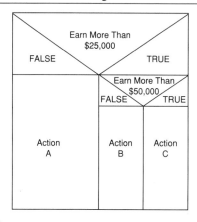

6.2.1   *Nested IF Statements*

Figure 6.14 shows a Nassi-Schneiderman chart for a nested selection structure in which life insurance premiums are computed at different rates based on age and sex considerations. The first level of decision involves age. If the owner of the insurance policy is over 35 years old, one course of action is specified over the other. For each course of action based on age, a determination of the owner's sex is then made. If the owner is male, one set of rates applies; if the owner is female, a second set of rates applies. The objective of the nested structure in this example is to divide the computation of the insurance premiums into four categories. This nested selection structure can be implemented in COBOL with a series of IF statements. Each decision box in Figure 6.14 requires an IF statement to implement the selection construct. Therefore, some IF statements will appear within the higher-order IF statements. In other words, the IF statements will also be nested.

Figure 6.14   *Nested Selection Structures*

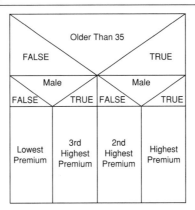

When coding, each successive level of nesting should be indented in order to improve the readability of the program code. It is important to indent the ELSE clause to the same position as its corresponding IF clause to denote the associated course of action for each outcome of the condition being tested. The code for the logic in Figure 6.14 is:

```
1000-DETERMINE-PREMIUM.
    IF CLIENT-AGE IS GREATER THAN 35
        IF CLIENT-SEX IS "MALE"
            MOVE HIGHEST-PREMIUM TO PREMIUM-RATE
        ELSE
            MOVE 2ND-HIGHEST-PREMIUM TO PREMIUM-RATE
    ELSE
        IF CLIENT-SEX IS "MALE"
            MOVE 3RD-HIGHEST-PREMIUM TO PREMIUM-RATE
        ELSE
            MOVE LOWEST-PREMIUM TO PREMIUM-RATE.
```

The first level of nesting is represented by the first IF statement. If the condition "older than 35" is true, the code specifying the corresponding course of action is indented under the IF clause. If the condition "older than 35" is false, the code specifying the course of action to be followed appears under the ELSE clause. The IF and ELSE that correspond to each level of selection should be written in the same margin to improve clarity and readability.

Nested IFs are interpreted by the following rules:

1. Every statement within a nested IF statement is controlled by the most recent IF or ELSE clause.
2. Each ELSE clause in a nested IF statement is matched with the most recent IF clause without an ELSE clause.
3. Each nested IF statement has only one period.
4. The END-IF terminates the previous IF.
5. A period terminates the entire compound statement.

When the above rules and consistent indentation are used, the logic of a nested IF is easier to read, follow, and debug. In the program of Figure 6.1, nested IFs are used to determine the discount points for the two purchase categories, DC-TOTAL-DOLLAR-PURCHASES (Lines 165 through 172) and DC-AVERAGE-DOLLAR-PURCHASES (Lines 173 through 178).

6.2.2   *The Case Control Structure*

Nested selection constructs can also be represented as a series of selection constructs using compound conditions to dictate the course of action to be taken at each level. For example, in the insurance premium computation example each premium computation could be perceived as four separate variations of the premium computation. This is illustrated in the Nassi Schneiderman chart in Figure 6.15. At each decision there are two paths, one of which specifies the course of action to be taken when the compound condition is true. The false path leads to another selection structure. A selection structure of this type is known as a *case structure*, a name derived from the way each "case" is explicitly set forth by a condition expression. Many programmers recognize the case structure as a fourth primitive structure because of its common occurrence in applications.

Figure 6.15   Nested Selections in a Case Structure

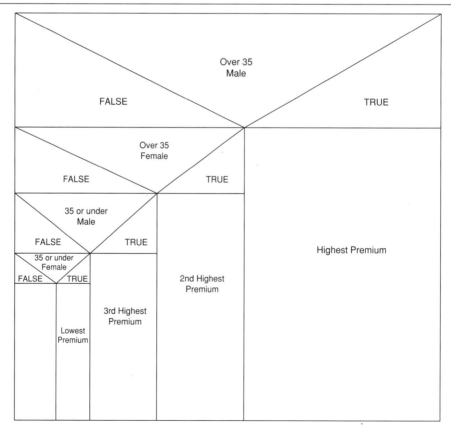

The COBOL code for the case structure for the insurance premium example is:

```
1000-DETERMINE-PREMIUM.
        IF CLIENT-AGE > 35 AND CLIENT-SEX = "MALE"
               MOVE HIGHEST-PREMIUM TO PREMIUM-RATE
        ELSE
               IF CLIENT-AGE > 35 AND CLIENT-SEX = "FEMALE"
                      MOVE 2ND-HIGHEST-PREMIUM TO PREMIUM-RATE
        ELSE
          IF CLIENT-AGE NOT < 35 AND CLIENT-SEX = "MALE"
               MOVE 3RD-HIGHEST-PREMIUM TO PREMIUM-RATE
        ELSE
          IF CLIENT-AGE NOT < 35 AND
               CLIENT-SEX = "FEMALE"
               MOVE LOWEST-PREMIUM TO PREMIUM-RATE.
```

Notice that the entire case structure was coded as one sentence. Each case of the premium computation is identified using complex conditions in the IF clauses. By isolating each case, the program becomes easier to read and follow.

Using this implementation of the case structure also allows for the specification of the action to be taken if an error condition occurs. To do this in the above example, it would be necessary to add an appropriate ELSE clause to the last IF statement. This is not always necessary, however. When the actions to be taken are mutually exclusive and no possible error conditions exist, each IF statement should be coded as a separate sentence. This has the effect of segmenting the four conditions and their respective actions as follows:

```
1000-DETERMINE-PREMIUM.
        IF CLIENT-AGE > 35 AND CLIENT-SEX = "MALE"
               MOVE HIGHEST-PREMIUM TO PREMIUM-RATE.
        IF CLIENT-AGE > 35 AND CLIENT-SEX = "FEMALE"
               MOVE 2ND-HIGHEST-PREMIUM TO PREMIUM-RATE.
        IF CLIENT-AGE NOT < 35 AND CLIENT-SEX = "MALE"
               MOVE 3RD-HIGHEST-PREMIUM TO PREMIUM-RATE.
        IF CLIENT-AGE NOT < 35 AND CLIENT-SEX = "FEMALE"
               MOVE LOWEST-PREMIUM TO PREMIUM-RATE.
```

Often, selecting the appropriate action to take in a case construct can be based on the value of a single variable. In the insurance premium example a single-digit numeric code, IP-CODE, may denote the class of premiums available. The Nassi-Schneiderman chart for the premium calculation case structure using an IP-CODE would be represented as in Figure 6.16. This representation of the case structure easily accommodates unknown or error conditions. Of course, in place of the single digit code, the explicit conditions could appear in the Nassi-Schneiderman chart in place of the numeric code.

Figure 6.16   ***Case Structure for Computation of Insurance Premiums***

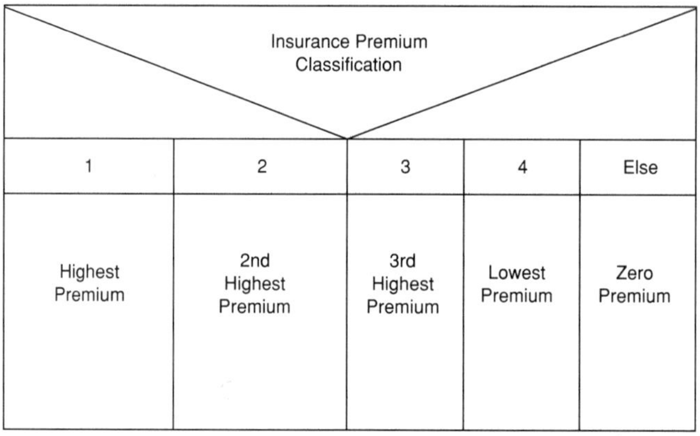

The COBOL implementation of the case structure in Figure 6.16 follows:

```
IF IP-CLASS = 1
     MOVE HIGHEST-PREMIUM TO PREMIUM-RATE
ELSE
     IF IP-CLASS = 2
     MOVE 2ND-HIGHEST-PREMIUM TO PREMIUM-RATE
ELSE
     IF IP-CLASS = 3
     MOVE 3RD-HIGHEST-PREMIUM TO PREMIUM-RATE
ELSE
     IF IP-CLASS = 4
     MOVE LOWEST-PREMIUM TO PREMIUM-RATE
ELSE
     MOVE ZERO TO PREMIUM-RATE.
```

An alternate approach using 88 levels could appear:

```
     05      IP-CLASS  PIC 9.
     88      1ST-RATE  VALUE 1.
     88      2ND-RATE  VALUE 2.
     88      3RD-RATE  VALUE 3.
     88      4TH-RATE  VALUE 4.


IF 1ST-RATE
     MOVE HIGHEST-PREMIUM TO PREMIUM-RATE
ELSE
     IF 2ND-RATE
```

```
          MOVE 2ND-HIGHEST-PREMIUM TO PREMIUM-RATE
ELSE
          IF 3RD-RATE
          MOVE HIGHEST-PREMIUM TO PREMIUM-RATE
ELSE
          IF 4TH-RATE
          MOVE LOWEST-PREMIUM TO PREMIUM-RATE
ELSE
          MOVE ZERO TO PREMIUM-RATE.
```

6.2.3 *The EVALUATE Statement*

COBOL provides a statement that directly implements the case structure. It is the EVALUATE statement. Its simplified format and rules are:

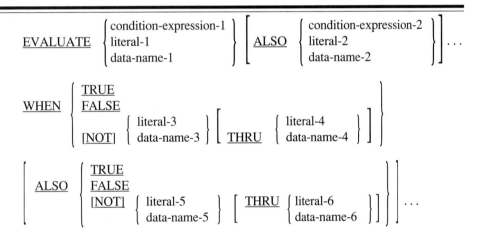

imperative-statement-1 . . .
[WHEN OTHER {imperative-statement-2} . . .]
[END-EVALUATE]

1. When condition-expression-1 or -2 is used, the option in the WHEN clause must be either the TRUE or FALSE option.
2. The words TRUE and FALSE are used to test the truth values of condition-expression-1 and -2.
3. When literal-1 and -2 are used, the associated entries in the WHEN clause must be data-names.
4. The THRU option allows testing for a range of values on data-name-1 or data-name-2.
5. Data-name-1 and data-names-3 and -4 must be of the same type.

The ALSO clause permits multiple items to be tested for specific values. A WHEN clause is specified for each case outcome and its associated action. The condition-expressions are evaluated as TRUE or FALSE. Literal-1 and -2 are compared to data-name-3 and -5 for equality of values. Data-name-1 and -2 are compared to a specific value for equality or to determine if they fall within a range specified by the THRU clause. The WHEN OTHER clause specifies the action to be taken for an unidentified case. The EVALUATE statement to implement the insurance premium case structure in Figure 6.16 would be coded as follows:

```
EVALUATE CLIENT-AGE > 35 ALSO CLIENT-SEX
        WHEN TRUE ALSO "MALE"
                MOVE HIGHEST-PREMIUM TO PREMIUM-RATE
        WHEN TRUE ALSO "FEMALE"
                MOVE 2ND-HIGHEST-PREMIUM TO PREMIUM-RATE
        WHEN FALSE ALSO "MALE"
                MOVE 3RD-HIGHEST-PREMIUM TO PREMIUM-RATE
        WHEN FALSE ALSO "FEMALE"
                MOVE LOWEST-PREMIUM TO PREMIUM-RATE
        WHEN OTHER
                MOVE ZERO TO PREMIUM-RATE
```

The program of Figure 6.1 also uses the EVALUATE statement. Starting on Line 179, the EVALUATE relates the points acquired by a customer to the next months discount percentage.

6.3   *Additional Statements for Program Control*

Program instructions are executed one after another in sequential fashion unless the order is altered. Changing the flow of control from one location in the program to another is called *branching*. The ability to modify the order of execution of instructions in a program is fundamental to programming.

Some instructions cause branching whenever they are executed. Transferring control to another location in the program with automatic return to the branching point is known as *conditional branching*. In COBOL, conditional branching is implemented using the PERFORM statement. It causes the execution of instructions in a separate paragraph before returning control to the PERFORM statement.

Transferring control to another paragraph without returning to the point where the branch occurred is called *unconditional branching*. Unconditional branching is not supported in structured programming, although COBOL provides a statement for its implementation. Unconditional branching is regarded with disdain by programmers who adhere to structured programming concepts, and with good reason. With unconditional branching, the rules of modularized programming using the three primitive structures can be easily violated. Figure 6.17 shows a flowchart with an unconditional branch. The structure looks like a combination of a selection and an iteration structure. However, it violates the single entry/single exit rule of structured programming. The decision box (a) representing a selection structure has one entry and two exits. The overall iteration structure controlled by (b) has one entry and no exit! Therefore, unconditional branching should be avoided.

Figure 6.17   **Unconditional Branching**

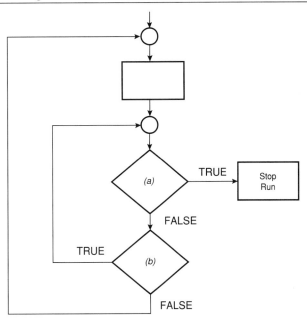

A flowchart was used in Figure 6.17 to illustrate unconditional branching. A Nassi-Schneiderman chart cannot show an unconditional branch without explicitly stating the branch. It is thus impossible to accidentally design an unconditional branch using Nassi-Schneiderman charts, which is another good reason to use them instead of flowcharts.

6.3.1   The GO TO Statement

The unconditional branch is implemented in COBOL with the *GO TO* statement. The GO TO statement transfers control to the first sentence in the paragraph named by the GO TO statement. No further imperative statements may appear in sequence following the GO TO in a sentence. The format and rules for the statement are:

GO TO paragraph-name.

1.   The paragraph may be any paragraph in the PROCEDURE DIVISION.
2.   The GO TO must be the last in a consecutive sequence of imperative statements in a sentence.

A GO TO statement may be used to bypass a sequence of instructions that is not relevant for a specific branch of a selection structure. The logic of Figure 6.18 may be implemented with the GO TO statement using the following code:

```
100-DETERMINE-PAST-DUE.
     COMPUTE BALANCE-DUE - AMOUNT-OF-BILL - AMOUNT-PAID.
     IF BALANCE-DUE NOT > ZERO OR
          BILL-DATE-MONTH NOT < CURRENT-MONTH - 2
          GO TO 300-ALL-OK.
200-ISSUE-PAST-DUE
     .
     .
     .

300-ALL-OK
     .
     .
     .
```

The code with the GO TO statement takes advantage of the fact that, unless otherwise specified, paragraphs are executed in physical order of appearance. In the example, the statement GO TO 300-ALL-OK transfers control to paragraph 300-ALL-OK. Control does not return to 100-DETERMINE-PAST-DUE.

Figure 6.18   A Selection Structure with Action on the True Branch

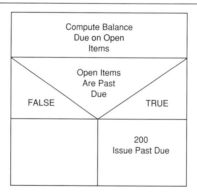

GO TO statements have generated much heated debate among programmers. The judicious and careful use of GO TO statements does not have to violate the rules of structured program design, but their use does tend to blur the direct relationship between the code and the design. The Nassi-Schneiderman chart in Figure 6.18 represents a structured design. However, the code using the GO TO statement has two entry points into the third paragraph and thus does not conform to the rules of structured programming. When the GO TO statement is used, the relationship between the programming code and the design is lost. Another reason for programmers' disdain of the GO TO statement is that historically the statement has been abused, resulting in unstructured programs that are very difficult to read and modify. Therefore, it is generally agreed that the evils of the GO TO statements outweigh their benefits and that their use should be limited to situations in which no structured alternative is available.

6.3.2   *The PERFORM THRU and EXIT Statements*

Another branching instruction in COBOL is a variation of the PERFORM statement. The rules and format for the PERFORM THRU statement are:

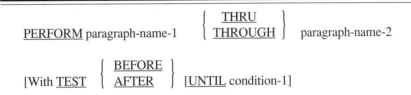

$$\underline{\text{PERFORM}} \text{ paragraph-name-1} \left\{ \begin{array}{l} \underline{\text{THRU}} \\ \underline{\text{THROUGH}} \end{array} \right\} \text{ paragraph-name-2}$$

$$\text{[With } \underline{\text{TEST}} \left\{ \begin{array}{l} \underline{\text{BEFORE}} \\ \underline{\text{AFTER}} \end{array} \right\} \text{ [}\underline{\text{UNTIL}} \text{ condition-1]}$$

1. There must be a logical adjacent path in the code from paragraph-name-1 to paragraph-name-2. This is called the range of the PERFORM.
2. If the range of the PERFORM contains a second PERFORM, the range of the second PERFORM must be wholly contained in the range of the first, or wholly outside the range of the first.
3. Condition-1 is any conditional expression. It is tested first to determine whether control is transferred, unless WITH TEST AFTER is used, when the condition is tested after the range of the PERFORM is complete.
4. After the range is executed, control passes to the statement following the PER-FORM THRU.

The *PERFORM THRU* statement transfers control to the first statement of paragraph-name-1 in the PERFORM clause. Then all the paragraphs physically appearing in the path to paragraph-name-2 in the THRU clause up to and including the last sentence in paragraph-name-2 are executed. If the UNTIL clause is not present, the PERFORM statement will execute the range only once. Control will then pass to the statement following the PERFORM. If the UNTIL clause is present, condition-1 will first be tested. If it is true, no transfer of control will take place and control will pass to the statement following the PERFORM THRU. If condition-1 is false, the range of the PERFORM will be executed and control will return to the PERFORM THRU so that condition-1 can be tested again.

This variation of the PERFORM statement allows the programmer to specify the execution of several paragraphs arranged in physical sequence using a single PERFORM statement. The following code executes numerous paragraphs in physical sequence using simple PERFORM statements.

```
PERFORM 200-CHECK-NUMERICS.
PERFORM 300-CHECK-ALPHAS.
PERFORM 400-CHECK-RANGES.
PERFORM 500-CHECK-SIGNS.
PERFORM 600-CHECK-LIMITS.
PERFORM 700-CHECK-PRESENCE.
```

The number of statements may be reduced by using the PERFORM THRU statement as follows:

```
PERFORM 200-CHECK-NUMERICS THRU 700-CHECK-PRESENCE.
```

The paragraphs to be executed must appear in sequence at a different point in the code. Thus, the PERFORM THRU statement imposes a physical dependence on the execution of the code since that execution is dependent on the physical appearance of the paragraph in the PERFORM range. In our programs, with the exception of the first paragraph, we have been ordering the paragraphs in numerical sequence based on the numbers assigned to the modules in the hierarchy chart. However, if the PERFORM THRU statement is used, it requires that the paragraphs be arranged in the order in which they should be executed, thereby imposing a physical restriction on the logical flow of control in the program.

The *EXIT* statement is used in the last paragraph of the range specified in a PERFORM THRU statement as a shared ending point. The EXIT statement is composed of the reserved word EXIT followed by a period. For example, for the statement

```
PERFORM 1000-PREPARE-INPUT THRU 4000-END-PROCESSING.
```

the last paragraph in the PERFORM range would be

```
4000-END-PROCESSING.
    EXIT.
```

If a paragraph name is assigned to a common point in the program, control can be transferred to that point. For the PERFORM THRU example, the statement

```
GO TO 4000-END-PROCESSING.
```

in any of the paragraphs within the range will transfer control to the end of the range. This has the effect of allowing the program to break out of the PERFORM range and return control to the statement following the PERFORM THRU statement or to the PERFORM statement if it is a PERFORM THRU UNTIL. Using a PERFORM THRU UNTIL statement in conjunction with an EXIT statement may appear as follows:

```
COPY-FILE.
    OPEN INPUT INPUT-FILE.
    PERFORM 100-READ-INPUT-FILE THRU 300-EXIT
        UNTIL EOF-IN-FILE = "YES"
    CLOSE INPUT-FILE.
    CLOSE OUTPUT-FILE.
    STOP RUN.
100-READ-INPUT-FILE.
    READ INPUT-FILE
        AT END MOVE "YES" TO EOF-IN-FILE
            GO TO 300-EXIT.
```

```
200-WRITE-OUTPUT.
      MOVE INPUT-RECORD TO OUTPUT-RECORD.
      WRITE OUTPUT-RECORD.
300-EXIT.
      EXIT.
```

Note that when the paragraph containing the EXIT statement is executed, control returns to the statement

```
PERFORM 100-READ-INPUT-FILE THRU 300-EXIT UNTIL EOF-IN-FILE = "YES".
```

In this example, the PERFORM UNTIL in conjunction with the EXIT statement eliminates the need for a priming read in the program. This is accomplished by breaking out of the processing sequence in the paragraph 100-READ-INPUT-FILE via a GO TO statement if the record read is an end-of-file record. With this combination of statements, the logic of the program follows a more natural repetitive process of input (READ), process, output (WRITE) rather than starting with a priming read and continuing with the repetition of a process-WRITE-READ iteration. Thus the use of the GO TO and PERFORM THRU statements avoids the need for a priming read. With each method, eliminating undesirable features requires using different unfavorable techniques. However, the priming read method is more common and is more flexible when multiple files are being processed, making it the better approach.

Many business firms provide programming standards that recommend a particular method for handling end-of-file conditions, have policies regarding the use of controversial statements, such as GO TO and PERFORM THRU, and indicate other programming features that standardize code and facilitate maintenance.

6.3.3   *The PERFORM VARYING Statement*

Another variation of the PERFORM statement is the *PERFORM VARYING* statement. This statement implements the iteration construct and controls the number of times a paragraph or range of paragraphs is performed. The format and rules for the PERFORM VARYING statement are:

PERFORM paragraph-name-1 $\left[\left\{ \begin{array}{c} \underline{\text{THRU}} \\ \underline{\text{THROUGH}} \end{array} \right\} \text{paragraph-name-2} \right]$

[With TEST $\left\{ \begin{array}{c} \underline{\text{AFTER}} \\ \underline{\text{BEFORE}} \end{array} \right\}$]

$\underline{\text{VARYING}}$ data-name-1

$\underline{\text{FROM}} \left\{ \begin{array}{c} \text{data-name-2} \\ \text{literal-1} \end{array} \right\} \underline{\text{BY}} \left\{ \begin{array}{c} \text{data-name-3} \\ \text{literal-2} \end{array} \right\} \underline{\text{UNTIL}} \text{ condition-1}$

$\left[\quad \underline{\text{AFTER}} \text{ data-name-4} \right.$

$$\text{FROM} \left\{ \begin{array}{l} \text{data-name-5} \\ \text{literal-3} \end{array} \right\} \underline{\text{BY}} \left\{ \begin{array}{l} \text{data-name-6} \\ \text{literal-4} \end{array} \right\} \underline{\text{UNTIL}} \text{ condition-2} \bigg] \dots$$

1. The value after the FROM clause must be integer.
2. The value after the BY clause must be positive integer.
3. The AFTER clauses allow nested variations such that the latter AFTER conditions are met prior to allowing the first AFTER to begin.
4. There may be up to six AFTER phrases.

Data-name-1 serves as a counter whose initial value is the value of data-name-2 or literal-1 in the FROM clause. This counter is incremented (or decremented) by the value of the data-name-3 or literal-2 in the BY clause. The specified paragraph is performed until condition-1 in the UNTIL clause is true. The AFTER clauses allow multiple data items to be varied. (They are discussed in depth in Chapter 9.) The PERFORM VARYING statement essentially counts the number of times the paragraph is executed. This allows the programmer to control a paragraph by specifying that number. Furthermore, he may use the data item in the VARYING clause anywhere in the program. For example, in

```
PERFORM 1000-READ-SUPPLIER-RECORD

     VARYING SUPPLIER-COUNT FROM 0 BY 1
          UNTIL EOF-SUPP-FILE.
```

1000-READ-SUPPLIER-RECORD is the paragraph to be executed repeatedly. SUPPLIER-COUNT is the counter that will be incremented by 1 after the paragraph is executed but before the test of the condition. Its starting value is zero. When the end of the supplier file is reached, the PERFORM will terminate. SUPPLIER-COUNT could then be displayed at the end of the program to cross reference the value to some control count of suppliers.

The PERFORM VARYING statement may be used to control iterations of known duration when the value of an incremented variable is important. For example, the code to project sales for a company would probably be executed a given number of times. The following code computes the forecast:

```
0-SALES-FORECAST.
     PERFORM 10-OBTAIN-INPUT.
     PERFORM 20-FORECAST
          VARYING WS-YEAR FROM START-YEAR
          BY 1 UNTIL WS-YEAR > STOP-YEAR.
10-OBTAIN-INPUT.
     DISPLAY "ENTER GROWTH RATE".
     ACCEPT GROWTH-RATE.
     DISPLAY "ENTER START YEAR".
     ACCEPT START-YEAR.
     DISPLAY "ENTER-STOP YEAR".
     ACCEPT STOP-YEAR.
```

```
            DISPLAY "ENTER STARTING SALES".
            ACCEPT STARTING-SALES.
            ADD 1 TO START-YEAR.
            DISPLAY "YEAR SALES".
    20-FORECAST.
            COMPUTE STARTING-SALES ROUNDED =
                  STARTING-SALES * (1 + GROWTH-RATE).
            DISPLAY WS-YEAR, STARTING-SALES.
```

If the forecast is to be for five years, the paragraph should be performed five times, with each pass through the iteration representing one year further into the future. Several input values to the sample code and the results that would be displayed at the end of the program are:

```
IF STARTING VALUES ARE:

    GROWTH RATE IS 10%

    START YEAR IS 1984

    STOP YEAR IS 1988

    STARTING SALES IS $100,000.00

RESULTS DISPLAYED WILL BE:

    YEAR          SALES

    1985          110000.00

    1986          121000.00

    1987          133100.00

    1988          146410.00
```

The PERFORM . . . VARYING is used in line 148 of Figure 6.1 as follows:

```
PERFORM 210-ACCUMULATE-CUSTOMER-BILLS WITH TEST AFTER
        VARYING DC-NUMBER-OF-PURCHASES FROM 1 BY 1
              UNTIL CB-CUSTOMER-NBR NOT = DB-CUSTOMER-NBR.
```

In this case, the VARYING serves to count the number of purchases (bills) for a single customer (UNTIL CB-CUSTOMER-NBR NOT = DB-CUSTOMER-NBR). The count (DC-NUMBER-OF PURCHASES) is later used in line 163 to compute an average purchase value.

6.3.4   Conditional Delimiters

COBOL also has delimiters for ending conditional statements. Conditional statements include the IF and PERFORM UNTIL statements and statements in which the truth or falsity of a very specific condition determines the action taken. For example, READ . . . AT END is a conditional statement in which the only allowable condition is the detection of the end-of-file record. Arithmetic statements using the ON SIZE ERROR clause are also considered conditional statements. In this case the condition is whether a result value exceeds the size of the result field.

All open conditional statements are terminated by a period. Optionally, a single conditional statement may be ended by using a delimiter such as the following:

END-ADD	END-IF
END-COMPUTE	END-PERFORM
END-DIVIDE	END-READ
END-MULTIPLY	END-WRITE
END-SUBTRACT	END-EVALUATE

Other delimiters are available for statements not yet covered.

Delimiters provide clarity and simplification of code. For example, in the nested IF:

```
IF STATE-CODE = "AZ"
      PERFORM 50-COMPUTE-AZ-TAX
ELSE
      IF STATE-CODE = "TX"
            PERFORM 60-COMPUTE-TX-TAX
            IF EMPLOYEE-AGE > 40
                  PERFORM 70-COMPUTE-RETIREMENT
            ELSE NEXT SENTENCE
      ELSE
            PERFORM 00-NO-TAX.
```

an additional ELSE is required to denote the fact that the statement IF EMPLOYEE-AGE < 40 does not have an action associated with the false branch. However, by using the END-IF delimiter the code can be written as:

```
IF STATE-CODE = "AZ"
      PERFORM 50-COMPUTE-AZ-TAX
ELSE
      IF STATE-CODE = "TX"
            PERFORM 60-COMPUTE-TX-TAX
            IF EMPLOYEE-AGE > 40
                  PERFORM 70-COMPUTE-RETIREMENT
            END-IF
      ELSE
            PERFORM 00-NO-TAX
```

```
          END-IF
END-IF.
```

The END-IF delimiters clearly define the end of the range for each IF statement and keep the sequencing of the ELSE clauses more natural. The more complex nested IF statements become, the more useful the delimiters.

The delimiters for the arithmetic statements are even more useful. Assume that several arithmetic statements are part of an IF statement as follows:

```
IF STATE-CODE = "MO"
     COMPUTE GROSS-PAY =
          SALARY + DIVIDENDS + BONUS
     COMPUTE TAXES =
          GROSS-PAY * MO-RATE
     COMPUTE NET-PAY =
          GROSS-PAY - TAXES.
```

Assume further that an ON SIZE ERROR clause needs to be added to the GROSS-PAY computation. Changing the CODE to:

```
IF STATE-CODE = "MO"
     COMPUTE GROSS-PAY =
          SALARY + DIVIDENDS + BONUS
          ON SIZE ERROR PERFORM 300-ERR
     COMPUTE TAXES =
          GROSS-PAY * MO-RATE
     COMPUTE NET-PAY =
          GROSS-PAY - TAXES.
```

would be faulty because the last two COMPUTE statements would become part of the action taken by a SIZE ERROR condition in the first COMPUTE statement. The problem can be corrected by moving these statements to a separate paragraph as separate sentences and then altering the IF statement as follows:

```
IF STATE-CODE = "MO"
     PERFORM 90-MO-TAXES.
```

However, a delimiter may also correct the problem as follows:

```
IF STATE-CODE = "MO"
     COMPUTE GROSS-PAY =
          SALARY + DIVIDENDS + BONUS
          ON SIZE ERROR PERFORM 300-ERR
     END-COMPUTE
     COMPUTE TAXES =
```

```
                    GROSS-PAY * MO-RATE
        COMPUTE NET-PAY =
                    GROSS-PAY - TAXES.
```

The program of Figure 6.1 uses delimiters in lines 127, 133, and 188 to help clarify the code.

Case Study: CDL's Categorize Daily Mail Revisited

Charlene Hilton made a big mistake in the Categorize Daily Mail program. Sometimes even the best analysts err, and the programmer often pays the price. In this case justice was served since Charlene is both the programmer and the analyst. She mistakenly designed the Categorize Daily Mail program so that only the error checks previously made on the data in the manual system were performed. However, in the conversion to the new system, different types of errors have been introduced and new features can be used to validate the data in a more comprehensive manner. The original program and supporting documentation appear in Chapter 3.

After conferring with the data entry and payment clerks, Charlene rewrites the program specifications to include the maintenance of control counts and to validate the customer number and payment field. This is described in the program summary in Figure 6.19. These changes do not affect the files used by the program, nor do they change the structure of the program. Only two modules have to be changed to accommodate the new requirements. These are illustrated in the Nassi-Schneiderman charts in Figure 6.20.

Figure 6.19   Additions to CDL's "Categorize Daily Mail" Specifications

PROGRAM SUMMARY

TITLE: *Additions to Categorize Daily Mail*

PREPARED BY: *C. Hilton*

DATE: *6-24-93*

FILES USED		
FILE NAME	MEDIA	ORGANIZATION

DESCRIPTION

A count of total input records must be kept and displayed.

The payment records must be verified as follows:

1. The payment must be numeric and nonzero.

2. The customer number must be numeric.

3. The customer numbers must start with 100001 as the lower limit.

Figure 6.20   Revisions to CDL's "Categorize Daily Mail"

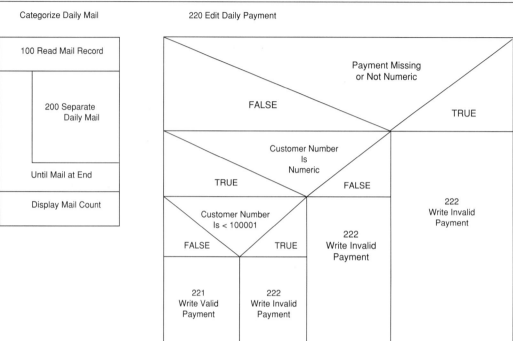

The main module "Categorize Daily Mail" now includes a DISPLAY of the input record count before the program terminates. The count is easily maintained by adding a VARYING clause to the PERFORM UNTIL statement that controls the main processing loop "200-Separate-Daily-Mail." The code additions are shown in Figure 6.21. Note that no ADD or COMPUTE statements are required. The module "220-Edit-Daily-Payment" has to be changed to incorporate all numeric and range checks. If any test fails, the module "222-Write-Invalid-Payment" is invoked. Otherwise the module "221-Write-Valid-Payment" is executed. Paragraph 220-EDIT-DAILY-PAYMENT uses nested IF statements to implement the nested selection structure.

Because she uses modular design for her programs, Charlene found it easy to implement the changes to the Categorize Daily Mail program. Although the changes seemed complex, only two modules had to be modified.

Figure 6.21 Revisions to CDL's "Categorize Daily Mail" COBOL Code

SYSTEM | PUNCHING INSTRUCTIONS | PAGE OF
PROGRAM | GRAPHIC | CARD FORM NUMBER
PROGRAMMER | DATE | PUNCH

SEQUENCE | CONT | A | B | COBOL STATEMENT | IDENTIFICATION

```
             (IN WORKING STORAGE ADD:)

       01  COUNTERS
           05  COUNT-INPUT-RECORDS    PIC 9(5).

             (IN PROCECURE DIVISION REPLACE:)

       CATEGORIZE-DAILY-MAIL
           OPEN INPUT PAYMENTS-AND-ORDERS-FILE.
           OPEN OUTPUT ORDERS-FILE.
           OPEN OUTPUT VALID-PAYMENTS-FILE.
           OPEN OUTPUT INVALID-PAYMENTS-FILE.
           PERFORM 100-READ-MAIL-RECORD.
           PERFORM 200-SEPARATE-DAILY-MAIL
               VARYING COUNT-INPUT-RECORDS FROM ZERO BY 1
               UNTIL EOF-PAYMENTS-AND-ORDERS = "TRUE".
           DISPLAY COUNT-INPUT-RECORDS.
           CLOSE PAYMENTS-AND-ORDERS-FILE
               ORDERS-FILE
               VALID-PAYMENTS-FILE
               INVALID-PAYMENTS-FILE.
            STOP RUN.
```

SYSTEM | PUNCHING INSTRUCTIONS | PAGE OF
PROGRAM | GRAPHIC | CARD FORM NUMBER
PROGRAMMER | DATE | PUNCH

SEQUENCE | CONT | A | B | COBOL STATEMENT | IDENTIFICATION

```
               (ALSO REPLACE:)

       220-EDIT-DAILY-PAYMENT.
           IF PAO-PAYMENT-AMOUNT IS NOT NUMERIC
               PERFORM 222-WRITE-INVALID-PAYMENT
           ELSE
               IF PAO-PAYMENT-AMOUNT IS ZERO
                   PERFORM 222-WRITE-INVALID-PAYMENT
               ELSE
                   IF PAO-PAYMENT-AMOUNT IS NOT NUMERIC
                       PERFORM 222-WRITE-INVALID-PAYMENT
                   ELSE
                       IF PAO-PAYMENT-AMOUNT IS LESS THAN 100001
                           PERFORM 222-WRITE-INVALID-PAYMENT
                       ELSE
                           PERFORM 222-WRITE-VALID-PAYMENT.
```

Summary

COBOL provides several enhancements to the basic statements used to support the three primary structures. COBOL's conditional expressions, ranging from simple conditions to combinations of conditions, allow the programmer to specify the circumstances under which different sets of action are to be carried out. Relation conditions test the stated relationship between two data items. Class conditions determine whether an item is numeric or alphabetic, and sign conditions test a numeric item to decide if it is positive, negative, or zero.

In the DATA DIVISION condition-names are level 88 entries that specify the values that a specific data item, known as the conditional variable, may have. They replace relation conditions and often improve the readability and maintainability of a program.

If simple conditions are insufficient for determining the special circumstances under which certain actions are taken, compound conditions may be formed by linking simple conditions with the logical operators AND and OR. When compound conditions themselves are combined, the determination of their truth value is based on specific rules of precedence of the operators. Conditional expressions allow the development of more complex structures such as nested selections and nested iterations. The conditional expressions also provide a means for restructuring nested selection structures into case structures. Although conditional expressions may be stated in many forms, they should be written in the form simplest to understand. This leads to more readable and maintainable code.

COBOL statements allow the programmer to control the sequence of execution of the program logic. The GO TO statement permits unconditional branching within a program, and the PERFORM THRU statement allows the execution of a set of paragraphs arranged physically in order of execution. The PERFORM THRU statement used in conjunction with the EXIT statement provides an alternative method of handling the priming READ in COBOL. The PERFORM VARYING statement is a useful implementation of the iteration structure that permits the programmer to count the number of times the repetition of a paragraph is executed.

The EVALUATE statement directly implements the case control structure. Another feature allows the use of delimiters for conditional statements. Often restrictions imposed by sentence structure in COBOL make it necessary to write more complex code to include longer sequences of statements as part of the imperative statement executed when a condition is met. With conditional delimiters such statement sequences can be delimited, thus clarifying and simplifying the code.

Key Terms

conditional statement	compound condition	unconditional branching
imperative statement	AND	GO TO
class condition	OR	PERFORM THRU
sign condition	nested selection structure	EXIT
condition-names	case structure	PERFORM VARYING
level 88	branching	
NOT	conditional branching	

Hints for Avoiding Errors

1. Often a program appears to work properly except at the very end when it seems to be trying to execute all over again. This is a frequent error, usually caused by the omission of the STOP RUN statement.

2. The NOT operator causes much confusion in complex conditions. Remember that NOT applies to the condition immediately following the NOT operator. If you want to negate multiple conditions, you must place the conditions within parentheses and the NOT operator outside and in front of the parentheses.

3. It is often simpler to use different forms of a condition when using the NOT operator. For example, the conditional expression NOT A OR NOT B is equivalent to the conditional expression NOT (A AND B). Use the expression that is most understandable in the code. Rephrasing conditions, however, is a major cause of program bugs, so be sure that the conditions are equivalent.

4. IF statements are sensitive to the placement of periods. Remember that a period terminates an IF sentence, thus affecting all IF statements in the sentence. An extra period will often change the intended selection structure without creating a syntax error.

5. Omission of a period from the end of an IF statement is also a common error. This results in including the statement following the IF sentence as part of the IF statement.

Exercises

6.1 Replace the nested IF statements in Figure 6.1 with EVALUATE statements. Replace the EVALUATE statement with a nested IF.

6.2 Show how the design and code of Figures 6.1 through 6.6 could be changed if exactly three billing records appear for every customer. Rewrite the code.

6.3 The EVALUATE statement can only replace up to 5 levels of nesting. True or false?

6.4 Assuming the following values:

A = 10, B = 8, C = 3, and D = 2,

and given the statements:

```
IF A NOT = 1 OR B > 10
      PERFORM PARA1
      IF C IS NUMERIC
            NEXT SENTENCE
      ELSE
            IF D < 5
                  PERFORM PARA2.
IF A = 10
      PERFORM PARA3.
```

what paragraphs will be executed?

6.5   If A = 1, B = 2, and C = 3, with which of the following statements will PAR-1 be executed?
    a.   IF A = 1 OR B = 2 AND C = 3 PERFORM PAR-1.
    b.   IF A = 1 AND B = 2 OR C = 3 PERFORM PAR-1.
    c.   IF A = 1 OR B = 2 OR C = 3 PERFORM PAR-1.
    d.   IF A = 1 AND B = 2 AND C = 3 PERFORM PAR-1.
    e.   All of the above

Use the following COBOL instructions to answer Exercises 6.6 through 6.8.

```
IF STATUS-CODE IS LESS THAN 6
      PERFORM A-PAR
      IF STATUS-CODE IS LESS THAN 3
            PERFORM B-PAR
      ELSE
            PERFORM C-PAR
ELSE
      PERFORM D-PAR.
IF STATUS-CODE = 6
      PERFORM E-PAR.
```

6.6   C-PAR will be performed when:
    a.   STATUS-CODE is greater than 6.
    b.   STATUS-CODE is less than 6 and greater than 3.
    c.   STATUS-CODE is less than 6.
    d.   STATUS-CODE is less than 6 and greater than or equal to 3.

6.7   Given that STATUS-CODE = 6, what paragraphs will be performed?
    a.   A-PAR, D-PAR, E-PAR
    b.   D-PAR, E-PAR
    c.   C-PAR, D-PAR
    d.   E-PAR

6.8   Given that STATUS-CODE = 4, what paragraph(s) will be performed?
    a.   C-PAR
    b.   A-PAR, B-PAR, E-PAR
    c.   A-PAR, C-PAR
    d.   A-PAR, E-PAR

6.9   The _____ command makes it possible to branch to a specified paragraph, execute it, and return to the statement following the command.

6.10   Given the statement:

```
PERFORM READ-RELEASE-PARA
      VARYING COUNT FROM 1 BY 2
      UNTIL COUNT > 10.
```

How many times will READ-RELEASE-PARA be performed?

    a.   0
    b.   9
    c.   10
    d.   5
    e.   None of the above

6.11   What will the value of K be after the following code sequence is executed?

```
MOVE ZERO TO K.
PERFORM TOTAL-PARA VARYING M FROM 1 BY 1
        UNTIL M = 3.
TOTAL-PARA.
    COMPUTE K = K + 1.
```

Refer to the following COBOL statement to answer Exercises 6.12 and 6.13.

```
PERFORM PARA-ONE
        VARYING SUB FROM 1 BY 1
        UNTIL SUB > 10.
```

6.12   The final value of SUB will be _____.

6.13   How many times will PARA-ONE be performed?

6.14   The GO TO statement represents a direct COBOL implementation of

    a.   the sequential structure.
    b.   the unconditional branch.
    c.   the selection structure.
    d.   the case structure.

6.15   The PERFORM THRU statement allows _____ execution of multiple paragraphs.

    a.   selective
    b.   repetitive
    c.   sequential
    d.   no

6.16   Through which of the following statement(s) can the case structure be implemented?

    a.   A sequence of PERFORM statements.
    b.   Nested IF statements.
    c.   The PERFORM THRU statement.
    d.   The EVALUATE statement.

6.17   An invalid sign condition test is

    a.   zero.
    b.   numeric.
    c.   positive.
    d.   negative.

6.18   Which is not a logical operator for conditions?
    a.   NOT
    b.   AND
    c.   NO
    d.   OR

6.19   Which does not represent a simple relation?
    a.   A IS NUMERIC
    b.   A IS ZERO OR A IS POSITIVE
    c.   88 EOF-CUSTOMER VALUE "Y".
    d.   B > A

6.20   The EXIT statement
    a.   ends a nested IF.
    b.   provides an end point for a series of paragraphs.
    c.   terminates a program.
    d.   is a clause of the PERFORM statement.

6.21   A compound condition requires the use of
    a.   an AND.
    b.   a NOT.
    c.   an OR.
    d.   Any one of the above

6.22   Simple conditions fall into four main categories:
    a.   comparison, class, value, condition-names
    b.   relation, class, sign, condition-names
    c.   sign, condition-names, relation, hybrid
    d.   class, sign, condition-names, numeric

6.23   The PERFORM THRU statement using the EXIT option provides an alternative method of handling the priming read in COBOL. True or false?

6.24   The GO TO statement represents conditional branching. True or false?

6.25   Level 88 entries may:
    a.   specify the values that a particular conditonal variable may have
    b.   replace relation conditions.
    c.   improve readability.
    d.   none of the above
    e.   all of the above

6.26   Compound conditions can be formed by linking simple conditions with the logical operators:
    a.   AND, OR, NOT.
    b.   EITHER, OR , BOTH.
    c.   NOT, BUT, AND.
    d.   NEITHER, NOR, BOTH.

6.27   The PERFORM THRU statement imposes a _____ restriction on the _____ flow of control in a program.
    a.   sequential, physical
    b.   logical, actual
    c.   physical, logical

6.28 What is the truth value of the expression A OR NOT B, if condition A is false and condition B is true?

    a. True

    b. False

    c. need parentheses to determine value

6.29 The following code:

```
100-DETERMINE-REPORT-ACCESS.
        IF EMP-SECURITY-LEVEL = "STRATEGIC"
            AND STATUS = "ACTIVE"
            PERFORM 350-OPEN-ACCESS-ALL.
        IF EMP-SECURITY-LEVEL = "TACTICAL"
            AND STATUS = "ACTIVE"
            PERFORM 400-OPEN-ACCESS-HIGH.
        IF EMP-SECURITY-LEVEL = "OPERATIONAL"
            AND STATUS = "ACTIVE"
            PERFORM 450-OPEN-ACCESS-RESTRICTED.
        IF EMP-SECURITY-LEVEL = "MANAGERIAL"
            AND STATUS = "ACTIVE"
            PERFORM 500-OPEN-ACCESS-DAILY-ONLY.
```

characterizes which structure?

    a. nested IF statements

    b. case control

    c. unconditional branching

    d. A and C

    e. none of the above

6.30 The sign condition can also test a numeric item to determine if its value is zero (0). True or false?

6.31 Condition-names are ideal for representing external sources of control. True or false?

6.32 By using statements such as the GO TO and PERFORM THRU the programmer can avoid making design tradeoffs by using these more efficient and logical coding methods. True or false?

6.33 The PERFORM THRU can be negated by the use of the operator NOT in conjunction with the GO TO and EXIT statements. True or false?

6.34 The arithmetic operators become conditional statements if the _____ clause is used.

6.35 The class condition determines whether an item is _____ or

_____.

6.36 The _____ statement directly implements the case control structure.

6.37 The _____ statement permits the programmer to count the number of times a paragraph is repetitively executed.

6.38 Changing the flow of control from one location in the program to another is called

_____.

6.39   Statements that specify an action to be taken without condition are referred to as
        _____ statements.

6.40   In COBOL, the reserved word _____ reverses the truth value of a stated
        condition.

6.41   The _____ statement can be altered using several options to construct a
        wide variety of iteration structures.

6.42   Why is it necessary to use combinations of conditions to control the flow of logic in a
        program?

6.43   List five condition delimiters.

6.44   Of what importance is a period (.) to an IF statement?

6.45   Why should GO TO statements be used as a last possible resort in COBOL programming?

PROGRAM INTEGRITY

Integrity, as applied to a program, relates to the program's soundness and completeness. Program integrity ensures that a program operates correctly. It is achieved by obtaining a working program, then continuing to monitor its performance in a production environment. This implies that the program is debugged, that adequate controls have been designed into the programs to detect errors, that such errors are eliminated, and that system controls are applied during production to ensure that no errors go undetected.

Up to this time, the text has concentrated on the process of designing and coding programs. In this chapter, however, the emphasis is on obtaining a running program that functions correctly. Any errors that inhibit the running of a program must be removed, and compliance with the program specifications must be reviewed.

7.1   Program Testing

Testing determines a program's correctness. Programs must be tested to ensure that they meet their functional specifications and that they do not malfunction. Test data and test cases are devised to determine whether the data are processed correctly. This type of testing requires the cooperation of the user, who is most familiar with what the system is supposed to do. Some methods of "testing" can be employed even before a program has been coded. We have already mentioned the use of structured *walkthroughs* for this purpose. They can determine whether the system and its programs meet the functional specifications.

Once the program is coded, users can provide feedback on whether the results are what they really wanted or if things were omitted. Many unspoken assumptions are often made by both sides during the specification of requirements, and it is not until there are tangible results that shortcomings are identified. Testing does not *prove* that a program is error-free; it indicates only that reasonable attempts have been made to find errors or bugs in a program.

Testing is extremely important because it can prevent failures or erroneous results during routine production. Remember that the cost of correcting errors rises as a project enters later phases of its development life cycle. Improper testing during the programming phase always manifests itself in the maintenance phase. Not only will the cost to correct errors be much higher at this time, but the consequences of such errors may be more critical. Imagine a situation in which skimpy testing of a banking system results in an inability to balance the books. Considering that some states require that banks balance their books before opening the following day, the cost of correcting the program would include not only programmer and computer time but also any lost business that might result. Problems have a tendency to feed on themselves, and failures in testing reveal themselves at the most inopportune times. As Murphy's law summarizes, "Anything that can go wrong will go wrong, and at the worst possible time."

We have stressed the importance of modular design because it makes a system easier to understand and develop. However, modular design also simplifies testing and debugging.

7.1.1   Top-Down Testing

The philosophy of top-down testing is analogous to that of top-down design. If testing is segmented and carried out module by module, it is easier to isolate potential problems. For instance, if a program is composed of 32 modules and you are going to test the entire system, there are 32 places in which an error can occur. Finding where it first appears is complicated proportionately.

Bottom-up testing involves at least three levels of testing progressing from the most detailed to the most general. All individual modules are tested first. Then modules are grouped into subsystems and tested. This tests the compatibility of individual modules, that is, that the data generated by one module and used as input to another module are as expected. Finally, the system is tested as a whole. The main problem with bottom-up testing is that all modules must be coded before testing begins. Therefore, there is no feedback until the job has been completed. This leads to a disproportionate expenditure of resources at the end when deadlines are supposed to be met. The testing may become haphazard, and improper testing almost certainly results.

When the top-down approach is used, however, testing can begin much earlier. In fact, it may begin as soon as the modules have been defined. New test cases can be developed as modules are added. Top-down testing is more manageable and provides faster feedback. It serves as an early warning system to discover errors in the system design. Additionally, with a top-down approach, the framework of the system is tested early and can be demonstrated to the user for feedback.

Top-down testing concentrates on a module-by-module approach beginning with the top module in the hierarchy. It begins with the coding of the top module using *dummy modules* for subordinates. Dummy modules, also called *stubs*, are module shells that stand in for modules that have not yet been coded. They do little or no processing, or they may simulate the processing that would occur when coded. For example, if a dummy module is supposed to read three fields from a record, it can be programmed with three constants representing each field. In top-down testing it is enough for the dummy module to print its name or display a value to verify the accuracy of the higher modules and the flow of control. Figure 7.1 illustrates the use of stubs in top-down testing.

Figure 7.1 **Top-Down Testing Strategy**

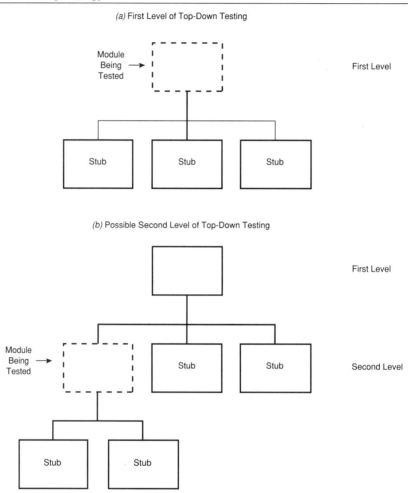

(a) First Level of Top-Down Testing

(b) Possible Second Level of Top-Down Testing

The choice of a module for the next level of testing is up to the programmer. For example, it might seem illogical to want to test the module that writes records out if the programmer has not yet read them in. On the other hand, it might enable the programmer to check the proposed report format and show it to the user. The strategy for choosing the next module to be tested is a personal choice, but it should be done piece by piece. Top-down testing is more a philosophy than a rigid methodology, so there should be flexibility in its implementation. It may be that some lower-level modules, such as reports, are necessary in order to have a good test. Thus, a programmer may still test components in isolation, especially if they perform complex logic. What is important to remember is that the interfaces between modules must also be tested.

One of the benefits of top-down testing is higher system or program reliability. As modules are added, the overall flow of control, especially of the higher-level modules, is tested and retested. Furthermore, the segmentation implied by this methodology makes it easier to locate an error because testing is done one module at a time.

7.1.2 Path Examination and Testing

A path in a program is a "route" taken by the program logic based on a combination of conditions that are met. For example, in Figure 7.2 we have identified six paths that the program can take based on whether an employee is salaried or receives hourly wages, earns commissions or not, and is enrolled in a health plan or not. Path A illustrates the path taken in the logic if an employee is salaried, receives commissions, and belongs to a health plan; B identifies a salaried employee who receives commissions but is not enrolled in a health plan; and C identifies a salaried employee who does not receive commissions and is enrolled in a health plan.

As you might guess, determining every path may be a very difficult task, especially when the program is large. It may be impossible to test every possible combination. At the very least, though, potentially troublesome paths should be identified and tested. These include paths that are contingent on a combination of conditions. For example, if only sales representatives receive transportation allowances, the payroll program should verify that the allowance is added to their pay only if the employees are salaried and on commission.

The iteration structure presents a special case of path determination, since the path taken may depend on which iteration is being executed. Always test the first and last iterations, since they will dictate that different processing logic be employed. Then test a middle iteration that outlines the normal logic path for all data in between. For example, the first time a program reads an input record it might be necessary to initialize a counter. For every subsequent iteration this counter might be incremented, and on the last iteration the counter value might be cross-checked to some predetermined value.

7.1.3 Test Plan

It is important to have a strategy for conducting the program testing. Work on this *test plan* can begin well in advance, when the programmers are still designing and coding their programs. Usually the user and the systems analyst generate the test plan, and much thought goes into designing the test cases.

First, the conditions to be tested in each module are documented. Ideally, the test plan should exercise all logic and paths in order to provide reasonable assurance that the program functions correctly. The plan should test one condition at a time and progress to more complex combinations. For example, care should be taken in testing editing procedures. Does the program catch all the data input errors or combinations of data input errors that might cause problems in later steps in the logic? Tests should check that fields are edited for appropriate character type. This prevents errors that happen when numbers and letters are added. Test that the values of important fields fall within given ranges and that values that should be positive are not negative. Test cases should also detect overflow and underflow conditions.

The next step is to create the test data and determine the output expected. Procedures for verifying the flow of control should first use valid data. Then "invalid" data that are designed to generate errors should test the program's reactions.

Figure 7.2   ***Path Determination***

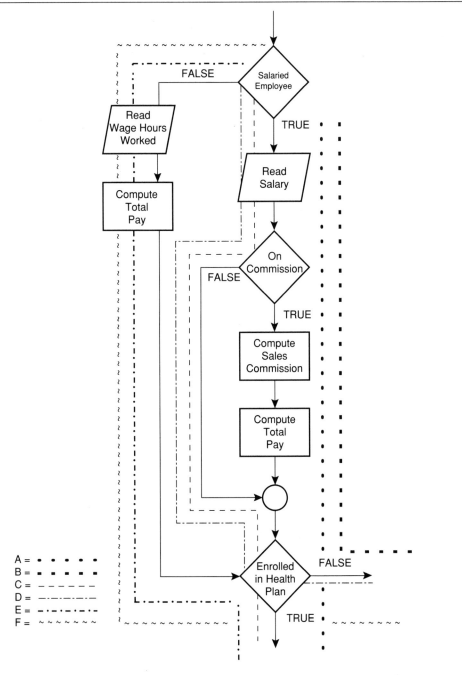

The third step should outline the actual testing procedures. Since commonly there is insufficient testing, the test plan should include multiple tests at various levels in the program structure. This can be incorporated into a top-down testing procedure. Test one or a few variables at a time by keeping others constant. In this way, cause-and-effect relationships can more easily be determined.

Compare actual test output with predicted output and document the results of the test. This may include output listings of sample runs with notes indicating whether the results are as expected or are incorrect. Listings of "before" and "after" file contents should be included with appropriate notes, too. The documentation should be reviewed either in a test walkthrough or by the person who will be in charge of the maintenance.

7.1.4   *Test Data*

The validity of a program test depends in great part on the test data used. Testing should start with valid data. Often it is possible to obtain existing data from current systems. Such data usually test typical conditions and make it easier to compare the actual results with predetermined results.

Exception conditions, however, are more likely to cause problems, and "bad" data should therefore be created to ensure that the program does not malfunction with such data. These data should test range limits. For example, how does a program that writes checks for paying suppliers handle a balance of $0.01? What is the upper bound? If nothing were owed, would the program write a check for $0.00? Often a good test of editing features is to have a novice user input the data to the program.

Test data should include very small, very large, and interim values for computations to test under- or overflows in resulting fields. The data should incorporate negative values, names with too many characters, and the like. For every test identified in the test plan, a good variety of test data should be available.

Some manufacturers provide utility programs that automatically generate test files based on parameters that describe the characteristics of the data. Test file generators should be used in conjunction with a representative sample of real data when at all possible. Some companies even maintain test-data banks or libraries that are used to test new programs or modifications to existing programs. This is especially useful where programs share data and are therefore interdependent. For example, an order entry program and an inventory management program both use and manipulate data on an inventory file. The test data generated to validate one program should prove useful in evaluating the other one.

7.2   *Debugging*

In the first part of this chapter we assumed that the programs had successfully compiled and run to normal termination, that is, that they did not end forcibly by intervention of the operating system. But getting a program to run is not always an easy task. In earlier chapters some debugging basics were presented. In this section we expand on these basics to build up your debugging skills. We will discuss some tools and techniques that help locate and correct two types of errors or bugs: those that prevent the program from running and those that yield erroneous results.

The greatest contributor to successful debugging is attitude. Programmers are renowned for their optimism. They believe that their programs cannot possibly have errors and that if something is amiss, it must surely be a problem with the hardware or the software. Such optimism is commendable. But the reality is that, except in the rarest of cases, it is the programs that have errors. A programmer who does not expect errors will not find them, and debugging will be a frustrating experience. Such a programmer will struggle through the debugging chore with little satisfaction, collecting perceived feedback to reinforce his preconceived notion. If, however, a programmer approaches debugging with an open mind, he can more easily detect and locate errors. Debugging is a challenge. But it can be tackled systematically much as a detective devises a scheme to solve a mystery. This implies that the programmer should develop a plan to deal with each error, carry it out, and document it.

The Golden Rule of debugging is to keep things simple. This means that the simple errors should be corrected first and also that errors should be tackled one at a time. Not only will this clear up many seemingly unrelated problems, but it will reinforce your positive attitude. Furthermore, as debugging tools and techniques become more powerful, they also become more complex, often requiring that the user learn how to use them and interpret their results. Therefore, always exhaust the simpler alternatives before progressing up the debugging aids ladder.

Documentation should be an integral part of debugging. This allows you to keep a record of problems you have encountered and their solutions. A simple debugging journal is adequate. It should describe a problem, note the fix, and detail any other worthwhile information. Figure 7.3 illustrates a sample entry from a debugging journal. Debugging tools and techniques will be explored in the context of three common cases of errors: compilation-time errors, run-time errors, and logic errors.

7.2.1   *Compilation-Time Errors*

In general, COBOL compilers detect and flag *compilation-time errors*, such as syntax errors and file usage errors. They also issue warnings about items that may present problems during execution but which are syntactically correct. Most of these errors are usually displayed or printed at the end of the listing of the compiled program. They usually denote the source-program line number where the error occurred along with a brief explanation of the error. Syntax errors are best explored in your computer system's COBOL documentation.

7.2.2   *Run-Time Errors*

Errors that occur during the execution of an already compiled program are known as *run-time errors*. Run-time errors cause premature termination of a program. Messages relating to such errors may be issued either by the compiler or by the operating system under which the compiler runs. Messages may range from a cryptic error code that must be looked up in the reference manual to a comprehensive message with obvious meaning.

A common symptom of run-time errors is that a program runs fine until the error occurs. By analyzing whatever output the program was able to generate, you may spot some clues. For example, if a payroll program appears to be performing payroll computations correctly until it tries to divide by the number of months, that might be a clue that the problem is in the division operation.

Figure 7.3   Entry in Debugging Journal

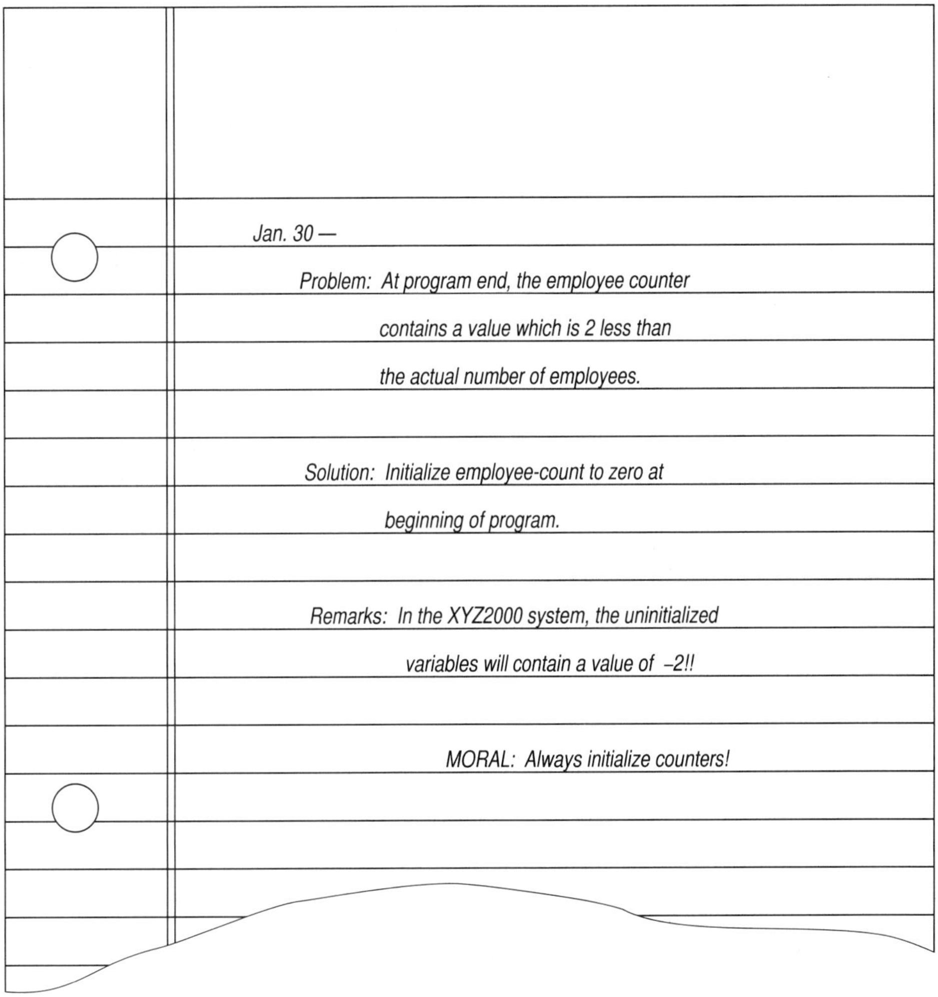

Jan. 30 —

> *Problem: At program end, the employee counter*
>
> *contains a value which is 2 less than*
>
> *the actual number of employees.*

> *Solution: Initialize employee-count to zero at*
>
> *beginning of program.*

> *Remarks: In the XYZ2000 system, the uninitialized*
>
> *variables will contain a value of –2!!*

> *MORAL: Always initialize counters!*

Run-time errors may seem more complex to resolve than syntax errors. However, such errors are usually caused by rule violations. A common violation is the *data exception* caused when arithmetic operations are attempted on nonnumeric data. Another violation that occurs during division usually involves an attempt to divide by zero. Overflows occur when a numeric result is too large for the receiving field. Underflows occur when the number is too small to be stored. Other common causes of run-time errors result from attempting some illegal operation, for example, attempting to access a file before it is opened or trying to read past the end of the file.

7.2.3   Logic Errors

Logic errors occur when the program runs to a normal termination but the output does not match the predicted output. These errors are the most challenging to debug. We begin by offering some techniques you should employ before considering the use of advanced debugging tools. You can probably debug your entire program by using your source code and flowcharts rather than a listing of the contents of memory.

Organize and plan a strategy. Concentrate on debugging one module at a time, beginning at the highest level. Try applying the system life cycle approach to your debugging. First you must identify the problem. It is important to wade through the symptoms or effect of the problem in order to discover the cause. Gather data about the problem. Check the obvious sources: hierarchy chart, flowcharts, program listing, output listings. They will provide you with the clues. Always work with the most recent copy of any documentation.

Analyze the data to identify where the error originated. For example, if the problem is that garbage is being printed for a certain field, it probably indicates that the field contained garbage before it was even printed. By studying your code, you might discover that you failed to move the field from a given record. When stepping through the program logic, use a "worksheet" to keep track of suspect variables, tables or arrays, indexes, and subscripts. It need not be a fancy form, just a sheet of paper to facilitate your tracking plan. It might look something like Figure 7.4, a crude form of tracing items manually that works very well. This is done by following the code and filling in the values of the variables as they are changed. As with most debugging tools, the debugging worksheet is designed to aid in identifying the location of an error.

Once it is located, design a fix for the bug. Review the revised program logic and do not forget to incorporate the change into the N-S charts. Change one thing at a time so that you can identify cause-and-effect relationships. If a substantial number of changes have to be made to correct some error, consider rewriting the module. Then pencil in the code on your source listing and save that version. Some fixes have a way of making things worse. By saving your old version, you can always backtrack.

Be sure you have a current listing of the source program to work with. Write in the changes you are going to make on the listing. If it is impractical to get a program listing every time you compile your program, write the next set of corrections in a different color of pencil. This way you can tell what version of changes you are on. As soon as your program listing starts getting hard to read, however, get a new listing. You should also get a new listing if you fix the problem.

When making changes to a program be aware that there is no such thing as a nonconsequential change. Any change in the logic alters the way the computer executes your program. The result may be obvious or may seem not to manifest itself at all. Many programmers who thought "that little line I added couldn't possibly have changed anything!" have been drastically wrong.

Once the bug is fixed, document it in your debugging journal. Nothing is more frustrating than facing a bug seen and fixed before and not remembering the solution! Be sure that all program documentation reflects the changes made to fix the problem, including hierarchy charts and logic charts.

Learn your limitations. If you have made an honest effort to debug your program and still cannot fix it, get help from a friend. Make sure you have the most recent listing of your program code, output, error messages, N-S charts, and hierarchy charts. It is a waste of the other person's time for you to come unprepared. Have a hypothesis about what the error is and a summary of the fixes you have tried and the results.

Figure 7.4 **"Worksheet" for Keeping Track of Suspect Data Items**

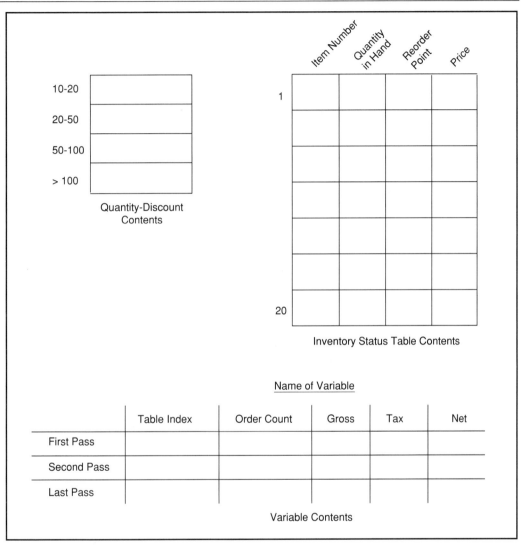

Sit down with your friend and walk through your logic, preferably at the highest level possible. For example, you might start with your hierarchy chart first. Logic errors are more easily detected when uncluttered by language specifics. Remember the rule about trying the simpler techniques first. Continue your walkthrough to the program listing if necessary. You will be surprised at how your own thinking becomes clearer when you have to explain your logic to someone else. More often than not, you will fix your own bug. If not, another person's perspective is bound to help.

If program-related possibilities are ruled out and the above sources yield no result, consult the system's technical personnel armed with meaningful documentation. If they locate a bug in the program, they have helped to solve the problem. If they locate a system fault, they will certainly be impressed with your deductive capabilities and organized detective work.

7.2.4   Debugging Aids

The following section surveys some of the more common debugging tools that exist as packages, or whose capabilities we can simulate by using ingenuity and a few common COBOL statements. We will use an example program containing a logic error and nondescript paragraph- and data-names to demonstrate the use of these tools and techniques in identifying the error. The purpose of the program is to make name tags to identify attendees at a party. The first and last names of those invited to the party are stored in a sequential file. There are two name labels per row on our output medium. Figure 7.5 shows the hierarchy chart for the program. Figure 7.6 shows the Nassi-Schneiderman charts for the modules "100-Read-Name-File", "200-Process", "210-Report", and "220-Print". Figure 7.7 shows the source listing of the program. The output obtained on a trial run with more than one name on the file is:

```
HELLO, MY NAME IS
SAM        JOHNSON
```

Notice that only one name tag was printed. Thus, there is an error.

Figure 7.5   **Hierarchy Chart for the "Party Labels" Program**

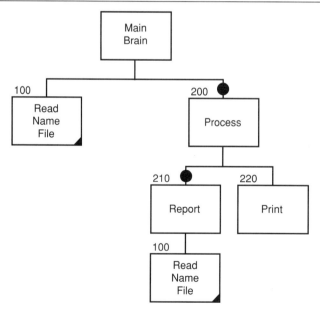

Figure 7.6   ***N-S Charts for the "Party Labels" Program***

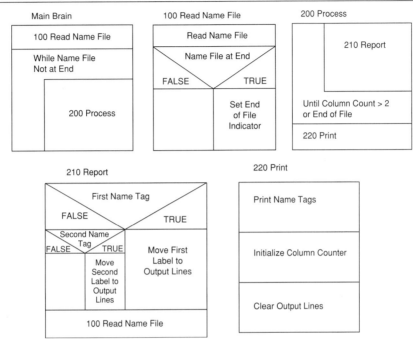

Figure 7.7   ***COBOL Listing of the "Party Labels" Program***

```
 1 IDENTIFICATION DIVISION
 2
 3 PROGRAM-ID. PARTY-LABELS.
 4 AUTHOR. AJT.
 5 DATE-COMPILED. 02-Sep-92 07:40.
 6
 7
 8 ENVIRONMENT DIVISION.
 9
10 CONFIGURATION SECTION.
11
12 SOURCE-COMPUTER. GENERIC-COMPUTER.
13 OBJECT-COMPUTER. GENERIC-COMPUTER.
14
15 INPUT-OUTPUT SECTION.
16
17 FILE-CONTROL.
```

Figure 7.7   *(continued)*

```
18        SELECT NAME-FILE  ASSIGN TO S-INPUT.
19        SELECT PRINT-FILE ASSIGN TO S-OUTPUT.
20
21
22 DATA DIVISION.
23
24 FILE SECTION.
25
26 FD   NAME-FILE
27      LABEL RECORDS ARE STANDARD.
28
29 01   NAME-REC.
30      05  IN-LAST                       PIC X(9).
31      05  IN-FIRST                      PIC X(9).
32
33 FD   PRINT-FILE
34      LABEL RECORDS ARE STANDARD.
35
36 01   PRINT-REC                         PIC X(80).
37
38 WORKING-STORAGE SECTION.
39
40 01   COL-COUNT       PIC 9      VALUE 1.
41 01   HELLO-MSG       PIC X(20)  VALUE "HELLO, MY NAME IS:  ".
42 01   EOF-FLAG        PIC X      VALUE "N".
43
44 01   DETAIL-1.
45      05  FILLER                        PIC X(10)  VALUE SPACES.
46      05  OUT-HELLO-1                   PIC X(20).
47      05  FILLER                        PIC X(20)  VALUE SPACES.
48      05  OUT-HELLO-2                   PIC X(20).
49      05  FILLER                        PIC X(10)  VALUE SPACES.
50
51 01   DETAIL-2.
52      05  FILLER                        PIC X(10)  VALUE SPACES.
53      05  OUT-FIRST-1                   PIC X(10).
54      05  OUT-LAST-1                    PIC X(10).
55      05  FILLER                        PIC X(20)  VALUE SPACES.
56      05  OUT-FIRST-2                   PIC X(10).
57      05  OUT-LAST-2                    PIC X(10).
58      05  FILLER                        PIC X(10)  VALUE SPACES.
59
```

Figure 7.7   *(continued)*

```
60
61 PROCEDURE DIVISION.
62
63 MAIN-BRAIN.
64     OPEN INPUT NAME-FILE.
65     OPEN OUTPUT PRINT-FILE.
66     PERFORM 100-READ-NAME-FILE.
67     PERFORM 200-PROCESS UNTIL EOF-FLAG = "Y".
68     CLOSE NAME-FILE.
69     CLOSE PRINT-FILE.
70     STOP RUN.
71
72 100-READ-NAME-FILE.
73     READ NAME-FILE AT END MOVE "Y" TO EOF-FLAG.
74
75 200-PROCESS.
76     PERFORM 210-REPORT UNTIL COL-COUNT > 2 OR EOF-FLAG = "Y".
77     PERFORM 220-PRINT.
78
79 210-REPORT.
80     IF COL-COUNT = 1
81         MOVE HELLO-MSG TO OUT-HELLO-1
82         MOVE IN-FIRST  TO OUT-FIRST-1
83         MOVE IN-LAST   TO OUT-LAST-1
84     ELSE
85         IF COL-COUNT = 2
86             MOVE HELLO-MSG TO OUT-HELLO-2
87             MOVE IN-FIRST  TO OUT-FIRST-2
88             MOVE IN-LAST   TO OUT-LAST-2.
89     PERFORM 100-READ-NAME-FILE.
90
91 220-PRINT.
92     WRITE PRINT-REC FROM DETAIL-1 AFTER 4.
93     WRITE PRINT-REC FROM DETAIL-2 AFTER 2.
94     MOVE 1 TO COL-COUNT.
95     MOVE SPACES TO DETAIL-1
96                    DETAIL-2.
```

Cross-References. Many compilers have a feature that makes *cross-references*, that is, it allows the programmer to display a list of all the paragraphs that make reference to a data-name or a paragraph-name. Once you have identified the data-name or paragraph-name that might be causing the problem, this feature can help you find every place in the program where it is used.

Thus, not only can you locate where the problem originates, but also what secondary effects it might have. Figure 7.8 shows a cross-reference listing for the program in Figure 7.7. For each data item, it first lists the line number and column where it is defined, followed by the line numbers of the statements where the item is referenced. A similar notation is used for cross-referencing paragraph-names. Note that some items have been defined but are not used. This may be important in your debugging task.

Figure 7.8   *Cross Reference Listing of the "Party Labels" Program*

```
                                CROSS-REFERENCE DICTIONARY

        DATA NAMES                DEFINE    REFERENCE


        NAME-FILE                 000018    000064    000068    000073
        NAME-REC                  000029
        IN-LAST                   000030    000083    000088
        IN-FIRST                  000031    000082    000087
        PRINT-FILE                000019    000065    000069    000092    000093
        PRINT-REC                 000036    000092    000093
        COL-COUNT                 000040    000076    000080    000085    000094
        HELLO-MSG                 000041    000081    000086
        EOF-FLAG                  000042    000067    000073    000076
        DETAIL-1                  000044    000092    000095
        OUT-HELLO-1               000046    000081
        OUT-HELLO-2               000048    000086
        DETAIL-2                  000051    000093    000095
        OUT-FIRST-1               000053    000082
        OUT-LAST-1                000054    000083
        OUT-FIRST-2               000056    000087
        OUT-LAST-2                000057    000088


        PROCEDURE NAMES           DEFINE    REFERENCE


        MAIN-BRAIN                000063
        100-READ-NAME-FILE        000072    000066    000089
        200-PROCESS               000075    000067
        210-REPORT                000079    000076
        220-PRINT                 000091    000077
```

Program Traces. Often compilers also have a *trace* capability that lists the paragraph names in the order in which they are executed. If this feature is not available on your system, you can make your own trace. Within each paragraph include some code that will print out the name of the paragraph or some message to indicate that control has passed to this point.

By following the trace, you know exactly which paragraphs are performed, how many times, and in what order. When testing the flow of control in your program, you might find it useful to compare a trace with your hierarchy chart. You can also use the trace to cross-check the control structures in your N-S chart. You can then use it to check problem areas. For example, if an iteration is to be executed 10 times, are there 10 instances of the paragraph name? If not, did the program stop too soon or too late?

A trace also offers clues about which paragraphs are not performed. If the program is supposed to print an error message but no message appears on the output, you might use a trace to find out if the paragraph that writes the error message was executed or not. Similar reasoning will be used to debug the program in Figure 7.7.

Figure 7.9 shows a trace of the program in Figure 7.7. Notice that control is passed to paragraph 220-PRINT only once. This accounts for the fact that only one name tag was printed. According to the N-S chart of the module "200-Process", module "220-Print" should be performed when the variable COL-COUNT is greater than two or when the end of the input file is reached. Since the trace shows many executions of paragraph 100-READ-NAME-FILE, we can rule out that the input file contained only one record. Therefore, the variable COL-COUNT is a suspect in the logic error. By consulting the cross-reference in Figure 7.8, we can find out where the variable is used.

Figure 7.9   *Trace of the "Party Labels" Program*

```
****   TRACE ON   ****
100-READ-NAME-FILE
200-PROCESS
210-REPORT
100-READ-NAME-FILE
210-REPORT
100-READ-NAME-FILE
210-REPORT
100-READ-NAME-FILE
210-REPORT
100-READ-NAME-FILE
210-REPORT
100-READ-NAME-FILE
210-REPORT
100-READ-NAME-FILE
210-REPORT
100-READ-NAME-FILE
300-PRINT
****  TRACE CLOSED  ****
```

Information Display. Another debugging technique that is fairly simple to use is to display the values of data items that are communicated between modules or variables that are tested in conditional statements. This is especially helpful when you have identified the variables that may be causing problems.

Since we determined that the variable COL-COUNT is a potential culprit for the nonexecution of paragraph 220-PRINT, we might want to display its value whenever control passes to paragraph 210-REPORT. The code alterations required to display the variable are:

```
210-REPORT.
DISPLAY "*** COL-COUNT= " COL-COUNT.
IF COL-COUNT = 1
        MOVE HELLO-MSG TO OUT-HELLO1
        MOVE IN-FIRST  TO OUT-FIRST-1
        MOVE IN-LAST   TO OUT-LAST-1
ELSE
        IF COL-COUNT = 2
                MOVE HELLO-MSG TO OUT-HELLO2
                MOVE IN-FIRST  TO OUT-FIRST-2
                MOVE IN-LAST   TO OUT-LAST-2.
        PERFORM 100-READ-NAME-FILE.
```

The resulting display would be:

```
*** COL-COUNT = 1
*** COL-COUNT = 1
*** COL-COUNT = 1
*** COL-COUNT = 1
*** COL-COUNT = 1
*** COL-COUNT = 1
*** COL-COUNT = 1
```

Notice that its value is always 1. COL-COUNT is not being incremented; therefore, it will never be greater than 1. This explains why paragraph 220-PRINT is executed only once when the end of the file is reached. The solution is reflected in the corrected N-S chart shown in Figure 7.10 and in the corrected code in Figure 7.11. Figure 7.12 shows the trace generated by the corrected program, and Figure 7.13 shows the correct output.

Figure 7.10   Revised Flowchart of Module "210-Report"

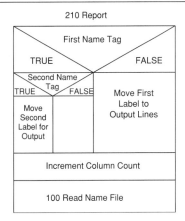

Figure 7.11   COBOL Code to Fix Error in the "Party Labels" Program

```
59
60
61 PROCEDURE DIVISION.
62
63 MAIN-BRAIN.
64     OPEN INPUT NAME-FILE.
65     OPEN OUTPUT PRINT-FILE.
66     PERFORM 100-READ-NAME-FILE.
67     PERFORM 200-PROCESS UNTIL EOF-FLAG = "Y".
68     CLOSE NAME-FILE.
69     CLOSE PRINT-FILE.
70     STOP RUN.
71
72 100-READ-NAME-FILE.
73     READ NAME-FILE AT END MOVE "Y" TO EOF-FLAG.
74
75 200-PROCESS.
76     PERFORM 210-REPORT UNTIL COL-COUNT > 2 OR EOF-FLAG = "Y".
77     PERFORM 220-PRINT.
78
79 210-REPORT.
80     IF COL-COUNT = 1
81         MOVE HELLO-MSG TO OUT-HELLO-1
82         MOVE IN-FIRST  TO OUT-FIRST-1
83         MOVE IN-LAST   TO OUT-LAST-1
```

Figure 7.11   (continued)

```
 84     ELSE
 85        IF COL-COUNT = 2
 86              MOVE HELLO-MSG TO OUT-HELLO-2
 87              MOVE IN-FIRST  TO OUT-FIRST-2
 88              MOVE IN-LAST   TO OUT-LAST-2.
 89     ADD 1 TO COL-COUNT.
 90     PERFORM 100-READ-NAME-FILE.
 91
 92 220-PRINT.
 93     WRITE PRINT-REC FROM DETAIL-1 AFTER 4.
 94     WRITE PRINT-REC FROM DETAIL-2 AFTER 2.
 95     MOVE 1 TO COL-COUNT.
 96     MOVE SPACES TO DETAIL-1
 97                    DETAIL-2.
```

➔ points to line 89

Figure 7.12   Trace of Corrected "Party Labels" Program

```
            ****   TRACE ON   ****
            100-READ-NAME-FILE
            200-PROCESS
            210-REPORT
            100-READ-NAME-FILE
            210-REPORT
            100-READ-NAME-FILE
            300-PRINT
            200-PROCESS
            210-REPORT
            100-READ-NAME-FILE
            210-REPORT
            100-READ-NAME-FILE
            300-PRINT
            200-PROCESS
            210-REPORT
            100-READ-NAME-FILE
            210-REPORT
            100-READ-NAME-FILE
            300-PRINT
            200-PROCESS
            210-REPORT
            100-READ-NAME-FILE
            300-PRINT
            **** TRACE CLOSED ****
```

Figure 7.13   *Correct Output of the "Party Labels" Program*

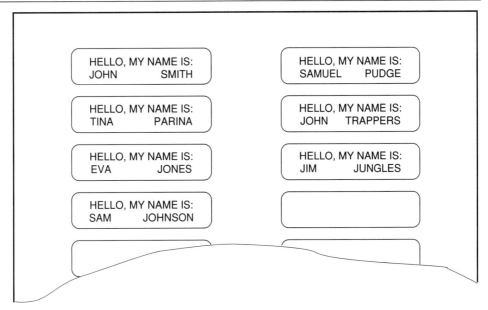

Before inserting DISPLAY statements generously throughout your program, keep in mind that you will have to interpret the output you generate. In other words, exercise common sense when displaying values. As always, plan your strategy. For example, if you have determined that "Net Pay" is a questionable variable, do you need to display both "Gross Pay" and "Deductions"? Do you need to display this variable in every paragraph that references it, or have you localized the problem to the "Net Pay" computation? When you display values, be sure to add some clarifying message such as "Gross Pay coming in to 100-Calculate-Net-Pay = " or "EOF flag is: ". Data are helpful only when they are meaningful and understandable.

Displaying the values of variables may soon generate much unneeded output. This is often true where there are nested iterations. One way to limit your output is to display values conditionally. Using DISPLAYs in this fashion is a simple application of the principle of "management-by-exception." For example, if errors are arising only for salaried employees, you may wish to display only the values associated with the salaried employees as follows:

```
IF SALARIED DISPLAY "NET PAY = " NET-PAY
```

If your report is exceeding the page size, you might want to display the line count by putting a DISPLAY of the line counter where the line count is tested for page controls:

```
DISPLAY "LINE COUNT" LINE-COUNT.
IF LINE-COUNT > THAN 55
     PERFORM 4130-NEW-PAGE.
```

Although we referred to printer output, other media might be better suited for displaying the desired values. For example, if the amount of output is relatively small, you might want it sent to the terminal screen. On the other hand, if the amount of output is very large, it is wise to send it to a disk file. This would have an added advantage: you could later browse through it and selectively print whatever you found helpful. Once your program is debugged, be sure to remove unnecessary DISPLAY statements from your program.

Interactive Debugging Features. Some systems offer software packages that facilitate debugging and may be used independently of the compiler or in conjunction with it. If you do not have access to such a debugging aid, it is possible to simulate some of its features using common COBOL statements or the COBOL debugging features. Interactive debuggers accept and display information in a conversational mode. They allow the programmer to control the execution of a program, set breakpoints, examine, and even change data values.

Breakpoints specify the location in the program where execution is to be suspended temporarily to allow other debugging commands to be used. This can be a particular line number or a particular paragraph. When the program's execution is suspended, the programmer can display the contents of a data item, change it, set a trace mode on, or turn the trace mode off. Then he can command the debugger to resume execution of the program.

Some debuggers allow the execution of a program to proceed statement by statement or paragraph by paragraph, or to continue until the next breakpoint. The programmer may even be able to specify at what location to resume execution, in essence altering the normal order of execution.

In the absence of such a ready-made tool, a programmer may construct a rudimentary debugger by using DISPLAY and ACCEPT statements. The programmer can set breakpoints through the use of ACCEPTs. An ACCEPT statement will halt the execution of the program and wait for input, thus setting breakpoints indirectly. Programmed breakpoints can be executed conditionally or unconditionally. Data must be input before execution is continued. We discussed the use of the DISPLAY statement for displaying the value of a data item or for generating a trace in the previous section.

Snapshots and Dumps. A *dump* is a listing of the contents of memory used by the program when the program terminates abnormally. It provides the memory addresses and contents of all program data and instructions and information on the state of a program at the time of termination. It also provides key information on the state of the system at the time the program terminated abnormally, such as the type of fault causing the termination or the instruction that caused the termination. Some systems even allow dumping selected parts of memory. A snapshot may be thought of as a dynamic dump taken during program execution. It provides much of the same information as the dump. Snapshots, however, can be obtained at different times during the execution, providing a trail of the state of the system and the program every time it is invoked.

Although they are comprehensive debugging tools, dumps and snapshots are not easy to interpret. Often the memory contents are printed as octal or hexadecimal numbers, making them even more difficult to read. "Reading" dumps requires training. Their use is best exploited by system programmers and software developers. Even trained COBOL programmers use them only after they have exhausted simpler tools.

7.3   The COBOL Debugging Feature

ANS COBOL has standard debugging features that are implemented to varying degrees on different computer systems. Because of the hardware dependency of the COBOL debugger implementation and the lack of inherent interactivity afforded by it, few systems utilize the entire range of debugging features recommended by ANS COBOL standards. With such restrictions, many vendors use their own debugging packages to handle COBOL debugging. Some, however, have implemented a large portion of the COBOL debugger, and more will probably do so in the future. Thus, it is advantageous to understand the use of the COBOL debugger, even though most of its features can be duplicated with the techniques mentioned earlier.

7.3.1   Debugging Lines

Currently, much of the information required during debugging sessions is obtained through the use of extra statements included in the program. These usually simulate a trace feature or display certain values. The difficulties involved with such a technique include the identification and removal of these extra statements once the debugging tasks are completed. This task is simplified if the statements are identified. But what if these statements could be left in the program and not be executed after it had been debugged? This would further simplify matters. COBOL debugging lines accomplish just this. They are activated only when the programmer specifies and are ignored the rest of the time.

A debugging line is a line of code that contains a D in column 7, the comment column. Debugging lines are treated as comment entries under normal compilation and therefore are not executed. The line of code would not be compiled unless the program were set in *debugging mode*. This can be accomplished by adding the clause WITH DEBUGGING MODE to the SOURCE-COMPUTER paragraph in the ENVIRONMENT DIVISION. Its format is:

SOURCE-COMPUTER computer-name [WITH DEBUGGING MODE].

When the DEBUGGING MODE clause appears in the SOURCE-COMPUTER paragraph, the lines of code with a D in column 7 are compiled and treated as executable statements. When the clause is removed, the lines of code with the D are treated as comments and not as executable statements.

This COBOL debugging feature gives the programmer the luxury of integrating debugging code in a program, to be activated with a single clause. This is very convenient in case the debugging code is needed later when enhancements or modifications are being made. To deactivate the debugging lines once the program is debugged, the programmer merely alters a single line of code (the SOURCE-COMPUTER line) and recompiles the program. The disadvantage of the method is that the code may be cluttered with debugging statements that must be properly documented.

7.3.2   Debugging Sections

Although debugging lines are implemented on many machines, the implementation of debugging sections is less common. *Debugging sections* allow programmers to create separate regions of code that will perform the debugging tasks. This allows the programmer to create elaborate debugging reports and eliminates the need to clutter the source code with scattered debugging lines. Debugging sections allow the program to monitor files, paragraphs, and data items in the same fashion as the display statements and traces. Certain computer installations require special operating system commands in order to execute debugging sections. The programmer will have to examine the vendor-supplied documentation to find out how to establish the debugging sections.

Developing a Trace. The debugging sections may be established to monitor the execution of one or more paragraphs. This is similar to a trace. When the traced paragraph(s) are encountered, the execution of the program is changed to permit it to store certain values about the state of the program and to execute any special statements specified by the programmer. The program then continues, executing the instructions specified by the paragraph being traced. Thus, by using debugging sections, the programmer may code the necessary steps to produce a trace.

In this section we will discuss how you can trace your program by setting up the correct debugging sections. The simplified format for doing this is:

```
PROCEDURE DIVISION.
DECLARATIVES.
section-name   SECTION.              ⎧ [ALL] data-name-1 ⎫
                                     ⎪ file-name-1       ⎪
     USE FOR DEBUGGING ON            ⎨                   ⎬
                                     ⎪ procedure-name-1  ⎪
                                     ⎩ ALL PROCEDURES    ⎭
END DECLARATIVES.
```

All debugging sections are specified following the reserved word DECLARATIVES. Section-name is the name assigned to the debugging section. Data-name-1 denotes the name of the data item to be traced, file-name-1 the file to be traced, and procedure-name-1 the paragraph or section to be traced. The reserved word ALL implies that all occurrences of the data-name-1 are to be traced. ALL PROCEDURES implies that all paragraphs and sections are to be traced. The reserved words END DECLARATIVES end this special group of instructions.

Figure 7.14 shows how the trace would be set up for the program in Figure 7.11. The debugging section named GENERATE-A-TRACE SECTION produces a trace of all paragraphs or sections in the party label program. It is the first line of code following the word DECLARATIVES. For tracing one or more paragraphs the only sentence that appears following the section-name is the USE statement. In this context the format and rules are:

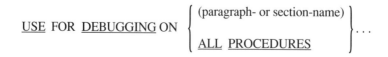

1. One or more paragraphs or sections may be specified.
2. ALL PROCEDURES sets the USE for every paragraph and section.

The establishment of the debugging section does not automatically display the paragraph names for the programmer. All displays are under the control of the programmer. Therefore, he may display only the name of the paragraph being executed, or he might format a whole debugging report to display them. This would be done by coding as many paragraphs as needed to accomplish this task within the debugging section. Each time the computer executes the paragraph(s) or section(s) being traced, the program transfers control to the associated debugging section, executes the entire section, and returns control to the normal flow of execution. In Figure 7.14 only the paragraph name is printed by the PRINT-PARAGRAPH-NAMES paragraph when the GENERATE-A-TRACE SECTION is executed. When DECLARATIVES are specified in a program, a section name must be specified to identify the rest of the program code. In the example, BEGIN-NAME-TAG denotes where the rest of the program starts. The normal program code appears following this header.

Figure 7.14   **Developing a Trace Using a Debugging Section**

```
PROCEDURE DIVISION.

DECLARATIVES.

GENERATE-A-TRACE SECTION.
    USE FOR DEBUGGING ALL PROCEDURES.
PRINT-PARAGRAPH-NAMES.
    IF DEBUG-CONTENTS NOT = "USE PROCEDURE"
        DISPLAY DEBUG-NAME

END DECLARATIVES.
BEGIN-NAME-TAG SECTION.
                    .
                    .
                    .
        (remainder of program code unchanged)
                    .
                    .
                    .
```

The names of the paragraphs are stored in a system-defined data item named DEBUG-NAME. Figure 7.14 illustrates an example of how DEBUG-NAME is used to display the name of the paragraphs being traced. DEBUG-NAME is a COBOL reserved word and may not be used by the programmer as one of the data items in the DATA DIVISION. DEBUG-NAME is part of a larger data group named DEBUG-ITEM, whose implicit system-defined description is:

```
01 DEBUG-ITEM.
02 DEBUG-LINE            PIC     X(6).
02 FILLER               PIC     X VALUE SPACE.
02 DEBUG-NAME           PIC     X(30).
02 FILLER               PIC     X VALUE SPACE.
02 DEBUG-SUB-1          PIC     S9999
                        SIGN IS LEADING SEPARATE CHARACTER.

02 FILLER               PIC     X VALUE SPACE.
02 DEBUG-SUB-2          PIC     S9999
                        SIGN IS LEADING SEPARATE CHARACTER.

02 FILLER               PIC     X VALUE SPACE.
02 DEBUG-SUB-3          PIC     S9999
                        SIGN IS LEADING SEPARATE CHARACTER.

02 FILLER               PIC     X VALUE SPACE.
02 DEBUG-CONTENTS PIC    X(*).
(* = VARIES BY SYSTEM AND APPLICATION)
```

When debugging sections are used in a program, the system automatically reserves the memory positions needed for DEBUG-ITEM in the format specified. Furthermore, its fields may only be accessed in the debugging sections. When a debugging section is executed, the fields of DEBUG-ITEM are filled automatically. For a USE procedure, DEBUG-LINE identifies the statement that caused execution of the USE procedure, DEBUG-NAME contains the name of the procedure, and DEBUG-CONTENTS contains the literal "USE PROCEDURE." Their contents vary with the type of element being debugged. Figure 7.15 specifies the contents of DEBUG-ITEM when the program is monitoring procedures.

Figure 7.15   *Actions Taken During Execution of a Debugging Section to Monitor Procedures*

When a procedure being monitored is executed, the following happens:

1. DEBUG-ITEM is filled as follows:
    a. Spaces are assigned to DEBUG-SUB-1, DEBUG-SUB-2, and DEBUG-SUB-3.
    b. The procedure name is assigned to DEBUG-NAME.
    c. The reason, or the control structure, is assigned to DEBUG-CONTENTS according to the table:

Debug Contents	Reason
1. "START PROGRAM"	First nondeclarative procedure is executed
2. "SORT INPUT" or "SORT OUTPUT"	INPUT or OUTPUT procedure of a SORT is executed
3. "PERFORM LOOP"	A PERFORM statement executed the procedure
4. "SPACES"	A GO TO caused the procedure to execute
5. "USE PROCEDURE"	A debug section was executed
6. " FALL THROUGH"	A procedure sequentially follows the end of a previous procedure

   d. The line number of the statement that transferred control to the procedure is assigned to DEBUG-LINE.
2. The associated debugging section is executed.
3. Control returns to the start of the procedure.

Monitoring a File. A debugging section may be used to monitor a file. In such a case, the USE FOR DEBUGGING statement would specify the files to be monitored. The format and actions of the USE FOR DEBUGGING statement for this purpose are:

USE FOR DEBUGGING ON {file-name-1}. . .

1. When an OPEN, CLOSE, DELETE, START, or READ statement is executed without finding the end of file, the DEBUGGING SECTION is executed.
2. DEBUG-ITEM is updated as follows:
    a. DEBUG-ITEM identifies the source statement that referenced the file.
    b. DEBUG-NAME contains the name of the file.
    c. DEBUG-CONTENTS is blank unless a READ was issued, in which case the record contents are stored.
3. Control returns to the statement following the statement that caused the DEBUG SECTION to execute.

The debugging section is established in the same fashion as in the example for monitoring paragraphs. Files are often monitored in order to examine the contents of certain input records.

Monitoring a Data Item. The USE FOR DEBUGGING statement may also be employed to monitor a specific data item by displaying its contents. The debugging section will be executed whenever the data-name specified is changed or referenced in the program. If only the data-name of the item being monitored is specified, the debugging section will be executed only when the data-name is explicitly written in the statement being executed, as in a MOVE statement. The format and actions for this use of the USE FOR DEBUGGING statement are:

USE FOR DEBUGGING ON [ALL REFERENCES OF] data-name-1 . . .

1. The ALL REFERENCES option causes the DEBUG section to be executed before any WRITE statement explicitly references the data item and after the execution of any other statement that explicitly references the data item.
2. DEBUG-ITEM is set to contain:
   a. the source statement number in DEBUG-LINE
   b. the data item name in DEBUG-NAME
   c. the value in DEBUG-CONTENTS
   d. if the data item is indexed or subscripted, the subscripts in DEBUG-SUB-1, DEBUG-SUB-2, and DEBUG-SUB-3 as needed, otherwise spaces in the three subscript locations. (Indexes and subscripts are discussed in Chapter 10.)
3. The DEBUG SECTION is executed before returning control to the normal execution stream.

The declaratives for a debugging section to monitor the data item COL-COUNT in the program in Figure 7.11 are:

```
PROCEDURE DIVISION.

DECLARATIVES.
DISPLAY-COL-COUNT SECTION.
     USE FOR DEBUGGING ON COL-COUNT.
COL-COUNT-DISPLAY.
     DISPLAY DEBUG-LINE DEBUG-CONTENTS
           "IS STATEMENT LINE AND VALUE OF COL-COUNT".
END DECLARATIVES.
```

Using the debugging section for monitoring data items replaces the need for incorporating code to display their values. However, all references to the variable being monitored will cause the section to be executed; whereas, using the DISPLAY statement, the programmer can limit the references by placing the DISPLAY statements in the desired locations in the code. An advantage of using debugging sections is that the line number of the statement referencing the monitored variable is available in DEBUG-ITEM. This enables the programmer to find exact locations in the program.

7.4   *System Controls to Maintain Program Integrity*

Other factors contribute to the smooth running of applications programs. These include software, hardware, and operational safeguards instituted at different levels to reduce to a minimum the probability of a program's malfunctioning.

7.4.1   *Built-in System Software Controls*

System software such as operating systems and compilers incorporates many mechanisms or controls for safeguarding its environment. It also offers the user many security features. As a programmer, you should be aware of these features and should use them to safeguard your applications.

The most general level of security exists at the user-identification level. Only valid users can access the system. Furthermore, each user can be restricted as to the amount of system resources he can use. These resources include processor time, amount of memory, disk space, and use of system programs. Other security features such as passwords restrict access to files. Passwords are a software lock for program or data files. Only persons who know the appropriate user-identification and password can manipulate a given account. It may be possible to have multiple passwords or to change them automatically based on some condition such as the time of day.

File protection features serve to limit the type of access allowed to a particular file. Permissions to read, write, modify, or execute a file may be granted by the owner of the file to other users in general, or be restricted to specific users. For example, if you have a program that compares a preprocess file with a postprocess file and lists the differences, you may want to allow everyone to execute your program file. You may, however, want no one but your closest friends to read it and no one else to modify it. You would protect your file accordingly. Some software systems even keep a log of all users who have accessed a file, at what time, and where they are logged on.

A useful protection technique when you are creating or modifying your source program is for the system to automatically save your program file at specified intervals. Horror stories abound of unsuspecting novices who lost entire programs during a momentary power failure because they had not implemented this feature. In the same vein, many systems automatically create backup versions of programs before changes are applied. This is a lifesaver when all those changes you just made to your program made it worse, and you wish you had your "old" program back. With this feature you can always go back to the version without the changes. Many systems allow you to specify how many versions you want to retain.

Some systems offer the programmer the capability of creating checkpoints. These are snapshots of the data during its run that save sufficient information from the program to completely restore and continue the run at a later time. Checkpoints are used to restart the program from that point. This is an important feature for long or critical programs.

7.4.2   *Hardware*

Many hardware features are aimed at maintaining the integrity of the physical system. Whenever it can, the operating system issues tests of hardware components and logs the results for later examination by the field engineer. Independent devices also test the components of the system on an ongoing basis.

Systems have devices that protect them from voltage surges. They may also have battery backup systems that provide power in case of power failures. Furthermore, with the continuing trend in microprocessor technology in which more intelligence is packed on chips, testing features such as automatic diagnostics can test each one of the control devices or components. Not only can they detect faults, but they can also isolate faulty components and provide information about their location to the field engineer.

In data transfers, the system performs parity checking. Parity checks are a technique whereby the computer adds a 1-bit to a character's binary representation in order to make the number of 1-bits odd (or even, as the case may be). Whenever there is a transfer of information, whether from a disk to the memory or from one memory location to another, the parity is checked. Most modern systems can detect and correct simple parity errors.

Still other hardware features include the parallel execution of instructions by a pair of microprocessors. Intermediate and final results are cross-checked to ensure validity. In case of a discrepancy, the instruction is repeated. If the results still differ, a process of autodiagnosis begins that identifies the fault and logs the information for the engineer. In multiprogramming environments checks are made to ensure that branches stay within each program's upper and lower memory limits. If any attempt is made to access a location outside these limits, the hardware can detect it and return control to the operating system for remedial action.

Often in organizations where continuous processing is crucial, hardware components are duplicated so that if one malfunctions, the other can continue without interruption. This might be the case in a banking operation where the communications processors are duplicated to ensure that the bank's branches always have access to the computer.

7.4.3   Control Department

Other controls such as accounting controls are exerted in organizations by a department that serves as a front end to the actual data processing operations. The tasks of the control department include numbering checks, editing both input and output data, cross-checking computed totals to manually determined totals, verifying that the number of records input to a process is equal to the number of records processed, and implementing double-entry bookkeeping methods in which transactions affect offsetting accounts so that their results are equal. Other controls on the data and programs include reporting exceptions and authorizing any adjustments. For example, if a payroll check is misaligned in the printer and is not printed correctly, there should be a procedure for authorizing the destruction of that check, which in turn is taken into account when the employee count is compared with the check count.

Input controls are developed to provide assurance that the data to be processed have been properly authorized and accurately converted to machine-readable form. Errors found in the original input should be reviewed by the user in charge. Errors in conversion should be reviewed by a person in charge of control within the data-processing department. This delegates the responsibility for correcting errors to the area where the error originated. Likewise, output controls strive to ensure that output results are accurate.

7.4.4   Operational Controls

Still other safeguards relate to the actual organization of the management information systems (MIS) department and the operation of the computer center. For control purposes, the MIS department should be organized in a way that promotes the division of duties and responsibilities. Systems analysts should not have access to the computer or to the tape and program libraries, nor should they write applications programs. Persons who have access to the hardware should not also have access to the programs and data files, and vice versa. This implies that operations personnel should not do systems design or systems maintenance activities. Access to tape libraries, programs, files, and computer hardware should be restricted. The physical environment of the computer center should be conducive to ensuring its security and safety.

Formal procedures should be defined for almost every activity in the computer room. All changes and modifications to programs should follow some defined procedure and be authorized. Procedures should exist and be followed for maintaining all existing disk files. These may include performing backups and purging files. At least one copy of the backups should be stored off-premises in a fireproof vault. Procedures for recovering from hardware, software, and operator errors should be built into the program or outlined in a procedure to the operator.

Case Study: CDL's Order Extension

Charlene is having problems getting the order extension program illustrated in Chapter 5 to work. In trying to find the problem she has exhausted the standard debugging methods, but she continues to get results indicating size errors during testing. This means that one or more of the computations in paragraph 2110-DETERMINE-TOTAL-COST is achieving a result too large for the result item. Charlene decides to use the COBOL debugging features to aid her in tracking down the bug. She inserts a debugging section into the code as shown in Figure 7.16. Its purpose is to display all the input values when the computation paragraph 2110-DETERMINE-TOTAL-COST is entered.

Figure 7.16   CDL's "Order Extension" Program Using Debugging Mode

```
1 IDENTIFICATION DIVISION.
2 PROGRAM-ID.  EXTEND-ORDERS.
3*  THIS PROGRAM TAKES THE ORDERS SEPARATED BY THE CATEGORIZE DAILY
4*  MAIL PROGRAM AND EXTENDS THE AMOUNT TO BE BILLED THE CUSTOMER
5 AUTHOR.        C HILTON
6 DATE-WRITTEN.  JUNE 29, 1995
7 DATE-COMPILED. 15-Mar-93 07:12.
10 ENVIRONMENT DIVISION.
11
12 CONFIGURATION SECTION.
13 SOURCE-COMPUTER.  GENERIC-COMPUTER WITH DEBUGGING MODE.
14 OBJECT-COMPUTER.  GENERIC-COMPUTER.
15
16 INPUT-OUTPUT SECTION.
17 FILE-CONTROL.
18    SELECT ORDERS-FILE ASSIGN TO "ORDER.DAT"
19        ORGANIZATION IS LINE SEQUENTIAL.
20    SELECT EXTENDED-ORDERS-FILE ASSIGN TO "EXORDR.DAT"
21        ORGANIZATION IS LINE SEQUENTIAL.
22
```

Figure 7.16   *(continued)*

```
23
24 DATA DIVISION.
25
26 FILE SECTION.
27
28 FD   ORDERS-FILE
29      LABEL RECORDS ARE STANDARD.
30
31 01   CUSTOMER-ORDER-REC.
32      05   CO-CUSTOMER-ID    PIC 9(6).
33      05   CO-CD-NUMBER      PIC 9(6).
34      05   CO-QUANTITY       PIC 99.
35      05   CO-ORDER-NUMBER   PIC 9(6).
36      05   CO-CD-PRICE       PIC 9(6)V99.
37
38 FD   EXTENDED-ORDERS-FILE
39      LABEL RECORDS ARE STANDARD.
40
41 01   EXTENDED-CUSTOMER-ORDER-REC.
42      05   ECO-CUSTOMER-ID    PIC 9(6).
43      05   ECO-CD-NUMBER      PIC 9(6).
44      05   ECO-QUANTITY       PIC 99.
45      05   ECO-BILLING-AMOUNT PIC 9(6)V99.
46      05   ECO-ORDER-NUMBER   PIC 9(6).
47
48 WORKING-STORAGE SECTION.
49
50 01   WORK-AREA.
51      05   WA-BULK-MAIL      PIC 99.
52      05   WA-SINGLE-MAIL    PIC 99.
53      05   WA-SHIPPING-COST  PIC 9(6)V99.
54      05   WA-CD-COST        PIC 9(6)V99.
55      05   WA-COMBINED-COST  PIC 9(6)V99.
56
57 01   CONTROL-TOTALS.
58      05   CT-NUMBER-OF-CDS      PIC 9(5)      VALUE ZERO.
59      05   CT-NUMBER-OF-ORDERS   PIC 9(5)      VALUE ZERO.
60      05   CT-SHIPPING-COST      PIC 9(10)V99  VALUE ZERO.
61      05   CT-OVERALL-COST       PIC 9(10)V99  VALUE ZERO.
62
63 01   END-OF-FILE-INDICATORS.
64      05   EOF-ORDERS PIC X(5) VALUE "FALSE".
```

Figure 7.16 (continued)

```
65
66 01  COSTING-CONSTANTS.
67     05  CC-BULK-RATE         PIC 99V99 VALUE 3.95.
68     05  CC-SINGLE-RATE       PIC 99V99 VALUE 1.24.
69     05  CC-STANDARD-CD-PRICE PIC 99V99 VALUE 16.95.
70
71
72 PROCEDURE DIVISION.
73
74 DECLARATIVES.
75 DISPLAY-VALUES SECTION.
76     USE FOR DEBUGGING ON 2110-DETERMINE-TOTAL-COST.
77 DISPLAY-COMPUTE-VALUES.
78     DISPLAY " ".
79     DISPLAY "CD NUMBER IS ", CO-CD-NUMBER.
80     DISPLAY "CD QUANTITY IS ", CO-QUANTITY.
81     DISPLAY "CD PROCE IS ", CO-CD-PRICE.
82 END DECLARATIVES.
83
84 ORDER-EXTENSION SECTION.
85
86 EXTEND-CUSTOMER-ORDER.
87     OPEN INPUT ORDERS-FILE.
88     OPEN OUTPUT EXTENDED-ORDERS-FILE.
89     PERFORM 1000-READ-CUSTOMER-ORDER.
90     PERFORM 2000-ATTACH-BILLING-AMOUNT UNTIL EOF-ORDERS = "TRUE "
91     PERFORM 3000-DISPLAY-CONTROL-TOTALS.
92     CLOSE ORDERS-FILE.
93     CLOSE EXTENDED-ORDERS-FILE.
94     STOP RUN.
95
96 1000-READ-CUSTOMER-ORDER.
97     READ ORDERS-FILE AT END MOVE "TRUE " TO EOF-ORDERS.
98
99 2000-ATTACH-BILLING-AMOUNT.
100     PERFORM 2100-CALCULATE-BILLING-AMOUNT.
101     PERFORM 2200-WRITE-EXTENDED-ORDER.
102     PERFORM 1000-READ-CUSTOMER-ORDER.
103
104 2100-CALCULATE-BILLING-AMOUNT.
105     PERFORM 2110-DETERMINE-TOTAL-COST.
106     PERFORM 2120-MAINTAIN-CONTROL-TOTALS.
```

Figure 7.16   *(continued)*

```
107
108 2110-DETERMINE-TOTAL-COST.
109     IF CO-CD-PRICE = ZERO
110         MOVE CC-STANDARD-CD-PRICE TO CO-CD-PRICE.
111     COMPUTE WA-CD-COST = CO-CD-PRICE * CO-QUANTITY
112         ON SIZE ERROR PERFORM 2111-DISPLAY-SIZE-MESSAGE.
113     DIVIDE 5 INTO CO-QUANTITY GIVING WA-BULK-MAIL
114         REMAINDER WA-SINGLE-MAIL
115         ON SIZE ERROR PERFORM 2111-DISPLAY-SIZE-MESSAGE.
116     COMPUTE WA-SHIPPING-COST = WA-BULK-MAIL * CC-BULK-RATE
117         + WA-SINGLE-MAIL * CC-SINGLE-RATE
118         ON SIZE ERROR PERFORM 2111-DISPLAY-SIZE-MESSAGE.
119     COMPUTE WA-COMBINED-COST = WA-SHIPPING-COST + WA-CD-COST
120         ON SIZE ERROR PERFORM 2111-DISPLAY-SIZE-MESSAGE.
121
122 2111-DISPLAY-SIZE-MESSAGE.
123     DISPLAY "   ".
124     DISPLAY "SIZE ERROR FOUND DURING COMPUTATIONS!".
125
126 2120-MAINTAIN-CONTROL-TOTALS.
127     ADD 1                TO CT-NUMBER-OF-ORDERS.
128     ADD CO-QUANTITY      TO CT-NUMBER-OF-CDS.
129     ADD WA-SHIPPING-COST TO CT-SHIPPING-COST.
130     ADD WA-CD-COST       TO CT-OVERALL-COST.
131     ADD WA-SHIPPING-COST TO CT-OVERALL-COST.
132
133 2200-WRITE-EXTENDED-ORDER.
134     MOVE CO-CUSTOMER-ID   TO ECO-CUSTOMER-ID.
135     MOVE CO-CD-NUMBER     TO ECO-CD-NUMBER.
136     MOVE CO-QUANTITY      TO ECO-QUANTITY.
137     MOVE CO-ORDER-NUMBER  TO ECO-ORDER-NUMBER.
138     MOVE WA-COMBINED-COST TO ECO-BILLING-AMOUNT.
139     WRITE EXTENDED-CUSTOMER-ORDER-REC.
140
141 3000-DISPLAY-CONTROL-TOTALS.
142     DISPLAY " ".
143     DISPLAY "THE NUMBER OF ORDERS IS "  CT-NUMBER-OF-ORDERS.
144     DISPLAY "THE NUMBER OF CDS ORDERED IS " CT-NUMBER-OF-CDS.
145     DISPLAY "THE TOTAL SHIPPING COSTS ARE " CT-SHIPPING-COST.
146     DISPLAY "THE TOTAL AMOUNT BILLED IS " CT-OVERALL-COST.
```

The first few results of the debugging run are printed in Figure 7.17. Charlene is surprised to find that the price being input from the test data is so large that the extended price is overflowing. She does not recall having had such high prices, so she examines the test file. Some of the test records are shown in Figure 7.18. She notices that the test data do indeed have values high enough to cause an overflow because she keyed the test data with all the digits before the decimal point. Thus, the error is in her creation of the test data and not in the program. But an interesting point is raised by the situation. If a large value should accidentally be entered into the system during production, an error would result!

Figure 7.17   *Results from a Debugging Run of CDL's "Order Extension" Program*

```
CD NUMBER IS      943200
CD QUANTITY IS    01
CD PRICE IS       001595.00

CD NUMBER IS      962100
CD QUANTITY IS    95
CD PRICE IS       000000.00

CD NUMBER IS      976431
CD QUANTITY IS    80
CD PRICE IS       011195.00

SIZE ERROR FOUND DURING COMPUTATIONS
                    .
                    .
                    .
```

Figure 7.18   *Test Data Records Used in CDL's "Order Extension" Program*

```
17432194320001000159500
18923196210095000000000
74231097643180011119500
```

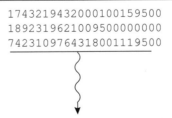

She confers with management to find a remedy. She is told that the price entered by the system should represent a discount price. If that price is ever higher than the standard price, the standard price should be substituted. Charlene changes the program to reflect this by changing the first line of the code in paragraph "2110-DETERMINE TOTAL-COST" from

```
IF CO-CD-PRICE = ZERO . . .
```

to

```
IF CO-CD-PRICE = ZERO OR CO-CD-PRICE > CC-STANDARD-CD-PRICE . . .
```

Of course, she also changes the documentation to reflect the change in code, removes the WITH DEBUGGING MODE from the ENVIRONMENT DIVISION, and notes the error in her personal debugging log for future reference.

Summary

The road from coding a program to obtaining a functional product involves compilation, testing, and debugging. Before embarking on this task, the programmer should do some desk verification to ensure that the program works "on paper." This involves reviewing the code for obvious syntax errors and walking through the program logic in much the same way the computer would. The latter step has been formalized in some organizations as a structured walkthrough.

Program testing serves to test a program for compliance to functional specifications and to identify errors. Shortcuts in testing will manifest themselves in greater magnitude during production, and their correction will be more costly. Testing should follow a top-down approach where the general integration of the modules is tested first and should proceed module by module to the detailed levels. Testing should be done according to a specified plan that outlines the conditions to be tested, the expected results, and the procedures to be used.

Care should be taken when developing tests to ensure that all logic is tested. As many paths as possible should be tested to provide reasonable assurance of the program's integrity. Valid data test the normal operation of the program while invalid data test its reactions and identify errors.

Debugging should be approached in an organized fashion. Following an approach similar to the life cycle is helpful. Debugging aids range from simple techniques resulting from the personal experiences of programmers to powerful, often automated tools. Cross-references list data-names and paragraph names and specify where they are defined and referenced. Program traces list the order of execution of program paragraphs. Interactive debugging aids and the COBOL debugging facility allow the programmer to examine the program as it is executing, often in a conversational mode. The programmer may display and change values. He may also control or change the order of execution of the program. The COBOL language itself has certain debugging facilities that are included to varying degrees on vendors' implementations of the language. They include debugging lines and debugging sections. To use these features, programs must include additional clauses and statements in the source program. COBOL debugging features allow the programmer to produce traces and display and/or change data items as specified in the debugging instructions.

Other features contribute to preserving the integrity of programs and files. These are aimed at preserving the integrity of the environment in which the programs run. They include security and reliability features that are inherent in the system software and hardware and control checks to ensure the validity of the input data, their processing, and their output. Procedures that outline the tasks of each individual involved with the system and the division of duties in the data processing department further aid in the prevention and detection of errors.

Key Terms

testing	run-time error	dump
walkthrough	data exception	debugging line
top-down testing	logic error	debugging mode
dummy module (stub)	cross reference	debugging section
test plan	trace	controls
compilation-time error	breakpoint	

Exercises

7.1   Using the information given in Figure 7.19, the code in Figure 7.20, and the trace listing in Fig ure 7.21, determine what error exists. How could you correct the program?

Figure 7.19   Specification for Exercise 7.1

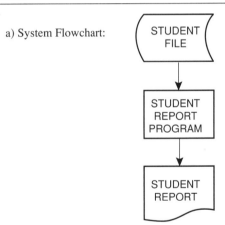

a) System Flowchart:

b) File Description of Student File:

```
FD  STUDENT-FILE . . . .
01  STUDENT-REC.
    05  IN-MATRIC   PIC X(6).
    05  IN-LAST     PIC X(15).
    05  IN-FIRST    PIC X(15).
    05  IN-MAJOR    PIC X(15).
```

Figure 7.19 **(continued)**

---

c) The Student File Contains the Following Records:

```
                1           2           3           4           5
12345678901234567890123456789012345678901234567890 1

111111THUMB            TOM           ACCOUNTING
222222SMITH            CORNELIUS     MIS
XYZXYZSTONE            SARA          EDUCATION
```

Figure 7.20 **PROCEDURE DIVISION for Exercise 7.1**

```
PROCEDURE DIVISION

A000-MAIN-BRAIN.
    OPEN INPUT STUDENT-FILE.
    OPEN OUTPUT PRINT-FILE.
    PERFORM A200-PROCESS UNTIL EOF = "Y".
    CLOSE STUDENT-FILE PRINT-FILE.
    STOP RUN.

A200-PROCESS.
    PERFORM B100-READ.
    PERFORM B200-WRITE.

B100-READ.
    READ STUDENT-FILE AT END MOVE "Y" TO EOF.

B200-WRITE.
    MOVE IN-MATRIC TO OUT-MATRIC.
    MOVE IN-LAST TO OUT-LAST.
    MOVE IN-FIRST TO OUT-FIRST.
    MOVE IN-MAJOR TO OUT-MAJOR.
    WRITE PRINT-REC FROM DETAIL-LINE.
```

Figure 7.21   *Trace of Program for Exercise 7.1*

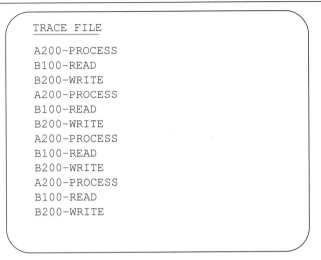

```
TRACE FILE

A200-PROCESS
B100-READ
B200-WRITE
A200-PROCESS
B100-READ
B200-WRITE
A200-PROCESS
B100-READ
B200-WRITE
A200-PROCESS
B100-READ
B200-WRITE
```

Figure 7.22   *Systems Flowchart and PROCEDURE DIVISION for Exercise 7.2*

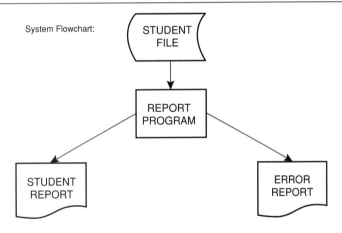

```
PROCEDURE DIVISION.

A000-MAIN-SECTION.
    OPEN INPUT STUDENT-FILE OUTPUT PRINT-FILE.
    PERFORM A100-INIT.
    PERFORM A200-PROCESS UNTIL EOF-FLAG = "Y".
    CLOSE STUDENT-FILE PRINT-FILE.
    STOP RUN.

A100-INIT.
```

Figure 7.22   (continued)

```
                MOVE "N" TO EOF-FLAG.
                PERFORM B100-READ.

            A200-PROCESS.
                MOVE "N" TO ERR-FLAG.
                PERFORM B200-EDIT-RECORD.
                IF ERR-FLAG = "Y"
                    PERFORM B300-PRINT-ERROR
                ELSE
                    PERFORM B400-PRINT-RECORD.

            B100-READ.
                READ STUDENT-FILE AT END MOVE "Y" TO EOF-FLAG.

            B200-EDIT-RECORD.
                IF MATRIC NOT NUMERIC
                    MOVE "Y" TO ERR-FLAG.
                IF IN-LAST = SPACES
                    MOVE "Y" TO ERR-FLAG.
                IF IN-FIRST = SPACES
                    MOVE "Y" TO ERR-FLAG.
                IF IN-MAJOR = SPACES
                    MOVE "Y" TO ERR-FLAG.

            B300-PRINT-ERROR.
                WRITE ERROR-REC FROM STUDENT-REC AFTER 2.

            B400-PRINT-RECORD.
                MOVE   IN-MATRIC TO OUT-MATRIC.
                MOVE   IN-LAST   TO OUT-LAST.
                MOVE   IN-FIRST  TO OUT-FIRST.
                MOVE   IN-MAJOR  TO OUT-MAJOR.
                WRITE  PRINT-REC FROM DETAIL-LINE AFTER 2.
                PERFORM B100-READ.
```

7.2   Conduct a structured walkthrough to examine the logic for the program in Figure 7.22.
7.3   Alter the code in Figure 7.20 to generate a trace using the COBOL DEBUGGING MODE.

For Exercises 7.4, 7.5, and 7.6 assume the following code:

```
PROCEDURE DIVISION
BEGIN-HERE.
      PERFORM A100-INIT.
      PERFORM A200-MAIN UNTIL EOF = "Y".
      PERFORM A300-END.
      STOP RUN.
A100-INIT.
      OPEN INPUT MASTER-FILE.
      OPEN OUTPUT PRINT-FILE.
      MOVE "N" TO EOF.
      PERFORM B100-READ.
A200-MAIN.
      PERFORM B100-READ.
A300-END.
      CLOSE MASTER-FILE PRINT-FILE.
B100-READ.
      READ MASTER-FILE AT END MOVE "Y" TO EOF.
```

7.4   Assuming that MASTER-FILE is empty, what paragraph names will be found in a trace file of the entire program's execution?

7.5   Assuming that MASTER-FILE contains three records, what paragraph names will the trace file contain?

7.6   Assuming that MASTER-FILE contains three records, what will happen if the B100-READ paragraph is changed to:

```
READ MASTER-FILE AT END MOVE "K" TO EOF.
```

7.7   The USE FOR DEBUGGING clause must appear as part of
       a.   a SECTION name.
       b.   a PARAGRAPH name.
       c.   the PROCEDURE DIVISION statement.

7.8   DEBUG-ITEM is filled
       a.   by the programmer.
       b.   automatically according to the USE type.
       c.   in the DEBUGGING lines.

7.9   Debugging lines are compiled
       a.   at all times.
       b.   when WITH DEBUGGING MODE is specified.
       c.   along with DEBUG-ITEM.

7.10   Program integrity implies that:
        a.   the program is debugged.
        b.   error controls have been designed and implemented.
        c.   errors are eliminated.
        d.   system controls are applied for error detection.
        e.   all of the above
        f.   A, B, and D

7.11   Testing proves that a program is error-free. True or false?

7.12   Testing should start with _____ data.
        a.   range
        b.   valid
        c.   stepped
        d.   keyed
        e.   bad

7.13   It is usually possible to test every possible path available in a program, therefore path testing should always be thoroughly completed before using alternative testing methods. True or false?

7.14   It is important, especially in organizations, to have a plan for conducting program testing. True or false?

7.15   The greatest contributor to debugging is:
        a.   planning.
        b.   documentation.
        c.   top-down design.
        d.   attitude.
        e.   optimism.

7.16   A _____ allows the programmer to look at all the paragraphs that refer to a data-name or paragraph-name.
        a.   cross-reference
        b.   compilation
        c.   trace file
        d.   debug line

7.17   For reason of complexity, it is impossible to emulate the operation of COBOL's interactive debug facility using standard coding techniques. True or false?

7.18   All debugging sections are specified following the reserved word DECLARATIVES. True or false?

7.19   The USE FOR DEBUGGING statement can be used to monitor a data item but not a file. True or false?

7.20   During coding, the programmer should be extremely aware of hardware diagnostics and should consult a systems operator about interfacing the program into the system's existing test procedures. True or false?

7.21   _____, also called _____, are module shells that stand in for modules that have not yet been coded.

7.22   The Golden Rule of debugging is _____ _____.

7.23 The three common cases of errors are:

    1. _____
    2. _____
    3. _____

7.24 A common run-time violation is the _____, caused when arithmetic operations are attempted on nonnumeric data.

7.25 A _____ offers clues as to what paragraphs are not performed during program execution.

7.26 The _____ statement can be used as a debugging method by identifying the values of selected variables during execution of a program.

7.27 A(n) _____ is a listing of the contents of memory (addresses, data, instructions, etc.) used by the program when it terminates abnormally.

7.28 Interactive program debugging can be implemented by adding the _____ clause to the _____ paragraph in the ENVIRONMENT DIVISION.

7.29 _____ checks are a technique whereby the computer adds a 1-bit to a character's binary representation in order to make the number of 1-bits odd (or even depending on the data).

7.30 What are the benefits, if any, to be gained by using top-down testing?

7.31 Of what use are system software safeguards to program integrity? Are they desirable?

7.32 Explain how operations management can be viewed as another method of program integrity.

7.33 Update this code, using COBOL debugging features, so that the contents of the input file and the running average can be monitored during an execution:

```
100-MAIN-LOGIC.
       OPEN INPUT GRADES-FILE.
       MOVE ZERO TO RUNNING-TOTAL TOTAL-COUNT
           CLASS-AVERAGE.
       PERFORM 200-READ-GRADES-FILE.
       PERFORM 300-PROCESS-AVERAGES
           UNTIL EOF-GRADES-FILE = "TRUE".
       WRITE OUTPUT-LINE FROM RUNNING-TOTAL.
       CLOSE GRADES-FILE.
       STOP RUN.
200-READ-GRADES-FILE.
       READ GRADES-FILE
           AT END MOVE "TRUE" TO EOF-GRADES-FILE.
300-PROCESS-AVERAGES.
       ADD GRADES-RECORD-LINE TO RUNNING-TOTAL.
       ADD 1 TO TOTAL-COUNT.
       DIVIDE RUNNING-TOTAL BY TOTAL-COUNT
           GIVING CLASS-AVERAGE.
```

7.34 Assuming that the GRADES-FILE in the previous exercise has three record lines, what paragraph-names would appear in a trace file of the program's execution?

C H A P T E R

8

REPORTING

In the rapidly changing business and computer environment, reporting systems must keep up with current needs and technology. Paper reports generated by many information reporting systems should be revised to meet changing user requirements. Traditional reports may be enhanced with terminal display and inquiry capabilities. The usefulness of a report depends on its intent and timing.

The intent dimension classifies reports into (1) action reports, (2) information reports, and (3) reference reports. Action reports initiate or control a needed procedure. The controlling program performs a specified action when a specified set of conditions exists. For example, the program could issue a past due notice. Information reports provide data for further analysis and control. The output of an information reporting program does not support specific decisions. Instead, it provides clues to management to direct its attention to the predefined content. For example, a sales report showing the confinement of a product to one region could clue management as to the need for a different distribution strategy. Reference reports consist of detailed histories of specified corporate functions. The information may be used to answer specific questions or to fill in details not provided by the other reports. For example, a complete listing of accounts receivable payments could be examined to track down a lost check.

Three basic timing environments classify reporting into (1) scheduled reporting, (2) exception reporting, and (3) demand reporting. Scheduled reports are issued to specified users at regular intervals. Examples are monthly journal reports, weekly sales representative expense reports, and daily cash flow reports. Exception reports are distributed to users when triggered by a predefined condition. Examples include low-inventory notifications, over-budget notices, and listings of projects behind schedule. Demand reports are generated only when a user requests their creation. Examples may include regional sales forecasts and analyses of raw material costs.

8.1   Report Formats

Although each reporting environment provides a unique set of information to management, the programming requirements are quite similar. The timing of reports affects scheduling more than programmers. The intent dimension implies subtle differences for an analyst, but the format and logic of business reports can be generalized. In this chapter, we explore the general structure of business reports and some of the basic COBOL features for implementing them.

8.1.1   Report Components

To generalize the structure of reports, we first need to identify the components of a report. Figure 8.1 outlines the different segments of a generalized report. The heart of a report is the *detail line*. It contains the lowest level of data occurring in the report. To illustrate, assume that there is a file containing information for a company's sales representatives. Each record in the file represents a sale to a customer and contains data about the office through which the sale was made, the sales representative's identification number, the customer who made the purchase, the date of sale, and the dollar total of the sale. Suppose we wish to produce a report each month to evaluate the performance of the sales force. The report could be as simple as the following listing of Figure 8.2. The lines on the listing are detail lines.

The listing contains the desired information, but it requires that an individual using the report organize and clarify the fields in the report to meet his needs. Features such as *headings* to identify the report contents would be useful. Column headings appearing immediately above each field in the detail lines identify the data. Page headings identify the report content and are printed at the top of each page. They are composed of report identification elements such as the company name, report title, report date, run date, distribution information, report identification number, and page numbers. The addition of headings is reflected in the sales report shown in Figure 8.3.

Figure 8.1   *Segments of a Generalized Report*

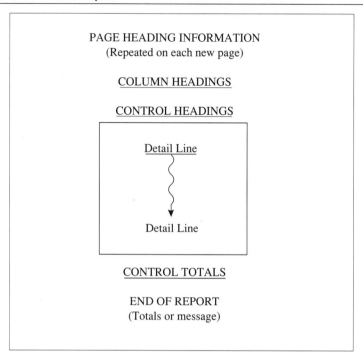

Figure 8.2   *Simple List of Sales Data*

```
L.A.      500-32-9738      602-884-8460      9/13/92      59.25
L.A.      500-32-9738      602-321-2768      9/14/92      72.30
L.A.      500-32-9738      314-747-1834      9/20/92     100.00
```

Figure 8.3   Sales Data List with Headings

```
REPORT #342                     HAROLD TUNA CO.                      PAGE 1

DISTRIBUTION CODE: A            MONTHLY SALES

RUN DATE:  12/12/93             NOVEMBER 1993

OFFICE      SALES REP.      CUSTOMER        SALES DATE    SALES AMOUNT
L.A.        500-32-9738     602-884-8460     9/13/92            59.85
L.A.        500-32-9738     602-321-2768     9/14/92            72.30
L.A.        500-32-9738     314-747-1834     9/20/92           100.00
L.A.        742-32-1924     314-167-9111     9/12/92          1010.00
L.A.        742-32-1924     314-167-9111     9/18/92          3217.00
```

Managers are also interested in the bottom line. Because of this, most reports contain summaries that condense important information into a few lines. If summaries are not printed at the end of a report, some other message should be used to signal the last page so that the recipient knows the report is complete. The sales report with totals may appear as shown in Figure 8.4.

Figure 8.4   Sales Data List with Summaries

```
REPORT #342                     HAROLD TUNA CO.                      PAGE 1

DISTRIBUTION CODE: A            MONTHLY SALES

RUN DATE:  12/12/93             NOVEMBER 1993

OFFICE      SALES REP.      CUSTOMER        SALES DATE    SALES AMOUNT
L.A.        500-32-9738     602-884-8460     9/13/92            59.85
L.A.        500-32-9738     602-321-2768     9/14/92            72.30
L.A.        500-32-9738     314-747-1834     9/20/92           100.00
L.A.        742-32-1924     314-167-9111     9/12/92          1010.00
L.A.        742-32-1924     314-167-9111     9/18/92          3217.00
TOTAL SALES                                                   4459.15
```

To present the information in a useful manner, long reports often require several logical breaks. Assume that the sales report is to be used by management to evaluate sales performance by regional office and within a regional office. The sales report should now include intermediate summary lines that show the total sales for each sales representative and for each regional office. These intermediate summary lines, which can appear within the body of the report, require headings and totals for each grouping. The summary lines are referred to as control breaks. The sales report with control break headings and totals would be as shown in Figure 8.5. Notice that control break headings appear in order of most inclusive (regional office) to least inclusive (sales representative) or from major heading to minor heading. The appearance of the totals, however, is the reverse, with the regional totals appearing at the end and the sales representative totals appearing first. Compare this to the general structure of Figure 8.1.

Figure 8.5   *Sales Data List with Control Breaks*

```
REPORT #342                      HAROLD TUNA CO.              PAGE 1

DISTRIBUTION CODE: A             MONTHLY SALES BY REGION

RUN DATE:  12/12/93              NOVEMBER 1993

                                 CUSTOMER      SALES DATE    SALE AMOUNT
OFFICE: L.A.

  REP. #500-32-9738

                                 602-884-8460   9/13/92            59.85
                                 602-321-2768   9/14/92            72.30
                                 314-747-1834   9/20/92           100.00

  TOTAL FOR REP. #500-32-9738

        231.55

REP. #742-32-1924

                                 314-167-9111   9/12/92          1010.00
                                 314-167-9111   9/18/92          3217.00

TOTAL FOR REP. 742-32-1924

  4,227.00

TOTAL FOR OFFICE: L.A.

        4,458.55

MONTHLY TOTAL IS 4,458.55
```

The term "control break" actually has a double meaning. From a manager's perspective, a control break represents a critical summary that breaks the report into controllable segments.

Often control break totals are used as important performance measures for various segments of the company. For example, a manager could use the sales report's control break on regional offices to evaluate the performance of a specific corporate office. He would use the control break on sales representatives to evaluate the performance of each sales representative.

From a programming standpoint, "control break" is a physical description. Since a report program lists detail lines in a systematic fashion, a repetitive structure controls the flow of the program. However, whenever a control break total is required, there must be an actual break in the repetitive logic to temporarily halt the printing of detail lines in order to print control break heading and totals.

8.1.2   Report Layout Design

A *report layout* is the arrangement of items on a sample report. The purpose of the report layout is to show the location and position of every item that is to appear on the report. The layout is reviewed by analysts, users, and programmers during the logical and physical design states of the systems development life cycle. It is a working document that can be changed during the design phases as users and analysts seek to improve report content and readability. Once approved, a report layout serves as a tool to guide the programmer in writing the programs.

The report layout form indicates precisely where data are to be presented, the spacing to be used, any headings and totals that are to appear, and any editing of data items that needs to be done. Figure 8.6 shows a typical report layout form. The form need not be a paper form; it may be the actual screen of the terminal. Some manufacturers have special software that allows a programmer to design reports at the terminal and make rapid changes to the layouts.

Figure 8.6   **Report Layout**

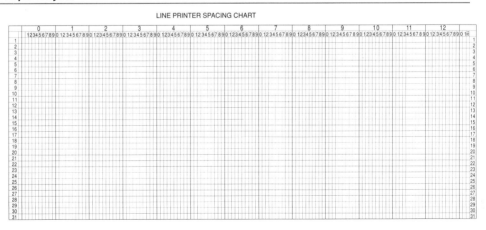

Report layout forms define the format of both printed and displayed reports. In this chapter, however, we will concentrate on printed reports. The notation used in designing a report layout includes: (1) Xs to denote that the computer is to print an alphanumeric data item, (2) 9s to indicate that it is to print a numeric data item, (3) editing characters such as the comma and zero suppression, and (4) constant information such as page headings that will not vary as the report progresses.

Figure 8.7   Report Layout for "Monthly Sales by Region" Report

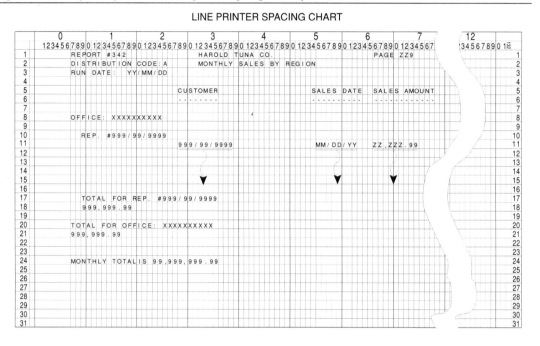

A layout for the last format of the sales report is shown in Figure 8.7. The report, column, and control headings are generally constant. They are printed on the report layout form as they are to appear. Since page numbers, office locations, and sales representative numbers vary, however, they are indicated by Xs, 9s, Zs, and commas on the report layout. Dates are specified by indicating the order of month, day, and year within the print location. The number of blank lines between heading types on the actual report are as shown unless otherwise noted. Column positioning is indicated by the column occupied by a certain character. Column numbers are indicated at the top of the report layout form. The lengths of the data items are exactly indicated by the number of Xs or 9s for each data item. For example, in Figure 8.7, page numbers can occupy three positions; thus they can range from 1 to 999. Row positions are indicated by the numbers circled on the left side of the form. In our sample layout column headings appear in the fifth row of each page. The detail lines and summary are also specified with exacting requirements. The completed form is circulated to the users for revision and approval before the programmer begins to code the report.

The layout in Figure 8.7 is the basis for the COBOL program of Figure 8.8. Figures 8.9 and 8.10 show the hierarchy chart and Nassi-Schneiderman charts, respectively. The program uses an input file, shown in Figure 8.11, to generate the listing. The input file must be in the sequence required for the report for this program to work.

Figure 8.8   *List Sales File Code*

```
 1 IDENTIFICATION DIVISION.
 2 PROGRAM-ID.  LIST-SALES-RECORDS.
 3*  THIS PROGRAM TAKES THE SALES FROM THE PRIOR MONTH AND
 4*  GENERATES A LISTING GROUPED BY REPRESENTATIVE AND OFFICE
 5 AUTHOR.        SELF.
 6 DATE-WRITTEN.  JUNE 12, 1996.
 7 DATE-COMPILED. 02-Sep-92 07:51.
10 ENVIRONMENT DIVISION.
11
12 CONFIGURATION SECTION.
13 SOURCE-COMPUTER.  GENERIC-COMPUTER.
14 OBJECT-COMPUTER.  GENERIC-COMPUTER.
15
16 INPUT-OUTPUT SECTION.
17 FILE-CONTROL.
18     SELECT MONTHLY-SALES-FILE ASSIGN TO DISK
19         ORGANIZATION IS SEQUENTIAL.
20     SELECT SALES-BY-REGION-FILE ASSIGN TO PRINTER
21         ORGANIZATION IS SEQUENTIAL.
22
23
24 DATA DIVISION.
25
26 FILE SECTION.
27
28 FD  MONTHLY-SALES-FILE
29     LABEL RECORDS ARE STANDARD.
30
31 01  MS-SALE-RECORD.
32     05  MS-OFFICE             PIC X(10).
33     05  MS-REPRESENTATIVE-ID  PIC 9(10).
34     05  MS-CUSTOMER-NBR       PIC 9(10).
35     05  MS-SALE-DATE          PIC 9(6).
36     05  MS-SALE-AMOUNT        PIC 9(5)V99.
37
38 FD  SALES-BY-REGION-FILE
39     LABEL RECORDS ARE OMITTED.
40
41 01  SBR-SALE-REC PIC X(80).
42
43 WORKING-STORAGE SECTION.
44
```

Figure 8.8 **(continued)**

```
45 01  PAGE-CONTROL-COUNTERS.
46     05  PC-LINE-COUNTER  PIC 99    VALUE 99.
47     05  PC-PAGE-NUMBER   PIC 9(4) VALUE ZERO.
48     05  PC-LINE-LIMIT    PIC 99    VALUE 55.
49
50 01  END-OF-FILE-INDICATORS.
51     05  EOF-MONTHLY-SALES-FILE PIC X VALUE "N".
52     88  MORE-SALES                    VALUE "N".
53     88  NO-MORE-SALES                 VALUE "Y".
54
55 01  SAVE-BREAK-VALUES.
56     05  SAVE-OFFICE           PIC X(10).
57     05  SAVE-REPRESENTATIVE   PIC X(10).
58
59 01  SALE-AMOUNTS.
60     05  SA-REPRESENTATIVE PIC 9(5)V99 VALUE ZERO.
61     05  SA-OFFICE         PIC 9(6)V99 VALUE ZERO.
62     05  SA-REPORT-TOTAL   PIC 9(8)V99 VALUE ZERO.
63
64 01  SBR-LAYOUT.
65     05  SBR-PAGE-HEADING-1.
66        10  FILLER      PIC X(6)  VALUE SPACES.
67        10  FILLER      PIC X(25) VALUE "REPORT #342".
68        10  FILLER      PIC X(34) VALUE "HAROLD TUNA CO.".
69        10  FILLER      PIC X(5)  VALUE "PAGE".
70        10  SBR-PAGE-NBR PIC ZZ9.
71     05  SBR-PAGE-HEADING-2.
72        10  FILLER PIC X(6) VALUE SPACES.
73        10  FILLER PIC X(25) VALUE "DISTIBUTION CODE: A".
74        10  FILLER PIC X(23) VALUE "MONTHLY SALES BY REGION".
75     05  SBR-PAGE-HEADING-3.
76        10  FILLER      PIC X(6) VALUE SPACES.
77        10  SBR-RUN-DATE PIC Z9/99/99.
78     05  SBR-COLUMN-HEADING-1.
79        10  FILLER PIC X(28) VALUE SPACES.
80        10  FILLER PIC X(16) VALUE "CUSTOMER".
81        10  FILLER PIC X(30) VALUE "SALES DATE  SALES AMOUNT".
82     05  SBR-COLUMN-HEADING-2.
83        10  FILLER PIC X(28) VALUE SPACES.
84        10  FILLER PIC X(16) VALUE "————".
85        10  FILLER PIC X(12) VALUE "————".
86        10  FILLER PIC X(12) VALUE ALL "-".
```

Figure 8.8   *(continued)*

```
 87      05  SBR-REGION-HEADING.
 88          10  FILLER         PIC X(6)  VALUE SPACES.
 89          10  FILLER         PIC X(8)  VALUE "OFFICE: ".
 90          10  SBR-REGION-1 PIC X(10).
 91      05  SBR-REPRESENTATIVE-HEADING.
 92          10  FILLER             PIC X(8) VALUE SPACES.
 93          10  FILLER             PIC X(6) VALUE "REP. #".
 94          10  SBR-REPRESENTATIVE PIC 999/99/9999.
 95      05  SBR-DETAIL.
 96          10  FILLER         PIC X(28) VALUE SPACES.
 97          10  SBR-CUSTOMER   PIC 999/99/9999.
 98          10  FILLER         PIC X(6)  VALUE SPACES.
 99          10  SBR-SALES-DATE PIC Z9/99/99.
100          10  FILLER         PIC X(4) VALUE SPACES.
101          10  SBR-SALE-AMOUNT PIC ZZ,ZZZ.99.
102      05  SBR-REPRESENTATIVE-TOTAL-1.
103          10  FILLER      PIC X(8)  VALUE SPACES.
104          10  FILLER      PIC X(16) VALUE "TOTAL FOR REP. #".
105          10  SBR-REP-NBR PIC 999/99/9999.
106      05  SBR-REPRESENTATIVE-TOTAL-2.
107          10  FILLER         PIC X(8)  VALUE SPACES.
108          10  SBR-REP-TOTAL PIC ZZ,ZZZ.99.
109      05  SBR-REGION-TOTAL-1.
110          10  FILLER         PIC X(6)  VALUE SPACES.
111          10  FILLER         PIC X(18) VALUE "TOTAL FOR OFFICE: ".
112          10  SBR-OFFICE-NBR PIC X(10).
113      05  SBR-REGION-TOTAL-2.
114          10  FILLER           PIC X(6)  VALUE SPACES.
115          10  SBR-OFFICE-TOTAL PIC ZZZ,ZZZ.99.
116      05  SBR-REPORT-TOTAL.
117          10  FILLER         PIC X(6)  VALUE SPACES.
118          10  FILLER         PIC X(17) VALUE "MONTHLY TOTAL IS".
119          10  SBR-MONTH-TOTAL PIC ZZ,ZZZ,ZZZ.99.
120
121
122 PROCEDURE DIVISION.
123 LIST-SALES-FILE.
124     OPEN INPUT MONTHLY-SALES-FILE.
125     OPEN OUTPUT SALES-BY-REGION-FILE.
126     PERFORM 1000-PREPARE-SALES-REPORT.
127     PERFORM 2000-ISOLATE-OFFICE-GROUP UNTIL NO-MORE-SALES.
128     PERFORM 3000-CONCLUDE-SALES-REPORT.
```

Figure 8.8   *(continued)*

```
129     CLOSE MONTHLY-SALES-FILE.
130     CLOSE SALES-BY-REGION-FILE.
131     STOP RUN.
132
133 1000-PREPARE-SALES-REPORT.
134     ACCEPT SBR-RUN-DATE FROM DATE.
135     PERFORM 1100-PRINT-PAGE-HEADINGS.
136     PERFORM 1200-READ-SALES-RECORD.
137
138 1100-PRINT-PAGE-HEADINGS.
139     IF PC-LINE-COUNTER > PC-LINE-LIMIT
140         ADD 1 TO PC-PAGE-NUMBER
141         MOVE PC-PAGE-NUMBER TO SBR-PAGE-NBR
142         WRITE SBR-SALE-REC FROM SBR-PAGE-HEADING-1 AFTER PAGE
143         WRITE SBR-SALE-REC FROM SBR-PAGE-HEADING-2
144         WRITE SBR-SALE-REC FROM SBR-PAGE-HEADING-3
145         WRITE SBR-SALE-REC FROM SBR-COLUMN-HEADING-1
146             AFTER ADVANCING 2 LINES
147         WRITE SBR-SALE-REC FROM SBR-COLUMN-HEADING-2
148         MOVE 6 TO PC-LINE-COUNTER.
149
150 1200-READ-SALES-RECORD.
151     READ MONTHLY-SALES-FILE AT END
152         MOVE "Y" TO EOF-MONTHLY-SALES-FILE
153         MOVE HIGH-VALUES TO MS-SALE-RECORD.
154
155 2000-ISOLATE-OFFICE-GROUP.
156     PERFORM 2100-BEGIN-OFFICE-BREAK.
157     PERFORM 2200-ISOLATE-REPRESENTATIVE-GP
158         UNTIL MS-OFFICE NOT EQUAL SAVE-OFFICE.
159     PERFORM 2300-END-OFFICE-BREAK.
160
161 2100-BEGIN-OFFICE-BREAK.
162     MOVE MS-OFFICE TO SAVE-OFFICE.
163     PERFORM 1100-PRINT-PAGE-HEADINGS.
164     PERFORM 2110-PRINT-OFFICE-HEADINGS.
165
166 2110-PRINT-OFFICE-HEADINGS.
167     MOVE MS-OFFICE TO SBR-REGION-1.
168     WRITE SBR-SALE-REC FROM SBR-REGION-HEADING
169         AFTER ADVANCING 2 LINES.
170     ADD 2 TO PC-LINE-COUNTER.
```

Figure 8.8   (continued)

```
171
172 2200-ISOLATE-REPRESENTATIVE-GP.
173     PERFORM 2210-BEGIN-REPRESENTATIVE-BRK.
174     PERFORM 2220-FORMAT-DETAIL-LINE
175         UNTIL MS-REPRESENTATIVE-ID NOT EQUAL SAVE-REPRESENTATIVE.
176     PERFORM 2230-END-REPRESENTATIVE-BREAK.
177
178 2210-BEGIN-REPRESENTATIVE-BRK.
179     MOVE MS-REPRESENTATIVE-ID TO SAVE-REPRESENTATIVE.
180     PERFORM 1100-PRINT-PAGE-HEADINGS.
181     PERFORM 2211-PRINT-REP-HEADINGS.
182
183 2211-PRINT-REP-HEADINGS.
184     MOVE MS-REPRESENTATIVE-ID TO SBR-REPRESENTATIVE.
185     WRITE SBR-SALE-REC FROM SBR-REPRESENTATIVE-HEADING
186         AFTER ADVANCING 2 LINES.
187     ADD 2 TO PC-LINE-COUNTER.
188
189 2220-FORMAT-DETAIL-LINE.
190     PERFORM 1100-PRINT-PAGE-HEADINGS.
191     PERFORM 2221-PRINT-DETAIL-LINE.
192     ADD MS-SALE-AMOUNT TO SA-REPRESENTATIVE.
193     PERFORM 1200-READ-SALES-RECORD.
194
195 2221-PRINT-DETAIL-LINE.
196     MOVE MS-CUSTOMER-NBR TO SBR-CUSTOMER.
197     MOVE MS-SALE-DATE     TO SBR-SALES-DATE.
198     MOVE MS-SALE-AMOUNT   TO SBR-SALE-AMOUNT.
199     WRITE SBR-SALE-REC FROM SBR-DETAIL.
200     ADD 1 TO PC-LINE-COUNTER.
201
202 2230-END-REPRESENTATIVE-BREAK.
203     PERFORM 2231-PRINT-REPRESENTATIVE-TOTS.
204     PERFORM 2232-MAINTAIN-OFFICE-TOTALS.
205
206 2231-PRINT-REPRESENTATIVE-TOTS.
207     MOVE SAVE-REPRESENTATIVE TO SBR-REP-NBR.
208     MOVE SA-REPRESENTATIVE TO SBR-REP-TOTAL.
209     WRITE SBR-SALE-REC FROM SBR-REPRESENTATIVE-TOTAL-1
210         AFTER ADVANCING 2 LINES.
211     WRITE SBR-SALE-REC FROM SBR-REPRESENTATIVE-TOTAL-2.
212     ADD 3 TO PC-LINE-COUNTER.
```

Figure 8.8   **(continued)**

```
213
214 2232-MAINTAIN-OFFICE-TOTALS.
215     ADD SA-REPRESENTATIVE TO SA-OFFICE.
216     MOVE ZERO TO SA-REPRESENTATIVE.
217
218 2300-END-OFFICE-BREAK.
219     PERFORM 2310-PRINT-OFFICE-TOTALS.
220     PERFORM 2320-MAINTAIN-OVERALL-TOTALS.
221
222 2310-PRINT-OFFICE-TOTALS.
223     MOVE SAVE-OFFICE TO SBR-OFFICE-NBR.
224     MOVE SA-OFFICE TO SBR-OFFICE-TOTAL.
225     WRITE SBR-SALE-REC FROM SBR-REGION-TOTAL-1
226         AFTER ADVANCING 2 LINES.
227     WRITE SBR-SALE-REC FROM SBR-REGION-TOTAL-2.
228     ADD 3 TO PC-LINE-COUNTER.
229
230 2320-MAINTAIN-OVERALL-TOTALS.
231     ADD SA-OFFICE TO SA-REPORT-TOTAL.
232     MOVE ZERO TO SA-OFFICE.
233
234 3000-CONCLUDE-SALES-REPORT.
235     MOVE SA-REPORT-TOTAL TO SBR-MONTH-TOTAL.
236     WRITE SBR-SALE-REC FROM SBR-REPORT-TOTAL
237         AFTER ADVANCING 2 LINES.
```

Figure 8.9   *Hierarchy Chart for the "List Sales File" Program*

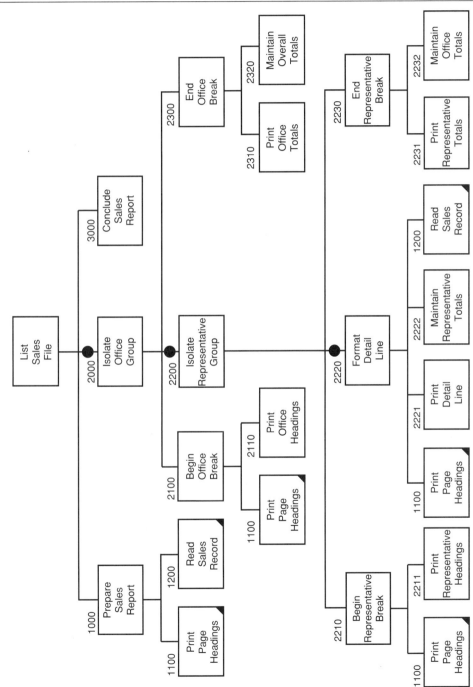

Figure 8.10   **List Sales File N-S Charts**

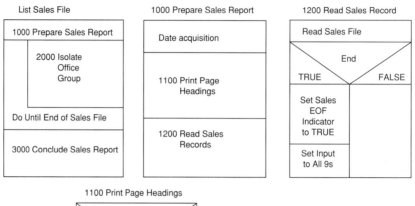

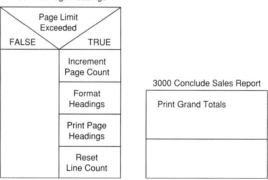

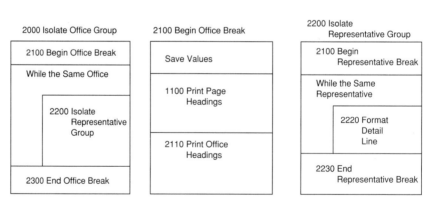

Figure 8.10   *(continued)*

2300 End Office Break

2310 Print Office Totals
2320 Maintain Overall Totals

2110 Print Office Headings

Move Office Information
Print Headings for an Office
Increment Line Counts

2310 Print Office Totals

Move Office Totals
Print Office Totals
Increment Line Counts

2320 Maintain Overall Totals

Add Office Totals to Overall Totals
Zero Out Office Totals

2210 Begin Representative Breaks

Save Values
1100 Print Page Headings
2211 Print Representative Headings

2220 Format Detail Line

1100 Print Page Headings
2221 Print Detail Line
Add Sale to Representative Totals
1200 Read Sales Record

2230 End Representative Break

2231 Print Representative Totals
2232 Maintain Office Totals

2211 Print Representative Headings

Move Representative Data
Print Representative Data
Increment Counter

2221 Print Detail Line

Move Detail Data to Print Line
Print Detail Line
Add to the Line Counter

2231 Print Representative Totals

Move Representative Total Data
Print Representative
Increment Line Counter

2232 Maintain Office Totals

Add Representative to Office Totals
Zero Out Representative Totals

Figure 8.11   Monthly Sales File Record Layout

RECORD LAYOUT SHEET

Record Name:			File Name:		
Prepared By:			Date:		
Key Fields:			Organization:		
Field	Description		Type*	Length	Decimal
	Office Location		A	10	
	Representative #		A	10	
	Customer #		N	10	
	Sale Date		N	6	
	Sale Amount		N	7	2

* A = alphanumeric
N = numeric

8.2   COBOL for Defining Report Formats

A report is nothing more than a file. Each line of a report is a record on that file. The physical representation of the report file varies from machine to machine, and this is reflected in the SELECT clause in the FILE-CONTROL SECTION of the ENVIRONMENT DIVISION. The device-name assigned to the report file also varies by manufacturer. In all cases, however, a SELECT statement must be included for each report generated by the program.

8.2.1   FILE SECTION for a Report

Since a report is a file, the DATA DIVISION must contain a file description (FD) entry for each physical report. The following is the FD entry and associated record definition for the sales report in Figure 8.7:

```
FD      SALES-BY-REGION-FILE
        LABEL RECORDS ARE OMITTED.


01      SBR-SALE-REC       PIC X(80).
```

Label records are meaningless for print files and are therefore omitted as seen in the FD. The record associated with a report file is commonly given only a name and length, but no field descriptions. The length of the record is the column width allowed by the output device such as a printer of display terminal. Since many different types of lines are printed on each report, the lines will be built in the WORKING-STORAGE SECTION of the program, then moved to the report file record immediately prior to writing that record to the file. Thus, we will concentrate on specifying report designs in WORKING-STORAGE SECTION entries.

8.2.2   *Defining Report Lines in WORKING-STORAGE*

Each report is composed of constants and variables representing a segment of the report as defined in Figure 8.1. It is good practice to group all line formats of a report into several consecutive 01 levels in the WORKING-STORAGE SECTION or as consecutive 05 levels under a single 01 entry. For the sales report example, the 05 entries appear as:

```
01  SBR-LAYOUT.
    05      SBR-PAGE-HEADING-1.
    05      SBR-PAGE-HEADING-2.
    05      SBR-PAGE-HEADING-3.
    05      SBR-COLUMN-HEADING-1.
    05      SBR-COLUMN-HEADING-2.
    05      SBR-REGION-HEADING.
    05      SBR-REPRESENTATIVE-HEADING.
    05      SBR-DETAIL.
    05      SBR-REPRESENTATIVE-TOTAL-1.
    05      SBR-REPRESENTATIVE-TOTAL-2.
    05      SBR-REGION-TOTAL-1.
    05      SBR-REGION-TOTAL-2.
    05      SBR-REPORT-TOTAL.
```

These entries were defined using the report layout form in Figure 8.7 and would have proper subordinate data items. Notice that each different line type on the report layout has an associated entry in the WORKING-STORAGE SECTION.

The report layout is then used to further specify the COBOL code required to print the desired information. At this point spacing across the page becomes important in the COBOL code. Each position on the layout must be accounted for in the associated DATA DIVISION entries to properly position the data on the report. Line spacing is handled in the PROCEDURE DIVISION, but column spacing is done in the WORKING-STORAGE SECTION. Let us define the entry for SBR-PAGE-HEADING-2, which is the second line printed at the top of each page of the report. This line contains only constants. The first constant appears in column 7. Thus we must "print" six spaces at the beginning of the line. To do this, we use the reserved word FILLER in conjunction with a VALUE clause of SPACES as the first entry under SBR-PAGE-HEADING-2. We mentioned previously that the COBOL reserved word SPACES fills the associated data field with blanks for the length specified in the associated PICTURE clause. The entry to account for the six spaces is:

```
10 FILLER PIC X(6) VALUE SPACES.
```

The first constant in the line is "Distribution Code:". This requires 20 positions on the print line and will thus appear as

```
10 FILLER PIC X(20) VALUE "DISTRIBUTION CODE: A".
```

Between the first and second constants five spaces are indicated on the report layout. This requires an entry to account for the SPACES. The description of the entire line appears as follows:

```
05   SBR-PAGE-HEADING-2.
     10   FILLER PIC X(6) VALUE SPACES.
     10   FILLER PIC X(20) VALUE "DISTRIBUTION CODE: A".
     10   FILLER PIC X(5) VALUE SPACES.
     10   FILLER PIC X(23) VALUE "MONTHLY SALES BY REGION".
```

We can take advantage of the property of left-justification of alphanumeric fields to reduce the length of the entry. A constant in a VALUE clause will be left-justified in an alphanumeric field; therefore, any blank needed after the constant may be accounted for by specifying a larger field size than actually needed for the constant. For example, the following code from Figure 8.8 is equivalent to the above entry for SBR-PAGE-HEADING-2:

```
05   SBR-PAGE-HEADING-2.
     10   FILLER PIC X(6) VALUE SPACES.
     10   FILLER PIC X(25) VALUE "DISTRIBUTION CODE: A".
     10   FILLER PIC X(23) VALUE "MONTHLY SALES BY REGION".
```

Other lines contain both variables and constants. SBR-REGION-HEADING, for example, begins in column 7 with the constant "OFFICE:" which requires eight positions. The office name is a variable and can be up to 10 positions long, as indicated by the report layout form. The WORKING-STORAGE SECTION entries for this report line appears:

```
05   SBR-REGION-HEADING.
     10   FILLER          PIC X(6) VALUE SPACES.
     10   FILLER          PIC X(8) VALUE "OFFICE: ".
     10   SBR-REGION-1    PIC X(10).
```

The actual value of SBR-REGION-1 will be determined in the PROCEDURE DIVISION.

8.2.3   Simple Editing

Let us return to the first line of the report in Figure 8.3. Recall that it contains both constant and variable information. An entry for this line is:

```
05    SBR-PAGE-HEADING-1.
      10    FILLER        PIC X(6) VALUE SPACES.
      10    FILLER        PIC X(25) VALUE "REPORT #342".
      10    FILLER        PIC X(34) VALUE "HAROLD TUNA CO.".
      10    FILLER        PIC X(5) VALUE "PAGE".
      10    SBR-PAGE-NBR  PIC 999.
```

The page number is to be printed using three positions. Unless leading zeros are replaced by blanks, page 3 will appear as "PAGE 003." The report would be more attractive if leading zeros were suppressed. This is accomplished by replacing each 9 character with a Z character in the PICTURE clause for every position where a blank is to appear in place of a leading zero. Remember that the Z does not cause all zeros to be replaced by blanks, only those at the beginning of the number. The editing will occur when the unedited field is moved to the edited field. The entry for the page number becomes:

```
      10 SBR-PAGE-NBR PIC ZZ9.
```

Now a page number of 3 will print as "PAGE 3."

When numeric data items are manipulated, decimal points are maintained through the use of the character V. The V, however, takes up no memory and therefore will not be printed on reports. To make numbers more readable, include a decimal point as an actual character by placing a period in the output data item's PICTURE clause where the decimal point belongs. Another similar feature involves the comma. When numeric output items are to include commas, simply write a comma in the PICTURE clause of the output data item in the position where the comma is to be inserted. If the numeric item does not have enough significant digits to need a comma, the comma will appear as a blank if used in conjunction with leading zero suppression. The decimal point and the comma each take up one print position. Therefore, these added positions must be accounted for in the PICTURE clauses. Figure 8.12 shows examples of moving numeric data fields to numeric edited fields that use decimal points and commas.

A slash (/) may also be used in edited numeric items. Each slash takes one print position and is placed in the edited field in the position in which it is desired. To develop the detail line entry for the date in the sales report, slashes are used to separate the month, day, and year. The entry would appear as:

```
SBR-SALE-DATE PIC 99/99/99.
```

The entire detail line of the sales report is in lines 95 through 101 of Figure 8.8.

Insertion Characters. The decimal point, the comma, and the slash are *insertion characters* that appear on the printed page as indicated by their position in the PICTURE clause. Insertion characters are also provided for blanks, zeros, algebraic signs, and accounting entries.

Figure 8.12   Simple Edits Using Z, (.), and (,)

Originating PICTURE	Originating Value	Receiving PICTURE	Receiving Value
9(6)	00032	Z(6)	32
9(6)	742153	Z(5)	42153
9(6)	004175	Z9(5)	04175
9(6)	002174	Z(6).99	2174.00
9(6)	000000	Z(6).ZZ	
9(6)	000000	Z(6).99	.00
9(6)	715234	ZZZ,ZZZ	715,234
S9(6)	+000124	ZZZ,ZZZ	124
S9(6)	−001759	ZZZ,ZZZ	1,759
S9(6)	−000321	999,999	000,321
S9(6)	+017421	ZZZ,ZZZ.ZZ	17,421.00
9(4)V99	034217	ZZZ,ZZZ	342
9(4)V99	049716	Z,ZZZ.99	497.16
9(4)V99	000000	Z,ZZZ.ZZ	
9(4)V99	172431	ZZ,ZZZ.ZZ	1724.310
9(4)V99	326414	9,999.99	3,264.14

Figure 8.13   Insertion Characters B and 0

Originating PICTURE	Originating Value	Receiving PICTURE	Receiving Value
9(4)	1024	990099	100042
9(4)	0612	9999000	0612000
9(4)	0112	9000	2000
X(4)	A124	X0XXX	A0124
X(4)	A321	XBXXX	A 321
X(10)	501234721	XXXBXXBXXXX	501 23 4721
X(8)	DALLASTX	X(6)BXX	DALLAS TX
9(4)	2734	99B99	27 34
9(4)V9	18752	9999BV9	1875 2
9(4)	0000	99BB99	00 00

Figure 8.14   Algebraic Insertion Edit Characters

Originating PICTURE	Originating Value	Receiving PICTURE	Receiving Value
S9(4)	−3271	9999−	3721−
S9(4)	+1492	9999−	1492
S9(4)	−8721	9999+	8721−
S9(4)	+1579	9999+	1579+
S9(4)V99	−712432	9(4).9(2)DB	7124.32DB
S9(4)V99	+712432	9(4).9(2)DB	7124.32
S9(4)V99	−169218	9(4).9(2)CR	1692.18CR
S9(4)V99	+169218	9(4).9(2)CR	1692.18

Blank characters can be inserted in any data item type. The edit character B is written in the PICTURE clause in every position where a space is desired. Zeros can be inserted in the same fashion. For example, accounting summaries are often cited in thousands of dollars. On the printed report, however, the missing zeros can be inserted with the edit character 0. Figure 8.13 shows how the edit characters B and 0 can be used in PICTURE clauses to improve readability.

Blanks, zeros, slashes, and commas can be inserted at any point in the data field. However, a decimal point can only appear once within a numeric edited field. The accounting insertion characters DB (debit) and CR (credit) and the algebraic insertion characters + (plus) and - (minus) may also appear only once when placed to the right of a numeric edited field. "DB", "CR", and "-" appear as specified on the printed report only if the numeric value is negative; otherwise spaces appear. A + edit character appears on the report as a "+" for positive values and as a "-" for negative values. Figure 8.14 illustrates the use of DB, CR, -, and + as insertion characters.

Floating Edit Characters. The Z edit character is an example of a *floating edit character* because each Z suppresses one instance of a leading zero until the first nonzero digit is found. Algebraic sign edit characters may also be used as floating edit characters. If specified to the left of a numeric edited item, the + and - edit characters may be used in a fashion similar to the Z edit character. This causes a "+" or "-" or blank to appear immediately before the first nonzero numeric position. Any other leading zeros are blank-filled. All floating edit characters may be used in combination with commas and decimal points and follow the same rules as the Z edit character. Other useful floating edit characters are the dollar sign ($) and the check protection character "*". The dollar sign follows the same rules as the Z, +, and - floating characters. The check protection character is similar; but, rather than filling the leftmost zeros with spaces, the zeros are replaced with the character "*". Figure 8.15 demonstrates various examples of the use of floating edit characters.

Figure 8.15   Floating Edit Characters

Originating PICTURE	Originating Value	Receiving PICTURE	Receiving Value
S9(4)V99	000000	$$$$$.$$	
S9(4)V99	124737	$(5).$$	$1247.37
S9(4)V99	074831	$$,$$$.$$	$748.31
S9(4)V99	−174831	$$,$$$.$$	$1748.31
S9(4)V99	923462	$$$$.$$	$234.62
S9(4)V99	−429614	− − − − −.− −	−4296.14
S9(4)V99	000000	− − − − −.− −	
S9(4)V99	429614	− − − − −.− −	4296.14
S9(4)V99	032112	++,+++.++	+321.12
S9(4)V99	197214	++,+++.++	+1,972.14
S9(4)V99	713428	****.**	7134.28
S9(4)V99	000000	****.**	*******
S9(4)V99	019732	****.**	*197.32
S9(4)V99	162143	*,***.**	1,621.43
S9(4)V99	097172	*,***.**	**971.72
S9(4)V99	000002	*,***.**	*****.02

Combining Edit Characters. The comma and the decimal point are often used in combination with floating edit characters. Special combinations exist that prove useful in printing reports, and special rules exist that govern the allowed combinations. When a decimal point is in the middle of a floating PICTURE description such as $$$.$$, the entire field is left blank when the data item value is zero. However, if the value is other than zero, the positions to the right of the decimal are treated as if they were a PICTURE of 9's. For example, the value 067 would appear as if its PICTURE clause were $$$.99 and would result in the printed field $.67.

Any insertion character may be used in combination with a floating edit character. When an insertion character appears to the right of the floating string, the floating character appears as close to the leading digit as possible and overlays the insertion character if necessary. Thus $$,$$$.$$ with a value of 342.12 will print as $342.12. The $ overlaid the , insertion character.

Combinations of floating strings are allowed. This may be accomplished by using a single floating character at the beginning of the PICTURE clause, followed by the desired number of the second character. Thus the PICTURE $***,***.99 forces the printing of the dollar sign in the first position, followed by a string of check protection characters. Figure 8.16 shows various combinations of editing characters. Following is a summary of useful characters that may appear in the PICTURE clause:

Figure 8.16   *Mixed Edit Characters*

Originating PICTURE	Originating Value	Receiving PICTURE	Receiving Value
S9(5)V99	0132152	$ZZ,ZZZ.ZZ	$ 1,321.52
S9(5)V99	–0791752	$ZZ,ZZZ.ZZDB	$ 7,917.52DB
S9(5)V99	0791752	$ZZ,ZZZ.ZZDB	$ 7,917.52
S9(5)V99	0000000	$**,***.**	$*********
S9(5)V99	0000000	$**,***.99	$*****.00
S9(5)V99	0134272	$**,***.99	$*1,342.72
S9(5)V99	0017842	+ZZ,ZZZZ.99	+ 178.42
S9(5)V99	–1243612	$$$,$$$.$$BDB	$12,436.12 DB

X   Represents one character of any kind.

9   Stands for a numeric digit.

S   Indicates a numeric value has a sign but is not stored as a position and will not print as a " + " or " - ".

V   Indicates the position of a decimal point in a number. The assumed decimal is not a character in storage.

Z   A leading zero suppression edit character.

B   Inserts a blank into the data field at the specified location.

/   Inserts a slash into the data field at the specified location.

0   Inserts a zero into the data field at the specified location.

,   Inserts a comma into a numeric edited data field at the specified location.

.   Represents an actual decimal point that would appear on a printed report.

*   A floating edit character used primarily for protection of the amount in the printing of checks.

$ A floating edit character that will insert a "$" in the last position suppressed and leave the preceding spaces blank.

DB Debit notation; used to the right of a numeric edited field and inserts a "DB" when the value of the data item is negative.

CR Credit notation; used to the right of a numeric edited field and inserts a "CR" when the value of the data item is negative.

+   The plus is used to the right of a numeric edited field and inserts a "+" when the value is positive or a "-" when the value is negative. Also used as a floating edit character that prints a " +" or "-" in the leftmost suppressed position and leaves the preceding zeros blank.

-    Used to the right of a numeric edited field and inserts a "-" when the value is negative or a blank when the value is positive. Also used as a floating edit character that prints a " - " or blank in the leftmost suppressed position and leaves the preceding zeros blank.

The MOVE statement is used to edit the data item; the unedited items must be moved to the edited item. Editing may also be accomplished by specifying an edited item as the result field. For example, when the GIVING option is used in the ADD, SUBTRACT, MULTIPLY, and DIVIDE statements, the data item specified in the GIVING clause may be a numeric edited item. The arithmetic operation is carried out and the result is essentially moved from a temporary storage location to the numeric edited item specified. This causes the editions specified in the PICTURE clause to take place. The COMPUTE statement also allows the specification of a numeric edited field as the receiving field for the result of the arithmetic expression specified. Numeric edited items may also be moved into numeric fields, resulting in the numeric value for use in computations. Figure 8.17 summarizes the rules governing the MOVEment of data items.

Figure 8.17   *Rules Governing Data Item MOVEs*

	Receiving Item			
Sending Item	Numeric	Numeric Edited	Alphanumeric	Alphanumeric Edited
Alphanumeric Groups, or Edited	AN	X	AN	AN
Edited Alphanumeric	X	X	AN	AN
Numeric Integer	N	N	AN	AN
Numeric Noninteger	N	N	X	X
Numeric Edited	N	N	AN	AN

AN = Handled as an alphanumeric move
N = Handled as a numeric move
X = Not allowed

8.3　*Report Logic*

Writing reports follows the same file transfer logic required to transfer records from one file to another that we presented in an earlier chapter. The program increases in length, however, primarily because of the increased number of MOVE statements required to set up the individual report lines. In addition, if totals are maintained for various fields, the program further increases in length but not in complexity. Other minor changes to the file transfer program logic result in large changes to its COBOL code. To better understand the logic for producing a report, let us develop the program for the Monthly Sales report of our earlier example.

Figure 8.9 illustrates the hierarchy chart for the program. The main module is called "List Sales File." The major repeating task is the isolation of each office grouping since the major control break in the report is by sales office. This task is indicated by the module "2000 Isolate Office Group." The processing required before we can group the file into offices is represented by the module "1000 Prepare Sales Report," which prints the first page headings, performs the priming read, and initializes variables. Module "3000 Conclude Sales Report" prints the final totals.

8.3.1　*Page Control Structure and Logic*

Page breaks differ from common control breaks in that page breaks are a physical requirement due to page length rather than a logical break in the report file. To handle page breaks, we introduce the module "1100 Print Page Headings." The module handles the paging, the update of the line and page counters, and the writing of the headings. The logic appears in Figure 8.10. This module may be performed from any point in the program when paging is appropriate, as at the beginning of a program or before each detail line is printed.

Coding the Page Control. For the page control logic function, a data item must be used to hold the page number that is to be printed at the top of each page. A line counter is also necessary to determine when the maximum number of lines per page has been reached. The entries from Figure 8.8 for these data items are the following:

```
WORKING-STORAGE SECTION.
01    PAGE-CONTROL-COUNTERS.
      05  PC-LINE-COUNTER   PIC 99 VALUE 99.
      05  PC-PAGE-NUMBER    PIC 9999 VALUE ZERO.
      05  PC-LINE-LIMIT     PIC 99 VALUE 55.
```

The page number is initialized to zero to start the count with page number 1 when the first page headings are written. A line counter is initialized to 99 so that when it is tested at the start of the report, the counter will test larger than the page length limit and cause the headings to be printed. A line limit is set to be 55 lines per page. This value would have been specified on the associated report layout. The code for a module to control paging using the logic in Figure 8.10 would be:

```
1100-PRINT-PAGE-HEADINGS.
    IF PC- LINE-COUNTER > PC-LINE-LIMIT
```

```
ADD 1 TO PC-PAGE-NUMBER
MOVE PC-PAGE-NUMBER TO SBR-PAGE-NBR
WRITE SBR-SALE-REC FROM SBR-PAGE-HEADING-1 AFTER PAGE
WRITE SBR-SALE-REC FROM SBR-PAGE-HEADING-2
WRITE SBR-SALE-REC FROM SBR-PAGE-HEADING-3
WRITE SBR-SALE-REC FROM SBR-COLUMN-HEADING-1
        AFTER ADVANCING 2 LINES
WRITE SBR-SALE-REC FROM SBR-COLUMN-HEADING-2
MOVE 6 TO PC-LINE-COUNTER.
```

8.3.2   *Automatic Page Control*

COBOL provides the optional facility to control the format of the page automatically. This is accomplished by the use of an additional clause in the file definition entry for the report file and an additional clause in the WRITE statement. For a report, the FD is extended to:

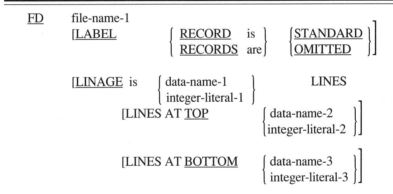

1. Data-names 1 through 3 must all be unsigned, integer elementary items.
2. Integer-literal 1 must be positive.
3. Integer-literals 2 and 3 must be nonnegative.
4. Data-names 1 through 3 are used to set and reset the page size when an OPEN . . . OUTPUT is executed or a WRITE . . . ADVANCING PAGE is executed.

The LINAGE clause allows the specification of a physical page length. The LINES AT TOP and LINES AT BOTTOM allow specification of the margins and define a logical page size. If the margin settings are omitted, the logical page defaults to the physical page. The LINAGE clause forces the automatic creation of a variable called LINAGE-COUNTER that may be referenced, but not changed, in the procedure division. LINAGE-COUNTER represents the line number at which the report is positioned within the logical page. If multiple reports appear in the program, references to LINAGE-COUNTER must be qualified by the file name.

The WRITE statement is also modified to incorporate the LINAGE feature. The additions are:

WRITE   record-name   [FROM identifier-1]

$$\left[\left\{ \begin{array}{c} \underline{\text{BEFORE}} \\ \underline{\text{AFTER}} \end{array} \right\} \text{ADVANCING} \left\{ \begin{array}{c} \left\{ \begin{array}{c} \text{identifier-2} \\ \text{integer-1} \\ \underline{\text{PAGE}} \end{array} \right\} \left\{ \begin{array}{c} \text{LINE} \\ \text{LINES} \end{array} \right\} \end{array} \right\}\right]$$

$$\left[\text{AT} \left\{ \begin{array}{c} \underline{\text{END-OF-PAGE}} \\ \underline{\text{EOP}} \end{array} \right\} \text{imperative-statement-1} \right]$$

$$\left[\underline{\text{NOT}} \text{ AT} \left\{ \begin{array}{c} \underline{\text{END-OF-PAGE}} \\ \underline{\text{EOP}} \end{array} \right\} \text{imperative-statement-2} \right]$$

1. ADVANCING PAGE and END-OF-PAGE (or EOP) cannot appear in the same statement.
2. If END-OF-PAGE (or EOP) is used, the LINAGE clause must appear in the FD for the associated file.
3. If the PAGE clause is used and the LINAGE clause is also used, the ADVANCING option causes the device to be positioned at the start of the logical page, not the physical page.

If the logical end of page is reached during the execution of a WRITE statement with the END-OF-PAGE phrase, imperative-statement-1 is executed. Thus, imperative-statement-1 is executed only after the record is written and the device has been repositioned. If the LINAGE clause is specified but the END-OF-PAGE option is not specified, the output file is positioned to the start of the next logical page. Thus, if the LINAGE option is used, it is strongly advisable to use the END-OF-PAGE option on all WRITE statements to the particular file, except for headings.

Using the automatic page controls would cause minor changes to be made in the design of the program. The "List Sales File" example will illustrate the changes. First, no change is needed in the hierarchy chart of Figure 8.9. In the Nassi-Schneiderman chart of Figure 8.10, the selection will have to be removed since COBOL will now be controlling the paging. The new file description would appear:

```
FD    SALES-BY-REGION-FILE

      LABEL RECORDS ARE OMITTED
      LINAGE IS 66 LINES
      LINES AT TOP 0
      LINES AT BOTTOM 11.
01    SBR-SALE-REC      PIC X(80).
```

The physical page is set to be the length of the computer paper and the desired 55 lines per logical page is set by the top and bottom margins. The WORKING-STORAGE page controls would now only require PC-PAGE-NUMBER. The module's code is now:

```
1100-PRINT-PAGE-HEADINGS.
        ADD 1 TO PC-PAGE-COUNTER.
        MOVE PC-PAGE-COUNTER TO SBR-PAGE-NBR.
        WRITE SBR-SALE-REC FROM SBR-PAGE-HEADING-1.
        WRITE SBR-SALE-REC FROM SBR-PAGE-HEADING-2.
        WRITE SBR-SALE-REC FROM SBR-PAGE-HEADING-3.
        WRITE SBR-SALE-REC FROM SBR-COLUMN-HEADING-1
                AFTER ADVANCING 2 LINES.
        WRITE SBR-SALE-REC FROM SBR-COLUMN-HEADING-2.
```

The LINAGE and END-OF-PAGE options can help reduce the coding burden to a small degree. More complex reports, however, often require more complete page control than is allowed by the rigid logical page definition. In this text we will stick with the more flexible approach of programmer-controlled paging until Chapter 13.

8.3.3   *Control Break Structure and Logic*

Figure 8.9 illustrates the entire hierarchy chart. Modules subordinate to module "2000 Isolate Office Group" contain the logic needed to process the control breaks. As the sales file is processed, it will be segmented into its major control break which, in this example, is at the individual sales office level. First, any headings associated with the highest-level group (the major control break) and any variable initializations are performed by module "2100 Begin Office Break." Second, the office divisions are subdivided into sales representative groups within each sales region. This secondary control break is module "2200 Isolate Representative Group." The third function ends the major control break by printing the office totals and maintaining overall totals. These functions are performed by "2300 End Office Break." If further control breaks were needed they would proceed in a similar fashion.

Once the second control break has been determined, the detail lines are processed by module "2200 Format Detail Line" and its subordinates. The Nassi-Schneiderman charts for the "List Sales File" program hierarchy chart are shown in Figure 8.10.

The overall totals for the example are kept in module "2320 Maintain Overall Totals" which adds the summary information for the major break level to the overall totals. In other words, the dollar sales for each office are added to the dollar sales of the entire company. Since the addition is performed at the time of the major break, the grand report totals need not be considered at the lower levels in the hierarchy. This helps keep the structure simpler by reducing the number of additions required at the detail level. For example, in module "2222 Maintain Representative Totals," the dollar amount from each input record is added to the totals for the representatives but not for office region totals and grand report totals. When a control break occurs, the appropriate totaling is accomplished. This method of maintaining totals at various levels is termed "rolling the totals," signifying that minor control break totals are rolled into major control break totals only when an actual break occurs in the process.

Another point worth noting is that, in this example, modules "2310 Print Office Totals" and "2231 Print Representative Totals" do not have subordinate paging considerations when printing the summary lines for the control breaks. This is due to the assumption that the user desires to keep the summary lines from appearing as the first line of a new page. User preferences should be taken into account in design decisions.

Control breaks occur when selected data items in the report detail record change value. In this example they occur when the sales representative number changes or the sales office identification changes. Control breaks are iteration structures in which detail lines continue to be printed uninterruptedly until a control break condition exists. In the Monthly Sales report example, detail lines are printed until a new representative record is found in the input file. Also, notice that sales representatives are processed until a new region or the end-of-file record is found in the input file. Thus, multiple control breaks are depicted as nested iteration structures. This can be seen in the Nassi-Schneiderman charts for modules "2000 Isolate Office Group" and "2200 Isolate Representative Group" in Figure 8.10.

The logic for each control break level may be summarized as follows:

1. Establish control break starting value.
2. Process next level until new value is found.
3. Write control break totals.

The next level could be a second control break, or the detail lines. Thus, for one control break and detail line, the logic in structured English is:

```
READ first record;
PERFORM program initializations;
REPEAT UNTIL file at end
     PERFORM work to start break;
     REPEAT UNTIL break is found
          process current record;
          READ next record;
     END-REPEAT;
     PERFORM wrapup for break;
END-REPEAT;
PERFORM wrapup for program.
```

The logic for processing two levels of control breaks is:

```
READ first record:
PERFORM program initialization;
REPEAT UNTIL file at end
  PERFORM work to start high-level break;
  REPEAT UNTIL high-level break found
       PERFORM work to start low-level break;
       REPEAT UNTIL low-level break found
            process current record;
            READ next record;
       END-REPEAT;
       PERFORM wrapup for low-level break;
  END-REPEAT;
  PERFORM wrapup for high-level break;
```

END-REPEAT;
PERFORM wrap up for program.

We have now completed the design for a report program that takes one input file and generates one report. Variations of the model might include the reproduction of more than one report, the use of more than one input file, or the updating of a master file during the report generation. Regardless of variations in the report, it is important to remember that control breaks represent levels in the hierarchy chart of a report.

Control Break Code. We mentioned before that an office or representative break should occur whenever the appropriate data items change. Therefore, the current values of the office and representative fields in the sales file must be compared with the previous record. However, we know that when a record is READ, the contents of the previous record are no longer available. This problem is resolved by using a save area in the WORKING-STORAGE SECTION to preserve the needed previous values. The entries to define the save areas are:

```
01    SAVE-BREAK-VALUES.
      05    SAVE-OFFICE              PIC X(10)
      05    SAVE-REPRESENTATIVE      PIC X(10)
```

The save areas are initialized in module "2100 Begin Office Break" when the control break begins. Thus, if the L.A. office is being processed, SAVE-OFFICE will be equal to "L.A." When the next office is found in the input record, a control break will take place. The code in the PROCEDURE DIVISION of Figure 8.8 appears as follows:

```
2100-BEGIN-OFFICE-BREAK.
      MOVE MS-OFFICE TO SAVE-OFFICE.
      PERFORM 1100-PRINT-PAGE-HEADINGS.
      PERFORM 2110-PRINT-OFFICE-HEADINGS.
```

The COBOL code of each module that directs a control break is nearly identical. For the office break the code appears as follows:

```
2000-ISOLATE-OFFICE-GROUP.
      PERFORM 2100-BEGIN-OFFICE-BREAK.
      PERFORM 2200-ISOLATE-REPRESENTATIVE-GP
            UNTIL MS-OFFICE NOT EQUAL SAVE-OFFICE.
      PERFORM 2300-END-OFFICE-BREAK.
```

The considerations at the end of each break would also be similar from one control break to the next. The code for the office break is:

```
2300-END-OFFICE-BREAK.
      PERFORM 2310-PRINT-OFFICE-TOTALS.
      PERFORM 2320-MAINTAIN-OVERALL-TOTALS.
```

A special condition arises when the program reaches the end of the file. Since we are comparing the current record contents stored in the save area, the current record will have no data, just an end-of-file mark. To force the execution of control breaks when we finish processing the input file we replace the end-of-file mark in the input record area. A good choice for a replacement character is all 9s for a numeric data item or the reserved word HIGH-VALUES for an alphanumeric field.

```
1200-READ-SALES-RECORD
      READ MONTHLY-SALES-FILE AT END
            MOVE "Y" TO EOF-MONTHLY-SALES-FILE
            MOVE ALL "9" TO MS-SALE-RECORD.
```

In this way, when processing continues, the fact that the sales representative ID number has changed will cause a proper control break for that group. Similarly, the change of office number will cause a control break for that group. An alternative method for dealing with this situation is to test for the end of the file whenever a control break is tested for.

In summary, no special COBOL commands are required to generate reports of moderate complexity. As with all programs, the critical factor is the design. By using iterative structures to manage control breaks, reports can be created to handle many business reporting systems.

Case Study: CDL's Accounts Receivable Listing

Management requires a simple report listing by customer of all CDL open accounts. The program specifications are given in Figure 8.18 and the record layout for the customer open items file is shown in Figure 8.19. Figure 8.20 shows the layout for this particular report. As you can see, control breaks are required on the order number and customer number. Grand totals also need to be maintained for the balance due.

Figure 8.18   CDL's "Accounts Receivable Listing" Program Specifications

TITLE: *List Accounts Receivable File*

PREPARED BY: *C. Hilton*

DATE: *6-30-93*

FILES USED		
FILE NAME	**MEDIA**	**ORGANIZATION**
Customer open items	*Disk*	*Sequential*
A/R Open Items List	*Printer*	*Sequential*

DESCRIPTION

Produce a complete listing of the accounts receivable file. Print only the dollar amounts due and the date in the detail lines. Break for major summary totals on customer number and secondly on order number. Grand totals are also desired.

Figure 8.19   Record Layouts for CDL's "Accounts Receivable Listing" Program

RECORD LAYOUT SHEET
Revised

Record Name: *A/R Open Item*		File Name: *Customer Open Items*			
Prepared By: *C. Hilton*		Date: *6-30-93*			
Key Fields:		Organization: *Sequential*			
Field	Description	Type*	Length	Decimal
Customer #	*Customer ID*	*N*	*6*	
Order Number	*Preprinted order number*	*N*	*6*	
Date	*MM / DD / YY of order*	*N*	*6*	
Billed amount	*Amount billed to customer*	*N*	*8*	*2*
Paid amount	*Partial payment received*	*N*	*8*	*2*

* A = alphanumeric
  N = numeric

Figure 8.20   Report Layout for CDL's "Accounts Recevable Listing" Program

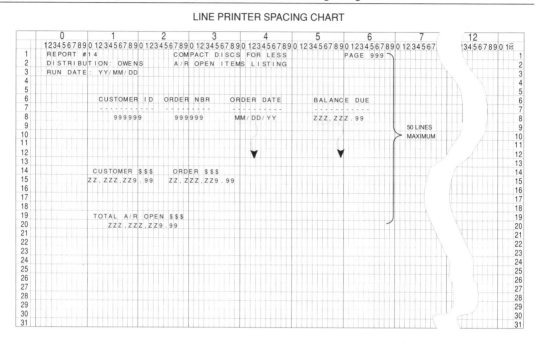

LINE PRINTER SPACING CHART

Charlene notices that the program is a simple listing of a sequential file with two control breaks. She pulls out her beginning COBOL class notes because she remembers that she was assigned a similar problem back then. After all, there is no need to waste effort in designing a program that thousands of other programmers, including herself, have successfully developed. Based on her class notes, Charlene develops the hierarchy chart illustrated in Figure 8.21. The Nassi-Schneiderman charts, shown in Figure 8.22, are also similar to the old design.

Figure 8.21 *Hierarchy Chart for "Accounts Receivable Listing" Program*

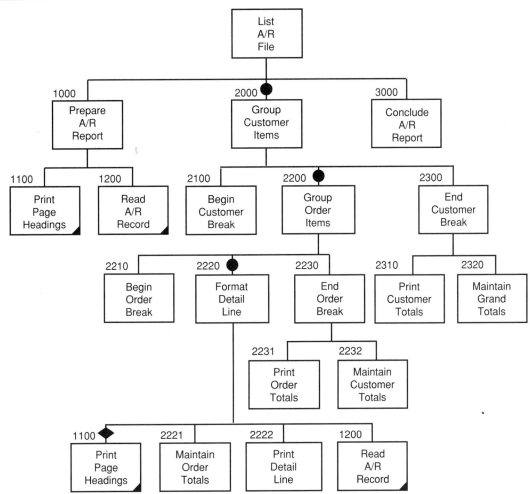

Figure 8.22   N-S Charts for CDL's "Accounts Receivable Listing" Program

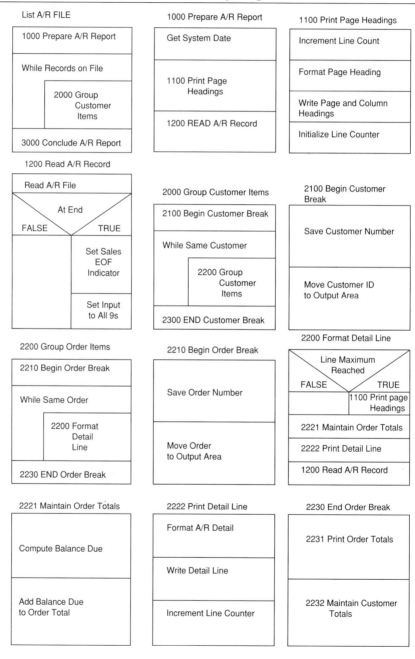

Figure 8.22 (continued)

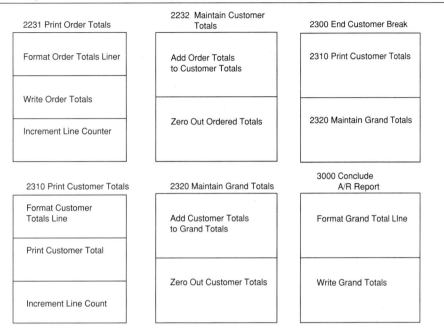

Compare modules "2100 Begin Customer Break" and "2210 Begin Order Break" with the generic report hierarchy chart of Figure 8.9. You will note some simplifications because the control breaks do not have any headings. Thus each module does not concern itself with the task of formatting and printing control break headings. This results in very short paragraphs in the COBOL code. Charlene considers eliminating the paragraphs but decides the savings in code is not worth the loss of modularity. There is no telling when someone might request that control break headings be added to the report.

The Nassi-Schneiderman chart for module "1200 Read A/R Record" adds an extra process to the end-of-file logic so that a control break occurs at the end of the file. Because the order and customer numbers in the input area will be compared with the order and customer numbers in the save area, Charlene moves a number different from a valid customer number and from valid order numbers to the input area. Her choice is a good one because neither a customer number nor an order number of all 9s may appear on the input file. The entire code for producing the open accounts report is shown in Figure 8.23.

Figure 8.23   **COBOL Code for CDL's "Accounts Receivable Listing" Program**

```
IDENTIFICATION DIVISION.
PROGRAM-ID.  LIST-ACCOUNT-RECEIVABLE-FILE
*      THIS PROGRAM USES THE A/R FILE TO PRODUCE A LISTING
*      WITH BREAKS ON CUSTOMER AN ORDER NUMBERS

AUTHOR    C. HILTON
DATE-WRITTEN    6/30/95
DATE-COMPILED   6/30/95



ENVIRONMENT DIVISION.


CONFIGURATION SECTION.

SOURCE-COMPUTER.   GENERIC-COMPUTER.
OBJECT-COMPUTER.   GENERIC-COMPUTER.

INPUT-OUTPUT SECTION.

FILE-CONTROL.
    SELECT AR-OPEN-ITEM-FILE ASSIGN TO DISK.
    SELECT OPEN-ITEM-LIST ASSIGN TO PRINTER.
```

```
DATA DIVISION


FILE SECTION

FD   OPEN-ITEM-LIST-FILE
     LABEL RECORDS ARE OMITTED

01   OIL-LINE   PIC X(80)


FD   AR-OPEN-ITEM-FILE
     LABEL RECORDS ARE STANDARD

01   AR-OPEN-ITEM-REC
     05   AR-CUSTOMER-NUMBER   PIC 9(6).
     05   AR-ORDER-NUMBER      PIC 9(6).
     05   AR-ORDER-DATE        PIC 9(6).
     05   AR-BILLED-AMOUNT     PIC 9(6)V99.
     05   AR-AMOUNT-PAID       PIC 9(6)V99.
```

Figure 8.23 (continued)

```
SYSTEM                                      PUNCHING INSTRUCTIONS              PAGE        OF
PROGRAM                                     GRAPHIC                           CARD FORM NUMBER
PROGRAMMER                         DATE      PUNCH

SEQUENCE   CONT  A   B                       COBOL STATEMENT                          IDENTIFICATION
1    3 4  6 7 8  12   16   20   24   28   32   36   40   44   48   52   56   60   64   68  72   76   80

              WORKING-STORAGE SECTION.

         01   END-OF-FILE-INDICATORS.
              05   EOF-AR   PIC X(5) VALUE "FALSE".


         01   SAVE-AREA.
              05   SAVE-CUSTOMER-NUMBER PIC 9(6).
              05   SAVE-ORDER-NUMBER     PIC 9(6).


         01   TOTALS.
              05   TOTAL-GRAND-AMOUNT-OWED        PIC 9(9)V99.
              05   TOTAL-AMOUNT-OPEN-ON-ORDER  PIC 9(8)V99.
              05   TOTAL-AMOUNT-CUSTOMER-OWES  PIC 9(8)V99.


         01   WORK-AREAS.
              05   WA-BALANCE-DUE   PIC 9(6)V99.
              05   WA-PAGE          PIC 999  VALUE ZERO.
              05   WA-LINES         PIC 99   VALUE ZERO.
              05   WA-DATE          PIC 9(6).
              05   WA-LINE-MAXIMUM  PIC 99   VALUE 50.
```

```
SYSTEM                                      PUNCHING INSTRUCTIONS              PAGE        OF
PROGRAM                                     GRAPHIC                           CARD FORM NUMBER
PROGRAMMER                         DATE      PUNCH

SEQUENCE   CONT  A   B                       COBOL STATEMENT                          IDENTIFICATION
1    3 4  6 7 8  12   16   20   24   28   32   36   40   44   48   52   56   60   64   68  72   76   80

         01   OIL-LINES

              05   OIL-COMPANY-TITLE.
                   10   FILLER               PIC X(31) VALUE
                                             "REPORT #19".
                   10   FILLER               PIC X(33) VALUE
                                             "COMPACT DISCS FOR LESS"
                   10   FILLER               PIC X(5)  VALUE "PAGE".
                   10   OIL-PAGE             PIC ZZ9.

              05   OIL-REPORT-TITLE.
                   10   FILLER               PIC X(31) VALUE
                                             "DISTRIBUTION OWENS".
                   10   FILLER               PIC X(22) VALUE
                                             "A/R OPEN ITEMS LISTING".

              05   OIL-DATE-TITLE.
                   10   FILLER               PIC X(10) VALUE "RUN DATE:".
                   10   OIL-RUN-DATE         PIC 99/99/99.
```

Figure 8.23 **(continued)**

```
05  OIL-COLUMN-HEADING.
    10  FILLER                      PIC X(11)  VALUE SPACE.
    10  FILLER                      PIC X(15)  VALUE "CUSTOMER ID".
    10  FILLER                      PIC X(13)  VALUE "ORDER NBR".
    10  FILLER                      PIC X(14)  VALUE "ORDER DATE".
    10  FILLER                      PIC X(11)  VALUE "BALANCE DUE".

05  OIL-UNDERLINE.
    10  FILLER                      PIC X(11)  VALUE SPACE.
    10  FILLER                      PIC X(15)  VALUE "-----------".
    10  FILLER                      PIC X(13)  VALUE "-----------".
    10  FILLER                      PIC X(14)  VALUE "-----------".
    10  FILLER                      PIC X(11)  VALUE "-----------".

05  OIL-DETAIL
    10  FILLER                      PIC X(14)  VALUE SPACE.
    10  OIL-CUSTOMER-NUMBER         PIC X(6)   VALUE SPACE.
    10  FILLER                      PIC X(8)   VALUE SPACE.
    10  OIL-ORDER-NUMBER            PIC X(6)   VALUE SPACE.
    10  FILLER                      PIC X(6)   VALUE SPACE.
    10  OIL-ORDER-DATE              PIC 99/99/99.
    10  FILLER                      PIC X(5)   VALUE SPACE.
    10  OIL-BALANCE-DUE             PIC ZZZ,ZZ9.99.
```

```
05  OIL-CUSTOMER-TOTAL-HEADING.
    10  FILLER                      PIC X(11)  VALUE SPACE.
    10  FILLER                      PIC X(30)  VALUE "CUSTOMER $$$".

05  OIL-CUSTOMER-TOTAL-DETAIL.
    10  FILLER                      PIC X(10)  VALUE SPACE.
    10  OIL-CUSTOMER-TOTAL          PIC ZZ,ZZZ,ZZ9.99.

05  OIL-ORDER-TOTAL-HEADING.
    10  FILLER                      PIC X(27)  VALUE SPACE.
    10  FILLER                      PIC X(10)  VALUE "ORDER $$$".

05  OIL-ORDER-TOTAL DETAIL.
    10  FILLER                      PIC X(24)  VALUE SPACE.
    10  OIL-ORDER-TOTAL             PIC ZZ,ZZZ,ZZ9.99.

05  OIL-GRAND-TOTAL-HEADING.
    10  FILLER                      PIC X(11)  VALUE SPACE.
    10  FILLER                      PIC X(20)  VALUE
                                    "TOTAL A/R OPEN $$$".

05  OIL-GRAND-TOTAL-DETAIL.
    10  FILLER                      PIC X(13)  VALUE SPACE.
    10  OIL-GRAND-TOTAL             PIC ZZZ,ZZZ,ZZ9.99.
```

Figure 8.23 (continued)

```
PROCEDURE DIVISION.

LIST-ACCOUNTS-RECEIVABLE-FILE.
    OPEN INPUT AR-OPEN-ITEM-FILE.
    OPEN OUTPUT OPEN-ITEM-FILE.
    PERFORM 1000-PREPARE-AR-REPORT.
    PERFORM 2000-GROUP-CUSTOMER-ITEMS UNTIL EOF-AR = "TRUE"
    PERFORM 3000-CONCLUDE-AR-REPORT.
    CLOSE AR-OPEN-ITEM-FILE.
    CLOSE OPEN-ITEM-LIST-FILE.
    STOP RUN.

1000-PREPARE-AR-REPORT.
    ACCEPT WA-DATE TO OIL-RUN-DATE.
    PERFORM 1100-PRINT-PAGE-HEADINGS.
    PERFORM 1200-READ-AR-RECORD.
```

```
1100-PRINT-PAGE-HEADINGS.
    ADD 1 TO WA-PAGE.
    MOVE WA-PAGE TO OIL-PAGE.
    WRITE OIL-LINE FROM OIL-COMPANY-TITLE
        AFTER ADVANCING PAGE.
    WRITE OIL-LINE FROM OIL-REPORT-TITLE.
    WRITE OIL-LINE FROM OIL-DATE-TITLE.
    WRITE OIL-LINE FROM OIL-COLUMN-HEADING
        AFTER ADVANCING 3 LINES.
    WRITE OIL-LINE FROM OIL UNDERLINE.
    MOVE SPACES TO OIL-LINE.
    WRITE OIL-LINE.
    MOVE 8 TO WA-LINES.

1200-READ-AR-RECORD.
    READ AR-OPEN-ITEM-FILEF.
        AT END MOVE "TRUE " TO EOF-AR
               MOVE ALL "9" TO AR-OPEN-ITEM.
```

Figure 8.23   (continued)

```
        2000-GROUP-CUSTOMER-ITEMS.
            PERFORM 2100-BEGIN-CUSTOMER-BREAK.
            PERFORM 2200-GROUP-ORDER-ITEMS
                UNTIL SAVE-CUSTOMER-NUMBER NOT = AR-CUSTOMER-NUMBER.
            PERFORM 2300-END-CUSTOMER-BREAK.

        2100-BEGIN-CUSTOMER-BREAK.
            MOVE AR-CUSTOMER-NUMBER TO SAVE-CUSTOMER-NUMBER
            MOVE AR-CUSTOMER-NUMBER TO OILE-CUSTOMER-NUMBER.

        2200-GROUP-ORDER-ITEMS.
            PERFORM 2210-BEGIN-ORDER-BREAK.
            PERFORM 2220-FORMAT-DETAIL0-LINE
                UNTIL SAVE-ORDER-NUMBER NOT = AR-ORDER-NUMBER.

        2210-BEGIN-ORDER-BREAK.
            MOVE AR-ORDER-NUMBER TO SAVE-ORDER-NUMBER.
            MOVE AR-ORDER-NUMBER TO OIL-ORDER-NUMBER.
```

```
        2220-FORMAT-DETAIL-LINE.
            IF WA-LINES NOT LESS THAN WA-LINE-MAXIMUM
                PERFORM 1100-PRINT-PAGE-HEADINGS.
            PERFORM 2221-MAINTAIN-ORDER-TOTALS.
            PERFORM 2222-PRINT-DETAIL-LINE.
            PERFORM 1200-READ-AR-RECORD.

        2221-MAINTAIN-ORDER-TOTALS.
            COMPUTE WA-BALANCE-DUE TO TOTAL-AMOUNT-OPEN-ON-ORDER.

        2222-PRINT-DETAIL-LINE.
            MOVE WA-BALANCE-DUE TO OIL-BALANCE-DUE.
            MOVE AR-ORDER-DATE   TO OIL-ORDER-DATE.
            WRITE OIL-LINE FROM OIL-DETAIL.
            MOVE SPACES TO OIL-DETAIL.
            ADD 1 TO WA-LINES.
```

Figure 8.23   (continued)

```
SYSTEM                                              PUNCHING INSTRUCTIONS          PAGE        OF
PROGRAM                                             GRAPHIC                        CARD FORM NUMBER
PROGRAMMER                                 DATE     PUNCH

SEQUENCE    C  A  B                         COBOL STATEMENT                                    IDENTIFICATION
1   3 4  6 7 8   12   16   20   24   28   32   36   40   44   48   52   56   60   64   68   72   76   80

            2230-END-ORDER-BREAK.
                PERFORM 2231-PRINT-ORDER-TOTALS.
                PERFORM 2232-MAINTAIN-CUSTOMER-TOTALS.


            2231-PRINT-ORDER-TOTALS.
                MOVE TOTAL-AMOUNT-OPEN-ON-ORDER TO OIL-ORDER-TOTAL
                WRITE OIL-LINE FROM OIL-ORDER-TOTAL-HEADING.
                WRITE OIL-LINE FROM OIL-ORDER-TOTAL-DETAIL.
                ADD 2 TO WA-LINES.


            2232-MAINTAIN-CUSTOMER-TOTALS.
                ADD TOTAL-AMOUNT-OPEN-ON-ORDER TO TOTAL-AMOUNT-CUSTOMER-OWES.
                MOVE ZERO TO TOTAL-AMOUNT-OPEN-ON-ORDER.


            2300-END-CUSTOMER-BREAK.
                PERFORM 2310-PRINT-CUSTOMER-TOTALS.
                PERFORM 2320-MAINTAIN-GRAND-TOTALS.
```

```
SYSTEM                                              PUNCHING INSTRUCTIONS          PAGE        OF
PROGRAM                                             GRAPHIC                        CARD FORM NUMBER
PROGRAMMER                                 DATE     PUNCH

SEQUENCE    C  A  B                         COBOL STATEMENT                                    IDENTIFICATION
1   3 4  6 7 8   12   16   20   24   28   32   36   40   44   48   52   56   60   64   68   72   76   80

            2310-PRINT-CUSTOMER-TOTALS.
                MOVE TOTAL-AMOUNT-CUSTOMER-OWES TO OIL-CUSTOMER-TOTAL.
                WRITE OIL-LINE FROM OIL-CUSTOMER-TOTAL-HEADING.
                WRITE OIL-LINE FROM OIL-CUSTOMER-TOTAL-DETAIL.
                ADD 2 TO WA-LINES.


            2320-MAINTAIN-GRAND-TOTALS.
                ADD TOTAL-AMOUNT-CUSTOMER-OWES TO TOTAL-GRAND-AMOUNT-OWED.
                MOVE ZERO TO TOTAL-AMOUNT-CUSTOMER-OWES.


            3000-CONCLUDE-AR-REPORT.
                MOVE TOTAL-GRAND-AMOUNT-OWED TO OIL-GRAND-TOTAL-HEADING.
                WRITE OIL-LINE FROM OIL-GRAND-TOTAL-HEADING.
                WRITE OIL-LINE FROM OIL-GRAND-TOTAL-DETAIL.
```

Summary

Report generation is a major function of business programs. Reports are used by all levels of management to view important information. The reports must be well designed to serve the information needs of the user. Once the specifications are complete, the programmer takes over.

Reports are files and require FD entries. Reports have various components that have standard programming considerations. Because headings, page breaks, control breaks, detail lines, and totals appear on most reports, a programmer must be prepared to handle these individual components.

Each report line must be coded in the WORKING-STORAGE SECTION of the DATA DIVISION. Each line is defined by allowing for proper spacing and inserting the required constants through the FILLER and VALUE clauses. Variables that are printed on the report may be edited so that they are easier to read through the use of COBOL editing characters. Insertion edit characters such as decimal points and floating edit characters such as zero suppression are used to make the report aesthetically pleasing.

Page breaks are controlled by the programmer to enforce physical page length restrictions on the report. This requires that the programmer establish a line counter and a page counter. Every time a line is to be printed, the line counter should be examined to determine if a page break is needed.

Control breaks segment large reports into more manageable pieces. Control breaks are determined by changes in specific fields of the report detail lines. Thus, a control break directs the flow of control in a program by requiring totals and headings based on certain conditions in the report.

Key Terms

detail line	report layout	page breaks
headings	insertion characters	LINAGE
control breaks	floating edit character	END-OF-PAGE

Hints for Avoiding Errors

1. COBOL does not set items in WORKING-STORAGE to any particular value. Therefore, remember to initialize all counters and totals with the VALUE clause or in the PROCEDURE DIVISION by moving initial values into them.
2. Control breaks should be carried out at the end of the report. When listing a file, move an appropriate value to the input area containing the end-of-file marker to force a control break; otherwise, the program will attempt to read past the end of the file.
3. Do not forget to increment the line counter for each line printed. Also remember to increment the page number and to move the new number to the page number output field before printing.
4. When printing a report with control breaks, the input file must be in the same order as the control breaks.

5. Spaces should be moved into a print line being built in the FILE SECTION before any data items are moved. Whatever characters were there before are "erased" by overlaying them with blanks so that you build the next record on a clean slate.

Exercises

8.1 Analyze, design, and code the program specified in Figures 8.24 and 8.25.

8.2 Design and code a program that generates a customer balance report as shown in Figure 8.26. The input file is in customer number order and has the following layout:

Customer Number	5	Numeric
Customer Name	15	Alphanumeric
Payment	8	Numeric (2 Decimal)
Payment-Date	6	MMDDYY
Purchase	8	Numeric (2 Decimal)
Purchase-Date	6	MMDDYY

Figure 8.24   Program Specifications for Exercise 8.1

PROGRAM SUMMARY

TITLE: *Population List*

PREPARED BY: *J. Hodd*

DATE: *6-19-93*

FILES USED		
FILE NAME	MEDIA	ORGANIZATION
Population	*Disk*	*Sequential*

DESCRIPTION

Produce a state population summary. Break on county and print county and grand totals. Design a new layout. The input file is in Figure 8.24.

Figure 8.25   **Record Layout for Exercise 8.1**

RECORD LAYOUT SHEET

Record Name: *City population*		File Name: *Population*		
Prepared By: *J. Hodd*		Date: *6-19-93*		
Key Fields:		Organization: *Sequential*		
Field	Description	Type*	Length	Decimal
City	*Name of city*	*A*	*20*	
County	*Name of county*	*A*	*10*	
Population	*Number as of last census*	*N*	*8*	*0*

* A = alphanumeric
N = numeric

Figure 8.26   **Customer Balance Report Layout**

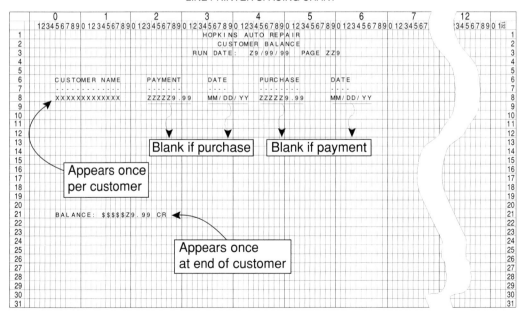

8.3 Use the file of Exercise 8.2, but assume the file is in order of payment or purchase date. Design a report to show total purchases and payments with a control break on DATE.

8.4 Which is not a consideration in designing a report layout?
   a. COBOL editing
   b. Good spacing
   c. Headings
   d. Totals
   e. User readability
   f. Size of WORKING-STORAGE
   g. Detail lines

For Exercises 8.5 through 8.9 assume that the sending area is TOTAL, the receiving area is TOTAL-OUT, and the following MOVE instruction has been executed:

```
MOVE TOTAL TO TOTAL-OUT.
```

After examining the data definitions in Exercises 8.5 through 8.9, choose the correct answer from the following answer set. (A "b" indicates a blank space.)
   a. b-12,345
   b. bbbbb$0.12
   c. *****12.34
   d. bb12,345.00
   e. -bb12,345
   f. $12,345.00
   g. $***12.34
   h. -b12,345.00
   i. bbb-123.34
   j. $****12.34

8.5   01   TOTAL   PIC   99V999 VALUE 12.345.
          01   TOTAL-OUT   PIC $**,**9.99.

8.6   01   TOTAL   PIC   S9(3)V99 VALUE   -123.34.
          01   TOTAL-OUT   PIC -,-.99.

8.7   01   TOTAL   PIC   S9(5) VALUE   -12345.
          01   TOTAL-OUT   PIC $$$,$$9.99.

8.8   01   TOTAL   PIC S9(5)   VALUE   -12345.
          01   TOTAL-OUT   PIC   -ZZZ,ZZ9.99.

8.9   01   TOTAL   PIC S9(5)   VALUE   -12345.
          01   TOTAL-OUT   PIC   -ZZZ,ZZZ.ZZ.

8.10   What character may be found in a numeric editing field?
    a.   the 9 picture character
    b.   the Z picture character
    c.   a decimal point
    d.   a + sign
    e.   all of the above

8.11   WORKING-STORAGE SECTION variables used in arithmetic computations may have a PICTURE clause defined with which of the following set of characters?
    a.   . 9 Z
    b.   9 X *
    c.   * 5 X
    d.   9 V S

For Exercises 8.12 through 8.15, assume that the following MOVE instruction is executed:

```
MOVE TOTAL TO TOTAL-OUT.
```

Given the sending area TOTAL and the receiving area TOTAL-OUT, what is the result?

8.12.
```
01    TOTAL PIC   S99V99  VALUE  -00.03.
01    TOTAL-OUT   PIC ZZZZ.ZZ-.
```

8.13.
```
01    TOTAL  PIC  999     VALUE 103.
      01    TOTAL-OUT    PIC    99090.
```

8.14.
```
01    TOTAL  PIC   S99V99          VALUE -0.03.
      01    TOTAL-OUT   PIC  $$,$$$.$$.
```

8.15.
```
01    TOTAL   PIC  S9(6) VALUE   -001030.
      01    TOTAL-OUT   PIC   ZZZZZZBCR.
```

8.16   Which edit character represents the credit symbol?

8.17   Which edit characters are floating string characters?
    a. $, + , DB
    b. $, Z, +
    c.   CR, DB
    d.   (.) and (,)

8.18   Which edit characters are insertion characters?
    a.   CR, Z, 1
    b.   Z, $, +
    c.   O, V, S
    d.   (,), / (,) DB

8.19 Which edit character prints when a signed numeric field is positive?
    a.   -
    b.   CR
    c.   DB
    d.   none of the above

8.20 Items that have edit characters in their PICTURE clauses:
    a.   may be used in calculations.
    b.   may not be used in any arithmetic statements.
    c.   may only be a result in an arithmetic statement.

8.21 Numeric edited items contain only insertion edit characters. True or false?

8.22 Reports can be classified into three types:
    a.   reference, on-file, action.
    b.   action, information, reference.
    c.   on-file, reference, information.
    d.   edited, nonedited, listing.

8.23 Each report line must be coded in the _____ SECTION.
    a.   WORKING-STORAGE
    b.   DECLARATIVES
    c.   LINKAGE
    d.   CONFIGURATION

8.24 Editing occurs when the unedited field is written out to a report line. True or false?

8.25 Line spacing is handled in the _____ DIVISION but column spacing is handled in the SECTION.
    a.   PROCEDURE, FILE
    b.   DATA, FILE
    c.   PROCEDURE, WORKING-STORAGE
    d.   DATA, WORKING-STORAGE

8.26 User preferences should be taken into account in report design decisions. True or false?

8.27 When a record is READ, the contents of the previous record are held in a COBOL buffer for the programmer to access. True or false?

8.28 The heart of the report is the _____ line.
    a.   title
    b.   header
    c.   detail
    d.   footer
    e.   none of the above

8.29 The period, comma, and slash are _____ characters.
    a.   insertion
    b.   accounting
    c.   floating edit
    d.   fixed edit

8.30 No special COBOL commands are required to generate reports of extremely high complexity. True or false?

8.31 COBOL automatically sets constant variables in the WORKING-STORAGE SECTION to their particular starting values. True or false?

8.32   A(n) _____ can only appear once within a numeric edited field.
      a. +
      b. *
      c. $
      d. .
      e. /

8.33   When printing a report with control breaks, the order of the input file *must* be in the same order as the control breaks. True or false?

8.34   Control breaks represent levels in the hierarchy chart of a _____ and _____ structure.
      a. program, layout
      b. report, program
      c. layout, file
      d. file, program
      e. none of the above

8.35   _____ are determined by changes in specific fields of the report detail lines.

8.36   The importance of a report is a function of _____ and timing.

8.37   Three basic timing environments classify reporting into _____ reporting, _____ reporting, and _____ reporting.

8.38   A(n) _____ is the arrangement of items on a sample report.

8.39   The _____ statement is used to edit of a data item.

8.40   Reports are _____ and require FD entries.

8.41   Report lines are defined and spaced using the _____ and _____ clauses in the WORKING-STORAGE SECTION.

8.42   If a page counter is to be used in a report, then a(n) _____ counter is required.

8.43   Explain the significance of combining traditional reports with terminal display and interactive design considerations.

8.44   What does a report provide?

8.45   What is the difference between page breaks and control breaks?

8.46   Describe the shortcomings of simple file-listing reports.

8.47   What would be the printed output of SECOND-ITEM given the following statements?

```
01 FIRST-ITEM   PIC S9(6)V99 VALUE -9473205.
01 SECOND-ITEM  PIC */**,***.ZZDB.
 .
 .
MOVE FIRST-ITEM TO SECOND-ITEM.
```

8.48   Alter the Sales Report design in Figures 8.10 through 8.16 to use the LINAGE and EOP options.

9

UPDATING SEQUENTIAL FILES

In the ever-changing business environment files constantly change to reflect new information. Sequential files present unique programming considerations in file update operations. In this chapter we study the specialized logic needed to handle the complexities of maintaining sequential files.

9.1   *Sequential Files*

Data stored on external memory are organized into files. These files are collections of records, each of which represents a logical grouping of information. Records in files can be organized in several different ways. *File organization* reflects the physical arrangement of records on an external storage medium. In this chapter we will be concerned only with the simplest file organization, sequential. More complex file structures will be covered in a later chapter.

9.1.1   *Sequential Organization*

Sequential files represent files whose order of records is in the sequence in which they were created. For example, when a secretary places business cards of vendors in a box, he is adding items to a sequential file of business cards. If the secretary were to sort the cards in the box according to some key file name, he would essentially be creating another sequential file whose items have a different order from the original file. In both cases the business card box file represents a stack of records that comprise the file.

Sequential files on external memory devices of a computer are conceptually similar to a business card box. Each time a program creates records for an existing sequential file, it places them on the stack of records already created. Later all the records may be sorted to create another sequential file of the same records but in a different order. A sequential file on an external memory device may only be accessed in sequential fashion. That is, in order to read the last record in the file, every record preceding it must be read. Whereas the secretary can thumb through the stack selectively and eliminate any business cards not required, the computer must read every record appearing before the desired record in a sequential file. Sequential files are not suitable for files in which only a small percentage of the records are needed at any one time. However, sequential files are adequate for applications in which most of the records require processing, as in payroll applications.

9.1.2   *The Physical Nature of Sequential Files*

Most external storage devices and peripherals permit sequential file processing. Magnetic disks are such devices. Other devices require that files be organized sequentially. Printer files and tape files require sequential organization. The characteristics of sequential files can be studied by examining the medium used for tape files.

Magnetic Tape. The magnetic tape used by computers is similar to the tape used by cassette recorders or reel-to-reel tape decks. In fact, many home computers use cassette tapes and cassette recorders for data storage. Suppose you wish to play a song from the middle of a cassette. You must first skip all the songs appearing before the one you wish to hear. This is due to the sequential nature of tape.

Data are recorded on the surface of the tape in patterns of magnetized spots representing bits. Figure 9.1 shows how the arrangements of the spots can indicate different characters on the tape. The vertical arrangement of the bits represents a character. As many characters as required are placed adjacent to one another to form a record in the file. Records are separated from each other with a space called the interrecord gap (IRG). The IRG allows the tape drive to decelerate and accelerate between records. As records are placed on the tape a sequential file is formed. The need to conduct inclusive reads in a sequential file to locate a specific record becomes apparent by studying the physical characteristics of magnetic tape.

Figure 9.1   Data Storage on Magnetic Tape

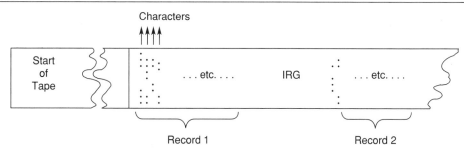

Magnetic tapes are read on tape drives that are functionally similar to tape decks for home use. Tape drives read and write to the magnetic tape. They perform their operations at various speeds depending on their price range. Tape drives are popular for applications that do not require great speed but need to store large amounts of data at a very low cost.

Label Records. COBOL allows the LABEL RECORDS clause to be used in the FD entry of every file. *Label records* are actual records on a tape file at the beginning and end of the file. Label records contain information about the file, but they do not form part of the file's contents. Figure 9.2 shows the placement of label records on a tape file. Each computer system varies with respect to the contents of the labels, but the label usually includes the value number associated with that reel, the file name, and the creation date. Specifying the LABEL RECORDS ARE STANDARD clause in the file description instructs the computer to consider the label records during the file preparation. The programmer need not consider label records further in the program.

Figure 9.2   Label Records on Magnetic Tape

When the program is run, the labels are checked by the operating system routines by comparing the tape label information with the job control instructions. This safeguards against the accidental destruction of tape files or the use of outdated or mistaken files. If the LABEL RECORDS ARE OMITTED clause is specified and label records exist, the program will attempt to read the label records as data records, and the results are unpredictable.

Blocking. Interrecord gaps take up space on the tape. The number of interrecord gaps may be controlled by blocking the records. Blocking allows the system to write multiple logical records between IRGs. A *block* is a physical record delimited by IRGs and may contain one or more logical records. Reducing the number of blocks reduces the number of IRGs, thereby increasing the amount of information that can be stored on a tape reel. The number of records between IRGs is referred to as the *blocking factor*.

Whenever the blocking factor of a sequential file is anything other than 1, it must be specified by the programmer. When a record is read an entire block is read and stored in main memory for use by subsequent reads and the number of physical reads is reduced. Figure 9.3 illustrates the concept of blocking on magnetic tape.

Figure 9.3 ***Blocked Records on Magnetic Tape***

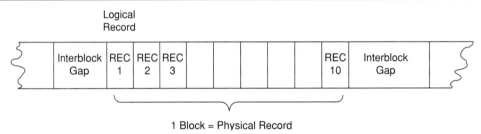

Buffers. When blocks containing more than one logical record are read from the storage device they no longer correspond to the READs issued by the program. A READ statement makes one logical record available to the program even though the computer may have read an entire block containing many records into memory. This area in internal memory is called a *buffer*. The desired record is stored as one of many records in the buffer. Assuming that a block contains 10 records, when the first READ is issued the buffer will hold the first 10 records as shown in Figure 9.4a. A pointer then points to the first logical record. This pointer keeps track of the record under consideration. With each successive READ the record pointer is automatically incremented. For example, when the fourth READ command is issued, the pointer will be indicating the fourth record in the buffer as shown in Figure 9.4b. Once all the records in the buffer have been processed, the subsequent READ will cause the computer to acquire the next block of 10 records from the external storage device and store them in the buffer. The buffer will then contain the second block of 10 records, and the pointer will be set to point to the first record in the buffer as illustrated in Figure 9.4c. This process continues until the file ends or the program stops.

Figure 9.4   **Buffering of Records**

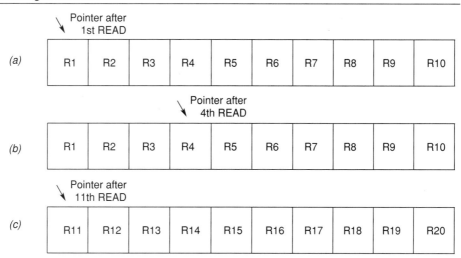

Most COBOL systems automatically use *double buffering*. In double buffering one block of data is read into a buffer while a block in a second buffer is being processed. This allows the overlapping of I/O operations and program execution as shown in Figure 9.5. Double buffering permits faster execution of a program.

9.2   Updating Sequential Files

Files containing company data must be changed as conditions warrant. External factors require that a file be updated. When customers mail in checks to a department store the store's records should be modified to reflect their new balances. When individuals send applications to a book club they expect to be added to the membership list. When members of a book club send in their resignations they expect to be eliminated from the club's mailing list. Internal factors also require that data in files be altered. A company must update its personnel files to reflect promotions, new hirings, and firings. Furthermore, a company must maintain its current inventory status of products by modifying its stock levels, adding new products to the files, and deleting products that are no longer produced.

Figure 9.5   Double Buffering of Records

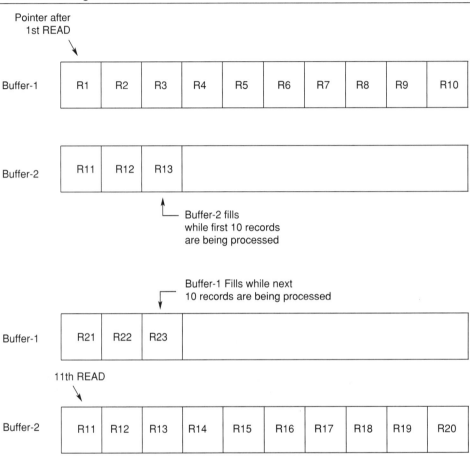

Pointer after
1st READ

Buffer-1 | R1 | R2 | R3 | R4 | R5 | R6 | R7 | R8 | R9 | R10

Buffer-2 | R11 | R12 | R13

Buffer-2 fills
while first 10 records
are being processed

Buffer-1 Fills while next
10 records are being processed

Buffer-1 | R21 | R22 | R23

11th READ

Buffer-2 | R11 | R12 | R13 | R14 | R15 | R16 | R17 | R18 | R19 | R20

9.2.1   Update Concepts

An information system must be able to update the files it retains. Files containing vital information such as customer mailing lists are maintained in current status through frequent file updates. A program usually maintains each file of importance to the organization. Figure 9.6 shows the system flowchart for a program that updates an inventory file. The old inventory file is updated or maintained by processing the changes stored in another file and creating a new current inventory file.

Figure 9.6   System Flowchart for a Master File Update

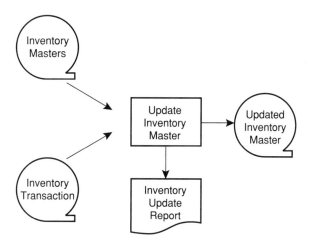

The file to be updated is referred to as a *master file*. A master file is usually a permanent file used by the organization to conduct major business functions. It contains information vital to the company, such as customer lists, accounts receivable, personnel records, or inventory records.

The file containing the changes to be applied is known as a *transaction file*. The various transactions may include additions, deletions, or modifications of items in the master file. Every business transaction indicates a required change to a master file.

The program that uses a transaction file to update a master file is called an update program or a file maintenance program. The update program reads the original master file and the transaction file, applies the indicated modification, and produces a new updated master file. The old master file is then retained for backup or historical information. Often a report of the changes made to the master file is also produced.

Each valid transaction dictates that one of three actions be taken with regard to the master file. A transaction may signal the addition of a record to the master file, as when a new customer is incorporated into the master file. It may result in the deletion of a record from the master file, as when a resigning employee is eliminated from the active employee file. It may also signal the replacement or modification of records or of certain fields in a record, as when a customer's address is changed in the customer master file or when the inventory level field is changed to reflect the arrival of materials.

Error situations that arise during file updates include the possibility of having invalid or erroneous transactions. Errors may occur when additions are specified for records that already exist on the file. A transaction in error may request the deletion of a nonexistent record. Errors also occur when transactions seek to modify or replace nonexistent records.

In file maintenance activities not all master file records will have a transaction applied to them and some master file records will have multiple transactions applied to them. For example, when the customer accounts for a major retail chain are updated, many customers will not have made payments or purchases and their records should therefore not be altered. Other customers, of course, will have made one or more purchases or payments. File update processes should allow for the possibility that a record on the master file may have no transactions, one transaction, or multiple transactions to be applied.

9.2.2   *Program Structure for Updating Sequential Files*

File update programs have common program structures. Figure 9.6 is a system flowchart for a generic file update process. We use the relationships of the files to develop a generic sequential file update program. The program structure for a file update program involving one master file, one transaction file, and one or more reports is represented by the hierarchy chart in Figure 9.7. The program structure does not depend on the organization of the file, although the detailed logic in the flowcharts will. The Nassi-Schneiderman charts to accompany the hierarchy are in Figure 9.8 and sample code is in the program of Figure 9.9.

Figure 9.7   *Hierarchy Chart for a File Update Program*

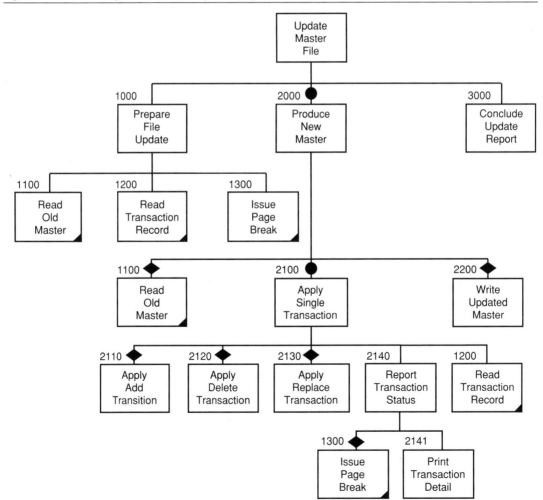

Figure 9.8   N-S Charts for a File Update Program

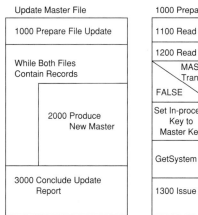

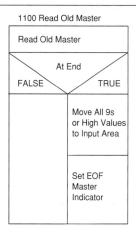

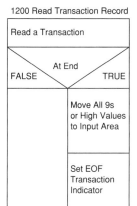

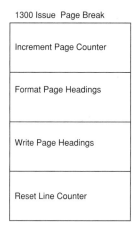

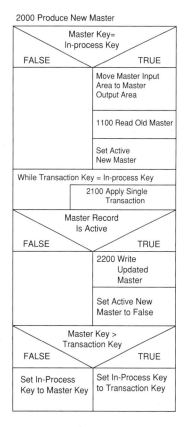

Figure 9.8   *(continued)*

2100 Apply Single Transaction

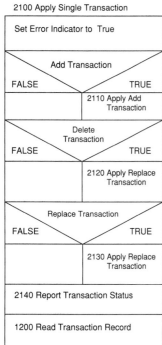

2110 Apply Add Transaction

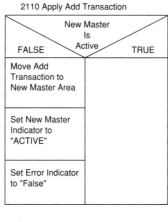

2120 Apply Delete Transaction

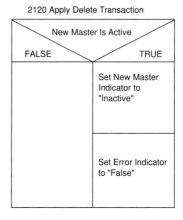

2130 Apply Replace Transaction

2140 Report Transaction Status

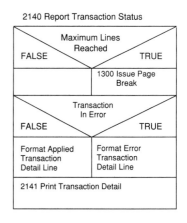

2141 Print Transaction Detail

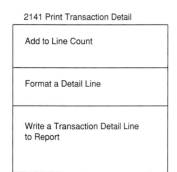

2200 Write Updated Master

3000 Conclude Update Report

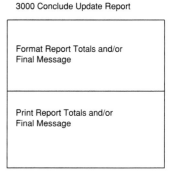

Figure 9.9 *Sample Code for a File Update Program*

```
 1
 2 IDENTIFICATION DIVISION.
 3 PROGRAM-ID.  GENERIC-SEQUENTIAL-UPDATE.
 4*   THIS PROGRAM TAKES A TRANSACTION-FILE AND
 5*   APPLIES THEM TO THE MASTER-FILE
 6
 7 AUTHOR.            SELF
 8 DATE-WRITTEN.      JULY 9, 1992
 9 DATE-COMPILED. 13-Jul-92 03:23.
11 ENVIRONMENT DIVISION.
12
13 CONFIGURATION SECTION.
14
15 SOURCE-COMPUTER.  GENERIC-COMPUTER.
16 OBJECT-COMPUTER.  GENERIC-COMPUTER.
17
18 INPUT-OUTPUT SECTION.
19
20 FILE-CONTROL.
21
22    SELECT TRANSACTION-FILE ASSIGN TO DISK
23        ORGANIZATION IS SEQUENTIAL
24        BLOCK CONTAINS 10 RECORDS.
25
26    SELECT MASTER-FILE ASSIGN TO DISK
27        ORGANIZATION IS SEQUENTIAL
28        BLOCK CONTAINS 10 RECORDS.
29
30    SELECT NEW-MASTER-FILE ASSIGN TO DISK
31        ORGANIZATION IS SEQUENTIAL
32        BLOCK CONTAINS 10 RECORDS.
33
34    SELECT UPDATE-REPORT ASSIGN TO PRINTER
35        ORGANIZATION IS SEQUENTIAL.
36
37 DATA DIVISION.
38
39 FILE SECTION.
40
41 FD  TRANSACTION-FILE
42     LABEL RECORDS ARE STANDARD.
43
```

Figure 9.9   *(continued)*

```
44 01  TRANSACTION-RECORD.
45     05  TRANSACTION-KEY-FIELD   PIC X(6).
46     05  TRANSACTION-TYPE        PIC X.
47         88  ADD-TRANSACTION      VALUE "A".
48         88  DELETE-TRANSACTION   VALUE "D".
49         88  REPLACE-TRANSACTION  VALUE "R".
50     05  TRANSACTION-MASTER-DATA PIC X(40).
51
52 FD  MASTER-FILE
53     LABEL RECORDS ARE STANDARD.
54
55 01  MASTER-RECORD.
56     05  MASTER-KEY-FIELD PIC X(6).
57     05  FILLER           PIC X(34).
58
59 FD  NEW-MASTER-FILE
60     LABEL RECORDS ARE STANDARD.
61
62 01  NEW-MASTER-RECORD.
63     05  NEW-MASTER-KEY-FIELD PIC X(6).
64     05  FILLER               PIC X(34).
65
66
67 FD  UPDATE-REPORT
68     LABEL RECORDS ARE OMITTED.
69
70 01  UPDATE-PRINT-LINE PIC X(80).
71
72
73 WORKING-STORAGE SECTION.
74
75 01  UPDATE-REPORT-LINES.
76     05  UP-REPORT-TITLE.
77         10  FILLER    PIC X(14) VALUE "REPORT #64".
78         10  FILLER    PIC X(38) VALUE
79                                  "MASTER FILE UPDATE".
80         10  FILLER    PIC X(5)  VALUE "PAGE".
81         10  UP-PAGE PIC ZZ9.
82     05  UP-DATE-LINE.
83         10  FILLER    PIC X(47)  VALUE "DISTRIBUTION".
84         10  FILLER    PIC X(5)   VALUE "DATE".
85         10  UP-DATE   PIC 99/99/99.
```

Figure 9.9   *(continued)*

```
86        05   UP-COLUMN-HEADING.
87             10   FILLER PIC X(15) VALUE "TRANSACTION".
88             10   FILLER PIC X(14) VALUE "KEY FIELD".
89             10   FILLER PIC X(09) VALUE "RECORD".
90        05   UP-DETAIL.
91             10   UP-CODE            PIC X(6).
92             10   UP-ERROR           PIC X(10).
93             10   UP-KEY             PIC 9(6).
94             10   FILLER             PIC X(4) VALUE SPACE.
95             10   UP-RECORD          PIC X(40).
96
97   01   END-OF-FILE-INDICATORS.
98        05   EOF-MASTER        PIC X(5) VALUE "FALSE".
99        05   EOF-TRANSACTION   PIC X(5) VALUE "FALSE".
100
101  01   PAGE-CONTROL-COUNTERS.
102       05   PCC-PAGE      PIC 999 VALUE ZERO.
103       05   PCC-LINE      PIC 99  VALUE 99.
104       05   PCC-MAX-LINE  PIC 99  VALUE 55.
105
106  01   PROCESS-INDICATORS.
107       05   ACTIVE-NEW-MASTER  PIC X(5) VALUE "FALSE".
108       05   IN-PROCESS-KEY     PIC X(6) VALUE SPACES.
109       05   ERROR-INDICATOR    PIC X(5) VALUE "TRUE".
110
111  PROCEDURE DIVISION.
112
113  UPDATE-MASTER-FILE.
114     OPEN INPUT MASTER-FILE.
115     OPEN INPUT TRANSACTION-FILE.
116     OPEN OUTPUT NEW-MASTER-FILE.
117     OPEN OUTPUT UPDATE-REPORT.
118     PERFORM 1000-PREPARE-FILE-UPDATE.
119     PERFORM 2000-PRODUCE-NEW-MASTER
120         UNTIL (EOF-MASTER = "TRUE" AND EOF-TRANSACTION = "TRUE").
121     PERFORM 3000-CONCLUDE-UPDATE-REPORT.
122     CLOSE MASTER-FILE.
123     CLOSE TRANSACTION-FILE.
124     CLOSE NEW-MASTER-FILE.
125     CLOSE UPDATE-REPORT.
126     STOP RUN.
127
```

Figure 9.9   (continued)

```
128 1000-PREPARE-FILE-UPDATE.
129     PERFORM 1100-READ-OLD-MASTER.
130     PERFORM 1200-READ-TRANSACTION-RECORD.
131     IF MASTER-KEY-FIELD < TRANSACTION-KEY-FIELD
132         MOVE MASTER-KEY-FIELD TO IN-PROCESS-KEY
133     ELSE
134         MOVE TRANSACTION-KEY-FIELD TO IN-PROCESS-KEY.
135     ACCEPT UP-DATE FROM DATE.
136     PERFORM 1300-ISSUE-PAGE-BREAK.
137
138 1100-READ-OLD-MASTER.
139     READ MASTER-FILE AT END MOVE "TRUE" TO EOF-MASTER
140         MOVE HIGH-VALUES TO MASTER-KEY-FIELD.
141
142 1200-READ-TRANSACTION-RECORD.
143     READ TRANSACTION-FILE AT END MOVE "TRUE" TO EOF-TRANSACTION
144         MOVE HIGH-VALUES TO TRANSACTION-KEY-FIELD.
145
146 1300-ISSUE-PAGE-BREAK.
147     ADD 1 TO PCC-PAGE.
148     MOVE PCC-PAGE TO UP-PAGE.
149     WRITE UPDATE-PRINT-LINE FROM UP-REPORT-TITLE AFTER PAGE.
150     WRITE UPDATE-PRINT-LINE FROM UP-DATE-LINE.
151     WRITE UPDATE-PRINT-LINE FROM UP-COLUMN-HEADING.
152     MOVE SPACES TO UPDATE-PRINT-LINE.
153     WRITE UPDATE-PRINT-LINE.
154     MOVE 4 TO PCC-LINE.
155
156 2000-PRODUCE-NEW-MASTER.
157     IF MASTER-KEY-FIELD = IN-PROCESS-KEY
158         MOVE MASTER-RECORD TO NEW-MASTER-RECORD
159         PERFORM 1100-READ-OLD-MASTER
160         MOVE "TRUE" TO ACTIVE-NEW-MASTER.
161     PERFORM 2100-APPLY-SINGLE-TRANSACTION
162         UNTIL TRANSACTION-KEY-FIELD > IN-PROCESS-KEY.
163     IF ACTIVE-NEW-MASTER = "TRUE"
164         PERFORM 2200-WRITE-UPDATED-MASTER
165         MOVE "FALSE" TO ACTIVE-NEW-MASTER.
166     IF MASTER-KEY-FIELD < TRANSACTION-KEY-FIELD
167         MOVE MASTER-KEY-FIELD TO IN-PROCESS-KEY
168     ELSE
169         MOVE TRANSACTION-KEY-FIELD TO IN-PROCESS-KEY.
```

Figure 9.9   (continued)

```
170
171 2100-APPLY-SINGLE-TRANSACTION.
172     MOVE "TRUE" TO ERROR-INDICATOR.
173     IF ADD-TRANSACTION      PERFORM 2110-APPLY-ADD-TRANSACTION.
174     IF DELETE-TRANSACTION  PERFORM 2120-APPLY-DELETE-TRANSACTION.
175     IF REPLACE-TRANSACTION PERFORM 2130-APPLY-REPLACE-TRANSACTION
176     PERFORM 2140-REPORT-TRANSACTION-STATUS.
177     PERFORM 1200-READ-TRANSACTION-RECORD.
178
179 2110-APPLY-ADD-TRANSACTION.
180     IF ACTIVE-NEW-MASTER = "FALSE"
181         MOVE TRANSACTION-MASTER-DATA TO NEW-MASTER-RECORD
182         MOVE "TRUE" TO ACTIVE-NEW-MASTER
183         MOVE "FALSE" TO ERROR-INDICATOR.
184
185 2120-APPLY-DELETE-TRANSACTION.
186     IF ACTIVE-NEW-MASTER = "TRUE"
187         MOVE "FALSE" TO ACTIVE-NEW-MASTER
188         MOVE "FALSE" TO ERROR-INDICATOR.
189
190 2130-APPLY-REPLACE-TRANSACTION.
191     IF ACTIVE-NEW-MASTER = "TRUE"
192         MOVE TRANSACTION-MASTER-DATA TO NEW-MASTER-RECORD
193         MOVE "FALSE" TO ERROR-INDICATOR.
194
195 2140-REPORT-TRANSACTION-STATUS.
196     IF PCC-LINE > PCC-MAX-LINE
197         PERFORM 1300-ISSUE-PAGE-BREAK.
198     IF ERROR-INDICATOR = "TRUE" MOVE "ERROR" TO UP-ERROR
199         ELSE MOVE SPACES TO UP-ERROR.
200     MOVE TRANSACTION-TYPE TO UP-CODE.
201     PERFORM 2141-PRINT-TRANSACTION-DETAIL.
202
203 2141-PRINT-TRANSACTION-DETAIL.
204     ADD 1 TO PCC-LINE.
205     MOVE TRANSACTION-MASTER-DATA TO UP-RECORD.
206     WRITE UPDATE-PRINT-LINE FROM UP-DETAIL.
207
208 2200-WRITE-UPDATED-MASTER.
209     WRITE NEW-MASTER-RECORD.
210
211 3000-CONCLUDE-UPDATE-REPORT.
212     MOVE "END OR REPORT" TO UPDATE-PRINT-LINE.
```

The main program module in Figure 9.7 is "Update Master File." Keep in mind that the name should actually be more meaningful, for example, "Update Customer Master." But for now, we will use generic names to describe the general program structure. This main module is divided into the three familiar modules representing the preprocessing, repetitive major processing, and postprocessing needed to accomplish the overall goal of the program. Module "1000 Prepare File Update" prints report headings and conducts the necessary priming reads. Module "3000 Conclude Update Report" prints the summary information. The major repetitive module that applies the transactions to the master file is "2000 Produce New Master." It generates a new master file from the old master file.

Module "2000 Produce New Master" is itself composed of a preprocessing, repetitive, and postprocessing module. Before a transaction can be applied by module "2100 Apply Single Transaction," the appropriate old master file record must be available. This is accomplished by module "1100 Read Old Master," which is performed selectively by its superior module. Once the transaction has been applied, the updated record is written to the new master file by module "2200 Write Updated Master."

Module "2100 Apply Single Transaction" is segmented into five subordinate modules. Each transaction type is represented by a separate module since the logic involved for each transaction type is different. Module "2140 Report Transaction Status" prints a detail line that indicates whether or not an error occurred. The next transaction record is read by module "1200 Read Transaction Record." The code is straightforward and found starting in lines 171, 195, and 142 respectively.

The program structure presented in the hierarchy chart is common to general file updates. Minor modifications may be made to accommodate such details as the physical restrictions of the file being modified, but the changes would extend to lower levels. The hierarchy chart shown serves as the beginning framework for all sequential file update programs.

9.2.3   Sequential File Update Logic

In this section we will develop the general design for updating a sequential master file. We will do so by expanding the framework given in the hierarchy chart of Figure 9.7 and taking into account the characteristics of sequential files.

Sequencing. The order of records in the files is critical in a sequential file update. The master file must be ordered in a specific sequence based on one or more key fields in the record. For example, a customer file containing the names and addresses of all customers may be ordered by customer identification numbers. In general, master files will already have a given sequence by the time they are to be updated. The actual key selected within a file is not important. What is important is that some sequence based on a unique identifier be determined and that the file be in the specified sequence. For example, the customer file could have been sorted by customer names.

Because of the restrictions inherent in a sequential file, the transaction file records must be in the same sequence as the master file records before the update process begins. If the transaction records were not in the same order as the master file records, a transaction for the fifth record in the master file might follow a transaction for the 500th record in the master file.

Figure 9.10 shows the records of a transaction file and a master file being used in an update as well as the resulting updated master file records. The transaction and key fields are listed for each transaction. The first transaction may be read as "Replace the information for customer number 209877 with the data contained in this transaction." The second transaction may be read as "Delete the customer with the number 298889." Each transaction may result in a successful application to the master file or in an error. The transactions flagged with an asterisk are errors. The errors are a result of attempting to add a record that already exists or delete/replace a record not on file.

Figure 9.10 *Records After File Update*

Original Master		Transaction File			Updated Master	
Key	**Rest of Record**	**Code**	**Key**	**Rest of Record**	**Key**	**Rest of Record**
184715	A . . .	REPLACE	209877	G . . . *	184715	A . . .
298889	B . . .	DELETE	298889	H . . .	321477	C . . .
321477	C . . .	ADD	321477	I . . . *	364711	D . . .
364711	D . . .	ADD	379155	J . . .	379155	J . . .
389211	E . . .	REPLACE	389211	K . . .	389211	K . . .
400001	F . . .	DELETE	458217	L . . . *	400001	F . . .

* Represents transaction error.

9.2.4   An Update Algorithm

The Nassi-Schneiderman charts to implement the generic file update of Figure 9.8 are shown in structured English in Figure 9.11. We will review the file update algorithm by following the logic specified in the relevant modules. The code of Figure 9.9 may be consulted as examples of implementing the logic.

Module "1000 Prepare File Update." The unique feature in this module is the selection of the "In-Process Key." The In-Process Key contains the key value of the record being processed. If the master file record key is less than the transaction file record key the master file record key becomes the In-Process Key to indicate that it must be processed next. If the transaction key is less than the master file record key, the transaction key becomes the In-Process Key, signaling that transactions must be processed before the next master file record is read. The In-Process Key will always contain the value of the item under current process. This allows the programmer to avoid frequent comparisons of the key fields in each file.

Figure 9.11   Sequential File Update Algorithm in Structured English

```
FILE-UPDATE-ALGORITHM
      READ a TRANSACTION-FILE record, setting indicator at end of file;
      READ a MASTER-FILE record, setting indicator at end of file;
      Set IN-PROCESS-KEY to the lower of the two file keys;
      REPEAT UNTIL both files at end
            IF OLD-MASTER-KEY = IN-PROCESS-KEY THEN
                  set ACTIVE-NEW-MASTER indicator to TRUE'
                  transfer OLD-MASTER-RECORD to NEW-MASTER-RECORD;
                  READ next MASTER-FILE record,
                        setting indicator at end of file;
            ELSE
                  set ACTIVE-NEW-MASTER indicator to FALSE;
            END-IF;
            REPEAT WHILE TRANSACTION KEY = IN-PROCESS KEY
                  IF TRANSACTION-CODE indicates an addition THEN
                        IF ACTIVE-NEW-MASTER indicator is TRUE THEN
                              PERFORM an error routine;
                        ELSE
                              build a NEW-MASTER-RECORD from the TRANSACTION record;
                        END-IF;
                  ELSE
                        IF TRANSACTION-CODE indicates a replace THEN
                              IF ACTIVE-NEW-MASTER indicator is TRUE THEN
                                    apply the replace;
                              ELSE
                                    PERFORM an error routine;
                              END-IF;
                        ELSE
                              IF TRANSACTION-CODE indicates a delete THEN
                                    IF ACTIVE-NEW-MASTER indicator is TRUE THEN
                                          set ACTIVE-NEW-MASTER indicator to FALSE;
                                    ELSE
                                          PERFORM an error routine;
                                    END-IF
                              ELSE
                                    PERFORM an invalid transaction routine;
                              END-IF
                        END-IF
                  END-IF
                  READ next TRANSACTION-FILE record,
                        setting indicator at end of file;
            END-REPEAT;
            IF ACTIVE-NEW-MASTER indicator is TRUE THEN
                  set ACTIVE-NEW-MASTER indicator to FALSE;
                  WRITE the NEW-MASTER-FILE record;
            END-IF;
            set IN-PROCESS-KEY to the lower of the two file keys;
      END REPEAT;
EXIT FILE-UPDATE-ALGORITHM
```

Module "1100 Read Old Master" and "1200 Read Transaction Record." When a program uses multiple files, as in an update program, it is highly unlikely that the number of records in all the files will coincide. More commonly one file will reach the end-of-file condition before the other. Provisions must be made to continue processing until the other file reaches the end-of-file condition. This ensures the completeness of the processing cycle. The program moves a very high value or a very low value (depending on the order of the records) into the key field when either file reaches the end to allow processing to continue until both files end. For example, in a file ordered by ascending key values the figurative constant HIGH-VALUES may be moved to an alphanumeric key field. If the key field is numeric, all 9s may be moved to the field. This permits the program to continue the update process when one file has ended but the other has not. In the resulting key comparisons, the value of the key field in the file that is not at the end will be less than the value of the key field in the file that is at the end. If the transaction file ends first, HIGH-VALUES should be moved to the transaction record's key field so that in subsequent comparisons the master file key field is lower than HIGH VALUES. This ensures that the remaining records in the master file are written to the new master file. Conversely, if the master file ends first, HIGH VALUES should be moved to the master file record's key field. Any comparison of the keys therefore shows the transaction key fields are less than the master file key. Thus any remaining records in the transaction file will be processed.

Module "2000 Produce New Master." The Nassi-Schneiderman chart indicates that the process of producing a new master file is controlled by a combination of a selection construct, followed by an iteration construct, followed by two selection constructs. The first selection construct tests whether the master file key is equal to the In-Process Key. If so, the old master file record is the next record to be written to the updated master file. It is therefore transferred to the output area of the updated master file, but the record is not written to the new file at this time because some transactions may need to be applied to it. Instead, the program sets an Active New Master indicator to true. This indicator signifies that a valid master record is in the output area.

A DO WHILE iteration construct controls the application of transactions to the master record in the output area. Transactions are applied as long as the transaction key is equal to the in-process key.

A selection structure tests whether the Active New Master indicator is on. If so, the record is written to the master file and the indicator is set to false. Finally, the last selection structure determines the new In-Process Key.

Module "2100 Apply Single Transaction." This module selects the proper transaction application module. It also sets a switch to indicate if a transaction is in error. This switch is used to alert the reporting module. Finally, the next transaction record is read and the cycle of applying transactions can begin again.

The Transaction Application Modules. Each transaction application module uses a selection structure to test for a transaction error immediately upon entrance. For example, the module "2110 Apply Add Transaction" examines the output area. If an active record exists in the output area it indicates that the record already exists and the transaction to add is an error. If the output area has the active new master indicator set to false, the add transaction is valid. The addition module then builds the new record in the output area and resets the indicators.

The transactions and master file records in Figure 9.8 may be used to follow the update algorithm logic. At the start, the first record of each file has been read. The master file key at 184715 is the lower key. It therefore becomes the first In-Process Key. Module "2000 Produce New Master" transfers the old master file record to the new master file output and sets the "active new master" indicator to true. Since the transaction key is not equal to the In-Process Key, the module "2100 Apply Single Transaction" is bypassed. The record is then written to the updated master file as the first record. Follow the process of the update to verify that all the transactions in Figure 9.8 are correctly applied.

The COBOL Code. No new COBOL statements are needed in the PROCEDURE DIVISION to perform a sequential file update. The code for the file update logic of Figures 9.7 and 9.8 could appear as shown in Figure 9.9. Notice in lines 140 and 144 of the code how HIGH-VALUES is used when the end of each file is reached. This will cause the key field of the exhausted file to test higher than the file with remaining records. The major iteration in the module UPDATE-MASTER-FILE is ended in line 120 only when both files are at the end. The IN-PROCESS-KEY of line 108 is used to determine which file to process in the module 2000-PRODUCE-NEW-MASTER starting in line 156.

The only additional code used in the example of Figure 9.9 is the BLOCK CONTAINS clause in lines 24, 28, and 32. When a blocking factor is other than 1, it is specified in the COBOL file description entry with the BLOCK CONTAINS clause. The format and rules for the clause are:

BLOCK CONTAINS integer { RECORDS | CHARACTERS }

1. The clause is required for all files not blocked at one record.
2. The RECORDS option may not be used for records larger than the block size or for variable-length records.

The blocking factor causes logical records to be placed adjacent to each other for the number specified in the BLOCK CONTAINS clause. This eliminates the need for many IRGs and cuts down on the space required to store the file. If the correct blocking factor is not specified by the programmer, the program will not work. In the example,

```
FD    EMPLOYER-MASTER

      LABEL RECORDS ARE STANDARD
      BLOCK CONTAINS 10 RECORDS.
```

the programmer is specifying a blocking factor of 10 logical records for each physical record.

9.3   *Sorting in COBOL*

We mentioned earlier that the transaction file must be in the same sequence as the master file to which it will be applied. Master files are usually kept in some determined sequence. However, transactions are generally entered into a computer as they occur and not in the order of the master file. Many vendors supply utility programs to sort files into a desired sequence. Such utility sorts generally take an unordered sequential file and produce an ordered sequential file by reorganizing the records into the desired sequence. This process involves reading the unordered file into a sort work area, sorting the records, and writing the sorted file to another storage device. This process is shown in Figure 9.12.

Figure 9.12   Sort Process

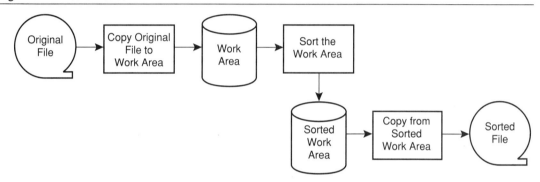

COBOL performs this same task. In addition, the COBOL sort has the added flexibility of allowing the programmer to intervene at any point in the process. To illustrate the advantage of this feature, Figure 9.13 shows how use of the COBOL sort may save a pass of the file once sorting has been done during an update. In Figure 9.13a, the process is divided into two subprocesses: (1) sorting the transactions and (2) applying the sorted transactions. Figure 9.13b illustrates a systems flowchart for the same general process but using the COBOL sort facility. Notice that an entire pass of the file may be saved by intervening during the transfer of the file to the sort area. On paper this may not appear to be a large savings, but in reality large file passes may take well over an hour. Thus, the COBOL sort feature often saves time.

Figure 9.13   Sorting with Updating

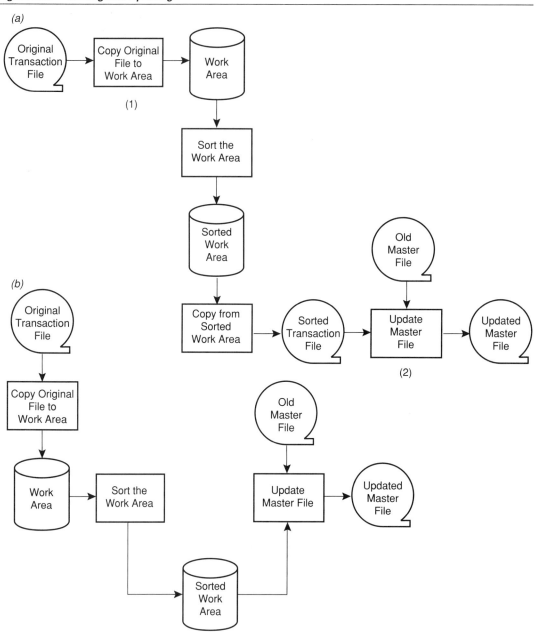

9.3.1   *The Simplified SORT Statement*

The COBOL statement that creates a sorted file is the SORT statement. The format for a simplified SORT statement is:

$$\underline{\text{SORT}} \text{ file-name-1 ON } \left\{ \left\{ \begin{array}{l} \underline{\text{ASCENDING}} \\ \underline{\text{DESCENDING}} \end{array} \right\} \text{ KEY } \{\text{data-name-1}\}\ldots \right\}\ldots$$

$$\begin{array}{ll} \underline{\text{USING}} & \{\text{file-name-2}\}\ldots \\ \underline{\text{GIVING}} & \text{file-name-3} \end{array}$$

1. File-name-2 and file-name-3 must be sequential files and may not be OPEN when the SORT is executed.
2. When the SORT is through, file-name-2, and file-name-3 are CLOSEd automatically.
3. File-name-1 must be described by an SD entry. File-name-2 and file-name-3 must be described by FD entries.

The COBOL SORT statement is actually a three step process. First, the SORT verb creates a sort work file identified by file-name-1 by transferring records from the input file denoted by file-name-2 to the sort work file. Second, the records in the sort file are sorted in accordance with the sequence specified, ASCENDING or DESCENDING, using the key field(s) specified by data-name-1. Finally, the sorted records are returned to the file specified as file-name-3 by the SORT for further processing by the program. In the example,

```
SORT TRAX-WORK-FILE ON ASCENDING KEY CUST-NO

     USING TRAX-MASTER-FILE
     GIVING SORTED-TRAX-FILE.
```

TRAX-MASTER-FILE is the input file containing the unsorted transactions, and SORTED-TRAX-FILE is the output file containing the sorted transactions. In the sort process the input records were copied to the TRAX-WORK-FILE from TRAX-MASTER-FILE. This work file will contain intermediate versions of the input file during the course of the sorting process. When the sort is complete, the input file will still be the original file and the output file SORTED-TRAX-FILE can be used for further processing.

The USING and GIVING Phrases. The USING phrase specifies the file used as input to the SORT. When the USING phrase is specified, the input file is automatically read into the sort work file. The programmer does not OPEN, READ, or CLOSE the input file. The SORT statement manipulates the file. The GIVING phrase specifies the file to which the sorted file sends the results. When the GIVING phrase is used, the file is not opened, written to, or closed by the programmer. Again the COBOL SORT will do this automatically. The files specified in the USING and GIVING clauses must be defined by FD entries in the DATA DIVISION. An example SORT statement using the USING and GIVING phrases is the following:

```
SIMPLE-SORT.
       SORT SORT-WORK-INVENTORY-FILE
            ON ASCENDING KEY SWINV-STOCK-NUMBER
            USING INVENTORY-FILE
            GIVING SORTED-INVENTORY-FILE.
       STOP RUN.
```

It is possible that a program may have been processing the file specified in the USING phrase prior to executing the SORT. If so, the file must be closed before the SORT is executed. Likewise, the file in the GIVING phrase may be opened and processed after the sort is complete.

The SELECT Clause. Like any other file, the sort work file must be associated with its physical medium. It therefore requires a SELECT statement in the ENVIRONMENT DIVISION. Because the ASSIGN TO clause used with sort files is system-dependent, you should consult your computer's COBOL documentation to specify the medium for the SORT file. SELECT statements must also appear for the input and output files. For the above example the SELECT clauses might appear as follows:

```
FILE-CONTROL.
       SELECT  INVENTORY-FILE ASSIGN TO DISK
            ORGANIZATION IS SEQUENTIAL.
       SELECT  SORT-WORK-INVENTORY-FILE
            ASSIGN TO SORT-WORK-DISK.
       SELECT  SORTED-INVENTORY-FILE ASSIGN TO DISK
            ORGANIZATION IS SEQUENTIAL.
```

The SD Entry. The use of an intermediate file known as the sort work file has been mentioned. This file is an actual physical file and is referred to by the file-name-1 used in the SORT statement. It must therefore be defined. Unlike other files, the SORT WORK file entry is not defined with an FD entry in the DATA DIVISION but is described with an SD entry following the FD entries in the DATA DIVISION. SD stands for sort description entry. SD entries are essentially the same as FD entries except that SD entries may not contain the LABEL RECORDS clause. Furthermore, the programmer may not specify the blocking factor of the sort work file because it is controlled by the system.

The SD entry describes the record layout of the sort work file. The key field used to order the file must be in the same location in the input file, the sort work file, and the output file when the USING and GIVING phrases are present. The record descriptions for the input file, the sort work file, and the output file are all similar. For the above inventory example, the FILE SECTION may appear as:

```
FILE SECTION.

FD    INVENTORY-FILE
      LABEL RECORDS ARE STANDARD.
01    INVENTORY-RECORD PIC X(80).

FD    SORTED-INVENTORY-FILE
      LABEL RECORDS ARE STANDARD.
01    SORTED-INVENTORY-RECORD PIC X(80).

SD    SORT-WORK-INVENTORY-FILE.
01    SORT-WORK-INVENTORY-RECORD.
      05    SWINV-STOCK-NUMBER       PIC X(5).
      05    SWINV-QOH                PIC 9(5).
      05    FILLER                   PIC X(70).
```

Since this example is simply sorting the input file, there is no need for us to refer to the individual fields making up the record. This is reflected in our description of both the input and the output files. Only SORT-WORK-INVENTORY-FILE is described more comprehensively, since the key SWINV-STOCK-NUMBER has to be accessible to order SORT-WORK-INVENTORY-FILE.

9.3.2   SORT Statement Using Procedures

The greatest single advantage of the COBOL SORT verb over a utility sort is the ability it offers the programmer to intervene at an intermediate step in the sorting process. This facility requires the use of the INPUT and/or OUTPUT PROCEDURE clauses in the SORT statement. The format and rules of the SORT statement incorporating these options are:

SORT file-name-1   {ON $\left[\begin{array}{l} \text{ASCENDING} \\ \text{DESCENDING} \end{array}\right]$ KEY {data-name-1}...}...

$\left\{\begin{array}{l} \text{INPUT \ PROCEDURE IS section-name-1} \\ \text{USING {file-name-2}...} \end{array}\right\}$
$\left\{\begin{array}{l} \text{OUTPUT PROCEDURE IS section-name-2} \\ \text{GIVING \ file-name-3} \end{array}\right\}$

1. All files names may not be OPEN when the SORT is executed.
2. All data-names specified as keys must be in a record that is part of an SD entry.
3. File-name-1 must be described by an SD entry; all other files must have an FD entry.

In the example,

```
SORT   SORT-WORK-INVENTORY-FILE
```

```
        ON ASCENDING KEY SWINV-STOCK-NUMBER
        INPUT PROCEDURE IS SORT-INPUT
        OUTPUT PROCEDURE IS SORT-OUTPUT.
```

SORT-WORK-INVENTORY-FILE is the sort work file, and the INPUT and OUTPUT PROCEDURE entries provide information as to where the instructions need by the SORT verb to carry out its sort process may be found.

Sections. Until now, sections have been extensively used in the ENVIRONMENT and DATA DIVISIONS. They were introduced as part of the PROCEDURE DIVISION for the purposes of debugging. It is necessary that a program be sectioned to implement the INPUT and OUTPUT PROCEDURES allowed by the SORT statement. The format for the INPUT and OUTPUT PROCEDURE options requires that a SECTION name be specified for that PROCEDURE. Recall that sections are used in the PROCEDURE DIVISION to group paragraphs into logical functions so that they form subdivisions of the PROCEDURE DIVISION. The format for specifying SECTIONs is:

       section-name <u>SECTION</u>.

It must be followed by a period, a space, and the paragraphs specifying the appropriate logic of the section.

    In the case of the SORT, the logical functions necessary to prepare records for sorting will appear in the INPUT PROCEDURE SECTION, whereas the logic necessary to process records that have already been sorted belongs in the OUTPUT PROCEDURE. The paragraphs in a SECTION must be physically contiguous, and all paragraphs must be contained in a SECTION. A section ends at the next section name or at the end of the PROCEDURE DIVISION. A paragraph belongs to the most recently specified SECTION in the code. SECTION names follow the same naming rules as do paragraphs. The only difference is that the word SECTION follows the section name.

    Figure 9.14 shows a PROCEDURE DIVISION with multiple SECTIONs. Section SORT-INPUT SECTION contains the paragraphs 100-CONTROL-SORT-INPUT, 110-READ-IN-VENTORY-RECORD, 120-SELECT-VALID-RECORDS, 121-RELEASE-SWINV-RECORD, and 130-EXIT-SORT-INPUT. As you can see, SECTIONs essentially divide a program into subunits resembling smaller programs.

Figure 9.14   *Use of SECTIONSs in PROCEDURE DIVISION*

```
        WORKING-STORAGE SECTION.


        01    EOF-INVENTORY                   PIC XXX VALUE "NO".
        01    EOF-SORT-WORK-INVENTORY         PIC XXX VALUE "NO".
        01    TOTAL-QOH                       PIC 9(10) VALUE ZERO.

        PROCEDURE DIVISION.
```

Figure 9.14   (continued)

```
SORT-CONTROL SECTION.
SIMPLE-SORT.
        OPEN INPUT INVENTORY-FILE.
        OPEN OUTPUT SORTED-INVENTORY-FILE.
        SORT SORT-WORK-INVENTORY-FILE
                ON ASCENDING KEY SWINV-STOCK-NUMBER
                INPUT PROCEDURE IS SORT-INPUT
                OUTPUT PROCEDURE IS SORT-OUTPUT.
        CLOSE INVENTORY-FILE.
        CLOSE SORT-INVENTORY-FILE.
        STOP RUN.


SORT-INPUT SECTION.

100-CONTROL-SORT-INPUT.
        PERFORM 110-READ-INVENTORY-RECORD.
        PERFORM 120-SELECT-VALID-RECORDS
                UNTIL EOF-INVENTORY = "YES".
        GO TO 130-EXIT-SORT-INPUT.

110-READ-INVENTORY-RECORD.
        READ INVENTORY AT END MOVE "YES" TO EOF-INVENTORY.

120-SELECT-VALID-RECORDS.
        MOVE INVENTORY-RECORD TO SORT-WORK-INVENTORY-RECORD.
        IF SWINV-STOCK-NUMBER NOT EQUAL ZERO
                PERFORM 121-RELEASE-SWINV-RECORD.
        PERFORM 110-READ-INVENTORY-RECORD.

121-RELEASE-SWINV-RECORD.
        RELEASE SORT-WORK-INVENTORY-RECORD.

130-EXIT-SORT-INPUT.
        EXIT.

SORT-OUTPUT SECTION.

200-CONTROL-SORT-OUTPUT.
        PERFORM 210-RETURN-SORTED-INVENTORY.
        PERFORM 220-ACCUMULATE-QOH
                UNTIL EOF-SORT-WORK-INVENTORY = "YES".
        DISPLAY "TOTAL QOH IS", TOTAL-QOH.
```

Figure 9.14   *(continued)*

```
        GO TO 240-EXIT-SORT-OUTPUT.
210-RETURN-SORTED-INVENTORY.
        RETURN SORT-WORK-INVENTORY-FILE
        AT END MOVE "YES" TO EOF-SORT-WORK-INVENTORY.

220-ACCUMULATE QOH.
        PERFORM 230-WRITE-SORTED-INVENTORY.
        ADD SWINV-QOH TO TOTAL-QOH.
        PERFORM 210-RETURN-SORTED-INVENTORY.

230-WRITE-SORTED-INVENTORY-FILE
        WRITE SORTED-INVENTORY-RECORD FROM
                SORT-WORK-INVENTORY-RECORD.

240-EXIT-SORT-OUTPUT.
        EXIT.
```

The INPUT PROCEDURE. An INPUT PROCEDURE is a set of statements that allow the programmer to specify the processing to be done before a file is sorted. The programmer opens the input file as usual. Then the input records are processed by executing the INPUT PROCEDURE section. When each record has been processed, it must be written to the sort work file so that is it available for sorting. However, COBOL does not allow the WRITE verb to be used for writing records to a sort file. Instead it provides the RELEASE verb to accomplish this action. Therefore, the processed record must be released to the sort work file. The format and rules for the RELEASE statement are:

RELEASE   record-name   [FROM data-name-1]

1.   Record-name must form part of an SD entry.
2.   The RELEASE must be a logical part of the INPUT PROCEDURE.
3.   The record-name must be the name of the logical record in the sort work file associated with the SORT statement.
4.   Once a record is RELEASEd, it is no longer available in the file's record area.

If the FROM phrase is specified, the contents of data-name-1 are first moved to record-name and the contents of record-name are released to the sort work file. Therefore, although the contents of record-name are no longer available, those of data-name-1 are. The FROM option in the RELEASE statement functions in the same way as in the WRITE statement.

After the INPUT PROCEDURE has been executed, only the records released to the sort work file are available for sorting. In Figure 9.14, SORT-INPUT is specified as the INPUT

PROCEDURE. It edits the records found in the input file for missing fields and then releases only those records that are valid. Thus invalid records will not be included in the sort and will not appear in the resulting sorted file.

When the INPUT PROCEDURE is specified, control passes from the SORT statement to the first paragraph in the SECTION named by the INPUT PROCEDURE, and returns to the SORT statement when the last sentence in the last paragraph of the SECTION has been executed. Thus the SECTION is similar to the PERFORM THRU structure. The same problems encountered with the PERFORM THRU apply to SECTIONs. It is necessary to bypass code that is not required at every iteration. For example, in the SORT-INPUT SECTION in Figure 9.14, paragraphs 110-READ-INVENTORY-RECORD, 120-SELECT-VALID-RECORDS, and 121-RELEASE-SWINV-RECORD should only be executed as long as there are records in the inventory file. To bypass this code when the end-of-file condition occurs on the inventory file, a GO TO statement transfers control to the end of the SECTION. This returns control to the SORT statement and program processing continues from that point.

The last paragraph in any SECTION should be a paragraph containing the EXIT statement. This provides a common exit point from the SECTION. It also allows the program to bypass code and branch to the last paragraph when the functions in the SECTION specified in the INPUT PROCEDURE have been completed. The code in Figure 9.14 uses the GO TO statement to bypass the remaining operations once the last record has been processed. This program unavoidably violates the one entry/one exit rule of structured programming because of the use of the GO TO statement for exiting the sections. This is a result of an idiosyncracy of the COBOL language and not one of program design.

The OUTPUT PROCEDURE. The OUTPUT PROCEDURE allows the programmer to specify the processing to be done using the sorted file while it is still an intermediate file. The sort work file will be opened automatically, making the sorted records available for further processing. COBOL does not allow the READ statement to be used to access the records in the sort-work-file. Instead it provides the RETURN statement. The RETURN statement functions just like a READ statement. Its format and rules are:

RETURN file-name RECORD [INTO data-name-1]
AT END imperative-statement-1
[NOT AT END: imperative-statement
[END-RETURN]

1. The file must be defined in an SD entry.
2. The RETURN must appear in the OUTPUT PROCEDURE of a SORT statement.

The file-name is the sort work file associated with the SORT statement and must be described by an SD entry. When the RETURN statement is executed, the next sorted record in the sort work file is made available in the sort record area.

If the INTO phrase is specified, the contents of the current record are moved to data-name-1. This makes the data available in the sort record area and in data-name-1. The INTO option in the RETURN statement functions in the same way as in the READ statement. The AT END clause allows the programmer to specify the action to be taken when the end of the sort work file is reached. In Figure 9.14, SORT-OUTPUT SECTION is specified as the OUTPUT PROCEDURE. It accumulates the total quantity-on-hand for all records and copies the sorted records to the output file SORTED-INVENTORY-FILE.

The RETURN verb causes the next sorted record to be available for processing. Thus the records need not ever be transferred to another file to be processed. Once the OUTPUT PROCEDURE has been executed, the sort work file is automatically closed. The sort work file is never opened or closed by the programmer. The same logic used to exit the INPUT PROCEDURE section must be employed to exit the OUTPUT PROCEDURE section.

Modifications to the Hierarchy Chart. The SORT statement causes only minor changes to the hierarchy chart for any program. This is because the sort is a preordering or postordering of the records in a file and does not influence the processing logic. To see how to incorporate the SORT into a hierarchy chart, examine Figure 9.15. The SORT appears in the top module of the hierarchy chart. The only programming tasks in the top module will be the SORT and the opening and closing of files. The second level modules represent the splitting of the sort into the INPUT PROCEDURE and OUTPUT PROCEDURE sections. Each procedure module is then identical to the structure of the program to accomplish the required tasks. If one or the other SECTIONs is not used, the respective module will not appear.

Figure 9.15   *Incorporating a SORT into a Hierarchy Chart*

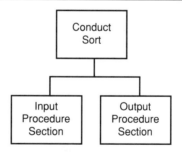

For example, the sort of the transaction file in the master file update shown in the system flowchart of Figure 9.13b requires only an OUTPUT PROCEDURE. A generic hierarchy chart would appear as in Figure 9.16. Notice that the only differences between Figures 9.7 and 9.16 are the extra module on top, the appearance of the module "4000 EXIT" to end the section, and the use of RETURN instead of READ in module "1200 Return Transaction Record". The code reflects these minor changes, as can be seen from the new code in Figure 9.17. The additional Nassi-Schneiderman charts are in Figure 9.18. The code of 9.17 also is an additional illustration of the changes required in the DATA DIVISION.

Figure 9.16   *Hierarchy Chart for "File Update" Program Incorporating a SORT*

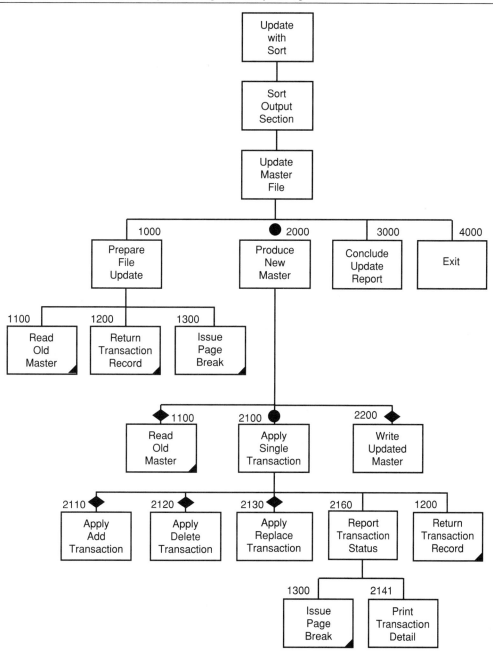

Figure 9.17   *"File Update" Code with Sort*

```
 1
 2 IDENTIFICATION DIVISION.
 3 PROGRAM-ID.  GENERIC-SEQUENTIAL-UPDATE.
 4*   THIS PROGRAM TAKES A TRANSACTION-FILE AND
 5*   APPLIES THEM TO THE MASTER-FILE
 6
 7 AUTHOR.           SELF
 8 DATE-WRITTEN.        JULY 9, 1992
 9 DATE-COMPILED. 13-Jul-92 04:21.
11 ENVIRONMENT DIVISION.
12
13 CONFIGURATION SECTION.
14
15 SOURCE-COMPUTER.  GENERIC-COMPUTER.
16 OBJECT-COMPUTER.  GENERIC-COMPUTER.
17
18 INPUT-OUTPUT SECTION.
19
20 FILE-CONTROL.
21
22    SELECT TRANSACTION-FILE ASSIGN TO DISK
23        ORGANIZATION IS SEQUENTIAL
24        BLOCK CONTAINS 10 RECORDS.
25
26    SELECT MASTER-FILE ASSIGN TO DISK
27        ORGANIZATION IS SEQUENTIAL
28        BLOCK CONTAINS 10 RECORDS.
29
30    SELECT NEW-MASTER-FILE ASSIGN TO DISK
31        ORGANIZATION IS SEQUENTIAL
32        BLOCK CONTAINS 10 RECORDS.
33
34    SELECT SORTED-TRANSACTIONS-FILE ASSIGN TO DISK.
35
36    SELECT UPDATE-REPORT ASSIGN TO PRINTER
37        ORGANIZATION IS SEQUENTIAL.
38
39 DATA DIVISION.
40
41 FILE SECTION.
42
43 FD  TRANSACTION-FILE
```

Figure 9.17   *(continued)*

```
44       LABEL RECORDS ARE STANDARD.
45
46 01   TRANSACTION-RECORD PIC X(47).
47
48 FD   MASTER-FILE
49       LABEL RECORDS ARE STANDARD.
50
51 01   MASTER-RECORD.
52       05   MASTER-KEY-FIELD PIC X(6).
53       05   FILLER           PIC X(34).
54
55 FD   NEW-MASTER-FILE
56       LABEL RECORDS ARE STANDARD.
57
58 01   NEW-MASTER-RECORD.
59       05   NEW-MASTER-KEY-FIELD PIC X(6).
60       05   FILLER               PIC X(34).
61
62
63 FD   UPDATE-REPORT
64       LABEL RECORDS ARE OMITTED.
65
66 01   UPDATE-PRINT-LINE PIC X(80).
67
68 SD   SORTED-TRANSACTIONS-FILE.
69
70 01   SORTED-TRANSACTION-RECORD.
71       05   TRANSACTION-KEY-FIELD   PIC X(6).
72       05   TRANSACTION-TYPE        PIC X.
73           88   ADD-TRANSACTION     VALUE "A".
74           88   DELETE-TRANSACTION  VALUE "D".
75           88   REPLACE-TRANSACTION VALUE "R".
76       05   TRANSACTION-MASTER-DATA PIC X(40).
77
78
79 WORKING-STORAGE SECTION.
80
81 01   UPDATE-REPORT-LINES.
82       05   UP-REPORT-TITLE.
83           10   FILLER    PIC X(14) VALUE "REPORT #64".
84           10   FILLER    PIC X(38) VALUE
85                                    "MASTER FILE UPDATE".
```

Figure 9.17   (continued)

```
 86             10  FILLER      PIC X(5)   VALUE "PAGE".
 87             10  UP-PAGE PIC ZZ9.
 88         05  UP-DATE-LINE.
 89             10  FILLER      PIC X(47)  VALUE "DISTRIBUTION".
 90             10  FILLER      PIC X(5)   VALUE "DATE".
 91             10  UP-DATE     PIC 99/99/99.
 92         05  UP-COLUMN-HEADING.
 93             10  FILLER PIC X(15) VALUE "TRANSACTION".
 94             10  FILLER PIC X(14) VALUE "KEY FIELD".
 95             10  FILLER PIC X(09) VALUE "RECORD".
 96         05  UP-DETAIL.
 97             10  UP-CODE          PIC X(6).
 98             10  UP-ERROR         PIC X(10).
 99             10  UP-KEY           PIC 9(6).
100             10  FILLER           PIC X(4) VALUE SPACE.
101             10  UP-RECORD        PIC X(40).
102
103 01  END-OF-FILE-INDICATORS.
104     05  EOF-MASTER        PIC X(5) VALUE "FALSE".
105     05  EOF-TRANSACTION   PIC X(5) VALUE "FALSE".
106
107 01  PAGE-CONTROL-COUNTERS.
108     05  PCC-PAGE      PIC 999 VALUE ZERO.
109     05  PCC-LINE      PIC 99  VALUE 99.
110     05  PCC-MAX-LINE  PIC 99  VALUE 55.
111
112 01  PROCESS-INDICATORS.
113     05  ACTIVE-NEW-MASTER   PIC X(5) VALUE "FALSE".
114     05  IN-PROCESS-KEY      PIC X(6) VALUE SPACES.
115     05  ERROR-INDICATOR     PIC X(5) VALUE "TRUE".
116
117
118 PROCEDURE DIVISION.
119
120 UPDATE-WITH-SORT.
121     OPEN INPUT MASTER-FILE.
122     OPEN OUTPUT NEW-MASTER-FILE.
123     OPEN OUTPUT UPDATE-REPORT.
124     SORT SORTED-TRANSACTIONS-FILE
125         ON ASCENDING KEY TRANSACTION-KEY-FIELD
126         USING TRANSACTION-FILE
127         OUPUT PROCEDURE IS UPDATE-MASTER-FILE-SECTION.
```

Figure 9.17   (continued)

```
128     CLOSE MASTER-FILE.
129     CLOSE NEW-MASTER-FILE.
130     CLOSE UPDATE-REPORT.
131     STOP RUN.
132
133
134 UPDATE-MASTER-FILE-SECTION SECTION.
135
136 UPDATE-MASTER-FILE.
137     PERFORM 1000-PREPARE-FILE-UPDATE.
138     PERFORM 2000-PRODUCE-NEW-MASTER
139         UNTIL (EOF-MASTER = "TRUE" AND EOF-TRANSACTION = "TRUE").
140     PERFORM 3000-CONCLUDE-UPDATE-REPORT.
141     GO TO 4000-EXIT.
142
143 1000-PREPARE-FILE-UPDATE.
144     PERFORM 1100-READ-OLD-MASTER.
145     PERFORM 1200-RETURN-TRANSACTION-RECORD.
146     IF MASTER-KEY-FIELD < TRANSACTION-KEY-FIELD
147         MOVE MASTER-KEY-FIELD TO IN-PROCESS-KEY
148     ELSE
149         MOVE TRANSACTION-KEY-FIELD TO IN-PROCESS-KEY.
150     ACCEPT UP-DATE FROM DATE.
151     PERFORM 1300-ISSUE-PAGE-BREAK.
152
153 1100-READ-OLD-MASTER.
154     READ MASTER-FILE AT END MOVE "TRUE" TO EOF-MASTER
155         MOVE HIGH-VALUES TO MASTER-KEY-FIELD.
156
157 1200-RETURN-TRANSACTION-RECORD.
158     RETURN SOTRTED-TRANSACTION-FILE AT END
159         MOVE "TRUE" TO EOF-TRANSACTION
160         MOVE HIGH-VALUES TO TRANSACTION-KEY-FIELD.
161
162 1300-ISSUE-PAGE-BREAK.
163     ADD 1 TO PCC-PAGE.
164     MOVE PCC-PAGE TO UP-PAGE.
165     WRITE UPDATE-PRINT-LINE FROM UP-REPORT-TITLE AFTER PAGE.
166     WRITE UPDATE-PRINT-LINE FROM UP-DATE-LINE.
167     WRITE UPDATE-PRINT-LINE FROM UP-COLUMN-HEADING.
168     MOVE SPACES TO UPDATE-PRINT-LINE.
169     WRITE UPDATE-PRINT-LINE.
```

Figure 9.17   (continued)

```
170      MOVE 4 TO PCC-LINE.
171
172  2000-PRODUCE-NEW-MASTER.
173      IF MASTER-KEY-FIELD = IN-PROCESS-KEY
174          MOVE MASTER-RECORD TO NEW-MASTER-RECORD
175          PERFORM 1100-READ-OLD-MASTER
176          MOVE "TRUE" TO ACTIVE-NEW-MASTER.
177      PERFORM 2100-APPLY-SINGLE-TRANSACTION
178          UNTIL TRANSACTION-KEY-FIELD > IN-PROCESS-KEY.
179      IF ACTIVE-NEW-MASTER = "TRUE"
180          PERFORM 2200-WRITE-UPDATED-MASTER
181          MOVE "FALSE" TO ACTIVE-NEW-MASTER.
182      IF MASTER-KEY-FIELD < TRANSACTION-KEY-FIELD
183          MOVE MASTER-KEY-FIELD TO IN-PROCESS-KEY
184      ELSE
185          MOVE TRANSACTION-KEY-FIELD TO IN-PROCESS-KEY.
186
187  2100-APPLY-SINGLE-TRANSACTION.
188      MOVE "TRUE" TO ERROR-INDICATOR.
189      IF ADD-TRANSACTION       PERFORM 2110-APPLY-ADD-TRANSACTION.
190      IF DELETE-TRANSACTION  PERFORM 2120-APPLY-DELETE-TRANSACTION.
191      IF REPLACE-TRANSACTION PERFORM 2130-APPLY-REPLACE-TRANSACTION
192      PERFORM 2140-REPORT-TRANSACTION-STATUS.
193      PERFORM 1200-RETURN-TRANSACTION-RECORD.
194
195  2110-APPLY-ADD-TRANSACTION.
196      IF ACTIVE-NEW-MASTER = "FALSE"
197          MOVE TRANSACTION-MASTER-DATA TO NEW-MASTER-RECORD
198          MOVE "TRUE" TO ACTIVE-NEW-MASTER
199          MOVE "FALSE" TO ERROR-INDICATOR.
200
201  2120-APPLY-DELETE-TRANSACTION.
202      IF ACTIVE-NEW-MASTER = "TRUE"
203          MOVE "FALSE" TO ACTIVE-NEW-MASTER
204          MOVE "FALSE" TO ERROR-INDICATOR.
205
206  2130-APPLY-REPLACE-TRANSACTION.
207      IF ACTIVE-NEW-MASTER = "TRUE"
208          MOVE TRANSACTION-MASTER-DATA TO NEW-MASTER-RECORD
209          MOVE "FALSE" TO ERROR-INDICATOR.
210
211  2140-REPORT-TRANSACTION-STATUS.
```

Figure 9.17   *(continued)*

```
212     IF PCC-LINE > PCC-MAX-LINE
213         PERFORM 1300-ISSUE-PAGE-BREAK.
214     IF ERROR-INDICATOR = "TRUE" MOVE "ERROR" TO UP-ERROR
215         ELSE MOVE SPACES TO UP-ERROR.
216     MOVE TRANSACTION-TYPE TO UP-CODE.
217     PERFORM 2141-PRINT-TRANSACTION-DETAIL.
218
219 2141-PRINT-TRANSACTION-DETAIL.
220     ADD 1 TO PCC-LINE.
221     MOVE TRANSACTION-MASTER-DATA TO UP-RECORD.
222     WRITE UPDATE-PRINT-LINE FROM UP-DETAIL.
223
224 2200-WRITE-UPDATED-MASTER.
225     WRITE NEW-MASTER-RECORD.
226
227 3000-CONCLUDE-UPDATE-REPORT.
228     MOVE "END OR REPORT" TO UPDATE-PRINT-LINE.
229     WRITE UPDATE-PRINT-LINE AFTER ADVANCING 2 LINES.
230
231 4000-EXIT.
```

Figure 9.18   Additions for "File Update" Sort

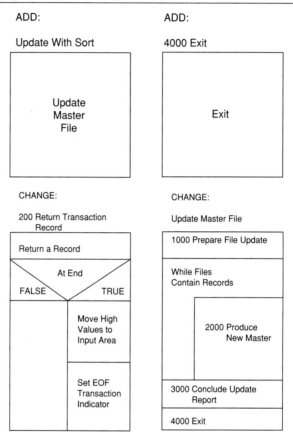

9.3.3   The MERGE Statement

Many business applications involve the combination of two or more input files into a single file where the files to be merged are already in the same sequence. For example, banking transactions may come in from the various branches of a bank to be *merged* into one transaction file that will be used to update the master file of accounts. The resulting merge file is just the aggregate of the input file records arranged in order based on some key field(s). To accomplish this process, COBOL provides the MERGE statement.

The MERGE statement is similar to the SORT statement. The format and rules for the MERGE statement are:

MERGE file-name-1 {ON $\left\{ \begin{array}{l} \underline{\text{ASCENDING}} \\ \underline{\text{DESCENDING}} \end{array} \right\}$ KEY {data-name-1}... }

      USING file-name-2 {file-name-3}...
      $\left\{ \begin{array}{l} \underline{\text{OUTPUT}} \quad \underline{\text{PROCEDURE}} \text{ IS section-name-1} \\ \underline{\text{GIVING}} \quad \text{file-name-4} \end{array} \right\}$

1. All files named may not be OPEN when the merge is executed.
2. Two or more files must be specified in the USING clause.
3. File-name-1 must be defined by an SD entry, all others by FD entries.
4. All data-names in the KEY clause must be defined in a record with the SD entry defining file-name-1.
5. Multiple keys may be specified.

File-name-1 identifies the merge work file whose description is contained in an SD entry in the DATA DIVISION. The data-names in the KEY clause must be defined in the record descriptions of the merge work file. They must identify the key fields to be used in merging the input files. The file(s) to be merged are specified in the USING clause and are described by FD entries in the DATA DIVISION. If an OUTPUT PROCEDURE is defined, the records of the merge work file are made available to the SECTION specified by section-name-1. The OUTPUT PROCEDURE uses RETURN statements to "read" the merged records. If the GIVING clause is chosen, file-name-4 is the file that will contain all the merged records of the merge work file. As in the SORT statement, all files must be CLOSEd before the MERGE statement is executed. The MERGE will automatically OPEN and CLOSE the relevant files. From a programming standpoint, merging programs is similar in structure and code to sorting programs.

Case Study: CDL's Update Accounts Receivable

Charlene now tackles the program that updates the accounts receivable file. The program should add the billed amount on each order to the amount due, reduce the amount due by the payments received, and make routing modifications. The system flowchart illustrated in Figure 9.19 depicts the files needed. The program specifications are described in Figure 9.20. Notice that the transactions must first be sorted and placed into a common format for updating the file. The record and report layouts are given in Figures 9.21 and 9.22, respectively.

Figure 9.19   System Flowchart for CDL's "A/R Update" Program

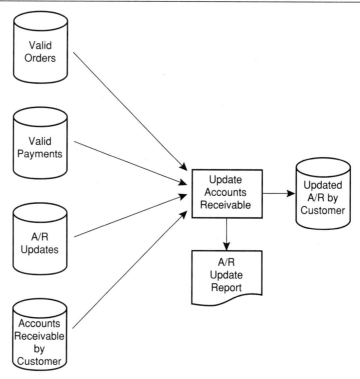

Figure 9.20 *CDL's "Update A/R" Program Specifications*

PROGRAM SUMMARY

TITLE: *Update Accounts Receivable*

PREPARED BY: *C. Hilton*

DATE: *7-8-93*

FILES USED

FILE NAME	MEDIA	ORGANIZATION
Valid orders	*Disk*	*Sequential*
Valid payments	*Disk*	*Sequential*
A/R updates	*Disk*	*Sequential*
A/R update report	*Printer*	*Sequential*
A/R by Customer	*Disk*	*Sequential*
Updated A/R by Cust.	*Disk*	*Sequential*

DESCRIPTION

The validated orders and validated payments must conform to the A/R updates format for subsequent processing. The orders, payments, and updates must then be sorted into customer number order. The A/R updates contain adds, deletes, and replacements to the A/R file. They have been validated prior to this program. "Adds" must have a new customer number. "Deletes" and "replacements" must have existing customer numbers. "Deletes" are also invalid if the customers owe money. The payments and orders become "change" transactions and may modify only the amount field upward.

All transactions appear on the update report. Five *s indicate a transaction in error. The old and new balance columns display the amount on the master file for account balances before and after the application of the transactions. No summary information is to be printed.

Note: 999999 is not a valid customer number.

Figure 9.21   Record Layouts for CDL's "Update A/R" Program

RECORD LAYOUT SHEET

Record Name: *Order*			File Name: *Orders/Extended Orders*		
Prepared By: *C. Hilton*			Date: *6-15-93*		
Key Fields:			Organization: *Sequential*		
Field	Description		Type*	Length	Decimal
Customer #	*A unique customer ID*		*N*	*6*	*0*
Disc number	*An identifier / stock number*		*N*	*6*	*0*
Quantity	*The number of CDs ordered*		*N*	*2*	*0*
Order #	*A preprinted order form no.*		*N*	*6*	*0*
Price	*Extended retail price*		*N*	*8*	*2*

* A = alphanumeric
  N = numeric

RECORD LAYOUT SHEET
Revised

Record Name: *Payments*			File Name: *Valid/Invalid Payment*		
Prepared By: *C. Hilton*			Date: *6-22-93*		
Key Fields:			Organization: *Sequential*		
Field	Description		Type*	Length	Decimal
Customer #	*A unique customer ID*		*N*	*6*	*0*
Payment amt.	*$*		*N*	*8*	*2*
Check ID	*The check number*		*A*	*8*	

* A = alphanumeric
  N = numeric

Figure 9.21 (continued)

RECORD LAYOUT SHEET

Record Name: *A/R Update*		File Name: *A/R Update*			
Prepared By: *C. Hilton*		Date: *7-8-93*			
Key Fields:		Organization: *Sequential*			
Field	Description	Type*	Length	Decimal	
Trans-ID	*Code for (A)dd*	*A*	*1*		
	(D)elete				
	(R)eplace				
	(C)hange amount				
Customer #	*A unique customer ID*	*N*	*6*	*0*	
Address	*Customer address*	*A*	*20*		
City	*Customer city*	*A*	*12*		
State	*Customer state*	*A*	*2*		
Zip	*Customer zip*	*N*	*5*	*0*	
Phone	*Customer phone*	*N*	*10*	*0*	
Balance	*Amount owed*	*N*	*8*	*2*	

* A = alphanumeric
  N = numeric

Figure 9.21 *(continued)*

RECORD LAYOUT SHEET

Record Name: *Customer A/R*		File Name: *Account Receivable*			
Prepared By: *C. Hilton*		Date: *7-8-93*			
Key Fields: *Customer ID*		Organization: *Sequential*			
Field	Description	Type*	Length	Decimal	
Customer #	*A unique customer ID*	*N*	*6*	*0*	
Cust. address	*Address field*	*A*	*20*		
City	*City of customer*	*A*	*12*		
State	*State code*	*A*	*2*		
Zip	*Zip code*	*N*	*5*	*0*	
Phone	*Phone number*	*N*	*10*	*0*	
Balance	*Amount owed*	*N*	*8*	*2*	

* A = alphanumeric
  N = numeric

Figure 9.22   CDL's "Update A/R" Report Layout

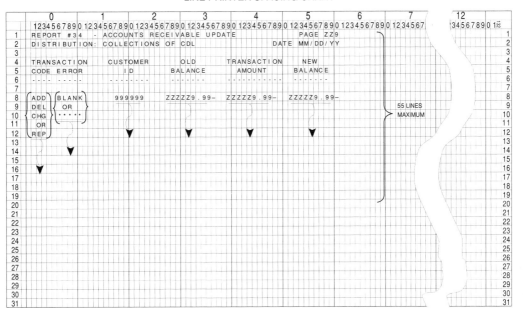

Charlene realizes that this file update application is a perfect opportunity for using the SORT verb with an input and an output procedure. The hierarchy chart in Figure 9.23 shows the program structure. Module "Update Accounts Receivable" represents the entire program and controls the updating process using the SORT statement. Module "10000 Transform Transaction Files" comprises the tasks to be accomplished prior to the actual updating of the accounts receivable master file. It represents the SORT input section and is divided into three subordinate modules. Module "11000 Prepare File Transform" performs the priming reads of the three input files. Module "12000 Transform Transaction Records" formats the records for use in subsequent processing, and module "13000 Exit Sort Input" terminates execution of the input section.

Module "20000 Update Master File" represents the tasks to be performed once the input records have been sorted. It represents the first paragraph in the SORT output section. Module "20000 Update Master File" essentially reads an update record, applies it to the old A/R master

Figure 9.23   Hierarchy Chart for CDL's "Update A/R" Program

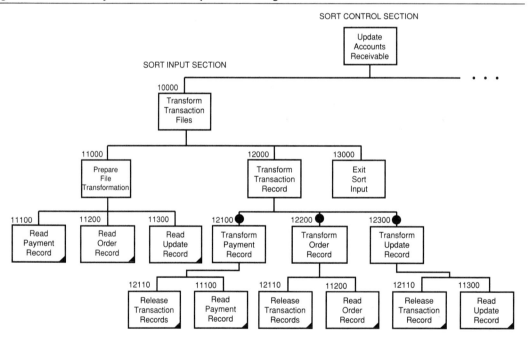

file, and produces the new updated A/R master. To decompose this module, Charlene consults a hierarchy chart she has that describes the program structure of an update algorithm presented in a COBOL text she used in college. There are three subordinate modules. Module "22000 Produce New Master" is the repetitive task needed to produce the updated master file. Before its execution, module "21000 Prepare File Update" prints report headings and performs the priming reads. Module "23000 Exit Sort Output" terminates the execution of the output section. The decomposition of the lower levels of "20000 Update Master File" is the same as that shown in Figure 9.7.

The Nassi-Schneiderman charts derived from the hierarchy chart are shown in Figure 9.24. The code is in Figure 9.25. The Nassi-Schneiderman charts developed by Charlene, for the most part, result in straightforward code. However, the logic encompassed in two of the logical functions requires more detail.

Figure 9.23   *(continued)*

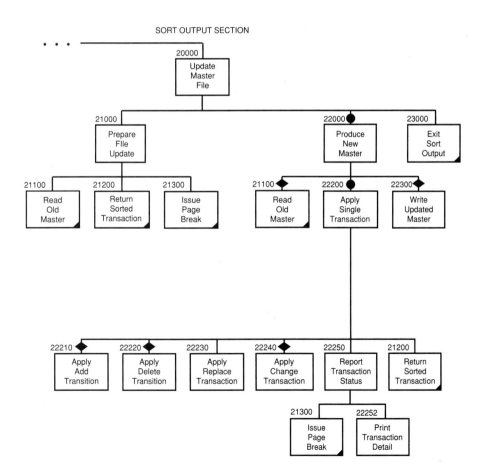

Figure 9.24   N-S Charts for CDL's "Update A/R" Program

Figure 9.24 *(continued)*

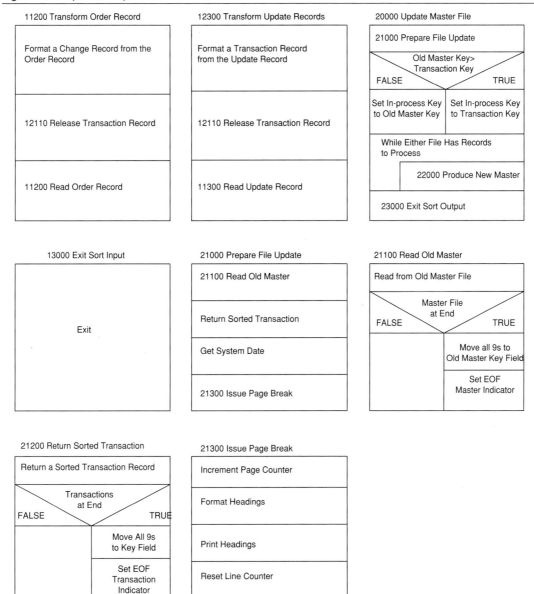

Figure 9.24   (continued)

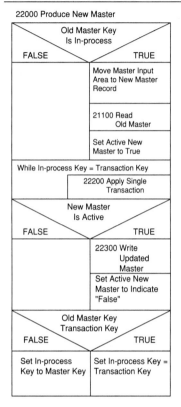

22000 Produce New Master

Old Master Key Is In-process

FALSE | TRUE

(TRUE) Move Master Input Area to New Master Record

21100 Read Old Master

Set Active New Master to True

While In-process Key = Transaction Key

22200 Apply Single Transaction

New Master Is Active

FALSE | TRUE

(TRUE) 22300 Write Updated Master

Set Active New Master to Indicate "False"

Old Master Key Transaction Key

FALSE | TRUE

Set In-process Key to Master Key | Set In-process Key = Transaction Key

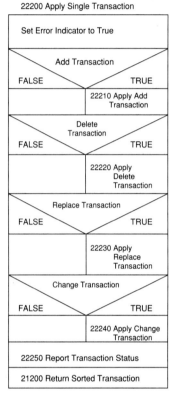

22200 Apply Single Transaction

Set Error Indicator to True

Add Transaction

FALSE | TRUE

22210 Apply Add Transaction

Delete Transaction

FALSE | TRUE

22220 Apply Delete Transaction

Replace Transaction

FALSE | TRUE

22230 Apply Replace Transaction

Change Transaction

FALSE | TRUE

22240 Apply Change Transaction

22250 Report Transaction Status

21200 Return Sorted Transaction

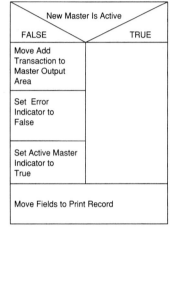

22210 Apply Add Transaction

New Master Is Active

FALSE | TRUE

Move Add Transaction to Master Output Area

Set Error Indicator to False

Set Active Master Indicator to True

Move Fields to Print Record

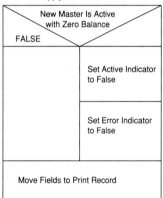

22220 Apply Delete Transaction

New Master Is Active with Zero Balance

FALSE

Set Active Indicator to False

Set Error Indicator to False

Move Fields to Print Record

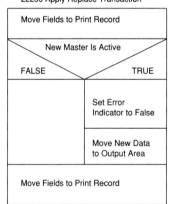

22230 Apply Replace Transaction

Move Fields to Print Record

New Master Is Active

FALSE | TRUE

Set Error Indicator to False

Move New Data to Output Area

Move Fields to Print Record

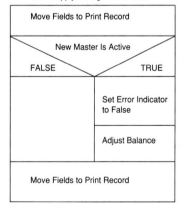

22240 Apply Change Transaction

Move Fields to Print Record

New Master Is Active

FALSE | TRUE

Set Error Indicator to False

Adjust Balance

Move Fields to Print Record

Figure 9.24   (continued)

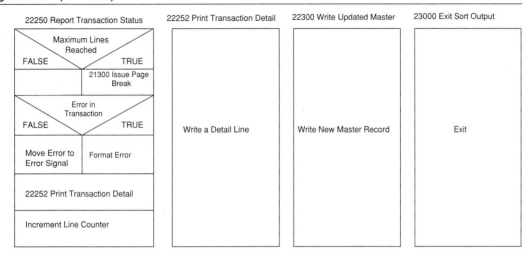

Figure 9.25   COBOL Code for CDL's "Update A/R" Program

```
 1
 2 IDENTIFICATION DIVISION.
 3 PROGRAM-ID. UPDATE-AR.
 4*    THIS PROGRAM TAKES ORDERS, PAYMENTS AND STANDARD UPDATES AND
 5*    APPLIES THEM TO THE ACCOUNTS RECEIVABLE FILE AFTER SORTING
 6
 7 AUTHOR.          C HILTON
 8 DATE-WRITTEN.    JULY 9, 1992
 9 DATE-COMPILED. 25-Jan-94 03:23.
13 ENVIRONMENT DIVISION.
14
15
16 CONFIGURATION SECTION.
17
18 SOURCE-COMPUTER.  GENERIC-COMPUTER.
19 OBJECT-COMPUTER.  GENERIC-COMPUTER.
20
21
22 INPUT-OUTPUT SECTION.
23
24 FILE-CONTROL.
25    SELECT ORDERS-FILE ASSIGN TO DISK
26        ORGANIZATION IS SEQUENTIAL.
```

Figure 9.25   *(continued)*

```
27      SELECT PAYMENTS-FILE ASSIGN TO DISK
28          ORGANIZATION IS SEQUENTIAL.
29      SELECT UPDATES-FILE ASSIGN TO DISK
30          ORGANIZATION IS SEQUENTIAL.
31      SELECT OLD-ACCOUNTS-RECEIVABLE-FILE ASSIGN TO DISK
32          ORGANIZATION IS SEQUENTIAL.
33      SELECT NEW-ACCOUNTS-RECEIVABLE-FILE ASSIGN TO DISK
34          ORGANIZATION IS SEQUENTIAL.
35      SELECT AR-UPDATE-REPORT-FILE ASSIGN TO DISK
36          ORGANIZATION IS SEQUENTIAL.
37      SELECT TRANSACTIONS-FILE ASSIGN TO DISK.
38
39
40
41
42
43 DATA DIVISION.
44
45
46 FILE SECTION.
47
48 FD ORDERS-FILE
49      LABEL RECORDS ARE STANDARD.
50
51 01  ORDER-REC.
52      05  O-CUSTOMER-NUMBER  PIC 9(6).
53      05  FILLER             PIC X(14).
54      05  O-PRICE            PIC 9(6)V99.
55
56 FD  PAYMENTS-FILE
57      LABEL RECORDS ARE STANDARD.
58
59 01  PAYMENT-REC.
60      05  P-CUSTOMER-NUMBER  PIC 9(6).
61      05  P-AMOUNT           PIC 9(6)V99.
62      05  FILLER             PIC X(8).
63
64 FD  UPDATES-FILE
65      LABEL RECORDS ARE STANDARD.
66
67 01  UPDATE-REC.
68      05  FILLER                PIC X(56).
```

Figure 9.25 **(continued)**

```
 69      05  UF-AMOUNT              PIC 9(6)V99.
 70
 71 FD  OLD-ACCOUNTS-RECEIVABLE-FILE
 72      LABEL RECORDS ARE STANDARD.
 73
 74 01  OLD-AR-ITEM-REC.
 75      05  OLDAR-CUSTOMER-NUMBER PIC 9(6).
 76      05  FILLER                PIC X(57).
 77
 78 FD  NEW-ACCOUNTS-RECEIVABLE-FILE
 79      LABEL RECORDS ARE STANDARD.
 80
 81 01  NEW-AR-ITEM-REC.
 82      05  NEWAR-CUSTOMER-NUMBER PIC 9(6).
 83      05  NEWAR-ADDRESS         PIC X(20).
 84      05  NEWAR-CITY            PIC X(12).
 85      05  NEWAR-STATE           PIC XX.
 86      05  NEWAR-ZIP             PIC 9(5).
 87      05  NEWAR-PHONE           PIC 9(10).
 88      05  NEWAR-BALANCE         PIC 9(6)V99.
 89
 90 FD  AR-UPDATE-REPORT-FILE
 91      LABEL RECORDS ARE OMITTED.
 92
 93 01  ARUP-LINE-REC PIC X(80).
 94
 95 SD  TRANSACTIONS-FILE.
 96
 97 01  TRANSACTION-REC.
 98      05  TRANS-CODE PIC X.
 99      88  ADD-TRANSACTION     VALUE "A".
100      88  DELETE-TRANSACTION  VALUE "D".
101      88  REPLACE-TRANSACTION VALUE "R".
102      88  CHANGE-TRANSACTION  VALUE "C".
103      05  TRANS-ACCOUNTS-RECEIVABLE-ITEM.
104          10  TRANS-CUSTOMER-NUMBER PIC 9(6).
105          10  FILLER                PIC X(49).
106          10  TRANS-AMOUNT          PIC S9(6)V99.
107
108 WORKING-STORAGE SECTION.
109
110 01  AR-UPDATE-REPORT-LINES.
```

Figure 9.25   (continued)

```
111     05   ARUP-REPORT-TITLE.
112          10   FILLER     PIC X(14) VALUE "REPORT #34".
113          10   FILLER     PIC X(38) VALUE
114                                    "ACCOUNTS RECEIVABLE UPDATE".
115          10   FILLER     PIC X(5)  VALUE "PAGE".
116          10   ARUP-PAGE  PIC ZZ9.
117     05   ARUP-DISTRIBUTION.
118          10   FILLER     PIC X(14)  VALUE "DISTRIBUTION".
119          10   FILLER     PIC X(33)  VALUE "COLLECTIONS OF CDL".
120          10   FILLER     PIC X(5)   VALUE "DATE".
121          10   ARUP-DATE PIC 99/99/99.
122     05   ARUP-COLUMN-1.
123          10   FILLER PIC X(15) VALUE "TRANSACTION".
124          10   FILLER PIC X(14) VALUE "CUSTOMER".
125          10   FILLER PIC X(09) VALUE "OLD".
126          10   FILLER PIC X(15) VALUE "TRANSACTION".
127          10   FILLER PIC X(03) VALUE "NEW".
128     05   ARUP-COLUMN-2.
129          10   FILLER PIC X(18) VALUE "CODE   ERROR".
130          10   FILLER PIC X(09) VALUE "ID".
131          10   FILLER PIC X(13) VALUE "BALANCE".
132          10   FILLER PIC X(11) VALUE "AMOUNT".
133          10   FILLER PIC X(07) VALUE "BALANCE".
134     05   ARUP-UNDERLINE.
135          10   FILLER PIC X(16) VALUE "—   —".
136          10   FILLER PIC X(10) VALUE "——".
137          10   FILLER PIC X(12) VALUE "———".
138          10   FILLER PIC X(12) VALUE "———".
139          10   FILLER PIC X(10) VALUE "———".
140     05   ARUP-DETAIL.
141          10   ARUP-CODE             PIC X(6).
142          10   ARUP-ERROR            PIC X(10).
143          10   ARUP-CUSTOMER-NUMBER  PIC 9(6).
144          10   FILLER                PIC X(4) VALUE SPACE.
145          10   ARUP-OLD-BALANCE      PIC ZZZZZ9.99-.
146          10   FILLER                PIC X(2) VALUE SPACE.
147          10   ARUP-TRANS-AMOUNT     PIC ZZZZZ9.99-.
148          10   FILLER                PIC X(2) VALUE SPACE.
149          10   ARUP-NEW-BALANCE      PIC ZZZZZ9.99-.
150
151 01  END-OF-FILE-INDICATORS.
152     05   EOF-ORDERS         PIC X(5) VALUE "FALSE".
```

Figure 9.25   (continued)

```
153     05  EOF-PAYMENTS        PIC X(5) VALUE "FALSE".
154     05  EOF-UPDATES         PIC X(5) VALUE "FALSE".
155     05  EOF-TRANSACTIONS    PIC X(5) VALUE "FALSE".
156     05  EOF-OLD-AR          PIC X(5) VALUE "FALSE".
157
158 01  PAGE-CONTROL-COUNTERS.
159     05  PCC-PAGE         PIC 999 VALUE ZERO.
160     05  PCC-LINE         PIC 99  VALUE 99.
161     05  PCC-MAX-LINE     PIC 99  VALUE 55.
162
163 01  SYSTEM-DATE.
164     05  SD-DATE      PIC 9(6).
165     05  SD-MM-DD-YY.
166         10  SD-MM    PIC XX.
167         10  SD-DD    PIC XX.
168         10  SD-YY    PIC XX.
169     05  SD-YEAR      PIC XX.
170
171 01  PROCESS-INDICATORS.
172     05  PI-ERROR-FOUND        PIC X(5) VALUE "FALSE".
173     05  PI-ACTIVE-NEW-MASTER  PIC X(5) VALUE "FALSE".
174     05  PI-IN-PROCESS-KEY     PIC 9(6) VALUE ZERO.
175
176 PROCEDURE DIVISION.
177
178
179 SORT-CONTROL SECTION.
180
181 UPDATE-ACCOUNTS-RECEIVABLE.
182     OPEN INPUT ORDERS-FILE.
183     OPEN INPUT PAYMENTS-FILE.
184     OPEN INPUT UPDATES-FILE.
185     OPEN INPUT OLD-ACCOUNTS-RECEIVABLE-FILE.
186     OPEN OUTPUT NEW-ACCOUNTS-RECEIVABLE-FILE.
187     OPEN OUTPUT AR-UPDATE-REPORT-FILE.
188     SORT TRANSACTIONS-FILE
189         ON ASCENDING KEY TRANS-CUSTOMER-NUMBER
190         INPUT PROCEDURE IS SORT-INPUT
191         OUTPUT PROCEDURE IS SORT-OUTPUT.
192     CLOSE ORDERS-FILE.
193     CLOSE PAYMENTS-FILE.
194     CLOSE UPDATES-FILE.
```

Figure 9.25   (continued)

```
195     CLOSE OLD-ACCOUNTS-RECEIVABLE-FILE.
196     CLOSE NEW-ACCOUNTS-RECEIVABLE-FILE.
197     CLOSE AR-UPDATE-REPORT-FILE.
198     STOP RUN.
199
200
201 SORT-INPUT SECTION.
202
203 10000-TRANSFORM-TRANS-FILES.
204     PERFORM 11000-PREPARE-FILE-TRANSFORM.
205     PERFORM 12000-TRANSFORM-TRANS-RECS.
206     GO TO 13000-EXIT-SORT-INPUT.
207
208 11000-PREPARE-FILE-TRANSFORM.
209     PERFORM 11100-READ-PAYMENT-RECORD.
210     PERFORM 11200-READ-ORDER-RECORD.
211     PERFORM 11300-READ-UPDATE-RECORD.
212
213 11100-READ-PAYMENT-RECORD.
214     READ PAYMENTS-FILE
215         AT END MOVE "TRUE" TO EOF-PAYMENTS.
216
217 11200-READ-ORDER-RECORD.
218     READ ORDERS-FILE
219         AT END MOVE "TRUE" TO EOF-ORDERS.
220
221 11300-READ-UPDATE-RECORD.
222     READ UPDATES-FILE
223         AT END MOVE "TRUE" TO EOF-UPDATES.
224
225 12000-TRANSFORM-TRANS-RECS.
226     PERFORM 12100-TRANSFORM-PAYMENT-RECS
227         UNTIL EOF-PAYMENTS = "TRUE".
228     PERFORM 12200-TRANSFORM-ORDER-RECS
229         UNTIL EOF-ORDERS = "TRUE".
230     PERFORM 12300-TRANSFORM-UPDATE-RECS
231         UNTIL EOF-UPDATES = "TRUE".
232
233 12100-TRANSFORM-PAYMENT-RECS.
234     MOVE "C" TO TRANSACTION-REC.
235     MOVE P-CUSTOMER-NUMBER TO TRANS-CUSTOMER-NUMBER.
236     COMPUTE TRANS-AMOUNT = 0.00 - P-AMOUNT.
```

Figure 9.25 (continued)

```
237      PERFORM 12110-RELEASE-TRANSACTION-REC.
238      PERFORM 11100-READ-PAYMENT-RECORD.
239
240 12110-RELEASE-TRANSACTION-REC.
241      RELEASE TRANSACTION-REC.
242
243 12200-TRANSFORM-ORDER-RECS.
244      MOVE "C" TO TRANSACTION-REC.
245      MOVE O-CUSTOMER-NUMBER TO TRANS-CUSTOMER-NUMBER.
246      MOVE O-PRICE TO TRANS-AMOUNT.
247      PERFORM 12110-RELEASE-TRANSACTION-REC.
248      PERFORM 11200-READ-ORDER-RECORD.
249
250 12300-TRANSFORM-UPDATE-RECS.
251      MOVE UPDATE-REC TO TRANSACTION-REC.
252      MOVE UF-AMOUNT TO TRANS-AMOUNT.
253      PERFORM 12110-RELEASE-TRANSACTION-REC.
254      PERFORM 11300-READ-UPDATE-RECORD.
255
256 13000-EXIT-SORT-INPUT.
257      EXIT.
258
259 SORT-OUTPUT SECTION.
260
261
262 20000-UPDATE-MASTER-FILE.
263      PERFORM 21000-PREPARE-FILE-UPDATE.
264      IF TRANS-CUSTOMER-NUMBER > OLDAR-CUSTOMER-NUMBER
265          MOVE OLDAR-CUSTOMER-NUMBER TO PI-IN-PROCESS-KEY
266      ELSE
267          MOVE TRANS-CUSTOMER-NUMBER TO PI-IN-PROCESS-KEY.
268      PERFORM 22000-PRODUCE-NEW-MASTER
269          UNTIL EOF-OLD-AR = "TRUE" AND EOF-TRANSACTIONS = "TRUE".
270      GO TO 23000-EXIT-SORT-OUTPUT.
271
272 21000-PREPARE-FILE-UPDATE.
273      PERFORM 21100-READ-OLD-MASTER.
274      PERFORM 21200-RETURN-SORTED-TRANS.
275      ACCEPT SD-DATE FROM DATE.
276      MOVE SD-DATE TO SD-MM-DD-YY.
277      MOVE SD-MM TO SD-YEAR.
278      MOVE SD-DD TO SD-MM.
```

Figure 9.25   (continued)

```
279     MOVE SD-YY TO SD-DD.
280     MOVE SD-YEAR TO SD-YY.
281     MOVE SD-MM-DD-YY TO SD-DATE.
282     MOVE SD-DATE TO ARUP-DATE.
283     PERFORM 21300-ISSUE-PAGE-BREAK.
284
285 21100-READ-OLD-MASTER.
286     READ OLD-ACCOUNTS-RECEIVABLE-FILE
287         AT END MOVE "TRUE" TO EOF-OLD-AR
288             MOVE 999999 TO OLDAR-CUSTOMER-NUMBER.
289
290 21200-RETURN-SORTED-TRANS.
291     RETURN TRANSACTIONS-FILE
292         AT END MOVE "TRUE" TO EOF-TRANSACTIONS
293             MOVE 999999 TO TRANS-CUSTOMER-NUMBER.
294
295 21300-ISSUE-PAGE-BREAK.
296     ADD 1 TO PCC-PAGE.
297     MOVE PCC-PAGE TO ARUP-PAGE.
298     WRITE ARUP-LINE-REC FROM ARUP-REPORT-TITLE
299         AFTER ADVANCING PAGE.
300     WRITE ARUP-LINE-REC FROM ARUP-DISTRIBUTION.
301     WRITE ARUP-LINE-REC FROM ARUP-COLUMN-1
302         AFTER ADVANCING 2 LINES.
303     WRITE ARUP-LINE-REC FROM ARUP-COLUMN-2.
304     WRITE ARUP-LINE-REC FROM ARUP-UNDERLINE.
305     MOVE SPACES TO ARUP-LINE-REC.
306     WRITE ARUP-LINE-REC.
307     MOVE 7 TO PCC-LINE.
308
309 22000-PRODUCE-NEW-MASTER.
310     IF OLDAR-CUSTOMER-NUMBER = PI-IN-PROCESS-KEY
311         MOVE OLD-AR-ITEM-REC TO NEW-AR-ITEM-REC
312         PERFORM 21100-READ-OLD-MASTER
313         MOVE "TRUE" TO PI-ACTIVE-NEW-MASTER.
314     PERFORM 22200-APPLY-SINGLE-TRANS
315         UNTIL PI-IN-PROCESS-KEY LESS THAN TRANS-CUSTOMER-NUMBER.
316     IF PI-ACTIVE-NEW-MASTER = "TRUE"
317         PERFORM 22300-WRITE-UPDATED-MASTER
318         MOVE "FALSE" TO PI-ACTIVE-NEW-MASTER.
319     IF OLDAR-CUSTOMER-NUMBER > TRANS-CUSTOMER-NUMBER
320         MOVE TRANS-CUSTOMER-NUMBER TO PI-IN-PROCESS-KEY
```

Figure 9.25   (continued)

```
321      ELSE
322          MOVE OLDAR-CUSTOMER-NUMBER TO PI-IN-PROCESS-KEY.
323
324 22200-APPLY-SINGLE-TRANS.
325    MOVE "TRUE" TO PI-ERROR-FOUND.
326    IF ADD-TRANSACTION
327        PERFORM 22210-APPLY-ADD-TRANS.
328    IF DELETE-TRANSACTION
329        PERFORM 22220-APPLY-DELETE-TRANS.
330    IF REPLACE-TRANSACTION
331        PERFORM 22230-APPLY-REPLACE-TRANS.
332    IF CHANGE-TRANSACTION
333        PERFORM 22240-APPLY-CHANGE-TRANS.
334    PERFORM 22250-REPORT-TRANS-STATUS.
335    PERFORM 21200-RETURN-SORTED-TRANS.
336
337 22210-APPLY-ADD-TRANS.
338    IF PI-ACTIVE-NEW-MASTER = "FALSE"
339        MOVE "FALSE" TO PI-ERROR-FOUND
340        MOVE "TRUE" TO PI-ACTIVE-NEW-MASTER
341        MOVE TRANS-ACCOUNTS-RECEIVABLE-ITEM TO NEW-AR-ITEM-REC.
342    MOVE "ADD" TO ARUP-CODE.
343    MOVE NEWAR-CUSTOMER-NUMBER TO ARUP-CUSTOMER-NUMBER.
344    MOVE ZERO TO ARUP-OLD-BALANCE.
345    MOVE TRANS-AMOUNT TO ARUP-TRANS-AMOUNT.
346    MOVE NEWAR-BALANCE TO ARUP-NEW-BALANCE.
347
348 22220-APPLY-DELETE-TRANS.
349    IF PI-ACTIVE-NEW-MASTER = "TRUE"
350        AND NEWAR-BALANCE = 0.00
351            MOVE "FALSE" TO PI-ERROR-FOUND
352            MOVE "FALSE" TO PI-ACTIVE-NEW-MASTER.
353    MOVE "DEL" TO ARUP-CODE.
354    MOVE NEWAR-CUSTOMER-NUMBER TO ARUP-CUSTOMER-NUMBER.
355    MOVE NEWAR-BALANCE TO ARUP-OLD-BALANCE.
356    MOVE ZERO TO ARUP-TRANS-AMOUNT.
357    MOVE NEWAR-BALANCE TO ARUP-NEW-BALANCE.
358
359 22230-APPLY-REPLACE-TRANS.
360    MOVE NEWAR-BALANCE TO ARUP-OLD-BALANCE.
361    IF PI-ACTIVE-NEW-MASTER = "TRUE"
362        MOVE "FALSE" TO PI-ERROR-FOUND
```

Figure 9.25   (continued)

```
363            MOVE TRANS-ACCOUNTS-RECEIVABLE-ITEM TO NEW-AR-ITEM-REC.
364        MOVE "REP" TO ARUP-CODE.
365        MOVE NEWAR-BALANCE TO ARUP-NEW-BALANCE.
366        MOVE NEWAR-BALANCE TO ARUP-TRANS-AMOUNT.
367        MOVE NEWAR-CUSTOMER-NUMBER TO ARUP-CUSTOMER-NUMBER.
368
369 22240-APPLY-CHANGE-TRANS.
370        MOVE NEWAR-BALANCE TO ARUP-OLD-BALANCE.
371        IF PI-ACTIVE-NEW-MASTER = "TRUE"
372            MOVE "FALSE" TO PI-ERROR-FOUND
373            ADD TRANS-AMOUNT TO NEWAR-BALANCE.
374        MOVE "CNG" TO ARUP-CODE.
375        MOVE NEWAR-BALANCE TO ARUP-NEW-BALANCE.
376        MOVE TRANS-AMOUNT TO ARUP-TRANS-AMOUNT.
377        MOVE NEWAR-CUSTOMER-NUMBER TO ARUP-CUSTOMER-NUMBER.
378
379 22250-REPORT-TRANS-STATUS.
380        IF PCC-LINE > PCC-MAX-LINE
381            PERFORM 21300-ISSUE-PAGE-BREAK.
382        IF PI-ERROR-FOUND = "TRUE"
383            MOVE "*****" TO ARUP-ERROR
384            MOVE ZERO TO ARUP-NEW-BALANCE
385            MOVE ZERO TO ARUP-OLD-BALANCE
386            MOVE TRANS-CUSTOMER-NUMBER TO ARUP-CUSTOMER-NUMBER
387        ELSE
388            MOVE SPACE TO ARUP-ERROR.
389        PERFORM 22252-PRINT-TRANSACTION-DETAIL.
390        ADD 1 TO PCC-LINE.
391
392 22252-PRINT-TRANSACTION-DETAIL.
393        WRITE ARUP-LINE-REC FROM ARUP-DETAIL.
394
395 22300-WRITE-UPDATED-MASTER.
396        WRITE NEW-AR-ITEM-REC.
397
398 23000-EXIT-SORT-OUTPUT.
399        EXIT.
```

Paragraph 12100-TRANSFORM-PAYMENT-RECORDS formats a "change" transaction from a payment record. The fields from the payment input area are moved to the sort work area, and the payment is negative so that the balance due amount is decreased. The formatted record is then sent to the sort file in paragraph 12110-RELEASE-TRANSACTION-RECORD.

Paragraph 11100-READ-PAYMENT-RECORD brings in the next payment. Paragraphs 12200-TRANSFER-ORDER-RECORD and 12300-TRANSFER-UPDATE-RECORD perform similar tasks for the order file and the update file, respectively.

An error flag is used in paragraph 22250-REPORT-TRANSACTION-STATUS to determine if an error signal, "*****", should be printed in the report detail line as indicated in the specifications. As with the generic update logic that Charlene uses, the formatting of each report detail line is accomplished by the appropriate transaction application modules. This is necessary because each transaction applied results in a slightly different format requirement. The test data and results are in Figure 9.26.

Figure 9.26   *Test Data and Results for CDL's "A/R Update" Program*

```
The ORDER file:

35765487654303876098000004299
18765409876501765432000001699
19837528746810654849000016990


The PAYMENT file:

10000100001492ZR101111
20000200001757ZX120912


The UPDATE records file:

A3412121200 BOOMDALE DRIVE ST. LOUIS   MO63124314987876500001990
A25199934 N. 15TH AVE.     LUBBOCK     NJ01765378564398700012999
D123456
D234567
D134211
R2134231433 BLOMSBUS DR.   NEW YORK    NY06543876342456709870000
R178271876 S. 10TH STREET  RUSTON      LA71270213765432100000000
C623145                                              00000100
C413213                                              00120000


The beginning A/R file:

1000011300 BOOMSTON        GLUSTER     NJ37465213122344400100000
12345623 N. HEATER         FINCH       WY89765737373737300000000
1876541098 MESSTRON        HARPER      CO76543987654324500000000
1983756745 QUEBE           ASTOR       MN86746563546457300100000
20000212455656343434344 1ST BANGOR     HI87654987654321300001757
```

Figure 9.26   (continued)

```
213423JSDKJSKJDJDJDJD       ETON         EN0000000000000000000000000
2345671299 ST. JOHN BLVD    MORTON       IL62134214675653400010000
2519991899 HORRID PLACE     TO LIVE      ND23456987657639800000010
357654999 E. A AVE.         NEWEST TOWN  AL99099999999999900000000
600000987 ALL OVER          AGAIN        NJ10298928763636600000000
62314515 HOME STREET        HOMETOWN USADC09876709876543210000000
```

The ending A/R file:

```
1000011300 BOOMSTON          GLUSTER     NJ37465213122344400098508
1876541098 MESSTRON          HARPER      CO76543987654324500001699
1983756745 QUEBE             ASTOR       MN86746563546457300116990
200002124556563434344 1ST BANGOR         HI87654987654321300000000
2134231433 BLOMSBUS DR.      NEW YORK    NY06543876342456709870000
2345671299 ST. JOHN BLVD     MORTON      IL62134214675653400010000
2519991899 HORRID PLACE      TO LIVE     ND23456987657639800000010
3412121200 BOOMDALE DRIVE ST. LOUIS      MO63124314987876500001990
357654999 E. A AVE.          NEWEST TOWN AL99099999999999900004299
600000987 ALL OVER           AGAIN       NJ10298928763636600000000
62314515 HOME STREET         HOMETOWN USADC09876709876543210000100
```

The TRANSACTION report:

```
REPORT #34    ACCOUNTS RECEIVABLE UPDATE            PAGE    1
DISTRIBUTION  COLLECTIONS OF CDL                DATE 01/25/94
```

TRANSACTION		CUSTOMER	OLD	TRANSACTION	NEW
CODE	ERROR	ID	BALANCE	AMOUNT	BALANCE
───	──	───	───	───	───
CNG		100001	1000.00	14.92-	985.08
DEL		123456	0.00	0.00	0.00
DEL	*****	134211	0.00	0.00	0.00
REP	*****	178271	0.00	0.00	0.00
CNG		187654	0.00	16.99	16.99
CNG		198375	1000.00	169.90	1169.90
CNG		200002	17.57	17.57-	0.00
REP		213423	0.00	98700.00	98700.00
DEL	*****	234567	0.00	0.00	0.00

Figure 9.26   (continued)

ADD	* * * * *	251999	0.00	129.99	0.00
ADD		341212	0.00	19.90	19.90
CNG		357654	0.00	42.99	42.99
CNG	* * * * *	413213	0.00	1200.00	0.00
CNG		623145	100000.00	1.00	100001.00

Summary

Data files must be constantly changed to reflect the state of the business environment. This requires that programmers be able to write programs that update existing files through deletions, additions, and changes.

A file to be updated is referred to as a master file. A master file is usually a permanent file that is used by the organization to conduct major business functions. The file containing the changes to be applied is referred to as the transaction file. Transactions may involve additions to or deletions from the master file, or modifications of items contained in the master file records. A program using transactions to update a master file is generally called an update program or a file maintenance program. The update program reads the original master file and the transaction file, applies the indicated modification to the master file, and produces a new updated master file.

Data stored on external memory are organized into files. Files are collections of records, each of which represents a logical grouping of information. Files may be organized in several different ways depending on the physical arrangement of the records on the external storage medium. Records on sequential files are arranged in order of some key field.

Most external storage devices and peripherals such as the magnetic disk allow sequential file processing. On the other hand, certain devices require that files be organized sequentially. For example, printer files must be organized sequentially. A mass storage device requiring a sequential organization for storing files is the tape drive. Tape files have label records at the beginning and end of the file. They contain information about the file contained therein but do not form part of the file's data. Specification of the LABEL RECORDS ARE STANDARD clause in the file description instructs the computer to consider the label records during the file preparation.

To use storage space on tape more efficiently, the programmer can control the number of interrecord gaps by blocking logical records. Whenever the blocking factor of a sequential file is anything other than 1, the blocking factor must be specified in the BLOCK CONTAINS clause of the file description entry.

The order of records in files is critical in sequential file updates. The master file and the transaction files must be ordered in a specific sequence based on one or more key fields in the record before updating can take place. COBOL provides a facility for ordering files via the SORT verb. The SORT statement allows the specification of an INPUT PROCEDURE to specify the processing of records prior to sorting or a USING option to sort without preprocessing. The OUTPUT PROCEDURE and GIVING options allow similar features for postprocessing of the sorted file. The INPUT and OUTPUT PROCEDUREs require that a program be sectioned.

The SORT allows the programmer to use any combination of USING/GIVING/INPUT PROCEDURE/OUTPUT PROCEDURE to meet the data-processing requirements of the program. However, if the USING/GIVING combination is used, the file will have as many passes as when using a utility sort and could probably be accomplished much more simply by using the utility. Therefore, well-written COBOL programs have one or both of the INPUT and OUTPUT PROCEDURES.

Key Terms

file organization	master file	INPUT PROCEDURE
label records	transaction file	OUTPUT PROCEDURE
block	SORT	RETURN
blocking factor	USING	MERGE
buffer	GIVING	RELEASE
double buffering	SD	

Hints for Avoiding Errors

1. Many programmers forget that a sort work file must not be opened, written to, read from, or closed. When they do remember, they often forget that normal files must be opened and closed.
2. Be careful when sectioning a program. Sections must be self-contained units. Avoid the use of GO TO statements in sections except when absolutely necessary. Such an exception is the branch to an exit paragraph appearing at the end of the section.
3. The use of HIGH-VALUES is restricted to nonnumeric comparisons. If you use HIGH-VALUES to determine the end of the file, be certain the fields under comparison are group items or are defined as PIC X. If the key field is numeric and you decide to use all 9s to indicate the end of file, be certain that all 9s is not a valid number for the key field.

Exercises

9.1   Design and code the program specified in Figure 9.27.

Figure 9.27   *Exercise 9.1 Specifications*

PROGRAM SUMMARY
TITLE: *Update Bank Accounts*
PREPARED BY: *J. Doe*
DATE: *9-7-93*

FILES USED		
FILE NAME	MEDIA	ORGANIZATION
Bank file	*Disk*	*Sequential*
Transaction File	*Disk*	*Sequential*

DESCRIPTION

        A bank file contains records with customer account numbers and account balances. A transaction file has also been created. Each record contains a customer account number and an amount. Both the amount field and balance field are signed. Negative customer balances are allowed. A negative amount should be subtracted from the balance in the bank file; a positive amount should be added. A customer may have 0, 1 or more transactions.

        Update the bank file and list its contents. Show errors on an error report.

Figure 9.27   (continued)

RECORD LAYOUT SHEET

Record Name: *Transaction-records*		File Name: *Transaction file*		
Prepared By: *J. Doe*		Date: *3-8-93*		
Key Fields: *Account number*		Organization: *Sequential*		
Field	Description	Type*	Length	Decimal
Account number	*Unique customer identifier*	*N*	*5*	
Amount	*Transaction amount (signed)*	*N*	*8*	*2*

* A = alphanumeric
  N = numeric

RECORD LAYOUT SHEET

Record Name: *Bank-record*		File Name: *Bank-file*		
Prepared By: *J.Doe*		Date: *3-8-93*		
Key Fields: *Account number*		Organization: *Sequential*		
Field	Description	Type*	Length	Decimal
Account number	*Unique customer identifier*	*N*	*5*	
Account balance	*Customer current balance (signed)*	*N*	*8*	*2*

* A = alphanumeric
  N = numeric

9.2   Change the program in Exercise 9.1 so that it first sorts the transactions into the required order.

9.3   Change the program in Exercise 9.1 so that the Bank File is OUTPUT in amount order and produces a listing of your design of all transactions in descending amount order for any amount over $1000.

9.4 Change the design and code of Figures 9.16 and 9.17 to preprocess the transaction file by eliminating any transactions without a proper code (A, D, or R). Place these on a separate listing of your design.

9.5 The RETURN verb
   a. causes one record to be read from the sort work file.
   b. is a control structure similar to the GO TO.
   c. can appear only in an INPUT PROCEDURE.
   d. ends a PERFORM statement range.

9.6 Determine which of the following is false when merging two files:
   a. Both files must have a common key.
   b. Both files must be in ascending order by the same key.
   c. Both files must be in the same order by the same key.

9.7 If the blocking factor of a file is 100, then:
   a. The programmer must write the logic to read 100 records consecutively and process each block.
   b. The programmer must write the logic to read one record at a time, just as if the file has not been blocked.
   c. With every READ command 100 records are transferred from the file to the main memory.

9.8 Given the following description in the FILE SECTION:

```
SD SORT-WORK-FILE.
01    SORT-WORK-REC.
```

Which of the following may appear in an OUTPUT PROCEDURE?
   a. OPEN OUTPUT SORT-WORK-FILE . . .
   b. RELEASE SORT-WORK-REC . . .
   c. RETURN SORT-WORK-REC . . .
   d. RETURN SORT-WORK-FILE . . .

Use the following SORT statement to answer Exercises 9.9 and 9.10:

```
SORT A-FILE ON ASCENDING X Y INPUT PROCEDURE IS P1 GIVING
B-FILE.
```

9.9 Which of the following is *not* true?
   a. The primary sort key is X.
   b. A-FILE and B-FILE must not be OPEN at the execution of this verb.
   c. Identifier names X and Y are used in all three files.

9.10. Which of the following is *not* performed automatically?
   a. A-FILE and B-FILE are opened for sorting.
   b. The records are moved to SORT-FILE for sorting.
   c. The sorted records are placed in B-FILE.

9.11   With respect to the SORT command, which statement is correct?
      a.   USING can only be used with the GIVING option.
      b.   INPUT PROCEDURE must be used with OUTPUT PROCEDURE.
      c.   GIVING may be accompanied by INPUT PROCEDURE.
      d.   INPUT PROCEDURE may be used with the USING option.

9.12   If a file is to be sorted using the SORT verb and the record items in the file are to be manipulated before sorting, which of the following must be used?
      a.   INPUT PROCEDURE
      b.   RETURN verb
      c.   GIVING option
      d.   OUTPUT PROCEDURE

For Exercises 9.13 and 9.14 use the following DATA DIVISION entries:

```
SD    SORT-FILE.
01    SORT-REC.
            05 GRADE              PIC 99.
            05 YEAR               PIC 9(4).
            05 ENROLLMENT         PIC 999.
FD    INPUT-FILE
      LABEL RECORDS ARE OMITTED.
01    REC
            05 GRADE              PIC 99.
            05 YEAR               PIC 9(4).
            05 ENROLLMENT         PIC 999.
```

and the following PROCEDURE DIVISION code:

```
SORT  SORT-FILE
      ON  ASCENDING KEY YEAR OF SORT-REC
          DESCENDING KEY GRADE OF SORT-REC
                USING INPUT-FILE
                GIVING OUTPUT-FILE.
```

Assume that INPUT-FILE contains

```
061972117
071975160
061973088
081975210
```

where each line represents one record with the first zero of each record in column 1.

9.13   What will be the first record in the sorted file?
9.14   What will be the last record in the sorted file?

Use the following to answer 9.15 and 9.16:

```
SORT A ON ASCENDING KEY A-KEY
            USING B
            GIVING C.
```

9.15   Which of the following is not automatically performed?
         a.   The unsorted records are placed in B.
         b.   The files are opened for sorting.
         c.   The records are moved to A where they are sorted.
         d.   The sorted records are placed in C.
         e.   A, B, and C are closed after sorting.

9.16   A-KEY appears in the record description for
         a.   A
         b.   B
         c.   C

9.17   File _____ reflects the physical arrangement of records on an external storage medium.
         a.   composition
         b.   content
         c.   organization
         d.   reference

9.18   Certain devices require that files be organized sequentially. True or false?

9.19   Most COBOL systems use _____ buffering.
         a.   single
         b.   double
         c.   triple
         d.   no

9.20   To use the COBOL SORT, a sort work file must be specified using a SELECT statement. True or false?

9.21   A _____ file is usually a permanent file used by the organization to conduct major business functions.
         a.   master
         b.   parent
         c.   transaction
         d.   key

9.22   The file containing changes to be applied is known as a _____ file.
         a.   master
         b.   parent
         c.   transaction
         d.   key

9.23   Every business transaction indicates a required change to a master file. True or false?

9.24   File update programs have widely varied program structures. True or false?

9.25   The detailed logic of a file update program does not depend on the organization of the file. True or false?

9.26   COBOL allows the _____ verb to write records to a sort work file as part of an output procedure.
        a.   WRITE
        b.   RETURN
        c.   SEND
        d.   RELEASE

9.27   When using the SORT command, the programmer must remember to also OPEN and CLOSE the input, output, and sort work files as part of the procedure. True or false?

9.28   The _____ of records is critical in sequential file updates.
        a.   order
        b.   number
        c.   size
        d.   content

9.29   The _____ clause must be present in every FD entry of every file.

9.30   _____ is used to control the number of inter-record gaps on a tape.

9.31   The last paragraph in any section should be a paragraph containing the _____ statement.

9.32   Records are separated from each other with a space called the _____.

9.33   The number of records between IRGs is referred to as the _____.

9.34   The figurative constant _____ permits the programmer to continue the update process when one file has ended but the other has not.

9.35   COBOL requires the _____ verb to READ records from a sort work file as part of an output procedure.

9.36   The _____ statement is similar to the SORT statement and given the programmer the ability to aggregate two or more files into a single input file.

9.37   The program that uses the transaction to modify the master file is called a(n) _____ program or _____ program.

9.38   A(n) _____ iteration construct controls the application of transactions to the master record in the output area.

9.39   Is the sequence, or order, of the files used in a sequential update program important? Why?

9.40   What benefits does the COBOL SORT offer over conventional sorts?

9.41   Is error-handling important to the sequential update process? If so, why?

MANIPULATING DATA
IN TABLES

Tables are a type of data structure used to store, accumulate, extend, and validate data. Tables are used extensively in business applications. For example, in payroll applications the amount of income tax withheld may be computed by consulting a table of withholding rates based on income range and number of dependents. Data may be stored in tables to provide additional information about a specific item, thereby enhancing or extending the information related to that specific item. Tables may also contain lists of items used to verify the accuracy of data input to a system.

10.1   Defining Tables

10.1.1   The Nature of Tables

The term *table* describes a sequence of consecutive memory locations having a common name. It represents a set of logically consecutive data items with a common name. Tables are also referred to as vectors, arrays, or matrices. Each data item within the sequence is called a *table element* and is distinguished by its position within the table.

A table is structurally similar to a sequential file containing only one record type. The table is analogous to the file, and each table element is analogous to a record in the file. The difference is that since a table resides in memory, a table element can be directly accessed if its position within the table is known whereas in a sequential file each record prior to the desired record must be accessed until the desired record is located, even if its position is known in advance. For example, assume we have a consecutive data group containing student numbers and student names as follows:

```
1342   JOHN JACOBS
1785   FRED GLOVER
2143   HELEN HARDIN
2297   MARY JONES
2482   ELLEN MATRY
3415   BING WATERS
3722   JULIE HAVENS
4215   MARK THOMAS
5001   JEFF DAVIS
```

In a sequential file if we needed the number and name of the eighth student, we would have to perform eight READs. In a table stored in computer memory, however, the program can locate the eighth student without examining the prior seven.

10.1.2   Uses of Tables

The purpose of a table is to present data in a tabular fashion by organizing the data items into repeating occurrences of the same data structure. For example, a table of the months of the year contains 12 occurrences of a single data item, month. Tables are also used to present information in a clear format. Most reports are created using a tabular form. Figure 10.1 shows a table presenting a comparison of different salespersons over five years. The table organizes the data so that the user can view the performance characteristics of each sales representative in relation to the other sales representatives and in relation to his performance over the years.

Sales (in thousands of dollars)				
1991	1992	1993	1994	1995
Joe	52	74	51	55	58
Fred	19	25	40	45	60
Harry	20	100	20	90	10
Arlene	70	60	62	65	64
Meg	10	40	30	20	10
John	75	62	70	102	97
Mary	102	33	95	84	71

Tables perform many functions in information systems and are incorporated into many programs. Computations can be performed with the data stored in tables. Input data can be validated against entries stored in tables. Tables can be used to attach prices to items ordered by mail or phone and are used to maintain exam and assignment scores of students. They are also used to organize reports. In every case the table is merely the data structure used to organize or present the information. The programmer is responsible for setting up the tables, organizing the table elements, and extracting the information.

A table may be used to perform data validation. For example, a table may contain all the valid part numbers for a mail-order auto parts store. When an order is received it can be checked against the table to determine whether the part number exists, thereby validating the order.

Data may be extended using tables as well. For instance, in the auto parts example the table could be expanded to store the price information shown in Figure 10.2. Thus, when an order for a part is received, the part may be found in the table and its price extracted and attached to the order. In this case the table has been used to extend our knowledge about a specific data item. If part inventories were maintained, data items in the table could preserve the quantity of each part in stock, thus accumulating data.

Figure 10.3 contains the program description for a program to validate auto parts orders using tables. The hierarchy chart for the program is shown in Figure 10.4. Figure 10.5 contains the record layout sheets. Figure 10.6 has the Nassi-Schneiderman charts and Figure 10.7 is the resulting code. The code features will be discussed in depth after we examine design features. The hierarchy chart in Figure 10.4 illustrates how the modules will accomplish the validation of the auto parts orders. Several modules imply some table operation. Module "1100 Load Parts Table" prepares the table for processing of the customer orders. The auto part ordered by the customer is validated by module "2120 Locate Part Entry." If the part is found in the table, the order is valid. If not, the order is invalid and is reported by module "2130 Write Invalid Order." Module "2200 Check Order Quantity" checks whether the part is in stock. This is done by checking the quantity of parts in stock once the part is located in the table. If the order can be filled, the quantity in stock is decremented by module "2210 Decrement Stock Quantity" to keep the inventory count current. Finally, if the part is valid but not in stock, module "2230 Write Backlogged Order" attaches the order to a backlog list.

Figure 10.2   Parts Table

Part #	Price	Quantity in Stock
1243	31.95	100
1972	18.75	34
3185	19.95	22

Figure 10.3   *Specifications for "Order Validation" Program*

PROGRAM SUMMARY

TITLE: *Verify Order Accuracy*

PREPARED BY: *Joe Gibbs*

DATE: *7-4-93*

FILES USED		
FILE NAME	**MEDIA**	**ORGANIZATION**
Part Table	*Disk*	*Sequential*
Order	*Disk*	*Sequential*
Invalid Orders	*Disk*	*Sequential*
Backlogged Orders	*Disk*	*Sequential*
Valid Orders	*Disk*	*Sequential*

DESCRIPTION

Orders are entered into the system through an order entry system. Orders are validated to make certain all fields are present. Each part is then verified against the parts table to make certain the part exists. If any errors occur up to this point, the order is written to an error file.

Remaining orders are checked against the quantity-on-hand element in the parts table. If the supply is gone, the order is written to the backlog file to be used as input at a later date.

All valid, fillable orders should have the current price attached; decrement the quantity on hand; and be written to a valid orders file for future processing.

Display control totals on backlog and orders filled at the end of the program.

Figure 10.4   Hierarchy Chart for "Order Validation" Program

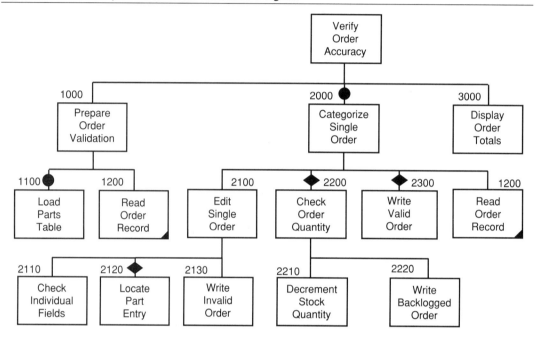

Figure 10.5   Record Layouts for "Order Validation" Program

RECORD LAYOUT SHEET

Record Name: *Part*		File Name: *Parts table*		
Prepared By: *Joe Gibbs*		Date: *7-4-93*		
Key Fields:		Organization: *Sequential*		
Field	Description	Type*	Length	Decimal
Part number	*Part number*	*N*	*4*	*0*
Price	*Retail price of the part*	*N*	*7*	*2*
QOH	*Quantity on hand*	*N*	*4*	*0*

* A = alphanumeric
  N = numeric

Figure 10.5   (continued)

RECORD LAYOUT SHEET

Record Name: *Order*		File Name: *Order/* (Valid, Invalid, Backlogged)		
Prepared By: *Joe Gibbs*		Date: *7-4-93*		
Key Fields:		Organization: *Sequential*		
Field	Description	Type*	Length	Decimal
Customer ID	*A unique customer number*	*N*	*6*	
Order number	*A purchase order number*	*N*	*6*	
Part number		*N*	*4*	*0*
Price	*Retail price of the part*	*N*	*7*	*2*
Quantity	*Quantity ordered*	*N*	*3*	*0*

* A = alphanumeric
  N = numeric

Figure 10.6   N-S Charts for "Order Validation" Program

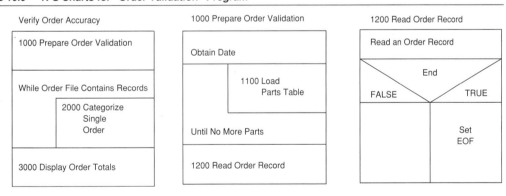

Figure 10.6   (continued)

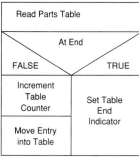

1100 Load Parts Table

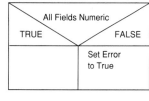

2110 Check Individual Fields

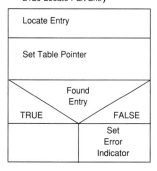

2120 Locate Part Entry

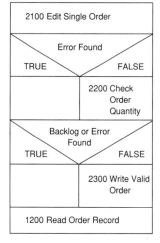

2000 Categorize Single Order

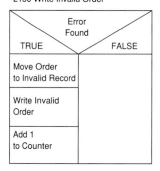

2130 Write Invalid Order

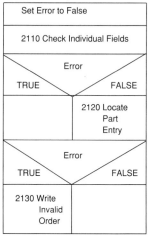

2100 Edit Single Order

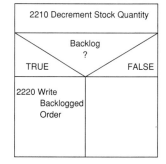

2200 Check Order Quantity

Figure 10.6   (continued)

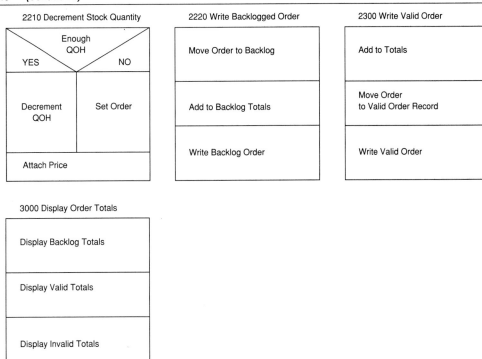

2210 Decrement Stock Quantity

Enough QOH

YES   NO

| Decrement QOH | Set Order |

Attach Price

2220 Write Backlogged Order

Move Order to Backlog

Add to Backlog Totals

Write Backlog Order

2300 Write Valid Order

Add to Totals

Move Order to Valid Order Record

Write Valid Order

3000 Display Order Totals

Display Backlog Totals

Display Valid Totals

Display Invalid Totals

Figure 10.7   Program Code for "Order Validation"

```
 1 IDENTIFICATION DIVISION.
 2 PROGRAM-ID.  VALIDATE-ORDERS.
 3*     THIS PROGRAM VALIDATES THE ORDERS FOR COMPLETENESS AND
 4*     TESTS THE PART NUMBERS AGAINST THE STOCK TABLE FOR
 5*     VALIDITY OF THE NUMBER AND IN HAVING ENOUGH ITEMS IN
 6*     STOCK.  AN ERROR FILE IS GENERATED FOR ALL INVALID
 7*     ORDERS.  VALID ORDERS HAVE THEIR PRICES ATTACHED AND ARE
 8*     WRITTEN TO A VALID ORDER FILE.  BACKLOGS ARE PUT ON A
 9*     SEPARATE FILE.
10
11 AUTHOR.          SELF
12 DATE-WRITTEN.     7-7-93.
13 DATE-COMPILED. 15-Jul-92 01:47.
15 ENVIRONMENT DIVISION.
16
```

Figure 10.7   (continued)

```
17 CONFIGURATION SECTION.
18
19 SOURCE-COMPUTER.  GENERIC-COMPUTER.
20 OBJECT-COMPUTER.  GENERIC-COMPUTER.
21
22 INPUT-OUTPUT SECTION.
23
24 FILE-CONTROL.
25     SELECT ORDERS-FILE ASSIGN TO DISK
26         ORGANIZATION IS SEQUENTIAL.
27     SELECT VALID-ORDERS-FILE ASSIGN TO DISK
28         ORGANIZATION IS SEQUENTIAL.
29     SELECT INVALID-ORDERS-FILE ASSIGN TO DISK
30         ORGANIZATION IS SEQUENTIAL.
31     SELECT BACKLOGGED-ORDERS-FILE ASSIGN TO DISK
32         ORGANIZATION IS SEQUENTIAL.
33     SELECT PARTS-TABLE-FILE ASSIGN TO DISK
34         ORGANIZATION IS SEQUENTIAL.
35
36 DATA DIVISION.
37
38 FILE SECTION.
39
40 FD  ORDERS-FILE
41     LABEL RECORDS ARE STANDARD.
42
43 01  ORDER-REC.
44     05  O-CUSTOMER-ID  PIC 9(6).
45     05  O-ORDER-NBR    PIC 9(6).
46     05  O-PART-NBR     PIC 9(4).
47     05  O-PART-PRICE   PIC 9(5)V99.
48     05  O-QUANTITY     PIC 9(3).
49
50 FD  VALID-ORDERS-FILE
51     LABEL RECORDS ARE STANDARD.
52
53 01  VALID-ORDER-RECORD  PIC X(26).
54
55 FD  INVALID-ORDERS-FILE
56     LABEL RECORDS ARE STANDARD.
57
58 01  INVALID-ORDER-REC PIC X(26).
```

Figure 10.7   *(continued)*

```
 59
 60 FD  BACKLOGGED-ORDERS-FILE
 61     LABEL RECORDS ARE STANDARD.
 62
 63 01  BACKLOGGED-ORDER-REC PIC X(26).
 64
 65 FD  PARTS-TABLE-FILE
 66     LABEL RECORDS ARE STANDARD.
 67
 68 01  PART-RECORD PIC X(15).
 69
 70
 71 WORKING-STORAGE SECTION.
 72
 73 01  NBR-OF-PARTS PIC 99 VALUE 0.
 74 01  PARTS-TABLE.
 75     05  PART OCCURS 1 TO 50 TIMES
 76         DEPENDING ON NBR-OF-PARTS
 77         ASCENDING KEY IS PTAB-PART-NBR
 78         INDEXED BY PART-INDEX.
 79             10  PTAB-PART-NBR    PIC 9(4).
 80             10  PTAB-PRICE       PIC 9(5)V99.
 81             10  PTAB-QOH         PIC 9999.
 82
 83 01  INDICATORS.
 84     05  EOF-ORDERS          PIC X(5) VALUE "FALSE".
 85     05  EOF-PART-TABLE      PIC X(5) VALUE "FALSE".
 86     05  ERR-CODE            PIC X(5) VALUE "FALSE".
 87
 88 01  CONTROL-TOTALS.
 89     05  CT-VALID-ORDER-COUNT      PIC 9(5) VALUE ZERO.
 90     05  CT-INVALID-ORDER-COUNT    PIC 9(5) VALUE ZERO.
 91     05  CT-BACKLOGGED-ORDER-COUNT PIC 9(5) VALUE ZERO.
 92     05  CT-EDIT                   PIC Z(4)9.
 93
 94
 95 PROCEDURE DIVISION.
 96
 97 VERIFY-ORDER-ACCURACY.
 98     OPEN INPUT ORDERS-FILE.
 99     OPEN INPUT PARTS-TABLE-FILE.
100     OPEN OUTPUT INVALID-ORDERS-FILE.
```

Figure 10.7   (continued)

```
101     OPEN OUTPUT VALID-ORDERS-FILE.
102     OPEN OUTPUT BACKLOGGED-ORDERS-FILE.
103     PERFORM 1000-PREPARE-ORDER-VALIDATION.
104     PERFORM 2000-CATEGORIZE-SINGLE-ORDER
105         UNTIL EOF-ORDERS = "TRUE".
106     PERFORM 3000-DISPLAY-ORDER-TOTALS.
107     CLOSE ORDERS-FILE.
108     CLOSE PARTS-TABLE-FILE.
109     CLOSE INVALID-ORDERS-FILE.
110     CLOSE VALID-ORDERS-FILE.
111     CLOSE BACKLOGGED-ORDERS-FILE.
112     STOP RUN.
113
114 1000-PREPARE-ORDER-VALIDATION.
115     PERFORM 1100-LOAD-PARTS-TABLE
116         VARYING NBR-OF-PARTS FROM 1 BY 1
117         UNTIL EOF-PART-TABLE = "TRUE".
118     SUBTRACT 1 FROM NBR-OF-PARTS.
119     PERFORM 1200-READ-ORDER-RECORD.
120
121 1100-LOAD-PARTS-TABLE.
122     READ PARTS-TABLE-FILE
123         AT END MOVE "TRUE" TO EOF-PART-TABLE.
124     IF EOF-PART-TABLE = "FALSE"
125         MOVE PART-RECORD TO PART (NBR-OF-PARTS).
126
127 1200-READ-ORDER-RECORD.
128     READ ORDERS-FILE
129         AT END MOVE "TRUE" TO EOF-ORDERS.
130
131 2000-CATEGORIZE-SINGLE-ORDER.
132     PERFORM 2100-EDIT-SINGLE-ORDER.
133     IF ERR-CODE = "FALSE" PERFORM 2200-CHECK-ORDER-QUANTITY.
134     IF ERR-CODE = "FALSE" PERFORM 2300-WRITE-VALID-ORDER.
135     PERFORM 1200-READ-ORDER-RECORD.
136
137 2100-EDIT-SINGLE-ORDER.
138     MOVE "FALSE" TO ERR-CODE.
139     PERFORM 2110-CHECK-INDIVIDUAL-FIELDS.
140     IF ERR-CODE = "FALSE" PERFORM 2120-LOCATE-PART-ENTRY.
141     IF ERR-CODE = "TRUE" PERFORM 2130-WRITE-INVALID-ORDER.
142
```

Figure 10.7   (continued)

```
143 2110-CHECK-INDIVIDUAL-FIELDS.
144     IF ORDER-REC NOT NUMERIC MOVE "TRUE" TO ERR-CODE
145     ELSE IF O-CUSTOMER-ID = ZERO MOVE "TRUE" TO ERR-CODE
146     ELSE IF O-ORDER-NBR = ZERO MOVE "TRUE" TO ERR-CODE
147     ELSE IF O-PART-NBR = ZERO MOVE "TRUE" TO ERR-CODE
148     ELSE IF O-QUANTITY = ZERO MOVE "TRUE" TO ERR-CODE.
149
150 2120-LOCATE-PART-ENTRY.
151     SET PART-INDEX TO 1.
152     SEARCH PART
153         AT END MOVE "TRUE" TO ERR-CODE
154         WHEN PTAB-PART-NBR (PART-INDEX) = O-PART-NBR
155             NEXT SENTENCE.
156
157 2130-WRITE-INVALID-ORDER.
158     ADD 1 TO CT-INVALID-ORDER-COUNT.
159     MOVE ORDER-REC TO INVALID-ORDER-REC.
160     WRITE INVALID-ORDER-REC.
161
162 2200-CHECK-ORDER-QUANTITY.
163     PERFORM 2210-DECREMENT-STOCK-QUANTITY.
164     IF ERR-CODE = "TRUE" PERFORM 2220-WRITE-BACKLOGGED-ORDER.
165
166 2210-DECREMENT-STOCK-QUANTITY.
167     IF O-QUANTITY <= PTAB-QOH (PART-INDEX)
168         SUBTRACT O-QUANTITY FROM PTAB-QOH (PART-INDEX)
169     ELSE
170         MOVE "TRUE" TO ERR-CODE.
171     MOVE PTAB-PRICE (PART-INDEX) TO O-PART-PRICE.
172
173 2220-WRITE-BACKLOGGED-ORDER.
174     ADD 1 TO CT-BACKLOGGED-ORDER-COUNT.
175     MOVE ORDER-REC TO BACKLOGGED-ORDER-REC.
176     WRITE BACKLOGGED-ORDER-REC.
177
178 2300-WRITE-VALID-ORDER.
179     ADD 1 TO CT-VALID-ORDER-COUNT.
180     MOVE ORDER-REC TO VALID-ORDER-RECORD.
181     WRITE-VALID-ORDER-REC.
182
183 3000-DISPLAY-ORDER-TOTALS.
184     MOVE CT-VALID-ORDER-COUNT TO CT-EDIT.
```

Figure 10.7   *(continued)*

```
185      DISPLAY "THE NUMBER OF VALID ORDERS IS " CT-EDIT.
186      MOVE CT-INVALID-ORDER-COUNT TO CT-EDIT.
187      DISPLAY "THE NUMBER OF INVALID ORDERS IS " CT-EDIT.
188      MOVE CT-BACKLOGGED-ORDER-COUNT TO CT-EDIT.
```

This program requires three table functions. First, the parts table must be initialized; that is, it must be brought into the computer's memory. Second, the table must be searched to find a specific entry. Third, the table must be manipulated to keep the quantity of parts in stock current. These table functions are very common and are similar from one program to another. In a hierarchy chart the modules representing the table function may appear at any level of a hierarchy chart and usually represent a complete module of code. We will conduct an in depth examination of the logic and code to accomplish these tasks in a later section of the chapter. First we will build a conceptual understanding of tables.

10.1.3   *Dimensionality of Tables*

Before a table can be used, its structure must be determined. The structure of a table in turn determines how it is defined in a COBOL program. Tables may vary in structure of *dimensionality* from a simple single-level table having multiple occurrences of one item type to tables within tables, or multilevel tables.

One-Dimensional Tables. A one-dimensional table is a list of items in the computer's internal memory. Following is a table containing a list of materials suppliers for a fictional company:

FRED'S STEEL INGOTS
AVERILL'S SIMULATORS
BUBBA'S CANNED AIR
HARRIET'S BUG KILLERS
GARY'S PAPER SUPPLIES

The list is simply a repetition of one data item type, suppliers. Each element in the list is identified by its position in the list. For example, BUBBA'S CANNED AIR is the third supplier for the company. The table presented is not arranged in any particular order. This is an *unordered table* in which sequence has no meaning. The table could be arranged so that it is in alphabetical order:

AVERILL'S SIMULATORS
BUBBA'S CANNED AIR
FRED'S STEEL INGOTS
GARY'S PAPER SUPPLIES
HARRIET'S BUG KILLERS

In this case, it is an *ordered table*. The position of BUBBA'S CANNED AIR is now second in the table.

The position of each element in the table becomes important when the programmer utilizes the data. In addition, the position of a single item within the table is used to represent the position of any related items. For example, if phone numbers and addresses were added to the table of suppliers, their position in the table would relate the elements to each other. In the following table:

SUPPLIER NAME	ADDRESS	PHONE NUMBER
AVERILL'S SIMULATORS	117 TAXCO HERSHEY NM	714-555-1212
BUBBA'S CANNED AIR	19 GRUB ST ALPHA MN	313-555-1212
FRED'S STEEL INGOTS	24 JOHN'S CIRCLE DOGG IA	422-555-1212
GARY'S PAPER SUPPLIES	3 INDUSTRIAL SQ LONGVIEW WA	991-555-1212
HARRIET'S BUG KILLERS	14141414 A ST GOSH MO	314-962-1212

BUBBA'S CANNED AIR is in the second position in the table. Its phone number is the second phone number in the table, and its address is the second address in the table. The integrity of the table is ensured by relating the items to each other by position within the table.

Addition of other fields to the table did not increase its dimension. It is still a one-dimensional table. We just increased the number of related elements within each element occurrence. In fact, we could view the table as a sequential file that is read into memory for convenience. The addition of the other elements to the table has effectively increased the number of elements that have single dimensionality. One way to determine the dimensionality of the table is to ask whether each item can be accessed by specifying a single position. In this case, since the address of any given supplier may be found by specifying its position in the table, and each phone number can be found by specifying a single position, and each supplier can be specified with a single position, it is a one-dimensional table. This positioning is shown in Figure 10.8.

Figure 10.8 **Position of Items in a One-Dimensional Table**

Supplier 1			Supplier 2			Supplier 3			Supplier 4			Supplier 5		
Name 1	Addr 2	Phone 3	Name 1	Addr 2	Phone 3	Name 1	Addr 2	Phone 3	Name 1	Addr 2	Phone 3	Name 1	Addr 2	Phone 3

Figure 10.9 **Memory Map of a One-Dimensional Table**

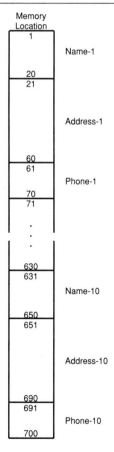

It is important to understand how memory is allocated to a table. Figure 10.9 shows the arrangement of the one-dimensional table in memory. Each occurrence of the table is allocated memory in the computer. Each data item that is part of each occurrence of the table appears in the order specified by the table definition. For example, in the supplier table the first element is the first occurrence of the supplier name, followed by the first occurrence of the supplier address, followed by the first occurrence of the supplier phone number. The second element is the second occurrence of the supplier name, supplier address, and supplier phone number. This order would be repeated 10 times to allow for all possible occurrences.

Two-Dimensional Tables. Two-dimensional tables result when multiple occurrences of a data item appear within one occurrence of a one-dimensional table entry. For example, a calendar for a single year is a two-dimensional table. Each month, of which there are 12 occurrences, has a repeated number of days. To specify a date within the year two positions are needed: the month and the day of the month. Thus, the month may be viewed as the first dimension and the day of the month as the second dimension. Figure 10.10 shows the annual calendar as a two-dimensional table.

Figure 10.10   *Two-Dimensional Calendar*

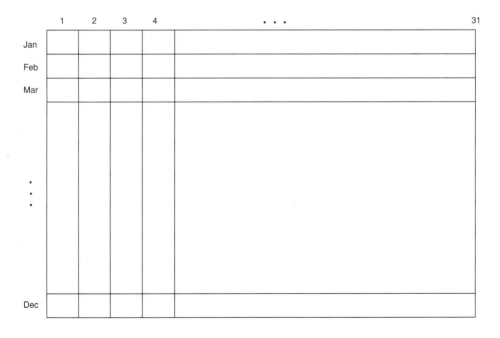

Figure 10.11   Two-Dimensional Parts Table

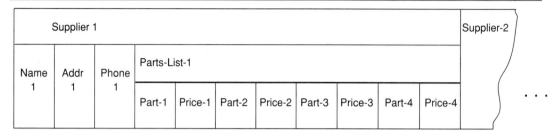

Two-dimensional tables may be more complex, as in Figure 10.11, which represents the supplier table. In this case, each element in the supplier table contains the name, address, telephone number, and product (part) provided by each supplier. Another table within each supplier element contains up to four elements describing the parts offered by that particular supplier. Each part is described by its name and price. Figure 10.12 shows this relationship in a data hierarchy chart. Since each supplier may supply more than one part, the list of the parts offered by each supplier is retained as a repeating data element within the repeating supplier list. In this case, to find the price for an item, both the supplier and the part must be identified. Thus, in Figure 10.13 to find the price of Ant Hotels from Harriet's Bug Killers, one must specify the proper supplier in the supplier list and the fourth part (product) in the parts list. Since two positions had to be specified, the table is a two-dimensional table. The repetition of elements adds to the dimensionality of a table, not the number of elements in each occurrence.

Figure 10.12   Data Hierarchy of the Two-Dimensional Parts Table

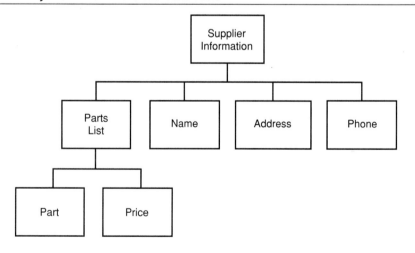

Figure 10.13 Two-Dimensional Parts Table with Multiple Data Items

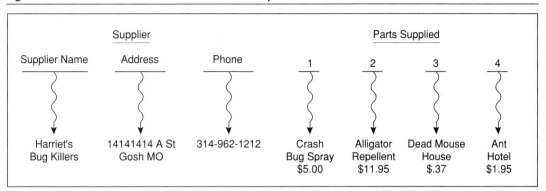

Memory allocation for tables of higher dimensions follows the same rules as for one-dimensional tables. Figure 10.14 shows how memory would be allocated to the two-dimensional table defined in Figure 10.13. Memory is allocated for the first occurrence of the supplier name, followed by the first occurrence of the supplier address, followed by the first occurrence of the supplier phone number, followed by the first occurrence of the entire parts list for the first supplier. Within the parts list each part will be completely specified before the next part receives any memory allocation. That is, each of the four part entries (name and price) for the first supplier will be allocated memory before memory is allocated for the second supplier. The allocation continues in sequential fashion for each supplier occurrence, until the last entry has been allocated memory.

Figure 10.14   Memory Map of Items in a Two-Dimensional Table

Memory Location	
1	Name-1
20	
21	Address-1
60	
61	Phone-1
70	
71	Part Name 1-1
90	
91	Price 1-1
98	
99	Part Name 1-2
118	
119	Price 1-2
126	
127	Part Name 1-3
146	
147	Price 1-3
154	
155	Part Name 1-4
174	
175	Price 1-4
182	
183	Name-2
202	
. . .	
	Price 10-4

Three-Dimensional Tables. Three-dimensional tables are an extension from the two-dimensional tables analogous to the extension that two-dimensional tables are from one-dimensional tables. That is, one of the elements in the second dimension has repeated occurrences. An example of a three-dimensional table is a complete calendar containing months, days, and years. Precise dates are identified by using the month, day, and year, as illustrated in Figure 10.15.

Figure 10.15   **Three-Dimensional Calendar**

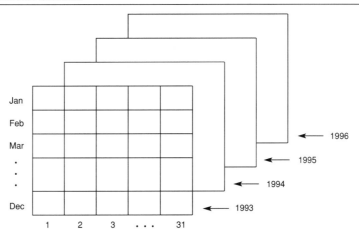

The third dimension in our supplier table may be the retention of data about the last three sales from each vendor. Assuming that purchase decisions are to be made based on the recent performance of the supplier with regard to delivery and quality, the table can be extended to include several instances of the supplier performance during the last three sales of the material supplied. This adds a third dimension to the supplier table, and now in order to pinpoint the delivery time of a product supplied by a certain supplier, we need to specify the supplier position, product position, and position of the most recent order. Figure 10.16 shows the addition of the third dimension to the supplier table. The data hierarchy is in Figure 10.17.

Figure 10.16 Three-Dimensional Parts Table

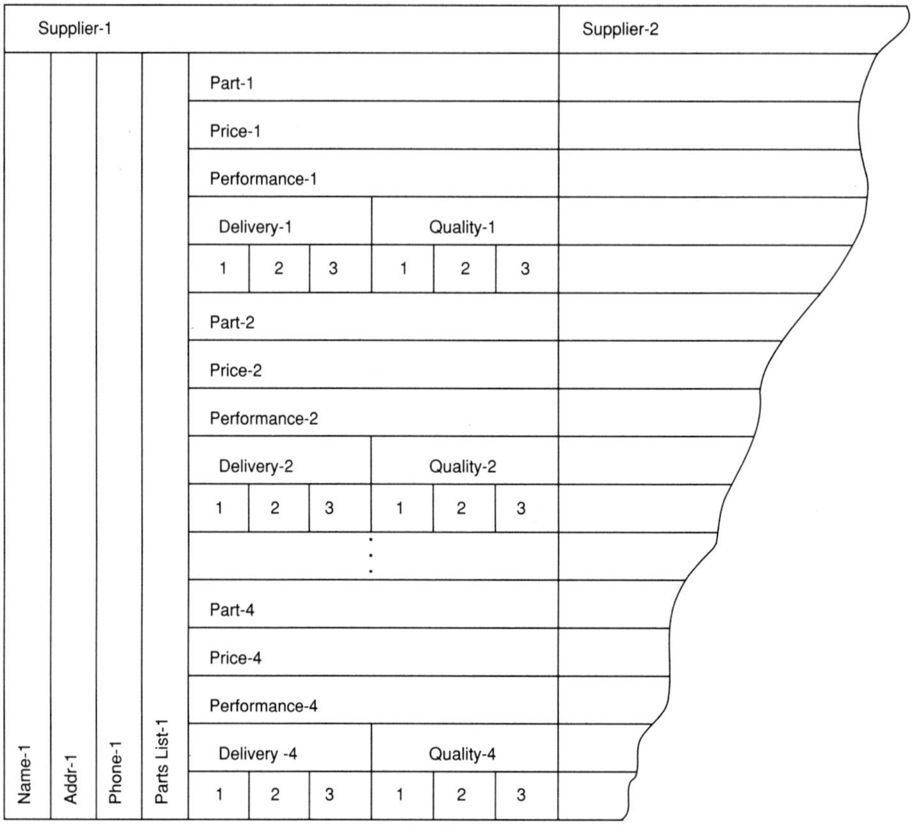

Figure 10.17   Data Hierarchy of the Three-Dimensional Parts Table

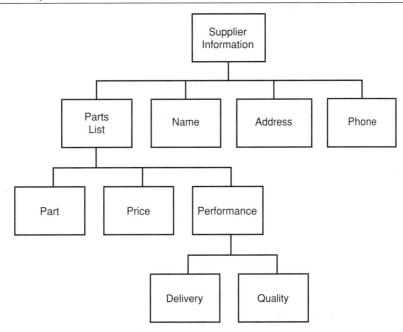

Theoretically, the dimensionality of tables may be extended forever. However, manipulating them becomes increasingly difficult. COBOL allows up to seven dimensions.

10.1.4   Defining Tables in COBOL

Tables are defined in the COBOL DATA DIVISION. When we defined a table earlier, we mentioned that it was a set of logically consecutive data items having a common name. In terms of the COBOL data hierarchy structure, the table corresponds to a group item and the table elements represent data items whose PICTURE description are identical. To define a table and specify the entry for the repeated data items we use the OCCURS clause. The *OCCURS* clause appears in the table's data description. It sets aside the memory area needed for the maximum number of elements to be stored. Since each element has an identical PICTURE clause, the OCCURS clause eliminates the need for making separate entries for each repeated data item in a table. The format and rules for the OCCURS clause are:

```
OCCURS integer-literal-1
    { TIMES                                                    }
    { TO integer-literal-2 TIMES DEPENDING ON data-name-1 }

    [ { ASCENDING  }                          ]
    [ { DESCENDING }  KEY IS data-name-2 ...  ] ...
    [ INDEXED BY  index-name-1 ...]
```

1. The subject of an entry containing an OCCURS clause and all subordinate data items, must be subscripted or indexed whenever referred to, except in a SEARCH statement.
2. KEY data-names are listed in order of decreasing significance.
3. KEY data items must be subordinate to the subject of the OCCURS.
4. No KEY item may contain an OCCURS clause.
5. The index-names must be unique.
6. The data-name-1 of the DEPENDING ON clause must not contain or be subordinate to an OCCURS clause.

Following is an entry for a sales quota table assigned to five sales representatives:

```
01   SALES-QUOTA-TABLE.

     05   SALES-QUOTA OCCURS 5 TIMES PIC 999.99.
```

The OCCURS clause can appear as part of any elementary or group items to define the number of occurrences of the item or group. For example, if we wanted to add another dimension to the above-described sales quota table, we might specify how the quota should be divided among three company products, In this case, the entry would become:

```
01   SALES-QUOTA-TABLE.
     05   SALES QUOTA OCCURS 5 TIMES.
          10    QUOTA-BY-PRODUCTS OCCURS 3 TIMES PIC 999.99.
```

The OCCURS clause may be used at the group level and have subordinate items or groups that in turn have OCCURS clauses. This is how multiple-dimensional tables are defined. The auto parts program of Figures 10.4 through 10.7 uses a single-dimensioned table. Its definition appears in lines 75 through 81 of Figure 10.7. It uses the more complex clauses that follow.

The number of occurrences of each item is specified by the integer literal following the word OCCURS when the DEPENDING ON clause is not used. The DEPENDING ON option allows the programmer to specify tables of variable length. In this case the programmer specifies the minimum number of occurrences with integer-literal-1 and the maximum number of occurrences with integer-literal-2. However, during execution of the program data-name-1 will contain the actual number of valid occurrences. Its value must be within the range of integer-literal-1 and integer-literal-2. For example,

```
05 NUM-PARTS                  PIC 99.
05 PARTS-TABLE OCCURS 1 TO 10 TIMES
      DEPENDING ON NUM-PARTS  PIC 9(5).
```

specifies that the size of the parts table may vary from 1 to 10 and its actual size will be found in the data item NUM-PARTS. The data item that establishes the size of the table must be initialized before the table can be used. The DEPENDING ON clause allows for more efficient table searching by allowing the programmer to utilize the actual size of a variable-size table. When a variable-size table is defined in memory, it is set up to hold the maximum contents, as defined by the literal value in the TO clause. But when the table is searched, the search is limited to the actual number of entries. If the programmer does not know the exact number of entries, he must determine the number of occurrences and initialize the DEPENDING ON data-name to that value as the table is created in memory. The code in Figure 10.7 uses the DEPENDING ON clause to specify the number of entries. The number of entries is later initialized in the PROCEDURE DIVISION.

The *KEY IS* phrase specifies the data items used to denote the sequence of the table elements. When multiple data items are listed as key fields, they are listed in order of decreasing significance for determining the order of the table elements. For example, if entries are ordered by REGION and by CITY within each REGION, the phrase is: KEY IS REGION CITY. The KEY IS phrase identifies the sequence of the data items within the table. It does not place the occurrences in order. COBOL assumes that the table is in the order specified (either ASCENDING or DESCENDING). KEY IS merely serves to document the table and to aid in searching the table for specific items when using COBOL search features. The auto parts example in Figure 10.7 uses the PART-NBR as the ASCENDING KEY (line 77).

The *INDEXED BY* phrase permits the programmer to specify an identifier for pointing to a specific occurrence within the table. The *index* points to the location of a table element in relation to the beginning of the table. The index-name selected may not appear elsewhere in the DATA DIVISION since it is a unique identifier for the table it is associated with and is bound to that table. An index does not have the same flexibilities as numeric data items do. It is not a data item and is not part of any data hierarchy, but it does provide a unique way to access items in the table. The auto parts table in Figure 10.7 is indexed in line 78 by a PART-INDEX established by the programmer.

We now turn our attention to defining the supplier table. The DATA DIVISION entries necessary for the one-dimensional supplier table are:

```
01   NBR-OF-SUPPLIERS  PIC 99 VALUE 10.
01   SUPPLIER-TABLE.
     05  SUPPLIER OCCURS 1 TO 10 TIMES
         DEPENDING ON NBR-OF-SUPPLIERS
         ASCENDING KEY IS SUP-NAME
         INDEXED BY SUPPLIER-INDEX.
         10   SUP-NAME  PIC X(20).
         10   SUP-ADDR  PIC X(40).
         10   SUP-PHONE PIC X(10).
```

In this table the suppliers are assumed to be in name sequence. The number of elements in the table varies and the actual count is stored in the elementary item named NBR-OF-SUPPLIERS. Finally, the index SUPPLIER-INDEX permits the programmer to refer to the specific items composing the table. Again, refer to lines 75 through 81 in Figure 10.7 to see the complete auto parts table definition.

The COBOL entries for the two-dimensional supplier table are:

```
01    SUPPLIER-TABLE.
      05    SUPPLIER OCCURS 10 TIMES
            ASCENDING KEY IS SUP-NAME
            INDEXED BY SUPPLIER-INDEX.
            10    SUP-NAME        PIC X(20).
            10    SUP-ADDR        PIC X(40).
            10    SUP-PHONE       PIC 9(10).
            10    PARTS-LIST OCCURS 4 TIMES
                  INDEXED BY PART-INDEX.
                  15    PART-NAME   PIC X(20).
                  15    PART-PRICE  PIC 9(6)V99.
```

In this case the number of items is shown to be fixed as indicated by the omission of the DEPENDING ON phrase. The COBOL entries for the three-dimensional supplier table are:

```
01    SUPPLIER-TABLE.
      05    SUPPLIER OCCURS 10 TIMES
            ASCENDING KEY IS SUP-NAME
            INDEXED BY SUPPLIER-INDEX.
            10    SUP-NAME        PIC X(20).
            10    SUP-ADDR        PIC X(40).
            10    SUP-PHONE       PIC 9(10).
            10    PARTS-LIST OCCURS 4 TIMES
                  INDEXED BY PART-INDEX.
                  15 PART-NAME       PIC X(20).
                  15 PART-PRICE      PIC 9(6)V99.
                  15 PART-DELIVERY  PIC 9
                     OCCURS 3 TIMES
                     INDEXED BY DELIVERY-INDEX.
                  15 PART-QUALITY    PIC X
                     OCCURS 3 TIMES
                     INDEXED BY QUALITY-INDEX.
```

In all three cases the sequence is known, and an index-name is provided. The index will not always be used within the program. Only certain COBOL statements require the specification of an index, whereas others allow its optional use.

10.2   Processing Tables

Tables must be manipulated to be useful. These manipulations will include arithmetic processing, initializations, and searches.

10.2.1   *Accessing Table Entries*

The programmer will need to refer to specific occurrences in the table to accomplish the tasks required by the program. A table element is designated by its occurrence number. This occurrence number is the same as the element's position in the table. For example, the first element has an occurrence number of 1.

Specifying an occurrence within the table is very simple in COBOL. The programmer need only specify the table name followed by the occurrence number in parentheses. This occurrence number can be denoted by an index defined in the INDEXED BY clause or by a *subscript* defined in the WORKING-STORAGE SECTION. The format and rules for accessing a single occurrence of a data item or data group within a table are:

$$
\text{data-name}\ \left[\ \left\{\ \begin{array}{l}\text{subscript-1 [,subscript-2...]} \\ \text{index-1 [\{\underline{+}\} literal-3] [index-2 \{\underline{+}\} literal-4]. . .]}\end{array}\ \right\}\ \right]
$$

1. Each subscript may be a positive integer literal or positive integer elementary item.
2. Subscripts and indexes may not be mixed.
3. Subscripts and indexes are used in order of less inclusive dimensions.
4. Index-n is specified in the INDEXED BY phrase of the OCCURS clause associated with the table.

For example, SUP-NAME (2) refers to the second occurrence of SUP-NAME, BUBBA'S CANNED AIR, in the one-dimensional supplier table. Two-dimensional tables require two subscripts or indexes to specify the occurrence in the table. For example, PART-NAME (2,4) refers to the fourth part supplied by the second supplier.

An index is the index-name associated with the table in the OCCURS clause. A subscript is a literal or an integer data item defined in the DATA DIVISION. The use of indexes and subscripts is almost interchangeable even though their use may not be mixed. Any time a data item in a table is referred to in the PROCEDURE DIVISION, the reference may be made using either a subscript or an index to specify the occurrence. However, certain statements in COBOL cannot be used with indexes, and others cannot be used with subscripts. These distinctions will become apparent when we discuss the PROCEDURE DIVISION entries used for manipulating tables.

10.2.2   *Initializing Tables*

If tables are to be used, they must first be initialized. We will present two procedures to initialize table values. One method is to read the table values from an external source into the table. The second method is to define table entries using literals in FILLER clauses.

Initializing a Table from an External File. Data may be read directly into a table if records in a sequential file are in the same format as the desired table. More often, however, a file is read into memory and the appropriate fields are moved into the table. Figure 10.18 contains a generic design of this process. In structured English the logic is:

Initialize table index;
READ first record;
REPEAT UNTIL file at end
    MOVE record to table entry indicated by index;
    READ next record;
    increment table index;
END-REPEAT.

Figure 10.18   Logic to Load a Table from an External File

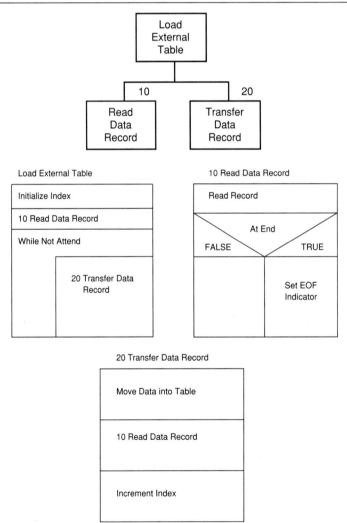

The COBOL entries necessary to describe the sample parts file and the sample parts table in the DATA DIVISION are:

```
FD   SUPPLIER-FILE
     LABEL RECORDS ARE STANDARD.
01   SUPPLIER-RECORD.
     05  SR-NAME     PIC X(20).
     05  SR-ADDRESS  PIC X(40).
     05  SR-PHONE    PIC X(10).
WORKING-STORAGE SECTION.
01   EOF-SUPPLIER-FILE  PIC X(5) VALUE "FALSE".
01   NBR-OF-SUPPLIERS  PIC  99.
01   SUPPLIER-TABLE.
     05  SUPPLIER OCCURS 1 TO 10 TIMES
       DEPENDING ON NBR-OF-SUPPLIERS
       ASCENDING KEY IS SUP-NAME
       INDEXED BY SUPPLIER-INDEX.
       10  SUP-NAME  PIC X(20).
       10  SUP-ADDR  PIC X(40).
       10  SUP-PHONE PIC 9(10).
```

The PROCEDURE DIVISION code used to initialize the SUPPLIER-TABLE from the SUPPLIER-FILE is based on Figure 10.16. The code is:

```
PROCEDURE DIVISION.

LOAD-SUPPLIER-TABLE.
       OPEN INPUT SUPPLIER-FILE.
       PERFORM 10-READ-SUPPLIER-RECORD.
       PERFORM 20-TRANSFER-SUPPLIER-ENTRY
          VARYING NBR-OF-SUPPLIERS FROM 1 BY 1
          UNTIL EOF-SUPPLIER-FILE = "TRUE".
       SUBTRACT 1 FROM NBR-OF-SUPPLIERS.
       CLOSE SUPPLIER-FILE.
       STOP RUN.

10-READ-SUPPLIER-RECORD.
    READ SUPPLIER-FILE
       AT END MOVE "TRUE" TO EOF-SUPPLIER FILE.

20-TRANSFER-SUPPLIER-ENTRY.
    MOVE SUPPLIER-RECORD TO SUPPLIER (NBR-OF-SUPPLIERS).
    PERFORM 10-READ-SUPPLIER-RECORD.
```

In the paragraph LOAD-SUPPLIER-TABLE, the PERFORM VARYING UNTIL state-ment loads the table from the file as long as there are records in the file. In this example the data-name used to indicate the number of records, NBR-OF-SUPPLIERS, is the data item being varied. Once the table is loaded, this data item will contain a value one more than the actual number of occurrences in the table, since the PERFORM VARYING statement increments the data item varied prior to testing the condition specified in the UNTIL clause. The module 1100-Load-Parts-Table in Figure 10.6 is a slight variation of the single dimensional table load.

To load a two-dimensional table two data items must be varied, one for each dimension. One way to think of these items is as a row data item and a column data item. The PERFORM VARYING statement with the AFTER clause allows the programmer to specify two or more data items or indexes to be varied.

When the AFTER clause is used to vary two or more items, condition-1 is the only criterion for leaving the control of the PERFORM. The other conditions serve to specify when the next level of varying is conducted, that is, when the next dimension is specified. For example, assume that we are filling a two-dimensional table consisting of three rows and four columns. The statement,

```
PERFORM FILL-IN-TABLE
        VARYING ROW FROM 1 BY 1
            UNTIL ROW > 3
        AFTER VARYING COL FROM 1 BY 1
            UNTIL COL > 4.
```

fills the table one row at a time. It does so by varying the data item COL from 1 to 4 prior to incrementing the data item ROW by one. When condition-2 (COL > 4) is met, the data item in the AFTER phrase (COL) is reset to 1 before the data item (ROW) in the previous VARYING phrase is varied. However, control will leave the PERFORM statement only when condition-1 (ROW > 3) is met. In other words, the data item specified by the AFTER phrase is completely varied UNTIL that condition is met before the data-item in the first VARYING is changed. The logic of a PERFORM VARYING with one AFTER clause is shown in the flowchart in Figure 10.19.

Figure 10.19   Logical Flow of a PERFORM VARYING . . . AFTER

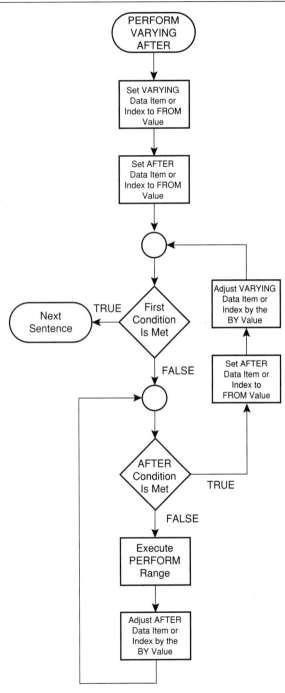

The data item varied first varies the most slowly, whereas the data item varied last varies the most rapidly. In the above example, the data item COL varied from 1 to 4 for each variation in the data item ROW.

If another dimension is added to the table, the order in which the three-dimensional table is filled depends on the order in which the data items are varied. Figure 10.20 shows a PERFORM VARYING statement containing two AFTER phrases and the values of the varied data items for each execution of the performed paragraph. Notice that the values of the varied data items of the AFTER phrases are reset when the condition (SCT-1 > 3) is met.

Figure 10.20 *Parameter Values of a PERFORM VARYING . . . AFTER . . . AFTER*

PERFORM 1010-SURVEY-CUSTOMER-TABLE

    VARYING SCT-1 FROM 1 BY 1

        UNTIL SCT-1 > 3

    AFTER VARYING SCT-2 FROM 1 BY 1

        UNTIL CST-2 > 2

    AFTER VARYING SCT-3 FROM 11 BY 2

        UNTIL SCT-3 = 15

| TIME | | VALUE OF | |
THROUGH	SCT-1	SCT-2	SCT-3
1	1	1	11
2	1	1	13
3	1	2	11
4	1	2	13
5	2	1	11
6	2	1	13
7	2	2	11
8	2	2	13
9	3	1	11
10	3	1	13
11	3	2	11
12	3	2	13
AT THE END	4	1	11

The index-name associated with the table can be used instead of a data-name in the VARYING clause of the PERFORM statement. This case is illustrated in the following example, in which a two-dimensional table is filled from an external file. Notice the same design of Figure 10.18 is used:

```
FD      SUPPLIER-FILE
        LABEL RECORDS ARE STANDARD.
01      SUPPLIER-RECORD.
        05    SR-NAME            PIC X(20).
        05    SR-ADDRESS         PIC X(40).
        05    SR-PHONE           PIC 9(10).
        05    SR-PART-NAME       PIC X(20).
        05    SR-PART-PRICE      PIC 9(6)V99.
WORKING-STORAGE SECTION.
01      EOF-SUPPLIER-FILE        PIC X(5) VALUE "FALSE".
01      SUPPLIER-TABLE.
        05    SUPPLIER OCCURS 10 TIMES
              ASCENDING KEY IS SUP-NAME
              INDEXED BY SUPPLIER-INDEX.
              10    SUP-NAME         PIC X(20).
              10    SUP-ADDR         PIC X(40).
              10    SUP-PHONE        PIC 9(10).
              10    PARTS-LIST OCCURS 4 TIMES
                    INDEXED BY PART-INDEX.
                    15    PART-NAME         PIC X(20).
                    15    PART-PRICE  PIC 9(6)V99.
01      SAVE-SUP-NAME      PIC X(20) VALUE SPACES.

PROCEDURE DIVISION.

LOAD-SUPPLIER-TABLE.
        OPEN INPUT SUPPLIER-FILE.
        PERFORM    10-READ-SUPPLIER-RECORD.
        PERFORM    20-TRANSFER-SUPPLIER-ENTRY
            VARYING SUPPLIER-INDEX FROM 1 BY 1
                  UNTIL EOF-SUPPLIER-FILE = "TRUE"
            AFTER VARYING PART-INDEX FROM 1 BY 1
                  UNTIL PART-INDEX > 4.
        CLOSE SUPPLIER-FILE.
        STOP RUN.

10-READ-SUPPLIER-RECORD.
        READ  SUPPLIER-FILE
              AT END MOVE "TRUE" TO EOF-SUPPLIER-FILE.
20-TRANSFER-SUPPLIER-ENTRY.
```

```
IF   SUP-NAME NOT = SAVE-SUP-NAME
     MOVE SR-NAME TO SAVE-SUP-NAME
     MOVE SR-NAME TO SUP-NAME (SUPPLIER-INDEX)
     MOVE SR-ADDRESS TO SUP-ADDR (SUPPLIER-INDEX)
     MOVE SR-PHONE TO SUP-PHONE (SUPPLIER-INDEX).
MOVE  SR-PART-NAME TO
     PART-NAME (SUPPLIER-INDEX, PART-INDEX).
MOVE  SR-PART-PRICE TO
     PART-PRICE (SUPPLIER-INDEX, PART-INDEX).
PERFORM  10-READ-SUPPLIER-RECORD.
```

The index can appear as part of the condition as in paragraph LOAD-SUPPLIER-TABLE. However, different rules apply when doing comparisons using indexes in conditions.

The rules for using indexes in conditions are:

1. The comparison of two indexes is treated as a comparison of the corresponding occurrence numbers.
2. The comparison of an index and a literal or an elementary integer item is treated as a comparison of the occurrence number and the value of the literal or elementary item.

Initializing Tables Within the Program. Table entries cannot be initialized at the time of their definition since a VALUE clause may not be specified in conjunction with an OCCURS clause. Furthermore, initializing the table in the PROCEDURE DIVISION with MOVE statements for each element in the table may require excessive code, especially if the table is large. Therefore, tables are usually initialized within the program through the use of the REDEFINES clause in the WORKING-STORAGE SECTION.

The *REDEFINES* clause is used to describe the same storage area by different data description entries. This is analogous to describing Mary Smith as Mary or as Ms. Smith. The format and rules for the REDEFINES clause are:

---

level-number data-name-1 <u>REDEFINES</u> data-name-2

1. Data-name-1 must describe an item of the same length as data-name-2.
2. The level-numbers for data-name-1 must be the same as those of data-name-2.
3. The level-number may not be 01 if used in the FILE SECTION.
4. Either data-name may be used to refer to the memory location.
5. No data description entry with a level-number equal to or less than that of data-name-1 may appear between data-name-2 and data-name-1.
6. No data item with a REDEFINES clause or subordinate to a REDEFINES clause may have a VALUE clause entry, except for 88 levels.
7. Data-name-2 may not have an OCCURS or REDEFINES clause.
8. Multiple REDEFINES are allowed, but they must all refer to the original data-name-2.

The REDEFINES clause allows the programmer not only to specify more than one data description for the same area in memory but also to initialize the storage area to the desired values. This implies that a memory area can be defined as a literal containing a set of values and redefined as a table. For example, the following entries:

```
WORKING-STORAGE SECTION.

01    ALPHABET    PIC   X(26) VALUE
      "ABCDEFGHIJKLMNOPQRSTUVWXYZ".


01    LETTER-TABLE REDEFINES ALPHABET.
      05   A-LETTER    PIC    X
           OCCURS 26 TIMES.
```

establish an area called ALPHABET whose description entry is PIC (26) and VALUE is "ABCDEFGHIJKLMNOPQRSTUVWXYZ." This occupies 26 successive locations in memory. LETTER-TABLE redefines this storage area as a one-dimensional table of 26 elements, each one character long. This permits accessing any letter by stating its position in the alphabet, in other words, its occurrence in the table. Since each entry in the table is one memory position long, the fifth letter can be obtained using the subscripted data-name A-LETTER (5). This acquires the value "E" since "E" is the fifth letter defined in the VALUE clause of the ALPHABET entry and occupies the fifth memory location. This is demonstrated as follows:

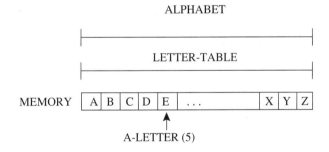

Now, using the memory map of the one-dimensional supplier table shown in Figure 10.9, let us initialize the table in the WORKING-STORAGE SECTION using FILLER data items in conjunction with VALUE clauses. Do not forget that every item in a table must have exactly the same number of positions. The storage area for the table is defined as follows:

```
WORKING-STORAGE SECTION
01    NBR-OF-SUPPLIERS    PIC    99      VALUE 5.
01    SUPPLIER-LIST.
      05   SUPPLIER-1.
           10    FILLER       PIC X(20)
                 VALUE "AVERILL'S SIMULATORS".
           10    FILLER       PIC X(40)
```

```
                            VALUE "117 TAXCO HERSHEY NM".
            10      FILLER          PIC 9(10)       VALUE  7145551212.


      05    SUPPLIER-2.
            10      FILLER          PIC X(20)
                            VALUE "BUBBA'S CANNED AIR".
            10      FILLER          PIC X(40)
                            VALUE "19 GRUB ST      ALPHA MN".
            10      FILLER          PIC 9(10)       VALUE 3135551212.


      05    SUPPLIER-3.
            10      FILLER          PIC X(20)       VALUE
                            "FRED'S STEEL INGOTS".
            10      FILLER          PIC X(40)       VALUE
                            "24 JOHN'S CIRCLE DOGG IA".
            10      FILLER          PIC 9(10)       VALUE 4225551212.


      05    SUPPLIER-4.
            10      FILLER          PIC X(20)       VALUE
                            "GARY'S PAPER SUPPLIES".
            10      FILLER          PIC X(40)       VALUE
                            "3 INDUSTRIAL SQ    LONGVIEW WA".
            10      FILLER          PIC 9(10)       VALUE 9915551212.


      05    SUPPLIER-5.
            10      FILLER          PIC X(20)       VALUE
                            "HARRIET'S BUG KILLERS".
            10      FILLER          PIC X(40)       VALUE
                            "14141414 A ST GOSH MO".
            10      FILLER          PIC 9(10)       VALUE 3149621212.


      05    FILLER                  PIC X(350) VALUE SPACES.
```

The following data description entry redefines the storage area as a table:

```
01    SUPPLIER-TABLE REDEFINES SUPPLIER-LIST.
      05    SUPPLIER OCCURS 1 TO 10 TIMES
            DEPENDING ON NBR-OF-SUPPLIERS
            ASCENDING KEY IS SUP-NAME
            INDEXED BY SUPPLIER-INDEX.
            10      SUP-NAME            PIC X(20).
            10      SUP-ADDR            PIC X(40).
            10      SUP-PHONE           PIC 9(10).
```

In general, tables that are small and static are described in the program using the REDEFINES clause. Tables that are dynamic or very large are usually kept on disk files because tables on files are easier to change than are programs. Furthermore, they can be used by more than one program without the need to code the actual table values into each program. Many information systems include table management programs that change tables stored on external media. Computer manufacturers and software houses often provide utilities to maintain tables stored as files.

10.2.3   *Searching Tables*

Tables would be of no use if specific entries in the table could not be located. For example, a part must be found in a parts table if its price is to be found. An instructor must find the student's entry in a grade table to record his exam grade. The process of finding a specific entry in a table is known as *searching*. COBOL provides three statements for searching tables. They are the PERFORM VARYING UNTIL statement, the SEARCH statement, and the SEARCH ALL statement.

Unordered Tables. Tables that are not sequenced in any specific order are called *unordered tables*. They must be completely searched to verify that an entry is not in the table. Figure 10.21 details the generic steps needed to locate an entry in an unordered table. The first step sets an indicator to flag when the search has ended. A pointer used to indicate the position of a table entry under investigation is initialized to a starting value. An iteration structure performs the search until the search is ended. The search may end because we have reached the end of the table or because the item has been found. If the search does not end during the current iteration, the pointer is incremented so that it points to the next entry in the table. In structured English, the logic for the process is:

```
Set end of search indicator to FALSE;
Set table index to first table position;
REPEAT UNTIL end of search
   IF index is past last table entry THEN
     set end of search indicator to TRUE;
     PERFORM missing item routine;
   ELSE
     IF item is found THEN
        set end of search indicator to TRUE;
        PERFORM found item routine;
     ELSE
        increment table index;
     END-IF;
   END-IF;
END-REPEAT.
```

Figure 10.21   Searching an Unordered Table

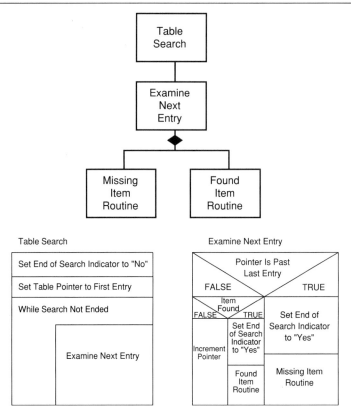

When the search ends, the entry may or may not have been located. If it was, a routine for a located entry will have been performed. If it was not, the pointer will point past the range of the number of table occurrences, and a routine to handle missing items will have been performed. It is advisable to allow for the possibility of missing entries. The COBOL code needed to implement a table search for the unordered one-dimensional supplier table using the PERFORM VARYING IS:

```
1000-LOCATE-SUPPLIER-ENTRY.
      MOVE "NO" TO SUPPLIER-SEARCH-OVER.
      PERFORM  1100-SEARCH-SUPPLIER-TABLE
         VARYING  SUPPLIER-POSITION FROM 1 BY 1
            UNTIL SUPPLIER-SEARCH-OVER = "YES".
1100-SEARCH-SUPPLIER-TABLE.
      IF SUPPLIER-POSITION > NBR-OF-SUPPLIERS
         MOVE "YES" TO SUPPLIER-SEARCH-OVER
         PERFORM 1200-REPORT-MISSING-ENTRY
      ELSE
```

```
        IF SUPPLIER-SEARCH-NAME =
           SUP-NAME (SUPPLIER-POSITION)
           MOVE "YES" TO SUPPLIER-SEARCH-OVER
           PERFORM 1300-REPORT-FOUND-ENTRY.
```

Note that the VARYING clause increments the pointer automatically, avoiding code for this design step in Figure 10.21.

Ordered Tables. When tables are arranged in order of a key field, the search logic can be modified to allow for an early termination. Figure 10.22 illustrates how a missing entry is identified in an ordered table. When the key field of a table entry is higher than the value being searched for, the item is determined to be missing from the table. The search logic to incorporate this change is shown in the N-S chart of Figure 10.23 and the following structured English:

```
Set end of search indicator to FALSE;
Set table index to first table position;
REPEAT UNTIL end of search
    IF index is past last table entry
      OR a higher key is found THEN
      set end of search indicator to TRUE;
      PERFORM missing item routine;
    ELSE
    IF item is found THEN
        set end of search indicator to TRUE;
        PERFORM found item routine;
    ELSE
        increment table index;
    END-IF;
  END-IF;
END-REPEAT.
```

Figure 10.22   Missing Entry in an Ordered Table

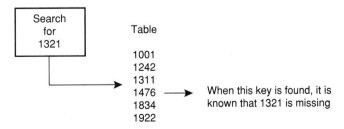

Figure 10.23   Searching an Ordered One-Dimensional Table

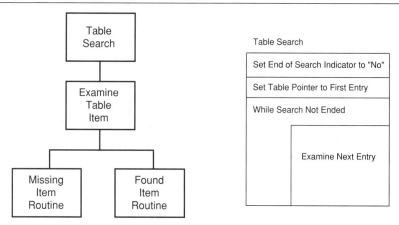

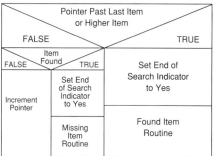

The difference between the unordered table search and the ordered table search lies exclusively in how the program determines whether or not an item has been found. If the pointer points to the correct entry, the item has been found. If the key field in the table is higher than the search field, the item has not been found. An end indicator is set to reflect that the search should end and the appropriate course of action should be taken.

As with an unordered table, separate courses of action should be specified for a missing item and a found item. Whether or not an entry has been found is determined by whether the pointer is pointing to the correct entry or not. The entire table need not be searched to determine that an item is missing. This may result in substantial savings in computer time. The COBOL code to implement the search logic depicted in Figure 10.23 is:

```
1000-LOCATE-SUPPLIER-ENTRY.
     MOVE "NO" TO SUPPLIER-SEARCH-OVER.
     PERFORM 1100-SEARCH-SUPPLIER TABLE
          VARYING SUPPLIER-INDEX FROM 1 BY 1
             UNTIL SUPPLIER-SEARCH-OVER = "YES".
```

```
1100-SEARCH-SUPPLIER-TABLE.
      IF SUP-NAME (SUPPLIER-INDEX) = SUPPLIER-SEARCH-NAME
          MOVE "YES" TO SUPPLIER-SEARCH-OVER
          PERFORM 1300-REPORT-ENTRY-FOUND
      ELSE
          IF SUP-NAME (SUPPLIER-INDEX) >
             SUPPLIER-SEARCH-NAME
          OR SUPPLIER-INDEX = NBR-OF-SUPPLIERS
                  MOVE "YES" TO SUPPLIER-SEARCH-OVER
                  PERFORM 1200-REPORT-MISSING-ENTRY.
```

Multidimensional Tables. The search logic for a multidimensional table incorporates a second and third search after the first dimension of the table has been searched. Figure 10.24 shows the logic in flowchart form for a two-dimensional ordered table search. The logic in structured English is:

```
Set end of search indicator to FALSE;
Set first dimension index to first position;
REPEAT UNTIL end of search
    IF index is past last table entry OR entry key is passed THEN
       Set end of search indicator to TRUE;
       PERFORM missing item routine;
    ELSE
       IF first dimension matches THEN
          Set second dimension index to first position;
          REPEAT UNTIL end of search indicator is TRUE
             IF index is past last table entry  OR entry key is passed THEN
                Set end of search indicator to TRUE;
                PERFORM missing item routine;
             ELSE
                IF item is found THEN
                   Set end of search indicator to TRUE;
                   PERFORM found item routine;
                ELSE
                   increment second dimension index;
                END-IF;
             END-IF;
          END-REPEAT;
       ELSE
          increment first dimension index;
       END-IF;
    END-IF;
END-REPEAT.
```

Figure 10.24   Two-Dimensional Search Logic for an Ordered Table

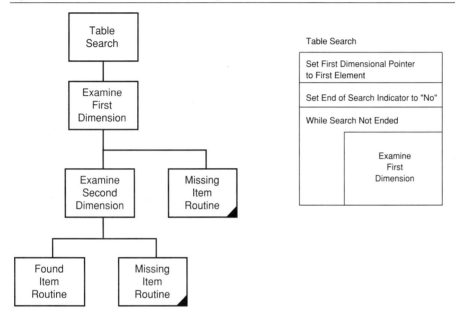

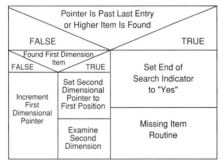

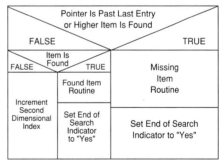

As you can see, the logic just repeats itself for the second dimension if the first dimension search is successful. This is also evident by the hierarchy chart in Figure 10.24 where an extra vertical level was added for the extra dimension. If either of the searches fails, the entry is missing. The COBOL code for the two-dimensional search is:

```
1000-LOCATE-SUPPLIER-ENTRY.
        MOVE "NO" TO SUPPLIER-SEARCH-OVER.
        PERFORM 1100-SEARCH-SUPPLIER-TABLE
        VARYING SUPPLIER-INDEX FROM 1 BY 1
            UNTIL SUPPLIER-SEARCH-OVER = "YES".
```

```
1100-SEARCH-SUPPLIER-TABLE.
      IF SUP-NAME (SUPPLIER-INDEX) = SUPPLIER-SEARCH-NAME
            PERFORM 1200-SEARCH-PARTS-LIST
                  VARYING PART-INDEX FROM 1 BY 1
                        UNTIL SUPPLIER-SEARCH-OVER = "YES"
      ELSE
            IF SUP-NAME (SUPPLIER-INDEX) <
                  SUPPLIER-SEARCH-NAME
                  OR SUPPLIER-INDEX = NBR-OF-SUPPLIERS
                        MOVE "YES" TO SUPPLIER-SEARCH-OVER
                        PERFORM 1300-REPORT-MISSING-ENTRY.
1200-SEARCH-PARTS-LIST.
      IF PART-NAME (SUPPLIER-INDEX, PART-INDEX)
            = PART-SEARCH-NAME
            MOVE "YES" TO SUPPLIER-SEARCH-OVER
            PERFORM 1400-REPORT-ENTRY-FOUND
      ELSE
            IF PART-NAME (SUPPLIER-INDEX, PART-INDEX)
                  < PART-SEARCH-NAME OR PART-INDEX = 4
                        MOVE "YES" TO SUPPLIER-SEARCH-OVER
                        PERFORM 1300-REPORT-MISSING-ENTRY.
```

10.2.4   *The COBOL SEARCH Statement*

COBOL provides a statement, appropriately called the SEARCH statement, to perform table searches. The SEARCH performs a sequential search of a table in the same fashion as the PERFORM VARYING statement. Thus the table may be ordered or unordered. The format for the SEARCH statement and its rules for construction are:

SEARCH table-name [VARYING data-name-1]
[AT END imperative-statement-1]

$$\left\{ \text{WHEN condition} \left\{ \begin{array}{c} \text{imperative-statement-2} \\ \text{NEXT SENTENCE} \end{array} \right\} \right\} \ldots$$

[END-SEARCH]

1.   The table-name must have an OCCURS and an INDEXED BY clause.
2.   The table-name must not be subscripted. If the table-name is higher-order dimension, the index must be set to the proper occurrence of the lower-order dimension.
3.   Data-name-1 is varied along with the index for the table-name.
4.   The index for table-name must be SET to a starting value before the SEARCH is executed.

5. If the search terminates without finding an element satisfying the search criteria, the AT END clause is executed.
6. If any WHEN condition is met, the SEARCH ends and the statement with the associated WHEN is executed.
7. The WHEN conditions are tested in order of appearance.
8. The conditions are restricted to simple conditions.

The *SEARCH* verb scans a table serially beginning at the location in the table where its associated index currently points. Therefore, the SEARCH statement requires that the table being searched contain an INDEXED BY clause in its description. If the VARYING clause is specified, data-name-1 must be an index data item that is incremented by the same amount as the primary index, or an elementary integer data item that is incremented by one each time the table index is incremented. The AT END clause in the SEARCH statement allows the programmer to specify the course of action to be taken if the SEARCH conditions are never met; that is, no element in the table satisfies the specified condition. If no AT END clause is specified, control passes to the sentence following the SEARCH statement. The WHEN clause allows an action to be specified when some condition is met. Multiple WHEN clauses may be specified. If any of the WHEN conditions are satisfied, the SEARCH terminates.

Since a table SEARCH begins where the table index is pointing, it must be set to a value before the search begins. Since an index is not a data item, we cannot MOVE an initial value to it. However, COBOL provides a special statement to initialize the index, the *SET* statement. The SET statement format and rules are:

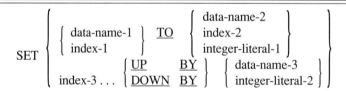

1. All data-names must be elementary positive integers.
2. Integer literals must be positive (>0).
3. The following actions are taken for various SET . . . TO statements.

	TO	
SET	integer-literal or data-name-2	index-2
data-name-1	not valid for integer data-names	data-name-1 is set to the occurrence number indicated by the index
index-1	index-1 is set to the occurrence number indicated by data-name-2 or integer-literal	index-1 is set to the occurrence number of index-2. They need not be indexes for the same table.

Indexes may be SET to values corresponding to occurrence numbers. For example,

```
SET-SUPPLIER-INDEX TO 1
```

initializes the table index to point to the first occurrence in the table. Indexes may be incremented or decremented by an integer number corresponding to that number of occurrences. For example,

```
SET SUPPLIER-INDEX UP BY 2
```

increments the table index so that it points to an occurrence two elements later in the table.

The SET and SEARCH statements can accomplish the same function as the PERFORM VARYING statement. The code to implement the one-dimensional ordered table search of Figure 10.23 using the SEARCH statement is:

```
1000-LOCATE-SUPPLIER-ENTRY.
        SET SUPPLIER-INDEX TO 1.
        SEARCH SUPPLIER
              AT END PERFORM 1200-REPORT-MISSING-ENTRY
              WHEN SUPPLIER-SEARCH-NAME
                   = SUP-NAME (SUPPLIER-INDEX)
                   PERFORM 1300-REPORT-FOUND-ENTRY
              WHEN SUPPLIER-SEARCH-NAME
                   < SUP-NAME (SUPPLIER-INDEX)
                   PERFORM 1200-REPORT-MISSING-ENTRY.
```

Notice how one paragraph now performs the work of two paragraphs when the PERFORM VARYING was used. A hierarchy chart using a SEARCH would have one less horizontal level than for the PERFORM VARYING. Figure 10.25 shows how the logic is greatly simplified using the SEARCH since the statement automatically conducts the varying of the pointers and the examination of the fields. The SET and SEARCH statements initialize and increment the index, as did the PERFORM VARYING UNTIL, but do not require an additional paragraph to control the termination of the search.

Figure 10.25   One-Dimensional Search with the COBOL SEARCH Statement

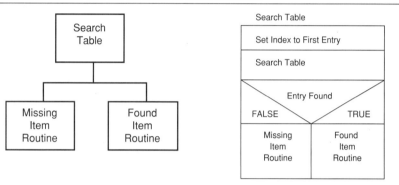

Furthermore, the SEARCH statement also provides different clauses to examine the different conditions of the table. For example, rather than testing for the presence or absence of the correct occurrence after the table search is performed, the AT END clause allows the specification of the action to be taken if an entry is missing and the WHEN clause is used to determine if the entry is missing in a table before examining every entry. Unordered tables cannot use the second WHEN clause in this specific example since every occurrence must be examined to determine if an occurrence is present. Using the SET and SEARCH statements eliminates the extra paragraph containing the selection structure needed when the PERFORM VARYING UNTIL statement is used. These COBOL verbs are used in the parts example code, lines 151 and 152 of Figure 10.7.

Multidimensional tables must be searched using successive SEARCH statements. In essence, each SEARCH statement allows the programmer to search one dimension at a time. Because of this, when searching multidimensional tables the programmer should ensure that the indexes for each dimension in the table are set to their proper values. Following is the code required to SEARCH the two-dimensional supplier table using the reduced logic shown in Figure 10.26. Notice how once again a horizontal level is removed from the logic of Figure 10.24.

```
1000-LOCATE-SUPPLIER-ENTRY.
     SET SUPPLIER-INDEX TO 1.
     SEARCH SUPPLIER
          AT END PERFORM  1200-REPORT-MISSING-ENTRY
          WHEN SUPPLIER-SEARCH-NAME
               = SUP-NAME (SUPPLIER-INDEX)
               PERFORM 1100-LOCATE-PART.
1100-LOCATE-PART.
     SET  PART-INDEX TO 1.
     SEARCH  PARTS-LIST
```

```
AT END PERFORM 1200-REPORT-MISSING-ENTRY
WHEN PART-SEARCH-NAME
       = PART-NAME (SUPPLIER-INDEX, PART-INDEX)
       PERFORM 1300-REPORT-ENTRY-FOUND.
```

Figure 10.26   Two-Dimensional Search Logic with the COBOL SEARCH Statement

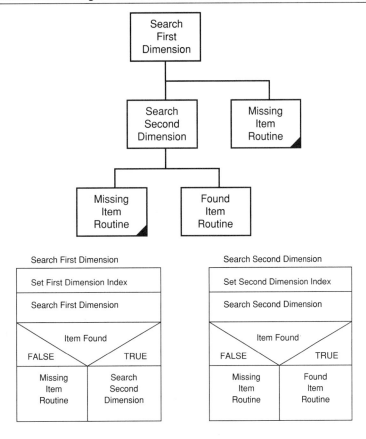

Note that in paragraph 1100-LOCATE-PART, we are searching the second dimension of the supplier table and that the value of SUPPLIER-INDEX has been determined in paragraph 1000-LOCATE-SUPPLIER-ENTRY.

10.2.5   The COBOL SEARCH ALL Statement

The third method of searching a table employs the SEARCH ALL statement. The SEARCH ALL statement performs a *binary search* of an ordered table. A binary search is a much more efficient method of searching a table since it eliminates half of the available occurrences to be searched during each successive pass. The table is divided into two halves (thereby "binary") and the desired key is compared with the midpoint key value to determine whether a match exists, or whether the desired key value is above or below the midpoint value. Based on that result the upper or lower half of the table is again divided into two halves and the desired key value is compared with the new midpoint key value. The process of halving the table and comparing it with the midpoint key value continues until the key is matched or it is determined that the entry does not exist.

The SEARCH ALL verb automatically performs a binary search. Thus, for larger tables the SEARCH ALL statement is much more efficient than the SEARCH statement. The format and rules for the SEARCH ALL statement are:

SEARCH ALL table-name
        [AT END imperative-statement-1]

WHEN $\begin{Bmatrix} \text{data-name-1} \\ \text{condition-name-1} \end{Bmatrix}$ $\begin{Bmatrix} \text{IS EQUAL TO} \\ \text{IS =} \end{Bmatrix}$ $\begin{Bmatrix} \text{literal-1} \\ \text{data-name-2} \\ \text{arithmetic-expression-1} \end{Bmatrix}$

$\left[\text{AND} \begin{Bmatrix} \text{data-name-3} \\ \text{condition-name-2} \end{Bmatrix} \begin{Bmatrix} \text{IS EQUAL TO} \\ \text{IS =} \end{Bmatrix} \begin{Bmatrix} \text{literal-2} \\ \text{data-name-4} \\ \text{arithmetic-expression-2} \end{Bmatrix} \right]$

$\begin{Bmatrix} \text{imperative-statement-2} \\ \text{NEXT STATEMENT} \end{Bmatrix}$

[END SEARCH]

1. If the condition in the WHEN clause cannot be met, the statement following the AT END clause is executed.
2. The table-name must have the INDEXED BY, KEY, and OCCURS clauses.
3. One of the data-names from the KEY clause must appear as data-name-1 or data-name-3 or must be associated with one of the condition names.
4. Data-name-2 and data-name-4 must not contain a KEY item or the table's index.

The WHEN clause specifies the conditions that must be met for a match. Since the search process is nonserial, the SEARCH ALL requires that the table be organized in the sequence specified by the ASCENDING or DESCENDING KEY clause in the table description. The SEARCH ALL ends if the conditions in the WHEN clause are satisfied; otherwise, if the entry is not found in that table, the statement indicated by the AT END clause will be executed. The SEARCH ALL statement for searching the one-dimensional supplier table is:

```
SEARCH ALL SUPPLIER
        AT END PERFORM  1200-REPORT-MISSING-ENTRY
        WHEN SUP-NAME (SUPPLIER-INDEX) IS
                EQUAL TO SUPPLIER-SEARCH-NAME
                PERFORM  1300-REPORT-FOUND-ENTRY.
```

10.2.6   *Performing Operations on Table Elements*

Once the entry of interest is found in a table, its data items can be manipulated like any other data item in the DATA DIVISION. Actually, the difficult part of performing mathematical operations on table data items is in locating the proper entry. The logic for locating entries for mathematical manipulation is identical to that presented for other table data items. The thing to remember is to refer to data items within the table using the proper subscripts of index levels. Then the data items within a table can be treated the same as any other data item in the PROCEDURE DIVISION. For example, see lines 168 and 171 of Figure 10.7, where table data is manipulated arithmetically and transferred to another location.

Some applications require that items within a table be summed across the table. For example, suppose a table contains sales figures for sales representatives grouped by offices and the offices grouped by region. The data descriptions entry is as follows:

```
01    SALES-TABLE.
      05    REGIONS OCCURS 10 TIMES.
            10    OFFICE OCCURS 20 TIMES.
                  15    SALES-REP PIC 9(5)V99
                        OCCURS 50 TIMES.
```

To find the total sales figure we use the PERFORM VARYING statement as follows:

```
MOVE ZERO TO TOTAL-SALES.
PERFORM 100-ADD-SALES
     VARYING REGION-SUBSCRIPT FROM 1 BY 1
          UNTIL REGION-SUBSCRIPT > 10
     AFTER VARYING OFFICE-SUBSCRIPT FROM 1 BY 1
          UNTIL OFFICE-SUBSCRIPT > 20
     AFTER VARYING REP-SUBSCRIPT FROM 1 BY 1
          UNTIL REP-SUBSCRIPT > 50.
100-ADD-SALES
     ADD SALES-REP (REGION-SUBSCRIPT, OFFICE-SUBSCRIPT,
          REP-SUBSCRIPT) TO TOTAL-SALES.
```

Case Study: CDL's Extend CD Orders

After reviewing the order validation program, Charlene decides that looking up the CD numbers in a table should be incorporated in the order extension program. The program specification is given in Figure 10.27 and the report layouts are in Figure 10.28. The validation table is stored in a file named "Compact Disc Stock Table." The invalid orders should be reported as shown in the report layout in Figure 10.29, whereas the valid orders should be written to an "Extended Order" file.

Figure 10.27   "Extend CD Orders" Program Specifications

PROGRAM SUMMARY
TITLE: *Extend CD Orders*
PREPARED BY: *C. Hilton*
DATE: *6-15-93*

FILES USED		
FILE NAME	MEDIA	ORGANIZATION
Order	Disk	Sequential
Extended Order	Disk	Sequential
Invalid Orders	Printer	Sequential
CD Stock Table	Disk	Sequential

DESCRIPTION

The orders from the order entry process are validated for nonzero entries and for valid stock numbers. If the CD number does not appear in the compact disc stock table, it is an invalid stock number. Error codes for the report are:

1. Field value zero

2. Invalid stock number

3. Both errors 1 and 2

4. Valid item, but not in stock

5. Both errors 1 and 4

If the entry is valid, the price from the table is used to compute the total amount due based on the quantity ordered. The total price is placed into the output record for the extended orders file. Shipping costs are added to the total price. Bulk rates require shipping 5 CDs; single rates are for 1 CD.

Figure 10.28 "Extend CD Orders" Record Layouts

RECORD LAYOUT SHEET

Record Name: Order		File Name: Orders/Extended Orders		
Prepared By: C. Hilton		Date: 6-15-93		
Key Fields:		Organization: Sequential		
Field	Description	Type*	Length	Decimal
Customer ID	A unique customer number	N	6	0
Disc number	An identifier/stock number	N	6	0
Quantity	The number ordered	N	2	0
Order #	A preprinted order form #	N	6	0
Price	Retail price	N	8	2

* A = alphanumeric
  N = numeric

RECORD LAYOUT SHEET

Record Name: CD Stock		File Name: CD stock table		
Prepared By: C. Hilton		Date: 7-7-93		
Key Fields:		Organization: Sequential		
Field	Description	Type*	Length	Decimal
Disc number	A unique stock number	N	6	0
Price	Price of item	N	6	2
Quantity	Quantity on hand	N	4	0

* A = alphanumeric
  N = numeric

Figure 10.29   "Extend CD Orders" Report Layout

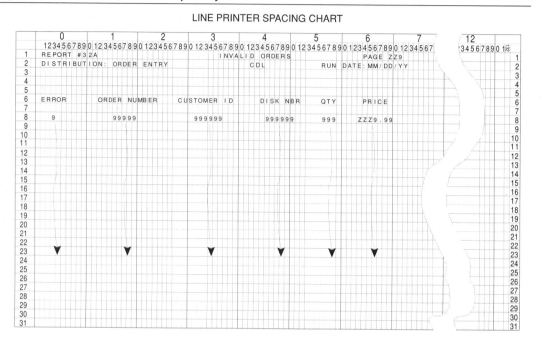

Figure 10.30   "Extend CD Orders" Hierarchy and N-S Charts

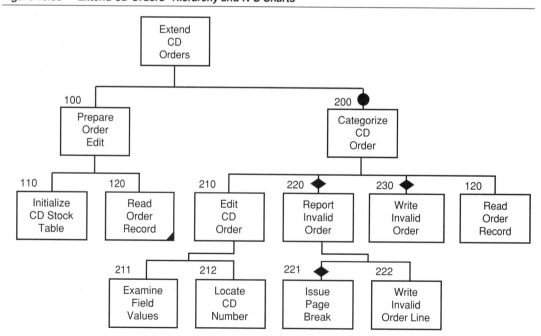

Figure 10.30 *(continued)*

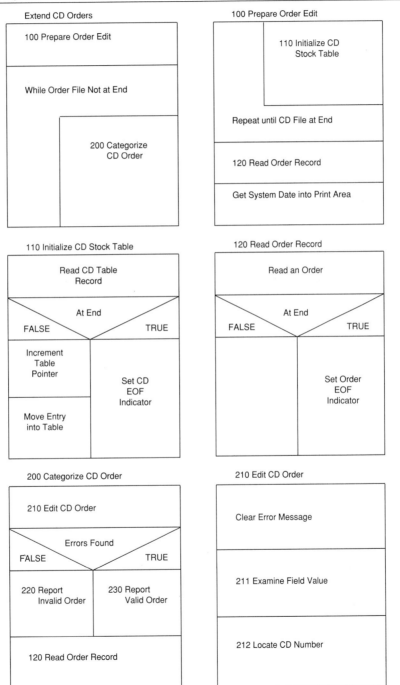

Figure 10.30   (continued)

211 Examine Field Value

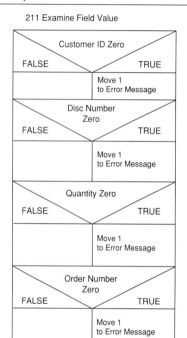

212 Locate CD Number

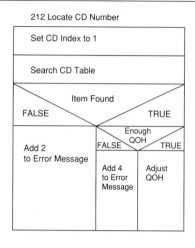

220 Report Invalid Order

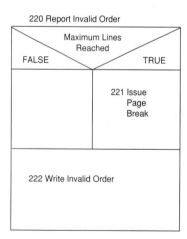

221 Issue Page Break

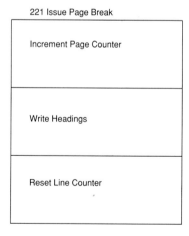

Figure 10.30   (continued)

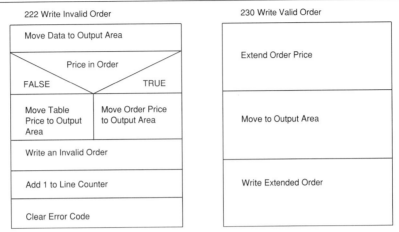

The hierarchy and Nassi-Schneiderman charts developed by Charlene are illustrated in Figure 10.30. The logic of most of the modules is straightforward. However, notice how the error code is used as a flag between the modules. In the N-S chart for module "211 Examine Field Value," a value of 1 is moved into the error code if any field in the order is zero; otherwise the error code remains at its present value of zero. In "212 Locate CD Number," a value of 2 is added to the error code if the CD number is invalid. This way if error type 1 and error type 2 are present, the error code will be 3 as per the program specifications. If the CD number is valid but there is not enough stock to fill the order, a value of 4 is added to the error code. The value of the error code is then used to determine whether the order is valid or not in module "200 Categorize CD Order."

The complete program is illustrated in Figure 10.31. Charlene uses a PERFORM VARY-ING UNTIL statement to load the CD stock table and to maintain the number of entries in the table in paragraph 100-PREPARE-ORDER-EDIT. In paragraph 212-LOCATE-CD-NUM-BER, Charlene uses the SEARCH statement to find the entry in the ordered table. Test data and results are in Figure 10.32.

Figure 10.31   "Extend CD Orders" Code

```
1 IDENTIFICATION DIVISION.
2 PROGRAM-ID.  EXTEND-ORDERS.
3*      THIS PROGRAM VALIDATES THE ORDERS FOR COMPLETENESS AND
4*      TESTS THE CD NUMBERS AGAINST THE CD IN STOCK TABLE FOR
5*      VALIDITY OF THE NUMBER AND IN HAVING ENOUGH ITEMS IN
6*      STOCK.  AN ERROR REPORT IS GENERATED FOR ALL INVALID
7*      ORDERS.  VALID ORDERS HAVE THEIR PRICES EXTENDED AND ARE
8*      WRITTEN TO A VALID ORDER FILE.
9
```

Figure 10.31   (continued)

```
10 AUTHOR.            C HILTON
11 DATE-WRITTEN.       7-7-93.
12 DATE-COMPILED. 25-Jan-94 07:35.
16 ENVIRONMENT DIVISION.
17
18
19 CONFIGURATION SECTION.
20
21 SOURCE-COMPUTER.  GENERIC-COMPUTER.
22 OBJECT-COMPUTER.  GENERIC-COMPUTER.
23
24
25 INPUT-OUTPUT SECTION.
26
27 FILE-CONTROL.
28     SELECT ORDERS-FILE ASSIGN TO "ORDER.DAT"
29         ORGANIZATION IS LINE SEQUENTIAL.
30     SELECT EXTENDED-ORDERS-FILE ASSIGN TO "EXORDR.DAT"
31         ORGANIZATION IS LINE SEQUENTIAL.
32     SELECT INVALID-ORDERS-FILE ASSIGN TO "REPORT.DAT"
33         ORGANIZATION IS LINE SEQUENTIAL.
34     SELECT COMPACT-DISC-STOCK-TABLE-FILE ASSIGN TO "CD.TAB"
35         ORGANIZATION IS LINE SEQUENTIAL.
36
37
38
39
40 DATA DIVISION.
41
42
43 FILE SECTION.
44
45 FD  ORDERS-FILE
46     LABEL RECORDS ARE STANDARD.
47
48 01  ORDER-REC.
49     05  O-CUSTOMER-ID   PIC 9(6).
50     05  O-DISC-NUMBER   PIC 9(6).
51     05  O-QUANTITY      PIC 99.
52     05  O-ORDER-NUMBER  PIC 9(6).
53     05  O-PRICE         PIC 9(6)V99.
54
```

Figure 10.31   (continued)

```
55 FD   EXTENDED-ORDERS-FILE
56      LABEL RECORDS ARE STANDARD.
57
58 01   EXTENDED-ORDER-REC.
59      05   EO-CUSTOMER-ID   PIC 9(6).
60      05   EO-DISC-NUMBER   PIC 9(6).
61      05   EO-QUANTITY      PIC 99.
62      05   EO-ORDER-NUMBER  PIC 9(6).
63      05   EO-TOTAL-PRICE   PIC 9(6)V99.
64
65 FD   INVALID-ORDERS-FILE
66      LABEL RECORDS ARE OMITTED.
67
68 01   INVALID-ORDER-REC PIC X(80).
69
70 FD   COMPACT-DISC-STOCK-TABLE-FILE
71      LABEL RECORDS ARE STANDARD.
72
73 01   CD-STOCK-REC.
74      05   CD-DISC-NUMBER PIC 9(6).
75      05   CD-PRICE       PIC 9(4)V99.
76      05   CD-QOH         PIC 9999.
77
78
79 WORKING-STORAGE SECTION.
80
81 01   NBR-OF-COMPACT-DISCS PIC 99 VALUE 0.
82 01   COMPACT-DISC-TABLE.
83      05   COMPACT-DISC OCCURS 1 TO 50 TIMES
84           DEPENDING ON NBR-OF-COMPACT-DISCS
85           ASCENDING KEY IS CDTAB-DISC-NUMBER
86           INDEXED BY CD-INDEX.
87              10   CDTAB-DISC-NUMBER PIC 9(6).
88              10   CDTAB-PRICE       PIC 9(4)V99.
89              10   CDTAB-QOH         PIC 9999.
90
91 01   PAGE-CONTROL-COUNTERS.
92      05   PCC-LINE         PIC 99  VALUE 99.
93      05   PCC-PAGE         PIC 999 VALUE ZERO.
94      05   PCC-MAX-LINES    PIC 99  VALUE 55.
95
96 01   SYSTEM-DATES.
```

Figure 10.31   (continued)

```
97      05   SD-DATE           PIC 9(6).
98      05   SD-MM-DD-YY.
99           10   SD-MM        PIC XX.
100          10   SD-DD        PIC XX.
101          10   SD-YY        PIC XX.
102     05   SD-YEAR           PIC XX.
103
104 01  POSTAL-RATES.
105     05   PR-BULK           PIC 99.
106     05   PR-SINGLE         PIC 99.
107     05   PR-BULK-RATE      PIC 99V99 VALUE 3.95.
108     05   PR-SINGLE-RATE    PIC 99V99 VALUE 1.24.
109
110 01  INDICATORS.
111     05   EOF-ORDERS        PIC X(5) VALUE "FALSE".
112     05   EOF-CD-TABLE      PIC X(5) VALUE "FALSE".
113     05   ERR-CODE          PIC 9    VALUE ZERO.
114     05   MAX-LINE          PIC 99   VALUE 55.
115
116 01  TOTAL-PRICE   PIC 9(6)V99.
117
118 01  INVALID-ORDERS-LISTING.
119     05   IOL-REPORT-TITLE.
120          10   FILLER       PIC X(35) VALUE "REPORT #32A".
121          10   FILLER       PIC X(28) VALUE "INVALID ORDERS".
122          10   FILLER       PIC X(5)  VALUE "PAGE".
123          10   IOL-PAGE     PIC ZZ9.
124     05   IOL-RUN-DATE.
125          10   FILLER       PIC X(40) VALUE
126                            "DISTRIBUTION:  ORDER ENTRY".
127          10   FILLER       PIC X(15) VALUE "CDL".
128          10   FILLER       PIC X(10) VALUE "RUN DATE:".
129          10   IOL-DATE     PIC 99/99/99.
130     05   IOL-COLUMNS.
131          10   FILLER       PIC X(11) VALUE "ERROR".
132          10   FILLER       PIC X(16) VALUE "ORDER NUMBER".
133          10   FILLER       PIC X(16) VALUE "CUSTOMER ID".
134          10   FILLER       PIC X(12) VALUE "DISC NUMBER".
135          10   FILLER       PIC X(8)  VALUE "QTY".
136          10   FILLER       PIC X(5)  VALUE "PRICE".
137     05   IOL-UNDERLINE.
138          10   FILLER       PIC X(11) VALUE "—".
```

Figure 10.31 (continued)

```
139          10  FILLER           PIC X(16) VALUE "————".
140          10  FILLER           PIC X(16) VALUE "————".
141          10  FILLER           PIC X(12) VALUE "————".
142          10  FILLER           PIC X(8)  VALUE "—".
143          10  FILLER           PIC X(8)  VALUE "————".
144      05  IOL-DETAIL.
145          10  FILLER           PIC X(2)  VALUE SPACE.
146          10  IOL-ERROR        PIC 9.
147          10  FILLER           PIC X(11) VALUE SPACE.
148          10  IOL-ORDER-NUMBER PIC 9(6).
149          10  FILLER           PIC X(10) VALUE SPACE.
150          10  IOL-CUSTOMER-ID  PIC 9(6).
151          10  FILLER           PIC X(8)  VALUE SPACE.
152          10  IOL-DISC-NUMBER  PIC 9(6).
153          10  FILLER           PIC X(5)  VALUE SPACE.
154          10  IOL-QUANTITY     PIC ZZ9.
155          10  FILLER           PIC X(5)  VALUE SPACE.
156          10  IOL-PRICE        PIC ZZZ,ZZ9.99.
157
158 PROCEDURE DIVISION.
159
160 EXTEND-CD-ORDERS.
161     OPEN INPUT ORDERS-FILE.
162     OPEN INPUT COMPACT-DISC-STOCK-TABLE-FILE.
163     OPEN OUTPUT INVALID-ORDERS-FILE.
164     OPEN OUTPUT EXTENDED-ORDERS-FILE.
165     PERFORM 100-PREPARE-ORDER-EDIT.
166     PERFORM 200-CATEGORIZE-CD-ORDER UNTIL EOF-ORDERS = "TRUE".
167     CLOSE ORDERS-FILE.
168     CLOSE COMPACT-DISC-STOCK-TABLE-FILE.
169     CLOSE INVALID-ORDERS-FILE.
170     CLOSE EXTENDED-ORDERS-FILE.
171     STOP RUN.
172
173 100-PREPARE-ORDER-EDIT.
174     PERFORM 110-INITIALIZE-CD-STOCK
175         VARYING NBR-OF-COMPACT-DISCS FROM 1 BY 1
176         UNTIL EOF-CD-TABLE = "TRUE".
177     SUBTRACT 1 FROM NBR-OF-COMPACT-DISCS.
178     PERFORM 120-READ-ORDER-RECORD.
179     ACCEPT SD-DATE FROM DATE.
180     MOVE SD-DATE TO SD-MM-DD-YY.
```

Figure 10.31   (continued)

```
181        MOVE SD-MM TO SD-YEAR.
182        MOVE SD-DD TO SD-MM.
183        MOVE SD-YY TO SD-DD.
184        MOVE SD-YEAR TO SD-YY.
185        MOVE SD-DATE TO IOL-DATE.
186
187 110-INITIALIZE-CD-STOCK.
188        READ COMPACT-DISC-STOCK-TABLE-FILE
189            AT END MOVE "TRUE" TO EOF-CD-TABLE.
190        IF EOF-CD-TABLE = "FALSE"
191            MOVE CD-STOCK-REC TO
192                COMPACT-DISC (NBR-OF-COMPACT-DISCS).
193
194 120-READ-ORDER-RECORD.
195        READ ORDERS-FILE
196            AT END MOVE "TRUE" TO EOF-ORDERS.
197
198 200-CATEGORIZE-CD-ORDER.
199        PERFORM 210-EDIT-CD-ORDER.
200        IF ERR-CODE = ZERO
201            PERFORM 230-REPORT-VALID-ORDER
202        ELSE
203            PERFORM 220-REPORT-INVALID-ORDER.
204        PERFORM 120-READ-ORDER-RECORD.
205
206 210-EDIT-CD-ORDER.
207        MOVE ZERO TO ERR-CODE.
208        PERFORM 211-EXAMINE-FIELD-PRESENCE.
209        PERFORM 212-LOCATE-CD-NUMBER.
210
211 211-EXAMINE-FIELD-PRESENCE.
212        IF O-CUSTOMER-ID = ZERO
213            MOVE 1 TO ERR-CODE.
214        IF O-DISC-NUMBER = ZERO
215            MOVE 1 TO ERR-CODE.
216        IF O-QUANTITY = ZERO
217            MOVE 1 TO ERR-CODE.
218        IF O-ORDER-NUMBER = ZERO
219            MOVE 1 TO ERR-CODE.
220
221 212-LOCATE-CD-NUMBER.
222        SET CD-INDEX TO 1.
```

Figure 10.31 (continued)

```
223     SEARCH COMPACT-DISC
224         AT END ADD 2 TO ERR-CODE
225         WHEN CDTAB-DISC-NUMBER (CD-INDEX) = O-DISC-NUMBER
226             NEXT SENTENCE.
227     IF ERR-CODE < 2
228         IF CDTAB-QOH (CD-INDEX) < O-QUANTITY
229             ADD 4 TO ERR-CODE
230         ELSE
231             SUBTRACT O-QUANTITY FROM CDTAB-QOH (CD-INDEX).
232
233 220-REPORT-INVALID-ORDER.
234     IF PCC-LINE > PCC-MAX-LINES PERFORM 221-ISSUE-PAGE-BREAK.
235     PERFORM 222-WRITE-INVALID-ORDER.
236
237 221-ISSUE-PAGE-BREAK.
238     ADD 1 TO PCC-PAGE.
239     MOVE PCC-PAGE TO IOL-PAGE.
240     WRITE INVALID-ORDER-REC FROM IOL-REPORT-TITLE
241         AFTER ADVANCING PAGE.
242     WRITE INVALID-ORDER-REC FROM IOL-RUN-DATE.
243     WRITE INVALID-ORDER-REC FROM IOL-COLUMNS
244         AFTER ADVANCING 3 LINES.
245     WRITE INVALID-ORDER-REC FROM IOL-UNDERLINE.
246     MOVE SPACE TO INVALID-ORDER-REC.
247     WRITE INVALID-ORDER-REC.
248     MOVE 6 TO PCC-LINE.
249
250 222-WRITE-INVALID-ORDER.
251     MOVE O-CUSTOMER-ID  TO IOL-CUSTOMER-ID.
252     MOVE ERR-CODE       TO IOL-ERROR.
253     MOVE O-DISC-NUMBER  TO IOL-DISC-NUMBER.
254     MOVE O-QUANTITY     TO IOL-QUANTITY.
255     MOVE O-ORDER-NUMBER TO IOL-ORDER-NUMBER.
256     IF ERR-CODE NOT = 2 AND ERR-CODE NOT = 3
257         MOVE CDTAB-PRICE (CD-INDEX) TO IOL-PRICE
258     ELSE
259         MOVE O-PRICE TO IOL-PRICE.
260     WRITE INVALID-ORDER-REC FROM IOL-DETAIL.
261     ADD 1 TO PCC-LINE.
262     MOVE ZERO TO ERR-CODE.
263
264 230-REPORT-VALID-ORDER.
```

Figure 10.31   (continued)

```
265      DIVIDE 5 INTO O-QUANTITY GIVING PR-BULK REMAINDER PR-SINGLE.
266      COMPUTE TOTAL-PRICE =
267          O-QUANTITY * CDTAB-PRICE (CD-INDEX) +
268          PR-BULK * PR-BULK-RATE +
269          PR-SINGLE * PR-SINGLE-RATE.
270      MOVE ORDER-REC TO EXTENDED-ORDER-REC.
271      MOVE TOTAL-PRICE TO EO-TOTAL-PRICE.
272      WRITE EXTENDED-ORDER-REC.
```

Figure 10.32   Test Data and Results for CDL's "Extend CD Orders"

The ORDER file:

```
198765123456029876540000000
000000123456015435670000000
323212999888017543270000000
000000998899016543560000000
654323234567019876540000000
545678234567020000000000000
```

The CD table:

```
1234560009991000
2345670010000000
3456780024990233
```

The EXTENDED ORDER file:

```
198765123456029876540000002246
```

Figure 10.32   (continued)

The ORDER ERROR report:

```
REPORT #32A                       INVALID ORDERS                PAGE   1
DISTRIBUTION:   ORDER ENTRY            CDL            RUN DATE: 94/01/25


ERROR      ORDER NUMBER      CUSTOMER ID      DISC NUMBER    QTY        PRICE
---        -----------       -----------      -----------    ---        -----


 1            543567            000000           123456        1          9.99
 2            754327            323212           999888        1          0.00
 3            654356            000000           998899        1          0.00
 4            987654            654323           234567        1         10.00
 5            000000            545678           234567        2         10.00
```

Summary

Many programs use tables to store, accumulate, extend, and validate data. The tables may have one or multiple dimensions and can be initialized, searched, and manipulated.

To define tables in the DATA DIVISION, the OCCURS clause is used to indicate the repeating data items or groups. If repeating items are ordered, their order is specified through the ASCENDING/DESCENDING KEY option. An index may be associated with the table by using the INDEXED BY clause. This index is used to refer to a specific occurrence of an item or group in the PROCEDURE DIVISION. A subscript, however, may be used instead of the index in the PROCEDURE DIVISION.

A table may be initialized from an external file through COBOL code in the PROCEDURE DIVISION. The PERFORM VARYING statement loads the table from a file. The table may also be initialized in the DATA DIVISION using the REDEFINES option.

To search a table for a specific entry, COBOL provides the SEARCH and SEARCH ALL statements. The SEARCH statement sequentially examines each entry in a table until some predetermined condition has been met or the last entry has been examined. The SEARCH ALL statement conducts a binary search on an ordered table.

Key Terms

tables	OCCURS	REDEFINES
table elements	KEY IS	searching
dimensionality	INDEXED BY	SEARCH
unordered table	index	SET
ordered table	subscript	binary search

Hints for Avoiding Errors

1. The SEARCH statement requires that the associated index be preset to the occurrence number of the first item to be searched. If it is not SET before executing the SEARCH statement, the SEARCH will appear to work normally, but the search will start wherever the index happens to point in the table and the item being searched for may not be found.
2. COBOL will not catch an error in the redefinition of tables. If the program appears to be working correctly except that report fields are off by a few spaces or items are appearing in the wrong columns, the REDEFINES clause may not be properly established or the internal table definition may be in error.
3. Remember that subscripts and indexes do not mix. Improper use of either item may cause the table to be improperly searched or loaded.
4. If a subscript is out of range, not all machines or COBOL compilers will catch the error. If you are acquiring bad data from a valid table, be sure that your subscripts are not pointing past the end of the table or to a memory location before the table. It is wise to check the range of the subscripts during testing and debugging.

Exercises

10.1   A major retail store is organized by region. Each region has a central office with a central telephone number. The regional offices handle all correspondence with the credit customers. Within each regional office each major department has a manager with his own telephone. The corporate sales are to be accumulated by month for each department by regions. Define a table that can be used to store the information described and to accumulate the monthly sales. Department and region codes are each four numeric digits long.

10.2   Assume that input records contain daily sales summaries for each department within each region. The record contains the day from 1 to 31, the month number from 1 to 12, the region code, the department code, and a dollar amount in 9(6)V99 format. Write a program to accept this unordered input, and update the table created in Exercise 10.1. Generate a report that summarizes the table entries accumulated.

10.3   When a table is searched, how would duplicate keys alter any search logic? Redraw the Nassi-Schneiderman charts in Figure 10.24 to indicate the required changes.

10.4   The WORKING-STORAGE SECTION entry:

```
01    STUDENT-INFO.
      03   NAME OCCURS 400 TIMES PICTURE X(20).
      03   COLLEGE PICTURE X(20).
```

allocates computer storage for:

    a.   400 student names and 400 colleges
    b.   8,000 student names
    c.   400 colleges only
    d.   400 names and one college
    e.   One name and 400 colleges

10.5   How many characters are defined by the following WORKING-STORAGE SECTION entries?

```
01      AREA-1.
        03   FIELD-1  PIC 99.
        03   FIELD-2  PIC 9(5).
        03   FIELD-3 REDEFINES FIELD-2  PIC X(5).
        03   FIELD-4  PIC X(5).
01      AREA-2 REDEFINES AREA-1  PIC X(12).
```

10.6   If an unsuccessful search of a table is made during either the SEARCH or SEARCH ALL statement,
    a.   the program continues with the next sentence.
    b.   the program stops.
    c.   control passes to the statement indicated by AT END.
    d.   none of the above

10.7   Which of the following is true about the SEARCH ALL statement?
    a.   No initial setting of index names in the program is needed.
    b.   The table must be ordered.
    c.   If the search is unsuccessful the value of the final index is unpredictable.
    d.   all of the above

10.8   Given the description:

```
01      NUMBERS.
        05 FILLER              PIC X VALUE "A".
        05 FILLER              PIC X VALUE "B".
        05 FILLER              PIC X VALUE "C".
01      FILLER REDEFINES NUMBERS.
            05 TABLE OCCURS 3 TIMES.
                06 TABLE-ITEM     PIC X.
```

What value will TABLE-ITEM (3) have?

10.9   When accessing data from a table using the SEARCH verb, the SET command is used to:
    a.   increment the value of the index while searching the table.
    b.   initialize the table.
    c.   initialize the value of the index before a table lookup.

10.10   Given the description:

```
01 FISH-STORES.

    02 FILLER PIC X (10) VALUE "SLOBOK."
    02 FILLER PIC X (10) VALUE "SALMON."
    02 FILLER PIC X (10) VALUE "HALIBUT."
    01 FISHS REDEFINES FISH-STORES.
        02 FISHIES OCCURS 3  TIMES  PIC X (10).
```

What is the value of FISHIES (2)?

10.11   Given the descripton:

```
01 TABLEA.
    02 A-LABEL OCCURS 15 TIMES.
        03 ONE PIC 9.
        03 TWO PIC 9.
01 TABLEB.
    02 SCORE OCCURS 5 TIMES.
        03 BITS PIC 99 OCCURS 3 TIMES.
```

How many dimensions does TABLEA have? TABLEB?

10.12   Data-names defined under the OCCURS clause must always be subscripted or indexed when used in the PROCEDURE DIVISION of a COBOL program. True or false?

10.13   A subscripted variable in COBOL is restricted to a maximum of four subscripts. True or false?

10.14   Which of the following claims is (are) true?
        a.   A subscript may be a data item.
        b.   A subscript must be an integer.
        c.   A subscript may be a figurative constant.

10.15   When using the INDEXED BY option of the OCCURS clause, the index data-name must be defined in the WORKING STORAGE section. True or false?

10.16   Which option(s) are used with the SEARCH statement?
        a.   SET
        b.   INDEXED BY
        c.   PERFORM
        d.   WHEN

10.17   The REDEFINES clause is used to
        a.   process tables.
        b.   search tables.
        c.   initialize tables.
        d.   read tables.

10.18   A single binary SEARCH ALL statement
      a.   must include a KEY in the OCCURS clause.
      b.   may search multidimensional tables.
      c.   must follow a SET statement.
      d.   a and b

10.19   A subscript
      a.   may be zero.
      b.   may be negative.
      c.   may have a decimal point.
      d.   must be integer.

10.20   The SET statement may be used to:
      a.   decrement an index.
      b.   increment an index.
      c.   initialize an index.
      d.   all of the above

10.21   If the number of elements in a table is not known, the OCCURS clause is often used with the _____ option.

10.22   Tables are rarely used in business applications. True or false?

10.23   What are the data items in a table called?
      a.   table subunits
      b.   index pointers
      c.   sequence values
      d.   table elements

10.24   Tables may be used to:
      a.   perform data validation.
      b.   extend data.
      c.   create reports.
      d.   handle pricing.
      e.   a, b, and c
      f.   all of the above

10.25   COBOL only allows the programmer to use one- or two-dimensional tables. True or false?

10.26   Adding fields to a one-dimensional table increases the number of related elements within each occurrence. True or false?

10.27   The _____ phrase specifies the data items used to denote the sequence of table elements.
      a.   PICTURE IS
      b.   KEY IS
      c.   INDEX IS
      d.   ELEMENT IS

10.28   Tables must be _____ to be of use.
      a.   manipulated
      b.   two-dimensional
      c.   ascending
      d.   indexed
      e.   a and d
      f.   none of the above

10.29   Theoretically the dimensionality of tables can be extended forever. True or false?

10.30   The process of finding a specific entry in a table is known as:
    a.   searching.
    b.   sorting.
    c.   stepped-indexing.
    d.   calling.

10.31   In COBOL the programmer is not permitted to manually set the pointer location in an index. True or false?

10.32   The following statement is syntactically correct. True or false?

```
MOVE "JURISPRUDENCE" TO LAW-ITEM (3,4,2)(LEGAL-INDEX).
```

10.33   _____ tables result when multiple occurrences of a data item appear within one occurrence of a one-dimensional table entry.

10.34   Tables are defined and memory is allocated by using the _____ clause.

10.35   The _____ phrase allows the programmer to specify an identifier for pointing to a specific occurrence within a table.

10.36   A(n) _____ describes a sequence of consecutive memory locations having a common name.

10.37   A(n) _____ table is one in which sequence has no meaning.

10.38   The _____ option allows the programmer to specify tables of varying length.

10.39   A(n) _____ is used to locate single occurrences within a table.

10.40   The _____ clause allows the programmer to initialize the storage to the desired values.

10.41   The SEARCH ALL command conducts a(n) _____ on a(n) _____ table, whereas the SEARCH statements performs a sequential search on any table.

10.42   Repeating, ordered items are specified using the _____ or _____ KEY option.

10.43   Tables can be loaded from external files by using the _____ statement.

10.44   Of what use are tables to business applications programs?

10.45   How does the nature of data to be used in a table affect the design of the table? The program?

10.46   Code an indexed table that allows for the following: ABC Company wants to use an interactive system to handle customer orders over the phone. Access will be needed to the parts file which lists a part number, description, quantity on hand, reorder point, retail price, suppliers of the part (1 to 5) and a lead time for each supplier to determine delivery dates for customers who order backlogged items. The total number of part records varies due to frequent new additions made by the purchasing department, but is never more than 500. The parts file is kept in the order of part numbers, from low to high.

10.47   Code the modules that will load the previous table into the internal memory of a COBOL program.

11

DOCUMENTATION
AND MAINTENANCE

Two complementary tasks associated with programming that are not usually given the attention they deserve are documentation and maintenance. Not only are they viewed as necessary evils, but management policies often discriminate against such tasks. Certainly everyone agrees as to the need for good program documentation, but this assertion usually goes no further than the words avowing it. Maintenance is often assigned to naughty programmers or new initiates.

When programs are designed better to start with, the time exerted on documentation and maintenance is minimized. Through better design, documentation can be developed in conjunction with the system rather than as an afterthought. This facilitates the programming step since the program code is a derivative of the design documentation. If good design is an initial consideration, the effort expended on maintenance can be reduced, since there will be fewer errors in the resulting code.

11.1   *Documentation*

System documentation describes the information system from start to finish. During the system development life cycle, much information pertaining to the system is generated and collected. Unless this information is classified in an organized fashion, it is likely that the documentation will end up being filed in some dusty cabinet in the company's basement. Sometimes companies may go overboard and require that every single facet of the system from problem recognition to last rites be documented with volumes of worthless data. When every step in the process requires many completed forms, it is no wonder that programmers develop an aversion to this activity. Documentation becomes a tedious job left as the last step in each of the phases of the life cycle and, of course, when a system starts falling behind schedule, documentation is the first activity cut from the schedule.

This is not a desirable situation. Documentation is necessary to the future of an information system. It provides the reasoning behind the system, and as such is the most important factor in understanding the system, modifying it, and developing guidelines for developing new systems. A maintenance programmer who needs to modify existing programs should be able to refer to the documentation to understand its purpose, its context, and its impact. It is difficult at best to glean this information when only the source code is available. Since file descriptions, report layouts, hierarchy charts, and Nassi-Schneiderman charts are documents used to create a program, these same documents should be available when changing program code. Thus, documentation should be developed as the system evolves to aid in the design of the system as well as its maintenance.

Documents are tools for the programmer. If the documentation has been used in creating program code, it will reflect the code. In this chapter we will study some of the components and characteristics of good documentation that can help in the original creation of the program, are readily updated, and can support the maintenance phase of the system's life cycle.

11.1.1   *Identifying Good Documentation*

The major criterion for evaluating documentation is its need. Certain documents are always of value. For example, hierarchy charts and file layouts provide critical information to a programmer. Other documents vary in importance from one program to another. Programs need not be overdocumented. Overdocumentation requires programmer effort to develop and maintain. If too much is required, few or no changes will be made and soon even the needed documentation will become outdated. Rigid documentation regulations by a company are of benefit up to a point, but some judgment should be left to the analysts and programmers to identify the subset actually needed for each project and program.

A second criterion is the accuracy of the documentation. Documentation should promote an understanding of the system or program; inaccurate documentation only detracts from that understanding. This implies that a programmer should maintain the documentation so that it reflects any fixes and changes made to the program during coding or debugging. Often a programmer forgets to change the design documentation, such as an N-S chart, to reflect the correction, thus propagating an error. This is similar to neglecting to change the N-S charts during maintenance activities.

The third major criterion is targeting the documentation to the appropriate audience.

Eliminate computer jargon from the documentation as far as possible. When record layouts are described, give proper names and descriptions for each data element. Nassi-Schneiderman charts should specify the design logic, not the computer instructions needed for the program. A good test for determining this is to ask whether a noncomputer user could view the Nassi-Schneiderman charts and understand the process. Avoid language dependencies. There is nothing valuable in a Nassi-Schneiderman chart that follows the program code line by line with identical language. A Nassi-Schneiderman chart must describe the logical process of the program, not its syntactical structure. These distinctions are shown in Figure 11.1. The first Nassi-Schneiderman chart is logic-oriented; the other one is computer-oriented. Language-specific or code-oriented N-S charts are usually a sign that the chart was developed after the program was written!

Figure 11.1   Logic-and-Code-Oriented N-S Charts

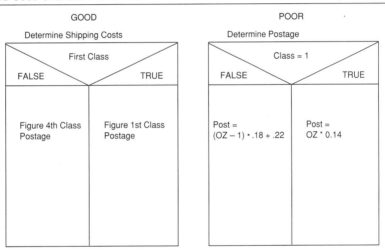

A fourth important criterion of good documentation is consistency. Data names should be standardized and documented to avoid using different names in the program for the same data item. Documentation forms should be used to maintain consistency. Not only do forms ensure similarity, they also save programmer effort, prod the programmer for the information required, and standardize the documents. The forms, therefore, aid in the understanding of the program. Furthermore, guidelines should be established to promote the consistent use of design methodologies. If flowcharts are used, all programmers should use identical boxes for the same functions. Likewise, module naming conventions and numbering standards should be established and followed on the hierarchy charts.

A final criterion of good documentation is availability. Several individuals work hard to produce the documentation for a program. It is a waste of their effort to provide inadequate facilities for distribution and storage. When a maintenance programmer requests the documentation for a program, it should be complete and available in one known location. Availability is also important in keeping documentation current since a programmer should be responsible for keeping the central source current.

Several common-sense practices also contribute to producing good documentation. One is to keep documentation neat. This does not mean that you have to typewrite every document or use computer aided document preparation. It does mean that you should use clear handwriting and avoid coffee stains. The proliferation of word processing systems makes their use in documentation very commonplace. Not only do they contribute to neatness, they also allow quick and easy changes to be made. Another practice is to label and date the program documents, including file layouts, report layouts, and source code. The date may help later to indicate which document reflects the most recent changes.

11.1.2   System Documentation

Documentation is developed and maintained throughout the system development life cycle. Certain documents, such as cost estimates, are not used by the programmer. However, other documents, such as the system dictionary and data flow diagrams, are used by the programmer as the specification requirements for each program.

The tools of documentation used by the analyst provide the programmer with exacting details on the function of each program. The programmer then uses the specifications to design and code each program. Many of the documentation methods used by analysts have been so fully developed that program design is a direct product of the system specifications. These methods are usually covered in system analysis and design courses.

11.1.3   Program Documentation

Even though the scope of this book covers the programming phase of the system development life cycle, remember that each phase is tied in to previous and succeeding phases. Thus, the specifications developed in the early phases are used to develop program documentation, whether they use functional decomposition or more rigid design methodologies. Also, the program documentation is used in program maintenance and so must be complete and available.

When program documentation is complete, it should be collected and stored in a central location with copies maintained off-site, in case of a disaster. A complete documentation package for a program can contain many different documents. Some of the more common ones are discussed below.

Cover Sheet. Maintenance programmers often do not have the time to investigate a complete set of documentation to understand the purposes and general function of a program. The *cover sheet* provides the programmer with an overview of the program on a single page. It should contain critical information about the program, including identification information, a brief description of the program's purpose, and a listing of required files. By reviewing the cover sheet, a programmer can more quickly locate a program that performs a particular function. Figure 11.2 shows a sample cover sheet.

Figure 11.2   Sample Program Cover Sheet

PROGRAM COVER SHEET

ID/TITLE _____

ORGANIZATION _____

                                                        NAME | DATE

_____   PREPARED BY _____

SYSTEM _____   REVIEWED BY _____

	DESCRIPTION OF PROGRAM	

FILES USED				
FILE NAME	MEDIA	ORGANIZATION	ACCESSING	I/O

Documentation Index. An index to the program documentation should be provided with each set of documentation. Preprinted index forms such as the one shown in Figure 11.3 help maintain documentation standards and ensure that a common order of documents is followed. If a particular document is not in the program's set, it may be crossed off the preprinted form. The main purpose of the documentation index is to indicate the documents actually included in the set. This alerts a programmer to the contents of the documentation package and to its completeness.

Figure 11.3   Sample Program Documentation Index

PROGRAM DOCUMENTATION INDEX

ID/TITLE _____

ORGANIZATION _____		NAME	DATE
_____	PREPARED BY _____		
SYSTEM _____	REVIEWED BY _____		

Program Documents

1. Cover Sheet

2. Document Index

3. System Flowchart

4. I/O Specifications

5. Program Summary

6. Report Layouts

7. Hierarchy Charts

8. Nassi-Schneiderman Charts

9. Error Messages

10. External Routines

11. Data Definition Summary

12. Test Plan

13. Listing

14. Change Requests

System Flowchart. A high-level system flowchart depicting input and output files used by a program should be included for each program. The symbols used identify the devices used for the files. For example, in Figure 11.4 the transaction file is on magnetic tape and the customer master file is on disk. The report is hard-copy printer output.

Figure 11.4   Sample Program Systems Flowchart

PROGRAM SYSTEM FLOWCHART

ID/TITLE _____

ORGANIZATION _____   NAME | DATE

_____   PREPARED BY _____

SYSTEM _____   REVIEWED BY _____

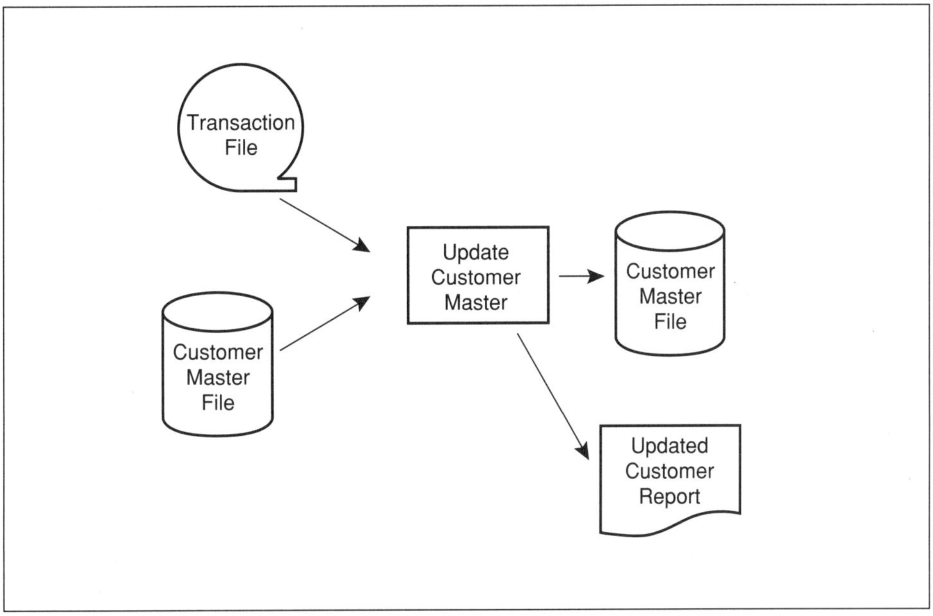

Although a complete system flowchart would show all the programs and files within the system, the system flowchart included as documentation for a program would only include the files affected or used by the program. Thus, the program's system flowchart demonstrates how the system components are affected by that particular program.

Input and Output Specifications. Before a program can be coded the files, records, and data items used as input to or output from the system must be completely specified. File description forms such as the one shown in Figure 11.5 can be used to communicate important structural information about files. It contains the information needed to code the ENVIRONMENT DIVISION, to identify all the records that may be present in that file, and to provide a cross listing to all the record types in the file. Record descriptions are some of the most important documents a programmer uses. Figure 11.6 shows a record layout form for specifying the order and descriptions of the fields within the record. These are required to code the FILE SECTION of a COBOL program. Data items within the records should be explicitly defined in a data element description form such as the one shown in Figure 11.7. However, data item descriptions are not necessary for many programs. In fact, it is often best to keep item descriptions in a central location as part of a comprehensive data item dictionary and to include them as part of the program documentation only for validation programs. The information provided in the data element description should include information about valid values for the items. These values are important for editing the data items. Cross-references serve to assess the impact that changes to data items have throughout the system and should be included in the form.

Program Summary. The written word is still an effective form of communication, and the original program specifications are generally given in narrative form. Throughout the text such *program narratives* have been specified on program summary forms such as the one in Figure 11.8. The program summary should be understandable by anyone and should provide a simple description of the program's purpose. As with all documents described to this point, the program summary should be developed by the analyst before a programmer is assigned to the specific program.

Figure 11.5   Sample File Description Form

FILE DESCRIPTION

PROGRAM ID _____

ORGANIZATION _____   NAME | DATE

_____   PREPARED BY _____|_____

SYSTEM _____   REVIEWED BY _____|

FILE NAME _____
CONTENT DESCRIPTION:
RECORDS CONTAINED IN FILE:
ORGANIZATION:
MEDIA:
KEY FIELD:
ACCESS MODE:
CONTROL AND UPDATE PROCEDURE
COMMENTS:

Figure 11.6   Sample Record Layout Form

RECORD LAYOUT SHEET

PROGRAM ID _____

Record Name:		File Name:			
Prepared By:		Date:			
Key Fields:		Organization:			
Field	Description		Type*	Length	Decimal

* A = alphanumeric
N = numeric

Figure 11.7   Sample Program Data Element Description Form

PROGRAM DATA ELEMENT DESCRIPTION

ID/TITLE _____

ORGANIZATION _____   NAME | DATE

_____   PREPARED BY _____|_____

SYSTEM _____   REVIEWED BY _____|_____

ELEMENT NAME	
ELEMENT ID	ELEMENT NUMBER

DEFINITION	
VALUES	SIZE

EDIT CRITERIA

CROSS-REFERENCES

COMMENTS

Figure 11.8   Sample Program Summary Form

PROGRAM SUMMARY
TITLE:
PREPARED BY:
DATE:

FILES USED		
FILE NAME	MEDIA	ORGANIZATION

DESCRIPTION_____

Report Layout. Also in the category of documents prepared prior to actual program design is the report layout. An example layout form is shown in Figure 11.9. The report layout describes the appearance of reports that a program should produce, whether hard copy or screen output.

Figure 11.9   ***Sample Report Layout Form***

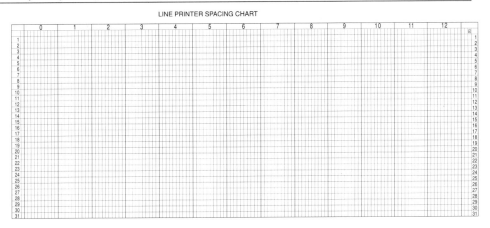

Hierarchy Charts. Hierarchy charts are a critical part of program documentation. A hierarchy chart is a working tool used to describe the structure of a program. As part of the documentation package, the hierarchy chart presents a brief overall view of the program.

Many companies have shifted to using structure charts other than hierarchy charts to represent the program structure. *Structure charts* are similar in appearance to hierarchy charts, but are more detailed. They display the passing of data between modules. This increase in detail reduces the need for detailed logic charts.

Nassi-Schneiderman Charts. Nassi-Schneiderman charts specify the program logic. They are a common development tool that a programmer uses to design a program prior to coding. Nassi-Schneiderman charts explain the sequence of operation and decision-making logic, that is, how and when things are done. Other logic representation tools, such as structured English and flowcharts, are often used in place of Nassi-Schneiderman charts. Each method has unique advantages.

As languages become more powerful, less detail may be required on the Nassi-Schneiderman charts, since several logical functions may be combined into a single program statement. Many organizations have also relaxed their standards on describing common, standard functions such as reading files. Reading a file is often a single module that does not vary by application. Therefore, the READ module Nassi-Schneiderman chart may be omitted from the program N-S charts. Such liberty should only be taken when permitted by the documentation standards of the organization, however.

Error Message Summary. Error messages presented to the user or computer operator should be specified in the early phases of the life cycle and should be included in the program specifications developed by the analyst. Other errors not specified by the analyst, such as ON

SIZE ERRORs for mathematical operations and AT END errors during searches should be identified during the development of the program flowcharts and documented in error message summaries. Figure 11.10 shows an error summary form to list all programmer-identified error conditions, the message displayed to the operator, and the course of action to be taken for each error.

Figure 11.10   Sample Program Error Summary Form

PROGRAM ERROR SUMMARY

ID/TITLE _____

ORGANIZATION _____   NAME | DATE

_____   PREPARED BY _____

SYSTEM _____   REVIEWED BY _____

ERROR MESSAGE	ACTION

External Routines. If a program uses subprograms, the *external routine* documentation should identify each subprogram called. An easy way of doing this is to include a copy of the cover sheet for each subprogram called. In this way, the external routine documentation can be collected as the needed routines are identified.

Internal Data Summary. Data items defined in the WORKING-STORAGE SECTION should also be documented in an *internal data summary*. The form used to describe data elements used for input and output, illustrated in Figure 11.7, could also be used to specify the meaning of each item in the WORKING-STORAGE SECTION and should be developed when the programmer is developing the WORKING-STORAGE SECTION. The more obvious items, such as report formats, require little explanation. Indicators and codes, however, often have uses not immediately evident to other programmers and require further explanation of their meaning and use. Descriptions of internal data, in contrast to input and output data, should form a part of the program's documentation rather than being centralized in a data dictionary.

Test Plan and Results. As we mentioned in the chapter on testing and debugging, a test data record should be created to test each branch and each condition in a program. The expected results must be determined. These test items should be placed in a checklist format similar to the one shown in Figure 11.11. Then when a test is run, the test items can be easily checked off. Each test run should be considered separately, since interactions caused by debugging changes are often unpredictable.

Program Listings. A complete current listing of each program should be included as part of the documentation package. This listing will save time during maintenance, since a programmer can begin to work immediately without having to wait for a listing to be produced. Furthermore, a listing including cross-references of data items and paragraphs provides helpful information about a program. Comments in the code that explain difficult algorithms greatly aid the programmer whose job it is to make corrections or changes.

Change Requests. Every change made to a program requires changes to the previous documentation so that it reflects the new code. To document the evolution of a program, each change should come on a formal request form similar to the one shown in Figure 11.12. By including *change requests* as part of the program documentation the history of the program is preserved. The superseded documentation should be attached to the change request. This facilitates backtracking to earlier versions if necessary. However, once a change is implemented, all documentation should be updated.

Figure 11.11   Sample Test Result Checklist

TEST RESULT CHECKLIST

ID/TITLE _____

ORGANIZATION _____

_____

SYSTEM _____

PREPARED BY _____

REVIEWED BY _____

	NAME	DATE

RECORD	RESULT	CORRECT (√)

Figure 11.12 Sample Program Change Request Form

PROGRAM CHANGE REQUEST

ID/TITLE _____

ORGANIZATION _____

	NAME	DATE
PREPARED BY _____		
REVIEWED BY _____		

_____

SYSTEM _____

REASON FOR CHANGE

DESCRIPTION OF CHANGE

DOCUMENTATION ATTACHED

CHANGES REQUIRED

ITEM	PERFORMED BY	DATE COMPLETED	ITEM	PERFORMED BY	DATE COMPLETED
☐ PROGRAM—————	———	———	☐ RUN INSTRUCTIONS ———	———	
☐ PROGRAM DOCUMENTATION	———	———	☐ USER PROCEDURES	———	
☐ FILE —————	———	———	☐	———	
☐ FILE DOCUMENTATION	———	———	☐	———	
☐ PRINTER LAYOUT	———	———	☐	———	
☐ DATA ELEMENT DICTIONARY	———	———	☐	———	
☐ TEST DATA & RUN	———	———	☐	———	

ASSIGNED TO: BEGIN DATE:

ESTIMATED COMPLETION TIME: COMPLETION DATE:

ESTIMATED COST: PRIORITY:

REQUESTED BY	DATE	CHANGED BY	DATE	APPROVED BY	DATE

11.1.4 *Automated Documentation*

Many documentation tools are currently available on-line. *Automated documentation* helps enforce many of the benefits of documentation while improving the productivity of the person developing the documentation. Automation enforces completeness and checks for accuracy. Input is restricted to maintain standards. When documentation resides on the computer it is available to more individuals. The documentation is easier to produce and maintain and is therefore more likely to be current. In essence, automated documentation achieves greater accuracy, completeness, standardization, availability, and productivity. Automated documentation for programming and other phases of the system development life cycle is often part of CASE (computer-assisted system engineering) packages available today.

11.2   *Maintenance*

In an earlier chapter we discussed maintenance in the context of the system development life cycle. Recall that *maintenance* arises to correct errors in the system, adapt a system to changes in the environment, and enhance the system. Program maintenance occupies a large portion of a programmer's effort as more and more systems go into production. As a matter of fact, the resources devoted to the maintenance of programs have already expanded beyond most expectations. In a way, this is encouraging because it indicates that the systems in production are worth keeping. It also indicates that programmers are likely to spend part of their careers making changes to someone else's code.

Errors that remain dormant in a system for years may surface when program thresholds are approached. For example, increases in the volume of data processed may cause tables to overflow. Program changes may result from factors in the external environment, such as changes in company policy, new tax laws, or mergers. Internal environment factors, such as new pricing structures or hardware acquisitions, may also cause the requirements of a program to change. Adding new functionality or improving the efficiency of programs dictate changes to existing programs. Thus, maintenance is a necessary, recurring process that has become a fact of life for today's programmers.

11.2.1 *Request the Change*

Changes should be initiated through a formal process on forms similar to the one shown in Figure 11.12. Changes initiate a life cycle of their own and the change requests identify the particular problem or enhancement desired of the system. A formal process for requisitioning changes minimizes the informal lines between user and programmer and reduces unauthorized changes. It is usually the unauthorized changes that result in outdated documentation and wasted programmer time.

The change request should identify the originator of the request and the description of the desired change. It should include a section detailing time and cost estimated to implement the change and should identify a projected initiation date, the programmer responsible for the change, and its priority. The user and the maintenance manager should sign off to confirm that both parties agree to the change. As the change is made, the programmer should record the actual effort expended. When the maintenance has been completed, the originator should sign off to indicate that the change has been implemented satisfactorily. The form should then be attached to the program documentation.

As stated above, a change initiates a miniature life cycle. Therefore, when the programming department receives a change request, it should be studied to determine the amount of effort and resources it will require. Any detrimental effects should also be noted. For example, if the change results from a change in the environment, an analysis of the environmental impact on the system should be conducted. If the change is an enhancement, a study should be made as to the impact and value of the enhancement, much as the impact and value of a new system is studied.

11.2.2 Prioritize the Requests

Many change requests are valid, needed, or desirable. Others are silly requests born of indifference, ignorance, triviality, or even malice. Thus, it is important that all changes be prioritized by a central authority. Certain changes deserve high priority. For example, a change in the payroll program due to tax law changes is a necessity. Others can be delayed. For example, changing the column alignment in an annual report is of low priority. Most, however, will fall between these extremes and should therefore be prioritized, usually based on a cost-benefit analysis.

11.2.3 Assign Responsibility

When a change request is approved, it should be assigned to a programmer familiar with the program. Companies often preassign programs to programmers for maintenance purposes. The responsible programmer should familiarize himself with the program by consulting the available documentation and if possible by talking to analysts, users, and operations personnel.

11.2.4 Perform Maintenance

Once assigned, the change must be documented, coded, and tested. Often the same test used in the original application may be used to test the change. It is important to retest the entire program and sometimes the entire system to ensure that the change implemented has no adverse effects on the unchanged portion. Remember, a change in one module can affect other modules that share data with the changed module.

11.2.5 Emergency Maintenance

Maintenance to correct errors does not come in a change request. Usually it takes the form of a phone call from bewildered operations personnel informing the programmer that the program "blew up" or from irate users complaining of garbage results. In this case, rather than having a formal request identify the desired change, the programmer identifies the problem and submits the change request.

In addition, error correction takes top priority. Furthermore, the responsibility for the system is well known to the programmer, the users, and the operations personnel. The programmer is usually placed "on call" when "his" program is run.

The maintenance required to correct errors is reduced to determining what caused the problem, correcting it, and testing it. This type of maintenance activity is similar to program development in that a programmer uses many of the same debugging techniques. Once the programmer has debugged the program, he must document whatever changes he made.

Case Study: CDL's List Inventory Quantity on Hand

Charlene instructed her system users on the procedure necessary to implement changes. Even before she had completed the system, Charlene received her first change request. It is shown in Figure 11.13. The request is a result of the need for a hard copy of the current number of CDs in stock. This will be used to verify customers' purchase requests and backlogged orders. The request represents an enhancement to the existing system. Fortunately, the listing can easily be generated from the CD-In-Stock Table. However, an entire new program must be added. Charlene treats the request as an addition to the system and develops the program documentation and code in Figures 11.14 through 11.22. The program test data and results are in Figure 11.23.

Figure 11.13   Change Request for CDL's "List Inventory QOH"

PROGRAM CHANGE REQUEST

ID/TITLE _Inventory List_

ORGANIZATION _CDL_

	NAME	DATE
PREPARED BY	F. Glover	9-13-93
REVIEWED BY		

SYSTEM _____

REASON FOR CHANGE   *When backlogged orders are processed there is no hard copy of the inventory to determine when an item is in stock*

DESCRIPTION OF CHANGE

Provide a daily listing of the items in stock for the backlog clerk to use to clear backlogged orders

DOCUMENTATION ATTACHED

CHANGES REQUIRED

ITEM	PERFORMED BY	DATE COMPLETED	ITEM	PERFORMED BY	DATE COMPLETED
☒ PROGRAM	CH	9-20-93	☐ RUN INSTRUCTIONS		
☒ PROGRAM DOCUMENTATION	CH	9-20-93	☐ USER PROCEDURES		
☐ FILE			☐		
☐ FILE DOCUMENTATION			☐		
☐ PRINTER LAYOUT			☐		
☐ DATA ELEMENT DICTIONARY			☐		
☒ TEST DATA & RUN	CH	9-20-93	☐		

ASSIGNED TO: *C. Hilton*   BEGIN DATE: *9-14-93*

ESTIMATED COMPLETION TIME: *5 days*   COMPLETION DATE: *9-25-93*

ESTIMATED COST: *$550*   PRIORITY: *Top*

F. Glover	9-13-93	C. Hilton	9-20-93	F. Glover	9-22-93
REQUESTED BY	DATE	CHANGED BY	DATE	APPROVED BY	DATE

Figure 11.14   Cover Sheet for CDL's "List Inventory QOH" Program

---

PROGRAM COVER SHEET

ID/TITLE   *List-Inventory-QOH*

ORGANIZATION   *CDL*

SYSTEM   *Inventory*

	NAME	DATE
PREPARED BY	*C. Hilton*	*9-15-93*
REVIEWED BY	*C. Hilton*	*9-15-93*

	DESCRIPTION OF PROGRAM	
	Provide a daily listing of the Quantity On Hand table.	

FILES USED				
FILE NAME	MEDIA	ORGANIZATION	ACCESSING	I/O
QOH - List	*Printer*	*Sequential*	—	*Output*
Compact disc stock table	*Disk*	*Sequential*	*Sequential*	*Input*

Figure 11.15   Documentation Index for CDL's "List Inventory QOH" Program

PROGRAM COVER SHEET

ID/TITLE *List-Inventory-QOH*

	NAME	DATE
ORGANIZATION *CDL*		
PREPARED BY *C. Hilton*	*9-15-93*	
SYSTEM *Inventory* REVIEWED BY		

Program Documents

1. Cover Sheet

2. Document Index

3. System Flowchart

4. I/O Specifications

5. Program Summary

6. Report Layouts

7. Hierarchy Charts

8. Nassi-Schneiderman Charts

9. Listing

10. Change Requests

Figure 11.16   System Flowchart for CDL's "List Inventory QOH" Program

PROGRAM COVER SHEET

ID/TITLE __List-Inventory-QOH__

ORGANIZATION __CDC__

	NAME	DATE
PREPARED BY	C. Hilton	9-15-93
REVIEWED BY		

SYSTEM _____

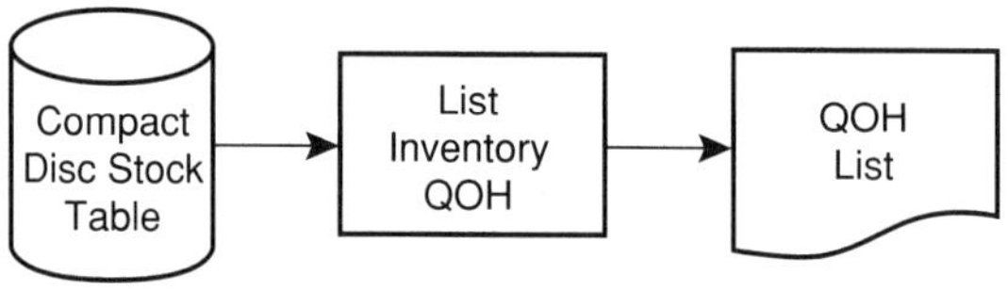

Figure 11.17   Layout Sheet for CDL's CD Stock Table Record

RECORD LAYOUT SHEET

Record Name: *CD Stock*		File Name: *Compact Disc Stock Table*		
Prepared By: *C. Hilton*		Date: *7-7-93*		
Key Fields:		Organization: *Sequential*		
Field	Description	Type*	Length	Decimal
Disc number	*A unique stock number*	*N*	*6*	*0*
Price	*Price of an item*	*N*	*6*	*2*
Quantity	*Quantity on hand*	*N*	*4*	

* A = alphanumeric
N = numeric

Figure 11.18   Program Summary for CDL's "List Inventory QOH" Program

PROGRAM SUMMARY
TITLE: *List-Inventory-QOH*
PREPARED BY: *C. Hilton*
DATE: *9-15-93*

FILES USED

FILE NAME	MEDIA	ORGANIZATION

DESCRIPTION

Provide a listing of the quantity on hand for each item in stock. This must be generated daily.

Figure 11.19   Report Layout for CDL's "List Inventory QOH" Program

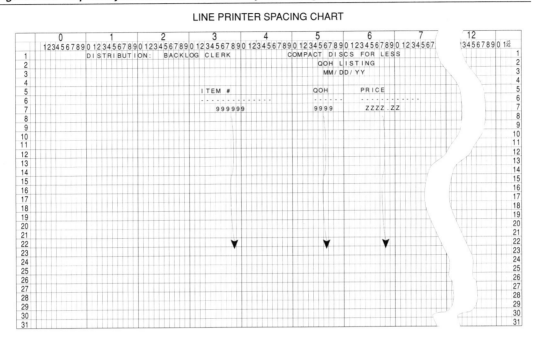

Figure 11.20   Hierarchy Chart for CDL's "List Inventory QOH" Program

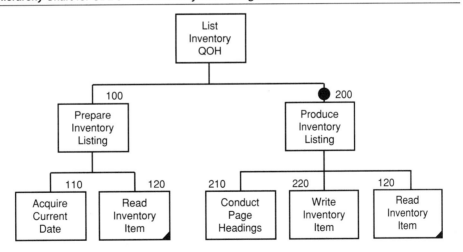

Figure 11.21   N-S Charts for CDL's "List Inventory QOH" Program

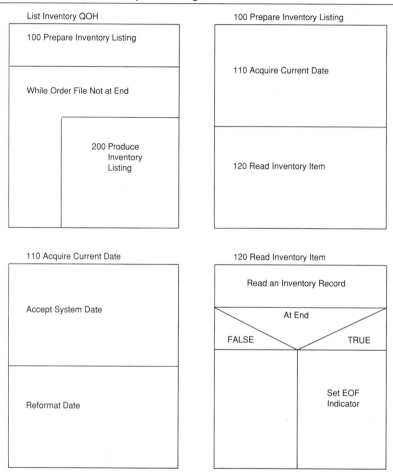

Figure 11.21   (continued)

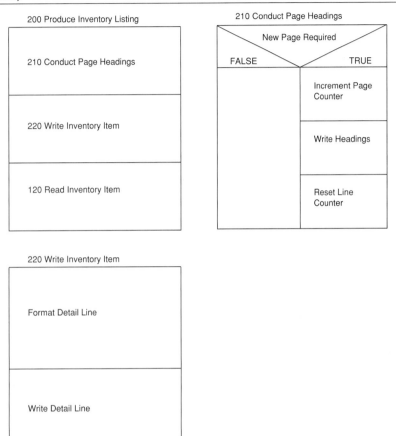

Figure 11.22   CDL's "List Inventory QOH" Program Code

```
 1 IDENTIFICATION DIVISION.
 2 PROGRAM-ID.  LIST-QOH.
 3*      THE DISK IN STOCK TABLE IS LISTED FOR THE BACKLOG CLERK
 4
 5 AUTHOR.          C HILTON
 6 DATE-WRITTEN.    9-17-93.
 7 DATE-COMPILED. 02-Feb-90 00:49.
11 ENVIRONMENT DIVISION.
12
```

Figure 11.22   (continued)

```
13
14 CONFIGURATION SECTION.
15
16 SOURCE-COMPUTER.   GENERIC-COMPUTER.
17 OBJECT-COMPUTER.   GENERIC-COMPUTER.
18
19
20 INPUT-OUTPUT SECTION.
21
22 FILE-CONTROL.
23     SELECT QOH-LISTING-FILE ASSIGN TO DISK
24         ORGANIZATION IS SEQUENTIAL.
25     SELECT COMPACT-DISC-STOCK-TABLE-FILE ASSIGN TO DISK
26         ORGANIZATION IS SEQUENTIAL.
27
28
29
30 DATA DIVISION.
31
32
33 FILE SECTION.
34
35 FD   QOH-LISTING-FILE
36      LABEL RECORDS ARE OMITTED.
37
38 01   QUANTITY-ON-HAND-RECORD PIC X(80).
39
40 FD   COMPACT-DISC-STOCK-TABLE-FILE
41      LABEL RECORDS ARE STANDARD.
42
43 01   CD-STOCK-RECORD.
44      05   CD-DISC-NUMBER PIC 9(6).
45      05   CD-PRICE        PIC 9(4)V99.
46      05   CD-QOH          PIC 9999.
47
48
49 WORKING-STORAGE SECTION.
50
51 01   WS-COUNTERS.
52      05   WS-LINE          PIC 99  VALUE 99.
53      05   WS-PAGE          PIC 999 VALUE ZERO.
54      05   WS-DATE          PIC 9(6).
```

Figure 11.22   (continued)

```
55      05  WS-MM-DD-YY.
56          10  WS-MM       PIC XX.
57          10  WS-DD       PIC XX.
58          10  WS-YY       PIC XX.
59      05  WS-YEAR         PIC XX.
60
61 01   INDICATORS.
62      05  EOF-CD-TABLE    PIC X(5) VALUE "FALSE".
63      05  MAX-LINE        PIC 99   VALUE 55.
64
65 01   COMPACT-DISC-QOH.
66      05  CDQ-REPORT-TITLE.
67          10  FILLER      PIC X(10) VALUE SPACES.
68          10  FILLER      PIC X(39) VALUE
69              "DISTRIBUTION: BACKLOG CLERK".
70          10  FILLER      PIC X(35) VALUE
71              "COMPACT DISCS FOR LESS".
72          10  FILLER      PIC X(5)  VALUE "PAGE".
73          10  CDQ-PAGE    PIC ZZ9.
74      05  CDQ-REPORT-NAME.
75          10  FILLER      PIC X(55) VALUE SPACE.
76          10  FILLER      PIC X(35) VALUE "QOH LISTING".
77      05  CDQ-RUN-DATE.
78          10  FILLER      PIC X(56) VALUE SPACE.
79          10  CDQ-DATE    PIC 99/99/99.
80      05  CDQ-COLUMNS.
81          10  FILLER      PIC X(32) VALUE SPACE.
82          10  FILLER      PIC X(22) VALUE "ITEM NUMBER".
83          10  FILLER      PIC X(9) VALUE "QOH".
84          10  FILLER      PIC X(5)  VALUE "PRICE".
85      05  CDQ-UNDERLINE.
86          10  FILLER      PIC X(32) VALUE SPACE.
87          10  FILLER      PIC X(22) VALUE "————".
88          10  FILLER      PIC X(9) VALUE "——".
89          10  FILLER      PIC X(12) VALUE "———".
90      05  CDQ-DETAIL.
91          10  FILLER         PIC X(35)  VALUE SPACE.
92          10  CDQ-ITEM-NUMBER PIC 9(6).
93          10  FILLER         PIC X(12) VALUE SPACE.
94          10  CDQ-QOH        PIC 9(4).
95          10  FILLER         PIC X(6)  VALUE SPACE.
96          10  CDQ-PRICE      PIC ZZZZ.ZZ.
```

Figure 11.22   (continued)

```
 97
 98
 99
100 PROCEDURE DIVISION.
101
102 LIST-INVENTORY-QOH.
103     OPEN INPUT COMPACT-DISC-STOCK-TABLE-FILE.
104     OPEN OUTPUT QOH-LISTING-FILE.
105     PERFORM 100-PREPARE-INVENTORY-LISTING.
106     PERFORM 200-PRODUCE-INVENTORY-LISTING
107         UNTIL EOF-CD-TABLE = "TRUE".
108     CLOSE QOH-LISTING-FILE.
109     CLOSE COMPACT-DISC-STOCK-TABLE-FILE.
110     STOP RUN.
111
112 100-PREPARE-INVENTORY-LISTING.
113     PERFORM 110-ACQUIRE-CURRENT-DATE.
114     PERFORM 120-READ-INVENTORY-ITEM.
115
116 110-ACQUIRE-CURRENT-DATE.
117     ACCEPT WS-DATE FROM DATE.
118     MOVE WS-DATE TO WS-MM-DD-YY.
119     MOVE WS-MM TO WS-YEAR.
120     MOVE WS-DD TO WS-MM.
121     MOVE WS-YY TO WS-DD.
122     MOVE WS-YEAR TO WS-YY.
123     MOVE WS-DATE TO CDQ-DATE.
124
125 120-READ-INVENTORY-ITEM.
126     READ COMPACT-DISC-STOCK-TABLE-FILE
127         AT END MOVE "TRUE" TO EOF-CD-TABLE.
128
129 200-PRODUCE-INVENTORY-LISTING.
130     PERFORM 210-CONDUCT-PAGE-HEADINGS.
131     PERFORM 220-WRITE-INVENTORY-ITEM.
132     PERFORM 120-READ-INVENTORY-ITEM.
133
134 210-CONDUCT-PAGE-HEADINGS.
135     IF WS-LINE IS LESS THAN MAX-LINE
136         ADD 1 TO WS-LINE
137     ELSE
138         ADD 1 TO WS-PAGE
```

Figure 11.22   (continued)

```
139          MOVE WS-PAGE TO CDQ-PAGE
140          WRITE QUANTITY-ON-HAND-RECORD FROM CDQ-REPORT-TITLE
141             AFTER ADVANCING PAGE
142          WRITE QUANTITY-ON-HAND-RECORD FROM CDQ-REPORT-NAME
143          WRITE QUANTITY-ON-HAND-RECORD FROM CDQ-RUN-DATE
144          WRITE QUANTITY-ON-HAND-RECORD FROM CDQ-COLUMNS
145             AFTER ADVANCING 3 LINES
146          WRITE QUANTITY-ON-HAND-RECORD FROM CDQ-UNDERLINE
147          MOVE SPACE TO QUANTITY-ON-HAND-RECORD
148          WRITE QUANTITY-ON-HAND-RECORD
149          MOVE 8 TO WS-LINE.
150
151 220-WRITE-INVENTORY-ITEM.
152     MOVE CD-DISC-NUMBER TO CDQ-ITEM-NUMBER.
153     MOVE CD-QOH        TO CDQ-QOH.
154     MOVE CD-PRICE      TO CDQ-PRICE.
155     WRITE QUANTITY-ON-HAND-RECORD FROM CDQ-DETAIL.
```

Figure 11.23   Test of "List Inventory QOH" Program

```
The CD TABLE:

1234560009991000
2345670010000000
3456780024990233



The REPORT:

        DISTRIBUTION: BACKLOG CLERK              COMPACT DISCS FOR LESS
                                                       QOH LISTING
                                                        90/02/02




                          ITEM NUMBER              QOH        PRICE
                          _____              ___        _____


                             123456               1000         9.99
                             234567               0000        10.00
                             345678               0233        24.99
```

Summary

Documentation and maintenance are two critical but often overlooked tasks related to programming. Documentation describes the program in complete terms. Maintenance changes the programs to correct bugs, adapt programs to new environments, or make improvements in existing programs.

Good documentation includes all the information needed to design, code, test, and maintain a program. Documentation should promote an understanding of the system or program. Some criteria of good documentation include accuracy, appropriateness, consistency, and availability. Documentation should reflect the actual status of a program. It should describe the system and the program to the appropriate audience, avoiding "computerese" and hardware and software dependencies. Consistency in documentation can be promoted through use of standardized forms, names, and numbering schemes. Availability of documentation can be ensured by keeping it complete and centrally located.

Maintenance is a phase in the systems development life cycle. Maintenance arises to correct errors in the system, to adapt a system to changes in its environment, and to enhance the system. Some errors may appear once a system is in production. They may result from system limitations, improper testing, or certain combinations of factors not tested or foreseen. Maintenance may result from external factors, internal policy changes, or changes in the hardware-software environment. Enhancements to a system may add new functionality or improve efficiency. Maintenance should follow formal change procedures in order to control the process. This forces priorities to be assigned to authorized changes, documents their cost and benefits,, and reduces needless or low-priority changes. Changes are approved, prioritized, assigned to a programmer, performed, and implemented. Errors should be afforded emergency maintenance, bypassing more formal change procedures that might be in place.

Key Terms

cover sheet	external routine	automated documentation
program narratives	internal data summary	maintenance
structure chart	change request	

Hints for Avoiding Errors

1. Before you design a program be certain that you have all the relevant documentation. Missing documents may cause you to make improper assumptions about the procedures involved.
2. Complete the design documentation before you code. Often when filling out a particular form, you are struck by an inconsistency that would have been a program bug.
3. When your program is completed, verify that your documentation is current. This will help you track down errors that become evident after the program is in production.

Exercises

11.1	Develop a complete documentation package for any one of your class assignments.
11.2	Since COBOL is a self-documenting language, the listing of the program itself is sufficient documentation. True or false?
11.3	Which is not a good program documentation tool?

       a.   system flowchart
       b.   current report layout
       c.   code-oriented flowchart
       d.   standardized change request

11.4   Structure charts are often used in place of
       a.   system flowcharts.
       b.   hierarchy charts.
       c.   program listings.
       d.   data flow diagrams.

11.5   Data items used by a single program and defined in WORKING-STORAGE should appear in _____.
       a.   an internal data summary.
       b.   an external routine document.
       c.   a change request.
       d.   no documentation except the program listing.

11.6   Maintenance does not arise from
       a.   an informal request from a user.
       b.   changes in the operating environment.
       c.   enhancements to a system.
       d.   errors in the system.

11.7   Approved program changes are
       a.   done immediately.
       b.   completed in the order received.
       c.   prioritized.
       d.   forgotten.

11.8   The major criterion for evaluating documentation is its _____.
       a.   image
       b.   need
       c.   history
       d.   content

11.9   Documentation is not concerned with promoting an understanding of the system or program. True or false?

11.10   An N-S flowchart must describe the logical process of the program. True or false?

11.11   Documentation is a tool for the programmer. True or false?

11.12   Documentation used to create programs should be:
       a.   technical.
       b.   scarce.
       c.   rigid.
       d.   accurate.

11.13   A _____ flowchart depicts input and output files to be used by a program and their related media devices.
    a.   hierarchy
    b.   unruled
    c.   system
    d.   indexed

11.14   Record descriptions are some of the least important documents a programmer may use. True or false?

11.15   A _____ is used to ascertain the structure of a program.
    a.   hierarchy chart
    b.   systems flowchart
    c.   program narrative
    d.   documentation index

11.16   The program narrative explains the sequence of operations and decision-making logic. True or false?

11.17   A complete current _____ of each program should be included as part of the documentation process.
    a.   dump
    b.   listing
    c.   snapshot
    d.   trace file

11.18   Maintenance is a recurring process. True or false?

11.19   A change indicates a _____ systems life cycle.
    a.   miniature
    b.   growing
    c.   fluctuating
    d.   different

11.20   A change in one module can never affect other modules that share data. True or false?

11.21   Flowcharts that contain "computer jargon" or computer instructions are said to be _____.

11.22   _____ is an important reason for keeping documentation current and in a central source location.

11.23   Using a(n) _____ may help later to indicate which documents reflect the most recent changes.

11.24   _____ documentation includes data flow diagrams, cost estimates, time reports, and feasibility reports.

11.25   The _____ _____ describes the appearances of reports a program should produce.

11.26   To document the evolution of a program, each _____ should come on a formal request form.

11.27   _____ may remain dormant in a system for years.

11.28   Changes in the _____ include new tax laws, mergers, and changes in company policy.

11.29   System _____ also include maintenance activities such as adding new functionality or improving efficiency.

11.30 How does documentation support the maintenance phase of the system development life cycle?

11.31 What is the importance of targeting documentation to an appropriate audience?

11.32 List examples of how to keep documentation consistent.

11.33 Name 9 of the 14 elements that should comprise a complete documentation package for a program.

11.34 Explain how an error message summary could be an effective documentation tool for an end-user.

12

MORE ON MODULARITY

The principal goal of structured design is to segment a system or a program into functional modules. This concept is known as *modularity*. It implies that program tasks are divided into well-defined segments each of which has a single, problem-related function and is therefore as independent of other modules as possible. Segregating tasks into modules leads to program designs that are easy to develop, enhance, and modify. But how do we judge modularity? It is one thing to preach, even to illustrate, the benefits of modular programs. Certainly there must be some measures that gauge how well a program's design conforms to structured design principles. In this chapter we discuss some of these measures and introduce subprograms as a method for enhancing modularity in COBOL programs.

12.1   *Evaluating Program Modularity*

Several criteria have been proposed for evaluating the quality of a program's design. Among them are more formal measures of program modularity, a key aspect of good design. These include the principles of coupling and cohesion that evaluate the decomposition of a program. Other measures of program design include span of control and scope of effect/scope of control, which assess a program's design using the hierarchy chart.

12.1.1   *Coupling*

Coupling evaluates module independence. It measures the strength of association among modules by examining the interaction or communication among them. Coupling analyzes a program decomposition to determine how well modules work apart. Good program design strives to minimize coupling, that is, to keep to a minimum the communication among modules. Modules that are "loosely coupled" exhibit a high degree of independence because the functions they represent do not depend on data from other modules. This independence reduces testing, debugging, and maintenance efforts. A programmer can concentrate on a single module without worrying about the functions that other modules perform.

Coupling is divided into different types with varying levels of severity. Figure 12.1 identifies data coupling, stamp coupling, control coupling, common coupling, and content coupling, ranging from low to high levels of coupling. The type of coupling can be determined by each relationship between modules. The basis for evaluating the degree of coupling in a program design is the hierarchy chart. Figure 12.2 illustrates the hierarchy chart for a company payroll program. Arrows represent the communication between modules and indicate the type of data being passed. A filled-in circle at the end of an arrow indicates an indicator or switch. An open circle at the end represents data. The direction of the arrow shows the direction of flow; that is, the circle represents the sender and the arrowhead the receiver.

Figure 12.1   Levels of Coupling

	Coupling	Definition
Low (Most Desirable)	Data	Only required data items are given to modules
	Stamp	Entire data structures are given to modules
	Control	Indicators that control program execution are passed among modules
	Common	All modules have access to a set of data
High (Least Desirable)	Content	Control is transferred or refers to the interior of another module

Figure 12.2   Examples of Coupling

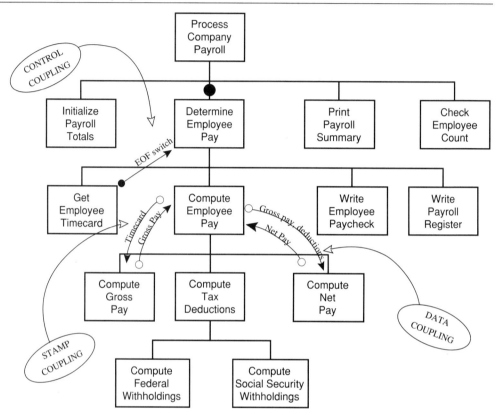

Data coupling, the passing of required data from one module to another, is illustrated in Figure 12.2 between modules "Compute Employee Pay" and "Compute Net Pay." In this case the higher-level module passes the gross pay and deduction data required by the lower-level module to compute the new pay. The subordinate module returns the value of the net pay to its superior module. Note that only the required data are passed. Data coupling is present in all programs because modules necessarily act on data.

Stamp coupling results when entire data structures such as records are passed between modules even though only a portion of the data structure is required. In Figure 12.2, the module "Compute Gross Pay" requires only the hours worked and the hourly salary to compute gross pay, but the superior module, "Compute Employee Pay," passes the entire timecard data. These data probably contain extra information such as employee name and department number that are unnecessary to the calculation. Stamp coupling permits modules to work on irrelevant data items, thus increasing the chances of program bugs and making it more difficult to find errors.

Two modules exhibit control coupling if a data item such as an indicator or flag intended to control the flow of execution of the program is passed. A common example of control coupling is shown in Figure 12.2 between the modules "Determine Employee Pay" and "Get Employee Timecard." The subordinate module sets a switch when the timecard file is empty to indicate that the end of the file has been reached. The end-of-file condition is then tested in the superior module to determine whether execution should proceed. Although control coupling occurs in many programs because of the physical nature of files, it should be kept to a minimum. An error in one module affects the performance of the module to which it is control coupled, thus making the program hard to debug and maintain.

In common coupling different modules can reference the same data items. With common coupling if an error is found in a data item, it is hard to determine what module caused the error since it could have occurred anywhere in the program. Furthermore, the impact of changing a data item during maintenance has to be traced through the entire program for possible undesirable effects rather than being confined to an identifiable module.

The COBOL language is inherently common-coupled because every paragraph in a program can access all the data items defined in the program's DATA DIVISION. Other languages allow the programmer to specify global and local variables in a program, thus eliminating common coupling. Global data are available throughout the program for use by any module. Local data are available only to the module where they are defined or to the modules to which the data are expressly communicated. While global data decrease the need for passing data between modules, they also allow any module to access them, thus increasing the probability of corrupting the data. If a programming language permits it, the programmer should define variables in a local fashion and pass only the data required by subordinate or superior modules. In COBOL the use of subprograms can diminish much language-dependent coupling.

Content coupling occurs when one module branches into the middle of a second module. Content coupling violates the single entry/single exit rule of structured programming and is easy to avoid by using structured programming techniques.

Coupling increases as the amount of data generated by one module but required by others increases. It is impossible to structure a program in which the modules are completely independent of each other. Data cannot be spontaneously generated as required by each module. Therefore, data may often be originated by one module, acted on by some, and reported by others. When data must be communicated between modules, it should be only between subordinates and superiors. The amount of data that has to be communicated between modules should be a minimal as possible because as intermodule data requirements increase, so does intermodule dependency.

12.1.2   *Cohesion*

Another criterion for evaluating functional decomposition and therefore a program's modularity is cohesion. *Cohesion* measures how well each module complies with its singleness of purpose, how strongly the elements of a single module relate to the completion of a single task. In the best case only one task is performed by a module, and all its component elements are directed toward accomplishing that task. Well-decomposed program designs exhibit high cohesion.

As with coupling, different types of cohesion exist displaying differing levels of severity. Figure 12.3 summarizes each type and provides examples of modules that fall within each category. The levels of cohesion are ordered from high to low, with the most desirable type of cohesion at the top and the least desirable at the bottom. We will see that this relates directly to a module's ease of maintainability. The basic tool for evaluating cohesion of program design is the hierarchy chart.

Figure 12.3   Levels of Cohesion

Cohesion	Definition	Sample Tasks
Functional	One and only one task is perfomed in the module.	Compute area of a triangle.
Sequential	The output from one task in the module is required to proceed with the next task.	Pick up exam. Read exam questions. Answer questions.
Communicational	All tasks in the module work with the same data.	Find shoe color. Find shoe size. Find shoe price.
Procedural	All tasks must be performed in a certain order, but they do not use the same data.	Find the bucket. Put soap in bucket. Fill bucket with water. Wash car.
Temporal	Tasks are related only by their approximate time of execution.	Brush teeth. Shower. Shave. Feed the dog.
Logical	Tasks are of the same general function.	Write mom. Write cousin Fred. Write a fan letter.
Coincidental	No meaningful relation from one task to another.	Wake up. Hunt for a job. Buy a Porsche.

High (most desirable)

↓

Low (least desirable)

A module exhibits *functional cohesion* if all its component elements contribute to the accomplishment of one and only one function. Functionally, cohesive modules are easy to maintain and debug because their function is easily identified and their logic involves only one task. The hierarchy chart in Figure 12.4 shows modules that exhibit functional cohesion. Note that each module performs a unique, complete task.

Figure 12.4   Functional Cohesion

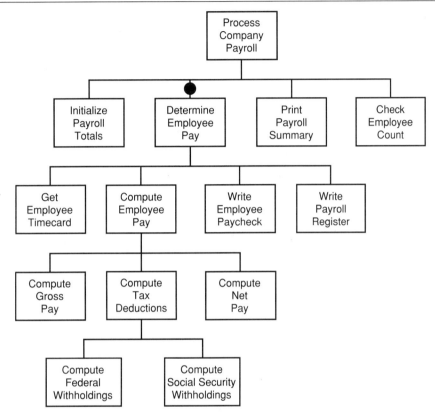

A module is *sequentially cohesive* if the output from one of its component tasks is the input to the next component task in the module. For example, the module "Write Net Pay to Check" in the revised payroll hierarchy chart in Figure 12.5 is sequentially cohesive. It includes two tasks to accomplish its function: calculating the net pay and printing the check, and the output from the first task is input to the second task. The accumulation of multiple tasks within the same module increases the difficulty of coding, testing, debugging, and maintenance.

Figure 12.5   Sequential Cohesion

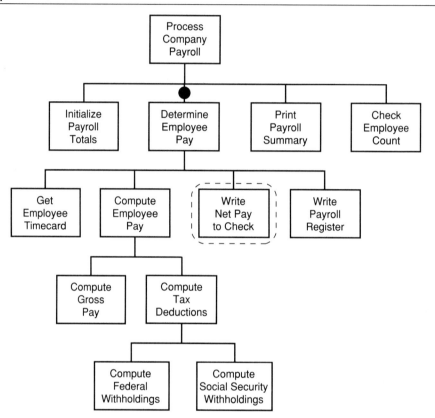

In *communicational cohesion* a module contains component tasks that work on the same data items. The module "Compute Tax Deductions" in the hierarchy chart in Figure 12.6 is communicationally cohesive. It has been modified to compute both social security and federal income tax withholdings. Although these computations can be performed in any order, both tasks require the same data item: gross pay.

Figure 12.6   *Communicational Cohesion*

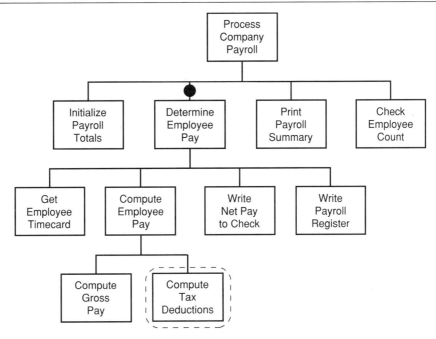

A module with *procedural cohesion* may be identified by noting that the flow of control passes from one component task in a module to the next task, although these tasks perform different activities. For example, a module that accumulates totals and acquires input is procedurally cohesive. The tasks are related only by the order in which they are carried out. One of the problems with procedurally cohesive modules is that the tasks may not all work on the same data. Thus if a data item is in error, it is difficult to locate it. In Figure 12.7 the module "Determine Gross Pay" illustrates procedural cohesion. The module tasks are to read the payroll record, compute the gross pay, and accumulate payroll totals.

Figure 12.7   Procedural Cohesion

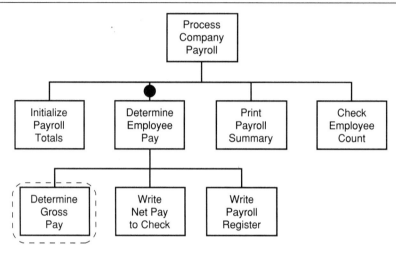

Temporal cohesion occurs when the tasks within a module are related by time. Modules that initialize variables at the beginning of a program are temporally cohesive modules, as are modules that prepare and print report summaries at the end. Temporally cohesive modules often combine too many unrelated tasks. This can cause problems when one is trying to locate a specific task within the program. In the hierarchy chart in Figure 12.8 the module "Terminate Process" exemplifies temporal cohesion. It consists of the tasks of producing a report summary and testing counts for end-of-program processing.

Figure 12.8   Temporal Cohesion

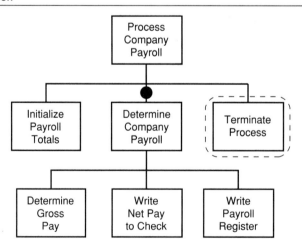

A module exhibits *logical cohesion* if it contains tasks of a similar nature, the selection of which depends on some action outside the module. For example, placing all program input and output tasks into a single module results in logical cohesion. The tasks are of the same type, but only one of them will be selected at any one time. Logical cohesion allows the sharing of constants, variables, and buffers, thus lowering memory requirements, but it often complicates the program code. Furthermore, a logically cohesive system tends to be inflexible. In the hierarchy chart in Figure 12.9 the module "Write Paychecks and Register" demonstrates logical cohesion because writing the paycheck and writing the payroll register are write functions combined in the same module. Should changes to the payroll register ever be required, the programmer will be unsure about whether he is making the changes to the register or to the paychecks.

Figure 12.9   *Logical Cohesion*

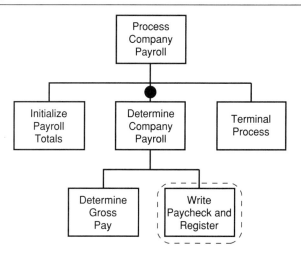

The worst level of cohesion is *coincidental cohesion*. Its existence in a module implies that the grouping of tasks within the module was indiscriminate. The hierarchy chart in Figure 12.10 contains a module with coincidental cohesion. A mixture of seemingly unrelated tasks has been grouped in a single module. They do not perform one well-defined function. The difficulty of coding, testing, debugging, and maintaining such a module should be evident.

Figure 12.10   *Coincidental Cohesion*

Process a Few
Accounting
Jobs

Coupling and cohesion evaluate a program design by examining the resultant decomposition. If we achieve the goal of segmenting a program into manageable modules, the program should exhibit a high level of cohesion. Cohesion seems to improve as the number of modules increases. However, as the number of modules increases, the communication between modules increases and coupling increases since there are more modules among which to pass data. Thus coupling and cohesion are opposing measures of functional decomposition, and the designer has to make trade-offs between them. In general, cohesion is considered to be the more critical measure.

12.1.3   Span of Control

The *span of control* of a module refers to the number of subordinates it has. In a company, managers are not required to supervise more individuals than they can reasonably handle. Conversely, managers are not usually needed for situations in which there is only one subordinate. In a program the concept is the same. It is not advisable to place too many modules subordinate to a controlling module because the program logic will be too long and difficult to follow. Neither is there much purpose in segmenting a module into one subordinate module. An important exception is in input and output operations where it is advisable to place each statement in a separate paragraph. An appropriate span of control ranges from two to five modules. It is possible, however, that in certain situations involving classifications up to nine subordinates are appropriate before becoming too complex. One example might be a transaction processing module in which there is one subordinate module for each type of transaction.

12.1.4   Scope of Effect and Scope of Control

The *scope of effect* of a module includes those modules that are affected by a decision made within that module. A module that sets a switch referenced by another module necessarily affects the second module regardless of its position in the hierarchy. The second module is said to be in the scope of effect of the first module. In Figure 12.2 module "Get Employee Timecard" sets an end-of file switch that is used by module "Determine Employee Pay" to control the execution of the other modules. In other words, module "Determine Employee Pay" is in the scope of effect of module "Get Employee Timecard."

The *scope of control* of a module includes not only itself but also all its subordinate modules at all levels of the hierarchy. Thus in Figure 12.2 the scope of control of module "Compute Tax Deductions" is three since it includes "Compute Tax Deductions," "Compute Federal Withholdings," and "Compute Social Security Withholdings." All modules in the hierarchy chart fall within the scope of control of the top module, "Process Company Payroll." In a well-designed program a module's scope of effect should be contained within the module's scope of control. Some exceptions do occur, however, because certain conditions affect the processing within a program. A notable example is the end-of-file indicator.

Other criteria for evaluating a program's design generally specify desirable features of the design. *Understandability* attempts to measure the level of complexity within a module. *Ease of coding* tries to measure how directly the design indicates the required code. *Accuracy* judges whether the proper lines of control are shown in the hierarchy chart. *Completeness* ventures to assess whether all modules are specified. Because these principles are rather subjective when applied as evaluators, they often serve better as guidelines than as measures of good design.

12.1.5   Segmenting Programming Tasks

In light of the above discussion, modularity is a measurable design goal that is highly desirable because it promotes ease of programming, testing, debugging, and maintenance. However, modularity has additional benefits. As programs grow larger and more complex, modular program design allows different programmers to work on different modules of the same program. If the design is truly modular, each programmer need not be concerned about the progress of the others. This permits programmers of differing levels of expertise to tackle modules of varying complexity. Furthermore, the overlapping development of modules greatly contributes to a decrease in total development time as measured from start to finish. In larger projects, such parallel development of the parts of a system is standard procedure.

Another advantage of modularity concerns programs in which certain tasks appear more than once in the program or, for that matter, in a business information system. Duplicating these repetitive tasks wastes programmer effort. Rather than completely rewriting each task every time it is needed, such effort could be saved by having the needed module already available. That way, a programmer could access the required module from his program to perform the desired task. If many such modules were available, there would be substantial savings in lines of new code. The advantage of having libraries of common code was certainly in the minds of the COBOL designers, because COBOL provides the means for accomplishing this through subprograms.

12.2   *COBOL Subprograms*

The concept of COBOL *subprograms* is similar to that of subroutines in other languages. The basis for segmenting a program into subprograms is an effective hierarchy chart. The coding of the modules in the hierarchy chart in Figure 12.2 conceivably might be divided among two programmers. One programmer codes the top three levels of the hierarchy chart as a main program and the other codes the remaining levels. In this case the modules subordinate to "Compute Employee Pay" are a subprogram. The main program will then utilize the subprogram to form an integrated functioning program. Figure 12.11 illustrates how a main program passes control to a subprogram and resumes control when the subprogram has finished executing its tasks.

Before the program can be executed, it is necessary to link together the separately coded modules, even though each module is developed and compiled separately. Compiled modules in object format are linked by invoking an operating system routine known as the linkage editor using the appropriate job control language. It is necessary that you consult your system manual to find out how to do this. During linkage, the modules are combined into one entity, and this unit may subsequently be executed.

A revision of the sample program from Chapter 6 serves as an example of the code concepts introduced in this chapter. The hierarchy chart is in Figure 12.12, the Nassi-Schneiderman charts are in Figure 12.13, the main program code is in Figure 12.14, the subprogram code is in Figure 12.15, and the code for a library entry is in Figure 12.16. Notice the "CALL" to the subprogram DETCLASS from line 152 of the main program in Figure 12.14. Recall that the purpose of the package of programs is to determine a discount classification for customers on a monthly basis. In this case the subprogram uses the customer purchases accumulated in the main program to determine the discount class.

Figure 12.11   Implementing a Module with a Subprogram

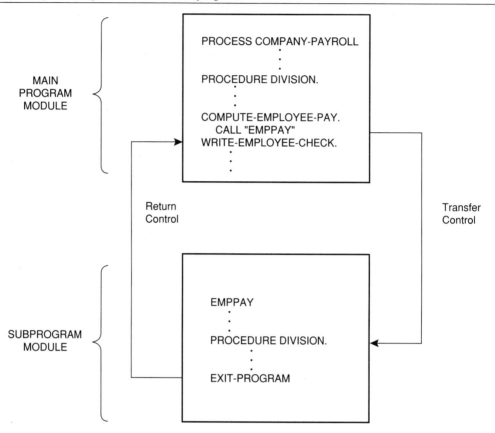

Figure 12.12   Hierarchy Chart for "Customer Discount Classification" Program

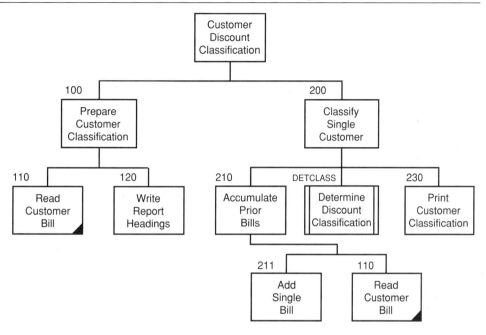

Figure 12.13   N-S Charts for "Customer Discount Classification" Program

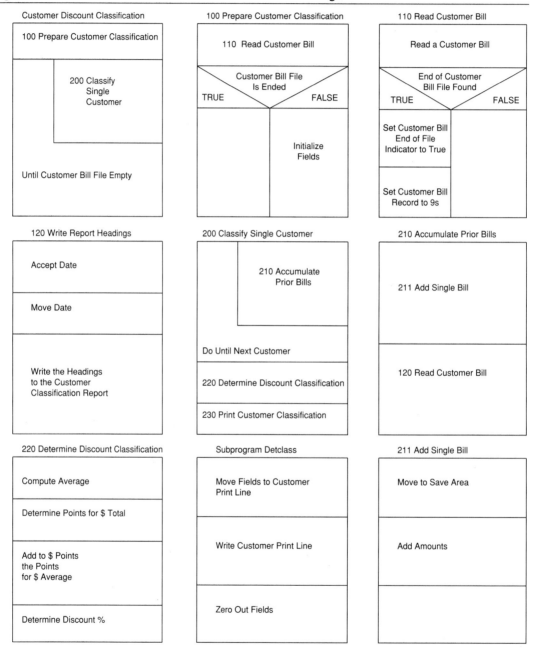

Figure 12.14   Program Code for "Customer Discount Classification"

```
 1 IDENTIFICATION DIVISION.
 2 PROGRAM-ID.  CUSTOMER-DISCOUNT-CLASSIFY.
 3*  THIS PROGRAM TAKES THE BILLS FROM THE PRIOR MONTH AND
 4*  COMPUTES THE DISCOUNT RATE FOR THE FOLLOWING MONTH
 5 AUTHOR.        SELF.
 6 DATE-WRITTEN.  JUNE 29, 1995.
 7 DATE-COMPILED. 16-Jul-92 01:08.
10 ENVIRONMENT DIVISION.
11
12 CONFIGURATION SECTION.
13 SOURCE-COMPUTER.  GENERIC-COMPUTER.
14 OBJECT-COMPUTER.  GENERIC-COMPUTER.
15
16 INPUT-OUTPUT SECTION.
17
18 FILE-CONTROL.
19     SELECT CUSTOMER-BILL-FILE ASSIGN TO DISK
20         ORGANIZATION IS SEQUENTIAL.
21     SELECT CUSTOMER-CLASS-LIST ASSIGN TO PRINTER
22         ORGANIZATION IS SEQUENTIAL.
23
24 DATA DIVISION.
25
26 FILE SECTION.
27
28 FD  CUSTOMER-BILL-FILE
29     LABEL RECORDS ARE STANDARD.
30
31 01  CUSTOMER-BILL-REC.
32     05  CB-CUSTOMER-NBR   PIC 9(3).
33     05  CB-CUSTOMER-NAME  PIC X(15).
34     05  CB-PURCHASE-AMT   PIC 9(6)V9(2).
35
36 FD  CUSTOMER-CLASS-LIST
37     LABEL RECORDS ARE OMITTED.
38
39 01  CUSTOMER-CLASS-LINE PIC X(80).
40
41 WORKING-STORAGE SECTION.
42
43 01  DUPLICATE-BILL.
44     05  DB-CUSTOMER-NBR   PIC 9(3).
```

Figure 12.14   (continued)

```
45      05   DB-CUSTOMER-NAME  PIC X(15).
46      05   DB-PURCHASE-AMT   PIC 9(6)V9(2).
47
48 01  TODAYS-DATE.
49      05   TD-MM                   PIC 9(2).
50      05   TD-DD                   PIC 9(2).
51      05   TD-YY                   PIC 9(2).
52
53 01  END-OF-FILE-INDICATORS.
54      05   EOF-BILLS PIC X(5) VALUE "FALSE".
55      88   MORE-BILLS VALUE "FALSE".
56      88   NO-MORE-BILLS VALUE "TRUE".
57
58 COPY DOLCOMPS.
59 01  DOLLAR-COMPUTATIONS.
60      05   DC-TOTAL-DOLLAR-PURCHASES   PIC 9(8)V9(2)   VALUE ZERO.
61           88   TOT-POINTS-0     VALUE 0.00 THRU 99.99.
62           88   TOT-POINTS-1     VALUE 100.00 THRU 499.99.
63           88   TOT-POINTS-2     VALUE 500.00 THRU 999.99.
64           88   TOT-POINTS-3     VALUE 1000.00 THRU 4999.99.
65           88   TOT-POINTS-4     VALUE 5000.00 THRU 99999999.99.
66      05   DC-NUMBER-OF-PURCHASES      PIC 99          VALUE ZERO.
67      05   DC-AVERAGE-DOLLAR-PURCHASES PIC 9(6)V9(2)    VALUE ZERO.
68           88   AVG-POINTS-0     VALUE 0.00 THRU 49.99.
69           88   AVG-POINTS-1     VALUE 50.00 THRU 99.99.
70           88   AVG-POINTS-2     VALUE 100.00 THRU 199.99.
71           88   AVG-POINTS-3     VALUE 200.00 THRU 999999.99.
72      05   DC-POINTS                   PIC 99          VALUE ZERO.
73      05   DC-DISCOUNT-RATE            PIC 99          VALUE ZERO.
74
75
76 01  CUSTOMER-CLASSIFICATION-REPORT.
77      05   CCR-HEADING-1.
78           10   FILLER PIC X(28) VALUE SPACE.
79           10   FILLER PIC X(40) VALUE "WHOLESALE SEAFOOD DISCOUNTS".
80      05   CCR-HEADING-2.
81           10   FILLER PIC X(30) VALUE SPACE.
82           10   FILLER PIC X(13) VALUE "MONTH ENDING ".
83           10   CCR-DATE.
84                15   CCR-MM PIC 99.
85                15   FILLER PIC X  VALUE "/".
86                15   CCR-DD PIC 99.
```

* appears at line 58

Figure 12.14   (continued)

```
87                 15  FILLER PIC X  VALUE "/".
88                 15  CCR-YY PIC 99.
89        05  CCR-HEADING-3  PIC X(80) VALUE SPACE.
90        05  CCR-HEADING-4.
91            10  FILLER PIC X(5)  VALUE SPACE.
92            10  FILLER PIC X(8)  VALUE "CUST #".
93            10  FILLER PIC X(18) VALUE "CUSTOMER NAME".
94            10  FILLER PIC X(12) VALUE "TOT PURCHASE".
95            10  FILLER PIC X(12) VALUE "AVG PURCHASE".
96            10  FILLER PIC X(10) VALUE "POINTS".
97            10  FILLER PIC X(15) VALUE "DISCOUNT AMT".
98        05  CCR-DETAIL-LINE.
99            10  FILLER             PIC X(8)  VALUE SPACE.
100           10  CCR-CUSTOMER-NBR   PIC 9(3).
101           10  FILLER             PIC X(3)  VALUE SPACE.
102           10  CCR-CUSTOMER-NAME  PIC X(18).
103           10  CCR-TOT-PURCHASES  PIC Z(8).99.
104           10  FILLER             PIC X(4)  VALUE SPACE.
105           10  CCR-AVG-PURCHASES  PIC Z(6).99.
106           10  FILLER             PIC X(6)  VALUE SPACE.
107           10  CCR-POINTS         PIC Z9.
108           10  FILLER             PIC X(6)  VALUE SPACE.
109           10  CCR-DISCOUNT-PCT   PIC Z9.
110
111
112 PROCEDURE DIVISION.
113
114 CUSTOMER-DISCOUNT-CLASS.
115    OPEN INPUT  CUSTOMER-BILL-FILE.
116    OPEN OUTPUT CUSTOMER-CLASS-LIST.
117    PERFORM 100-PREPARE-CUSTOMER-CLASS.
118    PERFORM 200-CLASSIFY-SINGLE-CUSTOMER UNTIL NO-MORE-BILLS.
119    CLOSE CUSTOMER-BILL-FILE.
120    CLOSE CUSTOMER-CLASS-LIST.
121    STOP RUN.
122
123 100-PREPARE-CUSTOMER-CLASS.
124    PERFORM 110-READ-CUSTOMER-BILL.
125    IF MORE-BILLS
126        PERFORM 120-WRITE-REPORT-HEADINGS
127        MOVE CUSTOMER-BILL-REC TO DUPLICATE-BILL
128    END-IF.
```

Figure 12.14   (continued)

```
129
130 110-READ-CUSTOMER-BILL.
131     READ CUSTOMER-BILL-FILE
132         AT END MOVE "TRUE" TO EOF-BILLS
133                 MOVE 999 TO CB-CUSTOMER-NBR
134     END-READ.
135
136 120-WRITE-REPORT-HEADINGS.
137     ACCEPT TODAYS-DATE FROM DATE.
138     MOVE TD-MM TO CCR-MM.
139     MOVE TD-DD TO CCR-DD.
140     MOVE TD-YY TO CCR-YY.
141     WRITE CUSTOMER-CLASS-LINE FROM CCR-HEADING-1
142         AFTER ADVANCING PAGE.
143     WRITE CUSTOMER-CLASS-LINE FROM CCR-HEADING-2.
144     WRITE CUSTOMER-CLASS-LINE FROM CCR-HEADING-3.
145     WRITE CUSTOMER-CLASS-LINE FROM CCR-HEADING-4.
146     WRITE CUSTOMER-CLASS-LINE FROM CCR-HEADING-3.
147
148 200-CLASSIFY-SINGLE-CUSTOMER.
149     PERFORM 210-ACCUMULATE-CUSTOMER-BILLS WITH TEST AFTER
150         VARYING DC-NUMBER-OF-PURCHASES FROM 1 BY 1
151             UNTIL CB-CUSTOMER-NBR NOT = DB-CUSTOMER-NBR.
152     CALL "DETCLASS" USING DOLLAR-COMPUTATIONS.
153     PERFORM 230-PRINT-CUSTOMER-CLASS.
154
155 210-ACCUMULATE-CUSTOMER-BILLS.
156     PERFORM 211-ADD-SINGLE-BILL.
157     PERFORM 110-READ-CUSTOMER-BILL.
158
159 211-ADD-SINGLE-BILL.
160     ADD CB-PURCHASE-AMT    TO DC-TOTAL-DOLLAR-PURCHASES.
161     MOVE CUSTOMER-BILL-REC TO DUPLICATE-BILL.
162
163 230-PRINT-CUSTOMER-CLASS.
164     MOVE DB-CUSTOMER-NBR              TO CCR-CUSTOMER-NBR.
165     MOVE DB-CUSTOMER-NAME             TO CCR-CUSTOMER-NAME.
166     MOVE DC-TOTAL-DOLLAR-PURCHASES    TO CCR-TOT-PURCHASES.
167     MOVE DC-AVERAGE-DOLLAR-PURCHASES TO CCR-AVG-PURCHASES.
168     MOVE DC-POINTS                    TO CCR-POINTS.
169     MOVE DC-DISCOUNT-RATE             TO CCR-DISCOUNT-PCT.
170     WRITE CUSTOMER-CLASS-LINE FROM CCR-DETAIL-LINE.
```

Figure 12.15   Subprogram Code

```
 1 IDENTIFICATION DIVISION.
 2 PROGRAM-ID.  DETCLASS.
 3*  THIS SUBPROGRAM TAKES THE DOLLAR VALUES FROM THE PRIOR MONTH AN
 4*  COMPUTES THE DISCOUNT RATE FOR THE FOLLOWING MONTH
 5 AUTHOR.        SELF.
 6 DATE-WRITTEN.  JUNE 29, 1995.
 7 DATE-COMPILED. 16-Jul-92 01:04.
10 ENVIRONMENT DIVISION.
11
12 CONFIGURATION SECTION.
13 SOURCE-COMPUTER.  GENERIC-COMPUTER.
14 OBJECT-COMPUTER.  GENERIC-COMPUTER.
15
16 DATA DIVISION.
17
18 LINKAGE SECTION.
19
20 COPY DOLCOMPS.
21 01   DOLLAR-COMPUTATIONS.
22     05   DC-TOTAL-DOLLAR-PURCHASES   PIC 9(8)V9(2)   VALUE ZERO.
23          88   TOT-POINTS-0      VALUE 0.00 THRU 99.99.
24          88   TOT-POINTS-1      VALUE 100.00 THRU 499.99.
25          88   TOT-POINTS-2      VALUE 500.00 THRU 999.99.
26          88   TOT-POINTS-3      VALUE 1000.00 THRU 4999.99.
27          88   TOT-POINTS-4      VALUE 5000.00 THRU 99999999.99.
28     05   DC-NUMBER-OF-PURCHASES     PIC 99          VALUE ZERO.
29     05   DC-AVERAGE-DOLLAR-PURCHASES PIC 9(6)V9(2)   VALUE ZERO.
30          88   AVG-POINTS-0      VALUE 0.00 THRU 49.99.
31          88   AVG-POINTS-1      VALUE 50.00 THRU 99.99.
32          88   AVG-POINTS-2      VALUE 100.00 THRU 199.99.
33          88   AVG-POINTS-3      VALUE 200.00 THRU 999999.99.
34     05   DC-POINTS                  PIC 99          VALUE ZERO.
35     05   DC-DISCOUNT-RATE           PIC 99          VALUE ZERO.
36
37
38 PROCEDURE DIVISION USING DOLLAR-COMPUTATIONS.
39
40 DETERMINE-CLASSIFICATION.
41     COMPUTE DC-AVERAGE-DOLLAR-PURCHASES ROUNDED =
42         DC-TOTAL-DOLLAR-PURCHASES / DC-NUMBER-OF-PURCHASES.
43     IF TOT-POINTS-1
44         ADD 1 TO DC-POINTS
```

*

Figure 12.15   (continued)

```
45      ELSE IF TOT-POINTS-2
46              ADD 2 TO DC-POINTS
47          ELSE IF TOT-POINTS-3
48                  ADD 3 TO DC-POINTS
49              ELSE IF TOT-POINTS-4
50                  ADD 4 TO DC-POINTS.
51      IF AVG-POINTS-1
52          ADD 1 TO DC-POINTS
53      ELSE IF AVG-POINTS-2
54              ADD 2 TO DC-POINTS
55          ELSE IF AVG-POINTS-3
56                  ADD 3 TO DC-POINTS.
57      EVALUATE DC-POINTS
58          WHEN 0 MOVE 0  TO DC-DISCOUNT-RATE
59          WHEN 1 MOVE 1  TO DC-DISCOUNT-RATE
60          WHEN 2 MOVE 2  TO DC-DISCOUNT-RATE
61          WHEN 3 MOVE 4  TO DC-DISCOUNT-RATE
62          WHEN 4 MOVE 7  TO DC-DISCOUNT-RATE
63          WHEN 5 MOVE 10 TO DC-DISCOUNT-RATE
64          WHEN 6 MOVE 15 TO DC-DISCOUNT-RATE
65          WHEN 7 MOVE 20 TO DC-DISCOUNT-RATE
66      END-EVALUATE.
67
68 EXIT-SUBROUTINE.
69      EXIT PROGRAM.
```

Figure 12.16   Library Entry Code

```
01  DOLLAR-COMPUTATIONS.
    05  DC-TOTAL-DOLLAR-PURCHASES    PIC 9(8)V9(2)    VALUE ZERO.
        88  TOT-POINTS-0        VALUE 0.00 THRU 99.99.
        88  TOT-POINTS-1        VALUE 100.00 THRU 499.99.
        88  TOT-POINTS-2        VALUE 500.00 THRU 999.99.
        88  TOT-POINTS-3        VALUE 1000.00 THRU 4999.99.
        88  TOT-POINTS-4        VALUE 5000.00 THRU 99999999.99.
    05  DC-NUMBER-OF-PURCHASES       PIC 99           VALUE ZERO.
    05  DC-AVERAGE-DOLLAR-PURCHASES PIC 9(6)V9(2)    VALUE ZERO.
        88  AVG-POINTS-0        VALUE 0.00 THRU 49.99.
        88  AVG-POINTS-1        VALUE 50.00 THRU 99.99.
        88  AVG-POINTS-2        VALUE 100.00 THRU 199.99.
```

Figure 12.16   (continued)

```
        88  AVG-POINTS-3       VALUE 200.00 THRU 999999.99.
    05  DC-POINTS              PIC 99              VALUE ZERO.
    05  DC-DISCOUNT-RATE       PIC 99              VALUE ZERO.
```

12.2.1   *Calling a Subprogram*

To transfer control to a subprogram, COBOL provides the *CALL* statement. The program containing the CALL statement is referred to as the *calling program*, and the subprogram specified in the CALL statement is the *called program*.

The format and rules for the CALL statement are:

CALL   literal-1   [USING   {data-name-1} . . .]

1.   Literal-1 contains the alphanumeric name of the called program.
2.   No recursive subprograms are allowed.
3.   Data-name-1 and all subsequent data-names must be 01 level data items in the calling program's FILE SECTION, WORKING-STORAGE SECTION, or LINKAGE SECTION of the DATA DIVISION.
4.   Data-name-1 and subsequent data-names must appear in the order of their corresponding items in the subprogram.

The literal specifies the subprogram being called. The USING phrase "passes" the data items to be acted upon by the subprogram. In essence, it is the way two modules communicate data. The USING phrase may only be specified if a USING phrase appears as part of the PROCEDURE DIVISION header of the called program. The data-names specified in the USING phrase designate the 01 data items of the calling program that the subprogram may access. They are the data items "passed" between called and calling program and are named a parameter list. The USING clause designates the data items that are common to both the calling program and the called program. The order of the data items specified in the USING clause is extremely important: The correspondence of data-names is by position and not by name. This means that they should be listed in the order expected by the subprogram. Figure 12.14, line 152 calls the subprogram "DETCLASS" USING the data elements stated by the PROCEDURE DIVISION on line 38 of Figure 12.15.

Assume that in the payroll example the module "Compute Employee Pay" has been coded as the subprogram EMPPAY and the program as PROCESS-COMPANY-PAYROLL. To pass control to the subprogram during execution, it must be CALLed by PROCESS-COMPANY-PAYROLL. In this example PROCESS-COMPANY-PAYROLL is the calling program and EMPPAY is the called program. The statement

```
    CALL "EMPPAY"  USING PAY-AMOUNTS.
```

calls the subprogram and specifies that PAY-AMOUNTS is the data item that the subprogram may access.

PAY-AMOUNTS must be an 01 level data item defined in PROCESS-COMPANY-PAYROLL. In this example the fields to be used by subprogram EMPPAY are the number of hours worked and the pay rate for calculation. Storage data items are also needed for returning the gross pay, taxes, and net pay calculated in EMPPAY. The 01 data entry description is:

```
WORKING-STORAGE SECTION.
01      PAY-AMOUNTS.
        05      PAY-HOURS     PIC     999.
        05      PAY-RATE      PIC     99V99.
        05      PAY-GROSS     PIC     9(5)V99.
        05      PAY-TAXES     PIC     9(4)V99.
        05      PAY-NET       PIC     9(5)V99.
```

Alternatively, each of the fields for wage calculation could have been defined as an 01 level data item. If so, the CALL statement would have been:

```
CALL "EMPPAY" USING  PAY-HOURS
                     PAY-RATE
                     PAY-GROSS
                     PAY-TAXES
                     PAY-NET.
```

The CALL statement transfers control to the first executable statement in the PROCE-DURE DIVISION of the subprogram. Once the subprogram is finished, control is returned to the statement immediately following the CALL statement. Hence, the CALL statement functions as the logical equivalent of a simple PERFORM statement. As with PERFORM statements, CALL does not allow recursion. For example, A may not CALL itself. Neither may it CALL another subprogram B which in turn CALLs subprogram A. However, CALLs can be nested. For example, program A may CALL subprogram B, which in turn CALLs subprogram C, and so on. In this case some subprograms become both calling and called programs.

CALL statements, like PERFORM statements, allow a programmer to implement modular programs. When subprograms are used in place of PERFORM statements coupling is improved, because the parameter list of the CALL statement limits the data items available to the subprogram. The subprogram then has access only to the data required rather than to every data item defined in the calling program.

12.2.2   *Defining a Subprogram*

Let us now turn our attention to the subprogram itself. Subprograms may be written in programming languages other than COBOL. This presents no problem because when linkage occurs both the calling program and the called subprogram are in object form. However, in this chapter we will limit our discussion to COBOL subprograms.

LINKAGE SECTION. A COBOL subprogram is very similar to a COBOL program with a few exceptions and additions. The first addition is the *LINKAGE SECTION* in the DATA DIVISION following the WORKING-STORAGE SECTION. It defines the data items specified in the USING phrase of the calling program's CALL statement. In other words it describes in the subprogram the data items referenced by both calling and called programs. Within the calling program such data items are defined in the DATA DIVISION. The data item descriptions in these two places should correspond. In the payroll subprogram example, "EMPPAY" would have the following LINKAGE SECTION:

```
LINKAGE SECTION.
        01    PAY-AMOUNTS.
              05 PAY-HOURS     PIC  999.
              05 PAY-RATE      PIC  99V99.
              05 PAY-GROSS     PIC  9(5)V99.
              05 PAY-TAXES     PIC  9(4)V99.
              05 PAY-NET       PIC  9(5)V99.
```

The LINKAGE SECTION of Figure 12.15 defines all variables used by both the main program and the subprogram. Notice that the names are identical, even though it is only necessary that the order and PICTURES be identical. It is good practice, however, to use identical names for standardization and to avoid confusion.

Data item definitions in the LINKAGE SECTION have these additional restrictions:

1. Data items in the LINKAGE SECTION can only be referred to in the called program's PROCEDURE DIVISION if they appear in the USING phrase or are subordinate to a data item in the USING phrase.
2. Data items in the LINKAGE SECTION cannot be associated with data items in the REPORT SECTION (defined in Chapter 13) of a calling program.
3. The VALUE clause may not appear in the LINKAGE SECTION except for 88-level condition entries.

PROCEDURE DIVISION Header. Another difference between a COBOL program and a subprogram is that the division header PROCEDURE DIVISION must be followed by a USING phrase to indicate that the called program is to function under the control of a CALL statement. The format is:

PROCEDURE DIVISION [USING {data-name-1} ...] .

Recall that the CALL statement also contains a USING phrase specifying the data items available to both programs. The data item list specified by the USING phrase in the PROCE-DURE DIVISION header should correspond to the data item list in the CALL statement of the calling program. This is how the association of data items in the called and calling program is accomplished. The subprogram considers data-item-1 of the PROCEDURE DIVISION header USING phrase and data-item-1 of the CALL statement USING phrase to be the same data item.

This logic extends to each remaining pair of data items. The important thing to remember is that the association of data items is positional.

The names of the data items in the USING phrases need not be identical in the program and subprogram. It is their positions that correspond. Therefore, it is important to verify that the lists of the passed or shared data items have identical PICTUREs. This correspondence is illustrated in Figure 12.17 for the payroll subprogram and the codes of Figures 12.14 and 12.15.

Figure 12.17   *Correspondence of Shared Data Items*

```
        CALLING PROGRAM

          WORKING-STORAGE SECTION.

          01 PAY-AMOUNTS
             05 PAY-HOURS PIC 999.
             05 PAY-RATE  PIC 99V99.
             05 PAY-GROSS PIC 9(5)V99.
             05 PAY-TAXES PIC 9(4)V99.
             05 PAY-NET   PIC 9(5)V99.
             .
             .
          PROCEDURE DIVISION
             .
             .
          CALL "EMPPAY"
            ( USING PAY-AMOUNTS. )   ◄─────┐
                                           │
                                           │
        CALLED PROGRAM                     │
                                           │
          LINKAGE SECTION.                 │  May be named differently.
                                           │  Must be in same order if
          01 PAY-AMOUNTS                   │  multiple items are listed.
             05 PAY-HOURS PIC 999.         │
             05 PAY-RATE  PIC 99V99.       │
             05 PAY-GROSS PIC 9(5)V99.     │
             05 PAY-TAXES PIC 9(4)V99.     │
             05 PAY-NET   PIC 9(5)V99.     │
             .                             │
             .                             │
          PROCEDURE DIVISION               │
                                           │
            ( USING PAY-AMOUNTS. )   ◄──────┘
```

EXIT PROGRAM Statement. The logical end of the subprogram is indicated by the *EXIT PROGRAM* statement. When the EXIT PROGRAM statement is encountered, control returns to the statement following the CALL statement in the calling program. The EXIT PROGRAM statement must be the only statement in the paragraph. The paragraph containing the statement may *not* be performed. Therefore, it is particularly important to determine its proper placement in the subprogram. Often the EXIT PROGRAM paragraph is placed immediately following the main processing paragraph of the subprogram. Control then falls through to the EXIT PROGRAM to terminate execution of the subprogram.

When it is exited, the called program will remain in the state it was when the EXIT PROGRAM statement was encountered. This is particularly important to note because it means that data values, indicator settings, and so on, will not be changed, nor will files be closed when the subprogram is exited.

The general code relating the program and the subprogram for the payroll example is shown in Figure 12.18. It also illustrates the similarity of the subprogram to the calling program and points out the differences, notably the USING phrase, the LINKAGE SECTION, and the EXIT PROGRAM statement. Line 69 of Figure 12.15 causes subprogram DETCLASS to return control to line 153 of the main program of Figure 12.14.

12.3   *The COPY Facility*

In business applications a small number of important files are used by a large number of programs. This implies that much programming effort is expended on coding similar file descriptions in program after program. However, just as COBOL provides a facility for increasing programmer productivity through the use of subprograms, it also provides a method for reducing the need to code file definitions repetitively.

The *COPY* facility allows sections of COBOL code to be stored in a library so that they may be copied into a new program as it is being developed. Not only can file and report descriptions be stored and subsequently copied, but any library text may be inserted into a source program at the time of compilation. That text is then treated as part of the program being compiled. The collection of insertable text is referred to as a *source library*.

The COPY facility provides further advantages for program maintenance. For example, by having one source of file descriptions, programs can be standardized to a great degree, since there will be uniformity of data item names and descriptions no matter what program is accessing them. This makes a program easier to debug or modify. Furthermore, whenever changes occur in the file, they can be centrally applied and will be reflected in all programs COPYing the description. This can lower the probability of errors significantly. The COPY facility may also be used to bring in small segments of PROCEDURE DIVISION code that are used often but are not complex enough to require a subprogram. Library entries may further be used for comment entries, literals, table descriptions, and debugging lines.

Figure 12.18   Relating COBOL Programs and Subprograms

```
                              CALLING PROGRAM

                              IDENTIFICATION DIVISION.
                              PROGRAM-ID. PROCESS-EMPLOYEE-PAYROLL.

                              WORKING-STORAGE SECTION.
                              01 PAY-AMOUNTS   PIC 999.
                                 05 PAY-HOURS  PIC 99V99.
                                 05 PAY-RATE   PIC 9(5)V99.
                                 05 PAY-GROSS  PIC 9(4)V99.
                                 05 PAY-TAXES  PIC 9(5)V99.
                                 05 PAY-NET
                                    .
                                    .
                              PROCEDURE DIVISION
                                    .
                                    .
                              CALL "EMPPAY"
                                 USING PAY-AMOUNTS.
                                    .
                                    .
                              STOP RUN.


                              CALLED PROGRAM

                              IDENTIFICATION DIVISION.
                              PROGRAM-ID. EMPPAY.
                                    .
                                    .
                              WORKING-STORAGE SECTION.
                                    .
                                    .
                              LINKAGE SECTION.
                              01 PAY-AMOUNTS.
                                 05 PAY-HOURS  PIC 999.
                                 05 PAY-RATE   PIC 99V99.
                                 05 PAY-GROSS  PIC 9(5)V99.
                                 05 PAY-TAXES  PIC 9(4)V99.
                                 05 PAY-NET    PIC 9(5)V99.

                              PROCEDURE DIVISION
                                 USING PAY-AMOUNTS.
                                    .
                                    .
                              EXIT-PARAGRAPH.
                              EXIT PROGRAM.
```

Returns control to calling program

Passes control to subprogram

Each manufacturer has a different method of establishing the source library. It is therefore necessary to consult your system's reference documentation for doing so. Once created, however, the source library can be exploited using the COBOL COPY statement. The simplified format and rules of the COPY statement are:

$$\underline{\text{COPY}} \text{ text-name} \quad \left[\left\{ \begin{array}{c} \underline{\text{OF}} \\ \underline{\text{IN}} \end{array} \right\} \text{ library-name} \right]$$

$$\left[\underline{\text{REPLACING}} \quad \left\{ \begin{array}{c} \text{identifier-1} \\ \text{literal-1} \\ \text{word-1} \end{array} \right\} \quad \underline{\text{BY}} \quad \left\{ \begin{array}{c} \text{identifier-2} \\ \text{literal-2} \\ \text{word-2} \end{array} \right\} \right] .$$

1. The text-name must be in a source library.
2. COPY statements may not be nested.
3. The COPY statement must be terminated by a period.
4. Word-1 or -2 may be any COBOL word except COPY.
5. The copied library text logically replaces the entire COPY statement.
6. If specified, the REPLACING option replaces each matched identifier, literal, or word with the corresponding identifier, literal or word.

Text-name identifies the name of the text entry in the source library. If multiple libraries exist, the OF (IN) clause qualifies the entry name by specifying the appropriate library to which it belongs. Within each library the text-name must be unique.

Suppose the following entry for the date exists in a source library as LIBRARY-DATE-CONVERSION:

```
01    DATE-CONVERSION.

      05  DC-MM-DD-YY.
          10   DC-MM    PIC XX.
          10   DC-DD    PIC XX.
          10   DC-YY    PIC XX.
      05  DC-YEAR       PIC XX.
```

To copy the entry to the WORKING-STORAGE SECTION of our program, we would use the following statement:

```
COPY LIBRARY-DATE-CONVERSION.
```

When the program is compiled, the library entry LIBRARY-DATE-CONVERSION will be copied into the program and will appear in the compilation listing as if it had been originally coded there. The resulting source listing for the WORKING-STORAGE SECTION would be:

```
COPY LIBRARY-DATE-CONVERSION.
01    DATE-CONVERSION.
      05  DC-MM-DD-YY.
          10   DC-MM    PIC XX.
          10   DC-DD    PIC XX.
          10   DC-YY    PIC XX.
      05  DC-YEAR       PIC XX.
```

When the date is accepted into DATE-CONVERSION it will have the format YYMMDD. It is so common to transform the system date from its YYMMDD format to a MMDDYY format that the following PROCEDURE DIVISION code could be stored in the source library as PD-DATE-CONVERSION to change the date format:

```
ACCEPT  DC-MM-DD-YY FROM DATE.
MOVE    DC-MM TO DC-YEAR.
MOVE    DC-DD TO DC-MM.
MOVE    DC-YY TO DC-DD.
MOVE    DC-YEAR TO DC-YY.
```

The resulting code in the PROCEDURE DIVISION would be:

```
COPY    PD-DATE-CONVERSION.
ACCEPT  DC-MM-DD-YY FROM DATE.
MOVE    DC-MM    TO  DC-YEAR.
MOVE    DC-DD    TO  DC-MM.
MOVE    DC-YY    TO  DC-DD.
MOVE    DC-YEAR  TO  DC-YY.
```

The REPLACING option allows the programmer to replace portions of the code to be copied with other code. This feature is useful to provide flexibility in the stored code. As an example, the first line of each report for a company may be standardized. The entry for REPORT-1ST-LINE may appear:

```
05   STANDARD-REPORT-FIRST-LINE
         10    FILLER    PIC  X(10)   VALUE SPACE.
         10    FILLER    PIC  X(9)    VALUE "REPORT #".
         10    FILLER    PIC  X(21)   VALUE "REPORT NUMBER".
```

For a program to utilize the standard line, the "REPORT NUMBER" literal would have to be changed. This could be handled by using the COPY and REPLACE in this fashion:

```
COPY REPORT-1ST-LINE REPLACING "REPORT NUMBER" BY "R247".
```

This would save the trouble of providing an identifier to the report number line and moving in a literal in the PROCEDURE DIVISION.

The advantages of using the COPY facility of COBOL to increase programmer productivity, program standardization, and program maintainability cannot be overemphasized. The main program of Figure 12.14 (line 58) and subprogram of Figure 12.15 (line 20) both copy in data descriptions for the required computations. The library entry of Figure 12.16 provides common names for both programs and guarantees that the PICTURE clauses and order of items is identical in both programs.

Case Study: CDL's Validate CD Orders

Charlene is convinced that the "Compact Disc Stock Table" used in the "Validate CD Orders" program will be used in more and more programs as new features, such as interactive order entry and validation, are added to the CDL system. Consequently, she decides to place the table description in a source library so that it can be copied into other programs. She further decides to create a subprogram to load the table into memory.

By creating the source library entry, Charlene establishes common names for the table that will propagate throughout the system. Furthermore, the table description may be brought into any program using only the COPY statement. Likewise, only a CALL statement is required to load the table into memory. A great savings of future coding effort can be realized at a small expense in current effort.

Charlene revises the program hierarchy chart so that it accounts for the subprogram. It is shown as a subordinate of module "100 Prepare Order Edit" in Figure 12.19. No other changes are required. The Nassi-Schneiderman charts for the subprogram are illustrated in Figure 12.20. Figure 12.21 contains the table description in the source library, and Figure 12.22 contains the subprogram code. Notice that the subprogram uses the COPY statement in the LINKAGE SECTION to obtain the table description from the source library. The copied variables are referenced in the PROCEDURE DIVISION USING clause.

Figure 12.19   Hierarchy Chart for CDL's "Validate CD Orders"

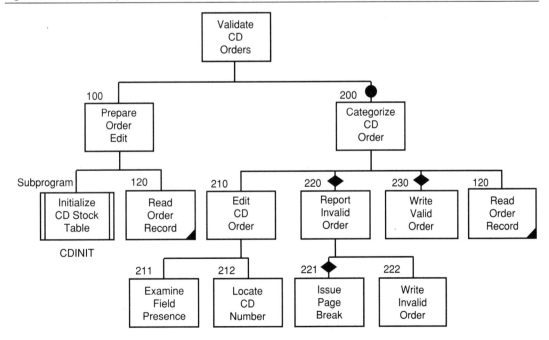

Figure 12.20   N-S Charts for CDINIT

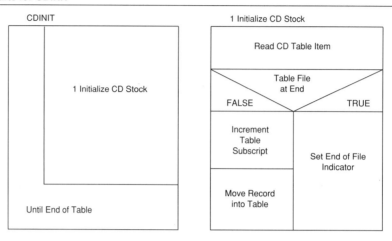

Figure 12.21   Compact Disc Table Entry in a Source Library

```
01   NBR-OF-COMPACT-DISCS PIC 99 VALUE 0.
01   COMPACT-DISC-TABLE.
     05   COMPACT-DISC OCCURS 1 TO 50 TIMES
          DEPENDING ON NBR-OF-COMPACT-DISCS
          ASCENDING KEY IS CDTAB-DISC-NUMBER
          INDEXED BY CD-INDEX.
              10   CDTAB-DISC-NUMBER PIC 9(6).
              10   CDTAB-PRICE       PIC 9(4)V99.
              10   CDTAB-QOH         PIC 9999.
```

Figure 12.22   CDINIT Subprogram for CDL's Order Validation

```
1 IDENTIFICATION DIVISION.
2 PROGRAM-ID. CDINIT.
3*     THIS PROGRAM IS TO BE USED AS A SUBROUTINE BY ANY PROGRAM.
4*     THE FUNCTION OF THE PROGRAM IS TO LOAD THE CD TABLE.
5
6 AUTHOR.          C HILTON
7 DATE-WRITTEN.      7-7-95
8 DATE-COMPILED. 30-Jan-93 01:02.
12 ENVIRONMENT DIVISION.
13
14
```

Figure 12.22   **(continued)**

```
15 CONFIGURATION SECTION.
16
17 SOURCE-COMPUTER.  GENERIC-COMPUTER.
18 OBJECT-COMPUTER.  GENERIC-COMPUTER.
19
20
21 INPUT-OUTPUT SECTION.
22
23 FILE-CONTROL.
24     SELECT COMPACT-DISC-STOCK-TABLE ASSIGN TO DISK
25         ORGANIZATION IS SEQUENTIAL.
26
27
28
29 DATA DIVISION.
30
31
32 FILE SECTION.
33
34 FD  COMPACT-DISC-STOCK-TABLE
35     LABEL RECORDS ARE STANDARD.
36
37 01  CD-STOCK.
38     05  CD-DISC-NUMBER PIC 9(6).
39     05  CD-PRICE       PIC 9(4)V99.
40     05  CD-QOH         PIC 9999.
41
42
43 WORKING-STORAGE SECTION.
44
45 01  EOF-CD-TABLE PIC X(5) VALUE "FALSE".
46
47
48 LINKAGE SECTION.
49
*    50 COPY CDTAB.
51 01  NBR-OF-COMPACT-DISCS PIC 99 VALUE 0.
52 01  COMPACT-DISC-TABLE.
53     05  COMPACT-DISC OCCURS 1 TO 50 TIMES
54         DEPENDING ON NBR-OF-COMPACT-DISCS
55         ASCENDING KEY IS CDTAB-DISC-NUMBER
56         INDEXED BY CD-INDEX.
```

Figure 12.22   (continued)

```
57              10  CDTAB-DISC-NUMBER PIC 9(6).
58              10  CDTAB-PRICE       PIC 9(4)V99.
59              10  CDTAB-QOH         PIC 9999.
60
61
62 PROCEDURE DIVISION
63    USING NBR-OF-COMPACT-DISCS COMPACT-DISC-TABLE.
64
65
66 INITIALIZE-CD-STOCK-TABLE.
67    OPEN INPUT COMPACT-DISC-STOCK-TABLE.
68    PERFORM 1-INITIALIZE-CD-STOCK UNTIL EOF-CD-TABLE = "TRUE".
69    CLOSE COMPACT-DISC-STOCK-TABLE.
70
71 EXIT-PROGRAM-PARAGRAPH.
72    EXIT PROGRAM.
73
74 1-INITIALIZE-CD-STOCK.
75    READ COMPACT-DISC-STOCK-TABLE
76        AT END MOVE "TRUE" TO EOF-CD-TABLE.
77    IF EOF-CD-TABLE = "FALSE"
78        ADD 1 TO NBR-OF-COMPACT-DISCS
79        MOVE CD-STOCK TO COMPACT-DISC (NBR-OF-COMPACT-DISCS).
```

The revised "Validate CD Orders" program appears in Figure 12.23. It also uses the COPY statement to define the table in the WORKING-STORAGE SECTION. The CALL statement in paragraph "100-Prepare-Order-Edit" calls the subprogram "CDINIT" to load the CD stock table. The test plan appears in Figure 12.24.

Figure 12.23   COBOL Code for Order Validation Program

```
 1 IDENTIFICATION DIVISION.
 2 PROGRAM-ID.  VALIDATE-ORDERS.
 3*      THIS PROGRAM VALIDATES THE ORDERS FOR COMPLETENESS AND
 4*      TESTS THE CD NUMBERS AGAINST THE CD IN STOCK TABLE FOR
 5*      VALIDITY OF THE NUMBER AND IN HAVING ENOUGH ITEMS IN
 6*      STOCK.  AN ERROR REPORT IS GENERATED FOR ALL INVALID
 7*      ORDERS.  VALID ORDERS HAVE THEIR PRICE ATTACHED AND ARE
 8*      WRITTEN TO A VALID ORDER FILE.
 9
10 AUTHOR.          C HILTON
11 DATE-WRITTEN.    7-7-95
```

Figure 12.23   (continued)

```
12 DATE-COMPILED. 30-Jan-93 01:13.
16 ENVIRONMENT DIVISION.
17
18
19 CONFIGURATION SECTION.
20
21 SOURCE-COMPUTER.  GENERIC-COMPUTER.
22 OBJECT-COMPUTER.  GENERIC-COMPUTER.
23
24
25 INPUT-OUTPUT SECTION.
26
27 FILE-CONTROL.
28     SELECT ORDERS-FILE ASSIGN TO DISK
29         ORGANIZATION IS SEQUENTIAL.
30     SELECT EXTENDED-ORDERS-FILE ASSIGN TO DISK
31         ORGANIZATION IS SEQUENTIAL.
32     SELECT INVALID-ORDERS-FILE ASSIGN TO PRINTER
33         ORGANIZATION IS SEQUENTIAL.
34
35
36
37
38 DATA DIVISION.
39
40
41 FILE SECTION.
42
43 FD  ORDERS-FILE
44     LABEL RECORDS ARE STANDARD.
45
46 01  ORDERS.
47     05  O-CUSTOMER-ID   PIC 9(6).
48     05  O-DISC-NUMBER   PIC 9(6).
49     05  O-QUANTITY      PIC 99.
50     05  O-ORDER-NUMBER  PIC 9(6).
51     05  O-PRICE         PIC 9(6)V99.
52
53 FD  EXTENDED-ORDERS-FILE
54     LABEL RECORDS ARE STANDARD.
55
56 01  EXTENDED-ORDER.
```

Figure 12.23   (continued)

```
57      05   EO-CUSTOMER-ID    PIC 9(6).
58      05   EO-DISC-NUMBER    PIC 9(6).
59      05   EO-QUANTITY       PIC 99.
60      05   EO-ORDER-NUMBER   PIC 9(6).
61      05   EO-TOTAL-PRICE    PIC 9(6)V99.
62
63 FD   INVALID-ORDERS-FILE
64      LABEL RECORDS ARE OMITTED.
65
66 01   INVALID-ORDER PIC X(80).
67
68
69 WORKING-STORAGE SECTION.
70
71 COPY CDTAB.
72 01   NBR-OF-COMPACT-DISCS PIC 99 VALUE 0.
73 01   COMPACT-DISC-TABLE.
74      05   COMPACT-DISC OCCURS 1 TO 50 TIMES
75           DEPENDING ON NBR-OF-COMPACT-DISCS
76           ASCENDING KEY IS CDTAB-DISC-NUMBER
77           INDEXED BY CD-INDEX.
78               10   CDTAB-DISC-NUMBER PIC 9(6).
79               10   CDTAB-PRICE       PIC 9(4)V99.
80               10   CDTAB-QOH         PIC 9999.
81
82 01   WS-COUNTERS.
83      05   WS-LINE           PIC 99  VALUE 99.
84      05   WS-PAGE           PIC 999 VALUE ZERO.
85      05   WS-TOTAL-PRICE    PIC 9(6)V99.
86      05   WS-DATE           PIC 9(6).
87      05   WS-MM-DD-YY.
88           10   WS-MM        PIC XX.
89           10   WS-DD        PIC XX.
90           10   WS-YY        PIC XX.
91      05   WS-YEAR           PIC XX.
92      05   WS-BULK           PIC 99.
93      05   WS-SINGLE         PIC 99.
94      05   WS-BULK-RATE      PIC 99V99 VALUE 3.95.
95      05   WS-SINGLE-RATE    PIC 99V99 VALUE 1.24.
96
97 01   INDICATORS.
98      05   EOF-CD-TABLE      PIC X(5) VALUE "FALSE".
99      05   EOF-ORDERS        PIC X(5) VALUE "FALSE".
```

`*` (line 71 marked with asterisk in left margin)

Figure 12.23   (continued)

```
100     05  ERR-CODE          PIC 9     VALUE ZERO.
101     05  MAX-LINE          PIC 99    VALUE 55.
102
103 01  INVALID-ORDERS-LISTING.
104     05  IOL-REPORT-TITLE.
105         10  FILLER              PIC X(35) VALUE "REPORT #32A".
106         10  FILLER              PIC X(28) VALUE "INVALID ORDERS".
107         10  FILLER              PIC X(5)  VALUE "PAGE".
108         10  IOL-PAGE            PIC ZZ9.
109     05  IOL-RUN-DATE.
110         10  FILLER              PIC X(40) VALUE
111                                 "DISTRIBUTION:  ORDER ENTRY".
112         10  FILLER              PIC X(15) VALUE "CDL".
113         10  FILLER              PIC X(10) VALUE "RUN DATE:".
114         10  IOL-DATE            PIC 99/99/99.
115     05  IOL-COLUMNS.
116         10  FILLER              PIC X(11) VALUE "ERROR".
117         10  FILLER              PIC X(16) VALUE "ORDER NUMBER".
118         10  FILLER              PIC X(16) VALUE "CUSTOMER ID".
119         10  FILLER              PIC X(12) VALUE "DISC NUMBER".
120         10  FILLER              PIC X(8)  VALUE "QTY".
121         10  FILLER              PIC X(5)  VALUE "PRICE".
122     05  IOL-UNDERLINE.
123         10  FILLER              PIC X(11) VALUE "—".
124         10  FILLER              PIC X(16) VALUE "————".
125         10  FILLER              PIC X(16) VALUE "———".
126         10  FILLER              PIC X(12) VALUE "———".
127         10  FILLER              PIC X(8)  VALUE "—".
128         10  FILLER              PIC X(8)  VALUE "———".
129     05  IOL-DETAIL.
130         10  FILLER              PIC X(2)  VALUE SPACE.
131         10  IOL-ERROR           PIC 9.
132         10  FILLER              PIC X(11) VALUE SPACE.
133         10  IOL-ORDER-NUMBER PIC 9(6).
134         10  FILLER              PIC X(10) VALUE SPACE.
135         10  IOL-CUSTOMER-ID  PIC 9(6).
136         10  FILLER              PIC X(8)  VALUE SPACE.
137         10  IOL-DISC-NUMBER  PIC 9(6).
138         10  FILLER              PIC X(5)  VALUE SPACE.
139         10  IOL-QUANTITY        PIC ZZ9.
140         10  FILLER              PIC X(5)  VALUE SPACE.
141         10  IOL-PRICE           PIC ZZZ9.99.
142
```

Figure 12.23   (continued)

```
143 PROCEDURE DIVISION.
144
145 VALIDATE-CD-ORDERS.
146     OPEN INPUT ORDERS-FILE.
147     OPEN OUTPUT INVALID-ORDERS-FILE.
148     OPEN OUTPUT EXTENDED-ORDERS-FILE.
149     PERFORM 100-PREPARE-ORDER-EDIT.
150     PERFORM 200-CATEGORIZE-CD-ORDER UNTIL EOF-ORDERS = "TRUE".
151     CLOSE ORDERS-FILE.
152     CLOSE INVALID-ORDERS-FILE.
153     CLOSE EXTENDED-ORDERS-FILE.
154     STOP RUN.
155
156 100-PREPARE-ORDER-EDIT.
157     CALL "CDINIT" USING NBR-OF-COMPACT-DISCS COMPACT-DISC-TABLE.
158     PERFORM 120-READ-ORDER-RECORD.
159     ACCEPT WS-DATE FROM DATE.
160     MOVE WS-DATE TO WS-MM-DD-YY.
161     MOVE WS-MM TO WS-YEAR.
162     MOVE WS-DD TO WS-MM.
163     MOVE WS-YY TO WS-DD.
164     MOVE WS-YEAR TO WS-YY.
165     MOVE WS-DATE TO IOL-DATE.
166
167 120-READ-ORDER-RECORD.
168     READ ORDERS-FILE
169         AT END MOVE "TRUE" TO EOF-ORDERS.
170
171 200-CATEGORIZE-CD-ORDER.
172     PERFORM 210-EDIT-CD-ORDER.
173     IF ERR-CODE IS EQUAL TO ZERO
174         PERFORM 230-REPORT-VALID-ORDER
175     ELSE
176         PERFORM 220-REPORT-INVALID-ORDER.
177     PERFORM 120-READ-ORDER-RECORD.
178
179 210-EDIT-CD-ORDER.
180     MOVE ZERO TO ERR-CODE.
181     PERFORM 211-EXAMINE-FIELD-PRESENCE.
182     PERFORM 212-LOCATE-CD-NUMBER.
183
184 211-EXAMINE-FIELD-PRESENCE.
```

Figure 12.23   (continued)

```
185     IF O-CUSTOMER-ID IS EQUAL TO ZERO
186         MOVE 1 TO ERR-CODE.
187     IF O-DISC-NUMBER IS EQUAL TO ZERO
188         MOVE 1 TO ERR-CODE.
189     IF O-QUANTITY IS EQUAL TO ZERO
190         MOVE 1 TO ERR-CODE.
191     IF O-ORDER-NUMBER IS EQUAL TO ZERO
192         MOVE 1 TO ERR-CODE.
193
194 212-LOCATE-CD-NUMBER.
195     SET CD-INDEX TO 1.
196     SEARCH COMPACT-DISC
197         AT END ADD 2 TO ERR-CODE
198         WHEN CDTAB-DISC-NUMBER (CD-INDEX) = O-DISC-NUMBER
199             NEXT SENTENCE.
200     IF ERR-CODE < 2
201         IF CDTAB-QOH (CD-INDEX) < O-QUANTITY ADD 4 TO ERR-CODE
202         ELSE SUBTRACT O-QUANTITY FROM CDTAB-QOH (CD-INDEX).
203
204 220-REPORT-INVALID-ORDER.
205     IF WS-LINE > MAX-LINE PERFORM 221-ISSUE-PAGE-BREAK.
206     PERFORM 222-WRITE-INVALID-ORDER.
207
208 221-ISSUE-PAGE-BREAK.
209     ADD 1 TO WS-PAGE.
210     MOVE WS-PAGE TO IOL-PAGE.
211     WRITE INVALID-ORDER FROM IOL-REPORT-TITLE
212         AFTER ADVANCING PAGE.
213     WRITE INVALID-ORDER FROM IOL-RUN-DATE.
214     WRITE INVALID-ORDER FROM IOL-COLUMNS
215         AFTER ADVANCING 3 LINES.
216     WRITE INVALID-ORDER FROM IOL-UNDERLINE.
217     MOVE SPACE TO INVALID-ORDER.
218     WRITE INVALID-ORDER.
219     MOVE 6 TO WS-LINE.
220
221 222-WRITE-INVALID-ORDER.
222     MOVE O-CUSTOMER-ID  TO IOL-CUSTOMER-ID.
223     MOVE ERR-CODE       TO IOL-ERROR.
224     MOVE O-DISC-NUMBER  TO IOL-DISC-NUMBER.
225     MOVE O-QUANTITY     TO IOL-QUANTITY.
226     MOVE O-ORDER-NUMBER TO IOL-ORDER-NUMBER.
```

Figure 12.23   (continued)

```
227     IF ERR-CODE NOT = 2 AND ERR-CODE NOT = 3
228         MOVE CDTAB-PRICE (CD-INDEX) TO IOL-PRICE
229     ELSE
230         MOVE O-PRICE TO IOL-PRICE.
231     WRITE INVALID-ORDER FROM IOL-DETAIL.
232     ADD 1 TO WS-LINE.
233     MOVE ZERO TO ERR-CODE.
234
235 230-REPORT-VALID-ORDER.
236     DIVIDE 5 INTO O-QUANTITY GIVING WS-BULK REMAINDER WS-SINGLE.
237     COMPUTE WS-TOTAL-PRICE =
238         O-QUANTITY * CDTAB-PRICE (CD-INDEX) +
239         WS-BULK * WS-BULK-RATE + WS-SINGLE * WS-SINGLE-RATE.
240     MOVE ORDERS TO EXTENDED-ORDER.
241     MOVE WS-TOTAL-PRICE TO EO-TOTAL-PRICE.
242     WRITE EXTENDED-ORDER.
```

Figure 12.24   Test Plan and Results for CDL's Order Validation Program

```
The ORDER file:

1987651234560298765400000000
0000001234560154356700000000
3232129999888017543270000000
0000009988990165435600000000
6543232345670198765400000000
5456782345670200000000000000


The CD table:

1234560009991000
2345670010000000
3456780024990233


The EXTENDED ORDER file:

1987651234560298765400002246
```

Figure 12.24   (continued)

```
The ORDER ERROR report:

REPORT #32A                        INVALID ORDERS              PAGE   1
DISTRIBUTION:   ORDER ENTRY             CDL          RUN DATE: 94/01/25


ERROR       ORDER NUMBER    CUSTOMER ID    DISC NUMBER    QTY        PRICE
-----       ------------    -----------    -----------    ---        -----

1              543567         000000         123456         1         9.99
2              754327         323212         999888         1         0.00
3              654356         000000         998899         1         0.00
4              987654         654323         234567         1        10.00
5              000000         545678         234567         2        10.00
```

Summary

The decomposition of programs into functional modules, a principle known as modularity, is the basis for developing structured programs. Modularity contributes to ease of programming, testing, debugging, and maintenance. Because of its importance, it is imperative to evaluate a program's design with regard to its modularity. Methods of evaluation include coupling, cohesion, span of control, and the scope of effect and scope of control criteria. All four methods employ the hierarchy chart as the basis for evaluating the program's decomposition.

Coupling, a measure of intermodule integrity, assesses the amount of communication between modules. The design objective is to minimize coupling by having highly independent modules. This results in reduction of the effort needed for testing, debugging, and maintenance. Several levels of coupling include data coupling, stamp coupling, control coupling, common coupling, and content coupling—depending on the communicational relationship between modules.

Cohesion, a measure of intramodule integrity, assesses the unity of task performed by an individual module. Levels of cohesion include functional cohesion, sequential cohesion, communicational cohesion, procedural cohesion, temporal cohesion, logical cohesion, and coincidental cohesion. The goal is to have highly cohesive modules whose component elements are directed toward accomplishing one function. As the number of modules decreases, however, cohesion worsens and coupling increases: these opposing measures of functional decomposition have design trade-offs. Generally, cohesion considerations should be afforded greater weight.

The span of control measure of functional decomposition evaluates the adequacy of the number of subordinate modules controlled by a single module. Generally, two to five modules are considered adequate. The scope of effect measure identifies the module that will be affected by a decision made within a particular module, and the scope of control measure refers to a particular module and all its subordinates. The design objective is to contain the module's scope of effect within its scope of control.

COBOL implements modularity not only through its paragraph structure but also through its subprogram facility. Before modules are linked together for execution, subprograms allow different modules to be coded and tested independently. Program control passes from a program to a subprogram via the CALL statement, which invokes the called subprogram and identifies the data items it may reference. This feature improves data coupling since only the data items specifically needed by the subprogram are made available.

To write COBOL subprograms, some additions to the standard COBOL statements are needed. In the DATA DIVISION a new section called the LINKAGE SECTION identifies the data items that can be referenced by both the subprograms and the calling program. Also, the PROCEDURE DIVISION header must incorporate the USING phrase that lists the same data items that appear in the calling program's CALL statement. The EXIT PROGRAM statement identifies the logical end of the subprogram.

Just as making subprograms available to all programmers introduces substantial savings in programming effort, COBOL reduces coding efforts through its COPY facility. When long file or report descriptions must be specified in multiple programs, COBOL allows text entries to be named and stored in centrally located source libraries. The COPY statement permits the programmer to name the library entry to be inserted into the source program at a particular place and then to be compiled as part of the original program. In addition to saving the labor associated with tedious coding, the COPY facility has the potential for creating uniformity, standardization, and centrally controlled descriptions and segments of code. Thus, COBOL's use of modularity in developing structured programs heightens a programmer's efficiency and lessens time and cost to the company.

Key Terms

modularity	coincidental cohesion	CALL
coupling	span of control	calling program
cohesion	scope of effect	called program
functional cohesion	scope of control	USING
sequential cohesion	understandability	parameter list
communicational cohesion	ease of coding	LINKAGE SECTION
procedural cohesion	accuracy	EXIT PROGRAM
temporal cohesion	completeness	COPY
logical cohesion	subprogram	source library

Hints for Avoiding Errors

1. Verify that the parameters specified by the USING clause are in identical order in both the CALL statement of the calling program and the PROCEDURE DIVISION of the called program. A difference could result in incorrect computations, incorrect reporting of data, or in abnormal program termination.

2. Make certain that the parameters being passed from a program to a subprogram have identical PICTUREs. If not, errors in the results will occur.
3. Use the COPY facility for file description entries where possible. This practice will result not only in always having the accurate clauses in the FD entries, but also in standardization of file names and data names.

Exercises

12.1 Write a subprogram to ACCEPT the system date and convert it to MM/DD/YY format. Pass only the result back to the calling program as a six-digit numeric field.

12.2 Develop a COPY item for the date conversion of Exercise 12.1. Show separate pieces of code for the necessary WORKING-STORAGE and PROCEDURE DIVISION entries.

12.3 Critique the CDL "Validate CD Order" program in terms of coupling, cohesion, and span of control.

12.4 Review all CDL programs and identify useful code segments for a COPY library.

12.5 A COPY statement can appear anywhere within a program where a character-string may occur, but not in _____.

12.6 The LINKAGE SECTION may not contain:
    a. data items requiring qualification.
    b. data items not included in the USING clause.
    c. data items defined in the REPORT SECTION.

12.7 The CALL statement transfers control to the _____ in the called subprogram.

12.8 The data items specified in the USING clause of the CALL statement can appear in a different sequence from those in the called program as long as the data-names are identical. True or false?

12.9 All data items in the LINKAGE SECTION must appear in the USING clause of the called program. True or false?

12.10 Which statement is not important in subprograms?
    a. CALL
    b. EXIT
    c. STOP

12.11 In the LINKAGE SECTION the VALUE clause may only appear in
    a. an 01 level.
    b. an 88 level.
    c. a 77 level.

12.12 The EXIT PROGRAM causes
    a. files to be closed.
    b. data values to reset.
    c. a return to the calling program.
    d. all of the above

12.13 A subprogram may issue a call to itself. True or false?

12.14 A subprogram may not contain a COPY statement. True or false?

12.15 Coupling is a measure of intramodule "goodness," whereas cohesion is a measure of intermodule "goodness." True or false?

12.16   Cohesion evaluates module independence. True or false?

12.17   The use of a switch or flag is an example of _____ coupling.
      a.   stamp
      b.   control
      c.   data
      d.   common

12.18   COBOL does not allow the programmer to specify global or local variables in a program, which would eliminate common coupling. True or false?

12.19   A module exhibits _____ cohesion if it contains component tasks that work on the same data items.
      a.   communicational
      b.   procedural
      c.   temporal
      d.   functional

12.20   Module independence is achieved by _____ coupling.
      a.   maximizing
      b.   optimizing
      c.   minimizing
      d.   measuring

12.21   It is impossible to structure a program in which the modules are completely independent of each other. True or false?

12.22   The _____ phase "passes" the data items to be acted upon by the subprogram.
      a.   CONTAINS
      b.   PASS
      c.   PARAMETER
      d.   USING

12.23   The following statement is a valid LINKAGE SECTION data entry. True or false?

```
01 GROSS-PAY-INDICATOR  PIC X(5) VALUE "FALSE".
```

12.24   The paragraph containing the _____ statement cannot be performed.
      a.   EXIT PROGRAM
      b.   CALL . . . USING
      c.   LINKAGE SECTION
      d.   COPY . . . IN
      e.   none of the above

12.25   Data items in the LINKAGE SECTION cannot be associated with data items in the _____SECTION of a calling program.
      a.   REPORT
      b.   COMMUNICATION
      c.   SCREEN
      d.   IDENTIFICATION

12.26   Any library text may be inserted into a source program at the time of compilation. True or false?

12.27 Two formal measures of program modularity are _____ and
_____.

12.28 _____ attempts to measure the level of complexity within a module.

12.29 _____ tries to measure how directly the design indicates the required code.

12.30 _____ judges whether the proper lines of control are shown in the hierarchy chart.

12.31 _____ is a measure of whether all required modules are specified.

12.32 To transfer control to a subprogram, COBOL provides the _____ statement.

12.33 A subprogram must contain a _____ SECTION following the WORKING-STORAGE SECTION.

12.34 The _____ facility of COBOL allows sections of code to be stored in a library so that they may be inserted into a new program as it is being developed.

12.35 The _____ identifies the modules that will be affected by a decision made within a particular module.

12.36 The _____ statement identifies the logical end of the subprogram.

12.37 What are the benefits to be gained from using COBOL features such as subprograms and the COPY facility?

SIMPLIFYING REPORTING WITH REPORT WRITER

13.1 Simplified Logic
  A Simplified Hierarchy Chart
  Logic Handled by the Report Writer
13.2 Coding the Report Writer
  The DATA DIVISION
  The PROCEDURE DIVISION
  Case Study: CDL's Accounts Receivable Listing Revisited
  Summary
  Hints for Avoiding Errors
  Exercises

Many languages require the logic developed in Chapter 8 to generate reports. COBOL, however, provides a powerful facility for producing reports called the *Report Writer*. The Report Writer feature greatly simplifies the logic needed to produce most reports. The trade-off, however, is that it involves additional coding in the DATA DIVISION. The Report Writer is a functioning feature of most COBOL compilers, although the extent of its implementation may vary among systems.

13.1 Simplified Logic

Language enhancements should either save coding time or provide more powerful commands to simplify a program's logical structure. The COBOL Report Writer does both. Much of the logic for report control is eliminated from the PROCEDURE DIVISION, reducing coding time. The Report Writer also simplifies the program design by providing powerful statements that perform page-break and control-break logic.

13.1.1   A Simplified Hierarchy Chart

The layout of the sales report example from Chapter 8 is replicated in Figure 13.1. This report is generated using records from a sequential file that contains an office identifier, a sales representative identifier, a customer number, a sales date, and a sales amount.

Figure 13.1   *Report Layout for "Monthly Sales by Region"*

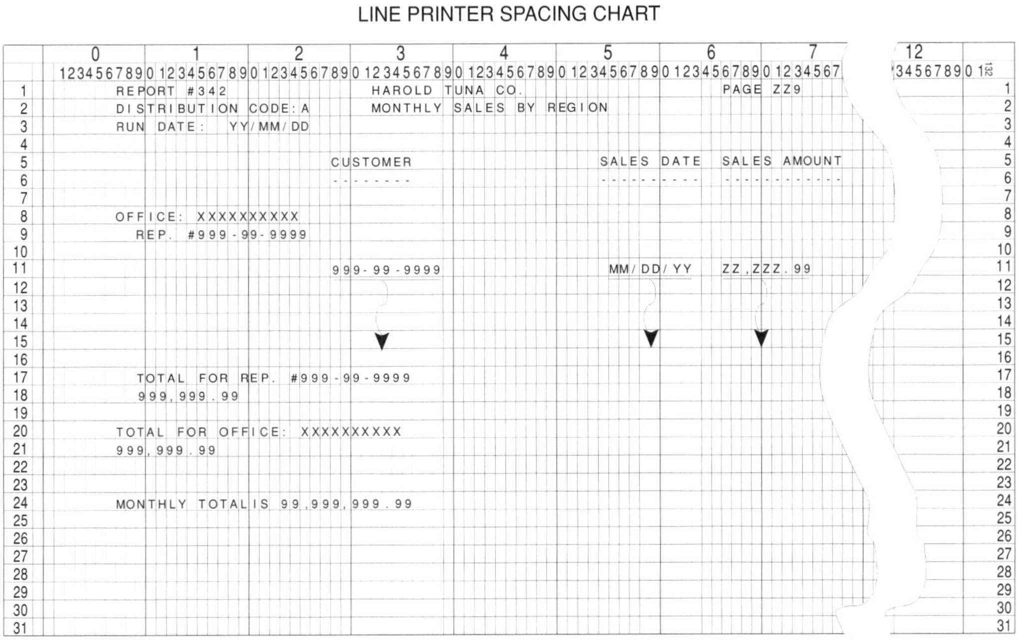

LINE PRINTER SPACING CHART

The hierarchy chart used to perform the reporting task in Chapter 8 is illustrated in Figure 13.2. Notice that the hierarchy chart contains 25 different modules. Only five of these modules actually perform the tasks of acquiring input records and preparing detail lines. The rest conduct control breaks, maintain report totals, and prepare new pages.

The five modules that perform the main activities are isolated from the large hierarchy chart and shown in Figure 13.3. We will use this hierarchy chart to develop reports using the Report Writer feature. The page breaks, control breaks, and totals will be automatically handled by the Report Writer through specifications in the DATA DIVISION. By eliminating much of the logic from the PROCEDURE DIVISION, the resulting code is shorter, simpler, and easier to maintain.

13.1.2   Logic Handled by the Report Writer

The Report Writer handles the logic eliminated from the larger hierarchy chart in Figure 13.2, resulting in the chart of Figure 13.3. The Nassi-Schneiderman charts for the design are in Figure 13.4 and the code is in Figure 13.5. To understand how this is done, it is necessary to study the general structure of the reports handled by the Report Writer. This general layout is depicted in Figure 13.6.

Figure 13.2   Hierarchy Chart for the "List Sales File" Program

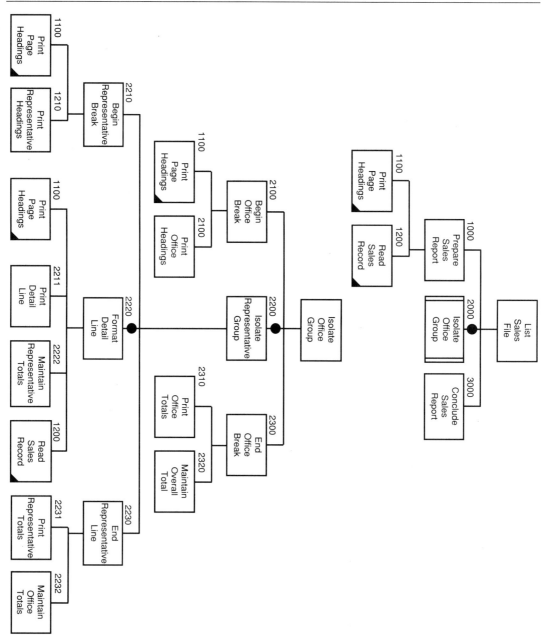

Figure 13.3   *Simplified Report Hierarchy Chart for the "List Sales File" Program*

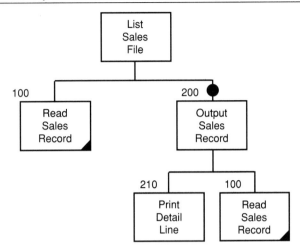

Figure 13.4   *N-S Charts for "List Sales File"*

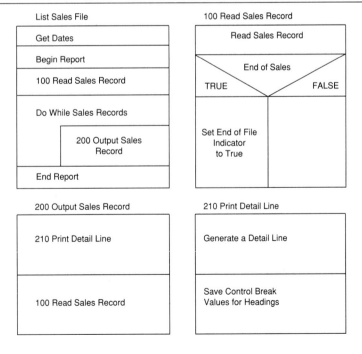

Figure 13.5   Code for "List Sales File"

```
 1 IDENTIFICATION DIVISION.
 2 PROGRAM-ID.  LIST-SALES-RECORDS.
 3*  THIS PROGRAM TAKES THE SALES FROM THE PRIOR MONTH AND
 4*  GENERATES A LISTING GROUPED BY REPRESENTATIVE AND OFFICE
 5 AUTHOR.         SELF.
 6 DATE-WRITTEN.  JUNE 12, 1996.
 7 DATE-COMPILED. 16-Jul-92 04:29.
10 ENVIRONMENT DIVISION.
11
12 CONFIGURATION SECTION.
13 SOURCE-COMPUTER.  GENERIC-COMPUTER.
14 OBJECT-COMPUTER.  GENERIC-COMPUTER.
15
16 INPUT-OUTPUT SECTION.
17 FILE-CONTROL.
18     SELECT MONTHLY-SALES-FILE ASSIGN TO DISK
19         ORGANIZATION IS SEQUENTIAL.
20     SELECT SALES-REPORT ASSIGN TO PRINTER
21         ORGANIZATION IS SEQUENTIAL.
22
23
24 DATA DIVISION.
25
26 FILE SECTION.
27
28 FD  MONTHLY-SALES-FILE
29     LABEL RECORDS ARE STANDARD.
30
31 01  MS-SALE-RECORD.
32     05  MS-OFFICE              PIC X(10).
33     05  MS-REPRESENTATIVE-ID  PIC 9(10).
34     05  MS-CUSTOMER-NBR       PIC 9(10).
35     05  MS-SALE-DATE          PIC 9(6).
36     05  MS-SALE-AMOUNT        PIC 9(5)V99.
37
38 FD  SALES-REPORT
39     LABEL RECORDS ARE OMITTED
40     REPORT IS MONTHLY-SALES-BY-REGION.
41
42 WORKING-STORAGE SECTION.
43
44 01  EOF-SALES PIC X VALUE "N".
```

Figure 13.5   *(continued)*

```
45
46 01  WS-DATE PIC 9(6).
47
48 01  SAVE-CONTROL-BREAKS.
49     05  SAVE-OFFICE         PIC 9(10).
50     05  SAVE-REPRESENTATIVE PIC 9(10).
51
52
53 REPORT SECTION.
54
55 RD  MONTHLY-SALES-BY-REGION
56     CONTROLS ARE MS-OFFICE MS-REPRESENTATIVE-ID FINAL
57     PAGE LIMIT IS 55 LINES
58     HEADING 1
59     FIRST DETAIL 8
60     LAST DETAIL 54
61     FOOTING 55.
62
63 01  TYPE PH.
64     05  LINE 1.
65         10  COLUMN 7 PIC X(10) VALUE "REPORT #342".
66         10  COLUMN 32 PIC X(15) VALUE "HAROLD TUNA COMPANY".
67         10  COLUMN 66 PIC X(5)  VALUE "PAGE".
68         10  COLUMN 71 PIC ZZ9 SOURCE PAGE-COUNTER.
69     05  LINE PLUS 1.
70         10  COLUMN 7 PIC X(19) VALUE "DISTIBUTION CODE: A".
71         10  COLUMN 32 PIC X(23) VALUE "MONTHLY SALES BY REGION".
72     05  LINE PLUS 1.
73         10  COLUMN 7 PIC X(9)  VALUE "RUN DATE:".
74         10  COLUMN 18 PIC Z9/99/99 SOURCE WS-DATE.
75     05  LINE PLUS 2.
76         10  COLUMN 29 PIC X(9) VALUE "CUSTOMER".
77         10  COLUMN 45 PIC X(30) VALUE "SALES DATE  SALES AMOUNT".
78     05  LINE PLUS 1.
79         10  COLUMN 29 PIC X(12) VALUE ALL "-".
80         10  COLUMN 45 PIC X(10) VALUE ALL "-".
81         10  COLUMN 57 PIC X(12) VALUE ALL "-".
82
83 01  TYPE CONTROL HEADING MS-OFFICE.
84     05  LINE PLUS 2.
85         10  COLUMN 7 PIC X(8)  VALUE "OFFICE: ".
86         10  COLUMN 15 PIC X(10) SOURCE MS-OFFICE.
```

Figure 13.5   (continued)

```
 87
 88 01   TYPE CONTROL HEADING MS-REPRESENTATIVE-ID.
 89      05   LINE PLUS 1.
 90          10   COLUMN 9  PIC X(6) VALUE "REP. #".
 91          10   COLUMN 14 PIC 999/99/9999
 92              SOURCE MS-REPRESENTATIVE-ID.
 93
 94 01   CUSTOMER-DATE-AMOUNT TYPE DE.
 95      05   LINE PLUS 1.
 96          10   COLUMN 29 PIC 999/99/9999 SOURCE MS-CUSTOMER-NBR.
 97          10   COLUMN 45 PIC Z9/99/99 SOURCE MS-SALE-DATE.
 98          10   COLUMN 57 PIC ZZ,ZZZ.99 SOURCE MS-SALE-AMOUNT.
 99
100 01   TYPE CF MS-REPRESENTATIVE-ID.
101      05   LINE PLUS 2.
102          10   COLUMN 9  PIC X(16) VALUE "TOTAL FOR REP. #".
103          10   COLUMN 25 PIC 999/99/9999 SOURCE SAVE-REPRESENTATIVE.
104      05   LINE PLUS 1.
105          10   MS-REPRESENTATIVE-TOTAL
106              COLUMN 9 PIC ZZ,ZZZ.99 SUM MS-SALE-AMOUNT.
107
108 01   TYPE CF MS-OFFICE.
109      05   LINE PLUS 2.
110          10   COLUMN 7  PIC X(15) VALUE "TOTAL FOR OFFICE: ".
111          10   COLUMN 25 PIC X(10) SOURCE SAVE-OFFICE.
112      05   LINE PLUS 1.
113          10   MS-OFFICE-TOTAL
114              COLUMN 7 PIC ZZZ,ZZZ.99 SUM MS-REPRESENTATIVE-TOTAL.
115
116 01   TYPE CF FINAL.
117      05   LINE PLUS 2.
118          10   COLUMN 7  PIC X(17) VALUE "MONTHLY TOTAL IS".
119          10   COLUMN 24 PIC ZZ,ZZZ,ZZZ.99 SUM MS-OFFICE-TOTAL.
120
121
122 PROCEDURE DIVISION.
123 LIST-SALES-FILE.
124      OPEN INPUT MONTHLY-SALES-FILE.
125      OPEN OUTPUT SALES-REPORT.
126      ACCEPT WS-DATE FROM DATE.
127      INITIATE MONTHLY-SALES-BY-REGION.
128      PERFORM 100-READ-SALES-RECORD.
```

Figure 13.5   (continued)

```
129     PERFORM 200-OUTPUT-SALES-RECORD UNTIL EOF-SALES = "Y".
130     TERMINATE MONTHLY-SALES-BY-REGION.
131     CLOSE MONTHLY-SALES-FILE.
132     CLOSE SALES-REPORT.
133     STOP RUN.
134
135 100-READ-SALES-RECORD.
136     READ MONTHLY-SALES-FILE AT END
137         MOVE "Y" TO EOF-SALES
138         MOVE HIGH-VALUES TO MS-SALE-RECORD.
139
140 200-OUTPUT-SALES-RECORD.
141     PERFORM 210-PRINT-DETAIL-LINE.
142     PERFORM 100-READ-SALES-RECORD.
143
144 210-PRINT-DETAIL-LINE.
145     GENERATE CUSTOMER-DATE-AMOUNT.
146     MOVE MS-OFFICE TO SAVE-OFFICE.
```

Figure 13.6   Generalized Structure of Reports

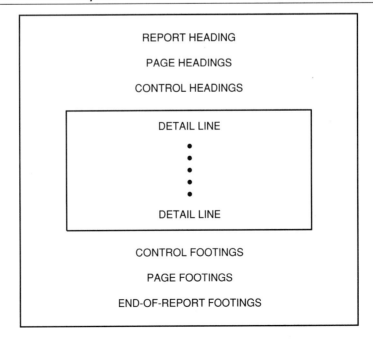

Report Heading. One or more lines of heading may be printed at the beginning of a report. In a conventional COBOL program the report heading is generated by the programmer in the preprocessing module, prior to performing the main iteration module. The Report Writer eliminates the need for code to print the heading in the PROCEDURE DIVISION. It allows the report heading to be one page in length. It may describe the contents of the report, list abbreviations used, provide a distribution list, or present any other information that needs to be printed only once at the beginning of the report.

Page Heading. The information presented at the top of each page of a report is known as a page heading. This implies that every page containing detail lines or summary information will contain page headings. A page heading usually includes the report title, run date, page number, and column headings for the detail lines. In Figure 13.1 the first six lines of the report comprise the page heading. Page numbers are maintained automatically by the Report Writer and new page headings are printed as needed. Therefore, the programmer does not need to conduct any page control activities in the PROCEDURE DIVISION, eliminating the need for the logic in module "1100-Print-Page-Headings."

Control Headings. Headings printed each time a control break is issued are known as control headings. The report in Figure 13.1 has control headings for each level of control break in lines 8 and 9. The Report Writer automatically prints any control headings specified in their appropriate places. The programmer does not have to write the code to determine where the control breaks occur. This represents substantial savings in code and logic by eliminating module numbers 2000, 2100, 2110, 2200, 2210, and 2211.

Detail Lines. Detail lines are still controlled by the programmer. Although the Report Writer formats the lines, a command must be issued to print each detail line. If desired, multiple detail lines may be used within a report, each of which is under the control of the programmer. This allows the programmer to establish a different format for different types of detail lines. For example, different transactions, errors, or conditions may require differing formats. Much of the logic in modules "2220 Format Detail Line" and "2221 Print Detail Line" is removed.

Control Footings (Control Totals). A control *footing* summarizes the contents of the detail lines in a control grouping. A control footing is presented at the end of the control group to which it belongs. In Figure 13.1 there are control footings for each sales representative and each office location. In conventional programs the programmer has to maintain the totals for each level of control break and test each control break item to determine when to print the control total or footing. By using the Report Writer, footing lines, tests for control breaks, and maintenance of totals are automatically conducted. Module numbers 2222, 2230, 2231, 2232, 2300, 2310, and 2320 in Figure 13.2 are thus eliminated.

Page Footings. With the exception of the report heading page, the bottom of each page may contain information, such as a summary or other information. The logic for keeping totals and writing page footings is handled automatically by the Report Writer. Since reports may contain both page headings and footings, care should be taken in the design phase to allow room for enough detail lines.

Report Footing. A report footing may be printed at the end of the entire report. It is analogous to the report heading and usually consists of overall summary information. The Report Writer prints the summary, relieving the programmer of this burden. This eliminates the need for module "3000 Conclude Sales Report."

13.2   Coding the Report Writer

In the previous section we emphasized that the Report Writer saves coding effort by greatly simplifying the logic structure of a report program. However, it is still necessary to specify the actions to be handled by the Report Writer. Much of this is done in the DATA DIVISION.

13.2.1   The DATA DIVISION

Using the Report Writer feature of COBOL requires making certain changes in the FILE and WORKING-STORAGE SECTIONs and adding a REPORT SECTION.

The FILE and WORKING-STORAGE SECTIONs. The first change is in the FD entry needed to describe the report's file in the FILE SECTION. The DATA RECORD clause is replaced with a REPORT clause that names the report(s) in the report file. The format and rules for the FD entry used with the Report Writer are:

FD file-name

$$\left[\text{ \underline{LABEL} \underline{RECORDS} ARE } \left\{\begin{array}{l}\underline{\text{OMITTED}}\\\underline{\text{STANDARD}}\end{array}\right\}\right]$$

$$\left\{\begin{array}{l}\underline{\text{REPORT}}\ \underline{\text{IS}}\\\underline{\text{REPORTS}}\ \underline{\text{ARE}}\end{array}\right\}\ \text{report-name-1 [report-name-2]} \ldots$$

1. The file-name must be defined by a SELECT clause.
2. The report-names must appear in the REPORT SECTION of the DATA DIVISION.

The FD entry in Figure 13.5 for the sales report example of Figure 13.1 is as follows:

```
FD      MONTHLY-SALES-REPORT

        LABEL RECORDS ARE OMITTED
        REPORT IS MONTHLY-SALES-BY-REGION.
```

No 01 level record entry follows the FD entry for a report. The entry that describes the actual report contents and layout appears in the REPORT SECTION, which we will examine shortly.

The WORKING-STORAGE SECTION requires no additions. In fact, the WORKING-STORAGE SECTION is greatly reduced because the descriptions of the accumulators, page counters, line counters, and the report layout appear in the REPORT SECTION. Notice in Figure 13.5, lines 44 through 50 contain only an end-of-file indicator, a date field, and two save areas. Compare this to the WORKING-STORAGE SECTION of the example in Chapter 8.

The REPORT SECTION. The REPORT SECTION follows the WORKING-STORAGE SECTION in the DATA DIVISION and must be specified prior to the PROCEDURE DIVISION. It defines all the reports to be generated by the Report Writer. The report formats for each type of report line are described in the REPORT SECTION. The page layouts and lengths, control breaks, and accumulators are also defined in this section.

RD Entries. Each report is defined by a report description, or RD entry, just as each file is defined by an FD or SD entry. The RD entry names and describes the report. A simplified format for the RD entry is:

RD report-name

$$\left[\left\{ \begin{array}{l} \underline{\text{CONTROL}} \text{ IS} \\ \underline{\text{CONTROLS}} \text{ ARE} \end{array} \right\} \quad \left\{ \begin{array}{l} \text{data-name-1[data-name-2]...} \\ \underline{\text{FINAL}} \text{ [data-name-1]...} \end{array} \right\} \right]$$

[PAGE LIMIT IS integer-1 LINES]
[HEADING integer-2]
[FIRST DETAIL integer-3]
[LAST DETAIL integer-4]
[FOOTING integer-5].

The various clauses provide information relevant to the formatting of the report. The CONTROL clause provides information about the control breaks. In other words, the control hierarchy for the report is established. The data items on which the levels of control depend are specified from the highest to the lowest, from major to minor. For example, in the sales report the control breaks are based on the entire report, the individual office, and the sales representatives as denoted by FINAL, MS-OFFICE, and MS-REPRESENTATIVE-ID. MS-OFFICE is considered the major control and MS-REPRESENTATIVE-ID is the minor control. The Report Writer tests these values every time a detail line is to be printed to determine if they have changed. If they have, a control break occurs. If the FINAL option is specified, it is the highest control level and must therefore precede the list of control items as in line 56 of Figure 13.5. The reserved word FINAL indicates that all detail lines are to be considered part of a larger group. Thus, a FINAL control break occurs once all records are processed. This allows report totals to be printed after all records have been processed.

The other clauses specify page formatting information. The PAGE LIMIT clause controls the number of lines allowed on each page. The HEADING clause specifies the line number where the page heading begins. If omitted, the first line is assumed. The FIRST DETAIL clause indicates the line where the first detail line may be printed on a page. The LAST DETAIL clause specifies the last line on which a detail line may be printed on the page. The FOOTING clause specifies the last line on the page where footings may be printed. The following is the RD entry for the sales report of Figure 13.5:

```
RD   MONTHLY-SALES-BY-REGION
     CONTROLS ARE MS-OFFICE MS-REPRESENTATIVE-ID
```

```
PAGE LIMIT IS 55 LINES
HEADING        1
FIRST DETAIL   8
LAST DETAIL    54
FOOTING        55.
```

This entry will cause control breaks on the office (region) and representative to be performed. The report page is restricted to 55 lines with the headings starting on the first line, the detail lines are restricted to lines 8 through 54, and one extra line of footings is being printed.

TYPE Entries. Each type of line in a particular report is known as a report group. Each report group corresponds to a line type specification and is described by a TYPE clause. Each report group is denoted with an 01-level entry following its corresponding RD entry in the REPORT SECTION. These are analogous to 01-level entries for records in the FILE SECTION. The simplified format and rules for the report group entry are:

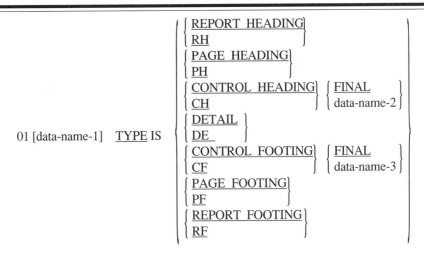

1. Data-name-1 must be supplied for type DETAIL.
2. Data-name-2, data-name-3, and FINAL must be in the CONTROL clause of the RD entry.

The Report Writer processes automatically each report group, with the exception of the DETAIL group. There can be only one REPORT HEADING group in a report, and it is processed once as the first group in the report. Only one PAGE HEADING may appear in the report description. It is processed automatically as the first group on each page. The CONTROL HEADING, if specified, is processed automatically at the beginning of the control group designated by a control data item in the report description (RD) entry. If FINAL is specified, the CONTROL HEADING group is processed when the first detail line for the report is generated. Only one CONTROL HEADING group per control item can be specified per report. A

CONTROL FOOTING group, if specified, is processed at the end of the control group designated by a control data item in the RD entry. Any control footing defined will be printed from minor to major up to and including the changed CONTROL data item. If FINAL is specified, the CONTROL FOOTING group is processed only once at the end of the report. Only one CONTROL FOOTING FINAL group can be specified per report. There can be only one PAGE FOOTING, and it is processed as the last group on each page. Only one REPORT FOOTING group may appear in a report description. It is processed once as the last group in the report. There is no limit to the number of DETAIL report groups in a report.

Each line type appearing in the report will have an 01 TYPE entry following the RD entry. Thus, the sales report will have an 01 TYPE DETAIL entry for the detail lines, an 01 TYPE CONTROL HEADING entry for each control break heading, and an 01 TYPE CONTROL FOOTING entry for the totals for each control break. The data-name-1 is optional for line types other than detail lines. However, it is required for detail lines so that the detail lines can be referenced by name in the PROCEDURE DIVISION, since the DETAIL report group is processed under the control of the programmer. TYPE entries for the sales report are:

```
01   TYPE   PAGE   HEADING
01   TYPE   CONTROL   HEADING   MS-OFFICE.
01   TYPE   CONTROL   FOOTING   MS-OFFICE.
01   TYPE   REPORT   FOOTING.
01   SALES-DETAIL   TYPE   DETAIL.
```

Line Specification. For each line type (report group), the position of the lines comprising it must be specified. For example, if a page heading is composed of three lines, there must be three line specification entries subordinate to the 01-level TYPE entry for it. It is good practice, but not a COBOL requirement, to define each line of the line type as a separate 05 entry in order of its appearance in the group. Following this guideline, a sample line type entry might appear as follows:

```
01   TYPE PAGE HEADING.
     05 (FOR FIRST LINE OF THE REPORT GROUP)
     05 (FOR SECOND LINE OF THE REPORT GROUP)
     05 (FOR THIRD LINE OF THE REPORT GROUP)
```

The simplified line specification format and rules are:

---

05 [data-name-1] <u>LINE</u> NUMBER IS $\begin{Bmatrix} \text{integer-1} \\ \underline{\text{PLUS}}\ \text{integer-2} \end{Bmatrix}$

1. Data-name-1 is optional and follows standard naming rules.
2. The PLUS option prints the line after integer-2 line feeds.
3. If integer-1 is specified, it must not be in conflict with the page controls specified in the RD entry or any other report line.

If the word LINE is followed immediately by a numeric literal, the report line will be printed at that specific line position on the page. For example, if the first line of a report were to appear on the third line of each page, the line specification would be:

```
01  TYPE PAGE HEADING
    05 LINE 3.
```

The LINE PLUS option specifies the number of lines to be skipped before the line is actually printed. It is similar to the AFTER ADVANCING clause in the WRITE statement. In the sales report example each one of the five report heading lines is specified with the LINE or LINE PLUS clause. The line specification for the lines in the page heading is:

```
01 TYPE  PAGE  HEADING.
   05 LINE 1.
   05 LINE PLUS 1.
   05 LINE PLUS 1.
   05 LINE PLUS 2.
   05 LINE PLUS 1.
```

The first heading line appears on the first line of the page. The second line immediately follows the first, as specified by the clause LINE PLUS 1. The fourth line leaves a blank line between itself and the third line.

Field Specification. Once the lines of the report group have been specified, their contents must be described. The individual fields making up the line are subgroups of the line. These subgroups are made up of individual data items and constants. For example, in the sales report the first line of the page heading is made up of the report number, the company name, and the page number. The items making up the subgroups should be coded in their order of appearance subordinate to the line they describe. For simplicity, we will always assign them as level-10 entries, but COBOL allows any level from 02 to 49. A typical line specification would appear as follows:

```
01 TYPE ...
   05  LINE  1.
       10  (FIRST SUBGROUP OF REPORT LINE)
       10  (SECOND SUBGROUP OF REPORT LINE)
       10  (THIRD SUBGROUP OF REPORT LINE)
```

The simplified format and rules for entering the line fields are:

```
10 [data-name-1]  [COLUMN NUMBER IS integer-1]
                  { PIC     } IS character-string
                  { PICTURE }
                  { SOURCE IS data-name-2           }
                  { VALUE IS literal                }
                  { SUM data-name-3 [data-name-4]...}
```

1. The character string of the PIC clause follows the rules established for the FILE and WORKING-STORAGE SECTIONs.
2. A SUM appearing in a TYPE CONTROL FOOTING is reset to zero after the control footing is printed.
3. In PAGE HEADING and PAGE FOOTING groups, SOURCE clauses must not reference control break data names.
4. In CONTROL FOOTING and REPORT FOOTING groups, SOURCE clauses must not reference group items containing control break data-names or data items subordinate to a control break data-name.

Each line type is defined by using the various field definition clauses. To specify an item on a line, its starting column, length, description, and value must be specified using the COLUMN, PICTURE, and VALUE, SOURCE, or SUM clauses.

The COLUMN NUMBER entry controls horizontal spacing of the report. Integer-1 specifies in what column a field begins. Since the Report Writer manages the spacing automatically and fills missing spaces with blanks, the programmer does not need to keep an exact count of the number of spaces in a print line. Each field within the line requires a PICTURE clause. It is formed in the same way as PICTURE clauses in the FILE and WORKING-STORAGE SECTIONs.

Each item may be filled using one of three options: VALUE, SOURCE, or SUM. The VALUE clause specifies the literal to be printed, such as VALUE "ABC COMPANY." The SOURCE clause specifies a previously defined data item, data-name-1, from which the value to be printed will be transferred. This implies that the value of the data item specified is automatically moved to the printable item prior to being printed. Data items defined in the DATA DIVISION or maintained by the Report Writer may be used in the SOURCE clause, except data items used in the CONTROL clause of the RD entry referred to in the PAGE HEADING or PAGE FOOTING. Furthermore, CONTROL FOOTING and REPORT FOOTING types may not use group items containing control data-names or data items subordinate to a control data-name in the SOURCE clause.

The following line type specification is for the first two lines in the page heading of the sample sales report:

```
01 TYPE  PH.
    05 LINE  1.
       10  COLUMN  7  PIC X(10)  VALUE    "REPORT #342".
       10  COLUMN 32  PIC X(15)  VALUE
           "HAROLD TUNA COMPANY".
       10  COLUMN 66  PIC X(5)  VALUE   "PAGE".
       10  COLUMN 71  PIC ZZ9 SOURCE PAGE-COUNTER.
    05  LINE PLUS  1.
       10  COLUMN  7  PIC X(19)  VALUE
           "DISTRIBUTION CODE: A".
       10  COLUMN 32  PIC X(23)  VALUE
           "MONTHLY SALES BY REGION".
```

Note that the page number is obtained from *PAGE-COUNTER*, which is a data item maintained by the Report Writer.

The *SUM* clause sets up a counter to which the values of the specified data items are added each time a detail line is printed. Thus, totals can be automatically maintained. If the field using the SUM clause is given a data-name, it may be used in other computations regardless of its PICTURE clause. This means that other fields in the REPORT SECTION can refer to this field to maintain higher levels of control totals. The line specifications for the detail line and control footings of the sales report are:

```
01 CUSTOMER-DATE-AMOUNT   TYPE  DE.
     05    LINE   PLUS  1.
           10  COLUMN   28  PIC X(12) SOURCE EDIT-CUSTOMER-ID.
           10  COLUMN   44  PIC 99/99/99 SOURCE MS-SALE-DATE.
           10  COLUMN   56  PIC  ZZ,119.99 SOURCE MS-SALE-AMOUNT.
01 TYPE  CF  MS-REPRESENTATIVE-ID.
     05    LINE   PLUS  1.
           10  COLUMN    9  PIC  X(15) VALUE "TOTAL FOR REP-".
           10  COLUMN   25  PIC  X(11) SOURCE SAVE-REPRESENTATIVE.
     05    LINE   PLUS  1.
           10  MS-REPRESENTATIVE-TOTAL   COLUMN 9 PIC ZZZ,ZZ9.99 SUM MS-
               SALE-AMOUNT.
01 TYPE  CF  MS-OFFICE.
     05    LINE   PLUS  1.
           10   COLUMN  7  PIC  X(18) VALUE "TOTAL FOR OFFICE:-".
     10    COLUMN 25 PIC  X(11)  SOURCE SAVE-OFFICE.
     05    LINE  PLUS  1.
           10  MS-OFFICE-TOTAL  COLUMN  7  PIC  ZZZ,ZZ9.99
               SUM  MS-REPRESENTATIVE-TOTAL.
```

The entire set of entries is in the REPORT SECTION of Figure 13.5.

The SUM clauses in the CONTROL FOOTING line types are used for the MS-REPRE-SENTATIVE-ID control break and the MS-OFFICE control break to represent the sales for the month. In the MS-REPRESENTATIVE-ID control break, MS-REPRESENTATIVE-TOTAL in the CONTROL FOOTING TYPE entry is the counter to which the MS-SALE AMOUNT is automatically summed and the numeric value is edited prior to printing. The value is automatically reset to zero to accumulate the total for the next representative. The totals for the office are handled in the CF TYPE entry for MS-OFFICE using SUM MS-REPRESENTATIVE-TOTAL. This causes MS-REPRESENTATIVE TOTAL to be rolled into MS-OFFICE-TOTAL as appropriate. Again, this is done automatically.

Although COBOL provides additional features in the Report Writer, we have limited our discussion to the most common ones. Many vendors have supplemented their report writers with their own enhancements. To discover the full features and complete syntax structure of your system's Report Writer you must consult the COBOL Reference Manual or User's Guide provided by your vendor.

13.2.2   *The PROCEDURE DIVISION*

It is still necessary to OPEN and CLOSE the files associated with the FD entries containing the reports. However, no WRITE statements need to be issued. Instead the Report Writer uses the INITIATE, GENERATE, and TERMINATE statements to produce the report.

The INITIATE Statement. The *INITIATE* statement causes the Report Writer to begin the processing of a report. The COBOL-supplied variable PAGE-COUNTER is initialized to one and the SUM counters to zero. Report headings, if specified, are printed. Each report, even if contained within the same file, must be initiated by the programmer. The format and rules of the INITIATE statement are:

INITIATE   { report-name } . . .

1.   Each report-name must have an RD entry.
2   The INITIATE must be conducted to a report-name that forms part of an OPEN file.

The INITIATE statement for the sales report (line 127 of Figure 13.5) is:

```
INITIATE MONTHLY-SALES-BY-REGION.
```

TERMINATE. The TERMINATE statement causes the Report Writer to conclude the processing of a report. TERMINATE should be the last command issued to a report. The TERMINATE statement causes final control breaks to be issued and report footings to be printed. Every report that has been initiated must be terminated. The format and rules for the TERMINATE statement are:

TERMINATE   { report-name } . . .

1.   Each report-name must be defined by an RD entry.
2.   The report-name must have been initiated.

The TERMINATE statement for the sales report of Figure 13.5 is:

```
TERMINATE MONTHLY-SALES-BY-REGION.
```

This causes the last representative totals, office totals, and report totals for the sales report to be printed.

The GENERATE Statement. The GENERATE statement is the driver that produces a report in accordance with the description in the REPORT SECTION of the DATA DIVISION. The format and rules of the GENERATE statement are:

Option 1: GENERATE data-name.
Option 2: GENERATE report-name.

1. The data-name must be a TYPE DETAIL in an RD entry.
2. The report-name must be defined by an RD entry.
3. The report must be initiated before executing a GENERATE statement.

If Option 1 is used, the GENERATE statement causes a detail line to be sent to the printer, control breaks to be tested, totals to be maintained, and page breaks to be checked. If any of the breaks are required to be performed, the GENERATE will perform them before the detail line is printed. Thus, this single statement performs the tasks previously performed by multitudes of ADDs, MOVEs, IFs, PERFORMs, and WRITEs. The programmer does not have to test for the control or page breaks, maintain totals, or MOVE fields to report lines.

The statement to GENERATE a detail line for the sales report of Figure 13.5 is:

```
GENERATE CUSTOMER-DATE-AMOUNT.
```

This statement causes the Report Writer to test for a page break and both control breaks. If a break occurs, the necessary totals, headings, and footings will be printed. In addition, the sales amount MS-SALE-AMOUNT from the detail line will be added to the sales representative total, MS-REPRESENTATIVE-TOTAL. The fields in the detail line entry 01 CUSTOMER-DATE-AMOUNT TYPE DE are moved to the appropriate location within the detail line. The detail line is then printed. All this is accomplished with one GENERATE statement.

If Option 2 of the GENERATE statement is used, a report-name is specified. This format prepares exactly the same report but suppresses the printing of all the detail lines, thus producing a summary report. For the sales report example, the statement would be

```
GENERATE MONTHLY-SALES-BY-REGION.
```

The resulting sales report would include only page headings, control headings, control footings, and report footings. This Report Writer feature is very useful for preparing summary reports for management. For example, if upper-level management requested a summary of a report that is given to a lower-level manager, the same program could be used to create both reports merely by changing one COBOL statement.

The Sales Report PROCEDURE DIVISION. The entire PROCEDURE DIVISION needed to create the sales report is:

```
PROCEDURE  DIVISION.
LIST-SALES-FILE.
```

```
      OPEN    INPUT    MONTHLY-SALES-FILE.
      OPEN    OUTPUT    SALES-REPORT.
      ACCEPT  WS-DATE    FROM    DATE.
      INITIATE  MONTHLY-SALES-BY-REGION.
      PERFORM  100-READ-SALES-RECORD.
      PERFORM  200-OUTPUT-SALES-RECORD UNTIL EOF-SALES = "Y".
      TERMINATE  MONTHLY-SALES-BY-REGION.
      CLOSE   SALES-REPORT.
      CLOSE   MONTHLY-SALES-FILE.
      STOP RUN.
  100-READ-SALES-RECORD.
      READ   MONTHLY-SALES-FILE.
          AT END MOVE "TRUE" TO EOF-SALES.
  200-OUTPUT-SALES-RECORD.
      PERFORM  210-PRINT-DETAIL-LINE.
      PERFORM  100-READ-MONTHLY-SALES.
  210-PRINT-DETAIL-LINE.
      GENERATE   CUSTOMER-DATE-AMOUNT.
      MOVE MS-OFFICE TO SAVE OFFICE.
      MOVE MS-REPRESENTATIVE-ID TO SAVE-REPRESENTATIVE.
```

The code is very compact and easy to follow. This has been accomplished with only a few additions to our subset of COBOL. As you can see, the COBOL Report Writer is a very powerful facility.

Case Study: CDL's Accounts Receivable Listing Revisited

Charlene is pleased that a new COBOL compiler containing the COBOL Report Writer is now available for her computer. She decides to redesign and code the listing of the accounts receivable file. The revised hierarchy chart appears in Figure 13.7. The number of modules has been reduced to five because the COBOL Report Writer handles the totals, control breaks, and line formatting and printing required in the program specifications. The Nassi-Schneiderman charts in Figure 13.8 further illustrate the simplification of the program compared with those in Chapter 8. Finally, the program code is illustrated in Figure 13.9. The PROCEDURE DIVISION is much shorter, and the REPORT SECTION has replaced most of the WORKING-STORAGE SECTION. The test data and results in Figure 13.10 demonstrate that Charlene's code is correct.

Figure 13.7   Revised Hierarchy Chart for CDL's "Accounts Receivable Listing" Program

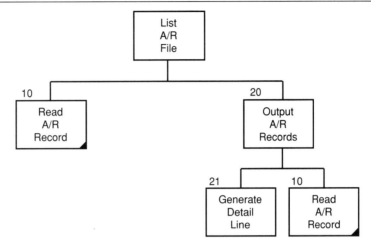

Figure 13.8   Revised N-S Charts for CDL's "Accounts Receivable Listing"

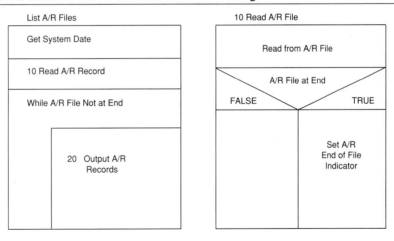

Figure 13.8   (continued)

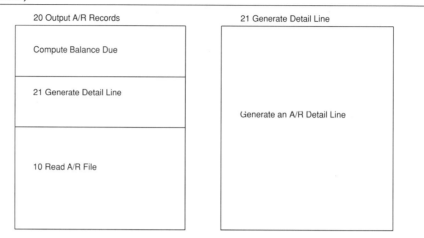

Figure 13.9   Program Code for "Accounts Receivable Listing"

```
 1 IDENTIFICATION DIVISION.
 2 PROGRAM-ID. LIST-AR.
 3*    THIS PROGRAM USES THE A/R FILE TO PRODUCE A LISTING
 4*    WITH BREAKS ON CUSTOMER AND ORDER NUMBERS
 5
 6 AUTHOR.  C HILTON
 7 DATE-WRITTEN.  3-1-94.
 8 DATE-COMPILED. 08-Mar-94 00:40.
12 ENVIRONMENT DIVISION.
13
14
15 CONFIGURATION SECTION.
16
17 SOURCE-COMPUTER.  GENERIC-COMPUTER.
18 OBJECT-COMPUTER.  GENERIC-COMPUTER.
19
20
21 INPUT-OUTPUT SECTION.
22
23 FILE-CONTROL.
24    SELECT AR-OPEN-ITEM-FILE ASSIGN TO DISK
25        ORGANIZATION IS SEQUENTIAL.
26    SELECT OPEN-ITEM-LIST-FILE ASSIGN TO PRINTER
27        ORGANIZATION IS SEQUENTIAL.
```

Figure 13.9 *(continued)*

```
28
29
30
31 DATA DIVISION.
32
33
34 FILE SECTION.
35
36 FD  OPEN-ITEM-LIST-FILE
37      LABEL RECORDS ARE OMITTED
38      REPORT IS AR-OPEN-ITEMS-LISTING.
39
40 FD  AR-OPEN-ITEM-FILE
41      LABEL RECORDS ARE STANDARD.
42
43 01  AR-OPEN-ITEM-REC.
44      05  AR-CUSTOMER-NUMBER  PIC 9(6).
45      05  AR-ORDER-NUMBER     PIC 9(6).
46      05  AR-ORDER-DATE       PIC 9(6).
47      05  AR-AMOUNT-BILLED    PIC 9(6)V99.
48      05  AR-AMOUNT-PAID      PIC 9(6)V99.
49
50 WORKING-STORAGE SECTION.
51
52 01  EOF-AR PIC X(5) VALUE "FALSE".
53
54 01  WORK-AREAS.
55      05  WA-DATE       PIC 9(6).
56      05  WA-MM-DD-YY.
57          10  WA-MM     PIC XX.
58          10  WA-DD     PIC XX.
59          10  WA-YY     PIC XX.
60      05  WA-YEAR       PIC XX.
61      05  WA-BALANCE    PIC 9(6)V99.
62
63
64 REPORT SECTION.
65
66 RD  AR-OPEN-ITEMS-LISTING
67      CONTROLS ARE FINAL AR-CUSTOMER-NUMBER AR-ORDER-NUMBER
68      PAGE LIMIT IS 55 LINES
69      HEADING 1
```

Figure 13.9   *(continued)*

```
70      FIRST DETAIL 9
71      LAST DETAIL 55.
72
73 01   TYPE PH.
74      05  LINE 1.
75          10   COLUMN 1  PIC X(10) VALUE "REPORT #19".
76          10   COLUMN 32 PIC X(22) VALUE "COMPACT DISCS FOR LESS".
77          10   COLUMN 65 PIC X(5)  VALUE "PAGE".
78          10   COLUMN 70 PIC ZZZZZZ9   SOURCE PAGE-COUNTER.
79      05 LINE PLUS 1.
80          10   COLUMN 1  PIC X(19) VALUE "DISTRIBUTION: OWENS".
81          10   COLUMN 32 PIC X(22) VALUE "A/R OPEN ITEMS LISTING".
82      05  LINE PLUS 1.
83          10   COLUMN 1  PIC X(09) VALUE "RUN DATE:".
84          05   COLUMN 11 PIC 99/99/99 SOURCE WA-DATE.
85      05  LINE PLUS 2.
86          10   COLUMN 12 PIC X(11) VALUE "CUSTOMER ID".
87          10   COLUMN 27 PIC X(09) VALUE "ORDER NBR".
88          10   COLUMN 40 PIC X(10) VALUE "ORDER DATE".
89          10   COLUMN 54 PIC X(11) VALUE "BALANCE DUE".
90      05  LINE PLUS 1.
91          10   COLUMN 12 PIC X(11) VALUE ALL "-".
92          10   COLUMN 27 PIC X(09) VALUE ALL "-".
93          10   COLUMN 40 PIC X(10) VALUE ALL "-".
94          10   COLUMN 54 PIC X(11) VALUE ALL "-".
95
96 01   TYPE CONTROL HEADING AR-ORDER-NUMBER.
97      05  LINE PLUS 2.
98          10   COLUMN 15 PIC 9(6) SOURCE AR-CUSTOMER-NUMBER.
99          10   COLUMN 29 PIC 9(6) SOURCE AR-ORDER-NUMBER.
100
101 01  DATE-BALANCE TYPE DETAIL.
102     05  LINE PLUS 1.
103         10   COLUMN 41 PIC Z9/99/99 SOURCE AR-ORDER-DATE.
104         10   COLUMN 54 PIC ZZZ,ZZ9.99 SOURCE WA-BALANCE.
105 01  TYPE CF AR-ORDER-NUMBER.
106     05  LINE PLUS 1.
107         10   COLUMN 28 PIC X(9) VALUE "ORDER $$$".
108     05  LINE PLUS 1.
109         10   T-ORDER COLUMN 25 PIC ZZ,ZZZ,ZZ9.99 SUM WA-BALANCE.
110
111 01  TYPE CF AR-CUSTOMER-NUMBER.
```

Figure 13.9   *(continued)*

```
112      05   LINE PLUS 1.
113           10   COLUMN 12 PIC X(12) VALUE "CUSTOMER $$$".
114      05   LINE PLUS 1.
115           10   T-CUSTOMER COLUMN 11 PIC ZZ,ZZZ,ZZ9.99 SUM T-ORDER.
116
117 01  TYPE CONTROL FOOTING FINAL.
118      05   LINE PLUS 4.
119           10   COLUMN 12 PIC X(20) VALUE "TOTAL A/R OPEN $$$".
120      05   LINE PLUS 1.
121           10   COLUMN 14 PIC ZZZ,ZZZ,ZZ9.99 SUM T-CUSTOMER.
122
123
124
125 PROCEDURE DIVISION.
126 LIST-AR-FILE.
127      OPEN INPUT AR-OPEN-ITEM-FILE.
128      OPEN OUTPUT OPEN-ITEM-LIST-FILE.
129      ACCEPT WA-DATE FROM DATE.
130      MOVE WA-DATE TO WA-MM-DD-YY.
131      MOVE WA-MM TO WA-YEAR.
132      MOVE WA-DD TO WA-MM.
133      MOVE WA-YY TO WA-DD.
134      MOVE WA-YEAR TO WA-YY.
135      MOVE WA-MM-DD-YY TO WA-DATE.
136      INITIATE AR-OPEN-ITEMS-LISTING.
137      PERFORM 10-READ-AR-RECORD.
138      PERFORM 20-OUTPUT-AR-RECORD
139          UNTIL EOF-AR = "TRUE".
140      TERMINATE AR-OPEN-ITEMS-LISTING.
141      CLOSE OPEN-ITEM-LIST-FILE.
142      CLOSE AR-OPEN-ITEM-FILE.
143      STOP RUN.
144
145 10-READ-AR-RECORD.
146      READ AR-OPEN-ITEM-FILE
147          AT END MOVE "TRUE" TO EOF-AR.
148
149 20-OUTPUT-AR-RECORD.
150      COMPUTE WA-BALANCE =  AR-AMOUNT-BILLED - AR-AMOUNT-PAID.
151      PERFORM 21-GENERATE-DETAIL-LINE.
152      PERFORM 10-READ-AR-RECORD.
153
```

Figure 13.9   *(continued)*

```
154 21-GENERATE-DETAIL-LINE.
155      GENERATE DATE-BALANCE.
```

Figure 13.10   *Test Plan*

```
Accounts Receivable Test Data

1111111000010915670000109900000999
1111111000010915670001299900000000
1111112000021015880000179900001099
1111112000021015880000099900000000
2222221000020915770000149900001283
2222222000030615870001678900000000
3333333000330415880000100000000000


A/R Report Results

REPORT #19                    COMPACT DISCS FOR LESS         PAGE       1
DISTRIBUTION: OWENS           A/R OPEN ITEMS LISTING
RUN DATE: 03/08/94


          CUSTOMER ID     ORDER NBR     ORDER DATE     BALANCE DUE
          -----------     ---------     ----------     -----------
            111111         100001
                                         9/15/67           1.00
                                         9/15/67         129.99
                          ORDER $$$
                            130.99


            111111         200002
                                        10/15/88           7.00
                                        10/15/88           9.99
                          ORDER $$$
                            16.99
          CUSTOMER $$$
              147.98


            222222         100002
                                         9/15/77           2.16
                          ORDER $$$
```

Figure 13.10 *(continued)*

```
                              2.16

           222222        200003
                                   6/15/87        167.89
                         ORDER $$$
                             167.89
         CUSTOMER $$$
              170.05

           333333        300033
                                   4/15/88         10.00
                         ORDER $$$
                              10.00
         CUSTOMER $$$
              10.00

         TOTAL A/R OPEN $$$
                 328.03
```

Summary

COBOL provides a powerful facility known as the Report Writer for developing reports. The Report Writer simplifies the logic required to produce most reports. It allows the programmer to describe a report by specifying its physical appearance in the REPORT SECTION of the DATA DIVISION. Each report is defined by an RD or report description entry, just as each file is defined by an FD or SD entry. The RD entry names the report, identifies the control breaks, and describes the physical characteristics of the report such as page length and layout. Following each RD entry is a report group description that specifies the types of lines that appear on a report and their characteristics. The Report Writer allows the following report groups: report heading, page heading, control heading, detail, control footing, page footing, and report footing. Each report group is further specified by describing the data items and constants that are the subgroups of the group. Their horizontal position, vertical position, description, and value are specified, as well as any accumulators that may be used.

In the PROCEDURE DIVISION three statements control the execution of the REPORT WRITER. They are the INITIATE, GENERATE, and TERMINATE statements. INITIATE begins the processing of the report and TERMINATE ends it. The programmer controls the printing of detail lines through the GENERATE statement. The GENERATE statement also allows the printing of summary reports in which no detail lines are printed but all headings and control breaks are maintained and printed.

The Report Writer automatically handles page breaks, control breaks, accumulation of totals, and the printing of headings. It simplifies the work needed to be done by the programmer and results in more compact, easy-to-follow code. The Report Writer is indeed a powerful facility.

Key Terms

Report Writer	TYPE	SUM
heading	VALUE	INITIATE
footing	SOURCE	TERMINATE
REPORT SECTION	PAGE-COUNTER	GENERATE
report description (RD)		

Hints for Avoiding Errors

1. The Report Writer feature of COBOL should be used for simple reports when the facility is available. Cutting down on the code required to maintain totals, test control breaks, and format reports cuts down on the opportunity for making errors.
2. The Report Writer is very flexible with respect to its true syntax. However, unless you follow a set of standards, you may create complexity and errors. Use the simplified standards suggested in this text for coding programs with the Report Writer.

Exercises

13.1   Identify the CDL programs that could benefit by using the Report Writer.
13.2   Apply the Report Writer to solve Exercise 8.1.
13.3   Apply the Report Writer to solve Exercise 8.2.
13.4   Apply the Report Writer to solve Exercise 8.3.
13.5   The INITIATE statement opens the report file for output. True or false?
13.6   The SUM clause indicates that the programmer
      a.   can only add to the data item.
      b.   is allowing automatic addition.
      c.   cannot specify an edit PICTURE clause.
13.7   List the valid TYPEs for report description entries.
13.8   A report will require entries in all of the following except:
      a.   FILE-CONTROL.
      b.   REPORT SECTION.
      c.   WORKING-STORAGE SECTION.
      d.   FILE SECTION.

13.9 The PICTURE clauses in the REPORT SECTION allow the same specifications as in the FILE SECTION. True or false?

13.10 A GENERATE statement that specifies a DETAIL TYPE causes
    a. SUM fields to be added.
    b. SOURCE fields to be moved.
    c. necessary control footings to be printed.
    d. all of the above

13.11 A control item is a data item that is tested each time
    a. a heading line is produced.
    b. a file is opened.
    c. a report is INITIATEd.
    d. a detail is GENERATEd.

13.12 The _____ clause specifies the purpose of each report line.
    a. TYPE
    b. PICTURE
    c. SUM
    d. SOURCE

13.13 The COLUMN clause indicates
    a. the first column used by a line.
    b. the leftmost position for each elementary item.
    c. the width of the report page.

13.14 PAGE-COUNTER
    a. must be maintained by the programmer.
    b. is maintained by the Report Writer.
    c. cannot appear in the source code.

13.15 By using Report Writer much of the logic for report control is eliminated from the DATA DIVISION. True or false?

13.16 The page layouts, lengths, control breaks, and accumulators are defined in the _____ SECTION.
    a. FILE
    b. WORKING-STORAGE
    c. REPORT
    d. COMMUNICATIONS

13.17 A _____ is required for detail lines so that they can be referenced by name in the PROCEDURE DIVISION.
    a. report-name
    b. data-name
    c. section-name
    d. procedure-name

13.18 Every report that has been initiated must be terminated. True or false?

13.19 The GENERATE report-name option is very useful for preparing summary reports for management. True or false?

13.20   Report Writer uses the _____, _____, and
_____ statements to control the execution of a report.
  a.   INITIATE, GENERATE, TERMINATE
  b.   START, REPEAT, STOP
  c.   INITIALIZE, DO WHILE, CONCLUDE
  d.   BEGIN, EXECUTE, FINAL

13.21   The _____ statement is the driver that produces a report in accordance
with the description in the REPORT SECTION of the DATA DIVISION.
  a.   EXECUTE
  b.   INITIATE
  c.   TERMINATE
  d.   GENERATE

13.22   The CONTROL FOOTING, if specified, is processed automatically at the beginning of the
control group designated by a control item in the RD entry. True or false?

13.23   The _____ entry controls horizontal spacing of the report.
  a.   SOURCE NUMBER
  b.   COLUMN NUMBER
  c.   PICTURE
  d.   SUM

13.24   Report Writer simplifies programming work, results in more compact code and actually
reduces the amount of code in some instances. True or false?

13.25   The COBOL-supplied variable PAGE-COUNTER must be initialized to 1 and the SUM
counters to zero by the programmer. True or false?

13.26   Report Writer automatically fills missing spaces with blanks when the COLUMN NUM-
BER clause is used. True or false?

13.27   Only one _____ may appear in the report description.
  a.   CONTROL FOOTING group
  b.   FINAL
  c.   DETAIL group
  d.   PAGE HEADING

13.28   Each report is defined by a(n) _____ entry which describes the
report.

13.29   The _____ clause provides information about control breaks.

13.30   The reserved word _____ indicates that all detail lines are to be
considered part of a larger group and occurs once all records are processed.

13.31   The _____ clause controls the number of lines allowed on each page.

13.32   The _____ option of Report Writer specifies the number of lines to be
skipped before the line is actually printed out.

13.33   When defining a report line, each item may be filled using three options:

  1. _____
  2. _____
  3. _____

13.34   The _____ clause sets up a pointer to which the values of the specified data items are added each time a detail line is printed.

13.35   The _____ clause indicates the line where the initial detail line may be printed on a page.

13.36   Report Writer reduces the most report-related code in the _____ DIVISION.

13.37   List the seven types of report lines.

13.38   Explain how the use of Report Writer enhances the principles of structured design.

14

HANDLING DIRECT ACCESS FILES

COBOL supports file structures other than sequential ones. A class of file structures that takes advantage of direct access storage devices is direct access files. Direct access files allow the selection of a specific record from a file without processing all the physically preceding records as in the case of sequential files. Based on a unique identifier, direct access files allow individual records to be read, written, or modified in any order. In this chapter we will study the characteristics, organizations, and processing modes of direct access files.

14.1   *Direct Access Storage Devices*

The properties of *direct access storage devices* are best illustrated by studying the physical characteristics of the disk drive and disk medium. Figure 14.1 illustrates a flexible disk known as a *diskette* used on most microcomputers and many larger systems as well. Physical data records are stored on the circular surface of the diskette as shown in Figure 14.2. The records consist of magnetized spots on the diskette surface in concentric circles called *tracks*. Tracks are analogous to the grooves in phonograph records. Each track is divided like a pie into *sectors*. The track and sector provide an *address* that is used to locate information as illustrated in Figure 14.3. When a disk file is created, the records are stored by filling one track after another.

Figure 14.1   *Diskette Storage Medium*

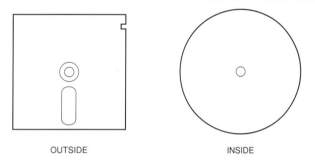

OUTSIDE   INSIDE

Figure 14.2   *Record Storage on Diskette*

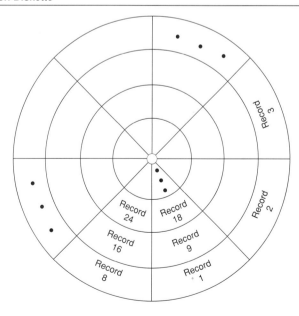

• Diskette records

Figure 14.3   *Locating Records on a Diskette*

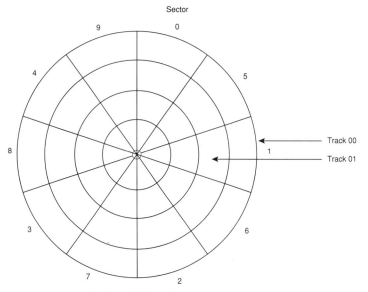

Tracks on a diskette surface

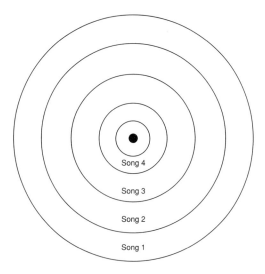

Tracks on a Phonograph record

Figure 14.4   Locating Specific Tracks on a Diskette

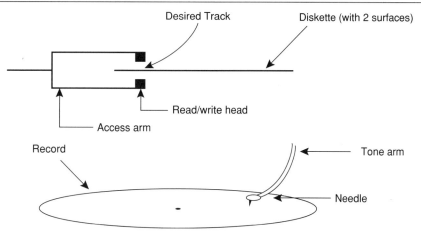

Diskettes are read and written on a device called a *disk drive*. As the disk drive rotates the disk at high speeds, its read/write heads access the records. These read/write heads are mounted in the disk drive unit on an access arm. There is one read/write head per recording surface. Figure 14.4 shows an access arm to which two read/write heads are attached. This accommodates double-sided diskettes that have two recording surfaces. The access arm moves over the tracks like a cartridge and needle on a turntable's tonearm moving over the record "tracks." The arm is moved from the edge to the interior of the diskette to position itself over the desired track, just as the tonearm is manually moved over a record to position it at a specific song. Once in position, the read/write heads can read records from the track.

At this point, the similarities between a tonearm and a disk drive access arm end. In a disk unit once the read/write heads are positioned over a specific track, the access arm does not move toward the interior or exterior of the disk unless commanded to do so. Furthermore, the records in a track can be read without moving the access arm. This is because the tracks on the diskette are concentric circles whereas a stereo record's track is a spiral.

In medium- and large-scale computer systems several nonflexible disks are integrated into a *disk pack*. Figure 14.5 shows a schematic illustration of a disk pack. Each disk in a disk pack is called a *platter*. The platters are stacked vertically and connected by a shaft. Each platter still has two recording surfaces, with the exception of the topmost and bottommost platters, which have only one. The read/write heads in the disk drive are mounted on an access mechanism, one head per recording surface. Since the access mechanism moves all access arms in parallel, the read/write heads are positioned over the same track on each surface. This stack of tracks forms a *cylinder*. Figure 14.6 shows the relationship between tracks and cylinders. In this illustration, all tracks numbered 50 become cylinder 50. The operating system takes advantage of this characteristic to reduce the time delay associated with repositioning, known as positioning time. After filling one track, the system continues filling the same track on the next surface rather than moving to an adjacent track, thus eliminating the time required to position the access arms.

Figure 14.5   *Side View of a Disk Pack*

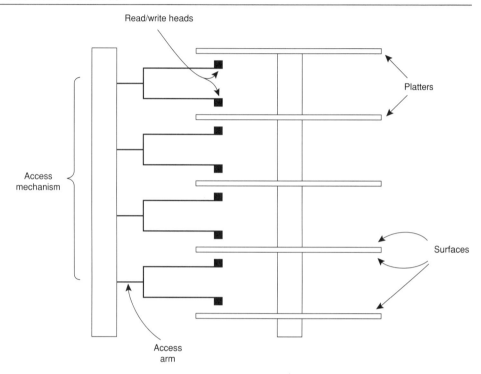

Figure 14.6   *Tracks and Cylinders on a Disk Pack*

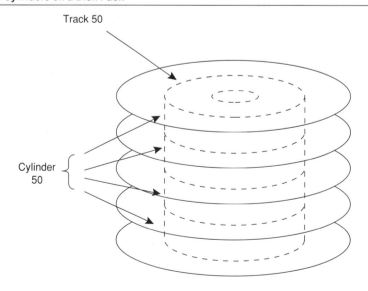

Data are stored on disks as a collection of magnetic spots representing different characters, as illustrated in Figure 14.7. This is similar to the way characters are stored on magnetic tape. The characters forming the data record are stored sequentially within the record. The total number of characters that can be stored on a disk varies not only with the storage device but also among manufacturers and can range from hundreds of thousands of bytes, or 8-bit characters, to thousands of millions of bytes.

Figure 14.7   *Data Storage on a Diskette or Disk*

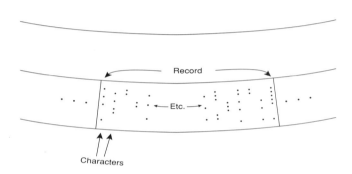

Since a record's location can be determined, it follows that the record can be accessed directly without the need to examine every previous record in the file. This capability is termed *direct access*. The computer system accesses a disk record by determining its surface, track, and record number. Once the read/write heads are positioned over the desired track, the system must wait for the appropriate record to pass under the read/write head as the platters rotate. This time is known as rotational delay or latency time. Latency and positional time together are known as the total access time.

14.2   *File Organization*

Organization refers to the logical structure of a file. In Chapter 9 we discussed sequential files. In the case of magnetic tape files both the physical and the logical file structures are in order of sequence. However, sequential organization is independent of storage medium, so sequential files can also exist on disk. In this chapter we will not pursue sequential file organization further but instead will discuss two other organizations that require mass storage devices and take advantage of their direct access capability. These organizations are relative and indexed files.

14.2.1   *Relative Files*

A *relative file* is a collection of records in which each record can be identified by its position in the file. The term "relative" refers to the fact that the relative position of a record within a file is directly related to a key field within the record. In other words, the key indicates the record position. We can access the first record, the 300th record, and so on. We can also access all the records from beginning to end. This implies that we can access the records in relative files randomly or sequentially. This characteristic allows the application to dictate the access method.

Relative files may be used if the records can be associated through ascending, consecutive numbers. To illustrate this, assume that parking spots in a company lot are assigned based on employee number and that employee numbers vary consecutively. Then employee number 231 should park in the 231st spot. The same rationale applies to records in a relative file. To access the records in a relative file, the computer must be able to determine the exact position of the record within the file. This is accomplished by using the record key as shown in Figure 14.8. The key value determines the position of the record in the relative file. For example, suppose that 200 records are stored in each track. Record number 231 would be the 31st record on the second track. Thus, positioning the read/write heads and reading the proper record within the track depends on a computation using the key value. This computation is very rapid. Many applications requiring fast access to files where the key is assigned in consecutive, ascending numbers use relative files.

Figure 14.8   Locating Records in a Relative File

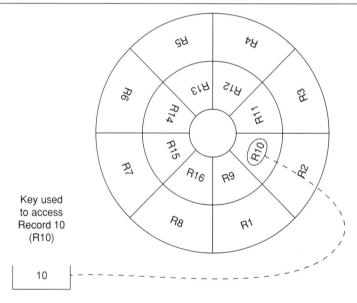

Key used
to access
Record 10
(R10)

| 10 |

The disadvantage of direct files lies in the selection of the key field. Unless the records have sequential, contiguous numbers, the processing of direct files may become tediously complex, or their size may become excessively large. To illustrate the latter, imagine a company whose employees are assigned parking spots based on their entire social security number. In order to assign each employee a unique parking spot in a manner analogous to a relative file, it would be necessary to have a spot in the parking lot for each social security number. Thus, 1,000,000,000 parking spots would be required to handle all the potential cars for the company!

It is possible to reduce the number of reserved spots needed by simplifying the key field. For example, the company might use only the last four digits of the social security number to assign spots. This would reduce wasted space, but another problem could arise: multiple employees might be assigned the same parking spot. In terms of a relative file, this results in *duplicate keys*. Since only one car can fit into one spot in the lot, just as only one record can be stored in a specific area on a disk, a simple solution, shown in Figure 14.9, is to assign one of the duplicate parking assignments to an open spot. This requires that the employee remember his new parking spot number. In a relative file, records with duplicate keys are assigned to "open" spots. Complications increase as the number of duplicate keys increases. To avoid these complications, we will assume the presence of small, unique keys for our discussion of relative files.

Figure 14.9   *Reassigning Duplicate Keys*

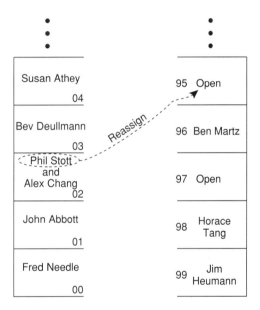

14.2.2   *Indexed Files*

Indexed file organization represents a compromise between sequential and relative file organizations. Each record in an indexed file is identified by a unique data field, called a *prime record key*, that provides a logical path to the record. Indexed organization allows the records to be accessed either sequentially or randomly, although it is not as efficient in either method as other file structures. Indexed file records are accessed by an *index*. The index contains the key field for each record and corresponding pointers containing the disk addresses for the records. The index is ordered by key value. By a search of the file index, the location of the desired record can be found and the record can then be accessed directly. This is analogous to an index in a book in which the entries are arranged alphabetically and the page numbers indicate the location of the topic entry. The organization of an indexed file is shown in Figure 14.10.

Figure 14.10   Indexed File Record Access

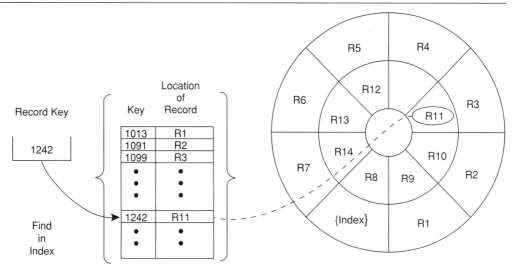

In our parking lot example an indexed organization would correspond to having an employee list in a predetermined sequence, such as social security number (keys), and assigning parking spots (addresses) based on that predetermined sequence. When an employee needs to find his parking spot, he would first consult the list and then go directly to the spot indicated in the index. Some overhead is required to examine the index, but it is much less than searching for a car in the parking lot in sequential fashion. Since it is no longer necessary that the key field be contiguous numbers, as in the case of relative files, the parking lot need only contain enough spots to meet its employees' needs. No empty spots would be necessary.

The advantages of indexed files are that they permit a sequential organization based on a key field, they allow rapid random access to records through the use of an index, and they utilize disk space effectively. The disadvantage is in the cost of maintaining the index and in the overhead associated with consulting the index each time a specific record is desired.

The index is often maintained in the computer's memory. When a record is required, the index is checked to find the location of the record on the disk. For large files, several levels of indexes may be required. This is like parking lots around a major shopping center. To find one's car, one must first know the proper lot number, then the proper aisle, then the spot where the car is parked.

14.2.3   Selecting the Appropriate File Organization

Selecting the appropriate file structure depends on the characteristics of the file and the processing requirements of the application. Sometimes file size may affect the choice of file organization. Large sequential files can be stored on less expensive storage media, thus reducing the amount of storage and overhead required during file processing. If, however, sequential files are to be processed in some order other than the preset sequence, it will be necessary to process each record up to the desired record.

Another factor in selecting file organization is the file's activity ratio. If numerous records are to be processed in sequential order, sequential organization is more appropriate. Files that change often are processed more efficiently if organized sequentially. Changes to relative files often result in increased duplicate keys. Changes to indexed files might cause the index to lose sequential organization, thus increasing processing overhead. If activity ratios are low, the converse of the above usually holds true. Figure 14.11 provides a comparison of the three file organizations supported by COBOL.

Figure 14.11   Comparison of File Organizations

File Organization	Sequential Update	Direct Update	Automatic Backup	Response Time	Cost	Update Code Difficulty
Sequential	Yes	No	Yes	Poor	Low	Complex
Indexed sequential	Yes	Yes	No	Good	High	Easy
Relative	Yes	Yes	No	Excellent	High	Varies

14.3   *Updating Direct Access Files*

Direct access files may be processed sequentially. If so, the file maintenance program designs of Chapter 9 are appropriate. However, to take advantage of the random access capabilities of direct access files, some changes are required to the program structure and logic. The changes required to the file update program structure to incorporate differing file organizations are minor. Most of the changes in the detailed design will be in the logic required to locate a specific record.

14.3.1   *Program Structure for Randomly Updating Direct Access Files*

To examine the changes required for processing direct access files, let us review the hierarchy chart used in Chapter 9 to update a sequential file. This is reproduced in Figure 14.12. In updating a sequential master file with a sequential transaction file, a new master file must be created, as illustrated in Figure 14.13. For direct access files, however, the master file is updated in the same area where it resides on the disk. That is, the master file is both input and output of the update process. This is illustrated in the system flowchart in Figure 14.14.

Figure 14.12   Hierarchy Chart for a Sequential File Update Program

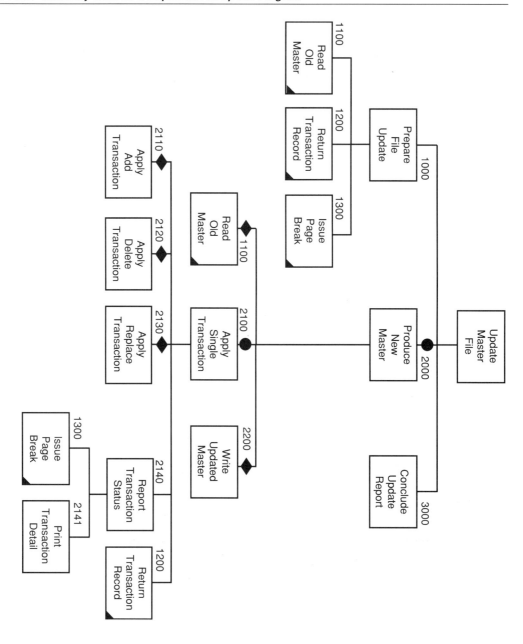

Figure 14.13   System Flowchart for a Sequential File Update

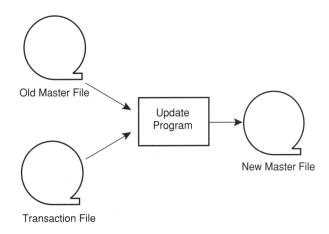

Figure 14.14   System Flowchart for a Direct Access File Update

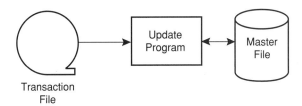

In the sequential file update hierarchy chart of Figure 14.12 the third level is dedicated to acquiring master records and writing them out to a different location. Because of the nature of sequential files, every master record in the file prior to the desired record must be read before a transaction can be applied. Then every transaction for the record must be applied before the new master record can be written to the updated file.

In direct access files the ability to access a desired record randomly allows transactions to be applied whenever they are encountered. This eliminates the need for the third level of the hierarchy chart from the update program. The resulting hierarchy chart is shown in Figure 14.15. Since a record is accessed only if a transaction applies to it, all input and output operations become part of the transaction modules. For example, the N-S chart for "2300 Apply Replace Transaction" in Figure 14.16 shows that the read of the Master Record is now part of the transaction logic.

Figure 14.15   Hierarchy Chart for a Direct Access File Update

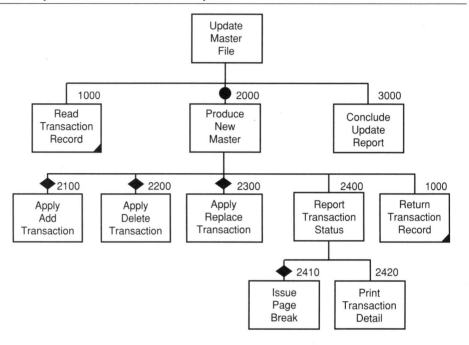

Figure 14.16   N-S Charts for a Direct Access File Update

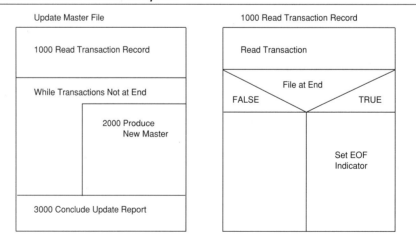

Figure 14.16   (continued)

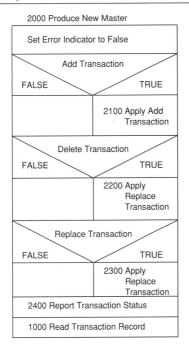

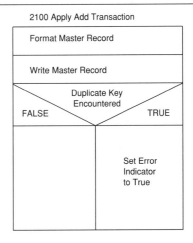

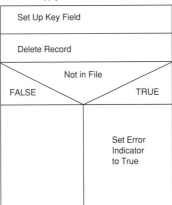

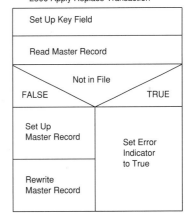

Figure 14.16 *(continued)*

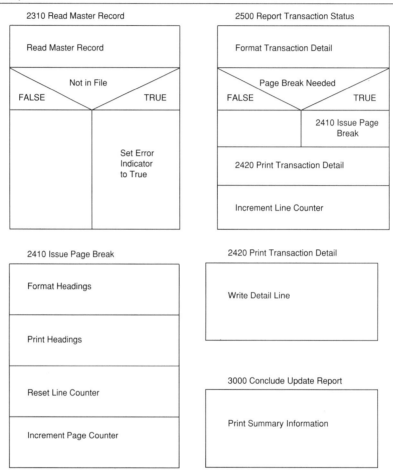

14.3.2 Program Logic for Randomly Updating Direct Access Files

To illustrate the simplification of the program logic, let us reexamine the modules that were eliminated from the hierarchy chart in Figure 14.12. In Figure 14.12, module "2000 Produce New Master" requires the testing of key fields to determine whether or not the next record is to be read. If the next old master record is to be read, the existing old master record has to be moved to the output area for the new master record to be written to the new master file. In Figure 14.15 the master file is read directly in module "2300 Apply Replace Transaction," thus eliminating the key matching logic; and because the same file area is used for input and output, the logic for moving a record from the input area to the output area is also eliminated.

Module "2200 Write Updated Master" no longer forms part of the main iterative module in Figure 14.15 because a new master file is no longer needed. The transactions are applied one at a time so that writing or rewriting a record is controlled by the individual transaction. There is no longer a need for maintaining an "active" record indicator, and the logic for determining the status of the transactions is reduced. In Figure 14.15 each transaction module controls the input and output to the master file. Similarly, the logic needed to compare transaction keys in the sequential update module "2100 Apply Single Transactions" is eliminated since the transactions affecting a master record need not be sequentially processed.

The major logic differences in randomly updating direct access files, as opposed to sequential files, are discussed below. The file update algorithm in structured English is:

```
FILE-UPDATE-ALGORITHM:
    READ a TRANSACTION-FILE
           record, setting indicator at end of file;
    REPEAT UNTIL TRANSACTION-FILE is at end
        set an error indicator to FALSE:
        IF TRANSACTION-CODE indicates an addition THEN
            build a MASTER record from the transaction record;
            WRITE the Record;
            IF the KEY is a duplicate THEN
                set the error indicator to TRUE;
            END-IF;
        END-IF;
        IF TRANSACTION-CODE indicates a deletion THEN
            delete the MASTER record;
            IF the KEY is missing THEN
                set the error indicator to TRUE;
            END-IF;
        END-IF;
        IF TRANSACTION-CODE indicates a replacement THEN
            READ the MASTER record;
            IF the KEY is missing THEN
                set the error indicator to TRUE;
            ELSE
                build the revised MASTER record;
                REWRITE the MASTER record;
            END-IF;
        END-IF;
        REPORT the TRANSACTION record status;
        READ next TRANSACTION-FILE record;
    EXIT REPEAT;
END FILE-UPDATE-ALGORITHM.
```

The Nassi-Schneiderman charts for updating direct access files are presented in Figure 14.16. The differences in the update logic between sequential and direct access files are summarized by module. The new code for the program using a direct file organization is in Figure 14.17.

Figure 14.17   Direct Access File Update Program Code

```
 1 IDENTIFICATION DIVISION.
 2 PROGRAM-ID.  GENERIC-DIRECT-ACCESS-UPDATE.
 3*   THIS PROGRAM TAKES A TRANSACTION-FILE AND
 4*   APPLIES THEM TO THE MASTER-FILE
 5
 6 AUTHOR.           SELF
 7 DATE-WRITTEN.     JULY 9, 1992
 8 DATE-COMPILED. 17-Jul-92 00:46.
10 ENVIRONMENT DIVISION.
11
12 CONFIGURATION SECTION.
13
14 SOURCE-COMPUTER.  GENERIC-COMPUTER.
15 OBJECT-COMPUTER.  GENERIC-COMPUTER.
16
17 INPUT-OUTPUT SECTION.
18
19 FILE-CONTROL.
20
21     SELECT TRANSACTION-FILE ASSIGN TO DISK
22         ORGANIZATION IS SEQUENTIAL.
23
24     SELECT MASTER-FILE ASSIGN TO DISK
25         ORGANIZATION IS RELATIVE
26         ACCESS MODE IS RANDOM
27         RELATIVE KEY IS MASTER-RELATIVE-KEY.
28
29     SELECT UPDATE-REPORT ASSIGN TO PRINTER
30         ORGANIZATION IS SEQUENTIAL.
31
32 DATA DIVISION.
33
34 FILE SECTION.
35
36 FD  TRANSACTION-FILE
37     LABEL RECORDS ARE STANDARD.
38
39 01  TRANSACTION-RECORD.
40     05  TRANSACTION-KEY-FIELD   PIC X(6).
41     05  TRANSACTION-TYPE        PIC X.
42         88  ADD-TRANSACTION     VALUE "A".
43         88  DELETE-TRANSACTION  VALUE "D".
```

Figure 14.17   (continued)

```
44          88  REPLACE-TRANSACTION VALUE "R".
45      05  TRANSACTION-MASTER-DATA PIC X(40).
46
47 FD  MASTER-FILE
48      LABEL RECORDS ARE STANDARD.
49
50 01  MASTER-RECORD.
51      05  MASTER-KEY-FIELD PIC X(6).
52      05  FILLER           PIC X(34).
53
54
55 FD  UPDATE-REPORT
56      LABEL RECORDS ARE OMITTED.
57
58 01  UPDATE-PRINT-LINE PIC X(80).
59
60
61 WORKING-STORAGE SECTION.
62
63 01  MASTER-RELATIVE-KEY PIC 9(6).
64
65 01  UPDATE-REPORT-LINES.
66      05  UP-REPORT-TITLE.
67          10  FILLER    PIC X(14) VALUE "REPORT #64".
68          10  FILLER    PIC X(38) VALUE
69                                  "MASTER FILE UPDATE".
70          10  FILLER    PIC X(5)  VALUE "PAGE".
71          10  UP-PAGE  PIC ZZ9.
72      05  UP-DATE-LINE.
73          10  FILLER    PIC X(47)  VALUE "DISTRIBUTION".
74          10  FILLER    PIC X(5)   VALUE "DATE".
75          10  UP-DATE   PIC 99/99/99.
76      05  UP-COLUMN-HEADING.
77          10  FILLER PIC X(15) VALUE "TRANSACTION".
78          10  FILLER PIC X(14) VALUE "KEY FIELD".
79          10  FILLER PIC X(09) VALUE "RECORD".
80      05  UP-DETAIL.
81          10  UP-CODE              PIC X(6).
82          10  UP-ERROR             PIC X(10).
83          10  UP-KEY               PIC 9(6).
84          10  FILLER               PIC X(4) VALUE SPACE.
85          10  UP-RECORD            PIC X(40).
```

Figure 14.17   (continued)

```
86
87 01  END-OF-FILE-INDICATORS.
88     05  EOF-TRANSACTION    PIC X(5) VALUE "FALSE".
89
90 01  PAGE-CONTROL-COUNTERS.
91     05  PCC-PAGE        PIC 999 VALUE ZERO.
92     05  PCC-LINE        PIC 99  VALUE 99.
93     05  PCC-MAX-LINE    PIC 99  VALUE 55.
94
95 01  PROCESS-INDICATORS.
96     05  ERROR-INDICATOR    PIC X(5) VALUE "TRUE".
97
98 PROCEDURE DIVISION.
99
100 UPDATE-MASTER-FILE.
101     OPEN I-O MASTER-FILE.
102     OPEN INPUT TRANSACTION-FILE.
103     OPEN OUTPUT UPDATE-REPORT.
104     PERFORM 1000-READ-TRANSACTION-RECORD.
105     PERFORM 2000-PRODUCE-NEW-MASTER
106         UNTIL EOF-TRANSACTION = "TRUE".
107     PERFORM 3000-CONCLUDE-UPDATE-REPORT.
108     CLOSE MASTER-FILE.
109     CLOSE TRANSACTION-FILE.
110     CLOSE UPDATE-REPORT.
111     STOP RUN.
112
113 1000-READ-TRANSACTION-RECORD.
114     READ TRANSACTION-FILE AT END MOVE "TRUE" TO EOF-TRANSACTION.
115
116 2000-PRODUCE-NEW-MASTER.
117     MOVE "FALSE" TO ERROR-INDICATOR.
118     IF ADD-TRANSACTION     PERFORM 2100-APPLY-ADD-TRANSACTION.
119     IF DELETE-TRANSACTION  PERFORM 2200-APPLY-DELETE-TRANSACTION.
120     IF REPLACE-TRANSACTION PERFORM 2300-APPLY-REPLACE-TRANSACTION
121     PERFORM 2400-REPORT-TRANSACTION-STATUS.
122     PERFORM 1000-READ-TRANSACTION-RECORD.
123
124 2100-APPLY-ADD-TRANSACTION.
125     MOVE TRANSACTION-MASTER-DATA TO MASTER-RECORD.
126     MOVE TRANSACTION-KEY-FIELD TO MASTER-RELATIVE-KEY.
127     WRITE MASTER-RECORD
```

Figure 14.17   (continued)

```
128          INVALID KEY MOVE "TRUE" TO ERROR-INDICATOR.
129
130 2200-APPLY-DELETE-TRANSACTION.
131    MOVE TRANSACTION-KEY-FIELD TO MASTER-RELATIVE-KEY.
132    DELETE MASTER-FILE
133          INVALID KEY MOVE "TRUE" TO ERROR-INDICATOR.
134
135 2300-APPLY-REPLACE-TRANSACTION.
136    MOVE TRANSACTION-KEY-FIELD TO MASTER-RELATIVE-KEY.
137    READ MASTER-FILE
138          INVALID KEY MOVE "TRUE" TO ERROR-INDICATOR.
139    IF ERROR-INDICATOR = "FALSE"
140       MOVE TRANSACTION-MASTER-DATA TO MASTER-RECORD
141       REWRITE MASTER-RECORD
142          INVALID KEY MOVE "TRUE" TO ERROR-INDICATOR.
143
144 2400-REPORT-TRANSACTION-STATUS.
145    IF PCC-LINE > PCC-MAX-LINE
146       PERFORM 2410-ISSUE-PAGE-BREAK.
147    IF ERROR-INDICATOR = "TRUE" MOVE "ERROR" TO UP-ERROR
148       ELSE MOVE SPACES TO UP-ERROR.
149    MOVE TRANSACTION-TYPE TO UP-CODE.
150    PERFORM 2420-PRINT-TRANSACTION-DETAIL.
151
152 2410-ISSUE-PAGE-BREAK.
153    ADD 1 TO PCC-PAGE.
154    MOVE PCC-PAGE TO UP-PAGE.
155    WRITE UPDATE-PRINT-LINE FROM UP-REPORT-TITLE AFTER PAGE.
156    WRITE UPDATE-PRINT-LINE FROM UP-DATE-LINE.
157    WRITE UPDATE-PRINT-LINE FROM UP-COLUMN-HEADING.
158    MOVE SPACES TO UPDATE-PRINT-LINE.
159    WRITE UPDATE-PRINT-LINE.
160    MOVE 4 TO PCC-LINE.
161
162 2420-PRINT-TRANSACTION-DETAIL.
163    ADD 1 TO PCC-LINE.
164    MOVE TRANSACTION-MASTER-DATA TO UP-RECORD.
165    WRITE UPDATE-PRINT-LINE FROM UP-DETAIL.
166
167 3000-CONCLUDE-UPDATE-REPORT.
168    MOVE "END OR REPORT" TO UPDATE-PRINT-LINE.
```

"Update Master File" Module. Little change is required to the major repetitive logic. The major difference is that processing is terminated when the end-of-file condition is reached in the transaction file rather than in both the master and transaction files.

"2100 Apply Add Transaction" Module. Since the keys are no longer compared prior to an output command, the record to be added is moved to the master record immediately prior to attempting to write to the file. If the attempt results in a duplicate key condition, the add transaction is invalid.

"2200 Apply Delete Transaction" Module. When using a direct access file, the key of the record to be deleted must be specified to the system. An attempt is then made to delete the record from the master file. If the record does not exist, the key will not appear in the master file and the delete transaction will be invalid.

"2300 Apply Replace Transaction" Module. The logic for replacing records is similar for both direct access and sequential files. The original record must first be located on the master file. If it exists, the record is replaced and the record is rewritten to the master file. If it does not exist, the transaction is in error.

Figure 14.18   System Flowchart for a Direct Access File Creation

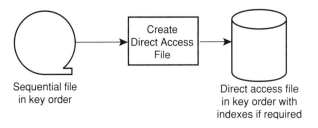

Sequential file
in key order

Create
Direct Access
File

Direct access file
in key order with
indexes if required

Figure 14.19   Hierarchy Chart for Direct Access File Creation

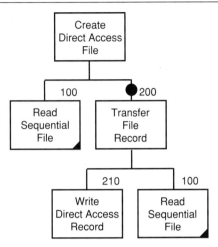

14.3.3   Creating Direct Access Files

Relative files and indexed files are usually created in a sequential fashion, and the sequentially organized file is then copied to a file with a relative or indexed organization. When the file is being copied, the computer automatically places the records in their appropriate location on disk, and builds the indexes for indexed files. A relative file is created in contiguous integer sequence beginning with 1. A relative file must initially be in key order and contain no missing keys. Figure 14.18 shows a system flowchart for creating a direct access file from a sequential file. The hierarchy chart for the file creation program appears in Figure 14.19. It is simply an iteration module that continually reads from a sequential file and transfers the records to the direct access file. The program logic is straightforward and appears in the Nassi-Schneiderman charts in Figure 14.20. The structured English would be:

```
CREATE-DIRECT-ACCESS-FILE ALGORITHM:
      READ A SEQUENTIAL-FILE record;
      REPEAT UNTIL SEQUENTIAL-FILE is at end
            build a DIRECT-ACCESS-FILE record from the SEQUENTIAL-FILE record;
            WRITE the DIRECT-ACCESS-FILE record;
            IF a KEY error occurs THEN
                  display an error message;
                  set end-of-file indicator;
            END-IF;
            READ next SEQUENTIAL-FILE record;
      END-REPEAT;
EXIT CREATE-DIRECT-ACCESS-FILE ALGORITHM.
```

Figure 14.20   N-S Charts for Direct Access File Creation

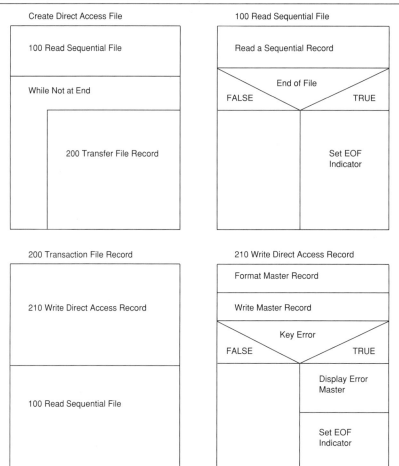

14.4   COBOL for Processing Direct Access Files

To process direct access files, we will introduce some variations to existing COBOL statements and add some new ones. These changes affect the ENVIRONMENT and PROCEDURE DIVISIONs.

14.4.1   Describing Direct Access Files

The first change occurs in the FILE CONTROL paragraph in the ENVIRONMENT DIVISION. The format and rules for the SELECT clause in the FILE CONTROL paragraph are:

SELECT file-name   <u>ASSIGN</u> <u>TO</u> implementor-name

$$\left[\underline{\text{ORGANIZATION}} \text{ IS } \left\{ \begin{array}{l} \underline{\text{SEQUENTIAL}} \\ \underline{\text{INDEXED}} \\ \underline{\text{RELATIVE}} \end{array} \right\} \right]$$

$$\left[\underline{\text{ACCESS}} \text{ MODE IS } \left\{ \begin{array}{l} \underline{\text{SEQUENTIAL}} \\ \underline{\text{RANDOM}} \end{array} \right\} \right]$$

$$\left[\left\{ \begin{array}{l} \underline{\text{RECORD}} \text{ KEY IS data-name-1} \\ \underline{\text{RELATIVE}} \text{ KEY IS data-name-2} \end{array} \right\} \right] .$$

1. The assumed values for the ORGANIZATION and ACCESS clauses are SEQUENTIAL unless otherwise specified.
2. If ORGANIZATION is SEQUENTIAL the ACCESS MODE must be SEQUENTIAL and the KEY clause is not specified.
3. If ORGANIZATION is INDEXED, the RECORD KEY must be specified.
4. If ORGANIZATION is RELATIVE, the RELATIVE KEY must be specified.
5. Data-name-1 must appear in the record description of the associated FD entry.
6. Data-name-2 must appear in the WORKING-STORAGE SECTION.

The ORGANIZATION clause specifies the logical structure of the file. ORGANIZATION may be SEQUENTIAL, INDEXED, or RELATIVE and relates directly to the file organizations discussed previously. By specifying the file ORGANIZATION the COBOL compiler automatically maintains the proper file structure for the programmer so that he need not be concerned with the physical characteristics of the file.

The ACCESS clause specifies the manner in which file records are to be accessed. The ACCESS mode indicates whether the file is to be processed sequentially or randomly. If ACCESS IS SEQUENTIAL is specified for sequential, indexed, or relative files, the file processing follows the logic for sequential files. If ACCESS IS RANDOM is specified for indexed or relative files, the processing proceeds in no particular order and each record is located as needed by the program.

The RECORD KEY clause is used for indexed files. The FD entry for the indexed file must contain the key specified in the RECORD KEY clause. The key field may be any item in the record as long as it is unique for each record.

The RELATIVE KEY clause is used for relative files. The key specified must be numeric, defined in the WORKING-STORAGE SECTION, and not part of the file's record description.

Following is the SELECT clause for an indexed file whose records are to be accessed on demand using the key field AR-NBR:

```
SELECT AR-CUSTOMER-FILE

    ASSIGN TO DISK
    ORGANIZATION IS INDEXED
```

```
        ACCESS IS RANDOM
        RECORD KEY IS AR-NBR.
```

Figures 14.21 and 14.22 illustrate the relationship between the SELECT statement and the key descriptions for indexed and relative files. The code in Figure 14.17 provides an example of the RELATIVE KEY in lines 27 and 63.

Figure 14.21   *Relationship of SELECT Clause and FD Entry for Indexed Files*

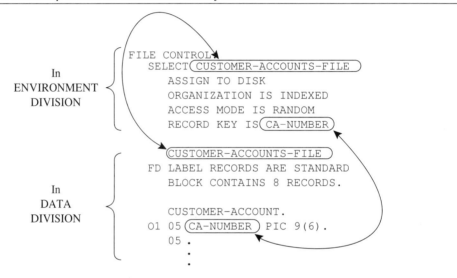

Figure 14.22   *Relationship of SELECT Clause and WORKING-STORAGE Entry for Relative Files*

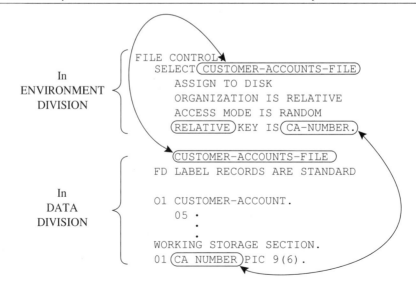

14.4.2   *Processing Direct Access Files Sequentially*

In this section we will discuss the group of valid statements that may be used for processing direct access files sequentially. Assume the following FILE CONTROL and DATA DIVISION entries:

```
FILE CONTROL.
    SELECT  AR-OPEN-ITEMS-FILE
        ASSIGN TO DISK
        ORGANIZATION IS RELATIVE
        ACCESS MODE IS SEQUENTIAL
        RELATIVE KEY IS KEY-ORDER-NUMBER.
            .
            .
            .
FD  AR-OPEN-ITEMS-FILE
    LABEL RECORDS ARE STANDARD.
01  AR-ITEM-REC.
    05  AR-CUSTOMER-ID    PIC 9(6).
    05  AR-ORDER-AMOUNT   PIC 9(5)V99.
WORKING-STORAGE SECTION.
    01  KEY-ORDER-NUMBER PIC 9(4).
```

The OPEN and CLOSE Statements. The format and rules for the OPEN statement for direct access files are:

$$\text{OPEN} \quad \left\{ \begin{array}{l} \underline{\text{INPUT}} \\ \underline{\text{OUTPUT}} \\ \underline{\text{I-O}} \end{array} \right\} \quad \{\text{file-name}\}\ldots$$

1. The file-name must be defined in a SELECT clause and FD entry.
2. A file must be OPENed before any operations are performed.

The direct access file may be opened for input only, output only, or for both input and output. By using the I-O option, a file can be updated into the same area on the storage device. This is the case in line 101 of Figure 14.17.

The format of the CLOSE statement remains the same as for sequential files. The OPEN and CLOSE statements for the AR-OPEN-ITEMS-FILE are:

```
OPEN I-O AR-OPEN-ITEMS-FILE.
```

and

```
CLOSE AR-OPEN-ITEMS-FILE.
```

The WRITE Statement. The format and rules for the WRITE statement for direct access files processed sequentially are:

WRITE record-name   [FROM data-name-1]
    INVALID KEY {imperative-statement} . . .
    [NOT INVALID KEY {imperative-statement}]
    [END-WRITE]

1.   Record-name must be an 01 level in an FD entry.
2.   The INVALID KEY clause is ended by a period.
3.   The RECORD KEY clause must contain a unique, valid key for indexed files.
4.   The RELATIVE KEY clause will be assigned a key for relative output files.
5.   Upon an INVALID KEY condition, the record is not written to the file and the imperative-statement is executed.

The INVALID KEY clause is executed for indexed files when the value of the RECORD KEY being written is not higher than the value of the record key of the previous record written. This indicates that there is a sequence error or a duplicate key. The INVALID KEY condition also occurs if the file has exhausted the disk space allocated to it. An error routine is usually performed as part of the INVALID KEY clause. For example,

```
WRITE AR-ITEM-REC INVALID KEY PERFORM 300-ERROR.
```

specifies that if the key value of the current record is not higher than the previous record's key value, paragraph 300-ERROR is performed.

The READ Statement. The READ statement for reading a direct access file sequentially does not change from the familiar sequential READ. The AT END clause still indicates that the file is exhausted. A successful read makes the contents of a record available in the file record area. The READ statement for the AR-OPEN-ITEM-FILE is:

```
READ AR-OPEN-ITEMS-FILE AT END MOVE "TRUE" TO EOF-AR.
```

The DELETE Statement. The DELETE statement logically removes from the file the record whose KEY appears in the RECORD KEY or RELATIVE KEY field. This means that the record cannot subsequently be accessed. The format and rules of the sequential DELETE statement are:

DELETE file-name RECORD

1.   The file-name must be defined in an FD entry and appear in a SELECT clause.
2.   The file-name must be a direct access file with SEQUENTIAL access mode.
3.   The file must be OPENed as I-O.
4.   The DELETE must follow a successful READ.

The statement

```
DELETE AR-OPEN-ITEMS-FILE RECORD.
```

logically deletes the most recently read record from AR-OPEN-ITEMS-FILE.

The REWRITE Statement. The *REWRITE* statement in sequential access mode logically replaces the last record successfully READ. The format and rules are:

REWRITE   record-name   [FROM data-name]
    INVALID KEY   {imperative-statement}...
    [NOT INVALID KEY {imperative-statement}]
    [END-REWRITE]

1. The record-name must be in an FD entry.
2. The REWRITE must follow a successful READ.
3. The INVALID KEY is not specified for a relative file accessed sequentially.
4. The file must have been OPENed for I-O.

An INVALID KEY condition occurs if the key field is not equal to the key of the record most recently READ. The statement

```
REWRITE AR-ITEM-REC

    INVALID KEY PERFORM 300-ERROR.
```

replaces the record just READ with the record currently defined in the record area. If the key differs, paragraph 300-ERROR is performed.

The START Statement. The START statement in sequential access mode allows a program to begin processing at any point in the file and continue processing sequentially from the current record forward. The format and rules for the START statement are:

START file-name

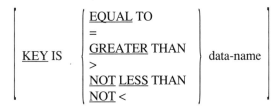

INVALID KEY {imperative-statement}...
[NOT INVALID KEY {imperative-statement}]
[END-START]

1. The file-name must be defined in an FD entry and SELECT clause.
2. The data-name must be the data-name in the KEY clause of the SELECT or, in indexed files, may be an alphanumeric item subordinate to the record key.
3. When specified, the KEY clause causes the file to be positioned at the first record that satisfies the condition.
4. The data-name must be initialized with the RELATIVE KEY or RECORD KEY prior to the START.
5. A key must have been properly established in the RECORD KEY or RELATIVE KEY data item.
6. If the KEY IS phrase is omitted, the first record found equal to the RECORD KEY or RELATIVE KEY data items is located.
7. The file must be OPENed for I-O or INPUT.

When the START statement is executed, the record that satisfies the condition specified in the KEY IS phrase will be the first record available to be processed. If the KEY IS phrase is not specified, the record available to be processed will be the first record that matches the value specified in the RECORD KEY or RELATIVE data item. If no record satisfies the stated condition or the previously specified key, an INVALID KEY condition occurs. For example,

```
START  AR-OPEN-ITEMS-FILE

    KEY  IS = KEY-ORDER-NUMBER
    INVALID KEY 300-ERROR-KEY.
```

will position the file AR-OPEN-ITEMS-FILE at the first record whose KEY value is equal to the value in KEY-ORDER-NUMBER. If the key is not found, paragraph 300-ERROR-KEY is performed.

14.4.3 Processing Direct Access Files Randomly

Most often, direct access files are processed randomly. This permits quick updates and rapid access to specific records. To examine the statements necessary to process direct access files randomly, assume the following FILE CONTROL and DATA DIVISION entries:

```
FILE CONTROL.
    SELECT  AR-OPEN-ITEMS-FILE
        ASSIGN TO DISK
        ORGANIZATION IS RELATIVE
        ACCESS MODE IS RANDOM
        RELATIVE KEY IS KEY-ORDER-NUMBER.
    SELECT  AR-TRANSACTIONS
        ASSIGN TO DISK.
```

```
    .
    .
    .
FD  AR-OPEN-ITEMS-FILE
    LABEL RECORDS ARE STANDARD.
01  AR-ITEM-REC.
    05  AR-CUSTOMER-ID    PIC 9(6).
    05  AR-ORDER-AMOUNT   PIC 9(5)V99.
FD  AR-TRANSACTIONS-FILE
    LABEL RECORDS ARE STANDARD.
01  AR-TRANSACTION-REC.
    05  ART-CODE PIC X.
    88  ART-ADD VALUE "A".
    88  ART-DELETE VALUE "D".
    88  ART-REPLACE VALUE "R".
    05  ART-ITEM.
        05  ART-ORDER-NBR     PIC 9(4).
        05  ART-CUSTOMER-ID   PIC 9(6).
        05  ART-AMOUNT        PIC 9(5)V99.
WORKING-STORAGE SECTION.
    01  KEY-ORDER-NUMBER  PIC 9(4).
    01  WS-ERROR          PIC X(4).
```

The OPEN and CLOSE statements for the randomly accessed files are the same as for sequentially accessed files. Other COBOL statements needed are discussed below.

The WRITE Statement. The format of the WRITE statement does not change from the sequential access WRITE statement. The file must be opened for output or for I-O. The key must be previously established in the data item designated as the RECORD KEY in the FILE SECTION if the file is indexed, or as the RELATIVE KEY in the WORKING-STORAGE SECTION if the file is relative. The INVALID KEY condition occurs if a WRITE is issued for a record that already exists on the file or if the file storage space has been exhausted. When the INVALID KEY condition arises, the record is not written to the file and the action specified in the INVALID KEY phrase is performed.

The WRITE statement for the AR-OPEN-ITEMS-FILE example is:

```
WRITE  AR-ITEM-REC INVALID KEY PERFORM  999-ERROR-KEY.
```

Record AR-ITEM-REC is written to the file in the position indicated by the key. If the key already appears in the file, 999-ERROR-KEY is performed. Line 127 contains the random WRITE statement for the program in Figure 14.17.

The DELETE Statement. The only change to the DELETE statement for randomly accessed files is that it contains an INVALID KEY phrase. The format and rules for this format of the DELETE statement are:

DELETE   file-name   RECORD
 INVALID KEY {imperative-statement}. . .
 [NOT INVALID KEY {imperative-statement}]
 [END-DELETE]

1. The file-name must be defined in an FD entry and appear in a SELECT clause.
2. The file-name must be a direct access file with RANDOM ACCESS MODE.
3. The file must be opened for I-O.

The INVALID KEY is activated by the absence of the desired record from the file. In the statement,

```
DELETE AR-OPEN-ITEMS-FILE INVALID KEY PERFORM  999-ERROR-KEY.
```

the appropriate AR-OPEN-ITEMS-FILE record is logically removed from the master file. If the record does not exist in the file, paragraph 999-ERROR-KEY is performed. In line 132 of Figure 14.17, the DELETE statement simply sets an error indicator if the record is not found.

The READ Statement. The READ statement for randomly accessed files varies from the statement used to process direct access files sequentially. The format and rules are:

READ file-name [INTO data-name]
 INVALID KEY {imperative-statement} . . .
 [NOT INVALID KEY {imperative-statement}]
 [END-READ]

1. The file-name must be specified in an FD entry and a SELECT clause.
2. The RELATIVE or RECORD KEY data item must contain the key of the record to be read.
3. The file must be OPENed as INPUT or I-O.

A successful READ makes the record whose key value is in the RELATIVE or RECORD KEY item available in the record input area. The INVALID KEY condition arises when the indicated record does not exist in the file. In the statement,

```
READ AR-OPEN-ITEMS-FILE INVALID KEY PERFORM  999-ERROR-KEY.
```

the record with the key whose value is specified in KEY-ORDER-NUMBER is READ. If the record is not found, paragraph 999-ERROR-KEY is performed. In line 137 of Figure 14.17, the READ sets an indicator if the record is missing.

The REWRITE Statement. The format of the REWRITE statement to handle randomly accessed files is the same as for sequentially accessed files. The INVALID KEY condition occurs when the desired record cannot be located in the file. The file must be opened as input-output. In the statement,

```
REWRITE  AR-ITEM-REC
      INVALID KEY  PERFORM 999-ERROR-KEY.
```

the record AR-ITEM-REC replaces the record with the same key value in the master file. If the record indicated by the key is not found, then paragraph 999-ERROR-KEY is performed. Line 141 contains the REWRITE statement in Figure 14.17.

14.4.4   *Implementing a Random Access Update*

Most direct access files are updated randomly. The program structure for doing this is the same as that illustrated in Figure 14.15. The logic, however, differs for the transaction application modules. We will develop the program code to implement these modules.

"2100 Apply Add Transaction" Module. Examine the Nassi-Schneiderman chart for module "2100 Apply Add Transaction" in Figure 14.26. The code to accomplish the logic using the previous file definitions is:

```
2100-APPLY-ADD-TRANSACTION.
      MOVE ART-CUSTOMER-ID TO AR-CUSTOMER-ID.
      MOVE ART-AMOUNT TO AR-ORDER-AMOUNT.
      MOVE ART-ORDER-NBR TO KEY-ORDER-NUMBER.
      WRITE AR-ITEM-REC
            INVALID KEY MOVE "TRUE" TO WS-ERROR.
```

The transaction data items are transferred to the record area. The record's number is moved to the RELATIVE KEY data item, KEY-ORDER-NUMBER. The WRITE statement then transfers the contents of the record area to the file. If the INVALID KEY condition occurs, an error flag is set. This is similar to the code of paragraph 2100-APPLY-ADD-TRANSACTION starting on line 124 of Figure 14.17.

"2200 Apply Delete Transaction" Module. The Nassi-Schneiderman code for module "2200 Apply Delete Transaction" appears:

```
2200-APPLY-DELETE-TRANSACTION.
      MOVE ART-ORDER-NBR TO KEY-ORDER-NUMBER.
      DELETE AR-OPEN-ITEMS-FILE RECORD
            INVALID KEY MOVE "TRUE" TO WS-ERROR.
```

The desired key is first moved to the RELATIVE KEY item. The DELETE is then issued. If the DELETE is successful, the routine exists normally. If the INVALID KEY condition occurs, an error flag indicates the error condition and the record remains intact. For another example, see lines 130 through 133 of Figure 14.17.

"2300 Apply Replace" and "2400 Change Transaction" Modules. The N-S chart for module "2300 Apply Replace Transaction" is almost identical to the N-S chart of module "2400 Apply Change Transaction." The code for the replace transaction is:

```
2300-APPLY-REPLACE-TRANSACTION.
        MOVE ART-ORDER-NBR TO KEY-ORDER-NUMBER.
        READ AR-OPEN-ITEMS-FILE INVALID KEY MOVE "TRUE" TO W-S ERROR.
        IF WS-ERROR = "FALSE"
                MOVE ART-CUSTOMER-ID TO AR-CUSTOMER-ID.
                MOVE ART-AMOUNT TO AR-ORDER-AMOUNT.
                REWRITE AR-ITEM-REC INVALID KEY MOVE "TRUE" TO WS-ERROR.
```

The key must be moved to the file record area. A READ statement acquires the record already on the file. If the entire contents of the record were to be replaced, the READ would not need to be conducted. In either case, the INVALID KEY condition indicates that the record is not on the file and therefore the transaction is in error. Figure 14.17 uses the same concepts in lines 135 through 142.

Case Study: CDL's Issue Purchase Requests

Charlene determines that the appropriate file organization of the permanent inventory file should be indexed sequentially. The program specifications are shown in Figure 14.23. It requires that purchase requests be optionally generated when the inventory file is updated with valid customer orders. The format for the files is shown in Figure 14.24. The purchase request form is shown in Figure 14.25.

Figure 14.23 Program Specifications for CDL's "Issue Purchase Request"

PROGRAM SUMMARY

TITLE: *Issue Purchase Requests*

PREPARED BY: *C. Hilton*

DATE: *7-14-93*

FILES USED		
FILE NAME	MEDIA	ORGANIZATION
Extended orders	*Disk*	*Sequential*
Inventory	*Disk*	*Index sequential*
Purchase requests	*Printer*	*Sequential*

DESCRIPTION

The extended, validated orders are used to alter the count of the quantity-on-hand field. If QOH falls below the reorder point, a purchase request for the order amount is generated and the current date is placed into the order date field. Do not issue a purchase request for any CD already ordered.

The purchases are recorded on preprinted forms whose format is attached. One purchase is issued per form. These are stuffed into windowed envelopes for mailing.

The extended orders are validated. If a key error occurs, display an appropriate error message and stop the execution of the program.

Figure 14.24   Record Layout for CDL's "Issue Purchase Request"

RECORD LAYOUT SHEET

Record Name: *Inventory item*			File Name: *Inventory*		
Prepared By: *C. Hilton*			Date: *7-14-93*		
Key Fields: *Disc NBR*			Organization: *Index sequential*		

Field	Description	Type*	Length	Decimal
Disc nbr	*A unique identifier*	*N*	*6*	*0*
Disc title	*Title of disc*	*A*	*20*	
Supplier	*Name of recording co.*	*A*	*20*	
Address	*Address of supplier*	*A*	*20*	
City	*City of supplier*	*A*	*12*	
State	*State of supplier*	*A*	*2*	
Zip	*Zip code of supplier*	*N*	*5*	*0*
QOH	*Quantity on hand*	*N*	*6*	*0*
ROP	*Reorder point*	*N*	*6*	*0*
Order date	*Date of purchase request*	*N*	*6*	*0*
Order amount	*Amount of order*	*N*	*6*	*0*
Price	*Price to customer*	*N*	*8*	*2*

* A = alphanumeric
  N = numeric

Figure 14.24   Record Layout for CDL's "Issue Purchase Request"

RECORD LAYOUT SHEET

Record Name: *Order*		File Name: *Orders/Extended Orders*		
Prepared By: *C. Hilton*		Date: *6-15-93*		
Key Fields:		Organization: *Sequential*		
Field	Description	Type*	Length	Decimal
Customer ID	*A unique customer number*	*N*	*6*	*0*
Disc number	*An identifier/stock number*	*N*	*6*	*0*
Quantity	*The number ordered*	*N*	*2*	*0*
Order #	*A preprinted order form*	*N*	*6*	*0*
Price	*Retail price*	*N*	*8*	*2*

* A = alphanumeric
  N = numeric

Figure 14.25   CDL's Purchase Request Form

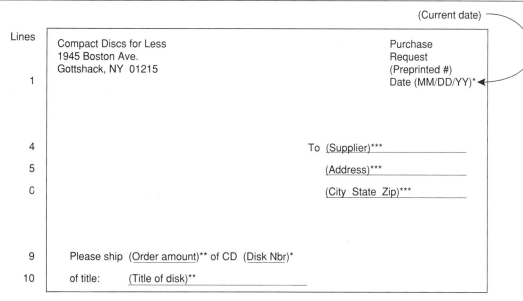

* Start in Col. 40
** Start in Col. 25
*** Start in Col. 30

Figure 14.26   Hierarchy Chart for CDL's "Issue Purchase Request"

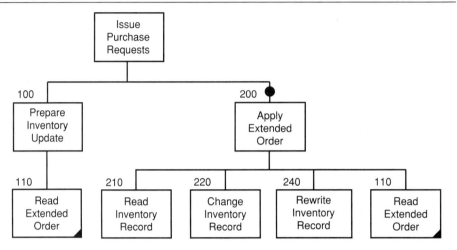

The hierarchy chart in Figure 14.26 shows the program structure to accomplish the required tasks. Only one type of transaction needs to be applied: the extension of orders. Module "Issue Purchase Requests" is segmented into the preliminary module "100 Prepare Inventory Update" and the repetitive module "200 Apply Extended Order."

Module "200 Apply Extended Order" reads an inventory record, alters the record, updates the inventory file, issues the required purchase requests, and reads an extended orders record. The program logic is illustrated by the Nassi-Schneiderman charts in Figure 14.27, the code appears in Figure 14.28, and the test plan with results are in Figure 14.29. The modules dealing with the direct access file are explained below.

Figure 14.27   N-S Charts for CDL's "Issue Purchase Requests"

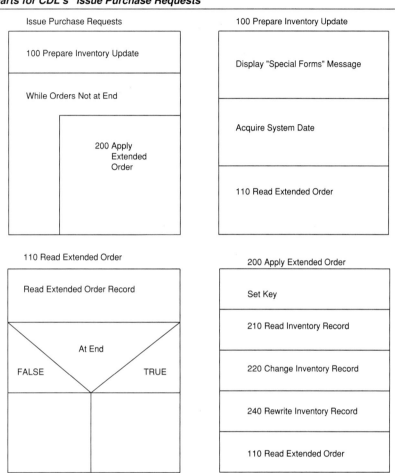

Figure 14.27   (continued)

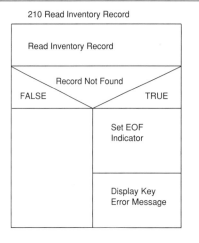

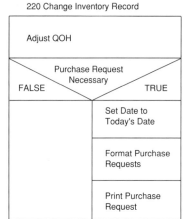

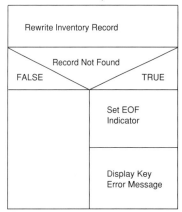

Figure 14.28   CDL's "Issue Purchase Requests" COBOL Code

```
 1 IDENTIFICATION DIVISION.
 2 PROGRAM-ID. PURCHASE-REQUESTS
 3*    THIS PROGRAM TAKES THE EXTENDED ORDERS, UPDATES THE QUANTITY
 4*    ON HAND AND ISSUES PURCHASE REQUESTS TO SUPPLIERS.
 5
 6 AUTHOR.          C HILTON.
 7 DATE-WRITTEN.    JULY 15, 1994.
 8 DATE-COMPILED. 08-Mar-94 02:23.
12 ENVIRONMENT DIVISION.
13
```

Figure 14.28   (continued)

```
14
15 CONFIGURATION SECTION.
16
17 SOURCE-COMPUTER.  GENERIC-COMPUTER.
18 OBJECT-COMPUTER.  GENERIC-COMPUTER.
19
20
21 INPUT-OUTPUT SECTION.
22
23 FILE-CONTROL.
24     SELECT EXTENDED-ORDERS-FILE ASSIGN TO DISK
25         ORGANIZATION IS SEQUENTIAL.
26     SELECT PURCHASE-REQUESTS-FILE ASSIGN TO PRINTER
27         ORGANIZATION IS SEQUENTIAL.
28     SELECT INVENTORY-FILE ASSIGN TO DISK
29         ORGANIZATION IS INDEXED
30         ACCESS MODE IS RANDOM
31         RECORD KEY IS INV-DISC-NBR.
32
33
34 DATA DIVISION.
35
36
37 FILE SECTION.
38
39 FD EXTENDED-ORDERS-FILE
40     LABEL RECORDS ARE STANDARD.
41
42 01  EXTENDED-ORDER-RECORD.
43     05  EO-CUSTOMER-NUMBER  PIC 9(6).
44     05  EO-DISC-NBR         PIC 9(6).
45     05  EO-QUANTITY         PIC 9(2).
46     05  EO-ORDER-NBR        PIC 9(6).
47     05  EO-PRICE            PIC 9(6)V99.
48
49 FD  INVENTORY-FILE
50     LABEL RECORDS ARE STANDARD.
51
52 01  INV-DISC-INFORMATION.
53     05  INV-DISC-NBR       PIC 9(6).
54     05  INV-DISC-TITLE     PIC X(20).
55     05  INV-SUPPLIER       PIC X(20).
```

Figure 14.28   (continued)

```
56      05   INV-ADDRESS         PIC X(20).
57      05   INV-CITY            PIC X(12).
58      05   INV-STATE           PIC X(2).
59      05   INV-ZIP             PIC 9(5).
60      05   INV-QOH             PIC 9(6).
61      05   INV-ROP             PIC 9(6).
62      05   INV-ORDER-DATE      PIC 9(6).
63      05   INV-ORDER-AMOUNT    PIC 9(6).
64      05   INV-PRICE           PIC 9(6)V99.
65
66 FD   PURCHASE-REQUESTS-FILE
67      LABEL RECORDS ARE OMITTED.
68
69 01   PR-LINE PIC X(60).
70
71
72 WORKING-STORAGE SECTION.
73
74 01   INDICATORS.
75      05   EOF-EXTENDED-ORDERS  PIC X(5) VALUE "FALSE".
76
77 01   WORKING-STORAGE-AREA.
78      05   WS-DATE     PIC 9(6).
79      05   WS-MM-DD-YY.
80           10   WS-MM   PIC XX.
81           10   WS-DD   PIC XX.
82           10   WS-YY   PIC XX.
83      05   WS-YEAR      PIC XX.
84
85 01   PURCHASE-REQUEST-LAYOUT.
86      05   PR-DATE-LINE.
87           10   FILLER     PIC X(39) VALUE SPACE.
88           10   PR-DATE    PIC Z9/99/99.
89      05   PR-SUPPLIER-LINE.
90           10   FILLER     PIC X(29) VALUE SPACE.
91           10   PR-SUPPLIER PIC X(20).
92      05   PR-ADDRESS-LINE.
93           10   FILLER     PIC X(29) VALUE SPACE.
94           10   PR-ADDRESS PIC X(20).
95      05   PR-CITY-STATE-ZIP.
96           10   FILLER     PIC X(29) VALUE SPACE.
97           10   PR-CITY    PIC X(13).
```

Figure 14.28 (continued)

```
 98          10  PR-STATE    PIC XXX.
 99          10  PR-ZIP      PIC 9(5).
100      05  PR-AMOUNT-NBR.
101          10  FILLER      PIC X(24) VALUE SPACE.
102          10  PR-AMOUNT   PIC Z(6).
103          10  FILLER      PIC X(9)  VALUE SPACE.
104          10  PR-DISC-NBR PIC 9(6).
105      05  PR-DISC-TITLE.
106          10  FILLER      PIC X(24) VALUE SPACE.
107          10  PR-TITLE    PIC X(20).
108
109
110 PROCEDURE DIVISION.
111
112 ISSUE-PURCHASE-REQUESTS.
113     OPEN INPUT EXTENDED-ORDERS-FILE.
114     OPEN I-O INVENTORY-FILE.
115     OPEN OUTPUT PURCHASE-REQUESTS-FILE.
116     PERFORM 100-PREPARE-INVENTORY-UPDATE.
117     PERFORM 200-APPLY-EXTENDED-ORDER
118         UNTIL EOF-EXTENDED-ORDERS EQUAL "TRUE".
119     CLOSE EXTENDED-ORDERS-FILE.
120     CLOSE INVENTORY-FILE.
121     CLOSE PURCHASE-REQUESTS-FILE.
122     STOP RUN.
123
124 100-PREPARE-INVENTORY-UPDATE.
125     DISPLAY "PURCHASE REQUEST FORMS REQUIRED.  PLEASE MOUNT.".
126     ACCEPT WS-DATE FROM DATE.
127     MOVE WS-DATE TO WS-MM-DD-YY.
128     MOVE WS-MM TO WS-YEAR.
129     MOVE WS-DD TO WS-MM.
130     MOVE WS-YY TO WS-DD.
131     MOVE WS-YEAR TO WS-YY.
132     MOVE WS-MM-DD-YY TO WS-DATE.
133     MOVE WS-DATE TO PR-DATE.
134     PERFORM 110-READ-EXTENDED-ORDER.
135
136 110-READ-EXTENDED-ORDER.
137     READ EXTENDED-ORDERS-FILE
138         AT END MOVE "TRUE" TO EOF-EXTENDED-ORDERS.
139
```

Figure 14.28   (continued)

```
140 200-APPLY-EXTENDED-ORDER.
141     MOVE EO-DISC-NBR TO INV-DISC-NBR.
142     PERFORM 210-READ-INVENTORY-RECORD.
143     PERFORM 220-CHANGE-INVENTORY-RECORD.
144     PERFORM 240-REWRITE-INVENTORY-RECORD.
145     PERFORM 110-READ-EXTENDED-ORDER.
146
147 210-READ-INVENTORY-RECORD.
148     READ INVENTORY-FILE
149         INVALID KEY
150             MOVE "TRUE" TO EOF-EXTENDED-ORDERS
151             DISPLAY EXTENDED-ORDER-RECORD
152             DISPLAY "KEY ERROR IN INVENTORY FILE".
153
154 220-CHANGE-INVENTORY-RECORD.
155     SUBTRACT EO-QUANTITY FROM INV-QOH.
156     IF INV-ORDER-DATE EQUAL ZERO AND INV-ROP GREATER INV-QOH
157         MOVE WS-DATE TO INV-ORDER-DATE
158         MOVE INV-SUPPLIER     TO PR-SUPPLIER
159         MOVE INV-ADDRESS      TO PR-ADDRESS
160         MOVE INV-CITY         TO PR-CITY
161         MOVE INV-STATE        TO PR-STATE
162         MOVE INV-ZIP          TO PR-ZIP
163         MOVE INV-ORDER-AMOUNT TO PR-AMOUNT
164         MOVE INV-DISC-NBR     TO PR-DISC-NBR
165         MOVE INV-DISC-TITLE   TO PR-TITLE
166         WRITE PR-LINE FROM PR-DATE-LINE AFTER ADVANCING PAGE
167         WRITE PR-LINE FROM PR-SUPPLIER-LINE AFTER ADVANCING 3
168             LINES
169         WRITE PR-LINE FROM PR-ADDRESS-LINE
170         WRITE PR-LINE FROM PR-CITY-STATE-ZIP
171         WRITE PR-LINE FROM PR-AMOUNT-NBR AFTER ADVANCING 3
172             LINES
173         WRITE PR-LINE FROM PR-DISC-TITLE.
174
175 240-REWRITE-INVENTORY-RECORD.
176     REWRITE INV-DISC-INFORMATION
177         INVALID KEY
178             MOVE "TRUE" TO EOF-EXTENDED-ORDERS
179             DISPLAY EXTENDED-ORDER-RECORD
180             DISPLAY "KEY ERROR IN INVENTORY UPDATE".
```

Figure 14.29 Test Plan

```
Inventory Test File:

111111BILLY SINGS GERSHWINCHEAP LABEL          1234 N. 1ST          ST. LOUIS
       MO63124000111000010000000000100000001299
222222HENRY SINGS GERSHWINCHEAP LABEL          1234 N. 1ST          ST. LOUIS
       MO63124000100000100121590000500000001599
333333FRED SINGS GERSHWIN CHEAP LABEL          1234 N. 1ST          ST. LOUIS
       MO63124000100000100000000000800000000999


Extended Order Test File:

1234561111110109876500000000
2345672222221093049000000000
3487653333332352355000009999


Resulting Purchase Order:

                                                3/08/94


                             CHEAP LABEL
                             1234 N. 1ST
                             ST. LOUIS    MO 63124



                           800         333333
                      FRED SINGS GERSHWIN
```

"210 Read Inventory Record." This module locates an inventory record in the indexed sequential file using the key given to it by its superior, "200 Apply Extended Order." If the INVALID KEY condition results, it means that the extended order does not have a valid CD number. However, since the extended orders have been validated before they were used in this program, only an extreme error would cause this condition to occur. Because of the seriousness of the error, Charlene decides that the appropriate course of action is to display the offending record contents with a message and to stop execution of the program by setting the end-of-file indicator for the Extended Orders File.

"240 Rewrite Inventory Record." This module performs the actual writing of the revised inventory file record. Again, since the possibility of error is so remote, the action taken on an

INVALID KEY condition is the same as that specified for the INVALID KEY in the READ module.

Summary

The two direct access file structures that are supported by COBOL are relative files and indexed sequential files. These file structures exploit the direct access capability of storage devices such as disks by allowing a record to be accessed directly since its location can be determined.

Relative files are organized in such a way that the relative position of a record is determined by a key field of the record. The selection of the key field is important in order to use storage space efficiently and reduce the number of duplicate records. In relative files the key is specified in the RELATIVE KEY clause. The key must be a data item that appears in the WORKING-STORAGE SECTION.

Indexed files combine the advantages of sequential and relative organization. The index entries contain the key field for the records and pointers to their corresponding disk locations. This allows the file to be accessed either sequentially or randomly. In indexed files the key used to locate the record is specified in the RECORD KEY clause. The key must be a data item appearing in the record description of the associated FD entry. The START verb allows the programmer to specify the starting point in the file from which sequential processing will take place.

The logic for processing relative and indexed files is similar, but simpler than the logic required for sequential files. Each transaction controls the input to and output from the file. A key data item is used to access the desired record. Since each record can be accessed directly, it is not necessary to sort the transactions and apply them in a batch process. They can be applied in whatever order the program encounters them.

COBOL provides the necessary statements to process direct access files. Direct access files are described by using additional COBOL phrases in the FILE CONTROL paragraph to specify the logical organization of the file and the manner in which it will be accessed. The WRITE statement adds new records to a direct access file. The REWRITE statement replaces an existing record, and the DELETE statement logically removes a record from the file. The INVALID KEY phrase specifies the action to be taken if the programmer attempts to write beyond the file's limits or if duplicate records are found. If the file is accessed randomly, the INVALID KEY phrase physically replaces the AT END phrase. It also specifies the action to be taken if the desired record is not found or an indexed file accessed sequentially is out of order. Before the program can randomly access a record in a direct access file, the desired key must be MOVEd to the RELATIVE KEY or RECORD KEY data item. Then the appropriate command can be issued.

Key Terms

direct access storage device	platter	indexed file
diskette	cylinder	prime record key
track	direct access	index
sector	organization	INVALID KEY
address	relative file	DELETE
disk drive	key value	REWRITE
disk pack	duplicate key	

Hints for Avoiding Errors

1. Be certain to MOVE in the correct key to the key field prior to conducting a random operation on a direct access file. Otherwise the incorrect record will be accessed.
2. Be aware that RELATIVE files created sequentially automatically assign the RELATIVE KEY value. This means that your file must be in the desired sequence prior to the start.
3. Always use the INVALID KEY phrase, even when it is optional. Many update programs assume transactions are properly applied when in fact they are not.
4. Verify file structure and blocking factors before coding any program. These errors are not caught by the compiler, but are found at the time of execution.

Exercises

14.1 Examine the files used by CDL. Which *could* be established as direct access files, and which *should* be established as direct access files?

14.2 Redo the program in Exercise 9-1 assuming the bank file is indexed with the account number as the key.

14.3 Design and code a program to create the bank file of Exercise 14.2 from the sequential file of Exercise 9-1.

14.4 A direct access file requires the clause ACCESS MODE IS RANDOM phrase following the SELECT statement when
    a. record keys are not known.
    b. processing transactions are not in sequence.
    c. the file is OPENed for OUTPUT.

14.5 Which of the following media is allowable for storing direct access files?
    a. Magnetic disk
    b. Magnetic tape
    c. Punched cards
    d. all of the above

14.6   Which types of files may be found on a disk device?
    a.   relative
    b.   direct access
    c.   indexed sequential
    d.   sequential
    e.   all of the above

14.7   Indexed sequential files can be
    a.   processed randomly.
    b.   processed sequentially.
    c.   timesaving in certain programs.
    d.   all of the above

14.8   When reading a direct access file in RANDOM fashion, the READ statement
    a.   requires the AT END clause.
    b.   requires the INVALID KEY clause.
    c.   requires a or b, but not both.

14.9   An advantage of DIRECT ACCESS MODE over SEQUENTIAL ACCESS MODE is that
    a.   less storage space is required for the file.
    b.   direct access is easier to process files sequentially.
    c.   direct access offers faster access to a particular record.

14.10   The INVALID KEY condition arises in a REWRITE when
    a.   the RECORD KEY or RELATIVE KEY does not exist on the file.
    b.   a sequential file is out of sequence.
    c.   an alphanumeric RECORD KEY is found in an indexed file.

14.11   List the file ORGANIZATION and ACCESS MODE combinations which may be used with a DELETE statement.

14.12   A relative file being sequentially accessed must be opened as _____ to issue a WRITE.
    a.   OUTPUT
    b.   INPUT
    c.   I-O
    d.   I-O or OUTPUT

14.13   A RELATIVE KEY must be numeric. True or false?

14.14   The RECORD KEY clause must be defined
    a.   in the WORKING-STORAGE SECTION.
    b.   in the record description of the file.
    c.   anywhere in the DATA DIVISION.

14.15   The key fields of the first few records in an indexed file are 1003, 1025, 1042, 1137 after the statement

```
START ILL-FILE KEY > 1025
    INVALID KEY PERFORM 100-XXX.
```

is executed. What record will be the first one accessed by a READ statement?

14.16   The data item in the RECORD KEY clause appears as part of the _____,
         and the data item in the RELATIVE KEY appears in the _____.
         a.   record description, FILE SECTION
         b.   WORKING-STORAGE SECTION, FILE SECTION
         c.   record description, WORKING-STORAGE SECTION

14.17   The _____ clause specifies the logical structure of a file.
         a.   RESERVE
         b.   ORGANIZATION
         c.   ACCESS MODE
         d.   KEY

For Exercises 14.18 through 14.21, assume that AQ-FILE is a randomly accessed indexed file opened
for I-O and contains the following records:

         RECORD-KEY-FIELD
               123456
               247191
               328761
               471534

Does an INVALID KEY condition occur with the following statements?

14.18   MOVE 471534 TO RECORD-KEY-FIELD.
             DELETE AQ-FILE RECORD
             INVALID   KEY PERFORM 999-ERR.

14.19   MOVE 123456 TO RECORD-KEY-FIELD.
             WRITE AQ-RECORD
             INVALID   KEY PERFORM 999-ERR.

14.20   MOVE 328760 TO RECORD-KEY-FIELD.
             DELETE   AQ-FILE RECORD
             INVALID   KEY PERFORM 999-ERR.

14.21   MOVE 328761 TO RECORD-KEY-FIELD.
             READ   AQ-FILE
             INVALID   KEY PERFORM 999-ERR.

14.22   A stack of tracks is referred to as a(n)   .
         a.   cone
         b.   cylinder
         c.   sector
         d.   address

14.23   Organization refers to the logical structure of a file. True or false?

14.24   Indexed file records are accessed by a(n) _____.
  a.   READ
  b.   KEY
  c.   INDEX
  d.   none of the above

14.25   If ORGANIZATION is INDEXED, the RELATIVE KEY must be specified. True or false?

14.26   If ORGANIZATION is SEQUENTIAL, the ACCESS MODE must be RANDOM. True or false?

14.27   The format of the WRITE statement does not change using random access files. True or false?

14.28   The logic for processing relative and indexed files is the same. True or false?

14.29   The _____ KEY is used for indexed files.
  a.   RECORD
  b.   INVALID
  c.   RELATIVE
  d.   INDEX

14.30   The _____ option must be used when updating direct access files using the REWRITE verb.
  a.   I/O
  b.   FROM
  c.   START
  d.   INTO

14.31   To incorporate differing file structures into an update program, most of the changes in the detailed design will be in the logic required to:
  a.   initialize the new files.
  b.   perform the update algorithm.
  c.   produce the required output.
  d.   locate a specific record.

14.32   Relative and indexed files are usually created in a sequential fashion and then copied to a file with a relative or indexed organization. True or false?

14.33   Relative files created sequentially automatically assign the relative key value. True or false?

14.34   The syntax of the following SELECT clause is valid. True or false?

```
SELECT MASTER-FILE ASSIGN TO DISK
    ORGANIZATION IS INDEXED
    ACCESS MODE IS SEQUENTIAL
    RECORD KEY IS EMPLOYEE-ID.
```

14.35   Concurrent circles of magnetized spots on a diskette surface are called _____.

14.36   Each track has a(n) _____,which is used to locate information.

14.37   In medium and large scale computer systems multiple disks are integrated into a(n) _____.

14.38   Each disk in a disk pack is called a(n) _____.

14.39   A(n) _____ file is a collection of records in which each record can be identified by its position in the file.

14.40   The _____ statement logically replaces the last record successfully READ.

14.41   The _____ statement in sequential access mode allows a program to begin processing at any point in the file and continue processing from the current record forward.

14.42   In relative files the RELATIVE KEY must be a data item that appears in the _____ SECTION.

14.43   Before a program can access a record in a direct access file randomly, the desired key must be _____ to the RELATIVE KEY or RECORD KEY data item.

14.44   What are the advantages and disadvantages of indexed files?

14.45   What should be taken into account when selecting an appropriate file organization?

14.46   How can direct access capabilities improve an organization's solution to its business problems?

WRITING INTERACTIVE PROGRAMS

Interactive systems are those in which the user and the computer act with one another through a terminal. This interaction is usually accomplished through a dialogue or through the choice of options on a displayed menu. The user enters data, queries, or responses and receives immediate feedback relative to his entry. More and more of today's business systems have interactive capabilities. One reason is productivity. By interacting with a personal computer or terminal connected to a mainframe, a user can obtain almost instantaneous information from the set of data available on the system. In addition, if data are validated as they are entered, their accuracy is improved, and turnaround time is faster since batch editing can be circumvented.

15.1   *Characteristics of an Interactive System*

Until now we have made no distinction between COBOL support for batch and for interactive systems. The features we discussed support both processing environments. However, certain characteristics of interactive systems require additional design and programming considerations. Furthermore, COBOL facilitates the handling of these systems through standard statements.

15.1.1   *Hardware*

Most of the hardware for batch and interactive systems is identical. A computer, mass storage devices, printers, and terminals are required to run each system. However, whereas in a batch system the computer operator usually initiates the execution of a program, in an interactive system the user initiates and controls the execution through an information exchange with the computer system. The computer responds to the user's requests immediately.

The interaction hardware device may be a terminal or a personal computer. The proliferation of interactive devices requires that they be considered during the design of software systems. With the distribution of hardware, the advantage of fast response to information needs becomes available to many individuals. Users no longer need to request the running of a batch job to generate desired information and wait long hours for the operations department to schedule their requests. They need not wait for reports to be sent through the company mail system in order to obtain their copy. With interactive processing, a user submits a request at his terminal and receives the output at his terminal. The distribution of hardware speeds up the dissemination of important information.

15.1.2   *Software*

Software for interactive systems is essentially the same as that for the batch environment. The same general tasks need to be performed. Many of the same structuring and logical design methodologies are appropriate for interactive systems' development cycles. The major design difference is in the inclusion of sophisticated interfaces to accommodate the interaction between the machine and the user.

In interactive systems input does not need to be collected over a period of time and subsequently input to the system at a single time. Instead, input can be generated on demand during the operating day and processed immediately. COBOL provides standard commands for simple formatting of screen input and output. More sophisticated screen communication is system-dependent and is accomplished with nonstandard extensions to various COBOL compilers.

15.1.3   *Applications*

Interactive systems are used for data entry, data retrieval, and file updates. Certain data entry systems use interactive procedures for collecting data that are to be input at a later time to a batch process. Such interactive data entry applications allow the computer to validate the data as they are entered into the system using specified validation rules. Data retrieval applications answer direct queries posed by users. When a question is asked, the appropriate files are queried to develop the response to be sent to the user's terminal.

File update applications using interactive systems take advantage of the fact that transactions can be applied immediately. A well-known interactive update application is that of airline reservations. A reservation clerk first queries the system to determine whether space is available on the requested flight. If so, the reservation is entered and applied to the file immediately. If it were entered through a batch processing system, reserved seats might be sold many times over.

15.2   *Interface Design Considerations*

Designing the input and output interfaces of an interactive system is the responsibility of the analyst. The programmer, however, should be aware of the different implementations. The quality of a system interface may be the difference between a system that is easy to use versus one that is hard to use; a system that is used versus a system that is ignored. By becoming aware of some major design guidelines for human-machine communication, a programmer should be able to detect flaws in the interface design and point out the problem to the analyst. In the following section we review some of the most commonly used means for implementing these interfaces.

15.2.1   *Menus*

A menu is much like a menu at a restaurant. It specifies the options available to the user. A sample menu is presented in Figure 15.1. In many restaurants customers can place orders by selecting the number of their choice. In an application *menu*, the user selects the desired option by keying in the appropriate keyword or number of the selection. Systems that utilize menus for user interaction are called menu-driven systems. Menu-driven systems are most appropriate for inexperienced users because of their simplicity and because they reduce the number of errors made by limiting the options available to the user. A sophisticated user, on the other hand, can feel restricted by menu-driven systems. Furthermore, more complex systems can become bogged down if implemented with menus. Given that only a limited number of options can appear on the terminal screen at any one time, it might be necessary to have several levels of menus to accommodate the available options.

Figure 15.1   An Application Menu

```
              SELECT THE DESIRED LANGUAGE COMPILER
                  1. COBOL
                  2. FORTRAN
                  3. PASCAL
                  4. EXIT THE SYSTEM

              TYPE THE NUMBER OF YOUR CHOICE ===>_
```

15.2.2   Commands

Command-driven systems are more common for experienced users. For example, many interactive operating systems on personal computers are command-driven. At any point in the system, the user might be required to enter a valid command. This gives the user much flexibility but requires much more error checking on the part of the system than does a menu-driven system. However, command-driven systems are seldom developed in-house for the users. For one thing, the programming overhead is very high from a validation standpoint. Command-driven systems are appropriate when the sophistication of the user is fairly high. Novices find command systems complicated and user-unfriendly. This often leads to an aversion to the system, as well as many errors when it is used. Generally, it is better to insult the intelligence of the few experienced users rather than to design command-driven systems for inexperienced users. If a system is certain to have only experienced users, however, a command-driven system may be the better alternative and the analyst should give it.

15.2.3   Formatted Screen Input

Fixed screen input is commonly used for many data entry applications. With fixed screen input a "form," analogous to a form one fills out, is displayed on the screen. Data entry clerks fill in the screen by keying in the requested information. Figure 15.2 shows a screen form for adding a new customer to a customer file. The form is fixed on the screen. As data are entered, the screen pointer, called a cursor, automatically moves from field to field awaiting data entry into the indicated field. For example, the cursor moves to the area where the customer address should be entered after the customer's name is entered. The data are usually validated as they are entered.

If an error is detected, a warning signal may be given requiring the data entry clerk to correct and reenter the invalid data item. When the form is completely filled, the keyed-in information is input to the application system by pressing a designated key. A new blank form appears on the screen ready for the next entry.

Figure 15.2   *A Fixed Screen Form*

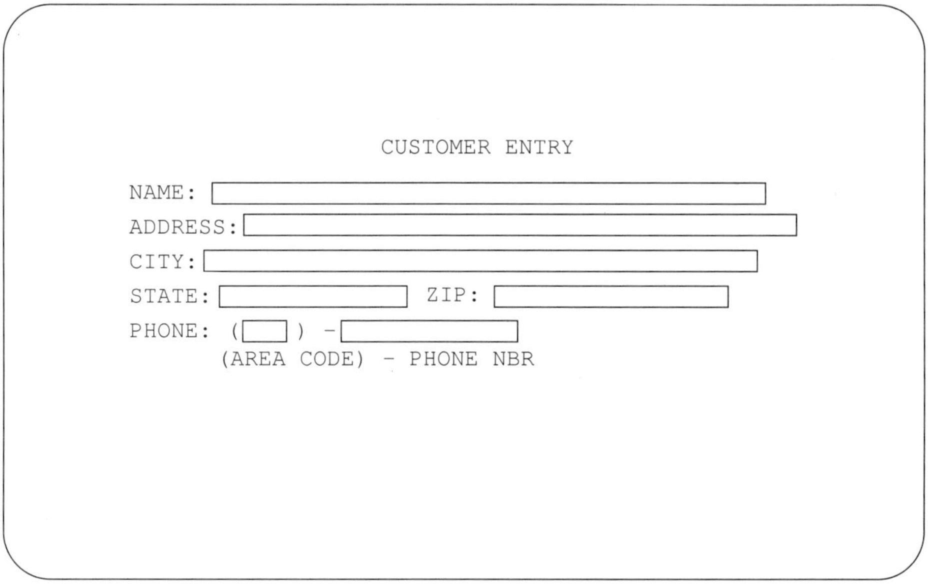

```
                              CUSTOMER ENTRY

         NAME:    [                                        ]
         ADDRESS: [                                          ]
         CITY:    [                                      ]
         STATE:   [                  ]   ZIP:  [               ]
         PHONE:   ([    ] ) -[                 ]
                  (AREA CODE) - PHONE NBR
```

The commands to format terminal screens are not standardized. Because of this, most vendors provide systems to develop programs for fixed screen input. These packages vary in complexity, comprehensiveness, and price. The better ones not only allow the analyst to design the screen but also permit the specification of the validation rules to be applied to the data, and automatically generate the programming code needed.

15.2.4   *Dialogues*

In many interactive systems the interface between the user and the computer is through a "conversation." Such an interface is called a *dialogue*. Dialogues must be carefully designed to convey proper messages. Good messages are appropriate, useful, and clear. They provide complete information and do not insult the user. In general, messages can be evaluated by asking whether the message (1) is complete and understandable, and (2) is properly and tactfully worded.

Message Length. Although messages should be concise and to the point, often they are too short. This is especially true in menu-driven systems. A user is to select from a list of choices, but the choices are often unclear. To illustrate this, examine the two menus in Figure 15.3. The options in menu (a) are too restricted. Menu (b) better explains the options by using phrases that are slightly longer.

Figure 15.3   *Comparison of Two Menus*

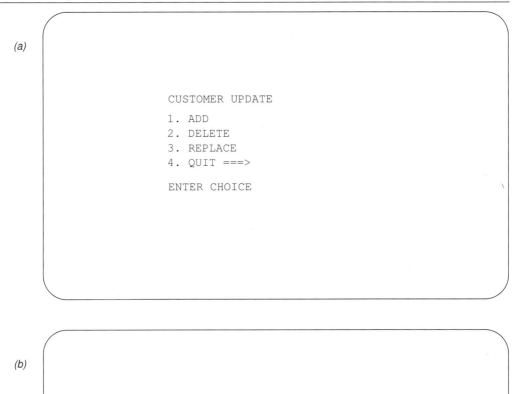

(a)

```
CUSTOMER UPDATE

1. ADD
2. DELETE
3. REPLACE
4. QUIT ===>

ENTER CHOICE
```

(b)

```
SELECT THE DESIRED TASK

1. ADD A NEW CUSTOMER
2. DELETE AN EXISTING CUSTOMER
3. REPLACE INFORMATION FOR A CUSTOMER
4. EXIT TO PREVIOUS MENU

PLEASE ENTER CHOICE ===>
```

Message Content. Messages should be written in terms familiar to the user. They should be relevant to the occasion and be useful to the user. Figure 15.4 shows two messages that inform the user of the same action. The message in Figure 15.4a contains computer terminology that the user may not understand and gives no indication of what the user can do about the situation. The message in Figure 15.4b provides the same information in common English and suggests a possible cause of the problem. If computer terminology is relevant, use it. If not, avoid it. For example, an accountant who keys in information does not need to know that the length of a field cannot exceed the maximum length for a COBOL numeric data item. He only needs to know that a number may not contain more than 18 digits.

Figure 15.4   *Comparison of User Messages*

```
(a)     ERROR FX971 ---> OBJ MISSING

(b)     FX971 ---> THE PROGRAM REQUESTED FOR
                   EXECUTION CANNOT BE LOCATED.
                   PLEASE VERIFY NAME.
```

Error Messages. Many users make errors when keying in information or commands. Not only should error messages be complete, they should also show proper respect. Positive reinforcement does wonders for user morale and inevitably influences whether the user feels threatened by the system or whether the system encourages its use. Figure 15.5 shows three error messages to the user. The message in Figure 15.5a demonstrates poor judgment in the selection of words; message 15–5b is meaningless to most users; but message 15–5c is clear and polite.

Proper grammatical structure and word usage are musts. The system under development may be for a friend in the organization, and it may seem cute to have the program address the user as "Ugly Face." However, the friend may not always be with the company, and other individuals who use it may not share your sense of humor.

Figure 15.5   *Comparison of Error Messages*

```
(a)     YOU GOOFED. CHECK THE NUMBER SIZE.

(b)     ACCEPT 9(9)V99 ONLY.

(c)     THE NUMBER MUST BE LESS THAN
        1,000,000,000.00 AND CONTAIN AT
        MOST 2 DECIMAL POSITIONS.
```

15.2.5   *Simple Data Entry*

Data entry programs are some of the more conceptually simple interactive programs. Such a program may not require access to any external files but may merely accept free-form input data and validate them. A hierarchy chart for such a program is shown in Figure 15.6. Several modules require interface considerations. For example, module "100 Present Process Instructions" provides instructions on how to operate the program. Module "211 Read User Input" interfaces with the user to obtain the necessary data. Module "212 Edit User Input" manipulates the character input to determine whether a valid entry was made. Module "300 Confirm Session Termination" informs the user that the session has been successfully completed.

Figure 15.6   **Hierarchy Chart for a Data Entry Program**

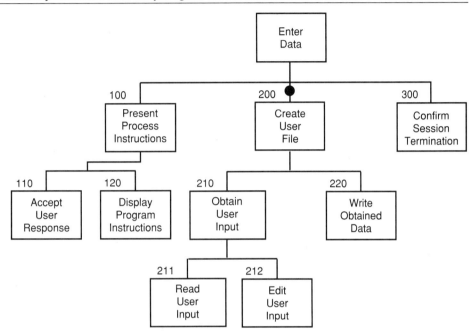

15.3   COBOL for Interactive Programs

Interactive programs dictate a variety of special programming considerations. Since rapid response is a prime consideration of interactive systems, files that are consulted are almost always direct access files. Character manipulation is another important design consideration. For example, when numeric input is accepted from a user, a difficulty arises in trying to accept the data as a valid COBOL number while allowing the user freedom in entering the number. A user may enter the value 121.00 as 121, 121., 0121.0, or even in another format, whereas the COBOL program may store the value in a data item with a PICTURE of 9(6)V99. Reconciling this difficulty requires the manipulation of the input into the format required by the computer. Character manipulation is also necessary to present computer data in a form understandable by the user.

15.3.1   Dialogues

In COBOL, dialogues are managed using DISPLAY and ACCEPT statements. A program that prompts the user for a line of information and then reads the response is coded as a sequence of DISPLAY and ACCEPT statements. The N-S chart for module "100 Present Process Instructions" in Figure 15.6 is presented in Figure 15.7. It displays introductory information and acquires starting values for the program. The associated code is:

```
100-PRESENT-PROCESS-INSTRUCTIONS.
    MOVE "X" TO ANS-INSTRUCTION.
    DISPLAY "DO YOU REQUIRE INSTRUCTIONS?".
    PERFORM 110-ACCEPT-USER-RESPONSE
        UNTIL ANS-INSTRUCTION = "Y"
        OR ANS-INSTRUCTION = "N".
    IF ANS-INSTRUCTION = "Y"
        PERFORM 120-DISPLAY-PROGRAM-INSTRUCTIONS.
110-ACCEPT-USER-RESPONSE.
    DISPLAY "RESPOND ""Y"" FOR YES, ""N"" FOR NO".
    ACCEPT ANS-INSTRUCTION.
120-DISPLAY-PROGRAM-INSTRUCTIONS.
    DISPLAY "IN ORDER TO ...".
```

Figure 15.7 **N-S Chart of Module "100 Present Process Instructions"**

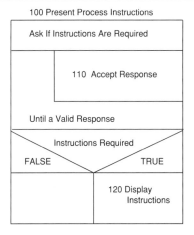

The DISPLAY statements send messages to the user's terminal, and the ACCEPT statements obtain the user's response. Errors in response input may be handled using the DO UNTIL structure as shown in the flowchart and the code prompting the user for the requested input until a valid entry is made. This prevents the program from proceeding with invalid data.

15.3.2   *Character Manipulation*

One of the major programming considerations concerns character manipulation. This is especially true for programs that allow free-format input or require validation of the data. Several COBOL statements support the required character manipulation. We will first examine simple versions of the statements.

The JUSTIFIED Clause. The data description of elementary items in the DATA DIVISION can be enhanced by using the JUSTIFIED clause. Its format is:

$$\left\{ \begin{array}{l} \underline{JUSTIFIED} \\ \underline{JUST} \end{array} \right\} \quad RIGHT$$

1. The data item must be an alphanumeric, alphabetic, or alphanumeric-edited elementary item.
2. Excess characters to the left are truncated.
3. Spaces are filled to the left when a sending field is shorter than a JUSTIFIED RIGHT receiving field.

The *JUSTIFIED* clause positions the characters within a receiving alphanumeric data item so that the rightmost character of the sending item is placed in the rightmost position of the receiving item, thus overriding the standard left justification. This permits the programmer to MOVE data into a field and to have the data right-justified as shown in Figure 15.8. A data item that is right-justified may look better when displayed. As we will see later, this clause is also very useful for determining the value of numbers entered in free format.

Figure 15.8   *Results of Using the JUSTIFIED RIGHT Clause*

		RIGHT JUSTIFIED	
Sending PICTURE	**Sending value**	**Receiving PICTURE**	**Receiving value**
X(5)	ABCDE	X(6)	♭ABCDE
X(5)	ABCDE	X(4)	BCDE
X(5)	ABCDE	X(5)	ABCDE

A Simple STRING Statement. When information is presented to the user, superfluous spaces should be removed from the stored values. For example, stored name and address fields of customers usually include all the blank spaces between the addressee's first and last names and the name of the city and the state. Without removing spaces, the displayed address would appear as in Figure 15.9. It is much more appealing and personal to have the information appear as in Figure 15.10, which requires the elimination of unnecessary spaces from the name and address lines.

Figure 15.9   An Address with Unnecessary Spaces

```
JOHN                    HUGS
1342    W.     BOODO    ST.
TUCSON          AZ          85721
```

Figure 15.10   An Address with Proper Spacing

```
JOHN HUGS
1342 W. BOODO ST.
TUCSON, AZ 85721
```

The COBOL *STRING* statement is used to perform this edit. It links together (concatenates) two or more data items into a single data item. The format of a simplified version of the STRING statement is:

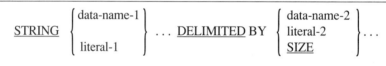

INTO data-name-3

1. No space-filling is provided.
2. A character-by-character alphanumeric to alphanumeric MOVE is conducted.
3. Each data-name-1 or literal-1 is moved to data-name-3 until the specified delimiter is reached.
4. All literals must be alphanumeric.
5. Data-name-1 and data-name-2 must be alphanumeric or numeric integer.
6. Data-name-3 must be alphanumeric, may not contain the JUST clause, and may not be reference modified.
7. If SIZE is specified, the entire contents of the sending item are sent to the receiving item.

Data-name-1 or literal-1 is the sending item; data-name-3 is the receiving item. Data-name-2 or literal-2 is the *delimiter* that indicates to the computer the character that signifies the end of the item being strung. For example, if the delimiter is a space, the sending field is transferred to the receiving field character by character until the first space in the sending field is found. If the delimiter SIZE is specified, the entire sending field is transferred to the receiving field regardless of contents. Figure 15.11 illustrates some examples of the use and effects of the STRING statement. Extensions to the STRING are explored in a later section.

Figure 15.11   **Results of Various STRING Statements**

NBR-1 PIC X(4)	NBR-2 PIC X(4)	NBR-3 PIC X(4)	Statement	RESULT-AREA PIC X(15) VALUE SPACES

AB/C	341B	?	STRING NBR-1 NBR-2
			  DELIMITED BY "/"
			  INTO RESULT-AREA.
				AB341Bbbbbbbbbb

AB/C	341B	2Q/4	STRING NBR-1 NBR-2 NBR-3
			  DELIMITED BY "*"
			  INTO RESULT-AREA.
				AB/C341BZQ/4bbb

AB/C	AB/D	/B*C	STRING NBR-1 DELIMITED BY "/"
			  NBR-2 DILIMTED BY SIZE
			  NBR-3 DELIMITED BY "8"
			  INTO RESULT-AREA.
				ABAB/D/Bbbbbbbb

b = space

Assume the following data descriptions:

```
01  NAME-ADDRESS
      05  NA-NAME-LINE         PIC   X(20).
      05  NA-ADDRESS-LINE      PIC   X(20).
      05  NA-CITY-STATE-ZIP    PIC   X(20).
01  CUSTOMER-ADDRESS-RECORD.
      05  CAR-NAME-FIRST       PIC   X(15).
      05  CAR-NAME-LAST        PIC   X(15).
      05  CAR-ADDRESS          PIC   X(20).
      05  CAR-CITY             PIC   X(12).
      05  CAR-STATE            PIC   X( 2).
      05  CAR-ZIP              PIC   9( 5).
```

The code to remove the extra spaces from the name and address lines is:

```
MOVE SPACE TO NA-CITY-STATE-ZIP.
MOVE SPACE TO NA-NAME-LINE.
STRING CAR-NAME-FIRST DELIMITED BY SPACE
    " " DELIMITED BY SIZE
    CAR-NAME-LAST DELIMITED BY SPACE
    INTO NA-NAME-LINE.
STRING
    CAR-CITY DELIMITED BY SPACE
    ", " DELIMITED BY SIZE
```

```
          CAR-STATE DELIMITED BY SIZE
          " " DELIMITED BY SIZE
          CAR-ZIP DELIMITED BY SIZE
          INTO NA-CITY-STATE-ZIP.
   MOVE CAR-ADDRESS TO NA-ADDRESS-LINE.
```

The literals " " and ", " in the STRING statement are the literals that provide spacing between the fields. Also notice that spaces were moved to the receiving fields since the STRING statement does not fill blanks.

The STRING statement can combine multiple data items and literals into a single data item and effect the requested editing. The STRING statement is helpful in formatting output for display on terminals or the printer. It is also used to reduce the size of fields to economize on the amount of storage space needed to save them.

A Simple UNSTRING Statement. The *UNSTRING* statement, the converse of the STRING statement, separates a character string into one or more components. It is especially useful for editing free-format commands or for transforming free-format numbers into valid numeric data items. The format and rules for a simplified UNSTRING statement are:

$$\underline{\text{UNSTRING}}\ \text{data-name-1}\ \left[\ \underline{\text{DELIMITED}}\ \text{BY}\ [\underline{\text{ALL}}]\ \left\{ \begin{array}{l} \text{data-name-2} \\ \text{literal-1} \end{array} \right\} \right.$$

$$\left. \left[\ \underline{\text{OR}}\ [\underline{\text{ALL}}] \left\{ \begin{array}{l} \text{data-name-3} \\ \text{literal-2} \end{array} \right\} \right] \dots \right]$$

$$\underline{\text{INTO}}\quad \{\text{data-name-4}\}\ \dots$$

1. Transfer of data-name-1 proceeds according to the MOVE rules for an alphanumeric field.
2. Data-name-1, -2, and -3 must be alphanumeric data items.
3. The reserved word ALL treats contiguous occurrences of the delimiter as a single occurrence.
4. If no delimiter is encountered, the UNSTRING stops at the end of the sending or last receiving field.
5. When multiple delimiters are specified, each occurrence of any one is considered a separate delimiter.
6. No character may be a part of more than one delimiter.
7. If the DELIMITED BY is left out, the UNSTRING will fill each entire receiving field.

Extensions to the simple UNSTRING statement will be presented later.

Figure 15.12 illustrates some examples of the simplified UNSTRING. Using the data descriptions given previously, the following UNSTRING statement would divide an address line into the elemental components of city, state, and zip:

```
UNSTRING NA-CITY-STATE-ZIP
    DELIMITED BY "," OR SPACE
    INTO CAR-CITY CAR-STATE CAR-ZIP.
```

Figure 15.12   *Results of Various UNSTRING Statements*

STARTING-ITEM PIC X(10)	Statement	NBR-1 PIC X(5)	NBR-2 PIC X(5)
ZW13/,ABCQ	UNSTRING STARTING-ITEM DELIMITED BY "/" OR "," INTO NBR-1 NBR-2.	ZW13ƀ	ƀƀƀƀƀ
ZW13/AB,CQ	SAME AS ABOVE	ZW13ƀ	ABƀƀƀ
X1//4321/B	UNSTRING STARTING-ITEM DELIMITED BY ALL "/" INTO NBR-1 NBR-2.	X1ƀƀƀ	4321ƀ

A Simple INSPECT Statement. The *INSPECT* statement replaces characters in a data item with other characters. The format for a simplified INSPECT statement is:

<u>INSPECT</u> data-name-1 <u>REPLACING</u>

$$\left\{ \left\{ \begin{array}{l} \underline{ALL} \\ \underline{LEADING} \\ \underline{FIRST} \end{array} \right\} \left\{ \begin{array}{l} \text{data-name-2} \\ \text{literal-1} \end{array} \right\} \quad \underline{BY} \quad \left\{ \begin{array}{l} \text{data-name-3} \\ \text{literal-2} \end{array} \right\} \right\}$$

1. The operation on data-name-1 proceeds from left to right.
2. Data-name-1 is treated as an alphanumeric data item regardless of its PICTURE.
3. If ALL is specified, every occurrence of data-name-2 or literal-1 is replaced by data-name-3 or literal-2.
4. If LEADING is specified, all occurrences of data-name-2 or literal-1 until another character is found are replaced.
5. If FIRST is specified, the leftmost occurrence of data-name-2 or literal-1 is replaced.

A common application of the INSPECT statement is in correcting data entry errors. For example, data entry personnel frequently key in the letter "O" when the actual value is a numeric 0 (zero). The code in Figure 15.13 corrects this error by replacing all occurrences of the letter "O" with a zero in the field intended to be numeric. We will cover extensions to the simple INSPECT statement in a later section.

Figure 15.13   Correcting a Common Data Entry Error Using an INSPECT Statement

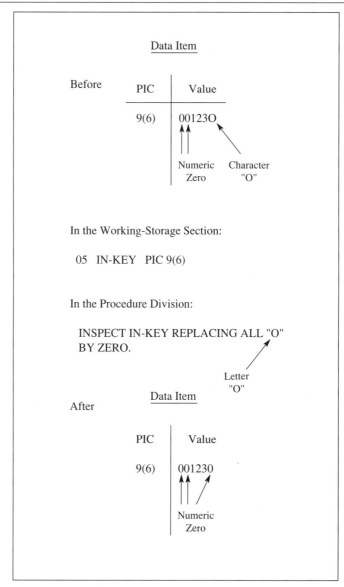

15.3.3   Free-Format Numeric Input

The character manipulation features discussed above can be used to convert a free-format numeric entry into a valid numeric data item used in computations. For example, assume that an unsigned positive dollar value is input in free-format and is to be converted to a numeric data item of PICTURE 9(6)V99. The COBOL code necessary to accomplish this task is:

In the WORKING-STORAGE SECTION:

```
05 NUMBER-IN                          PIC X(9).
05 NUMERIC-VALUE.
   05  BEFORE-DECIMAL                 PIC X(4)   JUST RIGHT.
   05  AFTER-DECIMAL                  PIC XX.
05 NUMERIC-RESULT REDEFINES NUMERIC-VALUE   PIC 9(4)V99.
```

In the PROCEDURE DIVISION:

```
ACCEPT NUMBER-IN.
INSPECT NUMBER-IN REPLACING ALL "$" BY SPACE.
UNSTRING NUMBER-IN DELIMITED BY "." OR " "
     INTO BEFORE-DECIMAL AFTER-DECIMAL.
INSPECT NUMERIC-VALUE REPLACING
     ALL SPACE BY ZERO.
IF NUMERIC-VALUE NOT NUMERIC
     MOVE ALL ZEROS TO NUMERIC-VALUE.
```

The INSPECT statement replaces a dollar sign that may or may not have been entered by the user. Next, the number is separated into the part before the decimal point and the part after the decimal point using the UNSTRING command. Notice that since the receiving field of the part before the decimal is JUSTIFIED RIGHT, the digits are transferred to the rightmost places in the data item. Another INSPECT statement is used to replace any blank characters in either part by zeros. Lastly, the data item is tested to ensure that all positions are numeric; otherwise it is zero-filled. In the data definition the number is redefined to be a numeric elementary data item that can be tested later to verify that a correct nonzero entry was made. Figure 15.14 shows results of using the above code.

Figure 15.14   *Handling Free-Format Numeric Input*

NUMBER-IN Value after ACCEPT	NUMBER-IN Value after 1st INSPECT	After UNSTRING		Numeric Value after 2nd INSPECT	Numeric Result After IF
		BEFORE-DECIMAL	AFTER-DECIMAL		
$19.45	b1945	bb19	45	001945	0019ᐃ45
$19.00	b19.00	bb19	00	001900	0019ᐃ00
$ZZbbb	bZZbbb	bZZb	bb	0ZZ000	0000ᐃ00
.35bbb	.35bbb	bbbb	35	000035	0000ᐃ35
100bbb	100bbb	b100	bb	010000	0100ᐃ00

b = blank   ∆ = implied decimal

15.3.4   The STRING Statement

The complete format of the STRING statement is shown below:

$$\underline{STRING} \quad \left\{ \left\{ \begin{array}{l} \text{data-name-1} \\ \text{literal-1} \end{array} \right\} \ldots \underline{DELIMITED} \text{ BY} \left\{ \begin{array}{l} \text{data-name-2} \\ \text{literal-2} \\ \underline{SIZE} \end{array} \right\} \right\} \ldots$$

> $\underline{INTO}$ data-name-3 [WITH $\underline{POINTER}$ data-name-4]
> [ON $\underline{OVERFLOW}$ imperative-statement-1]
> [$\underline{NOT}$ ON $\underline{OVERFLOW}$ imperative statement]
> [$\underline{END\text{-}STRING}$]

1. No space filling is provided.
2. A character-by-character alphanumeric to alphanumeric MOVE is conducted.
3. Each data-name-1 or literal-1 is moved until the specified delimiter is reached.
4. All literals must be alphanumeric.
5. Data-name-1 and data-name-2 must be alphanumeric or numeric integer.
6. Data-name-3 must be alphanumeric and may not contain the JUST clause.
7. Data-name-4 must be a numeric integer elementary item.

The *OVERFLOW* phrase allows the programmer to specify the action to be taken should the receiving field be too small. The *POINTER* phrase allows him to keep a count of the number of characters moved from the sending item to the receiving item, as well as to control the position of the entry in the sending item within the receiving item. Data-name-4 contains the value of the character position in the receiving item where the first character of the sending item will begin. It is up to the programmer to initialize data-name-4 with a value greater than zero prior to executing the STRING statement. Each character from the sending item is transferred to the receiving items, beginning at the position designated by data-name-4. The pointer is automatically incremented by one prior to moving the next character, thus allowing the programmer to determine the actual number of characters transferred. The example statement,

```
STRING  NBR-1  NBR-2  NBR-3

    DELIMITED  BY  "/"
    INTO RESULT-AREA
    WITH POINTER POINT-1.
```

results in the following values for the specified data items:

```
NBR-1          NBR-2          NBR-2
PIC X(4)       PIC X(4)       PIC X(4)
1234           AB/C           2Q/4
```

```
RESULT-AREA                BEGINNING   FINAL
PIC X(15) VALUE SPACE      POINT-1     POINT-1
   1234AB2Q                4           12
```

The pointer may be used to center an item in a display if the lengths of the item to be centered and the receiving field are known. Assume the following data descriptions in the WORKING-STORAGE SECTION:

```
05     CENTER-POINT     PIC   99.
05     DISPLAY-LINE     PIC   X(80).
05     DISPLAYED-ITEM   PIC   X(15).
05     LINE-LENGTH      PIC   99   VALUE 80.
05     DISPLAY-LENGTH   PIC   99   VALUE 15.
```

The following PROCEDURE DIVISION code centers the desired item on the display line.

```
COMPUTE CENTER-POINT =
    (LINE-LENGTH - DISPLAY-LENGTH + 1) / 2.
MOVE SPACE TO DISPLAY-LINE.
STRING DISPLAYED-ITEM
    DELIMITED BY SIZE
    INTO DISPLAY-LINE
    POINTER CENTER-POINT.
DISPLAY DISPLAY-LINE.
```

In this example the number of open positions in the receiving line is computed by finding the difference between the lengths of the two fields, and dividing the difference by 2. The pointer data item is set to this value to indicate the starting position in the receiving field. This causes the pointer to move over the correct number of spaces to center the sending item. If the length of the item to be displayed is unknown, the UNSTRING or INSPECT statement can be used to determine its length first.

15.3.5   *The UNSTRING Statement*

The complete format and rules of the UNSTRING statement are:

UNSTRING data-name-1

$$\left[\underline{\text{DELIMITED}} \text{ BY } [\underline{\text{ALL}}] \left\{ \begin{array}{l} \text{data-name-2} \\ \text{literal-1} \end{array} \right\} \left[\text{OR } [\underline{\text{ALL}}] \left\{ \begin{array}{l} \text{data-name-3} \\ \text{literal-2} \end{array} \right\} \right] \dots \right]$$

<u>INTO</u>   {data-name-4 [<u>DELIMITER</u> IN data-name-5] [<u>COUNT</u> IN data-name-6]} . . .
[WITH <u>POINTER</u> data-name-7]
[<u>TALLYING</u> IN data-name-8]
[ON <u>OVERFLOW</u> imperative-statement]
[<u>NOT</u> ON <u>OVERFLOW</u> imperative-statement]
[<u>END-UNSTRING</u>]

1. Transfer of data-name-1 proceeds according to the MOVE rules for an alphanumeric field.
2. Data-name-1, -2, and -3 must be alphanumeric data items.
3. The use of the ALL treats contiguous occurrences of the delimiter as a single occurrence.
4. If no delimiter is encountered, the UNSTRING stops at the end of the sending or last receiving item.
5. When multiple delimiters are specified, each occurrence of any one is considered a separate delimiter.
6. No character may be a part of more than one delimiter.
7. If the DELIMITED BY is left out, the UNSTRING will fill each entire receiving field.
8. Data-name-6, -7, -8 must be numeric integer.
9. Data-name-5 must be alphanumeric.
10. DELIMITER saves the delimiter that terminated a receiving field. If no delimiter is found, data-name-5 is space- or zero-filled.
11. DELIMITER can only be specified if the DELIMITED BY is specified.
12. COUNT saves the number of characters placed into data-name-4.
13. The pointer indicates the starting and ending position + 1 in data-name-7.
14. The TALLYING phrase identifies the data-item incremented for each receiving field. The programmer must initialize data-name-8.

The new optional clauses are especially helpful in doing more sophisticated character manipulations. They are very useful for interpreting data input at a terminal. The human-machine interface in interactive applications should be "user-friendly" and allow certain latitude to the user in making responses. Statements such as the UNSTRING statement help manipulate the user's input to meet the more rigid requirements of the computer.

The POINTER and OVERFLOW phrases of the UNSTRING are similar to those for the STRING statement. The starting value of the pointer indicates the position in the sending field to begin the unstringing process. The final value of the pointer will be equal to the initial value plus the number of characters examined during the execution of the UNSTRING. An OVERFLOW occurs when the pointer is less than 1 or greater than the length of data-name-1, or if all receiving items have been acted on prior to examining all the characters in the sending item.

The DELIMITER phrase allows the programmer to save in data-name-5 the specific delimiting character that ended a field. This may be useful when it is necessary to identify which of a number of delimiters actually terminated the receiving field. If the delimiting condition was the end of the sending item or two contiguous delimiters, data-name-5 will be space- or zero-filled depending on its PICTURE. Figure 15.15a illustrates the use and results of an UNSTRING statement with the DELIMITER phrase.

Figure 15.15   Results of Various UNSTRING Statements Using Optional Phrases

(a)

STARTING-ITEM PIC X(10)	Statement	NBR-1 PIC X(5)	NBR-2 PIC X(5)	Starting POINT-IT PIC 99	Ending POINT-IT PIC 99
34X1//*314	UNSTRING STARTING-ITEM DELIMITED BY "*" OR "/" INTO NBR-2 DELIMITER IN NBR-1 POINTER POINT-IT.	/ƀƀƀƀ	4X1ƀƀ	2	6

(b)

STARTING-ITEM PIC X(10)	Statement	NBR-1 PIC X(5)	NBR-2 PIC X(5)	COUNT-1 PIC 99	COUNT-2 PIC 99
1X1//43//2	UNSTRING STARTING-ITEM DELIMITED BY ALL "/" INTO NBR-1 COUNT COUNT-1 NBR-2 COUNT COUNT-2.	1X1ƀƀ	43ƀƀƀ	3	2

(c)

STARTING-ITEM PIC X(10)	Statement	NBR-1 PIC X(5)	NBR-2 PIC X(5)	TALLY-RESULT PIC 99
417////////	UNSTRING STARTING-ITEM DELIMITED BY ALL "/" INTO NBR-1 NBR-2 TALLYING IN TALLY-RESULT.	417ƀƀ		1

The *COUNT* phrase maintains in data-name-6 a count of the number of characters examined in data-name-1 exclusive of any delimiter characters. This is useful for validating the length of input values. For example, if part numbers for an inventory system are four characters long, the COUNT may be used to verify that no more than four characters are entered. Figure 15.15b shows an example of an UNSTRING statement using the COUNT phrase.

The *TALLYING* phrase allows data-name-8 to be incremented for each receiving item that is acted upon. This is convenient when a command at the terminal has multiple options. By TALLYING how many receiving items were actually used, one avoids the need to examine every possible receiving item. Figure 15.15c shows an example of an UNSTRING statement with the TALLYING option.

The options needed in an UNSTRING statement vary depending on the type of data entered. It may be necessary to determine the data type of an entered command before decomposing it. For example, assume that two types of transactions may be entered by the user at the terminal for an order entry application. The required fields for each transaction are shown in Figure 15.16. The command validation will differ greatly depending on whether the transaction adds or deletes an order. It would be wise to determine the type of transaction before attempting to validate it. This can be accomplished by unstringing the command into two fields: the type of transaction, and the rest of the command. The code to accomplish this task is the following:

In the WORKING-STORAGE SECTION:

```
01    TRANSACTION                PIC X(20).
01    T-POINTER                  PIC   99.
01    T-CODE                     PIC X(10).
```

In the PROCEDURE DIVISION:

```
ACCEPT TRANSACTION.
MOVE 1 TO T-POINTER.
UNSTRING TRANSACTION
    DELIMITED BY ALL "," OR ALL SPACE
    INTO T-CODE
    WITH POINTER T-POINTER.
```

After execution of the UNSTRING statement, the pointer indicates the position where the rest of the command begins, that is, the T-POINTER will be pointing to the next position in the sending item.

Assuming that the entry was:

```
ADD,17529,113.24,19
```

T-CODE will contain "ADD" and T-POINTER will have a value of 5.

Figure 15.16 *Required Entries for Two Transaction Types*

Pending Orders	
Add Transaction	**Delete Transaction**
Add Code ID Number Dollar Value Quantity	Delete Code ID Number

Once the transaction type is determined, the rest of the command may be unstrung into its components. This should begin at the position pointed to by T-POINTER. The code for UNSTRINGing the rest of the "ADD" transaction follows:

Additions to the WORKING-STORAGE SECTION:

```
01   T-ID                       PIC X( 8).
01   T-AMOUNT                    PIC X(10).
01   T-QTY                       PIC X(10).
01   T-TALLY                     PIC   99.
01   T-COUNT                     PIC   99.
```

Additions to the PROCEDURE DIVISION:

```
MOVE 1 TO T-TALLY.
UNSTRING TRANSACTION
    DELIMITED BY SPACE OR ","
    INTO T-ID COUNT T-COUNT
        T-AMOUNT
        T-QTY
    WITH POINTER T-POINTER
    TALLYING IN T-TALLY
    ON OVERFLOW PERFORM 110-ERROR.
IF T-TALLY NOT = 4 PERFORM 110-ERROR.
```

The TALLYING data item can be used to determine the validity of the transaction. For example, since the "ADD" transaction is assumed to have four parameters, then if more or fewer parameters exist, the transaction is in error. The data item indicated in the TALLYING IN phrase, T-TALLY, will be incremented by the number of fields actually unstrung by the second UNSTRING statement. If the number is not four, an error exists and the appropriate error action to be taken is specified later in the program.

The length of each field may be determined by using the UNSTRING command with the COUNT phrase. It, too, may be used to check the validity of a data item by determining whether a predetermined number of characters has been entered for the item. The COUNT phrase can additionally be used to determine the actual number of characters used in the field in order to accurately center the data item on the screen or a report. For example, if the ID Number in the previous example is required to be of a certain length, that length can be checked against the resulting value of T-COUNT.

15.3.6   The INSPECT Statement

The complete format and rules for the INSPECT statement are:

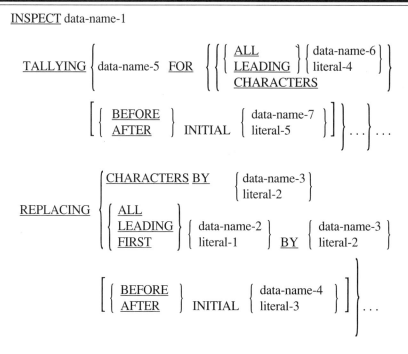

INSPECT data-name-1

$$\text{\underline{TALLYING}} \left\{ \text{data-name-5} \quad \underline{\text{FOR}} \quad \left\{ \left[\left\{ \begin{array}{l} \underline{\text{ALL}} \\ \underline{\text{LEADING}} \\ \underline{\text{CHARACTERS}} \end{array} \right\} \left\{ \begin{array}{l} \text{data-name-6} \\ \text{literal-4} \end{array} \right\} \right] \left[\left\{ \begin{array}{l} \underline{\text{BEFORE}} \\ \underline{\text{AFTER}} \end{array} \right\} \text{INITIAL} \left\{ \begin{array}{l} \text{data-name-7} \\ \text{literal-5} \end{array} \right\} \right] \right\} \dots \right\} \dots$$

$$\underline{\text{REPLACING}} \left\{ \begin{array}{l} \underline{\text{CHARACTERS}} \ \underline{\text{BY}} \left\{ \begin{array}{l} \text{data-name-3} \\ \text{literal-2} \end{array} \right\} \\ \left\{ \begin{array}{l} \underline{\text{ALL}} \\ \underline{\text{LEADING}} \\ \underline{\text{FIRST}} \end{array} \right\} \left\{ \begin{array}{l} \text{data-name-2} \\ \text{literal-1} \end{array} \right\} \underline{\text{BY}} \left\{ \begin{array}{l} \text{data-name-3} \\ \text{literal-2} \end{array} \right\} \\ \left[\left\{ \begin{array}{l} \underline{\text{BEFORE}} \\ \underline{\text{AFTER}} \end{array} \right\} \text{INITIAL} \left\{ \begin{array}{l} \text{data-name-4} \\ \text{literal-3} \end{array} \right\} \right] \end{array} \right\} \dots$$

1. The operation proceeds from left to right.
2. Data-name-1 is treated as an alphanumeric data item regardless of its PICTURE.
3. If ALL is specified, every occurrence of data-name-2 or literal-1 is replaced by data-name-3 or literal-2.
4. If LEADING is specified, all occurrences of data-name 2 or literal-1 until another character is found are replaced.
5. If FIRST is specified, the leftmost occurrence of data-name-2 or literal-1 is replaced.
6. All literals must be alphanumeric or alphabetic literals.
7. Both the TALLYING and REPLACING features may be used. If so, the TALLY-ING appears first and is executed first by the computer as if two separate commands were given.
8. The TALLYING places the resulting number into data-name-5, which must be an integer numeric elementary item.
9. Data-name-5 is not initialized by the INSPECT command.

The INSPECT statement allows the programmer to count and replace specified characters in a specified data field. The TALLYING option counts the number of occurrences of the specified characters and places the result in data-name-5. If the CHARACTERS option is used, TALLYING counts every character in the item, and can be used to determine the length of an entry. Figure 15.17 provides some examples and results of using the TALLYING option in the INSPECT statement.

Figure 15.17   Results of INSPECT Statements Using the TALLYING Option

NBR-1 PIC X(8)	Statement	TALLY-1 PIC 99	TALLY-2 PIC 99

742.1315	INSPECT NBR-1 TALLYING
	    TALLY-1 FOR CHARACTERS BEFORE "."
	    TALLY-2 FOR CHARACTERS AFTER ".".
		3	4

QQXQRB1Q	INSPECT NBR-1 TALLYING
	    TALLY-1 FOR ALL "B" AFTER "R"
	    TALLY-2 FOR LEADING "Q" BEFORE "X"
		1	2

The *REPLACING* option allows characters to be replaced so that undesired characters can be removed from the data item. If the ALL, LEADING, or FIRST options are used, these indicate the actual positions of the characters to be replaced. If the CHARACTERS option is used, every character in the field under inspection will be replaced. Figure 15.18 illustrates some examples and results of using the REPLACING option in the INSPECT statement.

Figure 15.18   Results of Various INSPECT Statements Using the REPLACING Options

Original NBR-1 PIC X(8)	Statement	Revised NBR-1	TALLY-1 PIC 99	TALLY-2 PIC 99

AB//B/BA	INSPECT NBR-1 REPLACING
	    ALL "A" BY "B"
	    ALL "//" BY "**".
		BB**B/BB		

AB//B/BA	INSPECT NBR-1 REPLACING
	    ALL "A" BY "B"
	    FIRST "/" BY "*". ·
		BB*/B/BB		

AB//B/BA	INSPECT NBR-1 REPLACING LEADING "A" BY "Q".	QB//B/BA		

QQXQRB1Q	INSPECT NBR-1
	    TALLYING TALLY-1 FOR ALL "Q"
	    REPLACING CHARACTERS BY "0".
		00000000	4	

The BEFORE and AFTER clauses allow the programmer to alter the range of inspection. By specifying the BEFORE phrase the range of inspection begins with the leftmost character of data-name-1 and ends with the character immediately to the left of the delimiting item specified as data-name-4 or -7, or literal-3 or -5. The AFTER phrase works similarly, limiting the inspection range to the area beginning with the character immediately to the right of the delimiting item. Figure 15.19 shows examples of how the range of inspection can be changed by using the BEFORE and AFTER clauses.

Figure 15.19 *Altering the Range of INSPECTion*

Data-name-1	Phrase	Range of Inspection
123XYZABC	BEFORE "Y"	123X
	AFTER "2"	3XYZABC
	BEFORE "1"	null
	AFTER "C"	null

The INSPECT statement is useful in determining field lengths, replacing invalid characters or leading characters in free-format input commands, or locating the position of a certain character in a field. For example, assume that the first nonzero position in a number is to be determined. The code to accomplish this task follows:

In the WORKING-STORAGE SECTION:

```
05   AR-ORDER-QTY          PIC 9(10).
05   AR-ORDER-QUANTITY-2 REDEFINES AR-ORDER-QTY PIC X(10).
05   AR-TALLY-QTY          PIC   99.
05   AR-QTY-MESSAGE        PIC X(50) VALUE SPACE.
```

In the PROCEDURE DIVISION:

```
INSPECT AR-ORDER-QUANTITY-2
     TALLYING AR-TALLY-QTY FOR LEADING ZERO.
```

Assuming that AR-ORDER-QTY is equal to 134, then AR-TALLY-QTY will be 7 after the INSPECT is executed.

Case Study: CDL's Enter Daily Mail

Charlene determines that free-format input would make the entry of daily payments and orders more "user-friendly." With this in mind, she develops the program specifications given in Figure 15.20. The program uses the file described in Figure 15.21. The hierarchy chart for the program is illustrated in Figure 15.22. Since no preprocessing or postprocessing is required, only the repetitive module "1000 Create Mail File" appears in the second level of the hierarchy chart.

Figure 15.20   *Program Specifications for CDL's "Enter Daily Mail" Program*

PROGRAM SUMMARY

TITLE: *Enter Daily Mail*

PREPARED BY: *C. Hilton*

DATE: *7-20-93*

FILES USED

FILE NAME	MEDIA	ORGANIZATION
Orders and payments	Disk	Sequential

DESCRIPTION

Allow for free-format entry of the daily mail payments and orders. Orders require an order code (0), a customer ID, a CD number, the quantity, and the order number. The order amount is optional. The payments require the purchase code (P), the customer ID, a check number, and the payment amount.

Each item will be keyed in as a single line at the terminal such as: P, cust ID, check nbr, amount; or: 0, cust ID, CD nbr, quantity, order nbr, amount. Validate each numeric entry and check for the presence of required fields.

Users will be experienced and trained; therefore no help or instructions are required. The session ends when the word "halt" is keyed in. Display any errors on the screen.

Figure 15.21   Record Layout for CDL's "Enter Daily Mail" Program

RECORD LAYOUT SHEET

Record Name: *Order/ Payment*			File Name: *Orders and Payments*		
Prepared By: *C. Hilton*			Date: *6-22-93*		
Key Fields:			Organization: *Sequential*		
Field	Description		Type*	Length	Decimal
Code	*"P" for payment, "O" for order*		*A*	*1*	
Amount	*Amount of P*		*N*	*8*	*2*
Customer nbr.	*A unique customer ID*		*N*	*6*	
Check #	*The check ID*		*A*	*8*	
Compact disc #	*The CD's stock number*		*N*	*6*	
Quantity	*The number ordered*		*N*	*2*	
Order number	*A preprinted no. from order form*		*N*	*6*	

* A = alphanumeric
  N = numeric

Module "1000 Create Mail File" is subdivided into "1100 Obtain Mail Record," which gets and edits the mail item from the data entry terminal, and "1200 Write Mail Record," which writes the record to the daily mail tape. The tasks of module "1100 Obtain Mail Record" are performed by its subordinate modules "1110 Accept Command Line" and "1120 Edit Mail Record." The N-S charts for the program are illustrated in Figure 15.23. The COBOL code appears in Figure 15.24. The test results are in Figure 15.25. Below we discuss in more detail the logic of selected modules.

Figure 15.22   Hierarchy Chart for CDL's "Enter Daily Mail" Program

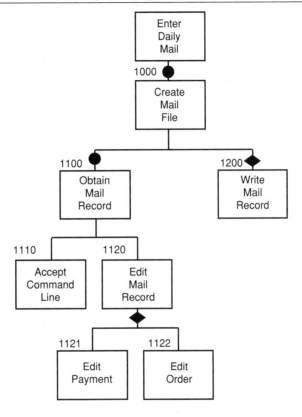

Figure 15.23   N-S Charts for CDL's "Enter Daily Mail"

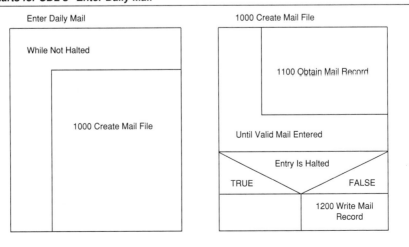

Figure 15.23   (continued)

1100 Obtain Mail Record

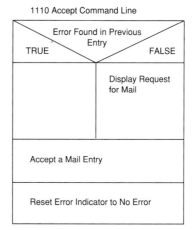

1110 Accept Command Line

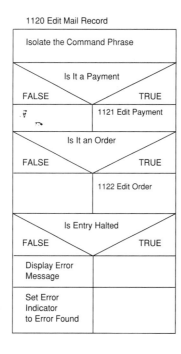

1120 Edit Mail Record

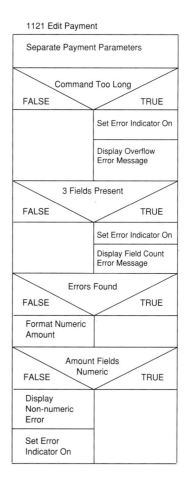

1121 Edit Payment

Figure 15.23 (continued)

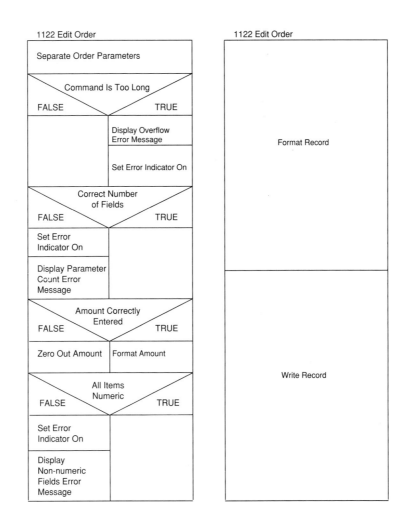

1122 Edit Order

Separate Order Parameters

Command Is Too Long

FALSE | TRUE

Display Overflow
Error Message

Set Error Indicator On

Correct Number
of Fields

FALSE | TRUE

Set Error
Indicator On

Display Parameter
Count Error
Message

Amount Correctly
Entered

FALSE | TRUE

Zero Out Amount | Format Amount

All Items
Numeric

FALSE | TRUE

Set Error
Indicator On

Display
Non-numeric
Fields Error
Message

1122 Edit Order

Format Record

Write Record

Figure 15.24 CDL's "Enter Daily Mail"

```
1 IDENTIFICATION DIVISION.
2 PROGRAM-ID.  ENTER-MAIL.
3*   THIS PROGRAM CREATES A FILE WITH ORDERS AND PAYMENTS
4*   AFTER HAVING ACCEPTED AND EDITED THEM FOR COMPLETENESS
5
6 AUTHOR. C. HILTON
```

Figure 15.24   (continued)

```
 7 DATE-WRITTEN. 6-22-94.
 8 DATE-COMPILED. 08-Mar-94 01:03.
12 ENVIRONMENT DIVISION.
13
14 CONFIGURATION SECTION.
15 SOURCE-COMPUTER.  GENERIC-COMPUTER.
16 OBJECT-COMPUTER.  GENERIC-COMPUTER.
17
18 INPUT-OUTPUT SECTION.
19 FILE-CONTROL.
20     SELECT PAYMENTS-AND-ORDERS-FILE ASSIGN TO DISK
21     ORGANIZATION IS SEQUENTIAL.
22
23
24
25 DATA DIVISION.
26 FILE SECTION.
27 FD  PAYMENTS-AND-ORDERS-FILE
28     LABEL RECORDS ARE STANDARD.
29 01  ORDER-OR-PAYMENT-REC.
30     05  PAO-CODE                PIC X.
31     05  PAO-PAYMENT-AMOUNT      PIC 9(6)V99.
32     05  PAO-CUSTOMER-NUMBER     PIC 9(6).
33     05  PAO-CHECK-NUMBER        PIC X(8).
34     05  PAO-ORDER-INFORMATION.
35         10  PAO-CD-STOCK-NUMBER  PIC 9(6).
36         10  PAO-QUANTITY-ORDERED PIC 99.
37         10  PAO-ORDER-NUMBER     PIC 9(6).
38
39
40 WORKING-STORAGE SECTION.
41 01  INDICATORS.
42     05  IND-ERROR PIC X(5) VALUE "FALSE".
43
44 01  STRING-RECORD PIC X(37).
45
46 01  UNSTRING-AREA.
47     05  UA-COMMAND-LINE     PIC X(80).
48     05  UA-POINT            PIC 99.
49     05  UA-TALLY            PIC 99.
50     05  UA-CODE.
51         10  UA-TYPE         PIC X.
```

Figure 15.24 (continued)

```
52          88  UA-PAYMENT       VALUE "P".
53          88  UA-ORDER         VALUE "O".
54          88  UA-HALT          VALUE "H".
55          10 FILLER            PIC X(9).
56      05  UA-CUSTOMER-NBR  PIC X(6).
57      05  UA-AMOUNT            PIC X(8).
58      05  UA-CHECK             PIC X(8).
59      05  UA-CD-NBR            PIC X(6).
60      05  UA-QUANTITY          PIC XX JUSTIFIED RIGHT.
61      05  UA-ORDER-NBR         PIC X(6).
62      05  UA-DECIMAL-AMOUNT    PIC X(9).
63      05  UA-FILLER            PIC X(10).
64      05  UA-SPLIT-AMOUNT.
65          10  UA-BEFORE-DECIMAL PIC X(6) JUSTIFIED RIGHT.
66          10  UA-AFTER-DECIMAL  PIC X(2).
67
68
69
70 PROCEDURE DIVISION.
71
72 ENTER-DAILY-MAIL.
73      OPEN OUTPUT PAYMENTS-AND-ORDERS-FILE.
74      PERFORM 1000-CREATE-MAIL-FILE
75          UNTIL UA-HALT.
76      CLOSE PAYMENTS-AND-ORDERS-FILE.
77      STOP RUN.
78
79 1000-CREATE-MAIL-FILE.
80      PERFORM 1100-OBTAIN-MAIL-RECORD.
81      PERFORM 1100-OBTAIN-MAIL-RECORD UNTIL IND-ERROR = "FALSE".
82      IF NOT UA-HALT PERFORM 1200-WRITE-MAIL-RECORD.
83
84 1100-OBTAIN-MAIL-RECORD.
85      PERFORM 1110-ACCEPT-COMMAND-LINE.
86      PERFORM 1120-EDIT-MAIL-RECORD.
87
88 1110-ACCEPT-COMMAND-LINE.
89      IF IND-ERROR = "FALSE"
90          DISPLAY " "
91          DISPLAY "PLEASE ENTER A PAYMENT, AN ORDER, OR HALT"
92          DISPLAY " ".
93      ACCEPT UA-COMMAND-LINE.
```

Figure 15.24 *(continued)*

```
 94      MOVE "FALSE" TO IND-ERROR.
 95
 96  1120-EDIT-MAIL-RECORD.
 97      MOVE 1 TO UA-POINT.
 98      UNSTRING UA-COMMAND-LINE DELIMITED BY "," OR " "
 99          INTO UA-CODE
100          WITH POINTER UA-POINT.
101      IF UA-PAYMENT PERFORM 1121-EDIT-PAYMENT.
102      IF UA-ORDER PERFORM 1122-EDIT-ORDER.
103      IF NOT UA-PAYMENT AND NOT UA-ORDER AND NOT UA-HALT
104          MOVE "TRUE" TO IND-ERROR
105          DISPLAY "INVALID COMMAND, MUST BE A HALT, A PAYMENT,"
106          DISPLAY "OR AN ORDER.  PLEASE REENTER. "
107          DISPLAY " ".
108
109  1121-EDIT-PAYMENT.
110      MOVE ZEROS TO UA-CD-NBR UA-QUANTITY UA-ORDER-NBR.
111      MOVE ZERO TO UA-TALLY.
112      UNSTRING UA-COMMAND-LINE DELIMITED BY ALL "," OR ALL " "
113          INTO UA-CUSTOMER-NBR
114                UA-CHECK
115                UA-DECIMAL-AMOUNT
116                UA-FILLER
117          WITH POINTER UA-POINT
118          TALLYING IN UA-TALLY
119          ON OVERFLOW MOVE "TRUE" TO IND-ERROR
120                    DISPLAY "COMMAND IS TOO LONG. "
121                            "PLEASE REENTER"
122                    DISPLAY " ".
123      IF IND-ERROR = "FALSE" AND UA-TALLY NOT = 3
124          MOVE "TRUE" TO IND-ERROR
125          DISPLAY "INCORRECT NUMBER OF PARAMETERS.  "
126                  "PLEASE REENTER."
127          DISPLAY " ".
128      IF IND-ERROR = "FALSE"
129          UNSTRING UA-DECIMAL-AMOUNT DELIMITED BY "." OR " "
130              INTO UA-BEFORE-DECIMAL UA-AFTER-DECIMAL
131          INSPECT UA-SPLIT-AMOUNT REPLACING ALL " " BY "0"
132          MOVE UA-SPLIT-AMOUNT TO UA-AMOUNT.
133      IF IND-ERROR = "FALSE" AND (UA-AMOUNT NOT NUMERIC OR
134          UA-CUSTOMER-NBR NOT NUMERIC)
135          MOVE "TRUE" TO IND-ERROR
```

Figure 15.24   (continued)

```
136            DISPLAY "REQUIRED NUMERIC FIELD CONTAINS NONNUMERIC "
137                    "CHARACTERS.   PLEASE RETRY."
138            DISPLAY " ".
139
140 1122-EDIT-ORDER.
141     MOVE SPACE TO UA-CHECK.
142     MOVE ZERO TO UA-TALLY.
143     UNSTRING UA-COMMAND-LINE DELIMITED BY ALL " " OR ALL ","
144         INTO UA-CUSTOMER-NBR
145             UA-CD-NBR
146             UA-QUANTITY
147             UA-ORDER-NBR
148             UA-DECIMAL-AMOUNT
149         WITH POINTER UA-POINT
150         TALLYING IN UA-TALLY
151         ON OVERFLOW MOVE "TRUE" TO IND-ERROR
152                     DISPLAY "COMMAND IS TOO LONG.  "
153                         "PLEASE REENTER."
154                     DISPLAY " ".
155     IF IND-ERROR = "FALSE" AND UA-TALLY LESS THAN 4
156         MOVE "TRUE" TO IND-ERROR
157         DISPLAY "TOO FEW PARAMETERS FOR THE ORDER."
158                 "  PLEASE REENTER."
159         DISPLAY " ".
160     IF IND-ERROR = "FALSE" AND UA-TALLY = 4
161         MOVE ZEROS TO UA-AMOUNT.
162     IF IND-ERROR = "FALSE" AND UA-TALLY = 5
163         UNSTRING UA-DECIMAL-AMOUNT DELIMITED BY "." OR " "
164             INTO UA-BEFORE-DECIMAL UA-AFTER-DECIMAL
165         INSPECT UA-SPLIT-AMOUNT REPLACING ALL " " BY "0"
166         MOVE UA-SPLIT-AMOUNT TO UA-AMOUNT.
167     INSPECT UA-QUANTITY REPLACING ALL " " BY "0".
168     IF IND-ERROR = "FALSE" AND (UA-AMOUNT NOT NUMERIC OR
169         UA-CUSTOMER-NBR NOT NUMERIC OR UA-QUANTITY NOT NUMERIC
170         OR UA-CD-NBR NOT NUMERIC OR UA-ORDER-NBR NOT NUMERIC)
171         MOVE "TRUE" TO IND-ERROR
172         DISPLAY "REQUIRED NUMERIC FIELD CONTAINS NONNUMERIC "
173                 "CHARACTERS.   PLEASE RETRY."
174         DISPLAY " ".
175
176 1200-WRITE-MAIL-RECORD.
177     STRING UA-TYPE
```

Figure 15.24   (continued)

```
178            UA-AMOUNT
179            UA-CUSTOMER-NBR
180            UA-CHECK
181            UA-CD-NBR
182            UA-QUANTITY
183            UA-ORDER-NBR
184            DELIMITED BY SIZE
185         INTO STRING-RECORD.
186      WRITE ORDER-OR-PAYMENT-REC FROM STRING-RECORD.
```

Figure 15.25   *Test Data and Results for CDL's "Enter Daily Mail"*

```
        Items to Enter:

        P,123456,567,45.88
        P,   (ERROR ON PARAMETER COUNT)
        P,456789, (ERROR ON PARAMETER COUNT)
        P,987654,987,76.00,100 (ERROR ON PARAMETER COUNT)
        P,YRTRBD,DLD,76.8   (ERROR ON NUMERIC ITEM)
        X (INVALID TRANSACTION CODE ERROR)
        O,987 (ERROR ON PARAMETER COUNT)
        O,765432,678976,12,876543
        O,123456,435645,08,545678,12.33



        The Resulting File:

        P00004588123456567      00000000000000
        O00000000765432         67897612876543
        O00001233123456         43564508545678
```

"1000 Create Mail File" Module. Module "1000 Create Mail File" controls the performance of module "1100 Obtain Mail Record" with a DO UNTIL structure. In this fashion Charlene forces the data entry clerk to enter a valid command. If a valid order or payment is entered, a record must be formatted and written to the PAYMENTS-AND-ORDERS-FILE by "1200 Write Mail Record."

"1120 Edit Mail Record" Module. "1120 Edit Mail Record" unstrings the command into two parts to determine the type of entry. Once determined, a detailed edit of the payment or order is conducted by "1121 Edit Payment" or "1122 Edit Order."

"1121 Edit Payment" Module. In module "1121 Edit Payment" the rest of the payment entry is unstrung. If the field overflows, the proper error message is displayed, the error indicator is set, and the module returns controls to its superior. The module also tests for the correct number of parameters by using the TALLYING option and verifies that certain fields are numeric. Similar logic is used to edit the orders in module "1122 Edit Order."

"1200 Write Mail Record" Module. Charlene uses the STRING statement to concatenate the mail record fields into the output area. By using the SIZE option, the STRING is equivalent to a series of moves when building the output record.

Summary

Interactive systems are those in which the user and computer communicate through a terminal. Interactive systems allow the proliferation of on-line, real-time applications calling for fast response times and immediate execution, such as airline reservation systems.

The software for interactive systems does not vary in functionality from that of batch systems since similar tasks need be performed in both environments. The difference lies almost exclusively in the interface between the computer and the user. Although the systems analyst is responsible for designing this interface, the programmer should be aware of the more common designs. Menus in which a user selects from a list of options are better for inexperienced users. They are easy to use and reduce the probability of errors. For data entry applications, fixed screen input allows the user to enter data by "filling in" a form displayed on the screen. In a dialogue, the computer and user interact through a series of questions and responses. Messages in dialogues should be appropriate, useful, and clear. Commands are another common form of human-machine communication. Such systems generally assume more experienced users and the programs for handling the commands are more complex.

Certain COBOL statements are especially useful in interactive programs. The DISPLAY and ACCEPT statements handle the input and output of data at the terminal. Other statements handle character manipulation typical in interactive applications. They allow the use of free-format input and permit data to be validated as they are entered. These statements include the STRING, UNSTRING, and INSPECT statements.

The STRING statement concatenates several fields into one to store them in less space or to display them in a more readable form. The POINTER option may be used to position the sending item in the receiving field or to indicate the last character placement within the field. By using the POINTER items may be centered prior to display.

The UNSTRING statement separates a data item into segments, allowing the programmer to handle each segment individually. This permits manipulation of the components of an input entry for validation.

The INSPECT statement counts and/or replaces specified characters in a data item. It may be used to determine field lengths, replace invalid or leading characters in free-format commands, or locate the position of a specified character in a field.

Key Terms

menu	STRING	POINTER
command-driven	delimiter	DELIMITER
fixed screen input	UNSTRING	COUNT
dialogue	INSPECT	TALLYING
JUSTIFIED	OVERFLOW	REPLACING

Hints for Avoiding Errors

1. It is important to properly initialize the POINTER data item when using it in the STRING and UNSTRING statements.
2. The STRING statement does not space-fill the resulting item. Therefore, values from a previous operation may linger and appear on reports or output files.
3. Be certain to specify character delimiters; numeric literals are invalid.
4. The logic involving the use of the POINTER may become complex when consecutive delimiters appear in a character string. In this case, avoid using the POINTER. Instead, first INSPECT the data item to find the first character after multiple consecutive delimiters.

Exercises

15.1 Examine the operating system commands and messages for your system. Discuss how they might be improved.

15.2 Develop the code required to accept free-format input for a signed dollar value that is to be stored in a numeric data item for later computation. Be sure to allow for every reasonable combination of entry formats.

15.3 Alter the CDL case to verify input field lengths and allow for the additional delimiter ":".

Use the following code segment to answer Exercises 15.4 through 15.9:

```
05   IN-POINT PIC 99 VALUE 3.
05   IN-TALLY PIC 99 VALUE ZERO.
05   IN-PART-1 PIC X(5) VALUE "971*0".
05   IN-PART-2 PIC X(5) VALUE "24*/A".
05   IN-TERM PIC X(10) VALUE "012*34*78".
```

State any changed data items and their contents after the execution of the following statements (answer each question independently):

15.4
```
STRING IN-PART-1 IN-PART-2
    DELIMITED BY "*" INTO IN-TERM
    POINTER IN-POINT.
```

15.5
```
STRING IN-PART-1 DELIMITED BY SIZE
      "1" DELIMITED BY SIZE
      IN-PART-2 DELIMITED BY "1"
      INTO IN-TERM.
```

15.6
```
INSPECT IN-PART-2
      REPLACING FIRST "0" BY "2" AFTER INITIAL "*".
```

15.7
```
INSPECT IN-TERM
      TALLYING IN-TALLY FOR CHARACTERS BEFORE FIRST "*".
```

15.8
```
UNSTRING IN-TERM
      DELIMITED BY "*" INTO IN-PART-1.
```

15.9
```
UNSTRING IN-TERM
      DELIMITED BY "*" OR "1" INTO IN-PART-1 IN-PART-2
      COUNT IN-TALLY
      WITH POINTER IN-POINT.
```

15.10   One of the uses of the INSPECT is to
        a.   count the occurrences of a certain character.
        b.   validate fields.
        c.   replace certain characters with others.
        d.   all of the above

15.11   The STRING statement causes
        a.   one data item to be transferred to another.
        b.   characters from multiple data fields to be sent to a single data field.
        c.   characters from one field to be sent to multiple fields.
        d.   none of the above

15.12   In the UNSTRING, the COUNT IN option
        a.   refers to an alphanumeric elementary item.
        b.   records the number of characters in a result field.
        c.   records the number of result fields.
        d.   all of the above

15.13   If the value 7 is moved to the pointer for an UNSTRING,
        a.   the 7th receiving field acquires all characters.
        b.   the UNSTRING stops at the 7th position.
        c.   the first 6 characters of the sending field are bypassed.
        d.   each result field has the first 6 characters blank-filled.

15.14   Most of the hardware for batch systems is incompatible with interactive systems. True or false?

15.15   The screen pointer on a terminal is called a:
   a.   marker.
   b.   cursor.
   c.   delimiter.
   d.   pointer.

15.16   "Good" messages are:
   a.   appropriate, useful, clear.
   b.   short, terse, direct.
   c.   thoughtful, technical, informative.
   d.   eye-catching, to-the-point, brash.

15.17   Character manipulation is a secondary design consideration. True or false?

15.18   The same general tasks need to be performed for both interactive and batch programs. True or false?

15.19   The commands to format terminal screens are not standardized in COBOL. True or false?

15.20   Data entry applications usually use _____ input, in which a "form" is displayed on the screen.
   a.   command
   b.   continuous feed
   c.   variable position
   d.   fixed screen

15.21   Programs that allow free-format input require data validation. True or false?

15.22   The _____ and _____ phrases of the STRING statement are the same as in the UNSTRING statement.
   a.   TALLYING, DELIMITER IN
   b.   COUNT, POINTER
   c.   POINTER, OVERFLOW
   d.   none of the above

15.23   Given the command:

```
UNSTRING USER-RESPONSE DELIMITED BY ALL ","
   INTO VALID-CHECK-FIELD
      DECIMAL-CHECK-FIELD COUNT IN VALID-COUNT.
```

   The COUNT phrase will maintain a count of characters on which data items?
   a.   USER-RESPONSE
   b.   VALID-CHECK-FIELD
   c.   DECIMAL-CHECK-FIELD
   d.   All of the above

15.24   The _____ and _____ clauses allow the programmer to alter the range of an inspection.
   a.   BEFORE, AFTER
   b.   START, STOP
   c.   BEGIN, END
   d.   none of the above

15.25 Numeric literals are invalid delimiters in COBOL. True or false?

15.26 The "conversation" interaction hardware may be a(n) _____ or

_____.

15.27 A(n) _____ is a dialogue interface that specifies the options available to the user.

15.28 _____ systems are more common dialogue interfaces for experienced users.

15.29 _____ statements send messages to the user's terminal.

15.30 The _____ statement is used to obtain user input from a terminal keyboard.

15.31 The _____ clause is used to position characters within a data field, usually to the right.

15.32 The _____ statement is used to remove superfluous spaces from stored values by concatenation.

15.33 The _____ statement separates a character string into one or more components.

15.34 A(n) _____ is any character used by the programmer to determine the boundaries of data fields when manipulating character strings.

15.35 The _____ statement replaces characters in a data item with other characters.

15.36 What is attractive about using an interactive design in business systems?

15.37 Explain the importance of data validation in an interactive program design.

15.38 Is communication with the end-user important when designing a dialog interface? If so, why?

15.39 Given the data items:

```
01  USER-INPUT              PIC X(50) VALUE
        "HUMPHREY          UDDOH*POINDEXTER*    ".
01  FIRST-NAME              PIC X(15).
01  MIDDLE-NAME             PIC X(10).
01  LAST-NAME               PIC X(15).
01  FIRST-NAME-COUNT        PIC 99 VALUE ZERO.
01  TALLY-FIELD            PIC 99 VALUE ZERO.
01  DELIMITER-HOLD          PIC X.
```

And the execution of the following command:

```
UNSTRING USER-INPUT
    DELIMITED BY ALL SPACE OR ALL "*"
    INTO FIRST-NAME COUNT IN FIRST-NAME-COUNT
        MIDDLE-NAME
        LAST-NAME DELIMITER IN DELIMITER-HOLD
    TALLYING IN TALLY-FIELD.
```

What will be the contents of each of the receiving fields and the COUNT, TALLY and DELIMITER fields?

A

FLOWCHART SYMBOLS

	Terminal	Shows the beginning and end of the flowchart.
Input/Output (I/O)	Indicates that data are input from an external source or are output to an external source.
Process	Indicates a single task or function.
Defined process	Indicates the use of a task defined in a different location within the same documentation. Defined processes include subroutines, external functions, or subtasks.
Decision	Indicates that a condition must be tested to determine the path to follow.
Connector	Merges multiple flows into a single flow.
Arrows	Indicate the direction of the flow.

Document   Represents a physical output,
                                usually a printed report.

Manual operation   Indicates an operation or task performed
                                independent of the system being described.

Magnetic Tape   Represents external storage in the form
                                of magnetic tape.

**Magnetic drum
and disk**   Represents external storage in the form
                                of a magnetic drum or disk.

**Communication
link**   Represents a physical link between the
                                computer and an input/output terminal.

Display   Represents an ouptut that is displayed
                                to an input/output terminal.

Off-page connector   Indicates that a flow continues in a different
                                location in the same documentation.

B

RESERVED WORD LIST

A

ACCEPT
ACCESS
ADD
ADVANCING
AFTER
ALL
ALPHABET
ALPHABETIC
ALPHABETIC-LOWER
ALPHABETIC-UPPER
ALPHANUMERIC
ALPHANUMERIC-EDITED
ALSO
ALTER
ALTERNATE
AND
ANY
ARE
AREA
AREAS
ASCENDING
ASSIGN
AT
AUTHOR

B

BEFORE
BINARY
BLANK
BLOCK
BOTTOM
BY

C

CALL
CANCEL
CD
CF
CH
CHARACTER
CHARACTERS
CLASS
CLOCK-UNITS
CLOSE
COBOL
CODE
CODE-SET
COLLATING
COLUMN

COMMA
COMMON
COMMUNICATION
COMP
COMPUTATIONAL
COMPUTE
CONFIGURATION
CONTAINS
CONTENT
CONTINUE
CONTROL
CONTROLS
CONVERTING
COPY
CORR
CORRESPONDING
COUNT
CURRENCY

D

DATA
DATE
DATE-COMPILED
DATE-WRITTEN
DAY

DAY-OF-WEEK
DE
DEBUG-CONTENTS
DEBUG-ITEM
DEBUG-LINE
DEBUG-NAME
DEBUG-SUB-1
DEBUG-SUB-2
DEBUG-SUB-3
DEBUGGING
DECIMAL-POINT
DECLARATIVES
DELETE
DELIMITED
DELIMITER
DEPENDING
DESCENDING
DESTINATION
DETAIL
DISABLE
DISPLAY
DIVIDE
DIVISION
DOWN
DUPLICATES
DYNAMIC

E

EGI
ELSE
EMI
ENABLE
END
END-ADD
END-CALL
END-COMPUTE
END-DELETE
END-DIVIDE
END-EVALUATE
END-IF
END-MULTIPLY
END-OF-PAGE
END-PERFORM
END-READ
END-RECEIVE
END-RETURN
END-REWRITE
END-SEARCH

END-START
END-STRING
END-SUBTRACT
END-UNSTRING
END-WRITE
ENTER
ENVIRONMENT
EOP
EQUAL
ERROR
ESI
EVALUATE
EVERY
EXCEPTION
EXIT
EXTEND
EXTERNAL

F

FALSE
FD
FILE
FILE-CONTROL
FILLER
FINAL
FIRST
FOOTING
FOR
FROM

G

GENERATE
GIVING
GLOBAL
GO
GREATER
GROUP

H – I

HEADING
HIGH-VALUE
HIGH-VALUES
I-O
I-O-CONTROL
IDENTIFICATION
IF

IN
INDEX
INDEXED
INDICATE
INITIAL
INITIALIZE
INITIATE
INPUT
INPUT-OUTPUT
INSPECT
INSTALLATION
INTO
INVALID
IS

J – L

JUST
JUSTIFIED
KEY
LABEL
LAST
LEADING
LEFT
LENGTH
LESS
LIMIT
LIMITS
LINAGE
LINAGE-COUNTER
LINE
LINE-COUNTER
LINES
LINKAGE
LOCK
LOW-VALUE
LOW-VALUES

M

MEMORY
MERGE
MESSAGE
MODE
MODULES
MOVE
MULTIPLE
MULTIPLY

N – O

NATIVE
NEGATIVE
NEXT
NO
NOT
NUMBER
NUMERIC
NUMERIC-EDITED
OBJECT-COMPUTER
OCCURS
OF
OFF
OMITTED
ON
OPEN
OPTIONAL
OR
ORDER
ORGANIZATION
OTHER
OUTPUT
OVERFLOW

P – Q

PACKED-DECIMAL
PADDING
PAGE
PAGE-COUNTER
PERFORM
PF
PH
PIC
PICTURE
PLUS
POINTER
POSITION
POSITIVE
PRINTING
PROCEDURE
PROCEDURES
PROCEED
PROGRAM
PROGRAM-ID
PURGE
QUEUE

QUOTE
QUOTES

R

RANDOM
RD
READ
RECEIVE
RECORD
RECORDS
REDEFINES
REEL
REFERENCE
REFERENCES
RELATIVE
RELEASE
REMAINDER
REMOVAL
RENAMES
REPLACE
REPLACING
REPORT
REPORTING
REPORTS
RERUN
RESERVE
RESET
RETURN
REVERSED
REWIND
REWRITE
RF
RH
RIGHT
ROUNDED
RUN

S

SAME
SD
SEARCH
SECTION
SECURITY
SEGMENT
SEGMENT-LIMIT
SELECT

SEND
SENTENCE
SEPARATE
SEQUENCE
SEQUENTIAL
SET
SIGN
SIZE
SORT
SORT-MERGE
SOURCE
SOURCE-COMPUTER
SPACE
SPACES
SPECIAL-NAMES
STANDARD
STANDARD-1
STANDARD-2
START
STATUS
STOP
STRING
SUB-QUEUE-1
SUB-QUEUE-2
SUB-QUEUE-3
SUBTRACT
SUM
SUPPRESS
SYMBOLIC
SYNC
SYNCHRONIZED

T

TABLE
TALLYING
TAPE
TERMINAL
TERMINATE
TEST
TEXT
THAN
THEN
THROUGH
THRU
TIME
TIMES
TO

TOP
TRAILING
TRUE
TYPE

U – V

UNIT
UNSTRING
UNTIL
UP
UPON
USAGE
USE
USING
VALUE
VALUES
VARYING

W – Z

WHEN
WITH
WORDS
WORKING-STORAGE
WRITE
ZERO
ZEROES
ZEROS

CHARACTERS

+
-
*
/
**
>
<
=
>=
<=

SELECT COBOL FORMATS

Formats for Identification Division

IDENTIFICATION DIVISION •
PROGRAM-ID • program-name •
[AUTHOR • [comment-entry] . . .]
[INSTALLATION • [comment-entry] . . .]
[DATE-WRITTEN • [comment-entry] . . .]
[DATE-COMPILED • [comment-entry] . . .]
[SECURITY • [comment-entry] . . .]

Formats for Environment Division

ENVIRONMENT DIVISION •
CONFIGURATION SECTION •
SOURCE-COMPUTER • computer-name [WITH DEBUGGING MODE] •
OBJECT-COMPUTER • computer-name
 [INPUT-OUTPUT SECTION •
 FILE-CONTROL •
    {file-control-entry} . . .

Format for File Control

Option 1

SELECT [OPTIONAL] file-name
    ASSIGN TO {implementor-name-1} . . .

$$\left[\text{RESERVE integer-1} \quad \left[\begin{array}{l} \text{AREA} \\ \text{AREAS} \end{array} \right] \right]$$

    [ORGANIZATION IS SEQUENTIAL]
    [ACCESS MODE IS SEQUENTIAL]
    [FILE STATUS IS data-name-1] •

Option 2

SELECT file-name
    ASSIGN TO {implementor-name-1} . . .

$$\left[\text{RESERVE integer-1} \quad \left[\begin{array}{l} \text{AREA} \\ \text{AREAS} \end{array} \right] \right]$$

    [ORGANIZATION IS RELATIVE]

$$\left[\text{ACCESS MODE IS} \quad \left\{ \begin{array}{l} \text{SEQUENTIAL} \\ \text{RANDOM} \\ \text{DYNAMIC} \end{array} \right\} \right]$$

    [RELATIVE KEY IS data-name-1] •

Option 3

SELECT file-name
    ASSIGN TO {implementor-name-1} . . .

$$\left[\text{RESERVE integer-1} \quad \left[\begin{array}{l} \text{AREA} \\ \text{AREAS} \end{array} \right] \right]$$

    [ORGANIZATION IS INDEXED]

$$\left[\text{ACCESS MODE IS} \quad \left\{ \begin{array}{l} \text{SEQUENTIAL} \\ \text{RANDOM} \\ \text{DYNAMIC} \end{array} \right\} \right]$$

    RECORD KEY IS data-name-1 •

Option 4

SELECT file-name ASSIGN TO {implementor-name-1} . . .

Format for Data Division

```
DATA DIVISION.
FILE SECTION.
FD file-name
```

$$\left[\underline{BLOCK} \text{ CONTAINS [integer-1 } \underline{TO}\text{] integer-2 } \left\{ \begin{array}{l} \underline{RECORDS} \\ CHARACTERS \end{array} \right\} \right]$$

[$\underline{RECORD}$ CONTAINS [integer-3 $\underline{TO}$] integer-4 CHARACTERS]

$$\left[\underline{LABEL} \left\{ \begin{array}{l} \underline{RECORD} \text{ IS} \\ \underline{RECORDS} \text{ ARE} \end{array} \right\} \left\{ \begin{array}{l} \underline{STANDARD} \\ \underline{OMITTED} \end{array} \right\} \right]$$

$$\left[\underline{VALUE} \ \underline{OF} \left\{ \text{implementor-name-1 IS} \left\{ \begin{array}{l} \text{data-name-1} \\ \text{literal-1} \end{array} \right\} \right\} \ldots \right]$$

$$\left[\underline{DATA} \left\{ \begin{array}{l} \underline{RECORD} \text{ IS} \\ \underline{RECORDS} \text{ ARE} \end{array} \right\} \{\text{data-name-3}\} \ldots \right]$$

$$\left[\underline{LINAGE} \text{ IS} \left\{ \begin{array}{l} \text{data-name-5} \\ \text{integer-5} \end{array} \right\} \text{LINES} \left[\text{WITH } \underline{FOOTING} \text{ AT} \left\{ \begin{array}{l} \text{data-name-6} \\ \text{integer-6} \end{array} \right\} \right] \right.$$

$$\left. \left[\text{LINES AT } \underline{TOP} \left\{ \begin{array}{l} \text{data-name-7} \\ \text{integer-7} \end{array} \right\} \right] \left[\text{LINES AT } \underline{BOTTOM} \left\{ \begin{array}{l} \text{data-name-8} \\ \text{integer-8} \end{array} \right\} \right] \right]$$

$$\left[\left\{ \begin{array}{l} \underline{REPORT} \text{ IS} \\ \underline{REPORTS} \text{ ARE} \end{array} \right\} \{\text{report-name-1}\} \ldots \right].$$

```
[record-description-entry] . . . ] . . .

[SD file-name]
```

[$\underline{RECORD}$ CONTAINS [integer-1 $\underline{TO}$] integer-2 CHARACTERS]

$$\left[\underline{DATA} \left\{ \begin{array}{l} \underline{RECORD} \text{ IS} \\ \underline{RECORDS} \text{ ARE} \end{array} \right\} \{\text{data-name-1}\} \right].$$

```
{record-description-entry} . . . ] . . .

[WORKING-STORAGE-SECTION •
```

$$\left[\begin{array}{l} \text{77-level-description-entry} \\ \text{record-description-entry} \end{array} \right] \ldots \right]$$

```
[LINKAGE SECTION •
```

$$\left[\begin{array}{l} \text{77-level-description-entry} \\ \text{record-description-entry} \end{array} \right] \ldots \right]$$

```
[REPORT SECTION •
  [RD report-name
```

$$\left[\left\{ \begin{array}{l} \underline{CONTROL} \text{ IS} \\ \underline{CONTROLS} \text{ ARE} \end{array} \right\} \left\{ \begin{array}{l} \{\text{data-name-1}\} \ldots \\ \underline{FINAL} \text{ [data-name-1]} \ldots \end{array} \right\} \right]$$

$$\left[\underline{\text{PAGE}} \begin{bmatrix} \text{LIMIT IS} \\ \text{LIMITS ARE} \end{bmatrix} \text{integer-1} \begin{bmatrix} \text{LINE} \\ \text{LINES} \end{bmatrix} [\underline{\text{HEADING}} \text{ integer-2}] \right.$$

[FIRST DETAIL integer-3] [LAST DETAIL integer-4]

[FOOTING integer-5]] •
{report-group-description-entry} . . .] . . .]

Format for Data Description Entry

Option 1

level-number $\left\{ \begin{array}{l} \text{data-name-1} \\ \underline{\text{FILLER}} \end{array} \right\}$

[REDEFINES data-name-2]

$$\left[\left\{ \begin{array}{l} \underline{\text{PICTURE}} \\ \underline{\text{PIC}} \end{array} \right\} \text{IS character-string} \right]$$

$$\left[[\underline{\text{USAGE}} \text{ IS}] \left\{ \begin{array}{l} \underline{\text{COMPUTATIONAL}} \\ \underline{\text{COMP}} \\ \underline{\text{DISPLAY}} \\ \underline{\text{INDEX}} \end{array} \right\} \right]$$

$$\left[[\underline{\text{SIGN}} \text{ IS}] \left\{ \begin{array}{l} \underline{\text{LEADING}} \\ \underline{\text{TRAILING}} \end{array} \right\} [\underline{\text{SEPARATE}} \text{ CHARACTER}] \right]$$

$$\left[\underline{\text{OCCURS}} \left\{ \begin{array}{l} \text{integer-1 } \underline{\text{TO}} \text{ integer-1 TIMES } \underline{\text{DEPENDING}} \text{ ON data-name-3} \\ \text{integer-2 TIMES} \end{array} \right. \right.$$

$$\left[\left\{ \begin{array}{l} \underline{\text{ASCENDING}} \\ \underline{\text{DESCENDING}} \end{array} \right\} \text{KEY IS \{data-name-4\} . . .} \right] . . .$$

[INDEXED BY {index-name-1} . . .]

$$\left[\left\{ \begin{array}{l} \underline{\text{SYNCHRONIZED}} \\ \underline{\text{SYNC}} \end{array} \right\} \begin{bmatrix} \underline{\text{LEFT}} \\ \underline{\text{RIGHT}} \end{bmatrix} \right]$$

$$\left[\left\{ \begin{array}{l} \underline{\text{JUSTIFIED}} \\ \underline{\text{JUST}} \end{array} \right\} \text{RIGHT} \right]$$

[BLANK WHEN ZERO]

[VALUE IS literal] •

Option 2

$$\text{66 data-name-1 } \underline{\text{RENAMES}} \text{ data-name-2 } \left[\left\{ \begin{array}{l} \underline{\text{THROUGH}} \\ \underline{\text{THRU}} \end{array} \right\} \text{data-name-3} \right] \right\} \dots \bullet$$

Option 3

$$\text{88 condition-name } \left\{ \begin{array}{l} \underline{\text{VALUE}} \text{ IS} \\ \underline{\text{VALUES}} \text{ ARE} \end{array} \right\} \left\{ \text{literal-1 } \left[\left\{ \begin{array}{l} \underline{\text{THROUGH}} \\ \underline{\text{THRU}} \end{array} \right\} \text{literal-2} \right] \right\} \dots \bullet$$

Format for Report Group Description Entry

Option 1

01 [data-name-1]

$$\left[\underline{\text{LINE}} \text{ NUMBER IS } \left\{ \begin{array}{l} \text{integer-1 [ON } \underline{\text{NEXT}} \text{ PAGE]} \\ \underline{\text{PLUS}} \text{ integer-2} \end{array} \right\} \right]$$

$$\underline{\text{TYPE}} \text{ IS } \left\{ \begin{array}{l} \left\{ \begin{array}{l} \underline{\text{REPORT}} \underline{\text{HEADING}} \\ \underline{\text{RH}} \end{array} \right\} \\ \left\{ \begin{array}{l} \underline{\text{PAGE}} \underline{\text{HEADING}} \\ \underline{\text{PH}} \end{array} \right\} \\ \left\{ \begin{array}{l} \underline{\text{CONTROL}} \underline{\text{HEADING}} \\ \underline{\text{CH}} \end{array} \right\} \left\{ \begin{array}{l} \text{data-name-2} \\ \underline{\text{FINAL}} \end{array} \right\} \\ \left\{ \begin{array}{l} \underline{\text{DETAIL}} \\ \underline{\text{DE}} \end{array} \right\} \\ \left\{ \begin{array}{l} \underline{\text{CONTROL}} \underline{\text{FOOTING}} \\ \underline{\text{CF}} \end{array} \right\} \left\{ \begin{array}{l} \text{data-name-3} \\ \underline{\text{FINAL}} \end{array} \right\} \\ \left\{ \begin{array}{l} \underline{\text{PAGE}} \underline{\text{FOOTING}} \\ \underline{\text{PF}} \end{array} \right\} \\ \left\{ \begin{array}{l} \underline{\text{REPORT}} \underline{\text{FOOTING}} \\ \underline{\text{RF}} \end{array} \right\} \end{array} \right\}$$

[[<u>USAGE</u> IS] <u>DISPLAY</u>]

Option 2

level-number [data-name-1]

    [<u>BLANK</u> WHEN <u>ZERO</u>]

    [<u>GROUP</u> INDICATE]

$$\left[\left\{ \begin{array}{l} \underline{\text{JUSTIFIED}} \\ \underline{\text{JUST}} \end{array} \right\} \text{RIGHT} \right]$$

$$\left[\underline{\text{LINE}} \text{ NUMBER IS } \left\{ \begin{array}{l} \text{integer-1 [ON } \underline{\text{NEXT}} \text{ PAGE]} \\ \underline{\text{PLUS}} \text{ integer-2} \end{array} \right\} \right]$$

[COLUMN NUMBER IS integer-3]

$$\left\{ \begin{array}{l} \underline{PICTURE} \\ \underline{PIC} \end{array} \right\} \text{IS character-string}$$

$$\left\{ \begin{array}{l} \underline{SOURCE} \text{ IS identifier-1} \\ \underline{VALUE} \text{ IS literal} \\ \{\underline{SUM} \text{ \{identifier-2\}} \dots [\underline{UPON} \text{ \{data-name-2\}} \dots] \} \dots \end{array} \right\}$$

$$\left[\underline{RESET} \text{ ON} \left\{ \begin{array}{l} \text{data-name-4} \\ \underline{FINAL} \end{array} \right\} \right]$$

[[USAGE IS] DISPLAY] •

Format for Procedure Division

Option 1

PROCEDURE DIVISION [USING {data-name-1} . . .] •
[DECLARATIVES •
{section-name SECTION [segment-number] • declarative-sentence •
[paragraph-name • [sentence] . . .] . . . } . . .
 END DECLARATIVES •]
{section-name SECTION [segment-number] •
[paragraph-name • [sentence] . . .] . . . } . . .

Option 2

PROCEDURE DIVISION [USING {data-name-1} . . .] •
[paragraph-name • [sentence] . . .] . . . } . . .

General Format for Verbs

ACCEPT identifier [FROM mnemonic-name]

$$\underline{ACCEPT} \text{ identifier } \underline{FROM} \left\{ \begin{array}{l} \underline{DATE} \\ \underline{DAY} \\ \underline{TIME} \end{array} \right\}$$

$$\underline{ADD} \left\{ \begin{array}{l} \text{identifier-1} \\ \text{literal-1} \end{array} \right\} \dots \underline{TO} \text{ \{identifier-m } \underline{ROUNDED}]\} \dots$$

[ON <u>SIZE ERROR</u> imperative-statement]
[<u>END-ADD</u>]

<u>ADD</u> $\begin{Bmatrix} \text{identifier-1} \\ \text{literal-1} \end{Bmatrix} \begin{Bmatrix} \text{identifier-2} \\ \text{literal} \end{Bmatrix}$ . . . <u>GIVING</u> {identifier-m <u>ROUNDED</u>]} . . .

[ON <u>SIZE ERROR</u> imperative-statement]
[<u>END-ADD</u>]

<u>CALL</u> $\begin{Bmatrix} \text{identifier-1} \\ \text{literal-1} \end{Bmatrix}$ <u>USING</u> {data-name-1} . . .]

<u>CLOSE</u> file-name-1 $\left[\begin{array}{l} \begin{Bmatrix} \underline{\text{REEL}} \\ \underline{\text{UNIT}} \end{Bmatrix} \begin{bmatrix} \text{WITH } \underline{\text{NO REWIND}} \\ \text{FOR } \underline{\text{REMOVAL}} \end{bmatrix} \\ \underline{\text{WITH}} \begin{Bmatrix} \underline{\text{NO REWIND}} \\ \underline{\text{LOCK}} \end{Bmatrix} \ldots \end{array} \right]$

<u>COMPUTE</u> {identifier-1 [<u>ROUNDED</u>]} . . . = arithmetic-expression
[ON SIZE ERROR imperative-statement]
[<u>END-COMPUTE</u>]

<u>COPY</u> text-name $\left[\begin{Bmatrix} \underline{\text{OF}} \\ \underline{\text{IN}} \end{Bmatrix} \text{library-name} \right]$

<u>DELETE</u> file-name RECORD [<u>INVALID</u> KEY imperative-statement]

<u>DISPLAY</u> $\begin{Bmatrix} \text{identifier-1} \\ \text{literal-1} \end{Bmatrix}$ . . . <u>UPON</u> mnemonic-name

<u>DIVIDE</u> $\begin{Bmatrix} \text{identifier-1} \\ \text{literal-1} \end{Bmatrix}$ <u>INTO</u> {identifier-2 [<u>ROUNDED</u>]} . . .
[ON <u>SIZE ERROR</u> imperative-statement] [<u>END-DIVIDE</u>]

<u>DIVIDE</u> $\begin{Bmatrix} \text{identifier-1} \\ \text{literal-1} \end{Bmatrix}$ <u>INTO</u> $\begin{Bmatrix} \text{identifier-2} \\ \text{literal-2} \end{Bmatrix}$ <u>GIVING</u> identifier-3 [<u>ROUNDED</u>]} . . .
[ON <u>SIZE ERROR</u> imperative-statement] [<u>END-DIVIDE</u>]

<u>DIVIDE</u> $\begin{Bmatrix} \text{identifier-1} \\ \text{literal-1} \end{Bmatrix}$ <u>BY</u> $\begin{Bmatrix} \text{identifier-2} \\ \text{literal-2} \end{Bmatrix}$ <u>GIVING</u> identifier-3 [<u>ROUNDED</u>]} . . .
[ON <u>SIZE ERROR</u> imperative-statement] [<u>END-DIVIDE</u>]

<u>DIVIDE</u> $\begin{Bmatrix} \text{identifier-1} \\ \text{literal-1} \end{Bmatrix}$ <u>INTO</u> $\begin{Bmatrix} \text{identifier-2} \\ \text{literal-2} \end{Bmatrix}$ <u>GIVING</u> identifier-3 [<u>ROUNDED</u>]} . . .
REMAINDER identifier-4 [ON <u>SIZE</u> <u>ERROR</u> imperative-statement] [<u>END-DIVIDE</u>]

DIVIDE $\left\{ \begin{array}{l} \text{identifier-1} \\ \text{literal-1} \end{array} \right\}$ BY $\left\{ \begin{array}{l} \text{identifier-2} \\ \text{literal-2} \end{array} \right\}$ GIVING identifier-3 [ROUNDED]} ...

REMAINDER identifier-4 [ON SIZE ERROR imperative-statement] [END-DIVIDE]

EVALUATE $\left\{ \begin{array}{l} \text{identifier-1} \\ \text{literal-1} \\ \text{expression-1} \end{array} \right\}$ ALSO $\left\{ \begin{array}{l} \text{identifier-2} \\ \text{literal-2} \\ \text{expression-2} \end{array} \right\}$ ...

{WHEN

$\left\{ \begin{array}{l} \text{TRUE} \\ \text{FALSE} \\ \text{[NOT]} \end{array} \right. \left\{ \begin{array}{l} \text{identifier-3} \\ \text{literal-3} \end{array} \right\} \left[\left\{ \begin{array}{l} \text{THROUGH} \\ \text{THRU} \end{array} \right\} \left\{ \begin{array}{l} \text{identifier-4} \\ \text{literal-4} \end{array} \right\} \right]$

[ALSO

$\left\{ \begin{array}{l} \text{TRUE} \\ \text{FALSE} \\ \text{[NOT]} \end{array} \right. \left\{ \begin{array}{l} \text{identifier-5} \\ \text{literal-5} \end{array} \right\} \left[\left\{ \begin{array}{l} \text{THROUGH} \\ \text{THRU} \end{array} \right\} \left\{ \begin{array}{l} \text{identifier-6} \\ \text{literal-6} \end{array} \right\} \right]$]

imperative-statement-1} ...

[WHEN OTHER imperative-statement-2]

[END-EVALUATE]

EXIT [PROGRAM] •

GENERATE $\left\{ \begin{array}{l} \text{data-name} \\ \text{report-name} \end{array} \right\}$

GO TO [procedure-name-1]

IF condition $\left\{ \begin{array}{l} \text{statement-1} \\ \text{NEXT SENTENCE} \end{array} \right\}$ $\left\{ \begin{array}{l} \text{ELSE statement-2} \\ \text{ELSE NEXT SENTENCE} \end{array} \right\}$

INITIATE {report-name-1} ...

INSPECT identifier-1 TALLYING

$\left\{ \text{identifier-2 FOR} \left\{ \left\{ \begin{array}{l} \text{ALL} \\ \text{LEADING} \\ \text{CHARACTERS} \end{array} \right\} \left\{ \begin{array}{l} \text{identifier-3} \\ \text{literal-1} \end{array} \right\} \right\} \left[\left\{ \begin{array}{l} \text{BEFORE} \\ \text{AFTER} \end{array} \right\} \text{INITIAL} \left\{ \begin{array}{l} \text{identifier-4} \\ \text{literal-2} \end{array} \right\} \right] \right\} ... \right\} ...$

INSPECT identifier-1 REPLACING

CHARACTERS BY $\left\{ \begin{array}{l} \text{identifier-6} \\ \text{literal-4} \end{array} \right\}$ $\left[\left\{ \begin{array}{l} \text{BEFORE} \\ \text{AFTER} \end{array} \right\} \text{INITIAL} \left\{ \begin{array}{l} \text{identifier-7} \\ \text{literal-5} \end{array} \right\} \right]$

$\left\{ \left\{ \begin{array}{l} \text{ALL} \\ \text{LEADING} \\ \text{FIRST} \end{array} \right\} \left\{ \begin{array}{l} \text{identifier-5} \\ \text{literal-3} \end{array} \right\} \text{BY} \left\{ \begin{array}{l} \text{identifier-6} \\ \text{literal-4} \end{array} \right\} \left[\left\{ \begin{array}{l} \text{BEFORE} \\ \text{AFTER} \end{array} \right\} \text{INITIAL} \left\{ \begin{array}{l} \text{identifier-7} \\ \text{literal-5} \end{array} \right\} \right] \right\} \ldots \right\} \ldots$

INSPECT identifier-1 TALLYING

$\left\{ \text{identifier-2 FOR} \left\{ \left\{ \begin{array}{l} \text{ALL} \\ \text{LEADING} \\ \text{CHARACTERS} \end{array} \right\} \left\{ \begin{array}{l} \text{identifier-3} \\ \text{literal-1} \end{array} \right\} \left[\left\{ \begin{array}{l} \text{BEFORE} \\ \text{AFTER} \end{array} \right\} \text{INITIAL} \left\{ \begin{array}{l} \text{identifier-4} \\ \text{literal-2} \end{array} \right\} \right] \right\} \ldots \right\} \ldots$

REPLACING

CHARACTERS BY $\left\{ \begin{array}{l} \text{identifier-6} \\ \text{literal-4} \end{array} \right\}$ $\left[\left\{ \begin{array}{l} \text{BEFORE} \\ \text{AFTER} \end{array} \right\} \text{INITIAL} \left\{ \begin{array}{l} \text{identifier-7} \\ \text{literal-5} \end{array} \right\} \right]$

$\left\{ \left\{ \begin{array}{l} \text{ALL} \\ \text{LEADING} \\ \text{FIRST} \end{array} \right\} \left\{ \begin{array}{l} \text{identifier-5} \\ \text{literal-3} \end{array} \right\} \text{BY} \left\{ \begin{array}{l} \text{identifier-6} \\ \text{literal-4} \end{array} \right\} \left[\left\{ \begin{array}{l} \text{BEFORE} \\ \text{AFTER} \end{array} \right\} \text{INITIAL} \left\{ \begin{array}{l} \text{identifier-7} \\ \text{literal-5} \end{array} \right\} \right] \right\} \ldots \right\} \ldots$

MERGE file-name-1 $\left\{ \text{on} \left\{ \begin{array}{l} \text{ASCENDING} \\ \text{DESCENDING} \end{array} \right\} \text{KEY \{data-name-1\}} \ldots \right\} \ldots$

USING file-name-2 (file-name-3) . . .

$\left\{ \begin{array}{l} \text{OUTPUT PROCEDURE IS section-name-1} \left[\left\{ \begin{array}{l} \text{THROUGH} \\ \text{THRU} \end{array} \right\} \text{section-name-2} \right] \\ \text{GIVING file-name-5} \end{array} \right\}$

MOVE $\left\{ \begin{array}{l} \text{identifier-1} \\ \text{literal} \end{array} \right\}$ TO {identifier-2} . . .

MULTIPLY $\left\{ \begin{array}{l} \text{identifier-1} \\ \text{literal-1} \end{array} \right\}$ BY {identifier-2 [ROUNDED]} . . .

[ON SIZE ERROR imperative-statement [END-MULTIPLY]

MULTIPLY $\left\{ \begin{array}{l} \text{identifier-1} \\ \text{literal-1} \end{array} \right\}$ BY $\left\{ \begin{array}{l} \text{identifier-2} \\ \text{literal-2} \end{array} \right\}$ GIVING {identifier-3 [ROUNDED]} . . .

[ON SIZE ERROR imperative-statement] [END-MULTIPLY]

$$
\text{OPEN} \left\{ \begin{array}{l} \underline{\text{OUTPUT}} \; \{\text{file-name-3} \; [\text{WITH} \; \underline{\text{NO}} \; \underline{\text{REWIND}}]\} \; \ldots \\ \underline{\text{I/O}} \; \{\text{FILE-NAME-5}\} \\ \underline{\text{EXTEND}} \; \{\text{file-name-7}\} \; \ldots \end{array} \right\}
$$

$$
\underline{\text{PERFORM}} \; \text{procedure-name-1} \; \left[\left\{ \begin{array}{l} \underline{\text{THROUGH}} \\ \underline{\text{THRU}} \end{array} \right\} \text{procedure-name-2} \right]
$$

$$
\underline{\text{PERFORM}} \; \text{procedure-name-1} \; \left[\left\{ \begin{array}{l} \underline{\text{THROUGH}} \\ \underline{\text{THRU}} \end{array} \right\} \text{procedure-name-2} \right] \left\{ \begin{array}{l} \text{identifier-1} \\ \text{integer-1} \end{array} \right\} \underline{\text{TIMES}}
$$

$$
\underline{\text{PERFORM}} \; \text{procedure-name-1} \; \left[\left\{ \begin{array}{l} \underline{\text{THROUGH}} \\ \underline{\text{THRU}} \end{array} \right\} \text{procedure-name-2} \right]
$$

$$
\left[\text{WITH} \; \underline{\text{TEST}} \; \left\{ \begin{array}{l} \underline{\text{BEFORE}} \\ \underline{\text{AFTER}} \end{array} \right\} \right] \underline{\text{UNTIL}} \; \text{condition-1}
$$

$$
\underline{\text{PERFORM}} \; \text{procedure-name-1} \; \left[\left\{ \begin{array}{l} \underline{\text{THROUGH}} \\ \underline{\text{THRU}} \end{array} \right\} \text{procedure-name-2} \right]
$$

$$
\left[\text{WITH} \; \underline{\text{TEST}} \; \left\{ \begin{array}{l} \underline{\text{BEFORE}} \\ \underline{\text{AFTER}} \end{array} \right\} \right]
$$

$$
\underline{\text{VARYING}} \left\{ \begin{array}{l} \text{identifier-2} \\ \text{index-name-1} \end{array} \right\} \underline{\text{FROM}} \left\{ \begin{array}{l} \text{identifier-3} \\ \text{index-name-2} \\ \text{literal-1} \end{array} \right\}
$$

$$
\underline{\text{BY}} \left\{ \begin{array}{l} \text{identifier-4} \\ \text{literal-3} \end{array} \right\} \underline{\text{UNTIL}} \; \text{condition-1}
$$

$$
\left[\underline{\text{AFTER}} \quad \left\{ \begin{array}{l} \text{identifier-5} \\ \text{index-name-3} \end{array} \right\} \underline{\text{FROM}} \left\{ \begin{array}{l} \text{identifier-6} \\ \text{index-name-4} \\ \text{literal-3} \end{array} \right\} \right.
$$

$$
\left. \underline{\text{BY}} \left\{ \begin{array}{l} \text{identifier-7} \\ \text{literal-4} \end{array} \right\} \underline{\text{UNTIL}} \; \text{condition-2} \right]
$$

$$
\left[\underline{\text{AFTER}} \quad \left\{ \begin{array}{l} \text{identifier-8} \\ \text{index-name-5} \end{array} \right\} \underline{\text{FROM}} \left\{ \begin{array}{l} \text{identifier-9} \\ \text{index-name-6} \\ \text{literal-5} \end{array} \right\} \right.
$$

$$
\left. \underline{\text{BY}} \left\{ \begin{array}{l} \text{identifier-10} \\ \text{literal-6} \end{array} \right\} \underline{\text{UNTIL}} \; \text{condition-3} \right]
$$

<u>READ</u> file-name[<u>NEXT</u>] RECORD[<u>INTO</u> identifier] [AT <u>END</u> imperative-statement] [<u>END-READ</u>]
<u>READ</u> file-name RECORD [<u>INTO</u> identifier] [<u>KEY</u> IS data-name]
      [<u>INVALID</u> KEY imperative-statement] [<u>END-READ</u>]
<u>RELEASE</u> record-name [<u>FROM</u> identifier]

RETURN file-name RECORD [INTO identifier] AT END imperative-statement [END-RETURN]
REWRITE record-name [FROM identifier]
[INVALID key imperative-statement] [END-REWRITE]

$$\text{SEARCH identifier-1} \left[\underline{\text{VARYING}} \quad \left\{ \begin{array}{l} \text{identifier-2} \\ \text{index-name-1} \end{array} \right\} \right] \text{[AT \underline{END} imperative-statement]}$$

$$\left\{ \underline{\text{WHEN}} \text{ condition-1} \left\{ \begin{array}{l} \text{imperative-statement-2} \\ \underline{\text{NEXT}} \ \underline{\text{SENTENCE}} \end{array} \right\} \right\} \dots \text{[\underline{END-SEARCH}]}$$

SEARCH ALL identifier-1 [AT END imperative-statement-1]

$$\underline{\text{WHEN}} \left\{ \begin{array}{l} \text{data-name-1} \quad \left\{ \begin{array}{l} \text{IS \underline{EQUAL} TO} \\ \text{IS =} \end{array} \right\} \left\{ \begin{array}{l} \text{identifier-3} \\ \text{literal-1} \\ \text{arithmetic-expression-1} \end{array} \right\} \\ \\ \text{condition-name-1} \end{array} \right\}$$

$$\underline{\text{AND}} \left\{ \begin{array}{l} \text{data-name-2} \quad \left\{ \begin{array}{l} \text{IS \underline{EQUAL} TO} \\ \text{IS =} \end{array} \right\} \left\{ \begin{array}{l} \text{identifier-4} \\ \text{literal-2} \\ \text{arithmetic-expression-2} \end{array} \right\} \\ \\ \text{condition-name-2} \end{array} \right\}$$

$$\left\{ \begin{array}{l} \text{imperative-statement-2} \\ \underline{\text{NEXT}} \ \underline{\text{SENTENCE}} \end{array} \right\}$$
[END-SEARCH]

$$\underline{\text{SET}} \quad \left\{ \begin{array}{l} \text{identifier-1} \\ \text{index-name-1} \end{array} \right\} \dots \underline{\text{TO}} \left\{ \begin{array}{l} \text{identifier-3} \\ \text{index-name-3} \\ \text{integer-1} \end{array} \right\}$$

$$\underline{\text{SET}} \ \{\text{index-name-4}\} \dots \quad \left\{ \begin{array}{l} \text{UP \underline{BY}} \\ \underline{\text{DOWN}} \ \underline{\text{BY}} \end{array} \right\} \left\{ \begin{array}{l} \text{identifier-4} \\ \text{integer-2} \end{array} \right\}$$

$$\underline{\text{SORT}} \text{ file-name-1} \left\{ \text{ON} \quad \left\{ \begin{array}{l} \underline{\text{ASCENDING}} \\ \underline{\text{DESCENDING}} \end{array} \right\} \text{KEY } \{\text{data-name-1}\} \dots \right\} \dots$$

$$\left\{ \begin{array}{l} \underline{\text{INPUT}} \ \underline{\text{PROCEDURE}} \text{ IS section-name-1} \quad \left[\left\{ \begin{array}{l} \underline{\text{THROUGH}} \\ \underline{\text{THRU}} \end{array} \right\} \text{ section-name-2} \right] \\ \\ \underline{\text{USING}} \ \{\text{file-name-2}\} \dots \end{array} \right\}$$

$$\left\{ \begin{array}{l} \underline{\text{OUTPUT}} \ \underline{\text{PROCEDURE}} \text{ IS section-name-3} \quad \left[\left\{ \begin{array}{l} \underline{\text{THROUGH}} \\ \underline{\text{THRU}} \end{array} \right\} \text{ section-name-4} \right] \\ \\ \underline{\text{GIVING}} \ \{\text{file-name-4}\} \dots \end{array} \right\}$$

$$\text{START file-name KEY} \left\{ \begin{array}{l} \text{IS } \underline{\text{EQUAL}} \text{ TO} \\ \text{IS } = \\ \text{IS } \underline{\text{GREATER}} \text{ THAN} \\ \text{IS } > \\ \text{IS } \underline{\text{NOT}} \underline{\text{LESS}} \text{ THAN} \\ \text{IS } \underline{\text{NOT}} < \end{array} \right\} \text{ data-name}$$

[INVALID KEY imperative-statement]

$$\underline{\text{STOP}} \left\{ \begin{array}{l} \underline{\text{RUN}} \\ \text{literal} \end{array} \right\}$$

$$\underline{\text{STRING}} \left\{ \left\{ \begin{array}{l} \text{identifier-1} \\ \text{literal-1} \end{array} \right\} \dots \underline{\text{DELIMITED}} \text{ BY} \left\{ \begin{array}{l} \text{identifier-3} \\ \text{literal-3} \\ \underline{\text{SIZE}} \end{array} \right\} \right\} \dots$$

INTO identifier-7 [WITH POINTER identifier-8]
[ON OVERFLOW imperative-statement]
[END-STRING]

$$\underline{\text{SUBTRACT}} \left\{ \begin{array}{l} \text{identifier-1} \\ \text{literal-1} \end{array} \right\} \dots \underline{\text{FROM}} \text{ identifier-m } [\underline{\text{ROUNDED}}]\} \dots$$

[ON SIZE ERROR imperative-statement] [END-SUBTRACT]

$$\underline{\text{SUBTRACT}} \left\{ \begin{array}{l} \text{identifier-1} \\ \text{literal-1} \end{array} \right\} \dots \underline{\text{FROM}} \left\{ \begin{array}{l} \text{identifier-m} \\ \text{literal-m} \end{array} \right\}$$

GIVING {identifier-n [ROUNDED]
[ON SIZE ERROR imperative-statement] [END-SUBTRACT]

$$\underline{\text{SUBTRACT}} \left\{ \begin{array}{l} \underline{\text{CORRESPONDING}} \\ \underline{\text{CORR}} \end{array} \right\} \text{ identifier-1 } \underline{\text{FROM}} \text{ identifier-2 } [\underline{\text{ROUNDED}}]\} \dots$$

[ON SIZE ERROR imperative-statement] [END-SUBTRACT]

TERMINATE {report-name-1} . . .
UNSTRING identifier-1

$$\left[\underline{\text{DELIMITED}} \text{ BY } [\underline{\text{ALL}}] \left\{ \begin{array}{l} \text{identifier-2} \\ \text{literal-1} \end{array} \right\} \left[\underline{\text{OR}} \; [\underline{\text{ALL}}] \left\{ \begin{array}{l} \text{identifier-3} \\ \text{literal-2} \end{array} \right\} \right] \dots \right\}$$

INTO {identifier-4 [DELIMITER IN identifier-5] [COUNT IN identifier-6] } . . .

[WITH POINTER identifier-10] [TALLYING IN identifier-11]
[ON OVERFLOW imperative-statement]
[END-UNSTRING]

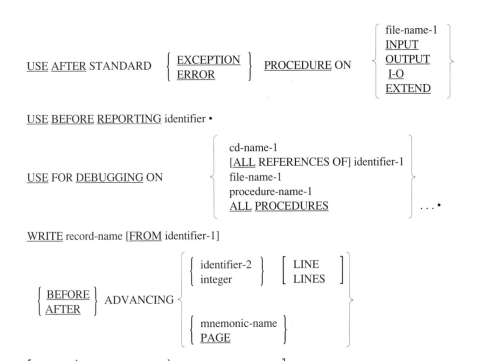

USE AFTER STANDARD $\left\{\begin{array}{l}\underline{EXCEPTION} \\ \underline{ERROR}\end{array}\right\}$ PROCEDURE ON $\left\{\begin{array}{l}\text{file-name-1} \\ \underline{INPUT} \\ \underline{OUTPUT} \\ \underline{I-O} \\ \underline{EXTEND}\end{array}\right\}$

USE BEFORE REPORTING identifier •

USE FOR DEBUGGING ON $\left\{\begin{array}{l}\text{cd-name-1} \\ [\underline{ALL} \text{ REFERENCES OF}] \text{ identifier-1} \\ \text{file-name-1} \\ \text{procedure-name-1} \\ \underline{ALL} \underline{PROCEDURES}\end{array}\right\}$ ... •

WRITE record-name [FROM identifier-1]

$\left\{\begin{array}{l}\underline{BEFORE} \\ \underline{AFTER}\end{array}\right\}$ ADVANCING $\left\{\begin{array}{l}\left\{\begin{array}{l}\text{identifier-2} \\ \text{integer}\end{array}\right\} \left[\begin{array}{l}\text{LINE} \\ \text{LINES}\end{array}\right] \\ \left\{\begin{array}{l}\text{mnemonic-name} \\ \underline{PAGE}\end{array}\right\}\end{array}\right\}$

$\left[\text{AT } \left\{\begin{array}{l}\underline{END-OF-PAGE} \\ \underline{EOP}\end{array}\right\} \text{imperative-statement}\right]$ [END-WRITE]

WRITE record-name [FROM identifier] [INVALID KEY imperative-statement] [END-WRITE]

Format for Conditions

Relation Condition

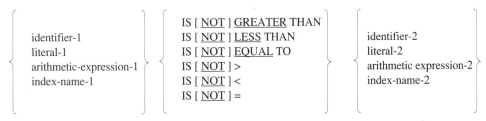

$\left\{\begin{array}{l}\text{identifier-1} \\ \text{literal-1} \\ \text{arithmetic-expression-1} \\ \text{index-name-1}\end{array}\right\}$ $\left\{\begin{array}{l}\text{IS [NOT] GREATER THAN} \\ \text{IS [NOT] LESS THAN} \\ \text{IS [NOT] EQUAL TO} \\ \text{IS [NOT] >} \\ \text{IS [NOT] <} \\ \text{IS [NOT] =}\end{array}\right\}$ $\left\{\begin{array}{l}\text{identifier-2} \\ \text{literal-2} \\ \text{arithmetic expression-2} \\ \text{index-name-2}\end{array}\right\}$

Class Condition

identifier IS [NOT] $\left\{\begin{array}{l}\underline{NUMERIC} \\ \underline{ALPHABETIC}\end{array}\right\}$

Sign Condition

$$\text{arithmetic-expression [} \underline{\text{NOT}} \text{]} \quad \left\{ \begin{array}{l} \underline{\text{POSITIVE}} \\ \underline{\text{NEGATIVE}} \\ \underline{\text{ZERO}} \end{array} \right\}$$

Condition-name Condition

condition-name

Switch-status Condition

condition-name

Negated Simple Condition

$\underline{\text{NOT}}$ simple-condition

Combined Condition

$$\text{condition} \quad \left\{ \left\{ \begin{array}{l} \underline{\text{AND}} \\ \underline{\text{OR}} \end{array} \right\} \text{ condition} \right\} \quad \ldots$$

Abbreviated Combined Relation Condition

$$\text{relation-condition} \quad \left\{ \left\{ \begin{array}{l} \underline{\text{AND}} \\ \underline{\text{OR}} \end{array} \right\} \text{ [} \underline{\text{NOT}} \text{] [relational-operator] object} \right\} \quad \ldots$$

INDEX

O

P